DK EYEWITNESS *TRAVEL GUIDES*

TURKEY

Main contributor: SUZANNE SWAN

DK PUBLISHING, INC.

LONDON • NEW YORK • MUNICH
MELBOURNE • DELHI

Produced by Struik New Holland Publishing (Pty) Ltd,
Cape Town, South Africa

MANAGING EDITORS Alfred LeMaitre, Laura Milton
MANAGING ART EDITOR Steven Felmore
EDITORS Amichai Kapilevich, Anna Tanneberger
EDITORIAL ASSISTANT Christie Meyer
DESIGNER Peter Bosman
MAP CO-ORDINATOR John Loubser
CARTOGRAPHER Carl Germishuys
PICTURE RESEARCHERS Sandra Adomeit, Karla Kik
DTP CHECK Damian Gibbs
PRODUCTION MANAGER Myrna Collins

MAIN CONTRIBUTOR
Suzanne Swan

OTHER CONTRIBUTORS
Rosie Ayliffe, Rose Baring, Barnaby Rogerson, Canan Sılay, Dominic Whiting

PHOTOGRAPHERS
Kate Clow, Terry Richardson, Anthony Souter, Dominic Whiting, Linda
Whitwam, Francesca Yorke

ILLUSTRATORS
Richard Bonson, Stephen Conlin, Gary Cross, Bruno de Robillard, Richard
Draper, Steven Felmore, Paul Guest, Ian Lusted,
Maltings Partnership, Chris Orr & Associates, David Pulvermacher, Paul
Weston, John Woodcock

Film outputting bureau Struik New Holland Publishing (Pty) Ltd
Reproduced by Unifoto (Cape Town)
Printed and bound by Toppan Printing Co. (Shenzhen Ltd)

First American Edition, 2003

02 03 04 05 10 9 8 7 6 5 4 3 2 1

Published in the United States by
DK Publishing, Inc., 375 Hudson Street,
New York, New York 10014

Copyright © 2003 Dorling Kindersley Limited, London

ALL RIGHTS RESERVED UNDER INTERNATIONAL AND PAN-AMERICAN COPYRIGHT
CONVENTIONS. NO PART OF THIS PUBLICATION MAY BE REPRODUCED, STORED
IN A RETRIEVAL SYSTEM, OR TRANSMITTED IN ANY FORM OR BY ANY MEANS,
ELECTRONIC, MECHANICAL, PHOTOCOPYING, RECORDING OR OTHERWISE WITHOUT
THE PRIOR WRITTEN PERMISSION OF THE COPYRIGHT OWNER.

Published in Great Britain by Dorling Kindersley Limited.
Library of Congress Cataloging-in-Publication Data
Swan, Suzanne.
DK Eyewitness travel guides: Turkey / main contributor, Suzanne Swan.
p. cm.
Includes index.
ISBN 0-7894-8329-7 (alk. paper)
1. Turkey--Guidebooks. 2. Turkey --Description and travel. I. Title:
Turkey. II. Title
DR416 .S88 2002
915.6104'4--dc21
2002019268

FLOORS ARE REFERRED TO THROUGHOUT IN ACCORDANCE WITH BRITISH USAGE;
IE THE "FIRST FLOOR" IS THE FLOOR ABOVE GROUND LEVEL.

See our complete product line at
www.dk.com

**The information in every
DK Eyewitness Travel Guide is checked regularly.**
Every effort has been made to ensure that this book is as up-to-date as
possible at the time of going to press. Some details, however, such as
telephone numbers, opening hours, prices, gallery hanging arrangements
and travel information are liable to change. The publishers cannot accept
responsibility for any consequences arising from the use of this book, nor
for any material on third party websites, and cannot guarantee that any
website address in this book will be a suitable source of travel information.
We value the views and suggestions of our readers very highly. Please write
to: Publisher, DK Eyewitness Travel Guides, Dorling Kindersley,
80 Strand, London WC2R 0RL, Great Britain.

◁ **Dramatic light accentuates the İşak Paşa Sarayı near Doğubeyazıt**

The village of Üçağız, on the
Mediterranean coast

CONTENTS

HOW TO USE
THIS GUIDE 6

INTRODUCING
TURKEY

PUTTING TURKEY
ON THE MAP 10

A PORTRAIT OF
TURKEY 12

Commagene stone head on Mount
Nemrut (Nemrut Dağı)

TURKEY THROUGH
THE YEAR 34

THE HISTORY OF
TURKEY 40

EYEWITNESS *TRAVEL GUIDES*

TURKEY

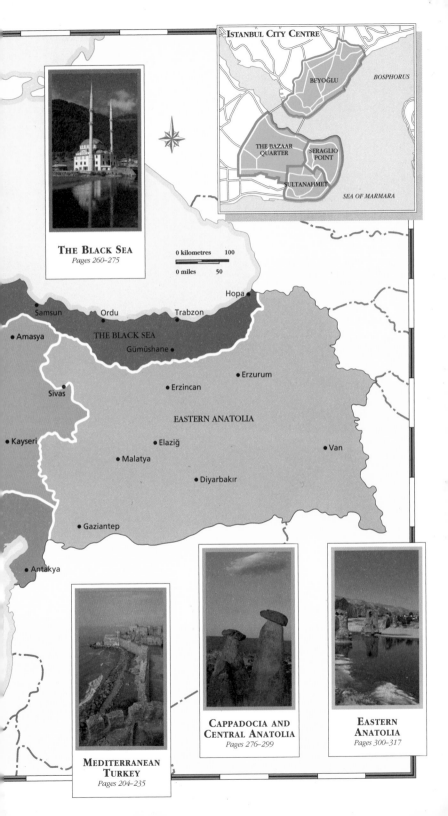

THE BLACK SEA
Pages 260–275

ISTANBUL CITY CENTRE

BEYOĞLU

BOSPHORUS

THE BAZAAR QUARTER

SERAGLIO POINT

SULTANAHMET

SEA OF MARMARA

Hopa

Samsun Ordu Trabzon

Amasya THE BLACK SEA

Gümüshane

Erzurum

Erzincan

Sivas

EASTERN ANATOLIA

Kayseri

Elaziğ

Van

Malatya

Diyarbakır

Gaziantep

Antakya

0 kilometres   100

0 miles   50

MEDITERRANEAN TURKEY
Pages 204–235

CAPPADOCIA AND CENTRAL ANATOLIA
Pages 276–299

EASTERN ANATOLIA
Pages 300–317

Emblems of Istanbul, the Haghia Sophia and Blue Mosque

Vendor selling *boza*, a drink made from lightly fermented grain

Example of Turkish weaving with geometric design

Sumela Monastery *(see p272)*

HOW TO USE THIS GUIDE

THIS GUIDE helps you to get the most from your stay in Turkey. It provides expert recommendations and detailed practical advice. *Introducing Turkey* locates the country geographically, and sets it in context. *Istanbul Area by Area* and *Turkey Region by Region* are the main sight-seeing sections, giving information on major sights, with photographs, maps and illustrations. Suggestions for restaurants, hotels, entertainment and shopping are found in *Travellers' Needs*, while the *Survival Guide* contains useful advice on everything from changing money to travelling by bus.

ISTANBUL AREA BY AREA

Turkey's largest city has been divided into four sightseeing areas. Each has its own chapter opening with a list of the sights that are described. The *Further Afield* section covers many peripheral places of interest. All sights are numbered and plotted on an *Area Map*. Information on the sights is easy to locate as it follows the numerical order used on the map.

Sights at a Glance lists the chapter's sights by category, such as Museums and Galleries, Mosques, Parks and Gardens and Historic Buildings.

2 Street-by-Street Map
This gives a bird's-eye view of the key areas in each sightseeing area.

Stars indicate the sights that no visitor should miss.

Story boxes explore specific subjects in detail.

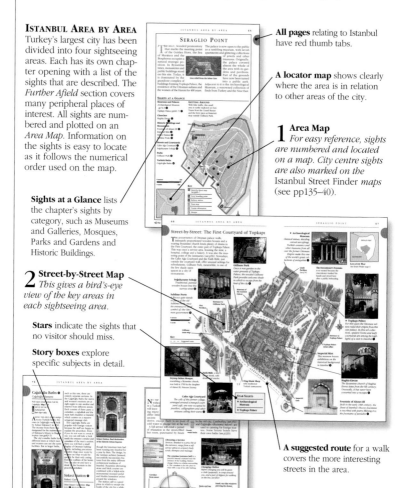

All pages relating to Istanbul have red thumb tabs.

A locator map shows clearly where the area is in relation to other areas of the city.

1 Area Map
For easy reference, sights are numbered and located on a map. City centre sights are also marked on the Istanbul Street Finder *maps (see pp135–40).*

A suggested route for a walk covers the more interesting streets in the area.

3 Feature
Each feature looks in detail at an important attraction, tracing its history or cultural context, and providing detailed information on what can be seen today.

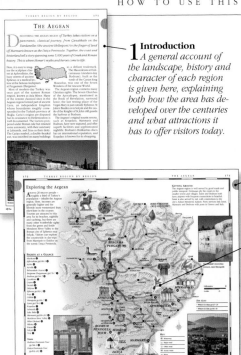

1 Introduction
A general account of the landscape, history and character of each region is given here, explaining both how the area has developed over the centuries and what attractions it has to offer visitors today.

TURKEY REGION BY REGION
Apart from Istanbul, the rest of the country is divided into seven regions, each with a separate chapter. The most interesting towns and sights to visit are numbered on a *Pictorial Map* at the beginning of each chapter.

Each area of Turkey can be easily identified by its colour coding, shown on the inside front cover.

2 Pictorial Map
This shows the main road network and gives an illustrated overview of the whole region. All interesting places to visit are numbered and there are also useful tips on getting to, and around, the region.

A town map shows the locations of all the sights described in the text.

3 Detailed Information
All the important towns and other places to visit are described individually. They are listed in order, following the numbering on the Pictorial Map. Within each entry, there is further detailed information on important buildings and other sights.

For all the top sights, a Visitors' Checklist provides the practical information you will need to plan your visit.

4 Turkey's Top Sights
The historic buildings are dissected to reveal their interiors; important archaeological sites have maps showing key sights and facilities. The most interesting towns or city centres have maps, with sights picked out and described.

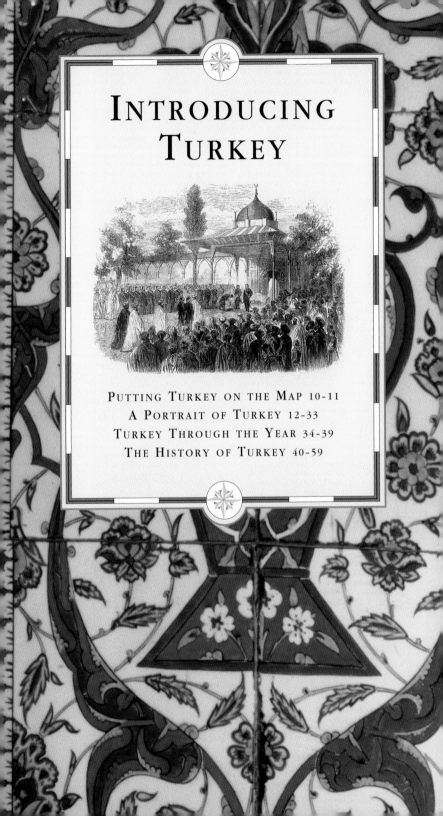

INTRODUCING
TURKEY

Putting Turkey on the Map

L YING BETWEEN Europe, Asia and the Middle East, Turkey is located midway between the equator and the North Pole. It covers an area of 810,000 sq km (503,334 sq miles). A small area called Thrace forms part of the European continent, while the larger section, Anatolia, forms part of Asia. The city of Istanbul is situated at the meeting point of Europe and Asia and is divided by the Bosphorus, the strait linking the Black Sea and the Sea of Marmara. Countries bordering Turkey are Greece and Bulgaria on the European side, and Georgia, Armenia, Iran, Iraq and Syria to the east and southeast.

KEY

✈ Airport

━━ Motorway

━━ Major road

══ Secondary road

─── Railway

- - - International boundary

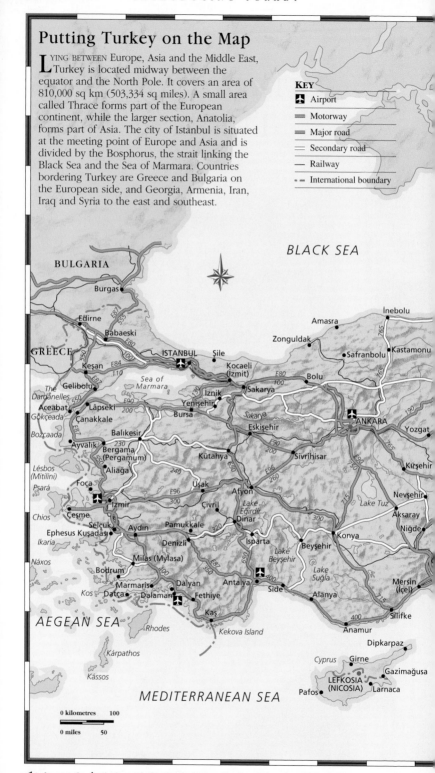

BLACK SEA

BULGARIA
Burgas
İnebolu
Edirne
Amasra
Babaeski
Zonguldak
Kastamonu
GREECE
İSTANBUL   Şile
Safranbolu
Keşan
Kocaeli (İzmit)
Bolu
The Dardanelles
Geliboulu
Sea of Marmara
İznik
Sakarya
ANKARA
Aceabat
Lâpseki
Yenişehir
Bursa
Sakarya
Yozgat
Gökçeada
Çanakkale
Eskişehir
Bozcaada
Balıkesir
Kütahya
Sivrihisar
Kırşehir
Ayvalık
Bergama (Pergamum)
Nevşehir
Lésbos (Mitilini)
Aliağa
Uşak
Lake Tuz
Psará
Foça
Afyon
Aksaray
Chios
İzmir
Çivril
Lake Eğirdir
Konya
Niğde
Çeşme
Selçuk
Pamukkale
Dinar
Ephesus Kuşadası
Aydın
İsparta
Beyşehir
Ikaria
Denizli
Lake Beyşehir
Náxos
Milas (Mylasa)
Lake Suğla
Mersin (İçel)
Bodrum
Antalya
Marmaris
Dalyan
Side
Alanya
Kos
Datça
Dalaman
Fethiye
Silifke
Kaş
Anamur

AEGEAN SEA
Rhodes
Kekova Island
Dipkarpaz
Kárpathos
Cyprus
Girne
Gazimağusa
Kássos
LEFKOSIA (NICOSIA)
Larnaca
Pafos

MEDITERRANEAN SEA

0 kilometres   100

0 miles   50

◁ **A close-up of an İznik tile panel, showing the intricate floral motifs known as arabesques**

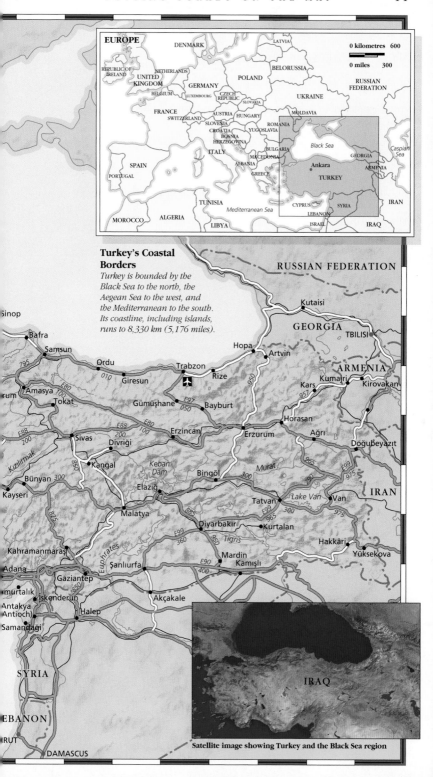

EUROPE

0 kilometres 600

0 miles 300

DENMARK

LATVIA

REPUBLIC OF IRELAND

UNITED KINGDOM

NETHERLANDS

BELGIUM

GERMANY

LUXEMBOURG

POLAND

BELORUSSIA

RUSSIAN FEDERATION

UKRAINE

FRANCE

SWITZERLAND

CZECH REPUBLIC

SLOVAKIA

AUSTRIA

HUNGARY

MOLDAVIA

SLOVENIA

CROATIA

BOSNIA HERZEGOVINA

ROMANIA

YUGOSLAVIA

Black Sea

GEORGIA

Caspian Sea

ITALY

BULGARIA

MACEDONIA

Ankara

ARMENIA

SPAIN

ALBANIA

GREECE

TURKEY

IRAN

PORTUGAL

TUNISIA

Mediterranean Sea

CYPRUS

LEBANON

SYRIA

MOROCCO

ALGERIA

LIBYA

ISRAEL

IRAQ

Turkey's Coastal Borders

Turkey is bounded by the Black Sea to the north, the Aegean Sea to the west, and the Mediterranean to the south. Its coastline, including islands, runs to 8,330 km (5,176 miles).

RUSSIAN FEDERATION

Kutaisi

GEORGIA

TBILISI

Sinop

Bafra

Samsun

Ordu

Giresun

Hopa

Artvin

ARMENIA

Trabzon

Rize

Kumajri

Kirovakan

795

010

E80

700

E80

Amasya

Tokat

rum

Gümüşhane

E97

Bayburt

050

Kars

957

Doğubeyazıt

E88

200

E80

100

Sivas

Erzincan

Erzurum

Horasan

Ağrı

200

Divriği

Kangal

Keban Dam

Bingöl

Murat

965

E99

975

Kızılırmak

850

Bünyan

300

Elazığ

300

300

Lake Van

Van

IRAN

Kayseri

Malatya

Tatvan

965

975

825

885

Diyarbakır

Kurtalan

E99

Kahramanmaraş

Euphrates

Şanlıurfa

360

E99

950

Tigris

Mardin

Hakkâri

Adana

Gaziantep

850

Kamışlı

E90

400

Yüksekova

murtalık

İskenderun

Akçakale

Antakya (Antioch)

Halep

SYRIA

Samandağı

IRAQ

EBANON

RUT

DAMASCUS

Satellite image showing Turkey and the Black Sea region

A Portrait of Turkey

THE POPULAR IMAGE *many visitors have of Turkey is one of idyllic Mediterranean beaches lapped by an azure sea. Sun and sand, however, barely hint at the riches this country has to offer. A bridge between Asia and Europe, Turkey is one of the great cradles of civilization – a proud country whose cultural and historic treasures will delight and inspire even seasoned travellers.*

Contrasts between old and new add greatly to the fascination that overwhelms visitors to Turkey. Istanbul, the metropolis of this fast-changing nation, displays all the hustle and bustle of a great world city, while only a few hours away rural people congregate around communal water supplies and collect wood to light their fires.

Tulips in bloom

The superb scenery and landscape reflect a remarkable geographical diversity. Beguiling seascapes, soft beaches and brooding mountains along the Mediterranean coast yield to the tranquillity of Turkey's Lake District, while the deep forests and cool *yayla* (plateaux) of the Black Sea region leave visitors unprepared for the vast empty steppes of the eastern provinces. Pictures can only hint at the enchantment that awaits travellers in Cappadocia. Here, centuries of underground activity have resulted in entire cities carved deep into the porous tuff, while eons of erosion have carved the landscape into fantastic fairytale-like mushroom formations.

Many of Turkey's national parks and wetland sanctuaries are a last refuge for species that are almost extinct elsewhere in Europe, and for botanists there is an amazing display of flora.

Add to this countless ancient ruins, and the friendliness and hospitality of the Turkish nation, and you are guaranteed an unforgettable holiday.

Looking out over the Bosphorus from Sultanahmet

◁ **Prayer on a holy Friday during Ramazan**

The Library at Ephesus *(see pp182–3)*, one of the most famous Roman sites in Turkey

HISTORICAL FRAMEWORK

Anatolia has seen the rise and fall of sophisticated civilizations, including that of the great Assyrians, Hittites, Phrygians and Urartians. Over the centuries, this land was populated almost continuously. The Hellenistic period produced some of the finest sites. Near Çanakkale, on the Aegean coast, lie the remains of ancient Troy *(see p174)*, and in the mountainous southwest are the ruined settlements of Lycia *(see p215)*, whose inhabitants left behind an assortment of unusual rock tombs.

In the early Christian era, St Paul travelled through Asia Minor, then part of the Roman empire, to preach the Gospel. Between the 3rd and 7th centuries, Christianity was a central force in the development of Anatolia. This was the period when the Byzantine empire attained the pinnacle of its glory. The Romans and Byzantines endowed Turkey with glorious archi-

Ottoman tilework at the Topkapı Palace, Istanbul

tectural masterpieces, remnants of which can still be seen at places like Ephesus *(see pp182–3)*, Aphrodisias *(see pp188–9)*, and in Istanbul, where the former church of Haghia Sophia has stood for 14 centuries *(see pp82–5)*.

The Seljuk Turks added their superb architectural patrimony, as did the Ottomans, whose empire at one point stretched from Hungary to Iraq. Many other peoples, among them Jews, Russians, Armenians and Greeks, have played an important part in Turkey's complex history. The fruits of this diversity can be seen in superb mosaics and frescoes, colourful tilework, underground cities, interesting historic and biblical sights, city walls and fortresses.

Turks are proud of the modern nation Atatürk *(see p58)* forged out of the ruined Ottoman empire. "*Ne Mutlu Türküm Diyene*" is a common Turkish phrase that means "happy is the person who can say he is a Turk."

RELIGION

Most of Turkey's population of 65 million people follow the Sunni branch of Islam, but other, lesser-known Muslim communities, such as the Alevis, also flourish.

Because the Turkish Republic is founded on secular principles, religion does not seem to hold the significance that it does in other Muslim countries. The devout do attend prayer times in the mosque five times daily as laid down by the Koran, but some Turkish Muslims do not go to mosque at all.

A department of religious affairs does exist, however. Its function is to exercise control over family morals and to safeguard the principles of Islam. Church and state are not separated by statute, and so the boundaries between them can be unclear at times. Invariably, Atatürk's principles are invoked as sacred when religion appears to steer too close to politics. The issue of Islamic dress is emotionally charged and a subject of debate.

A card game interrupted for a tray of *simit*

Byzantine mosaic, Haghia Sophia

Pockets of various Christian denominations, such as Greek and Armenian Orthodox, are found in larger cities, and members are allowed to worship freely within their own communities.

SOCIETY

The Turkish language is of Central Asian origin but uses the Latin alphabet. It has a natural vowel harmony that makes it sound melodic and soft. Turkish terms such as *divan* and *ottoman* have entered the English vocabulary, while Turkish borrows words like *tren* and *randevu* from English and French.

Turks have an uninhibited body language that is as emphatic as speech. They are unrestrained about enjoying themselves, but traditional segregation of the sexes means that groups of men sitting around smoking, drinking endless cups of *çay* (tea) and playing dominoes, cards or *tavla* (backgammon) are a common sight. A pronounced family ethos cements the generations, and festivals unite the extended family. It is all bound together by hospitality, an age-old Turkish tradition, in which food and drink play a central role.

Children are regarded as national treasures, but many families blame the advent of television in the 1950s for eroding the discipline and respect for elders that were once the norm.

The Blue Mosque *(see pp88–9)* **in Istanbul**

Turkey's gradual transition to a modern, Western society received a major boost in 1952 when it became a member of the North Atlantic Treaty Organization (NATO). This brought advances in communications, transport and its defence policy. New roads, highways and projects to improve the tourism infrastructure changed the face of the country.

Traditional juice vendor

Modernization continues to be an important hallmark of Turkish society. Today, remote villages can boast of high-speed, fibre-optic telephone connections, but may lack adequate water or reliable electricity supplies. The Internet and cellular telephones have become essential accessories, and new housing projects are quickly festooned with satellite TV dishes.

MODERN TURKEY

For most Turks, the modern version of their ancient country dates from the founding of the Turkish Republic in 1923. Its architect was Mustafa Kemal – better known as Atatürk – a decorated former army officer who became Turkey's first President.

Atatürk is the central figure in all the development of modern Turkey. His reforms, strictly enacted, set the country on the road to becoming European rather than Asian, and his status in the eyes of the Turkish nation has scarcely dimmed since his death. His picture is everywhere and his statue adorns almost every village square.

Few statesmen have matched his integrity and style, and the soldier-turned-politician model still appeals strongly to Turks.

Democracy has proved much more difficult to implement than Western theoretical models. Turkey's military leaders, who intervened in politics in 1960, 1971 and 1980, keep a close eye on political life. In 1997, democratically elected prime minister, Necmettin Erbakan, was ousted from office for his overt religious leanings, but few Turks would seriously challenge the idea of a secular safety net. Moreover, political parties have also acquired the knack of resorting to alliances with various coalition partners in order to gain a working majority, but coalitions are mercurial and shift constantly.

Soldiers mounting guard at the Atatürk Mausoleum *(see p244)*, Ankara

Children hard at work in school

POPULATION MOVEMENT

In the 1960s, many Turks left for Germany to work under a government scheme that offered remittances in foreign currency – still an important source of income. Many of them settled, and 2.2 million Turks now consider Germany their home. There are large Turkish communities in other EU states. Libya and Saudi Arabia have also employed Turks on construction projects.

In Ottoman times, the state provided an all-encompassing social service to its citizens, who willingly complied with its ordered governance. Today, the role of the state is being redefined. Officials are elected and democracy is the goal of society. The large state-owned monopolies that placed Turkey on its feet continue to resist privatization. Some wish to retain the status quo and maximize central power.

Within Turkey, the trend has been for rural people to leave the land and seek a more stable life in urban areas. Few plan to return, even if city life is not what they hoped for. Some of Turkey's best-known films, such as *Sürü* (The Herd), and *Eşkiya* (The Bandit), highlight the common themes of identity, lifestyle and poverty. Turkey's indomitable spirit and remarkable vitality are best seen and appreciated in its proud people. Journeys invariably result in friendships, some of them lasting. If a Turk declares himself your *arkadaş* (friend), he will be a steadfast soulmate long after your holiday memories have faded.

Folk dancers from the Black Sea

Maintaining the old-fashioned centralized state places a huge financial burden on Turks, who must pay for growing debts and international loans. The gap between rich and poor seems to be widening. This slows democratic reform, and increasingly leaves the state catering to an elite minority. Budgets for social services, health and education, for example, lag behind the defence budget. Many people hope that Turkey's planned entry as a full member of the European Union (EU) will even out such inequalities.

Fish sold on the quayside along Istanbul's Golden Horn (see p99)

Landscape and Geology

MOUNTAIN RANGES are Turkey's most distinctive geographic feature, with the Taurus and Pontic ranges enclosing the high Anatolian Plateau. The mountains are geologically young, and the many faulting and folding areas indicate that mountain building is still active. In fact, 80 per cent of the country lies in an extremely active tectonic zone, and earthquakes are frequent. Turkey has eight main drainage basins but the most important ones are the Euphrates (Fırat) and the Tigris (Dicle). About one quarter of Turkey is covered with forest, with stands of pine, spruce and cedar, as well as deciduous trees. About 13 per cent of this area is productive; erosion, logging and fires have all depleted forested areas.

Saklıkent Gorge *is typical of the Mediterranean coastal region, where steep valleys and gorges bisect elongated mountain ridges.*

İzmit, east of Istanbul, *was the epicentre of the 1999 earthquake that measured 7.4 on the Richter scale and claimed the lives of at least 25,000 people.*

PLATE MOVEMENTS

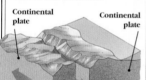

Continental plate   Continental plate

Strike-slip faulting *is found along the North Anatolian Fault. When rocks suddenly shift or move along such fault lines, the tension is released as an earthquake.*

New mountain range   Continental plate

Continental plate

Collisions *between two continental plates result in crust being pushed upwards to form mountain ranges.*

Istanbul
Eurasian Plate
Sea of Marmara
İzmit
North Anatolian Fault
Ankara
Anatolian Plate
Aegean Sea
MEDITER
African Plate

KEY

— Fault line

➡ Direction of plate movement

The Mediterranean *and Aegean coasts are characterized by mountain soils which are clay-based and red, brown and grey in colour. Plains around Adana and Antalya support extensive food, crop and horticultural production.*

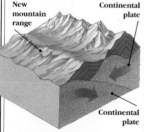

Lake Van lies in a crater-like depression that became landlocked when lava flows from the adjacent Pleistocene-era volcano blocked the flow of water. Today, drainage from feeder streams fills the lake and only evaporation sustains a constant water level. It has a surface area of 3,713 sq km (1,440 sq miles) and a very high level of sodium carbonate.

Pontic Mountains

BLACK SEA

Erzurum

Erzincan

Lake Van

Arabian Plate

Antakya

Adana

ANEAN SEA

Taurus Mountains

GEOLOGY AND EARTHQUAKES

Turkey lies between three converging continental plates – the Anatolian, Eurasian and Arabian plates. As the Arabian plate moves northward into the Eurasian plate, it pushes the Anatolian plate westward, causing earthquakes along the North Anatolian Fault. Further west, the African plate pushes beneath the Anatolian plate, stretching the crust under the Aegean Sea. Tectonic activity is prevalent throughout Turkey.

East of Adıyaman, the alluvial Mesopotamian plain lies between the Tigris and Euphrates rivers. This fertile area produces much of Turkey's wheat and cotton.

Isolated Mediterranean bays were, for centuries, havens for pirates. The Taurus Mountains made sections of the coast inaccessible, allowing peoples like the Lycians (1st and 2nd century BC) to resist Roman rule and retain their own language and culture. As harbours silted up, such civilizations declined.

SOUTHEAST ANATOLIAN PROJECT (GAP)

This showpiece project was conceived during the 1980s to produce hydroelectric power by harnessing the flow of the Tigris and Euphrates rivers. Plans involve the building of 22 dams and 19 power plants spread over more than 1.7 million hectares (4.2 million acres) of land. The project is intended to help develop Turkey's poor eastern provinces, but critics argue that flooding 300,000 sq km (115,800 sq miles) will submerge ancient cultural treasures and displace local people.

The massive Atatürk Dam

Flora and Fauna of Turkey

Turkey offers much for the naturalist, with rich marine ecosystems, abundant birdlife and elusive larger mammals. The rugged eastern provinces still harbour large mammals such as bear, jackal, and wolf. The country is also floristically rich, with more than 11,000 plant species recorded. The tulip is perhaps

Poppies, central Anatolia the most famous of these. The great diversity of plants stems from the variety of habitats – from arid plains to mountains and temperate woodland – but also from Turkey's position as a "biological watershed" at the crossroads of Europe and Asia. There are huge tracts of unspoiled countryside, some of which have been set aside as national parks.

The Anatolian lynx *can still be found in upland areas, although its habitat is under threat.*

THE MEDITERRANEAN COAST
Large areas of the Mediterranean and Aegean coast are dominated by evergreen scrub, with Jerusalem sage, kermes oak, broom and sun roses among the common species. More open scrub areas contain orchids, bulbs and annuals. Tucked under bushes are hellebores and Comper's orchid with its distinctive trailing tassels. Arum lilies exude a fetid odour to entice pollinators. Late summer brings the spires of sea squill and sea daffodil. The carob tree sheds its pods in autumn while colchicum and sternbergias unfold.

Common sternbergia

WETLANDS
Here, dragonflies hover over flowering rush, waterlilies and irises, while water meadows fill with buttercups, bellevalia, marsh orchids and pale blue asyneumas. Despite international recognition of their diversity, Turkish wetlands are under threat from dams, drainage, pollution and climatic change. Surviving examples are Sultansazlığı near Niğde *(see p289)*, Kuşcenneti National Park near Bursa *(see p157)*, and the Göksu Delta *(see p229)*.

Marsh orchid

WOODLANDS
Coniferous forests harbour stands of peonies, orchids, foxgloves, fritillaries and golden peas. The western Taurus range has an endemic subspecies of cedar of Lebanon, and in the north are forests of Oriental beech and fir, with rhododendron, ferns, lilies, primulas and campanulas. In autumn cyclamen and edible mushrooms appear. There are giant cedar at Dokuz Göl near Elmalı, endemic oak species at Kasnak near Eğirdir *(see p254)*, and ancient mixed woodland, now threatened by a dam, in the Fırtına valley.

Peony

STEPPE

Despite their sparse appearance, the broad expanses of the Anatolian Plateau support many flowering plants. Highlights include stately asphodelines, which reach 1.8 m (6 ft) in height, purple gladioli, flax in yellow, pink or blue, and the colourful parasite *Phelypaea coccinea*. On the eastern steppe are found the lovely white, purple or blue oncocyclus iris. Göreme National Park in Cappadocia and Nemrut Dağı National Park *(see p306)* are good places to see this flora. Deforestation and erosion have greatly altered the steppe, and intensive farming practices have accelerated this process.

Iberian oncocyclus

MOUNTAINS

In spring, subalpine meadows are carpeted with buttercups. Above the treeline, snow-drops, winter aconite and crocus crowd together near the snowmelt. These are

Snowdrop

followed by star-of-Bethlehem, grape hyacinth, fritillaries, foxtail lilies, asphode-lines and bright red tulips. Scree and rocky slopes are dotted with colourful alpine flowers like iris, rock jasmine and aubretia. Important mountain reserves include Kaçkar Mountains National Park near the Black Sea coast, Aladağlar National Park, Beyşehir Gölü National Park near Eğirdir *(see p254)* and the ski centres at Uludağ *(see p157)* and Erciyes *(see p288)*.

BIRDS OF ANATOLIA

More than 440 species of bird have been recorded in Turkey, which offers a range of habitats from woodlands and mountains to wetlands and steppe. The country's position on the migratory flyways makes its a paradise for bird-watchers. Autumn offers the spectacle of vast flocks of migrating storks and raptors over the Bosphorus. In winter, lakes and wetlands hold thousands of wintering wildfowl.

Alpine chough can be seen in the mountains, where they nest on ledges, nooks and crevices. They store food in cracks, which they cover with stones.

Adult golden eagles are resident, but the young of northern Europe migrate south in winter to the mountainous areas of the Mediterra-nean.

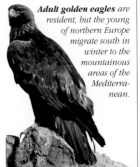

Chukar partridge is one of many game birds in Turkey, where hunting is a popular pastime.

Serin live in woodlands and vine-yards. Local populations are augmented by migra-tory birds in autumn.

Music and Dance

TURKISH MUSIC AND DANCE are deeply rooted in history and tradition, having been influenced by Ottoman classics, mystical Sufi chants and Central Asian folk tunes, as well as jazz and pop. The result is a vibrant mosaic of old and new culture, an eclectic mixture of styles. In Turkey, visitors are treated to variety, from the meditational trance of Whirling dervishes and the merry twirling of folk dancers to the steady beat of Mehter bands, undulating rhythms of belly dancers and the stirring strains of *zurna* buskers. The country offers a musical and dance extravaganza second to none.

Zither-like
kanun

The zurna (shawm) is a member of the oboe family. Its character-istic, strident sound features strongly in Turkish folk music.

TRADITIONAL INSTRUMENTS

Turkish instruments can be classified into three main groups. Stringed instruments include the *saz* and *ud*, winds the *kaval* and *ney*, and percussion the *davul* and *darbuka*.

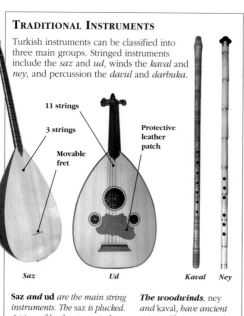

11 strings

3 strings

Movable fret

Protective leather patch

Saz

Ud

Kaval   Ney

Davul

Saz and ud *are the main string instruments. The saz is plucked. A piece of leather protects the belly of the ud from the strokes of the plectrum.*

The woodwinds, *ney and kaval, have ancient origins. The ney is made from reed, while the kaval is carved from the wood of the plum tree.*

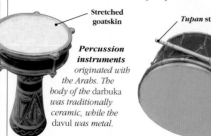

Stretched goatskin

Percussion instruments *originated with the Arabs. The body of the darbuka was traditionally ceramic, while the davul was metal.*

Tupan stick

Darbuka

Davul

*A **saz player** entertains villagers in this 1950s photograph. Although tastes have changed, Turks remain proud of their musical traditions.*

Sufi music uses the sounds of the ney, ud *and* kanun to interpret secular pieces based on the mode system and accompany poems that are chanted by a chorus. Through whirling motions, the dancers attain a trance-like state (see p255).

The **Kılıç Kalkan**, *or spoon dance, of the Black Sea region is performed to the rhythmic beating of two wooden spoons. Traditional folk dancing is an important part of Turkish culture, as are colourful regional costumes.*

Low G clarinet

Bagpipes (*tulum*) made from goatskin

Belly dancing is popular in Turkey and remains a firm favourite with tourists. The sensuous rippling body movements, and gyrations of the hips, require impressive muscle control.

Arabesque *and pop music* *are big business in Turkey, its heroes and heroines attaining cult status. Ibrahim Tatlıses is a much-loved performer of* arabesk, *Oriental-style music with lyrics that bemoan human hardship, while art-music trained Sezen Aksu is one of the top-selling pop stars.*

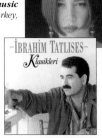

FASIL MUSIC

Fasıl music is considered semi-classical and is performed in *meyhane (see p337)* or concert halls. Its distinctive single harmony is similar to gypsy *(Çingene)* music, and both display a masterful control of traditional wind, string and percussion instruments. Fasıl music is intended to be listened to, but gypsy music is often accompanied by dancing.

MEHTER: MUSIC OF THE JANISSARIES

Mehter performance

From 1299 until the dissolution of the Janissary corps in 1826, *mehter* music accompanied the armies of the Ottoman empire into battle, with a distinctive marching step to the rhythm of the words, "Gracious God is good. God is compassionate." Today the revived Mehter band performs at the Istanbul Military Museum *(see pp120–21)* and at Topkapı Palace.

Hans and Caravanserais

Carved detail from the Sultanhanı

DOTTED ACROSS ANATOLIA are many *hans* (storage depots) and *caravanserais* (hostelries) built in Seljuk and Ottoman times to protect merchants travelling the caravan routes that crossed Anatolia along the Roman-Byzantine road system. From the 13th century, the Seljuks built more than 100 *hans* to encourage trade. It was under the Ottomans, though, that *hans* and *caravanserais* became a part of the state-sponsored social welfare system and played a key role in expanding Ottoman territory and influence. Several of these facilities can be visited today, and some have been turned into hotels or restaurants.

LOCATOR MAP

← *Major trade routes*

Camel caravans laden with silks and spices from China made their way through Anatolia to the great commercial centre of Bursa (see pp162–7). Slaves from the Black Sea hinterland were another important trading commodity.

Portal of the storage hall

A small mosque raised on arches stands in the centre of the courtyard.

A thick curtain wall surrounded the *caravanserai.*

The central gate provided the only entry to the fortified structure.

The central courtyard, *surrounded by arcades, provided shelter from the hot sun and contained apartments and a* hamam *(Turkish bath) to revive weary travellers.*

Corner turret for defence

The stone bridge over the Köprü River near Antalya was built by the Seljuks near the site of a Roman bridge. The structure has recently been restored.

Barrel-vaulted ceiling

A caravanserai at Mylasa, a bustling commercial centre in western Anatolia, is shown in this 19th-century oil painting by the English artist, Richard Dadd.

The octagonal lantern tower let light into the interior.

THE SULTANHANI

The Sultanhanı, near the central Anatolian city of Aksaray *(see pp292–3)*, is one of the best-preserved Seljuk *caravanserais.* Built between 1226 and 1229 for Sultan Alaeddin Keykubad *(see p250),* the complex consisted of a courtyard surrounded by various amenities – stables, mosque, Turkish bath and accommodation – for the use of travellers, and a covered hall in which trade goods could be safely stored.

Five-aisled storage hall

The Cinci Hanı (see p268) *was an important fixture of the busy trading centre of Safranbolu, which lay on the key Black Sea caravan route.*

Accommodation for travellers was provided in two tiers of rooms.

The Kızlarağası Hanı in İzmir (see p178) *is an Ottoman han dating from 1744. Hans had the same amenities found at a caravanserai, together with storerooms, offices and rows of cell-like workshops, all grouped around a courtyard. The restored Kızlarağası Hanı houses a variety of cafés, shops and craft workshops.*

Customs and Traditions

Turkish customs have been passed down from generation to generation and are integrated into contemporary life. Climate, geography and ethnic background play a significant role, but many customs have their origins in Islam and have changed little over the years. An enduring faith is attached to the blue bead, or *mavi boncuk*, an amulet that protects the wearer from the evil eye. It may be seen dangling wherever good luck is needed.

Mavi boncuk

Religious and social mores dictate separate lives for many men and women, so customs bring them together for celebrations such as weddings, births and rites of passage. Family life is pivotal to Turkish culture, and communities are strengthened by the social and economic ties of the extended family.

In Karagöz *shadow puppet theatre, a cast of stock characters enact satiric themes. The puppets are three-dimensional cut-outs made from camel skin.*

CIRCUMCISION

For the celebration of his *sünnet*, or circumcision ritual, a boy is dressed in the satin uniform of a sergeant major, and his parents throw as lavish a celebration as they can afford. Relatives and friends proffer money as gifts for the young man, and the whole event is often photgraphed for the family album.

Gold coins attached to ribbons

Offerings *pinned to a pillow symbolize the gifts the young man will take into manhood.*

In line with Islamic tradition, *Turkish boys are circumcised between the ages of seven and 10. A lavish uniform is worn for this special occasion.*

VILLAGE WEDDINGS

Celebrations such as weddings may last for several days and involve a number of individual rituals. In the rural areas, families often approve and sanction wedding partners. The bride always has a *çeyiz* (trousseau) comprising lovely, handcrafted articles she and her mother have made for the new home.

Headscarves are worn by many rural women.

Village square (meydan)

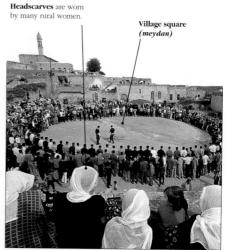

Making flat bread *for the marriage feast is the responsibility of the women of the family. The tradition of making katmer or gözleme (crepes) is being revived in some parts of Turkey.*

Wedding festivities *in the picturesque village of Midyat, near the Syrian border, bring a large and appreciative crowd out to watch dancers performing.*

HANDICRAFTS

Craft skills were handed down from the Ottoman guild system, and Turkey has many skilled craftspeople. One example is *oya*, or needle lace, which is noted for its intricate floral designs crocheted in silk. These were originally crafted for a bride's trousseau. As late as the 1920s, wives crocheted them as part of their husband's headdress. Quilt-making, on the other hand, was traditionally passed down from the father.

Weaving is a rural tradition and done mainly by women. Designs of carpets and kilims (see pp358–9) are handed down from one generation to the next.

***Copper and brass ware**, worked by hand, is an integral part of the Turkish household.*

***Local markets** are the best places to look for traditional crafts. Shown here are handmade linens in Kalkan.*

***Hand-printed textiles**, known as yazma, are a proud and venerable craft tradition in central Anatolian towns such as Tokat.*

***Woodworking skills** were handed down from the Ottomans. Unique wooden walking sticks are made in Devrek, near the Black Sea. These wooden bowls were produced near Adana.*

TRADITIONAL DRESS

Traditionally, Turkish women wove their clothing according to individual designs, and dyed them using plant extracts. Today, each region has its own styles of *şalvar* (trousers worn by women) and head coverings such as *başörtüsü* (scarves).

Printed skirt · Full robe · Decorative headdress

***A group of folk dancers** wear the traditional costume of the Van region. Folk dancing is hugely popular, with regional costumes as much a part of the show as music and laughter.*

NATIONAL SERVICE

All men over the age of 18 must serve 18 months of compulsory military service, and Turkish society still considers this to be a fundamental rite of passage to manhood. For rural youths, this may be their first time away from home, and *askerlik* (military service) fulfils a social role as a bridge to adulthood. The departing conscript may be required to visit friends and relatives to ask forgiveness for any wrongdoings and may be presented with gifts before he reports for duty.

Young soldiers of the Turkish Army on duty

Islamic Art in Turkey

Tile detail

IN ISLAMIC ART, the highest place is held by calligraphy, or the art of beautiful writing. This is because a calligrapher's prime task is writing the Holy Koran, believed by Muslims to be the word of God. In the purest forms of Islam, the use of animal forms in works of art is regarded as detracting from pious thoughts. Thus artists and craftsmen turned their talents to designs featuring geometric motifs and intricate foliage designs known as arabesques. As well as calligraphy, these highly disciplined forms included miniature paintings, jewellery, metal, tiles and ceramics, stone-carving and textiles. Under the Ottomans, the finest creations came from the Nakkaşhane, or sultan's design studio. Here, an apprentice system that lasted up to 10 years maintained the imperial traditions of excellence and innovation.

Calligraphic inscription in embossed metal

Ceramic tile panels contain messages taken from the Koran, executed in Arabic or Kufic script.

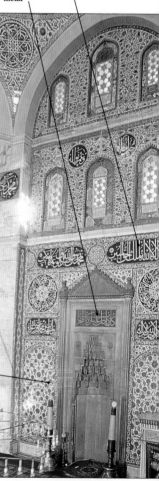

Floral decorations

*The sultan's **tuğra** was his personal monogram, used in place of his signature. It would be drawn by a calligrapher or engraved on a wooden block as a stamp. This example shows the tuğra of Abdül Hamit I (1774–89).*

Ornamental loops

Tile panel featuring plant motifs

Floral tile motif

Koranic texts provided templates for woodcarvers, metal-workers, weavers and ceramic painters. Although highly decorative, Islamic art is filled with meaning: the tulip (lâle), a much-used motif, is an anagram for Allah.

SOKOLLU MEHMET PAŞA MOSQUE, ISTANBUL

Designed by Sinan *(see p101)* in 1570 for a distinguished grand vizier, the oblong prayer hall features a beautiful *qibla* (wall of the mosque at right angles to the direction of Mecca). The calligraphic decoration includes exquisite tilework and stone-carving.

Inscription in metal

**Tilework on
squinches
supporting
the dome**

The minaret *of the Green
Mosque (Yeşil Camii) in İznik
(see p160) features complex
patterns of coloured tiles.
The mosque, which was
completed in 1378, takes
its name from the richly
decorated minaret.*

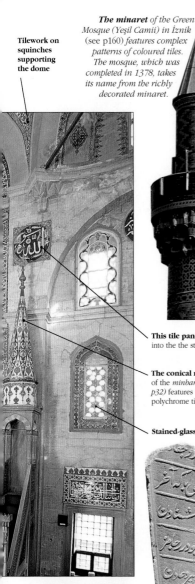

This tile panel is set
into the the stone wall.

The conical roof
of the *minbar (see
p32)* features
polychrome tiling.

Stained-glass windows

An Arabic inscription
*winds around a gravestone
in the grounds of the Alanya
Museum (see p226).*

A tile panel over the entrance
to the Mausoleum of Selim II, in
the precincts of Haghia Sophia
in Istanbul, shows a masterful
integration of calligraphy and
organic motifs.

THE ART OF THE OTTOMAN MINIATURE

Ottoman miniature painting
was primarily a courtly art
form which reached a peak
of development in the late
16th century during the rule
of Süleyman the Magnificent
(see p55). Miniature painting
was influenced by Persian
art, with many of the finest
Persian minaturists being
brought to work at the
court workshops of Topkapı
Palace *(see pp68–71).* As
well as illustrations for
manuscripts of Koranic texts
and Persian epics – Persian
was the language of the
Ottoman court – a unique
style was developed to
record the history of the
dynasty. This included battle
scenes, palace rituals, major
festivals and topographical
scenes. By the 17th century,
miniature painters had
mastered three-dimensional
representation, while the
18th century heralded a
more naturalistic style and a
broadening of subjects to
include landscapes, still lifes
and portraits. Although
there were a number of
celebrated miniature artists,
these exquisite works were,
for the most part, neither
signed nor dated.

**Early 17th-century miniature
showing Hasan, grandson of
Mohammed, on his deathbed**

Ottoman Architecture

İznik tile detail

F ROM ALBANIA TO TRIPOLI, and from Baghdad to Bosnia, the Ottomans left superb examples of their architectural skills. Nowhere is this more apparent than in Istanbul, where the sultans built beautiful mosques, palaces and *külliyes* (Islamic charitable institutions).

Ottoman architecture is marked by a strict hierarchy of forms, scales and materials, reflecting the rank of a building's patron. Mosques commissioned by members of the Ottoman family, for example, were the only ones entitled to two or more minarets. Another distinguishing feature is the influence of Byzantine architecture. Many architects, among them Mimar Sinan *(see p101)*, were of Greek or Armenian origin.

Ornamental fountains *(çeşme) were built in busy central squares or markets. This example is in the bazaar in Kayseri (see pp290–91).*

THE EARLY OTTOMAN MOSQUE

The earliest form of the Ottoman mosque consisted of a single large prayer hall covered by a hemispheric dome, with a covered porch and minaret outside. The Junior Hacı Özbek Mosque (1333) in İznik is considered the earliest example of this form. It was modified by adding bays (often covered by small domes) around the central dome, and by the addition of a covered portico and arcaded courtyard.

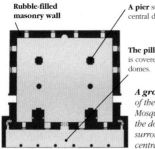

Rubble-filled masonry wall

A pier supports the central dome.

The pillared portico is covered by seven domes.

A ground plan *of the Selimiye Mosque shows the domed bays surrounding the central hall.*

The Selimiye Mosque, *in Konya (see pp250–51), was started in 1558 by Sultan Selim II when he was governor of Konya. It was finished in 1587. Clearly visible is the bulk of the central prayer hall, which is topped by a hemispheric dome. The mosque adjoins the Mevlâna Museum.*

THE LATER OTTOMAN MOSQUE

The form of the Ottoman mosque underwent a dramatic evolution in the years following the conquest of Constantinople. The Ottomans frequently converted Orthodox churches, notably Haghia Sophia *(see pp82–5)*, into mosques. Under the influence of such models, architects began to create higher, single-domed mosques, and greatly open up the interior space.

The Şehzade Mosque *(also called the Prince's Mosque) in Istanbul was the first imperial mosque built by the architect, Mimar Sinan (see p101). It was commissioned in 1543 by Süleyman the Magnificent.*

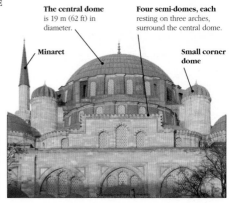

The central dome is 19 m (62 ft) in diameter.

Four semi-domes, each resting on three arches, surround the central dome.

Minaret

Small corner dome

FOUNTAINS (ŞADIRVAN)

Based on the Koranic principle that water is the source of life, the provision of public water supplies was a civic duty. Every town had its *çeşme* (public fountain), and *külliyes* offered *sebil* (free distribution of water). The *şadırvan* was placed in a mosque courtyard for the performance of ritual ablutions.

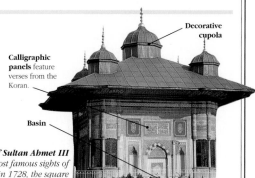

Decorative cupola

Calligraphic panels feature verses from the Koran.

Basin

The Fountain of Sultan Ahmet III is one of the most famous sights of Istanbul. Built in 1728, the square structure has basins on all sides.

THE KONAK

Like many other Ottoman buildings, the *konak* (mansion house) consisted of a wooden structure built on a foundation of stone and brick to withstand the cold Anatolian winter. The ground floor contained granaries, stables and storage areas. The kitchens and public rooms were on the first floor, with the private quarters on the top floor.

Pitched roof

Wooden upper floor

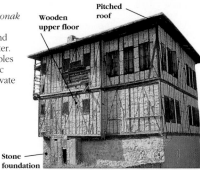

Living areas *had sofas (upholstered benches) along the walls. The nook shown here is in a konak that has been turned into a hotel in Safranbolu (see pp268–9).*

Stone foundation

A rural konak *in northern Turkey shows the typical three-storey form. Some had separate entrances for the harem (women's quarters) and selamlık (men's quarters).*

YALI

The *yalı* (waterfront villa), is found along the Bosphorus. Most *yalıs* were built during the 18th and 19th centuries as grand summer residences for wealthy citizens of Ottoman Istanbul. Sited to make maximum use of the waterside location, they also incorporated boathouses or moorings.

Wood was the main building material.

Decorative pilasters

The waterside location provided easy access and maximum visibility.

Yalıs were built *in a variety of forms and architectural styles, from simple wooden structures to this lavish Russian-style mansion.*

BUILDING TYPES

Bedesten Covered stone market

Çeşme Public water fountain

Daruşşifa Hospital

Hamam Bath house *(see p77)*

İmaret Soup kitchen

Külliye Educational/charitable complex surrounding a major mosque *(see pp32–3)*

Medrese Theological college *(see pp32–3)*

Mescit Small prayer hall

Tekke Monastery

Tımarhane Lunatic asylum

Türbe Tomb

Exploring Mosques

FIVE TIMES A DAY throughout Istanbul a chant is
broadcast over loudspeakers set high in the city's
minarets to call the faithful to prayer. Over 99 per cent
of the population is Muslim, though the Turkish state
is officially secular. Most belong to the Sunni branch
of Islam, but there are also a few Shiites. Both follow
the teachings of the Koran, the sacred book of Islam,
and the Prophet Mohammed (c.570–632), but Shiites
accept, in addition, the authority of a line of 12 imams
directly descended from Mohammed. Islamic mystics
are known as Sufis (*see p255*).

**Overview of the impressive
Süleymaniye Mosque complex**

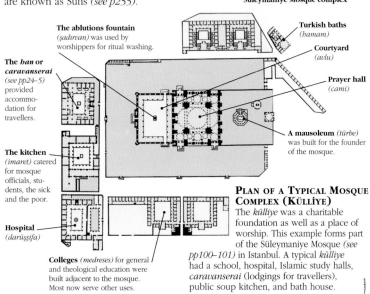

The ablutions fountain
(*şadırvan*) was used by
worshippers for ritual washing.

Turkish baths
(*hamam*)

Courtyard
(*avlu*)

**The *han* or
caravanserai**
(*see pp24–5*)
provided
accommo-
dation for
travellers.

Prayer hall
(*cami*)

A mausoleum (*türbe*)
was built for the founder
of the mosque.

The kitchen
(*imaret*) catered
for mosque
officials, stu-
dents, the sick
and the poor.

Hospital
(*darüşşifa*)

PLAN OF A TYPICAL MOSQUE COMPLEX (KÜLLİYE)

The *külliye* was a charitable
foundation as well as a place of
worship. This example forms part
of the Süleymaniye Mosque (*see
pp100–101*) in Istanbul. A typical *külliye*
had a school, hospital, Islamic study halls,
caravanserai (lodgings for travellers),
public soup kitchen, and bath house.

Colleges (*medreses*) for general
and theological education were
built adjacent to the mosque.
Most now serve other uses.

INSIDE A MOSQUE

The prayer hall of a great mosque can offer
visitors a soaring sense of space. Islam
forbids images of living things (human or
animal) inside a mosque, so there are never
any statues or figurative paintings, but the
geometric and abstract architectural details
of the interior can be exquisite. Men and
women pray separately. Women often
use a screened-off area or a balcony.

The müezzin mahfili *is a platform found in
large mosques. The muezzin (mosque official)
stands on this when chanting responses to the
prayers of the imam (head of the mosque).*

The mihrab, *a niche
in the wall, marks the
direction of Mecca.
The prayer hall is laid
out so that most people
can see the mihrab.*

The minbar *is a lofty
pulpit to the right of the
mihrab. This is used by
the imam when he
delivers the Friday
sermon* (khutba).

MUSLIM BELIEFS AND PRACTICES

Muslims believe in God (Allah), and the Koran shares many prophets and stories with the Bible. However, whereas for Christians Jesus is the son of God, Muslims hold that he was just one in a line of prophets – the last being Mohammed, who brought the final revelation of God's truth to mankind. Muslims believe that Allah communicated the sacred texts of the Koran to Mohammed through the archangel Gabriel.

Muslims have five basic duties. The first of these is the profession of faith: "There is no God but Allah, and Mohammed is his Prophet". Muslims are also enjoined to pray five times a day, give alms to the poor, and fast during the month of Ramazan *(see p36)*. Once during their lifetime, if they can afford it, they should make the pilgrimage *(haj)* to Mecca (in Saudi Arabia), the site of the Kaaba, a sacred shrine built by Abraham, and also the birthplace of the Prophet.

The call to prayer *used to be given by the muezzin from the balcony of the minaret. Nowadays loudspeakers broadcast the call. Only imperial mosques have more than one minaret.*

PRAYER TIMES

The five daily prayer times are calculated according to the times of sunrise and sunset, and thus change throughout the year. Exact times are posted on boards outside large mosques. Those given here are a guide.

Prayer	Summer	Winter
Sabah	5am	7am
Öğle	1pm	1pm
İkindi	6pm	4pm
Akşam	8pm	6pm
Yatsı	9:30pm	8pm

Ritual ablutions *must be undertaken before prayer. Worshippers wash their head, hands and feet either at the fountain in the courtyard or at taps set in a wall of the mosque.*

When praying*, Muslims face the Kaaba in Mecca, even if they are not in a mosque, where the mihrab indicates the right direction. Kneeling and lowering the head to the ground are gestures of humility and respect for Allah.*

VISITING A MOSQUE

Visitors are welcome at any mosque in Turkey, but non-Muslims should avoid visiting at prayer times, especially the main weekly congregation and sermon on Fridays at 1pm. Take off your shoes before entering the prayer hall. Shoulders and knees should be covered. Men must remove their hats. Women need to cover their hair, so take a light scarf when sightseeing. Do not eat, take photographs with a flash or stand very close to worshippers. A contribution to a donation box or mosque official is courteous.

Board outside a mosque giving times of prayers

The loge (hünkar mahfili) *provided the sultan with a screened-off balcony where he could pray, safe from would-be assassins.*

The kürsü*, seen in some mosques, is a throne used by the imam while he reads extracts from the Koran.*

TURKEY THROUGH THE YEAR

URKEY'S national and regional holidays fall into three categories: religious feasts celebrated throughout the Islamic world, festivities associated with events or people in Turkish history, and traditional festivals, usually with a seasonal theme. The joyful spirit is tangible on public holidays and religious feast days when old and young, rich and poor unite and extended families gather.

Folk dancers

Regional events celebrate Turkey's diverse origins in terms of music, folklore, sport and the performing arts. Urban centres like İzmir and Istanbul host well-publicized festivals, but smaller towns also stage lively celebrations. *Luna park* (fun fairs) are wildly popular. The passage of the seasons is important, as many venues are outdoors. In the eastern provinces, harsh winters restrict the types of events that can be staged.

SPRING

THIS IS THE BEST season for visiting Turkey. Temperatures are comfortable and the days longer and warmer. Many places receive a facelift after winter and restaurants arrange their tables outdoors. This is also the time to see Turkey's wild flower displays. Most tourist attractions, such as the historic sights, are far less crowded and thus more peaceful at this time of year.

Turkish children paying their respects to the memory of Atatürk

MARCH

International Film Festival *(late Mar–mid-Apr)*, Istanbul. Various cinemas in the city screen a selection of Turkish and foreign films.

APRIL

Tulip Festival *(late Apr)*, Emirgan, Istanbul. A colourful celebration of the flower that originated in Turkey, held in a chic suburb north of the Fatih Bridge.

Tulips in Emirgan Park, scene of the Tulip Festival in spring

National Sovereignty and Children's Day *(23 Apr)*. Anniversary of the first Grand National Assembly that convened in Ankara in 1920. Children from all around Turkey commemorate the life of the revered Atatürk.

ANZAC Day *(24–25 Apr)*, Çanakkale and Gallipoli Peninsula *(see pp168–9)*. Representatives from Australia, New Zealand and Turkey commemorate the courage in battle displayed by both sides in World War I.

MAY

Yunus Emre Culture and Art Week *(6–10 May)*, Eskişehir *(see p257)*. A week-long commemoration of the life and devotional love poetry of the 13th-century mystic, Yunus Emre.

Marmaris International Yachting Festival *(2nd week in May)*, at Marmaris *(see pp200–201)*. Mainly a convention for yacht owners, brokers and buyers, this event fills the marina with all kinds of vessels and is sure to appeal to anyone interested in yachting.

Memorial at Gallipoli

National Youth and Sports Day *(19 May)*. Celebrated all over the country to mark Atatürk's birthdate in 1881 and the anniversary of his arrival in the town of Samsun *(see p265)* in 1919 to plan the War of Independence.

Conquest of Istanbul *(May 29)*, Istanbul. The anniversary of Constantinople's capture by Sultan Mehmet the Conqueror in 1453.

Cirit Games *(May–Sep; see September p36)*.

Turkey's beaches, popular with locals and visitors in summer

SUMMER

Turks take their holidays seriously, and summer sees coastal areas of the Aegean and Mediterranean, in particular, crowded with university students and families on the move. Those city-dwellers lucky enough to own a summer house usually move to the coast to escape the oppressive heat when the school holidays begin in June.

Turkey's beaches offer opportunities for all kinds of activities, and resorts such as Bodrum and Marmaris are renowned for their active nightlife. Be on the look-out for impromptu festivals involving grease-wrestling or folk dancing, for example. Although local tourist offices have information on events in their area, these may not be well publicized and full details may be unavailable until just prior to the event.

JUNE

Hittite Festival *(15–20 Jun)*, Çorum *(see p294)*. Students of Hittite art and culture and enthusiasts from around the globe gather for this annual event to attend lectures, debates and related outings.
Lycia Culture and Art Festival *(last week Jun)*, Kaş *(see p214)*. Renowned for its superb performances of contemporary dance and theatre, as well as painting exhibitions. There are also street performances and many other art events.

Kafkasör Culture and Arts Festival *(last half of Jun)*, Artvin *(see p275)*. A festival in an alpine meadow that offers country handicrafts, folk dancing and singing, as well as bull wrestling.
Istanbul Festival of Arts and Culture *(mid-Jun–mid-Jul)*, venues around the city. A prestigious event for opera, theatre and ballet performances. Both Turkish and Western classical music are featured and the highlight is a one-night performance of Mozart's *Abduction from the Seraglio*, which is authentically staged at the Topkapı Palace.
International Opera and Ballet Festival *(Jun–mid-Jul)*, Aspendos *(see p221)*. The Roman theatre is the venue for thrilling, open-air performances of opera, ballet

International Opera and Ballet Festival poster, Aspendos

and orchestral music. Visitors can enjoy a picnic at the site before performances.
International İzmir Festival *(mid-Jun–mid-Jul)*, İzmir *(see pp178–9)*. On at the same time as the Istanbul Festival of Arts and Culture, this event offers the same programme for connoisseurs of music, ballet and theatre. Performances also take place at Çeşme and Ephesus.

JULY

Navy Day *(1 Jul)*. This holiday has some symbolism for Turks as it commemorates the anniversary of the end of the capitulations, or trade concessions, granted by the Ottoman sultans to a number of European powers from the mid-16th century onwards.
Kırkpınar Festival and Grease Wrestling Championship *(usually first week Jul)*, Edirne *(see pp152–3)*. A popular event with men, in which the contenders, in *kıspet* (leather breeches) and smeared with olive oil, compete for the coveted honour in this traditional national sport.

Grease-wrestling tournament

AUGUST

Troy Festival *(10–15 Aug)*, Çanakkale *(see p174)*. Dance, theatre and art events that attract foreign performers.
Hacı Bektaş Commemorative Ceremony *(mid-Aug)*, Avanos *(see p283)*. Held in remembrance of Hacı Bektaş Veli, the mystic and philosopher who founded an Islamic sect based on unity and human tolerance.
Victory Day *(30 Aug)*. This day, known as Zafer Bayramı, is celebrated throughout Turkey. It is an important anniversary that celebrates the victory of the Turkish Republican army over the Greeks at the battle of Dumlupınar in 1922 during the War of Independence.

Racing yachts competing in Marmaris Race Week

AUTUMN

AUTUMN IS AN IDEAL time for visiting Turkey. The rural regions have grape or wine festivals and many villages celebrate their successful harvests of wheat, apricots, cotton or other crops. In coastal regions, the sea is still quite warm and watersports can continue well into October. Along the south coast, warm weather can last until quite late in November.

Watermelon cart, Diyarbakır

SEPTEMBER

Cirit Games *(May–Sep)*, Erzurum *(see pp316–37)*. Cirit originated with nomads from Central Asia. It is a rough-and-tumble cross between

Horse and rider at the Cirit Games in Erzurum

polo and javelin-throwing in which horse and rider enjoy equal prestige. The games take place every Sunday.
Tango Festival *(second week in Sep)*, in Marmaris *(see pp200–201)*. An unusual six-day event in which couples follow the lead of professional dance couples and also participate in boat tours, street dancing, and other activities.
Watermelon Festival *(16–23 Sep)*, Diyarbakır *(see pp308–309)*. One of only a few festivals in eastern Turkey, this one revolves around the gigantic watermelons grown by the local farmers.
Cappadocia Grape Harvest Festival *(mid-Sep)*, Ürgüp *(see p283)*. Celebration of local food and wine in an area that has been called the birthplace of viticulture.

OCTOBER

Golden Orange Film Festival *(first week Oct)*, Antalya *(see pp218–19)*. Recently, Turkish-language films and those with a local flavour have begun to feature more prominently in this annual festival that has been going for over 20 years.
International Bodrum Cup Regatta *(third week of Oct)*, Bodrum *(see pp198–9)*. This regatta is open to several

classes of wooden yachts only. Both Turkish and foreign yachtsmen compete.
Race Week *(last week Oct to first week Nov)*, Marmaris *(see pp200–201)*. In- and offshore races held in three divisions under authority of the Turkish Sailing Federation. There is also a fancy-dress night, and cocktail and dinner parties.
Republic Day *(29 Oct)*. This important national holiday commemorates the proclamation of the Turkish Republic in 1923.

NOVEMBER

Atatürk Commemoration Day *(10 Nov)*. Atatürk's death in 1938 is recalled each year with a poignant one-minute silence. This show of respect is observed throughout the country at 9:05am, the exact moment the revered leader passed away in Istanbul's Dolmabahçe Palace *(see pp122–3)*. Everything in the country grinds to a halt – people and even the traffic stops – and visitors are advised to follow suit.

MUSLIM HOLIDAYS

The dates of the Muslim calendar and its holy days are governed by the phases of the moon and therefore change from year to year. In the holy month of **Ramazan**, Muslims do not eat or drink between dawn and dusk. Some restaurants are closed during the day and tourists should be discreet when eating in public. Straight after this follows the three-day **Şeker Bayramı** (Sugar Festival), when sweet-meats are prepared. Two months and 10 days later, a four-day celebration, **Kurban Bayramı** (Feast of the Sacrifice), commemorates the Koranic version of Abraham's sacrifice. This is the main annual public holiday in Turkey, and hotels, trains and roads are packed.

Whirling dervishes at the Mevlevi Monastery in Istanbul

WINTER

WHEN THE STREET vendors begin roasting chestnuts in Ankara and Istanbul, it is a sign that winter is near. Both cities can be damp and cold. Ankara frequently has temperatures below freezing and much snow. This is when coastal regions have their rainy season. Winter is a good time for visitors to explore Turkey's museums, as major sights are open and uncrowded. The ski centres *(see p362)* at Palandöken *(see p317)* and Uludağ *(see p157)* have their busiest season from December to April, and offer activities both on and off the slopes.

Turks do not celebrate Christmas, but most hotel chains offer a special menu on the day. New Year's Day, however, is an official holiday throughout Turkey. It is celebrated heartily in restaurants and at home, and a lavish meal is served. Often the main course is turkey! Visitors are always welcome to join in these celebrations, but advance booking is advisable for popular places. Some establishments that close for the winter open again just for the New Year's Eve celebrations.

DECEMBER

St Nicholas Symposium and Festival *(first week Dec)*, Demre *(see p216)*. Visitors who have an interest in the legend of Santa Claus will not want to miss this symposium and the discussions and ceremonies that accompany it. A host of related debates is organized, and pilgrimages are made to the 4th century church of St Nicholas in Demre, located near Antalya, and to the birthplace of Nicholas in Patara, near Kaş.
Mevlâna Festival *(10–17 Dec)*, Konya *(see pp250–51)*. A festival that commemorates Celaleddin Rumi *(see p255)*, the mystic who founded the Mevlevi order. This is the only time that the whirling dervishes are in residence in their home city and offers one of the best performances anywhere in Turkey.

JANUARY

New Year's Day *(1 Jan)*. A national holiday.
Camel Wrestling *(mid-Jan)*, Selçuk *(see p180)*. Premier championship event held in the ruined Roman theatre at Ephesus *(see pp182–3)*.

FEBRUARY

Camel Wrestling *(through Feb)*, Aydın, İzmir and other Aegean towns. Impromptu camel wrestling bouts *(deve güreşi)* that coincide with the mating season (Dec–Feb), after which male camels become docile again.

A champion camel, adorned with tassels and rugs

NATIONAL HOLIDAYS

New Year's Day (1 Jan)
National Sovereignty and Children's Day *Ulusal Egemenlik ve Çocuk Bayramı* (23 Apr)
National Youth and Sports Day *Gençlik ve Spor Günü* (19 May)
Conquest of Istanbul (May 29)
Navy Day *Denizcilik Günü* (1 Jul)
Victory Day *Zafer Bayramı* (30 Aug)
Republic Day *Cumhuriyet Bayramı* (29 Oct)
Atatürk Commemoration Day (10 Nov)

New Year's celebrations in Istanbul

The Climate of Turkey

TURKEY'S MOUNTAINOUS terrain and maritime influence have created diverse climatic regions. The Aegean and Mediterranean coasts enjoy mean temperatures of 29°C (84°F) in July and 9°C (48°F) in January. Rain falls mainly in winter; Antalya receives an annual average of 991 mm (39 in). Along the Black Sea, rainfall is heavier, averaging 2,438 mm (96 in) a year. The rugged northeast has warm summers, but severe winters, with temperatures averaging -9°C (16°F). Precipitation is more evenly spread throughout the year, and snow lasts 120 days. The central plateau has hot, dry summers averaging 23°C (73°F) and cold, moist winters, when temperatures average below 0°C (32°F).

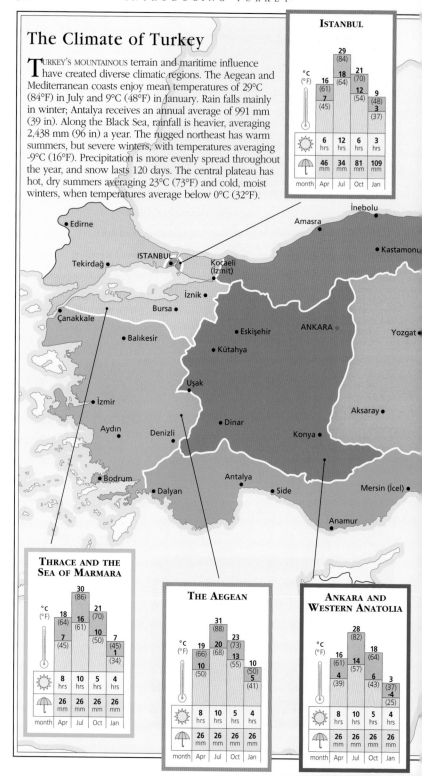

ISTANBUL

°C (°F)				
		29 (84)		
	16 (61)	18 (64)	21 (70)	
	7 (45)		12 (54)	9 (48)
				3 (37)
☼	6 hrs	12 hrs	6 hrs	3 hrs
☂	46 mm	34 mm	81 mm	109 mm
month	Apr	Jul	Oct	Jan

İnebolu
Edirne
Amasra
Kastamonu
Tekirdağ
ISTANBUL
Kocaeli (İzmit)
İznik
Bursa
Çanakkale
Eskişehir
ANKARA
Yozgat
Balıkesir
Kütahya
Uşak
İzmir
Aksaray
Aydın
Denizli
Dinar
Konya
Bodrum
Antalya
Dalyan
Side
Mersin (İcel)
Anamur

THRACE AND THE SEA OF MARMARA

°C (°F)				
		30 (86)		
	18 (64)	16 (61)	21 (70)	
	7 (45)		10 (50)	7 (45)
				1 (34)
☼	8 hrs	10 hrs	5 hrs	4 hrs
☂	26 mm	26 mm	26 mm	26 mm
month	Apr	Jul	Oct	Jan

THE AEGEAN

°C (°F)				
		31 (88)		
	19 (66)	20 (68)	23 (73)	
	10 (50)		13 (55)	10 (50)
				5 (41)
☼	8 hrs	10 hrs	5 hrs	4 hrs
☂	26 mm	26 mm	26 mm	26 mm
month	Apr	Jul	Oct	Jan

ANKARA AND WESTERN ANATOLIA

°C (°F)				
		28 (82)		
	16 (61)	14 (57)	18 (64)	
	4 (39)		6 (43)	3 (37)
				-4 (25)
☼	8 hrs	10 hrs	5 hrs	4 hrs
☂	26 mm	26 mm	26 mm	26 mm
month	Apr	Jul	Oct	Jan

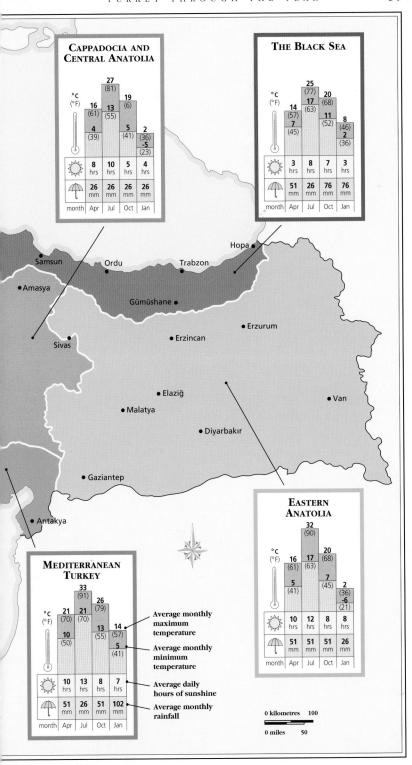

CAPPADOCIA AND CENTRAL ANATOLIA

°C (°F)				
	16 (61)	27 (81)	19 (6)	
	4 (39)	13 (55)	5 (41)	2 (36)
				-5 (23)
☀	8 hrs	10 hrs	5 hrs	4 hrs
☂	26 mm	26 mm	26 mm	26 mm
month	Apr	Jul	Oct	Jan

THE BLACK SEA

°C (°F)				
	14 (57)	25 (77)	20 (68)	8 (46)
	7 (45)	17 (63)	11 (52)	2 (36)
☀	3 hrs	8 hrs	7 hrs	3 hrs
☂	51 mm	26 mm	76 mm	76 mm
month	Apr	Jul	Oct	Jan

Hopa ·
Samsun · Ordu · Trabzon ·
Amasya ·
Gümüşhane ·
Erzurum ·
Sivas · Erzincan ·
Elazığ · Van ·
Malatya ·
Diyarbakır ·
Gaziantep ·
Antakya ·

EASTERN ANATOLIA

°C (°F)				
	16 (61)	32 (90)	20 (68)	
	5 (41)	17 (63)	7 (45)	2 (36)
				-6 (21)
☀	10 hrs	12 hrs	8 hrs	8 hrs
☂	51 mm	51 mm	51 mm	26 mm
month	Apr	Jul	Oct	Jan

MEDITERRANEAN TURKEY

°C (°F)				
	21 (70)	33 (91)	26 (79)	14 (57)
	10 (50)	21 (70)	13 (55)	5 (41)
☀	10 hrs	13 hrs	8 hrs	7 hrs
☂	51 mm	26 mm	51 mm	102 mm
month	Apr	Jul	Oct	Jan

Average monthly maximum temperature
Average monthly minimum temperature
Average daily hours of sunshine
Average monthly rainfall

0 kilometres 100
0 miles 50

THE HISTORY OF TURKEY

THE HISTORY OF TURKEY *is as ancient as that of humankind. Known as Anatolia and previously as Asia Minor, this land has witnessed the rise and fall of many great and advanced civilizations, from the early Hittites to the Persians, Lydians, Greeks, Romans, Byzantines and Ottomans. A singular heritage of splendid art and architecture bears the mark of an often tumultuous past.*

Long before great empires such as the Persian, Roman, Byzantine and Ottoman began to exploit the strategic position of Asia Minor, important ancient civilizations flourished in the fertile river valleys, on the windswept, arid interior plains and along the southern coastline of Anatolia.

The early communities were replaced by successive waves of migration that saw the rise and fall of new cultures, each of which left reminders of its dominance and glory and contributed to the astoundingly varied cultural tapestry that forms the basis of today's proud, modern republic.

Female figurine, Alacahöyük (c.1270 BC)

PREHISTORIC TURKEY

Stone tools as well as various other crude artifacts, animal bones and food fossils from the Old Stone Age that were found near Burdur north of Antalya *(see pp218–19),* prove that people have lived in Turkey since 20,000 BC. The earliest inhabitants were nomadic hunter-gatherers who migrated in response to changing weather patterns and seasons. They followed the wild animal herds they depended upon for their sustenance, clothing, tools and weapons.

THE FERTILE CRESCENT

The earliest permanent settlers were the prehistoric farming communities of Mesopotamia, living in the well-watered stretch of land between the Tigris and Euphrates rivers in what is now northern Syria and Iraq.

Around 10,000 BC groups of people began to settle in Anatolia, where they raised crops of wheat and barley. They also kept domestic animals such as sheep, goats and cattle, and used dogs to protect and herd their livestock. These early farmers were the first to venture beyond the boundaries of the Fertile Crescent, establishing communities along the Mediterranean and Red Sea, as well as around the Persian Gulf. Here, the archaeological remains of Neolithic villages date back to 8000 BC, and by 7000 BC countless thriving settlements had sprung up.

It was during this period that people discovered how to smelt metal and work with it. They developed methods of extracting and casting various useful objects such as weapons, as well as ornamental items. The earliest items cast from copper were made in Anatolia around 5000 BC.

TIMELINE

20,000 BC Old Stone Age settlement north of Antalya			*Hand axe* 		**10,000 BC** End of Old Stone Age in Anatolia	
20,000 BC	18,000 BC	16,000 BC	14,000 BC	12,000 BC	10,000 BC	8000 BC
Flint spear tips	**17,000 BC** Paleolithic hunter-gatherers fashion flint spear tips				**9000 BC** Emergence of modern humans in Anatolia	

◁ **Constantine IX Monomachus, ruler of the Byzantine Empire from 1042 to 1055**

THE FIRST TOWN

Together with Hacılar, Çatalhöyük (see p254) near Konya was possibly the world's first town. It had a population of around 5,000 people and is thought to have been the largest settlement at the time. Most of its inhabitants were farmers, but there was also brisk trade in obsidian (volcanic glass), brought into workshops from nearby volcanoes and used to fashion sharp cutting tools.

Archaeologists have been able to determine with certainty that Çatalhöyük's houses were sturdy structures built of brick and timber. The architectural designs also reflect the demands of an advanced culture that valued comfort. They typically feature separate living quarters and cooking areas, as well as several sheds and a number of store rooms.

Flint dagger with bone handle

Cattle seem to have played a rather important part in this ancient culture of Anatolia. This is evident from the fact that many of the rooms that were excavated at Çatalhöyük were decorated with elaborate wall paintings depicting cows, as well as clay heads with real horns moulded in relief onto the walls. Since Çatalhöyük's people had animistic beliefs, it has been suggested that the murals and bull's-head emblems could point to the practice of ritual or cult activities. Similarly, small terracotta figurines of a voluptuous female deity (the mother goddess) probably played a part in fertility rites, offerings or other religious ceremonies.

THE COPPER AGE

By the Copper Age (from about 5500 to 3000 BC), farming had become a way of life and people were raising crops and animals for a living. The increase in agricultural activity created a growing need for tools and implements. Methods for ore extraction and smelting were refined and passed on from father to son. Copper implements were widely used. Focal points of this period were Hacılar and Canhasan, both of which also manufactured fine pottery items, using advanced techniques. Their attractive clay vessels were decorated with distinctive multicoloured backgrounds.

THE BRONZE AGE

Between 3000–1200 BC, the Anatolian metalworkers began to experiment with various techniques and developed new skills. Their workshops produced a surplus of goods and a brisk trade began to flourish. Among these items were gold jewellery, ornaments, belts, drinking vessels and statuettes of the mother goddess.

Artist's impression of Çatalhöyük, possibly the world's first town

TIMELINE

8000 BC	7000 BC	6000 BC	5000 BC

8000 BC Start of the Neolithic period in Anatolia

Statuette of mother goddess, Çatalhöyük

5600 BC Fertility figurines made of terracotta at Hacılar and Çatalhöyük

7250–7500 BC Community at Cayonu near Diyarbakır farms with sheep and goats

6800 BC Çatalhöyük develops into a farming town of 5,000 people

Terracotta jar from Canhasan

5000 BC Pottery begins to combine functionality with attractive design

THE ASSYRIANS

The empire of Assyria developed in northern Mesopotamia sometime in the 3rd millennium BC. It expanded and, by about 1900 BC, a network of Assyrian trading colonies had been established. Commerce between northern Mesopotamia and Anatolia began to take shape.

As trade goods circulated, the demand for them quickly grew and merchants found themselves catering to a rapidly expanding market.

The Assyrians grasped the importance of keeping track of their transactions, and developed a writing system using cuneiform symbols to represent words. Their trade agreements and accounts were imprinted on clay tablets, several of which have been preserved. The commercial records that were found at the Assyrian trading colony at Kanesh (modern Kültepe, *see p291*)

Assyrian clay 'letter' and envelope

are the earliest examples of writing to have been discovered in Anatolia.

Lively trade meant increased travel and demands on transport. Some areas saw the introduction of simple taxation systems. For the first time in history, money came to be regarded as the primary source of wealth, and envy, conflict and violence ensued as communities sought to protect territories, routes and resources from outsiders.

Not all inhabitants of the area presently occupied by Turkey gathered in central Anatolia. The city of Troy, immortalized by Homer and Virgil, stood at the strategic entrance to the Dardanelles Straits (*see p168*). Some scholars believe that the fall of Troy, as told in Homer's *Iliad*, coincides with the end of the Bronze Age, an era that had helped to establish an artistic and civilized culture in which the next civilization, the Hittites, would thrive and flourish.

HELEN OF TROY

According to Greek mythology Helen was the most beautiful woman of the ancient world. She was the daughter of King Tyndareus and Leda, who had been seduced by Zeus. In childhood, Helen was abducted by Theseus, who hoped to marry her when the time came. After having been rescued by her twin brothers Castor and Pollux, King Tyndareus decreed that Helen should marry the man of her choice. Helen chose Menelaus, king of Sparta, and lived happily at his side until she met Paris. Her elopement with the Trojan prince resulted in a heated battle between Greece and Troy as Menelaus fought to free his wife. After nine years of futile warfare Menelaus and Paris agreed to meet in single combat. Paris died as a result of his wounds; the victorious Menelaus reclaimed his Helen and returned with her to Sparta, where they lived happily to an old age.

Beautiful Helen of Troy with Paris

4000–3000 BC Settlement at Alacahöyük flourishes		3000 BC Beginning of Bronze Age in Anatolia; Troy, Ephesus and Smyrna become important cities		1900 BC Brisk trade by Assyrian trading colonies	
	Gold cup, Alacahöyük				
4000 BC		**3000 BC**		**2000 BC**	
	3900 BC Cities begin to emerge and a simple form of writing develops	2500 BC Hatti civilization establishes city kingdoms	1900–2000 BC Arrival of Hittites from the Caucasus; rise of Hittite empire	*Assyrian cylinder seal made of serpentine*	

THE HITTITES

Historians are uncertain about the origins of the Hittites and how they got to Anatolia. It is clear that they arrived some time during the second millennium BC and were established at the time of the Assyrian trading colonies. Theirs was the first powerful empire to arise in Anatolia. Its capital was at Hattuşaş, present-day Boğazkale *(see pp296–7)*.

The Hittite language, which was written in both cuneiform script and hieroglyphics, is believed to be the oldest of the Indo-European languages and was deciphered only in 1915. A large collection of Hittite writings was discovered at Hattuşaş. It contained cuneiform texts on various subjects, such as religious rituals, omens, myths and prayers, as well as the writings of Anitta, an early Hittite king. The library is today preserved in the archives at Boğazkale.

Remains of Hittite relief, Boğazkale

Religion played an important role in the daily lives of the Hittites. They worshipped the "Thousand Gods of the Land of Hatti", an impressive pantheon led by the weather god Taru and his wife, the sun goddess Wurushemu.

An advanced people, Hittites knew the art of forging iron, an advantage that made them a powerful military force and allowed them to use horses and chariots in warfare. Their cuneiform texts also revealed a complex legal system and the fair treatment of criminals and prisoners.

King Anitta conquered large parts of central Anatolia, including the Assyrian trading colony at Kanesh. His conquests increased the might of the kingdom, but also led to decentralization. The empire splintered into several city-states, until King Huzziya began to reunite the independent elements and fought to regain parts of Anatolia.

King Huzziya's successor, Labarna Hattushili I, is considered to be the founder of the Old Hittite Empire. He had his eye on wealthy Syria, then an important centre of trade, crafts and agriculture, and in an effort to annex its city-states he began to extend his campaigns into northern Syria. One of his grandsons finally managed to conquer Babylon around 1530 BC, but the constant wars made expansion difficult, and in general, Hittite rulers repeatedly gained, lost and regained territories throughout the duration of their empire.

GOLDEN AGE OF THE HITTITES

The Hittite empire reached its peak around 1300 BC, when Hattushili II and Ramses II, the ruler of Egypt, signed an agreement of peace and friendship. As a result of this treaty, Hittite culture could flourish and the city of Hattuşaş grew rapidly. The Hittite empire entered its Golden Age. Hattuşaş grew into a large city. It was surrounded by sturdy walls and had an impressive temple and palace complex. The columns of the royal palace

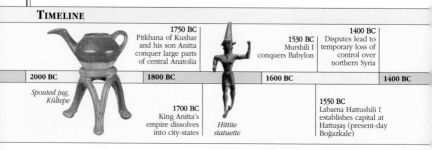

Carved reliefs on the Sphinx Gate at Alacahöyük

TIMELINE

2000 BC	1800 BC	1600 BC	1400 BC

1750 BC Pitkhana of Kushar and his son Anitta conquer large parts of central Anatolia

1530 BC Murshili I conquers Babylon

1400 BC Disputes lead to temporary loss of control over northern Syria

Spouted jug, Kültepe

1700 BC King Anitta's empire dissolves into city-states

Hittite statuette

1550 BC Labarna Hattushili I establishes capital at Hattuşaş (present-day Boğazkale)

were supported on bases in the shape of bulls and lions, while the city gates were decorated with elaborate relief sculptures of fantastic sphinxes and armed gods.

Relative peace and stability saw a flowering of Hittite culture. Elegant pottery items, metal figures, animal-shaped vessels and stamp seals bearing royal symbols were produced. They also collected the documents in picture and

Croesus, the wealthy king of the Lydians

cuneiform script that now provide valuable information about their culture for archaeologists. According to records written at the time, Hittite kingdoms flourished throughout Anatolia.

DECLINE OF THE HITTITES

In the early 12th century BC, the Sea Peoples migrated from the eastern Mediterranean. These migrations contributed to the collapse of several kingdoms, including that of the Hittites. Around 1220 BC, Mediterranean pirates harried the boundaries of the empire, while the empire was suffering under a terrible famine. Many people died or fled, leaving only vestiges of the former empire in Syria and southern Anatolia. The Assyrians, not affected by the migrations, used the sufferings of the Hittites to their advantage and incorporated many of their kingdoms. The remaining pieces of the former Hittite empire were occupied by the Phrygians, a Balkan tribe, who had invaded from the northwest.

Lydian coin from 700 BC

TOWARDS THE HELLENISTIC AGE

During the 7th century BC, Anatolia gradually became dominated by the Lydians, while the Lycian civilization flourished along the Mediterranean coastline. Their rock tombs (see p215) can still today be seen between Fethiye and Antalya (see pp218–19).

The Lydians, a powerful Hittite-related tribe, settled in western Anatolia. Under the leadership of their king, Croesus, they conquered and annexed many Anatolian city-states around 700 BC. Renowned silversmiths, they are credited with the invention of coinage.

In the meanwhile, the Ionian Renaissance saw a flowering of Greek culture and economy along the Aegean coast. Pioneers from Miletus (see pp190–91) established colonies along the shores of the Mediterranean and Black Sea. City-states such as Knidos and Halicarnassus flourished, setting the stage for the next act in Anatolia's history.

1274 BC War between Syria and Egypt	1000 BC Urartians establish a pic caption state near Lake Van	Assyrian-influenced statue of King Tarhunza	700 BC Remaining Hittite kingdoms annexed by Assyria
1200 BC	**1000 BC**	**800 BC**	
1259 BC War with Egypt ends with the first written peace treaty signed by Ramses II and Hittite king Hattushili II	Urartian gold button		800 BC Phrygians rise to power in central and southeastern Anatolia

The Hellenistic Age

EASTWARD EXPANSION of Greek influence, roughly between 330 BC and 132 BC, was led by Alexander the Great (356–324 BC). After the assassination of his father, Philip II of Macedon, the young Alexander first consolidated his position in Europe and then took on the might of the Persian Empire, which had absorbed most of Anatolia during the 5th century BC. He first **Alexander** invaded Anatolia and Phoenicia, proceeding **the Great** on to Egypt and India, setting up cities and leaving garrisons behind as he went. In Anatolia, the new colonists soon became the ruling class and imposed laws to promote Hellenization.

ALEXANDER'S EMPIRE

→ *Alexander's campaigns*

Sarisses **(spears)** used by the Macedonian phalanx (battle formation) were 5.5 m (18 ft) long.

Pergamum
This artist's impression shows what the hilltop city would have looked like in 200 BC. It depicts the magnitude of Alexander's vision to create Pergamum as the perfect Greek city.

Alexander is on his stallion, Bucephalus.

Perge
The city of Perge, reputedly founded by two Greek seers after the Trojan War, welcomed Alexander the Great in 333 BC and gave him guides for his journey from Phaselis to Pamphylia.

THE BATTLE AT ISSUS

After campaigning in Asia Minor for just one year, Alexander won his first major battle. In November 333 BC, he and the Persian king, Darius III, clashed for the second time. At a mountain pass at Issus (near İskenderun), Macedonian troops managed to encircle the Persian cavalry. When Darius saw Alexander cut through his men and head straight for him, he fled the field leaving his troops in disarray and his mother, wife and children as hostages. Victorious Alexander pressed on to Egypt and then across Persia to the Himalayas until a mutiny by his exhausted soldiers in 324 BC forced him to turn back. He died of a sudden fever in Babylon the following year, at the age of 32.

Alexander Sarcophagus
Dating from the late 4th century BC, this sarco-phagus is named after Alexander because he is depicted in the battle scene friezes. The carvings are regarded as being among the most exquisite examples of Hellenistic art ever discovered.

Gold Octodrachma
This coin was minted by one of Alexander's successors, King Seleukos III of Syria, who ruled from 226–223 BC.

Darius III

Golden chariot

The Lycian Sarcophagus and Harpy Tomb at Xanthos
Xanthos was the chief city of ancient Lycia. Ravaged by the Persians around 540 BC, it was rebuilt and soon regained its former prominence. The Lycian sarcophagus and the Harpy Tomb shown here date from this period. Together with Pinara and many other Lycian cities, Xanthos surrendered to Alexander the Great in 334 BC.

Alexander and the Gordian knot

THE GORDIAN KNOT

Zeus, the father of the gods, had decreed that the people of Phrygia should choose as their king the first person to ride a wagon to his temple. The unlikely candidate, according to legend, was a peasant by the name of Gordius. Hardly able to believe his good fortune, the newly crowned king dedicated his wagon to Zeus, tying it to a pillar of the temple with an intricate knot. A subsequent oracle prophesied that the person who managed to untie it would become ruler of all Asia. That honour fell to Alexander the Great, who cheated the oracle by using his sword to cut the strands.

ROME MOVES EASTWARD

The Roman Republic, established in central Italy around 500 BC, began a rapid expansion to the east during the 2nd century BC. After defeating their old enemies and rivals, the Carthaginians, the Roman armies defeated the Greeks at Corinth and Galatian forces in northern Anatolia. While the Romans were victorious in battle, the civilization of the Greeks in time exerted a great influence on Rome. This led the poet Horace to write *"Graecia capta ferum victorum cept"* (Greece took her fierce conqueror captive).

Marble head of a Greek youth

Greek art and culture dominated the Roman way of life. The Romans even adopted Greek as lingua franca in their newly acquired territories east of the Adriatic Sea.

Roman rule brought the benefits of Roman civilization, such as law, better hygiene and civil engineering. As they advanced, Roman armies built impressive military roads. These were of vital importance for trade. At the height of the Roman empire, it was possible to travel from the Adriatic coast to Syria on well-constructed, wide stone roads. The Stadiusmus (guidepost) monument at Patara (near Kalkan), possibly erected by Claudius, displays an inventory of roads and distances throughout Lycia.

ROMAN EXPANSION

The short-lived empire of Alexander the Great produced a number of successor states, including the Seleucid empire, which controlled much of Anatolia by the 2nd century BC. In two wars, known as the First and Second Macedonian Wars, Rome gained control of key city-states and kingdoms on the Mediterranean coast and in the Anatolian interior. Most submitted without resistance; others were simply handed over. King Atallus III of Pergamum, for example, simply left his kingdom to Rome in 133 BC when he realized that resistance was futile. Those who fought back, such as Mithridates VI of Pontus, were eventually defeated. But the wars against Mithridates marked the beginning of the turbulent Roman civil wars.

In 31 BC, Octavian, the nephew of Julius Caesar, emerged as victor of the civil wars. As a sign of its gratitude, the Roman Senate declared him emperor, and he was henceforth known as Augustus. Apart from extending the Roman territory and reorganizing the army, Octavian also established *colonia*, communal villages for retired soldiers. Examples of these can still be seen today, at Sagalassos and Antiocheia-in-Pisidia (near modern-day Eğirdir).

ROMAN RELIGION

The Romans worshipped an impressive array of gods. The greatest were Jupiter, his wife Juno, Minerva, the goddess of wisdom, and Mars, god of war. Apart from their own deities, the Romans also adopted those of the people they conquered, and allowed the

19th-century depiction of Mithradates VI of Pontus

Cyrus the Great	**546 BC** Sardis, captial of the Lydian Empire, is overthrown by the Persians under Cyrus the Great	**130 BC** The Roman province of Asia is created	*Emperor Hadrian*	**AD 96–180** Five good emperors rule Rome
600 BC	**400 BC**	**200 BC**		**AD 1**
560–546 BC King Croesus rules the Lydian empire	**334 BC** Alexander the Great claims Anatolian peninsula from the Persians	**68 BC** Pompey defeats the pirates *St Paul's Well in Tarsus*	**AD 1** St Paul (Saul of Tarsus) born in Cilicia	

local customs to continue. The people of Anatolia, therefore, continued to perform the fertility rites that were associated with the mother goddess, Cybele. Other, smaller sects and cults also flourished. Mithraism, originating with the Zoroastrian religion that was practised in Persia, was extremely influential, particularly among the soldiers of the Roman army. Many people, especially the poor, were drawn to the popular cult of the Egyptian god, Osiris.

Statuette of the Mother Goddess, Cybele

FIVE GOOD EMPERORS

By the 2nd century AD, peace and order again prevailed in Rome's outlying provinces. At home, the empire prospered under the rule of the "five good emperors" (Nerva, Trajan, Hadrian, Antonius Pius, and Marcus Aurelius with Lucius Verus). During this period of relative peace and prosperity, the Romans endowed their far-flung territories with countless sophisticated aqueducts and *nymphaea* (reservoir systems) to distribute fresh water and remove waste products. Theatres and council chambers were built, as were *stadia* and *gymnasia* to host the popular sporting events. When emperor Hadrian (AD 117–138) toured the remote provinces, the delighted citizens of Attaleia (modern Antalya) *(see p218–9)*, Termessos *(see p220)* and numerous

Hadrian, one of the "five good emperors"

other towns erected elaborate, beautiful memorial arches to honour the emperor and commemorate his visit.

CHRISTIANITY

St Paul, born Saul of Tarsus around AD 1, established the first churches in Asia Minor. Early Christian communities soon came into conflict with Roman authorities when they refused to make sacrifices to the emperor. However, all this changed in the 4th century AD, when Constantine, who ruled from AD 324 to 337, converted to Christianity. His conversion came about just before the Battle of the Milvian Bridge in AD 311, when he had a vision of a flaming cross inscribed with the words "in this sign, conquer".

In AD 324, Constantine founded the city of Constantinople (the site of modern-day Istanbul), and within six years had made it the capital and Christian centre of the empire. Massive walls enclosed its seven hills, and the emperor ordered the construction of a hippodrome, forum and public baths. Coastal cities were plundered for works of art to adorn the new capital, and new settlers were enticed by offers of bread and land. Constantine was succeeded by Theodosius, after whose death the empire was divided into two halves ruled by his sons, Arcadius and Honorius. The division sowed the seeds of Rome's eventual decline.

284–305 Diocletian divides the Roman Empire into east and west	324 Constantine becomes sole ruler of the Roman Empire	*Constantine and his wife, Helen*	641 Constantine III, born Heraclonas in 626, becomes co-ruler at age 15

200	400	600	800

141 Major earthquake in southern Asia Minor	311 Edict of tolerance towards Christianity	330 Constantinople is founded by emperor Constantine	*Justinian*	518 Dynasty of Justinian begins with the rule of Justin (518–527)	716 Treaty signed by Theodosius III and Bulgarian Khan Tervel establishes the border of Thrace

The Byzantine Empire

Greek cross

THE BYZANTINE EMPIRE reached its height under Justinian (AD 527–65), who reconquered much of North Africa, Italy and southern Spain and initiated major building programmes, including the construction of the Haghia Sophia *(see pp82–5)*. Under his rule, Constantinople was endowed with beautiful palaces, churches and public buildings. In the 8th century, the empire became wracked by the iconoclastic dispute, which centred on the role of images in religious life, and its territory steadily shrank under pressure from Arab expansion and the influx of the Seljuk Turks.

THE BYZANTINE EMPIRE

☐ *Extent in AD 565*

CONSTANTINOPLE IN 1200

For almost a thousand years, Constantinople was the richest city in Christendom. At its core were the church of Haghia Sophia, the Hippodrome *(see p90)* and the Great Palace *(see pp92–3)*. In 1204 a Crusader army sacked the city and carried off many of its treasures.

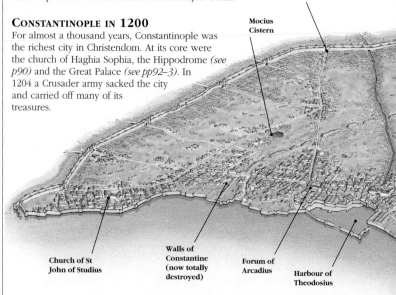

Gate of St Romanus

Mocius Cistern

Church of St John of Studius

Walls of Constantine (now totally destroyed)

Forum of Arcadius

Harbour of Theodosius

BYZANTINE CHURCH ARCHITECTURE

Early Byzantine churches were either basilical (such as St John of Studius, *see p116*) or built to a centralized plan (as in SS Sergius and Bacchus, *see p92*). From the 9th century, churches were built around four corner piers, or columns. Exteriors consisted mostly of unadorned brickwork, but the interiors were lavishly decorated with golden mosaics. Although the Ottoman sultans converted Constantinople's churches into mosques after their conquest of the city, many original features are still clearly discernible today.

TYPICAL LATE BYZANTINE CHURCH

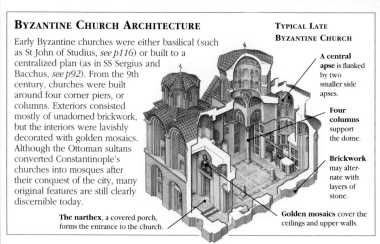

A central apse is flanked by two smaller side apses.

Four columns support the dome.

Brickwork may alternate with layers of stone.

Golden mosaics cover the ceilings and upper walls.

The narthex, a covered porch, forms the entrance to the church.

Walls of Theodosius
The land walls built by Theodosius II withstood many sieges until the Ottoman conquest in 1453.

"Greek Fire"
The Byzantines defended their shores using powerful ships called dromons, *oared vessels from which "Greek fire" (an early form of napalm) could be directed at enemy vessels.*

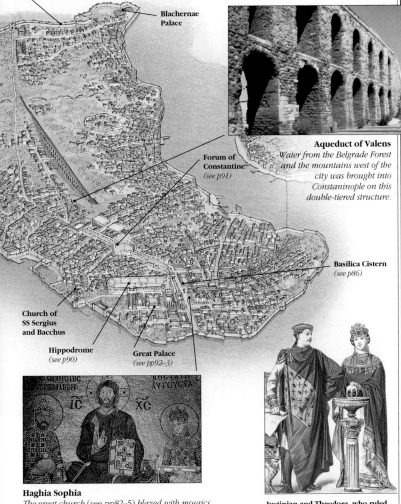

Blachernae Palace

Aqueduct of Valens
Water from the Belgrade Forest and the mountains west of the city was brought into Constantinople on this double-tiered structure.

Forum of Constantine
(see p91)

Basilica Cistern
(see p86)

Church of SS Sergius and Bacchus

Hippodrome
(see p90)

Great Palace
(see pp92–3)

Haghia Sophia
The great church (see pp82–5) blazed with mosaics, including this example showing Christ flanked by the Emperor Constantine IX and Empress Zoe.

Justinian and Theodora, who ruled the Byzantine Empire at its height

ORIGINS OF THE TURKS

The Turkish people are descended from tribes of Central Asian nomads, known as the Turkmen. In the 10th century, some of these tribes moved into Russia, China and India, while others began raiding Byzantine-ruled Anatolia. The attacks increased as the century progressed, until one group, the Seljuks, broke away and gradually began to move eastward.

In the mid-11th century, the Seljuk Turks crossed the Oxus River and invaded Persia. Baghdad fell in 1055, and it was here that Seljuk leader Tuğrul Bey, was crowned caliph – ruler of the Islamic world. Tuğrul Bey established the powerful Great Seljuk Sultanate which ruled much of the Islamic world, including Iran, Central Asia, Iraq, Syria and Palestine, from 1055 until 1156.

Seljuk manuscript depicting Aristotle and disciples

THE SELJUK RUM SULTANATE

Alp Arslan, nephew of Tuğrul Bey, succeeded him as sultan in 1063, and went on to occupy Syria and Armenia, and to launch various raids into Anatolia. In 1071, the Byzantines tried to defeat the Seljuks, but their army was destroyed at the Battle of Manzikert (Malazgirt) on 26 August 1071, a disaster which saw the capture of the emperor, Romanus IV Diogenes.

Romanus IV Diogenes (left), vanquished at Manzikert

Although the victorious Seljuks did not actively seek to govern Anatolia, the vacuum left by the Byzantine defeat resulted in the formation of a series of Islamic-Turkish states. The most famous of these states was the Seljuk Sultanate of Rum (1077–1308), initially based in Nicaea (modern-day İznik) *(see pp160–61)*. Other states established by the Seljuks were those of the Danışman at Sivas (1095–1175) and Saltuks (1080–1201) at Erzurum.

The period from the late 11th to late 12th century was one of turmoil in Anatolia. The arrival of the Crusaders, who seized Nicaea in 1097, and then Antioch (modern Antakya) the following year, altered the balance of power drastically. The Crusader influence was especially pronounced in southern Anatolia, where Crusader knights established the Principality of Antioch and the County of Edessa (centred on modern-day Şanlıurfa). The Seljuks moved their capital to Konya, and the Byzantines tried once more to repel the Seljuks, only to be soundly defeated at the Battle of Myriocephalon in 1176.

Under the rule of Kılıç Arslan II (1156–92), the Seljuk Sultanate of Rum became the most powerful state in Anatolia. The capture of Antalya

Seljuk stone bridge near Aspendos

Under the Rum Seljuks, science and literature flourished, together with painting and sculpture. This cultural renaissance was partly caused by an influx of skilled and educated people fleeing the advance of the Mongols from the east.

(see pp218–19) in 1207 gave access to the Mediterranean, and Seljuk Anatolia prospered. The capture of Sinop in 1214 secured trade across the Black Sea, and the capture of Alanya *(see p226)* in 1221 provided an additional boost to maritime trade.

WEALTH AND PROSPERITY

To consolidate their power, the Seljuks forged trade relations with other states signing agreements with Byzantium, Cyprus, Provence, Pisa, Venice, Florence and Genoa between 1207 and 1253. They constructed bridges to facilitate overland trade and built *hans* and *caravanserais* *(see pp24–5)* to provide shelter for travelling merchants and their goods.

The Seljuk empire reached its peak under Sultan Malik Şah (1072–92), who generously patronized the arts and sciences. Yet the hallmark of Seljuk civilization was their architecture, which reached a peak in the 13th century. The hospital complex at Divriği *(see p317)*, harbour fortifications at Alanya, the Sultanhanı near Aksaray *(see pp24–5)* and the Karatay theological college in Konya *(see pp250–51)* were all built during this efflorescence.

MONGOL DOMINATION

In 1243 Mongol forces defeated the Seljuk army at Kösedağ, and until 1308 the Seljuk sultans were reduced to the status of vassals under the Mongols. During the 13th and 14th centuries, many Christians converted to Islam, because the Mongols offered reduced taxation for Muslims.

The Mongols ruled Anatolia until 1335, when the first Beylik states were set up by rebel Turkmen. These included the Karamanids in the Taurus highlands and the Danişmandids in central Anatolia. However, it was the small emirate of Ertuğrul, based in Eskişehir, that triumphed. Ertuğrul's son, Osman, founded a dynasty known as the Ottomans, and created one of the greatest empires the world has known.

Mongol archers attacking Seljuk cavalry

Crusader

	1131 Sultan Mesut I establishes the Seljuk Rum sultanate with its capital at Konya	1204 Constantinople is besieged, sacked and looted during the Fourth Crusade	1326 Ottoman armies capture Bursa; Orhan Bey is the first Ottoman ruler to call himself sultan
1100		**1200**	**1300**
1100–1400 Start of the Crusades, undertaken to liberate the Holy Land	1176 Defeat of Byzantines at Myriocephalon	1243 Mongol invasion of Anatolia	1299 Osman Bey establishes Ottoman principalities in Söğüt and Domaniç

The Ottoman Empire

THE EXPANSION OF THE Ottoman lands accelerated during the late 13th century. A turning point was Mehmet II's capture of Constantinople in 1453. Constant wars advanced the imperial frontiers deep into the Balkans and the Middle East. Syria and Egypt fell in 1516–17, bringing the holy cities of Mecca and Medina under Ottoman control. By the mid-1500s the Ottoman sultan was the central figure of the (Sunni) Muslim world. The Ottoman Empire, though often associated with excessive opulence, was characterized also by its efficient administration, religious tolerance and immense military power.

Ottoman nargile

THE OTTOMAN EMPIRE

☐ *Maximum extent (1566)*

Osman I
The founder of the Ottoman dynasty ruled a small emirate on the frontiers of the declining Byzantine empire. Expansion of the Ottoman lands began under his son, Orhan.

Foot soldiers were often poorly trained auxiliaries.

The elite Janissaries *(see p56)* were professional soldiers.

Cannons were used in large numbers by the Ottoman armies.

The Fall of Constantinople
Constantinople, the last remnant of Byzantium, fell to the army of Mehmet II on 29 May 1453. This view shows the Turkish camp, and the bridge of boats built to cross the Golden Horn.

Mehmet II (The Conqueror)
The sultan safeguarded freedom of worship and successfully repopulated Constantinople.

Barbarossa
This ferocious and feared "pirate" became admiral of the Ottoman fleet in 1533. After his death the Ottomans never fully regained control of the Mediterranean.

Ottoman Cartography
In 1521, the Ottoman admiral and cartographer, Piri Reis, drew on the accounts of Spanish and Portuguese explorers and captured sailors to compile a remarkable map of the world on gazelle hide.

Horses were held in high regard. The banner of the sultan's troops was a horse-tail.

Ottoman soldiers were known for their skilful archery.

Sipahis fought on horseback.

Süleyman the Magnificent
One of the most enlightened sultans, Süleyman (1520–66) was a poet, lawmaker and patron of the arts. Art and architecture flourished during his prosperous rule.

THE BATTLE OF MOHACS

At Mohacs, on 28 August 1526, Süleyman the Magnificent led an army of 200,000 against the forces of Louis II, the 14-year-old king of Hungary. The Hungarian forces were out-manoeuvred by the Janissaries (see p56) and faltered under massed Ottoman artillery fire. Despite this great success, the expansion of the Ottoman empire into Europe came to an end three years later with the unsuccessful siege of Vienna.

The Battle of Lepanto, 1571
Ottoman sea power was fatally weakened after the defeat by Don John of Austria, commanding the fleet of the Holy League in the waters of the Gulf of Patros.

THE EMPIRE OF SÜLEYMAN

The Ottoman Empire reached its zenith under the leadership of Sultan Süleyman the Magnificent (1520–66). It stretched from the borderlands of southern Hungary to Yemen, and from the Crimea to Morocco.

This advance was aided by well-organized administration, as well as military organization. A key practice was *devşirme*, which required rural Christian subjects to give one son to the service of the sultan. The boys converted to Islam and were educated to become civil servants or Janissaries (soldiers).

Janissaries were subject to strict discipline, including celibacy, but could gain high-ranking privileges that were previously reserved for bureaucrats. As a result, an ambitious *kul* (slave) could attain powerful status. In fact, many grand viziers (prime ministers) were products of the *devşirme* system.

By the 18th century, however, the former elite corps had become a corrupt political power and a serious threat to the sultanate. Whenever the Janissaries felt that their privileges were under threat, they rioted violently and no-one dared to intervene.

Members of the Janissary corps

DISPLAYS OF WEALTH

After Süleyman's death, the empire was ruled by a succession of mediocre sultans who concentrated on enjoying their riches rather than ruling their vast territories. Selim II (Selim the Sot) was known more for his fondness for wine than his interest in the affairs of state. Thus the empire became easy prey for the plotting and intrigue of the Janissaries, as well as the expansionist ambitions of other powers.

At the signing of the Treaty of Karlowitz in 1699, the empire lost half its European possessions. This marked the beginning of the empire's decline and opened the way for Russian advances in the Black Sea region. Long years of war followed, forcing the state to reorganize its finances.

Families that could afford to buy state land began to accumulate great personal wealth. In imitation of Sultan Ahmed III (1703–30), the elite built palaces on the Bosphorus, sported the latest European fashions and lived in luxury. Corruption and nepotism affected the entire empire, while its borders were constantly threatened. In 1730, an uprising in Istanbul overthrew Ahmed III. In short wars with Russia, Venice, Austria and Persia, the empire continued to lose territory.

REVIVAL AND DECLINE

A period of peace, from 1739 to 1768, produced an economic upswing and a brief artistic renaissance that saw the completion of the Nurosmaniye in 1755 – the first sultanic mosque complex built in Istanbul since that of

Dolmabahçe Palace, a lavish display of opulence

TIMELINE

1300	1400		1500	1600
1335 Beginning of the Beylik Period	**1397** The first Ottoman siege of Constantinople		**1513** Piri Reis creates a map of the world	
1364 Sultan Orhan recaptures Edirne (Adrianople)	**1453** Constantinople falls to Mehmet II, the Conqueror, and is renamed Istanbul	*Mehmet the Conqueror*	**1533** Barbarossa becomes admiral of Ottoman fleet	**1569** Great fire of Istanbul destroys much of the city

Ahmed I in 1617. This interlude was shattered when Russian troops mobilized by Catherine the Great invaded the feeble Ottoman empire. In two periods of war (1768–74 and 1788–91), the Russians gained access to the Black Sea and managed to annex the Crimean region. This was the first Muslim territory lost by the Ottomans, and, to make it worse, they were also forced to pay reparations to Russia.

Abdül Hamit II, grieving as Crete is awarded to Greece

In 1826, Mahmud II suppressed the Janissaries in a massacre known as the "Auspicious Event" and reorganized the bureaucracy in an effort to modernize the empire. Russia, meanwhile, encouraged Greece, Serbia, Moldavia and the Ottoman vassal state of Wallachia (in modern Romania) to demand self-rule. Mahmud II hoped that by passing the Tanzimat edicts (1839 and 1856) he could ensure good government, equality for all and a stronger state. However, the edict of 1856, written under pressure from European powers after the disastrous Crimean War (1853–1856) and based on Western-style, secular ideals, was greeted with bitter resistance.

TIMES OF WAR

In the 1870s, a reformist movement known as the Young Ottomans began to press for a constitutional monarchy. Sultan Abdül Hamit II enacted some liberal reforms, but dissolved the infant parliament in 1878 as the country faced the bitter Russo-Ottoman war.

During the next few years, further debilitating wars took place, gradually ensuring the independence of the Balkan provinces. In 1908, a bitter group of officers formed the Committee for Unity and Progress, dubbed the Young Turks by Western observers. When Abdül Hamit II refused to accept a constitution, he was replaced by the weak Mehmet V. The committee took control of the government.

In 1912 and 1913, the empire lost most of its remaining European possessions in the Balkan Wars. Greatly weakened, it slid into World War I a year later on the side of Germany and Austria-Hungary. The cost of the war in economic and human terms was terrible. By 1918, only the heartland of Anatolia remained to the Ottomans. Foreign troops occupied Istanbul, İzmir and other cities. Turkish nationalists reacted by setting up an assembly in Ankara to plan for the future, but a bitter war of independence took place before modern Turkey was born.

Russian troops fighting Turkish forces in the Caucasus in 1914

1648 Great earthquake of Istanbul	1699 Treaty of Karlowitz		1807 Janissaries rebel against reforms to control their power	1881 Mustafa Kemal (later Atatürk) is born in Salonika	
	1700		**1800**	**1900**	
1686 Ottomans are forced to evacuate Hungary	1740 Stirrings of dissent in Egypt	1826 Mahmud II crushes the Janissaries in a bloody revolt	1840–1855 Tanzimat reforms attempt to modernize and revive the Ottoman Empire	1906 Early movement towards the Committee of Union and Progress (CUP)	

Atatürk

THE TREATY OF LAUSANNE

The disastrous losses of World War I and the subsequent occupation of parts of Turkey by powers such as Britain, France and Italy, fuelled Turkish nationalism. When Greek troops occupied İzmir on 15 May 1919 and pushed eastwards to Ankara, a bitter war ensued. Turkish efforts met with little success until Mustafa Kemal, an army officer respected for his heroism during the Gallipoli campaign of 1915–16, assumed the leadership.

Signatories at Lausanne, with Mussolini among them

Atatürk, father of the Turkish Republic

At nationalist congresses in Erzurum and Sivas, his calls for the establishment of a republic were greeted with enthusiasm. When the Greeks had been routed at the battle of Dumlupınar and all foreign forces had been expelled, peace returned to Anatolia and the republic was proclaimed. The Treaty of Lausanne (1923) recognized the new borders and territories of Turkey. Ankara became the capital of the new state.

As part of their peace settlement, Greece and Turkey agreed to an unusual clause that stipulated the exchange of populations. Around 1.25 million Greeks were returned to Greece from Anatolia, while roughly 450,000 Muslims were sent back to Turkey. The impact of having to accommodate such large numbers of refugees was considerable for both countries, and delayed their recovery from the years of war.

ATATÜRK'S VISION

Mustafa Kemal's election as leader of the new state came as no surprise. Known after 1935 as Atatürk (father of the state), he greatly admired European lifestyles and culture and envisaged a modern, westernized Turkish state. In 1926, he adopted legal codes used in Germany, Italy and Switzerland and abolished the traditional Muslim governing body, the caliphate. In 1928, the country was proclaimed a secular state with a Western-style constitution. The Islamic courts and religious schools were abolished and a Latin-based alphabet replaced Arabic and Persian ones. While most Turks supported these reforms, some resisted what they saw as a suppression of Islam.

Atatürk demonstrating the Latin alphabet

TIMELINE

Turkish flag

Atatürk memorial

1938 Atatürk dies

1900	1910	1920	1930	1940	1950

1915–16 Gallipoli campaign

1924 Caliphate abolished

1925–38 Atatürk introduces reforms destined to modernize Turkey

1950 Call to prayer returned to Arabic after 27 years in Turkish

1923 First Constitution implemented with the formation of the Republic

1952 Turkey becomes a member of NATO

BUILDING THE STATE

By the time Atatürk died in 1938, the foundations for a modern, secular state had been laid. Transportation had been improved and new industries set up, often under state control. Former prime minister and army chief İsmet İnönü took the reins of power, ruling until 1952.

In 1939 Turkey concluded an agreement with France that returned what is now the Hatay province to Turkish control. However, Turkey remained resolutely neutral during World War II. After the war, aid, loans and military assistance came from the United States and 5,500 Turkish troops participated in the Korean War (1950–54) under United Nations (UN) auspices. In 1952, the country joined the North Atlantic Treaty Organization (NATO), the military alliance of North American and European states, and permitted NATO forces to be stationed on its soil.

Veteran political leader Bülent Ecevit

TOWARDS DEMOCRACY

In 1950 the Democratic Party came to power. Prime Minister Adnan Menderes introduced schemes to improve living standards and open Turkey to foreign investment. This resulted in rapid economic development – and major social upheaval. Building programmes and increased migration saw rises in inflation, unrest, foreign debt and political repression. Between 1960 and 1980, the military intervened repeatedly to maintain control and safeguard the legacy of Atatürk. During this period, civilian leaders such as Süleyman Demirel and Bülent Ecevit grappled with the challenges of political instability and economic modernization.

In the 1970s and 1980s, the Kurdish minority began to rally against the state, and presented a bold challenge during the 1990s . The 1999 arrest and trial of PKK (Kurdish Workers' Party) leader Abdullah Öcalan brought the conflict to international attention. The issue remains sensitive.

Political violence and terrorism marred the 1980s. The armed forces took charge in 1981 and civilian rule was only gradually restored after 1982. The Motherland Party (ANAP) won the 1983 elections. Its leader, Turgut Özal, opened Turkey to foreign investment and free trade. Despite progress since then, Turkey, too, has felt the impact of recession, resulting in high inflation, debt and unemployment.

INTO THE 21ST CENTURY

In 1993, Tansu Çiller became the first female prime minister, a milestone for women's rights in Turkey, but tensions between religious and secular parties mounted. In 1995 the Islamist Welfare Party, the largest political bloc, assumed power. In 1996, it formed a coalition with the True Path Party, but was outlawed two years later for contravening secular principles. The gap between religious belief and Turkey's secular orientation remains a source of tension.

Students wearing traditional Islamic head covering

1960	1970	1980	1990	2000
1961 Second Constitution of the Republic	*NATO emblem* **1980** Military coup; third Constitution (1982)	**1996** Turkey enters European customs union, bringing potential trade advantages		**1999** Earthquake shatters İzmit
1971 Military coup **1960** First military coup	**1978** Kurdish Workers' Party (PKK) formed	**1991** As NATO partner, Turkey provides support for the US during the Gulf War	**2000** Ahmet Necdet Sezer is elected president	

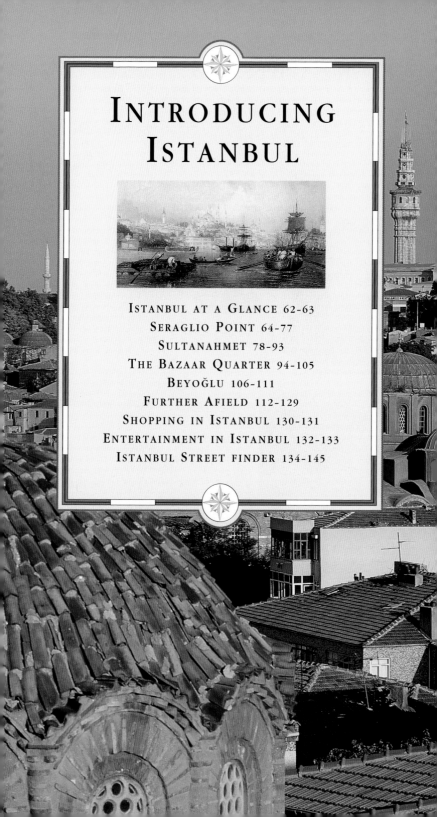

INTRODUCING ISTANBUL

Istanbul at a Glance

NUMEROUS INTERESTING places to visit in Istanbul are described in the *Area by Area* section of this book, which covers the sights of central Istanbul as well as those a short way out of the city centre. They range from mosques, churches, palaces and museums to bazaars, Turkish baths and parks. For a breathtaking view across the city, climb Galata Tower *(see p110–11)* or take a ferry ride *(see p385)* to the city's Asian shore. If you are short of time, you will probably want to concentrate on only the most famous monuments, namely Topkapı Palace, Haghia Sophia and the Blue Mosque, which are located conveniently close to each other.

The Church of St Saviour in Chora (see pp118–19) *contains some of the finest Byzantine mosaics and frescoes.*

A boat trip along the Bosphorus (see pp126–7) *is a wonderful way of viewing sights such as the 14th-century Genoese Castle (above the village of Anadolu Kavağı).*

THE BAZAAR QUARTER
(see pp94–105)

SULTANAHMET
(see pp78–93)

Süleymaniye Mosque (see pp100–101) *was built by the great architect, Sinan, in honour of his patron, Süleyman the Magnificent (see pp54–5).*

The Grand Bazaar (see pp104–105) *is a maze of shops under an intricately painted, vaulted roof. Shopkeepers are relentless, and bargaining (see p130) is a must.*

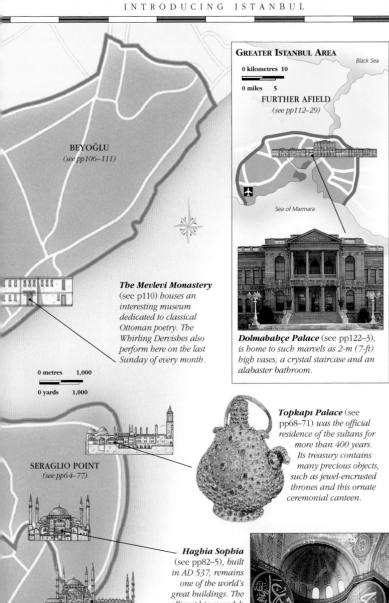

GREATER ISTANBUL AREA

0 kilometres 10

0 miles 5

Black Sea

FURTHER AFIELD
(see pp112–29)

Sea of Marmara

BEYOĞLU
(see pp106–111)

The Mevlevi Monastery
(see p110) *houses an interesting museum dedicated to classical Ottoman poetry. The Whirling Dervishes also perform here on the last Sunday of every month.*

0 metres 1,000

0 yards 1,000

Dolmabahçe Palace (see pp122–3), *is home to such marvels as 2-m (7-ft) high vases, a crystal staircase and an alabaster bathroom.*

SERAGLIO POINT
(see pp64–77)

Topkapı Palace (see pp68–71) *was the official residence of the sultans for more than 400 years. Its treasury contains many precious objects, such as jewel-encrusted thrones and this ornate ceremonial canteen.*

Haghia Sophia
(see pp82–5), *built in AD 537, remains one of the world's great buildings. The calligraphic roundels were added during the 19th century.*

The Blue Mosque
(see pp88–9) *was built by some of the same stonemasons who helped to build the Taj Mahal.*

SERAGLIO POINT

T HE HILLY, wooded promontory that marks the meeting point of the Golden Horn, the Sea of Marmara and the Bosphorus occupies a natural strategic position. In Byzantine times, monasteries and public buildings stood on this site. Today, it is dominated by the grandiose complex of

Lion relief from the Ishtar Gate

buildings forming Topkapı Palace, the residence of the Ottoman sultans and the women of the Harem for 400 years.

The palace is now open to the public as a rambling museum, with lavish apartments and glittering collections of jewels and other treasures. Originally, the palace covered almost the whole of the area with its gardens and pavilions. Part of the grounds have now been turned into a public park. Adjacent to it is the Archaeological Museum, a renowned collection of finds from Turkey and the Near East.

SIGHTS AT A GLANCE

Museums and Palaces
Archaeological Museum pp74–5 **2**
Topkapı Palace pp68–71 **1**

Churches
Haghia Eirene **4**

Historic Buildings and Monuments
Fountain of Ahmet III **5**
Imperial Mint **3**
Sirkeci Station **11**
Sublime Porte **9**

Streets and Courtyards
Cafer Ağa Courtyard **7**
Soğukçeşme Sokağı **6**

Parks
Gülhane Park **8**

Turkish Baths
Cağaloğlu Baths **10**

GETTING AROUND
With little traffic, this small area is easily explored on foot. Trams from the Grand Bazaar and the ferry piers at Eminönü stop outside Gülhane Park.

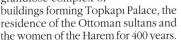

0 metres	400
0 yards	400

KEY

- ▢ Street-by-Street map *See pp66–7*
- 🚢 Ferry boarding point
- 🚉 Railway station
- 🚋 Tram stop
- ℹ️ Tourist information
- **C** Mosque
- — Walls

◁ **The Circumcision Pavilion in the third courtyard of Topkapı Palace**

Street-by-Street: The First Courtyard of Topkapı

THE JUXTAPOSITION of Ottoman palace walls, intimately proportioned wooden houses and a soaring Byzantine church lends plenty of drama to the First Courtyard, the outer part of Topkapı Palace. This was once a service area, housing the mint, a hospital, college and a bakery. It was also the mustering point of the Janissaries *(see p56)*. Nowadays, the Cafer Ağa Courtyard and the Fatih Büfe, just outside the courtyard wall, offer unusual settings for refreshments. Gülhane Park, meanwhile, is one of the few shady open spaces in a city of monuments.

Gülhane Park
Once a rose garden in the outer grounds of Topkapı Palace, the wooded Gülhane Park provides welcome shade in which to escape from the heat of the city ⑧

Soğukçeşme Sokağı
Traditional, painted wooden houses line this narrow street ⑥

Sublime Porte
A Rococo gate stands in place of the old Sublime Porte, once the entrance to (and symbol of) the Ottoman government ⑨

Museum of the Ancient Orient

Entrance to Gülhane Park

Alay Pavilion

```
0 metres        75
0 yards         75
```

ALEMDAR CAD

Gülhane tram stop

KEY

– – – Suggested route

SOĞUKÇEŞME CA

Zeynep Sultan Mosque, resembling a Byzantine church, was built in 1769 by the daughter of Ahmet III, Princess Zeynep.

Fatih Büfe, a tiny ornate kiosk, sells drinks and snacks.

Otag Music Shop sells traditional Turkish instruments.

Cafer Ağa Courtyard
The cells of this former college, arranged around a tranquil courtyard café, are now occupied by jewellers, calligraphers and other artisans selling their wares ⑦

STAR SIGHTS

★ **Archaeological Museum**

★ **Topkapı Palace**

★ Archaeological Museum

Classical statues, dazzling carved sarcophagi, Turkish ceramics and other treasures from all over the former Ottoman Empire make this one of the world's great collections of antiquities ❷

Çinili Pavilion
(see p74)

LOCATOR MAP
See Street Finder map 5

The Executioner's Fountain is so named because the executioner washed his hands and sword here after a public beheading.

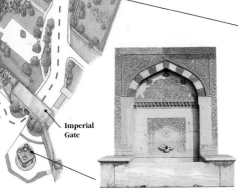

★ Topkapı Palace

For 400 years the Ottoman sultans ruled their empire from this vast palace. Its fine art collections, opulent rooms and leafy courtyards are among the highlights of a visit to Istanbul ❶

Entrance to Topkapı Palace

Topkapı Palace ticket office

Imperial Mint
This museum houses exhibitions on the historical background to Istanbul ❸

Haghia Eirene
The Byzantine church of Haghia Eirene dates from the 6th century. Unusually, it has never been converted into a mosque ❹

Imperial Gate

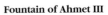

Fountain of Ahmet III
Built in the early 18th century, the finest of Istanbul's Rococo fountains is inscribed with poetry likening it to the fountains of paradise ❺

Topkapı Palace **❶**

Topkapı Sarayı

Süleyman I's *tuğra* over the main gate

Bᴇᴛᴡᴇᴇɴ 1459 and 1465, shortly after his conquest of Constantinople *(see p54)*, Mehmet II built Topkapı Palace as his principal residence. Rather than a single building, it was conceived as a series of pavilions contained by four enormous courtyards, a stone version of the tented encampments from which the nomadic Ottomans had emerged. Initially, the palace served as the seat of government and contained a school in which civil servants and soldiers were trained. In the 16th century, however, the government was moved to the Sublime Porte *(see p73)*. Sultan Abdül Mecid I abandoned Topkapı in 1853 in favour of Dolmabahçe Palace *(see pp122–3)*. In 1924 it was opened to the public as a museum.

★ Harem
The labyrinth of exquisite rooms where the sultan's wives and concubines lived can be visited on a guided tour (see p71).

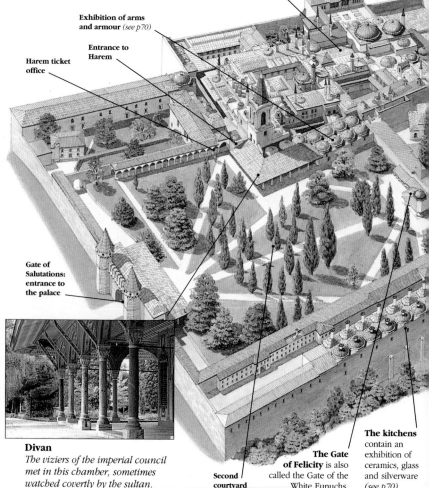

Exhibition of arms and armour *(see p70)*

Entrance to Harem

Harem ticket office

Gate of Salutations: entrance to the palace

Divan
The viziers of the imperial council met in this chamber, sometimes watched covertly by the sultan.

Second courtyard

The Gate of Felicity is also called the Gate of the White Eunuchs.

The kitchens contain an exhibition of ceramics, glass and silverware *(see p70).*

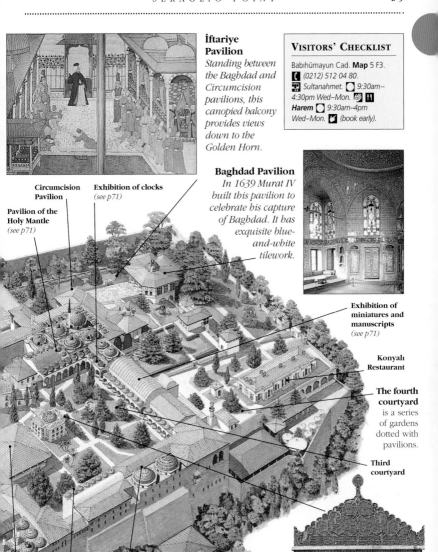

İftariye Pavilion
Standing between the Baghdad and Circumcision pavilions, this canopied balcony provides views down to the Golden Horn.

VISITORS' CHECKLIST

Babıhümayun Cad. **Map** 5 F3.
(0212) 512 04 80.
Sultanahmet. 9:30am–4:30pm Wed–Mon.
Harem 9:30am–4pm Wed–Mon. (book early).

Circumcision Pavilion

Exhibition of clocks
(see p71)

Pavilion of the Holy Mantle
(see p71)

Baghdad Pavilion
In 1639 Murat IV built this pavilion to celebrate his capture of Baghdad. It has exquisite blue-and-white tilework.

Exhibition of miniatures and manuscripts
(see p71)

Konyalı Restaurant

The fourth courtyard
is a series of gardens dotted with pavilions.

Third courtyard

Library of Ahmet III
Erected in 1719, the library is an elegant marble building. This ornamental fountain is set into the wall below its main entrance.

Exhibition of imperial costumes
(see p70)

Throne Room

★ Treasury
This 17th-century jewel-encrusted jug is one of the precious objects exhibited in the former treasury (see pp70–71).

STAR FEATURES

★ **Harem**

★ **Treasury**

Exploring the Palace's Collections

DURING THEIR 470-YEAR REIGN, the Ottoman sultans amassed a glittering collection of treasures. After the foundation of the Turkish Republic in 1923 *(see p58)*, this was nationalized and the bulk of it put on display in Topkapı Palace. As well as diplomatic gifts and articles commissioned from the craftsmen of the palace workshops, many of the items in the collection were the booty from successful military campaigns. Many date from the massive expansion of the Ottoman Empire during the reign of Selim the Grim (1512–20), when Syria, Arabia and Egypt were conquered.

CERAMICS, GLASS AND SILVERWARE

THE KITCHENS contain the palace's ceramics, glass and silverware collections. Turkish and European pieces are massively overshadowed by the vast display of Chinese (as well as Japanese) porcelain. This was brought to Turkey along the Silk Route, the overland trading link between the Far East and Europe. Topkapı's collection of Chinese porcelain is the world's second best, after China.

The Chinese porcelain on display spans four dynasties: the Sung (10–13th centuries), followed by the Yüan (13–14th centuries), the Ming (14–17th centuries) and the Ching (17–20th centuries). Celadon, the earliest form of Chinese porcelain collected by the sultans, was made to look like jade, a stone believed by the Chinese to be lucky. The Ottomans prized it because it was said to neutralize poison in food. More delicate than these are a number of exquisite blue-and-white pieces, mostly of the Ming era.

Chinese aesthetics were an important influence on Ottoman craftsmen, particularly in the creation of designs for their fledgling ceramics industry at İznik *(see p161)*. Although there are no İznik pieces in the Topkapı collection, many of the tiles on the palace walls originated there. These clearly show the influence of designs used for Chinese blue-and-white porcelain, such as stylized flowers and cloud scrolls. Much of the later porcelain, particularly the Japanese Imari ware, was made for the export market. The most obvious examples of this are some plates decorated with quotations from the Koran. A part of the kitchens, the old confectioners' pantry, has been preserved as it would have been when in use. On display are huge cauldrons and other utensils wielded by the palace's chefs as they prepared to feed its 12,000 residents and guests.

Japanese porcelain plate

ARMS AND ARMOUR

TAXES AND TRIBUTES from all over the empire were once stored in this chamber, which was known as the Inner Treasury. Straight ahead as you enter are a series of horse-tail standards. Carried in processions or displayed outside tents, these proclaimed the rank of their owners. Viziers *(see p56–7)*, for example, merited three, and the grand vizier five, while the sultan's banner would flaunt nine.

The weaponry includes ornately embellished swords and several bows made by sultans themselves (Beyazıt II was a particularly fine craftsman). Seen next to these exquisite items, the huge iron swords used by European crusaders look crude by comparison.

Also on view are pieces of 15th-century Ottoman chainmail and colourful shields. The shields have metal centres surrounded by closely woven straw painted with flowers.

IMPERIAL COSTUMES

A COLLECTION of imperial costumes is displayed in the Hall of the Campaign Pages, whose task was to look after the royal wardrobe. It was a palace tradition that on the death of a sultan his clothes were carefully folded and placed in sealed bags. As a result, it is possible to see a perfectly preserved kaftan once worn by Mehmet the Conqueror *(see p54)*. The reforms of Sultan Mahmut II included a revolution in the dress code. The end of an era came as plain grey serge replaced the earlier luxurious silken textiles.

Sumptuous silk kaftan once worn by Mehmet the Conqueror

TREASURY

OF ALL THE exhibitions in the palace, the Treasury's collection is the easiest to appreciate, glittering as it does with thousands of precious and semi-precious stones. Possibly the only surprise is that there are so few women's jewels here. Whereas the treasures of the sultans and viziers were owned by the state, reverting to the palace on their deaths, those belonging to the women of the court did not.

In the first hall stands a diamond-encrusted suit of chainmail, designed for Mustafa III (1757–74) for ceremonial use. Diplomatic gifts include a fine pearl statuette of a prince seated beneath a canopy, which was sent to Sultan Abdül Aziz (1861–76) from India. The greatest pieces are to be seen in the second hall. Foremost among these is the Topkapı dagger (1741). This splendid object was commissioned by the sultan from his own jewellers. It was intended as a present for the Shah of Persia, but he died before it reached him. Among the exhibits are a selection of bejewelled *aigrettes* (plumes) which were used to add splendour to imperial turbans.

The Topkapı dagger

In the third hall is the 86-carat Spoonmaker's diamond, said to have been discovered in a rubbish heap in Istanbul in the 17th century, and bought from a scrap merchant for three spoons. The gold-plated Bayram throne was given to Murat III by the Governor of Egypt in 1574 and used for state ceremonies.

The throne in the fourth hall, a gift from the Shah of Persia, was acknowledged by the equally magnificent gift of the Topkapı dagger. In a cabinet near the throne is an unusual relic: a case containing bones said to be from the hand of St John the Baptist.

MINIATURES AND MANUSCRIPTS

IT IS POSSIBLE to display only a tiny fraction of Topkapı's total collection of over 13,000 miniatures and manuscripts at any one time. Highlights include a series of depictions of warriors and fearsome creatures known as *Demons*

and Monsters in the Life of Nomads, which was painted by Mohammed Siyah Qalem, possibly as early as the 12th century. It is from this Eastern tradition of miniature painting, which was also prevalent in Mogul India and Persia, that the ebullient Ottoman style of miniatures *(see p29)* arose.

Also on show are some fine examples of calligraphy *(see pp28–9)*, including copies of the Koran, manuscripts of poetry and several *firmans*, the imperial decrees by which the sultan ruled his empire.

CLOCKS

EUROPEAN CLOCKS given to, or bought by, various sultans form the majority of this collection, despite the fact that there were makers of clocks and watches in Istanbul from the 17th century. The clocks range from simple, weight-driven 16th-century examples to an exquisite 18th-century English mechanism encased in mother-of-pearl and featuring a German organ which played tunes every hour, on the hour. The only male European eyewitness accounts of life in the Harem were written by mechanics who serviced the clocks. The exhibition closed temporarily in 2002.

17th-century watch made of gold, enamel and precious stones

PAVILION OF THE HOLY MANTLE

SOME OF THE HOLIEST relics of Islam are displayed in these five domed rooms, which are a place of pilgrimage for Muslims. Most of the relics found their way to Istanbul as a result of the conquest by Sultan Selim the Grim of Egypt and Arabia, and his assumption of the caliphate (the leadership of Islam) in 1517.

The most sacred treasure is the mantle once worn by the Prophet Mohammed. Visitors cannot actually enter the room in which it is stored; instead they look into it from an antechamber through an open doorway. Night and day, holy men chant passages from the Koran over the gold chest in which the mantle is stored. A stand in front of the chest holds two of Mohammed's swords.

Behind a glass cabinet in the anteroom are hairs from the beard of the Prophet, a tooth, a letter written by him and an impression of his footprint.

In other rooms are some of the ornate locks and keys for the Kaaba (Muslim shrine in Mecca) which were sent to Mecca by successive sultans.

LIFE IN THE HAREM

Apart from the sultan's mother, the most powerful woman in the Harem, and the sultan's daughters, the women of the Harem were slaves, gathered from the furthest corners of the Ottoman Empire and beyond. Their dream was to become a favourite of the sultan and bear him a son, which, on some occasions, led to marriage. Competition was stiff, however, for at its height the Harem contained over 1,000 concubines, many of whom never rose beyond the service of their fellow captives. The last women eventually left the Harem in 1909.

A Western view of life in the Harem, from a 19th-century engraving

Archaeological Museum ❷

See pp74–5.

Imperial Mint ❸
Darphane-i Amire

First courtyard of Topkapı Palace.
Map 5 E4. 🚇 *Gülhane or Sultanahmet.*

THE OTTOMAN MINT opened here in 1727, but most of what can be seen today dates from the reign of Mahmut II (1808–39), when the complex was extended. In 1967, the mint moved to a new location. The buildings now house laboratories for the state restoration and conservation department, but visitors can look around the outside of the building during office hours.

Haghia Eirene ❹
Aya İrini Kilisesi

First courtyard of Topkapı Palace.
Map 5 E4. 📞 *(0212) 522 17 50.*
🚇 *Gülhane or Sultanahmet.*
◻ *for concerts.*

THOUGH THE present church dates only from the 6th century, it is at least the third building to be erected on what is thought to be the oldest site of Christian worship in Istanbul. Within a decade of the Muslim conquest of the city in 1453 *(see pp54)* it had

One of the four elaborately decorated sides of the Fountain of Ahmet III

been incorporated within the Topkapı Palace complex and pressed into use as an arsenal. Today the building, which has good acoustics, is the setting for concerts during the Istanbul Music Festival *(see p35)*.

Inside are three fascinating features that have not survived in any other Byzantine church in the city. The *synthronon*, the five rows of built-in seats hugging the apse, were occupied by clergy officiating during services. Above this looms a simple black mosaic cross on a gold background, dating from the iconoclastic period in the 8th century, when figurative images were forbidden. At the back of the church is a cloister-like courtyard where deceased Byzantine emperors once lay in their porphyry sarcophagi. Most have been moved to the Archaeological Museum.

Fountain of Ahmet III ❺
Ahmet III Çeşmesi

Junction of İshak Paşa Cad & Babıhümayun Cad. **Map** 5 E4.
🚇 *Gülhane or Sultanahmet.*

BUILT IN 1728, the most beautiful of Istanbul's countless fountains survived the violent deposition of Sultan Ahmet III two years later. Many other monuments constructed by the sultan during his reign, which has become known as the Tulip Period, were destroyed. The fountain is in the delicate Turkish Rococo style, with five small domes, mihrab-shaped niches and dizzying floral reliefs.

Ottoman "fountains" do not spout jets of water, but are more like ornate public taps. They sometimes incorporated a counter, or *sebil*, from which refreshments would be served.

In this case, each of the fountain's four walls is equipped with a tap, or *çeşme*, above a carved marble basin. Over each tap is an elaborate calligraphic inscription by the 18th-century poet Seyit Vehbi Efendi. The inscription, in gold on a blue-green background, is in honour of the fountain and its founder. At each of the four corners there is a *sebil* backed by three windows covered by ornate marble grilles. Instead of the customary iced water, passers-by at this fountain would have been offered sherbets and fla-voured waters in silver goblets.

The apse of Haghia Eirene, with its imposing black-on-gold cross

Soğukçeşme Sokağı ❻

Map 5 E4. 🚇 *Gülhane.*

CHARMING OLD wooden houses line this narrow, sloping cobbled lane ("the street of the cold fountain"), which squeezes between the outer walls of Topkapı Palace and the towering minarets of Haghia Sophia. Traditional houses like these were built in the city from the late 18th century onwards.

The buildings in the lane were renovated by the Turkish Touring and Automobile Club (TTOK, *see p385*) in the 1980s. Some of them now form the Ayasofya Pansiyonları, a series of attractive pastel-painted guesthouses popular with tourists. Another building has been converted by the TTOK into a library of historical writings on Istanbul, and archive of engravings and photographs of the city. A Roman cistern towards the bottom of the lane has been converted into the attractive Sarnıç restaurant.

Traditional calligraphy on sale in Cafer Ağa Courtyard

Cafer Ağa Courtyard ❼
Cafer Ağa Medresesi

Caferiye Sok. **Map** 5 E3.
🚇 *Gülhane.* ⏰ *8:30am–8pm daily.*

THIS PEACEFUL courtyard at the end of an alley was built in 1559 by the architect Sinan *(see p101)* for the chief black eunuch as a *medrese* (theological college, *see p32*). Sinan's bust presides over the café tables in the courtyard. The former students' lodgings

Restored Ottoman house on Soğukçeşme Sokağı

are now used to display a variety of craft goods typically including jewellery, silk prints, ceramics and calligraphy.

Gülhane Park ❽
Gülhane Parkı

Alemdar Cad. **Map** 5 E3.
🚇 *Gülhane.* ⭕ *daily.* 📷

GÜLHANE PARK occupies what were the lower grounds of Topkapı Palace. Today it has a neglected air but it is still a shady place to stroll that also includes a couple of interesting landmarks.

The park no longer contains a zoo, but seek out the aquarium in the disused cascade on the right. It is housed in the cavernous vaults of a Roman water cistern. At the far end of the park is the Goths' Column, a well-preserved 3rd-century victory monument, surrounded by a cluster of clapboard teahouses. Its name comes from the Latin inscription on it which reads: "Fortune is restored to us because of victory over the Goths".

Across Kennedy Caddesi, the main road running along the northeast side of the park, there is a viewpoint over the busy waters where the Golden Horn meets the Bosphorus.

OTTOMAN HOUSES

The typical, smart town house of 19th-century Istanbul had a stone ground floor above which were one or two wooden storeys. The building invariably sported a *çıkma*, a section projecting out over the street. This developed from the traditional Turkish balcony, which was enclosed in the northern part of the country because of the colder climate. Wooden lattice covers, or *kafesler*, over the windows on the upper storeys ensured that the women of the house were able to watch life on the street below without being seen themselves. Few wooden houses have survived. Those that remain usually owe their existence to tourism and many have been restored as hotels. While the law forbids their demolition, it is very hard to obtain insurance for them in a city that has experienced so many fires.

Sublime Porte ❾
Bab-ı Ali

Alemdar Cad. **Map** 5 E3.
🚇 *Gülhane.*

FOREIGN AMBASSADORS to Ottoman Turkey were known as Ambassadors to the Sublime Porte, after this monumental gateway which once led into the offices and palace of the grand vizier. The institution of the Sublime Porte filled an important role in Ottoman society because it could often provide an effective counterbalance to the whims of sultans.

The Rococo gateway you see today was built in the 1840s. Its guarded entrance now shields the offices of Istanbul's provincial government.

Rococo decoration on the roof of the Sublime Porte

Archaeological Museum ❷
Arkeoloji Müzesi

A<small>LTHOUGH</small> THIS collection of antiquities was begun only in the mid-19th century, provincial governors were soon sending in objects from the length and breadth of the Ottoman Empire. Today the museum has one of the world's richest collections of classical artifacts, and also includes treasures from the pre-classical world. The main building was erected under the directorship of Osman Hamdi Bey (1881–1910), to house his finds. This archaeologist, painter and polymath discovered the exquisite sarcophagi in the royal necropolis at Sidon in present-day Lebanon. A new four-storey wing of the museum was opened in 1991.

Roman statue of Apollo

★ **Alexander Sarcophagus**
This fabulously carved marble tomb from the late 4th century BC is thought to have been built for King Abdalonymos of Sidon. It is called the Alexander Sarcophagus because Alexander the Great is depicted on it winning a victory over the Persians.

KEY

- ☐ Classical Archaeology
- ☐ Children's Museum
- ☐ Thracian, Bithynian and Byzantine Collections
- ☐ Istanbul Through the Ages
- ☐ Anatolia and Troy
- ☐ Anatolia's Neighbouring Cultures
- ☐ Turkish Tiles and Ceramics
- ☐ Museum of the Ancient Orient
- ☐ Non-exhibition space

GALLERY GUIDE
The 20 galleries of the main building house the museum's important collection of classical antiquities. The new wing has displays on the archaeology of Istanbul and nearby regions, and includes the Children's Museum. There are two other buildings within the grounds: the Çinili Pavilion, which contains Turkish tiles and ceramics, and the Museum of the Ancient Orient.

Sarcophagus of the Mourning Women

The porticoes of the museum take their design from the 4th-century BC Sarcophagus of the Mourning Women.

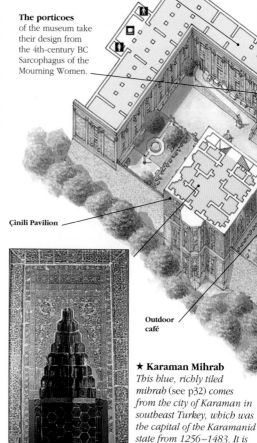

Çinili Pavilion

Outdoor café

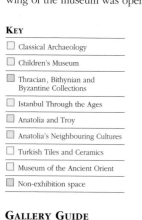

STAR EXHIBITS

- ★ Alexander Sarcophagus
- ★ Karaman Mihrab
- ★ Treaty of Kadesh

★ **Karaman Mihrab**
This blue, richly tiled mihrab (see p32) comes from the city of Karaman in southeast Turkey, which was the capital of the Karamanid state from 1256–1483. It is the most important artistic relic of that culture.

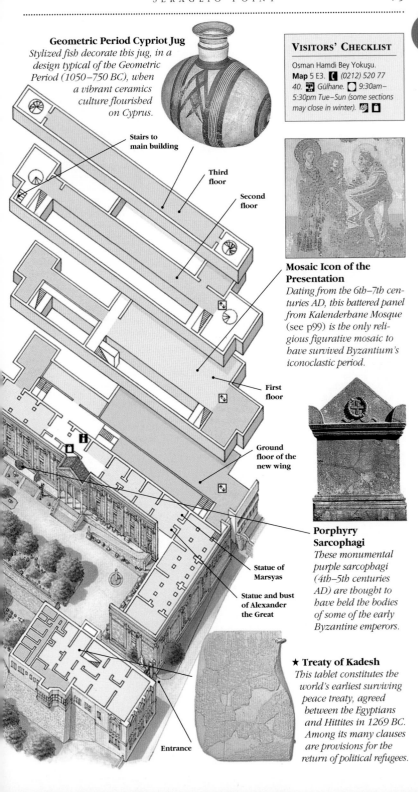

Geometric Period Cypriot Jug
Stylized fish decorate this jug, in a design typical of the Geometric Period (1050–750 BC), when a vibrant ceramics culture flourished on Cyprus.

VISITORS' CHECKLIST

Osman Hamdi Bey Yokuşu.
Map 5 E3. (0212) 520 77
40. Gülhane. 9:30am–
5:30pm Tue–Sun (some sections
may close in winter).

Stairs to main building

Third floor

Second floor

Mosaic Icon of the Presentation
Dating from the 6th–7th centuries AD, this battered panel from Kalenderhane Mosque (see p99) is the only religious figurative mosaic to have survived Byzantium's iconoclastic period.

First floor

Ground floor of the new wing

Porphyry Sarcophagi
These monumental purple sarcophagi (4th–5th centuries AD) are thought to have held the bodies of some of the early Byzantine emperors.

Statue of Marsyas

Statue and bust of Alexander the Great

★ Treaty of Kadesh
This tablet constitutes the world's earliest surviving peace treaty, agreed between the Egyptians and Hittites in 1269 BC. Among its many clauses are provisions for the return of political refugees.

Entrance

Cağaloğlu Baths ⓾
Cağaloğlu Hamamı

Prof Kazım İsmail Gürkan Cad 34, Cağaloğlu. **Map** 3 E4 (5 D3).
 (0212) 522 24 24.
 Sultanahmet. 8am–8pm daily (women), 8am–10pm daily (men).

AMONG THE city's more sumptuous Turkish baths, the ones in Cağaloğlu were built by Sultan Mahmut I in 1741. The income from them was designated for the maintenance of Mahmut's library in Haghia Sophia *(see pp82–5)*.

The city's smaller baths have different times at which men and women can use the same facilities. But in larger baths,

Corridor leading into the Cağaloğlu Baths, built by Mahmut I

such as this one, there are entirely separate sections. In the Cağaloğlu Baths the men's and women's sections are at right angles to one another and entered from different streets. Each consists of three parts: a *camekan*, a *soğukluk* and the main bath chamber or *hararet*, which centres on a massive octagonal massage slab.

The Cağaloğlu Baths are popular with foreign visitors because the staff are happy to explain the procedure. Even if you do not want to sweat it out, you can still take a look inside the entrance corridor and *camekan* of the men's section. Here you will find a small display of Ottoman bathing regalia, including precarious wooden clogs once worn by women on what would frequently be their only outing from the confines of the home. You can also sit and have a drink by the fountain in the peaceful *camekan*.

Sirkeci Station ⓫
Sirkeci Garı

Sirkeci İstasyon Cad, Sirkeci. **Map** 3 E3 (5 E1). (0212) 520 65 75.
 Sirkeci. daily.

THIS MAGNIFICENT railway station was built to receive the long-anticipated Orient Express from Europe. It was officially opened in 1890, even

Sirkeci Station, final destination of the historic Orient Express

though the luxurious train had been running into Istanbul for a year by then. The design, by the German architect Jasmund, successfully incorporates features from the many different architectural traditions of Istanbul. Byzantine alternating stone and brick courses are combined with a Seljuk-style monumental recessed portal and Muslim horseshoe arches around the windows.

The station café is a good place in which to escape the bustle of the city for a while. Sirkeci serves Greece and other destinations in Europe as well as the European part of Turkey. Istanbul's other mainline railway station is Haydarpaşa *(see p125)*, on the Asian side of the city.

THE WORLD-FAMOUS ORIENT EXPRESS

The Orient Express made its first run from Paris to Istanbul in 1889, covering the 2,900-km (1,800-mile) journey in three days. Both Sirkeci Station and the Pera Palas Hotel *(see p108, 110, 326)* in Istanbul were built especially to receive its passengers. The wealthy and often distinguished passengers of "The Train of Kings, the King of Trains" did indeed include kings among the many presidents, politicians, aristocrats and actresses. King Boris III of Bulgaria even made a habit of taking over from the driver of the train when he travelled on it through his own country.

A byword for exoticism and romance, the train was associated with the orientalist view of Istanbul as a treacherous melting pot of diplomats and arms dealers. It inspired no fewer than 19 books – *Murder on the Orient Express* by Agatha Christie and *Stamboul Train* by Graham Greene foremost among them – six films and one piece of music. During the Cold War standards of luxury crashed, though a service of sorts, without even a restaurant car, continued twice weekly to Istanbul until 1977.

A 1920s poster for the Orient Express, showing a romantic view of Istanbul

Turkish Baths

No trip to Istanbul is complete without an hour or two spent in a Turkish bath (*hamam*), which will leave your whole body feeling rejuvenated. Turkish baths differ little from the baths of ancient Rome, from which they derive, except there is no pool of cold water to plunge into at the end.

A full service will entail a period of relaxation in the steam-filled hot room, punctuated by bouts

Ornate wash basin

of vigorous soaping and massaging. There is no time limit, but allow at least an hour and a half for a leisurely bath. Towels and soap will be provided, but you can take special toiletries with you. Two historic baths located in the old city, Çemberlitaş (*see p91*) and Cağaloğlu (illustrated below), are used to catering for foreign tourists. Some luxury hotels have their own baths (*see p320*).

Choosing a Service
Services, detailed in a price list at the entrance, range from a self-service option to a luxury body scrub, shampoo and massage.

The *camekan* (**entrance hall**) is a peaceful internal courtyard near the entrance of the building. Bathers change clothes in cubicles surrounding it. The *camekan* is also the place to relax with a cup of tea after bathing.

Changing Clothes
Before changing you will be given a cloth (peştemal), to wrap around you, and a pair of slippers for walking on the hot, wet floor.

Corridor from street

Basin and tap for washing

Small, star-like windows piercing the domes

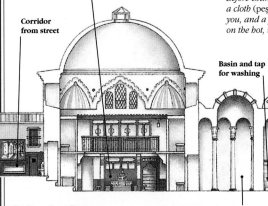

Cağaloğlu Baths
The opulent, 18th-century Turkish baths at Cağaloğlu have separate, identical sections for men and women. The men's section is shown here.

The *soğukluk* (**intermediate room**) is a temperate passage between the changing room and the *hararet*. You will be given dry towels here on your way back to the *camekan*.

In the *hararet* (**hot room**), the main room of the Turkish bath, you are permitted to sit and sweat in the steam for as long as you like.

The Exfoliating Body Scrub
In between steaming, you (or the staff at the baths) scrub your body briskly with a coarse, soapy mitt (kese).

The Body Massage
A marble plinth (göbek taşı) occupies the centre of the hot room. This is where you will have your pummelling full-body massage.

SULTANAHMET

TWO OF THE city's most significant monuments face each other across gardens, known as Sultanahmet Square. The Blue Mosque was built by Sultan Ahmet I, from whom this part of the city gets its name. Opposite is Haghia Sophia, an outstanding example of early Byzantine architecture, and still regarded as one of the world's most remarkable churches. A square next to the Blue Mosque marks the site of the Hippodrome, a chariot-racing stadium built by the Romans in about AD 200. On the other side of the Blue Mosque, the city slopes down to the Sea of Marmara in a jumble of alleyways. Traditional-style Ottoman houses have been built over the remains of the Great Palace of the Byzantine emperors.

Mosaic of Empress Irene in Haghia Sophia

SIGHTS AT A GLANCE

Mosques and Churches
Blue Mosque pp88-9 **7**
Church of SS Sergius and Bacchus **14**
Haghia Sophia pp82-5 **1**
Sokollu Mehmet Paşa Mosque **13**

Museums
Mosaics Museum **6**
Museum of Turkish and Islamic Arts **8**
Vakıflar Carpet Museum **5**

Squares and Courtyards
Hippodrome **9**
Istanbul Crafts Centre **3**

Historic Buildings and Monuments
Basilica Cistern **2**
Baths of Roxelana **4**
Bucoleon Palace **15**
Cistern of 1001 Columns **10**
Constantine's Column **12**
Tomb of Sultan Mahmut II **11**

KEY

▨	Street-by-Street map *See pp80–81*
⊞	Tram stop
ℹ	Tourist information
C	Mosque
—	Walls

GETTING AROUND
Trams from Eminönü and Beyazıt stop in Sultanahmet by the Firuz Ağa Mosque on Divanyolu Caddesi. From there, most of the sights are easily reached on foot.

0 metres	250
0 yards	250

◁ **The elegant domes of the Blue Mosque, catching the evening sun**

Street-by-Street: Sultanahmet Square

T WO OF ISTANBUL'S most venerable monuments,
the Blue Mosque and Haghia Sophia, face each
other across a leafy square, informally known as
Sultanahmet Square (Sultanahmet Meydanı), next to
the Hippodrome of Byzantium. Also in this fascinating historic quarter are a handful of museums,
including the Mosaics Museum, built over part of
the old Byzantine Great Palace (see pp92–3), and
the Museum of Turkish and Islamic Arts. No less
diverting than the cultural sights are the cries of
the *simit* (bagel) hawkers and carpet sellers, and
the chatter of children selling postcards.

Tomb of Sultan Ahmet I
Stunning 17th-century İznik tiles
(see p161) adorn the inside of
this tomb, which is part of the
outer complex of the Blue Mosque.

★ Blue Mosque
Towering above
Sultanahmet Square
are the six beautiful
minarets of this world-
famous mosque. It was
built in the early 17th
century for Ahmet I **7**

**Sultanahmet
tram stop**

**Firuz Ağa
Mosque**

**Fountain
of Kaiser
Wilhelm II**

**Museum of Turkish
and Islamic Arts**
Tents and rugs used by Turkey's
nomadic peoples are included in
this impressive collection **8**

**Egyptian
Obelisk**

KEY

— — — Suggested route

**Serpentine
Column**

**Brazen
Column**

ATMEYDANI SOK

ATMEYDANI SOK

TAVUKHANE SOK

TORUN SOK

DİV

Hippodrome
This stadium was the city's
focus for more than 1,000
years before it fell into ruin.
Only a few sections, such
as the central line of
monuments, remain **9**

**Vakıflar
Carpet Museum**
Part of the Blue
Mosque complex, this
museum displays fine
antique carpets **5**

Mosaics Museum
Hunting scenes are one of the
common subjects that can be
seen in some of the mosaics
from the Great Palace **6**

0 metres   75
0 yards   75

★ Basilica Cistern
This marble Medusa head is one of two classical column bases found in the Basilica Cistern. The cavernous cistern dates from the reign of Justinian I (see p49) in the 6th century ❷

A stone pilaster next to the remains of an Ottoman water tower is all that survives of the Milion, a triumphal gateway.

LOCATOR MAP
See Street Finder, maps 4 and 5

★ Haghia Sophia
The supreme church of Byzantium is over 1,400 years old but has survived in a remarkably good state. Inside it are several glorious figurative mosaics ❶

Baths of Roxelana
Sinan (see p101) designed these beautiful baths in the mid-16th century. They no longer serve their original function, however, having been converted into a state-run carpet shop ❹

Yeşil Ev Hotel
(see p325)

Istanbul Crafts Centre
Visitors have a rare opportunity here to observe Turkish craftsmen practising a range of skills ❸

Cavalry Bazaar
Eager salesmen will call you over to peruse their wares – mainly carpets and handicrafts – in this bazaar. With two long rows of shops on either side of a lane, the bazaar was once a stable yard.

STAR SIGHTS
- ★ Blue Mosque
- ★ Basilica Cistern
- ★ Haghia Sophia

Haghia Sophia ①

Aya Sofya

THE "CHURCH OF HOLY WISDOM", Haghia Sophia is among the world's greatest architectural achievements. More than 1,400 years old, it stands as a testament to the sophistication of the 6th-century Byzantine capital and had a great influence on architecture in the following centuries. The vast edifice was built over two earlier churches and inaugurated by Emperor Justinian in 537. In the 15th century the Ottomans converted it into a mosque: the minarets, tombs, and fountains date from this period. To help support the structure's great weight, the exterior has been buttressed on numerous occasions, which has partly obscured its original shape.

Print of Haghia Sophia from the mid-19th century

Seraphims adorn the pendentives at the base of the dome.

Calligraphic roundel

Kürsü *(see p33)*

Byzantine Frieze
Among the ruins of the monumental entrance to the earlier Haghia Sophia (dedicated in AD 415) is this frieze of sheep.

Buttress

Imperial Gate

Entrance

Outer narthex

Inner narthex

The galleries were originally used by women during services.

HISTORICAL PLAN OF HAGHIA SOPHIA

Nothing remains of the first 4th-century church on this spot, but there are traces of the second one from the 5th century, which burned down in AD 532. Earthquakes have taken their toll on the third structure, strengthened and added to many times.

KEY

☐ 5th-century church

▨ 6th-century church

☐ Ottoman additions

STAR FEATURES

★ **Nave**

★ **The Mosaics**

★ **Ablutions Fountain**

★ **Nave**
Visitors cannot fail to be staggered by this vast space which is covered by a huge dome reaching to a height of 56 m (184 ft).

VISITORS' CHECKLIST

Ayasofya Meydanı, Sultanahmet.
Map 5 E4. [(0212) 522 17 50.
Sultanahmet.
9:15am–4:30pm Tue–Sun.
ground floor only.

Brick minaret

★ **The Mosaics**
The church's splendid Byzantine mosaics include this one at the end of the south gallery. It depicts Christ flanked by Emperor Constantine IX and his wife, the Empress Zoe.

Sultan's loge

Müezzin mahfili
(see p32)

The Coronation Square served for the crowning of emperors.

Mausoleum of Mehmet III

Library of Sultan Mahmut I

Mausoleum of Selim II
The oldest of the three mausoleums was completed in 1577 to the plans of Sinan (see p101). Its interior is entirely decorated with İznik tiles (see p161).

The mausoleum of Murat III was used for his burial in 1599. Murat had by that time sired 103 children.

Exit

The Baptistry, part of the 6th-century church, now serves as the tomb of two sultans.

★ **Ablutions Fountain**
Built around 1740, this fountain is an exquisite example of Turkish Rococo style. Its projecting roof is painted with floral reliefs.

Exploring Haghia Sophia

Calligraphic roundel

Designed as an earthly mirror of the heavens, the interior of Haghia Sophia succeeds in imparting a truly celestial feel. The artistic highlights are a number of glistening figurative mosaics – remains of the decoration that once covered the upper walls but which has otherwise mostly disappeared. The remarkable works of Byzantine art date from the 9th century or later, after the iconoclastic era. Some of the patterned mosaic ceilings, however, particularly those adorning the narthex and the neighbouring Vestibule of the Warriors, are part of the cathedral's original 6th-century decoration.

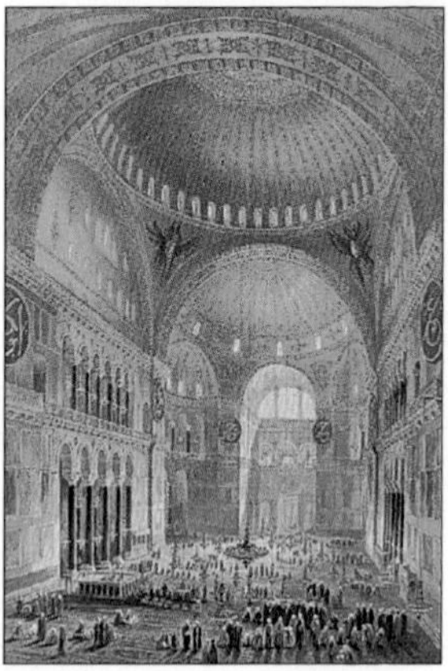

Interior as it looked after restoration in the 19th century

Ground Floor

The first of the surviving Byzantine mosaics can be seen over the Imperial Gate. This is now the public entrance into the church, although previously only the emperor and his entourage were allowed to pass through it. The mosaic shows **Christ on a throne with an emperor kneeling beside him** ① and has been dated to between 886 and 912. The emperor is thought to be Leo VI, the Wise.

The most conspicuous features at ground level in the nave are those added by the Ottoman sultans after the conquest of Istanbul in 1453, when the church was converted into a mosque.

The **mihrab** ②, the niche indicating the direction of Mecca, was installed in the apse of the church directly opposite the entrance. The **sultan's loge** ③, on the left of the mihrab as you face it, was built by the Fossati brothers. These Italian-Swiss architects undertook a major restoration of Haghia Sophia for Sultan Abdül Mecit in 1847–9.

To the right of the mihrab is the ***minbar*** ④, or pulpit, which was installed by Murat III (1574–95). He also erected four ***müezzin mahfilis*** ⑤, marble platforms for readers of the Koran *(see p32)*. The largest of these is adjacent to the *minbar*. The patterned marble **coronation square** ⑥ next to it marks the supposed site of the Byzantine emperor's throne, or omphalos (centre of the world). Nearby, in the south aisle, is the **library of Mahmut I** ⑦, which was built in 1739 and is entered by a decorative bronze door.

Across the nave, between two columns, is the 17th-century marble **preacher's throne** ⑧, the contribution of Murat IV (1623–40). Behind it is one of several ***maqsuras*** ⑨. These low, fenced platforms were placed beside walls and pillars to provide places for elders to sit, listen and read the Koran.

In the northwestern and western corners of the church are two **marble urns** ⑩, thought to date from the Hellenistic or early Byzantine period. A rectangular pillar behind one of the urns, the **pillar of St Gregory the Miracle-Worker** ⑪, is believed to have healing powers.

As you leave the church you pass through the Vestibule of the Warriors, so called because the emperor's bodyguards would wait here for him when he came to worship. Look behind you as you enter it at the wonderful mosaic of the **Virgin with Constantine and Justinian** ⑫ above the door. It shows Mary seated

Floorplan of Haghia Sophia

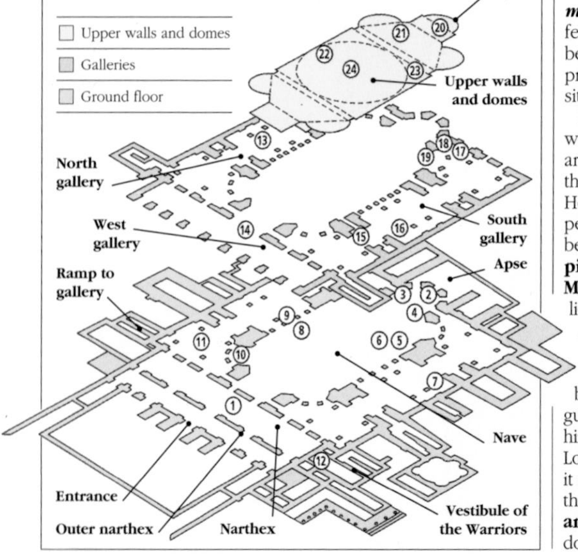
Upper walls and domes
Galleries
Ground floor
Apse
Upper walls and domes
North gallery
West gallery
South gallery
Ramp to gallery
Apse
Nave
Entrance
Outer narthex
Narthex
Vestibule of the Warriors

on a throne holding the infant Jesus and flanked by two of the greatest emperors of the city. Constantine, on her right, presents her with the city of Constantinople, while Justinian offers her Haghia Sophia. This was made long after either of these two emperors lived, probably in the 10th century, during the reign of Basil II (see p52). Visitors exit the church by the door that was once reserved for the emperor, due to its proximity to the Great Palace (see pp92–3).

Figure of Christ, detail from the Deësis Mosaic in the south gallery

GALLERIES

A RAMP LEADS from the ground floor to the north gallery. Here, on the eastern side of the great northwest pier, you will find the 10th-century mosaic of **Emperor Alexander holding a skull ⑬**. On the west face of the same pier is a medieval drawing of a galleon in full sail. The only point of interest in the west gallery is a green marble disk marking the location of the Byzantine **Empress's throne ⑭**.

There is much more to see in the south gallery. You begin by passing through the so-called **Gates of Heaven and Hell ⑮**, a marble doorway of which little is known except that it predates the Ottoman conquest.

Around the corner to the right after passing through this doorway is the **Deësis Mosaic ⑯** showing the Virgin Mary and John the Baptist with Christ Pantocrator (the All-Powerful). Set into the floor opposite it is the tomb of Enrico Dandalo, the Doge of Venice responsible for the sacking of Constantinople in 1204 (see p53).

In the last bay of the south gallery there are two more mosaics. The right-hand one of these is of the **Virgin holding Christ, flanked by Emperor John II Comnenus and Empress Irene ⑰**. The other shows **Christ with Emperor Constantine IX Monomachus and Empress Zoe ⑱**. The faces of the emperor and empress have been altered.

Eight **wooden plaques ⑲** bearing calligraphic inscriptions hang over the nave at the level of the gallery. An addition of the Fossati brothers, they bear the names of Allah, the Prophet Mohammed, the first four caliphs and Hasan and Hussein, two of the Prophet's grandsons who are revered as martyrs.

Mosaic depicting the archangel Gabriel, adorning the lower wall of the apse

UPPER WALLS AND DOMES

T HE APSE is dominated by a large and striking mosaic showing the **Virgin with the infant Jesus on her lap ⑳**. Two other mosaics in the apse show the archangels **Gabriel ㉑** and, opposite him, Michael, but only fragments of the latter now remain. The unveiling of these mosaics on Easter Sunday 867 was a triumphal event celebrating victory over the iconoclasts.

Three mosaic portraits of **saints ㉒** adorn niches in the north tympanum and are visible from the south gallery and the nave. From left to right they depict: St Ignatius the Younger, St John Chrysostom and St Ignatius Theophorus.

In the four pendentives (the triangular, concave areas at the base of the dome) are mosaics of six-winged **seraphim ㉓**. The ones in the east pendentives date from 1346–55, but may be copies of much older ones. Those on the west side are 19th-century imitations that were added by the Fossati brothers.

The great **dome ㉔** itself is decorated with Koranic inscriptions. It was once covered in golden mosaic and the tinkling sound of pieces dropping to the ground was familiar to visitors until the building's 19th-century restoration.

Mosaic of the Virgin with Emperor John II Comnenus and Empress Irene

The cavernous interior of the Byzantine Basilica Cistern

Basilica Cistern ❷

Yerebatan Sarayı

13 Yerebatan Cad, Sultanahmet.
Map 5 E4. ⬛ *(0212) 522 12 59.* ▦
Sultanahmet. ◯ *8:30am–5:30pm
daily (Oct–Apr 8:30am–4pm).* ▨

T HIS VAST underground
water cistern, a beautiful
piece of Byzantine engineering,
is the most unusual tourist
attraction in the city. Although
there may have been an earlier,
smaller cistern here, this
cavernous vault was laid out
under Justinian in 532, mainly
to satisfy the growing demands
of the Great Palace *(see
pp92–3)* on the other side of
the Hippodrome *(see p90).* For
a century after the conquest
(see p54), the Ottomans did
not know of the cistern's
existence. It was rediscovered
after people were found to be
collecting water, and even fish,
by lowering buckets through
holes in their basements.

Visitors tread walkways, to
the mixed sounds of classical
music and dripping water.
The cistern's roof is held up
by 336 columns, each over
8 m (26 ft) high. Only about
two thirds of the original

structure is visible today, the
rest having been bricked up
in the 19th century.

In the far left-hand corner
two columns rest on Medusa
head bases. These bases are
evidence of plundering by the
Byzantines from earlier
monuments. They are thought
to mark a *nymphaeum,* a
shrine to the water nymphs.

Istanbul Crafts Centre ❸

Mehmet Efendi Medresesi

Kabasakal Cad 5, Sultanahmet.
Map 5 E4. ⬛ *(0212) 517 67 82.*
▦ *Adliye.* ◯ *8:30am–5:15pm daily.*

I F YOU ARE INTERESTED in
Turkish craftwork, this former Koranic college is worth
a visit. You can watch skilled
artisans at work: they may be
binding a book, executing an
elegant piece of calligraphy
or painting glaze onto ceramics. All the pieces that are
produced here are for sale.
Other good buys include
exquisite dolls, meerschaum
pipes and jewellery based on
Ottoman designs.

Next door is the Yeşil Ev
Hotel *(see p325),* a restored
Ottoman building with a
pleasant café in its courtyard.

Baths of Roxelana ❹

Haseki Hürrem Hamamı

Ayasofya Meydanı, Sultanahmet.
Map 5 E4. ⬛ *(0212) 638 00 35.* ▦
Sultanahmet. ◯ *9am–5pm
Wed–Mon.*

T HESE BATHS were built for
Süleyman the Magnificent
(see pp54–5) by Sinan *(see
p101),* and are named after
Roxelana, the sultan's devious
wife. They were designated

ROXELANA

Süleyman the Magnificent's
power-hungry wife Roxelana
(1500–58, Haseki Hürrem
in Turkish), rose from being
a concubine in the imperial
harem to become his chief
wife, or first *kadın (see p71).*
Thought to be of Russian
origin, she was also the first
consort permitted to reside
within the walls of Topkapı
Palace *(see pp68–71).*

Roxelana would stop at
nothing to get her own way.
When Süleyman's grand vizier and friend from youth,
İbrahim Paşa, became a threat to her position, she
persuaded the sultan to have him strangled. Much later,
Roxelana performed her *coup de grâce.* In 1553 she
persuaded Süleyman to have his handsome and popular
heir, Mustafa, murdered by deaf mutes to clear the way
for her own son, Selim, to inherit the throne.

The 16th-century Baths of Roxelana, now housing an exclusive carpet shop

for the use of the congregation of Haghia Sophia (*see pp82–5*) when it was used as a mosque. With the women's entrance at one end of the building and the men's at the other, their absolute symmetry makes them perhaps the most handsome baths in the city.

The building is now a government-run carpet shop, but the baths' original features are still clearly visible. A look around it is a must for those who have no intention of baring themselves in a public bath, but are curious about what the interior of a Turkish bath (*see p77*) is like.

Each end starts with a *camekan*, a massive domed hall which would originally have been centred on a fountain. Next is a small *soğukluk*, or intermediate room, which opens into a *hararet*, or steam room. The hexagonal massage slab in each *hararet*, the *göbek taşı*, is inlaid with coloured marbles, indicating that the baths are of imperial origin.

Vakıflar Carpet Museum **5**
Vakıflar Halı Müzesi

Imperial Pavilion, Blue Mosque, Sultanahmet. **Map** 5 E5.
(*(0212) 518 13 30.* Sultanahmet.
○ *9am–noon & 1–4pm Tue–Sat.*
● *public & religious hols.*

A RAMP TO THE LEFT of the main doorway into the Blue Mosque (*see pp88–9*) leads up to the Vakıflar Carpet

Museum. It has been installed in what was formerly the mosque's imperial pavilion. This pavilion was built by Ahmet I and used on Fridays by him and his successors when they attended prayers.

The carpets (*see pp358–9*) are hidden from potentially destructive sunlight by stained-glass windows. They date from the 16th to the 19th centuries and are mostly from the western Anatolian regions of Uşak, Bergama and Konya. For many years mosques have played a vital role in the preservation of early rugs: all the carpets in this museum lay inside mosques until recently.

Detail of a 5th-century mosaic in the Mosaics Museum

Mosaics Museum **6**
Mozaik Müzesi

Arasta Çarşısı, Sultanahmet.
Map 5 E5. (*(0212) 518 12 05.*
Sultanahmet. ○ *9am–4pm Tue–Sun.*

THIS MUSEUM was created simply by roofing over a part of the Great Palace of the Byzantine Emperors (*see pp92–3*) which was discovered in the 1930s. In its heyday the palace boasted hundreds of rooms, many of them glittering with gold mosaics.

The surviving mosaic floor shows a lively variety of wild and domestic beasts and includes some hunting and fighting scenes. It is thought to have adorned the colonnade leading from the royal apartments to the imperial enclosure beside the Hippodrome, and dates from the late 5th century AD.

Blue Mosque **7**

See pp88–9.

Museum of Turkish and Islamic Arts **8**
Türk ve İslam Eserleri Müzesi

Atmeydanı Sok, Sultanahmet.
Map 5 D4. (*(0212) 518 18 05/06.*
Sultanahmet. ○ *9:30am–5:30pm Tue–Sun.* w *www.tiem.org*

O VER 40,000 items are on display in the former palace of İbrahim Paşa (c.1493–1536), the most gifted of Süleyman's many grand viziers. The collection was begun in the 19th century and ranges from the earliest period of Islam, under the Omayyad caliphate (661–750), through to modern times.

Each room concentrates on a different chronological period or geographical area of the Islamic world, with detailed explanations in both Turkish and English. The museum is particularly renowned for its collection of rugs. These range from 13th-century Seljuk fragments to the palatial Persian silks that cover the walls from floor to ceiling in the palace's great hall.

On the ground floor, an ethnographic section focuses on the lifestyles of different Turkish peoples, particularly the nomads of central and eastern Anatolia. The exhibits include recreations of a round felt *yurt* (Turkic nomadic tent) and a traditional brown tent.

Recreated *yurt* interior, Museum of Turkish and Islamic Arts

Blue Mosque 🌀
Sultan Ahmet Camii

THE BLUE MOSQUE, which takes its name from the mainly blue İznik tilework *(see p161)* decorating its interior, is one of the most famous religious buildings in the world. Serene at any time, it is at its most magical when floodlit at night, its minarets circled by keening seagulls. Sultan Ahmet I commissioned the mosque during a period of declining Ottoman fortunes, and it was built between 1609–16 by Mehmet Ağa, the imperial architect. The splendour of the plans pro-voked great hostility at the time, because a mosque with six minarets was considered a sacrilegious attempt to rival the architecture of Mecca.

A 19th-century engraving showing the Blue Mosque viewed from the Hippodrome *(see p90)*

Thick piers support the weight of the dome.

Mihrab

The loge *(see p33)* accommodated the sultan and his entourage during mosque services.

The Imperial Pavilion now houses the Vakıflar Carpet Museum *(see p87).*

Minbar
The 17th-century minbar is intricately carved in white marble. It is used by the imam during prayers on Friday (see p32).

Prayer hall

Exit for tourists

Müezzin mahfili *(see p32)*

Entrance to courtyard

★ İznik Tiles
No cost was spared in the decoration. The tiles were made at the peak of tile production in İznik (see p161).

STAR FEATURES

★ Inside of the Dome

★ İznik Tiles

★ View of the Domes

★ **Inside of the Dome**
Mesmeric designs employing flowing arabesques are painted onto the interior of the mosque's domes and semidomes. The windows which pierce the domes no longer have their original 17th-century stained glass.

VISITORS' CHECKLIST

Sultanahmet Meydanı. **Map** 5 E5.
(0212) 518 13 19; or (0212) 513 36 08 for permission to visit minarets and domes. Sultan-ahmet. 9am–5pm daily. prayer times. **Son et Lumière** May–Sep: daily after dusk.

★ **View of the Domes**
The graceful cascade of domes and semidomes makes a striking sight when viewed from the courtyard below.

Over 250 windows
allow light to flood into the mosque.

Entrance

Ablutions Fountain
The hexagonal şadırvan is now purely ornamental since ritual ablutions are no longer carried out at this fountain.

Each minaret
has two or three balconies.

Exit to Hippodrome

The courtyard covers an area the same size as the prayer hall, balancing the whole building.

Washing the Feet
The Muslim's ritual ablutions conclude with the washing of the feet (see p33). Taps outside the mosque are used by the faithful for this purpose.

Egyptian Obelisk and the Serpentine Column in the Hippodrome

Hippodrome 𝟵

At Meydanı

Sultanahmet. **Map** 3 E4 (5 D4).
🚊 *Sultanahmet.*

LITTLE IS LEFT of the gigantic stadium which once stood at the heart of the Byzantine city of Constantinople *(see pp50–1)*. It was originally laid out by Emperor Septimus Severus during his rebuilding of the city in the 3rd century AD. Emperor Constantine I *(see p49)* enlarged the Hippodrome and connected its *kathisma*, or royal box, to the nearby Great Palace *(see pp92–3)*. It is thought that the stadium held up to 100,000 people. The site is now an elongated public garden, At Meydanı, the Square of the Horses. There are, however, enough remains of the Hippodrome to get a sense of its scale and importance.

The road running around the square almost directly follows the line of the chariot racing track. You can also make out

Relief carved on the base of the Egyptian Obelisk

some of the arches of the *sphendone* (the curved end of the Hippodrome) by walking a few steps down İbret Sokağı. Constantine adorned the *spina*, the central line of the stadium, with obelisks and columns from Ancient Egypt and Greece, importing a sense of history to his new capital. Conspicuous by its absence is the column which once stood on the spot where the tourist information office is now located. This was topped by four bronze horses which were pillaged during the Fourth Crusade *(see p52)* and taken to St Mark's in Venice. Three ancient monuments remain, however. The **Egyptian Obelisk**, which was built in 1500 BC, stood outside Luxor until Constantine had it brought to his city. This beautifully carved monument is broken and is probably only one third of its original height. It stands on a base, made in the 4th century AD, showing Theodosius I *(see p49)* and his family in the *kathisma*

watching various events. The four sides depict a chariot race; Theodosius preparing to crown the winner with a wreath of laurel; prisoners paying homage to the emperor; and the erection of the obelisk itself.

Next to it is the **Serpentine Column**, believed to date from 479 BC, which was shipped here from Delphi. The heads of the serpents were knocked off in the 18th century by a drunken Polish nobleman. One of them can be seen in the Archaeological Museum *(see pp74–5)*.

Another obelisk still standing, but of unknown date, is usually referred to as the **Column of Constantine Porphyrogenitus**, after the emperor who restored it in the 10th century AD. It is also sometimes called the Brazen Column, because it is thought to have once been sheathed in a case of bronze. Its dilapidated state owes much to the fact that young Janissaries *(see p56)* would routinely scale it as a test of their bravery.

The only other structure in the Hippodrome is a domed fountain which commemorates the visit of Kaiser Wilhelm II to Istanbul in 1898.

The Hippodrome was the scene of one of the bloodiest events in Istanbul's history. In 532 a brawl between rival chariot-racing teams developed into the Nika Revolt, during which much of the city was destroyed. The end of the revolt came when an army of mercenaries, under the command of Justinian's general Belisarius, massacred an estimated 30,000 people trapped in the Hippodrome.

Cistern of 1,001 Columns 𝟭𝟬

Binbirdirek Sarnıcı

Klodfarer Cad, Sultanahmet. **Map** 3 D4 (5 D4). 🚊 *Çemberlitaş.*

THIS CISTERN dates back to around the 4th century AD, and was second in size only to the nearby Basilica Cistern *(see p86)*. It was also known as the Cistern of Philoxenus and measured 64 m (210 ft) by 56 m (184 ft).

CEREMONIES IN THE HIPPODROME

Beginning with the inauguration of Constantinople on 11th May 330 *(see p49)*, the Hippodrome formed the stage for the city's greatest public events for the next 1,300 years. The Byzantines' most popular pastime was watching chariot racing in the stadium. Even after the Hippodrome fell into ruins following the Ottoman conquest of Istanbul *(see p54)*, it continued to be used for great public occasions. This 16th-century illustration depicts Murat III watching the 52-day-long festivities staged for the circumcision of his son Mehmet. All the guilds of Istanbul paraded before the Sultan displaying their crafts.

Sultan Murat III

Palace of İbrahim Paşa (Museum of Turkish and Islamic Arts, *see p00*)

Column of Constantine Porphyrogenitus **Serpentine Column** **Egyptian Obelisk**

It could hold enough water to supply a population of 360,000 for about 10 days.

The herring-bone brick roof vaults are supported by 264 marble columns – the 1,001 columns of its name is poetic exaggeration. Interestingly, due to its dampness, the cistern building proved to provide the ideal atmosphere for the silk weaving process and, for many decades, it was thus used by Istanbul's silk weavers as a workplace.

Tomb of Sultan Mahmut II ❶

Mahmut II Türbesi

Divanyolu Cad, Çemberlitaş.
Map 3 D4 (4 C3). 🚊 Çemberlitaş.
◯ 9:30am–4:30pm daily.

THIS LARGE octagonal mausoleum is in the Empire style (modelled on Roman architecture), made popular by Napoleon. It was built in 1838, the year before Sultan Mahmut II's death and is shared by sultans Mahmut II, Abdül Aziz and Abdül Hamit II *(see pp57)*. Within, Corinthian pilasters divide up walls which groan with symbols of prosperity and victory. The huge tomb dominates a cemetery that has beautiful headstones, a fountain and, at the far end, a good café.

Constantine's Column ❶

Çemberlitaş

Yeniçeriler Cad, Çemberlitaş.
Map 3 D4 (4 C3).
🚊 Çemberlitaş.
Çemberlitaş Baths Vezirhanı Cad 8.
◯ 6am–midnight daily.

A SURVIVOR OF both storm and fire, this 35-m (115-ft) high column was constructed in AD 330 as part of the celebrations to inaugurate the new Byzantine capital *(see p49)*. It once dominated the magnificent Forum of Constantine.

Made of porphyry brought from Heliopolis in Egypt, it was originally surmounted by a Corinthian capital bearing a statue of Emperor Constantine dressed as Apollo. This was brought down in a storm in 1106. Although what is left is relatively unimpressive, it has been carefully preserved. In the year 416 the 10 stone drums making up the column were reinforced with metal rings. These were renewed in 1701 by Sultan Mustafa III, and consequently the column is known as Çemberlitaş (the

Constantine's Column

Hooped Column) in Turkish. In English it is sometimes referred to as the Burnt Column because it was damaged by several fires, especially one in 1779 which decimated the Grand Bazaar *(see pp104–5)*.

A variety of fantastical holy relics were supposedly entombed in the base of the column, which has since been encased in stone to strengthen it. These included the axe which Noah used to build the ark, Mary Magdalen's flask of anointing oil, and remains of the loaves of bread with which Christ fed the multitude.

Next to Constantine's Column, on the corner of Divanyolu Caddesi, stand the Çemberlitaş Baths. This splendid *hamam* complex *(see p79)* was commissioned by Nur Banu, wife of Sultan Selim II, and built in 1584 to a plan by the great Sinan *(see p101)*. Although the original women's section no longer survives, the baths still have separate facilities for men and women. The staff are used to foreign visitors, so this is a good place for your first experience of a Turkish bath.

Sokollu Mehmet Paşa Mosque ⑬

Sokollu Mehmet
Paşa Camii

Şehit Çeşmesi Sok, Sultanahmet.
Map 5 D5. ☎ (0212) 518 16 33.
🚊 Çemberlitaş or Sultanahmet.
◯ daily. 💰 donation.

Built by the architect Sinan (see p101) in 1571–2, this mosque was commissioned by Sokollu Mehmet Paşa, grand vizier to Selim II. The simplicity of Sinan's design solution for the mosque's sloping site has been widely admired. A steep entrance stairway leads up to the mosque courtyard from the street, passing beneath the teaching hall of its *medrese (see p32)*. Only the tiled lunettes above the windows in the portico give a hint of the jewelled mosque interior to come.

Inside, the far wall around the carved mihrab is entirely covered in İznik tiles (see p161) of a sumptuous green-blue hue. This tile panel, designed specifically for the space, is complemented by six stained-glass windows. The "hat" of the *minbar* is covered with the same tiles. Most of the mosque's other walls are of plain stone, but they are enlivened by a few more tile panels. Set into the wall over the entrance there is a small piece of greenish stone which is supposedly from the Kaaba, the holy stone at the centre of Mecca.

Interior of the 16th-century Sokollu Mehmet Paşa Mosque

The Byzantine Church of SS Sergius and Bacchus, now a mosque

SS Sergius and Bacchus' Church ⑭

Küçük Ayasofya Camii

Küçük Ayasofya Cad. **Map** 5 D5.
🚊 Çemberlitaş or Sultanahmet.
◯ daily. ♿

Commonly referred to as "Little Haghia Sophia", this church was built in 527, a few years before its namesake (see pp82–5). It too was founded by Emperor Justinian (see p51), together with his empress, Theodora, at the beginning of his long reign. Ingenious and highly decorative, the church gives a somewhat higgledy-piggledy impression both inside and out and is one of the most charming of all the city's architectural treasures.

Inside, an irregular octagon of columns on two floors supports a broad central dome composed of 16 vaults. The

RECONSTRUCTION OF THE GREAT PALACE

In Byzantine times, present-day Sultanahmet was the site of the Great Palace, which, in its heyday, had no equal in Europe and dazzled medieval visitors with its opulence. This great complex of buildings – including royal apartments, state rooms, churches, courtyards and gardens – extended over a sloping, terraced site from the Hippodrome to the imperial harbour on the shore of the Sea of Marmara. The palace was built in stages, beginning under Constantine in the 4th century. It was enlarged by Justinian following the fire caused by the Nika Revolt in 532. Later emperors, especially the 9th-century Basil I, extended it further. After several hundred years of occupation, it was finally abandoned in the second half of the 13th century in favour of Blachernae Palace.

The Mese was a colonnaded street lined with shops and statuary.

Hippodrome (see p90)

Hormisdas Palace

Church of SS Peter and Paul

Church of SS Sergius and Bacchus

mosaic decoration which once adorned some of the walls has long since crumbled away. However, the green and red marble columns, the delicate tracery of the capitals and the carved frieze running above the columns are original features of the church.

The inscription on this frieze, in boldly carved Greek script, mentions the founders of the church and St Sergius, but not St Bacchus. The two saints were Roman centurions who converted to Christianity and were martyred. Justinian credited them with saving his life when, as a young man, he was implicated in a plot to kill his uncle, Justin I. The saints supposedly appeared to Justin in a dream and told him to release his nephew.

The Church of SS Sergius and Bacchus was built between two important edifices to which it was connected, the Palace of Hormisdas and the Church of SS Peter and Paul, but has outlived them both. After the conquest of Istanbul in 1453 (see p54) it was converted into a mosque.

Bucoleon Palace ⓕ
Bukoleon Sarayı

Kennedy Cad, Sultanahmet.
Map 5 E5. 🚇 *Sultanahmet.*

F INDING THE SITE of what remains of the Great Palace of the Byzantine emperors requires precision. It is not advisable to visit the ruins alone as they are usually inhabited by tramps.

Take the path under the railway from the Church of SS Sergius and Bacchus, turn left and walk beside Kennedy Caddesi, the main road along the shore of the Sea of Marmara, for about 400 m (450 yards). This will bring you to a stretch of the ancient sea walls, constructed to protect the city from a naval assault. Within these walls you will find a creeper-clad section of stonework pierced by three vast windows framed in

marble. This is all that now survives of the Bucoleon Palace, a maritime residence that formed part of the sprawling Great Palace. The waters of a small private harbour lapped right up to the palace and a private flight of steps led down into the water, allowing the emperor to board imperial *caïques*. The ruined tower just east of the palace was a lighthouse, called the Pharos, in Byzantine times.

Wall of Bucoleon Palace, the only part of the Byzantine Great Palace still standing

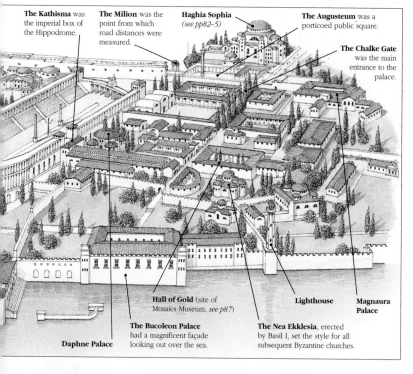

The Kathisma was the imperial box of the Hippodrome.

The Milion was the point from which road distances were measured.

Haghia Sophia (see pp82–5)

The Augusteum was a porticoed public square.

The Chalke Gate was the main entrance to the palace.

Hall of Gold (site of Mosaics Museum, see p87)

Lighthouse

Magnaura Palace

The Bucoleon Palace had a magnificent façade looking out over the sea.

The Nea Ekklesia, erected by Basil I, set the style for all subsequent Byzantine churches.

Daphne Palace

THE BAZAAR QUARTER

TRADE HAS always been important in a city straddling the continents of Asia and Europe. Nowhere is this more evident than in the warren of streets lying between the Grand Bazaar and Galata Bridge. Everywhere, goods tumble out of shops onto the pavement. Look through any of the archways in between shops and you will discover courtyards or *hans (see pp24–5)* containing feverishly

Window from Nuruosmaniye Mosque

industrious workshops. With its seemingly limitless range of goods, the labyrinthine Grand Bazaar is at the centre of all this commercial activity. The Spice Bazaar is equally colourful but smaller and more manageable.

Up on the hill, next to the university, is Süleymaniye Mosque, a glorious expression of 16th-century Ottoman culture. It is just one of numerous beautiful mosques in this area.

SIGHTS AT A GLANCE

Mosques and Churches
Kalenderhane Mosque **7**
New Mosque **1**
Prince's Mosque **6**
Rüstem Paşa Mosque **3**
Sülemaniye Mosque pp100–101 **5**
Tulip Mosque **8**

Bazaars, Hans and Shops
Book Bazaar **11**
Grand Bazaar pp104–105 **13**
Spice Bazaar **2**
Valide Hanı **12**

Museums and Monuments
Forum of Theodosius **9**

Squares and Courtyards
Beyazıt Square **10**
Çorlulu Ali Paşa Courtyard **14**

Waterways
Golden Horn **4**

KEY

▦	Street-by-Street map *See pp96–97*
⚓	Ferry boarding point
🚊	Tram stop
🚌	Main bus stop
C	Mosque

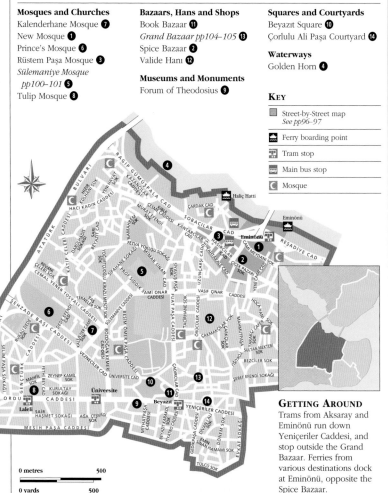

GETTING AROUND

Trams from Aksaray and Eminönü run down Yeniçeriler Caddesi, and stop outside the Grand Bazaar. Ferries from various destinations dock at Eminönü, opposite the Spice Bazaar.

0 metres	500
0 yards	500

◁ **The inside of the Grand Bazaar, always thronging with bargain-hunters**

Street-by-Street: Around the Spice Bazaar

THE NARROW STREETS around the Spice Bazaar encapsulate the spirit of old Istanbul. From here buses, taxis and trams head off across the Galata Bridge and into the interior of the city. The blast of ships' horns signals the departure of ferries from Eminönü to Asian Istanbul. It is the quarter's shops and markets, though, that are the focus of attention for the eager shoppers who crowd the Spice Bazaar and the streets around it, sometimes breaking for a leisurely tea beneath the trees in its courtyard. Across the way, and entirely aloof from the bustle, rise the domes of the New Mosque. On one of the commercial alleyways that radiate out from the mosque, an inconspicuous doorway leads up stairs to the terrace of the serene, tile-covered Rüstem Paşa Mosque.

Nargile on sale near the Spice Bazaar

★ **Rüstem Paşa Mosque**
The interior of this secluded mosque is a brilliant pattern-book made of İznik tiles (see p161) of the finest quality ❸

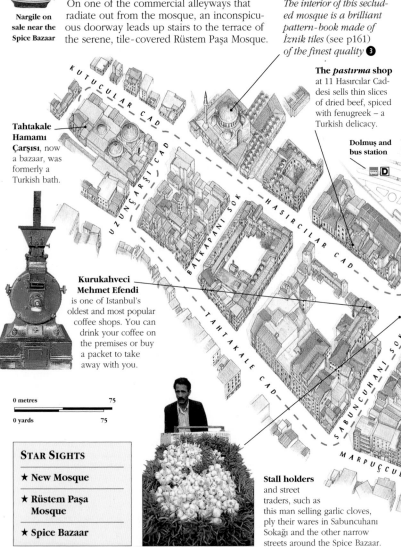

The *pastırma* shop at 11 Hasırcılar Caddesi sells thin slices of dried beef, spiced with fenugreek – a Turkish delicacy.

Dolmuş and bus station

Tahtakale Hamamı Çarşısı, now a bazaar, was formerly a Turkish bath.

Kurukahveci Mehmet Efendi is one of Istanbul's oldest and most popular coffee shops. You can drink your coffee on the premises or buy a packet to take away with you.

KUTUCULAR CAD

UZUNÇARŞILI CAD

BALKAPANI SOK

HASIRCILAR CAD

TAHTAKALE CAD

SABUNCUHANI SOK

MARPUÇCUL

0 metres 75
0 yards 75

Stall holders and street traders, such as this man selling garlic cloves, ply their wares in Sabuncuhanı Sokağı and the other narrow streets around the Spice Bazaar.

STAR SIGHTS

★ New Mosque

★ Rüstem Paşa Mosque

★ Spice Bazaar

Eminönü is the port from which ferries depart to many destinations and also for trips along the Bosphorus (*see pp126–7*). It bustles with activity as traders compete to sell drinks and snacks.

LOCATOR MAP
See Street Finder maps 4 and 5

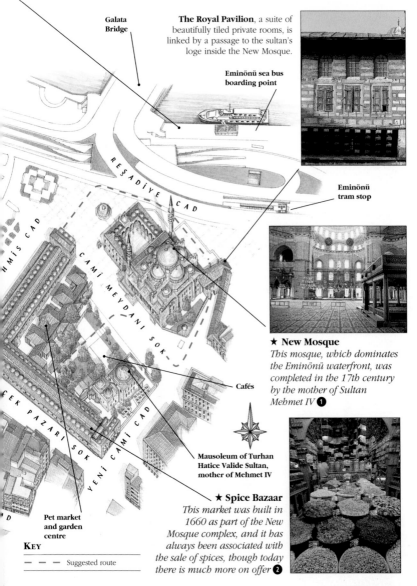

Galata Bridge

The Royal Pavilion, a suite of beautifully tiled private rooms, is linked by a passage to the sultan's loge inside the New Mosque.

Eminönü sea bus boarding point

Eminönü tram stop

★ **New Mosque**
This mosque, which dominates the Eminönü waterfront, was completed in the 17th century by the mother of Sultan Mehmet IV ❶

Cafés

Mausoleum of Turhan Hatice Valide Sultan, mother of Mehmet IV

★ **Spice Bazaar**
This market was built in 1660 as part of the New Mosque complex, and it has always been associated with the sale of spices, though today there is much more on offer ❷

Pet market and garden centre

KEY

– – – Suggested route

New Mosque ❶
Yeni Cami

Yeni Cami Meydanı, Eminönü.
Map 5 D2. 🚇 *Eminönü.* ⭘ *daily.*

SITUATED AT the southern end of Galata Bridge, the New Mosque is one of the most prominent mosques in the city. It dates from the time when a few women from the harem became powerful enough to dictate the policies of the Ottoman sultans.

The mosque was started in 1597 by Safiye, mother of Mehmet III, but building was suspended on the sultan's death as his mother then lost her position. It was not completed until 1663, after Turhan Hatice, mother of Mehmet IV, had taken up the project.

Though the mosque was built after the classical period of Ottoman architecture, it shares many traits with earlier imperial foundations, including a monumental courtyard. The mosque once had a hospital, school and public baths.

The turquoise, blue and white floral tiles decorating the interior are from İznik *(see p161)* and date from the mid-17th century, though by this time the quality of the tiles produced there was already in decline. More striking are the tiled lunettes and bold Koranic frieze decorating the porch between the courtyard and the prayer hall.

At the far left-hand corner of the upper gallery is the sultan's loge *(see p33)*, which is linked to his personal suite of rooms.

A selection of nuts and seeds for sale in the Spice Bazaar

Spice Bazaar ❷
Mısır Çarşısı

Cami Meydanı Sok. **Map** 5 D2.
🚇 *Eminönü.* ⭘ *8am–7pm Mon–Sat.*

THIS CAVERNOUS, L-shaped market was built in the early 17th century as an extension of the New Mosque complex. Its revenues once helped maintain the mosque's philanthropic institutions.

In Turkish the market is named the Mısır Çarşısı – the Egyptian Bazaar – because it was built with money paid as duty on Egyptian imports. In English it is usually known as the Spice Bazaar. From medieval times spices were a vital and expensive part of cooking and they became the market's main produce. The bazaar came to specialize in spices from the Orient, taking advantage of Istanbul's site on the trade route between the East (where most spices were grown) and Europe.

Stalls in the bazaar stock spices, herbs and other foods such as honey, nuts, sweetmeats and *pastırma* (dried beef). Today's expensive Eastern commodity, caviar, is also available, the best variety being Iranian. Nowadays an eclectic range of items can be found in the Spice Bazaar, from household goods, toys and clothes to exotic aphrodisiacs. The square between the two arms of the bazaar is full of commercial activity, with cafés, and stalls selling plants and pets.

Floral İznik tiles adorning the interior of Rüstem Paşa Mosque

Rüstem Paşa Mosque ❸
Rüstem Paşa Camii

Hasırcılar Cad, Eminönü.
Map 4 C2. 🚇 *Eminönü.* ⭘ *daily.*

RAISED ABOVE the busy shops and warehouses around the Spice Bazaar, this mosque was built in 1561 by the great architect Sinan *(see p101)* for Rüstem Paşa, son-in-law of and grand vizier to Süleyman I *(see p55)*.

The staggering wealth of its decoration says something about the amount of money that the corrupt Rüstem managed to salt away. Most of the interior is covered in İznik tiles of the highest quality. The four piers are adorned with tiles of one design, but the rest of the prayer hall is a riot of different patterns, from abstract to floral. Some of the finest tiles can be found on the galleries, making it the most magnificently tiled mosque in the city.

The New Mosque, a prominent feature on the Eminönü waterfront

Golden Horn ❹

Haliç

Map 4 C1. 🚇 *Eminönü.*
🚌 *55T, 99A.*

OFTEN DESCRIBED as the world's greatest natural harbour, the Golden Horn is a flooded river valley that flows southwest into the Bosphorus. The estuary attracted settlers to its shores in the 7th century BC and later enabled Constantinople to become a rich and powerful port. According to legend, the Byzantines threw so many valuables into it during the Ottoman conquest *(see p54)* that the waters glistened with gold. Today, however, it has become polluted by the numerous nearby factories.

Spanning the mouth of the Horn is the Galata Bridge, which joins Eminönü to Galata. The bridge, built in 1992, opens in the middle to allow access for tall ships. It is a good place from which to appreciate the complex geography of the city and admire the minaret-filled skyline. Fishermen's boats selling mackerel sandwiches are usually moored at each end.

The present Galata Bridge replaced a pontoon bridge with a busy lower level of restaurants. The old bridge has been reconstructed further up the Golden Horn, just south of the Rahmi Koç Museum.

Süleymaniye Mosque ❺

See pp100–101.

Prince's Mosque ❻

Şehzade Camii

70 Şehzade Başı Cad, Saraçhane.
Map 4 B3. 🚇 *Laleli.* 🔲 *daily.*
Tombs 🔲 *9am–5pm Tue–Sun.*

THIS MOSQUE complex was erected by Süleyman the Magnificent *(see p55)* in memory of his eldest son by Roxelana, Şehzade (Prince) Mehmet, who died of smallpox at the age of 21. The building was Sinan's *(see p101)*

Dome of the Prince's Mosque, Sinan's first imperial mosque

first major imperial commission and was completed in 1548. The architect used a delightful decorative style in this mosque before abandoning it in favour of the classical austerity of his later work. The mosque is approached through an elegant porticoed inner courtyard, while the other institutions making up the mosque complex, including a *medrese (see p32)*, are enclosed within an outer courtyard. The mosque's interior is unusual and was something of an experiment: symmetrical, it has a semi-dome on all four sides.

The three tombs to the rear of the mosque, belonging to Şehzade Mehmet himself and grand viziers İbrahim Paşa and Rüstem Paşa, are the finest in the city. Each has beautiful İznik tiles *(see p161)* and original stained glass. That of Şehzade Mehmet also boasts the finest painted dome in Istanbul.

On Fridays you may notice a crowd of women flocking to another tomb within the complex, that of Helvacı Baba. This has been done traditionally for over 400 years. Helvacı Baba is said to miraculously cure crippled children, solve any fertility problems and find husbands or accommodation for those who beseech him.

Kalenderhane Mosque ❼

Kalenderhane Camii

16 Mart Şehitleri Cad, Saraçhane.
Map 4 B3. 🚇 *Üniversite.*
🔲 *prayer times only.*

SITTING IN THE LEE of the Valens Aqueduct, on the site where a Roman bath once stood, is this Byzantine church with a chequered history. Built and rebuilt several times between the 6th and 12th centuries, it was converted into a mosque shortly after the conquest in 1453 *(see p54)*. The mosque is named after the Kalender brotherhood of dervishes, who used the church as its headquarters for some years after the conquest.

The building has the cruciform layout characteristic of Byzantine churches of the period. Some of the decoration remaining from its last incarnation, as the Church of Theotokos Kyriotissa (her Ladyship Mary, Mother of God), also survives in the prayer hall with its marble panelling and in the fragments of fresco in the narthex (entrance hall).

A shaft of light illuminates the interior of Kalenderhane Mosque

Süleymaniye Mosque ❺
Süleymaniye Camii

ISTANBUL'S MOST IMPORTANT MOSQUE is both a tribute to its architect, the great Sinan, and a fitting memorial to its founder, Süleyman the Magnificent (see p55). It was built above the Golden Horn in the grounds of the old palace, Eski Saray, between 1550 and 1557. Like the city's other imperial mosques, the Süleymaniye Mosque was not only a place of worship, but also a charitable foundation, or külliye (see p32). The mosque is surrounded by its former hospital, soup kitchen, schools, caravanserai and bath house. This complex provided a welfare system which fed over 1,000 of the city's poor – Muslims, Christians and Jews alike – every day.

Courtyard
The ancient columns that surround the courtyard are said to have come originally from the kathisma, the Byzantine royal box in the Hippo-drome (see p90).

Muvakkithane Gateway
The main courtyard entrance (now closed) contained the rooms of the mosque astronomer, who determined prayer times.

Minaret

Tomb of Sinan

The caravanserai provided lodging and food for travellers and their animals.

İmaret Gate

Café in a sunken garden

İmaret
The kitchen – now a restaurant – fed the city's poor as well as the mosque staff and their families. The size of the millstone in its courtyard gives some idea of the amount of grain needed to feed everyone.

★ Mosque Interior

A sense of soaring space and calm strikes you as you enter the mosque. The effect is enhanced by the fact that the height of the dome from the floor is exactly double its diameter.

VISITORS' CHECKLIST

Prof Sıddık Sami Onar Caddesi, Vefa. **Map** 4 C3. **(** (0212) 513 36 08. 🚋 Beyazıt or Eminönü. ◯ daily; phone first for permission to visit interior. ● at prayer times.

The Tomb of Roxelana contains Süleyman's beloved Russian-born wife.

Entrance

Graveyard

★ Tomb of Süleyman

Ceramic stars said to be set with emeralds sparkle above the coffins of Süleyman, his daughter Mihrimah and two of his successors, Süleyman II and Ahmet II.

These marble benches were used to support coffins before burial.

"Addicts Alley" is so called because the cafés here once sold opium and hashish as well as coffee and tea.

The *medreses* to the south of the mosque house a library containing 110,000 manuscripts.

Former hospital and asylum

SINAN, THE IMPERIAL ARCHITECT

Like many of his eminent contemporaries, Koca Mimar Sinan (c.1491–1588) was brought from Anatolia to Istanbul in the *devşirme*, the annual roundup of talented Christian youths, and educated at one of the elite palace schools. He became a military engineer but won the eye of Süleyman I, who made him chief imperial architect in 1538. With the far-sighted patronage of the sultan, Sinan – the closest Turkey gets to a Renaissance architect – created masterpieces which demonstrated his master's status as the most magnificent of monarchs. Sinan died aged 97, having built 131 mosques and 200 other buildings.

Bust of the great architect Sinan

STAR FEATURES

★ Mosque Interior

★ Tomb of Süleyman

Tulip Mosque ❽
Laleli Camii

Ordu Cad, Laleli. **Map** 4 B4.
🚊 *Laleli*. ⭘ *prayer times only.*

BUILT IN 1759–63, this mosque complex is the city's best example of the Baroque style, of which its architect, Mehmet Tahir Ağa, was the greatest exponent. A variety of gaudy, coloured marble covers all of its surfaces. Underneath the body of the mosque is a great hall, supported on eight piers with a fountain in the middle, used as a market and packed with Eastern Europeans and Central Asians haggling over clothing.

The nearby Büyük Taş Hanı, or Big Stone Han, probably part of the mosque's original complex *(see pp32–3)*, now houses shops and a restaurant. To get to it, turn left outside the mosque into Fethi Bey Caddesi, and take the second left into Çukur Çeşme Sokağı. The main courtyard of the han is at the end of a long passage off this lane.

The Baroque Tulip Mosque, housing a marketplace in its basement

Forum of Theodosius ❾

Ordu Cad, Beyazıt. **Map** 4 C4.
🚊 *Üniversite or Beyazıt.*

THE CITY OF Constantinople *(see pp50–51)* was built around large public squares or forums, the largest of which stood on the site of Beyazıt Square. It was once known as the Forum Tauri (Forum of the Bull) because of the huge bronze bull in which sacrificial animals, and sometimes

Peacock feather design on a column at the Forum of Theodosius

criminals, were roasted. The huge columns, decorated with a motif reminiscent of a peacock's tail, are particularly striking. When the forum became derelict these columns were reused in the city, some in the Basilica Cistern *(see p86)*, and fragments from the forum were built into Beyazıt Hamamı, a Turkish bath *(see p77)* further west down Ordu Caddesi, now a bazaar.

Beyazıt Square ❿
Beyazıt Meydanı

Ordu Cad, Beyazıt. **Map** 4 C4.
🚊 *Beyazıt.*

ALWAYS FILLED with crowds of people and huge flocks of pigeons, Beyazıt Square is the most vibrant space in the old part of the city. During the week the square is the venue for a flea market, with carpets *(see pp358–9)*, silks and general bric-a-brac on sale and many cafés located beneath shady plane trees.

On the northern side of the square is the Moorish-style gateway leading into Istanbul University. Within the wooded grounds rises **Beyazıt**

Tower, a marble fire-watching station built in 1828 on the site of Eski Saray, the palace first inhabited by Mehmet the Conqueror *(see p54)*. A climb of 180 steps leads to a panoramic view over Istanbul.

On the square's eastern side is **Beyazıt Mosque**. Completed in 1506, it is the oldest surviving imperial mosque in the city. Behind the impressive outer portal is a harmonious courtyard with an elegant domed fountain at its centre. The layout of its interior is heavily inspired by the design of Haghia Sophia *(see pp82–5)*.

Beyazıt Tower, within the wooded grounds of Istanbul University

Book Bazaar ⑪
Sahaflar Çarşısı

Sahaflar Çarşısı Sok, Beyazıt.
Map 4 C4. 🚇 *Üniversite.*
🕐 8am–8pm daily. ♿

THIS CHARMING book-sellers' courtyard, on the site of the Byzantine book and paper market, can be entered either from Beyazıt Square or from inside the Grand Bazaar *(see pp104–105)*. Early in the Ottoman period *(see pp54–5)*, printed books were seen as a corrupting influence and were banned in Turkey, so the bazaar sold only manuscripts. On 31 January 1729 İbrahim Müteferrika (1674–1745) produced the first printed Turkish book, an Arabic dictionary, and today his bust stands in the centre of the market. Book prices are fixed and cannot be haggled over.

Customers browsing in the Book Bazaar (Sahaflar Çarşisi)

Valide Han ⑫
Valide Hanı

Junction of Çakmakçılar Yokuşu & Tarakçılar Sok, Beyazıt. **Map** 4 C3.
🚇 *Beyazıt, then 10 mins' walk.*
🕐 9:30am–5pm Mon–Sat.

IF THE GRAND BAZAAR *(see pp104–105)* seems large, it is sobering to realize that it is only the covered part of a huge area of seething commercial activity which reaches all the way to the Golden Horn. Most of the manufacturing and trade takes place in *hans (see pp24–5)* hidden away from the street behind shaded gateways.

The largest han in Istanbul is Valide Han, built in 1651 by Kösem, the mother of Sultan Mehmet IV. You enter it from Çakmakçılar Yokuşu through a massive portal, pass through an irregularly shaped forecourt, and come out into a large courtyard centring on a Shiite mosque. This was built when the han became the centre of Persian trade in the city. The han now throbs to the rhythm of hundreds of weaving looms.

A short walk further down Çakmakçılar Yokuşu is Büyük

Yeni Han, hidden behind another impressive doorway. This 1764 Baroque han has three arcaded levels. In the labyrinth of streets around the hans, artisans are grouped according to their wares.

Grand Bazaar ⑬

See pp104–105.

Çorlulu Ali Paşa Courtyard ⑭
Çorlulu Ali Paşa Külliyesi

Yeniçeriler Cad, Beyazıt. **Map** 4 C4.
🚇 *Beyazıt.* 🕐 *daily.*

LIKE MANY OTHERS in the city, the *medrese (see p32)* of this mosque complex outside the Grand Bazaar has become the setting for a tranquil outdoor café. It was built for Çorlulu Ali Paşa, son-in-law

of Mustafa II, the grand vizier under Ahmet III.

The complex is entered from Yeniçeriler Caddesi by two alleyways. Several carpet shops now inhabit the *medrese* and rugs are hung and spread all around for prospective buyers. The carpet shops share the *medrese* with a *kahve*, a traditional café, which is popular with locals and university students. It advertises itself irresistibly as the "Traditional Mystic Water Pipe and Erenler Tea Garden" where you can sit, drink tea and perhaps smoke a *nargile* (bubble pipe), while deciding which carpet to buy *(see pp358–9)*.

Situated across Bileycıler Sokak, an alleyway off Çorlulu Ali Paşa Courtyard, is the Koca Sinan Paşa tomb complex, the courtyard of which is another tea garden. The charming *medrese*, mausoleum and *sebil* (a fountain where water was handed out to passersby) were built in 1593 by Davut Ağa, who succeeded Sinan *(see p101)* as chief architect of the empire. The tomb of Koca Sinan Paşa, grand vizier under Murat III and Mehmet III, is a striking 16-sided structure.

Just off the other side of Yeniçeriler Caddesi is Gedik Paşa Hamamı, probably the city's oldest working Turkish baths *(see p77)*, built around 1475 for Gedik Ahmet Paşa, grand vizier under Mehmet the Conqueror *(see p54)*.

Carpet shops in Çorlulu Ali Paşa Courtyard

The Grand Bazaar ⓭
Kapalı Çarşı

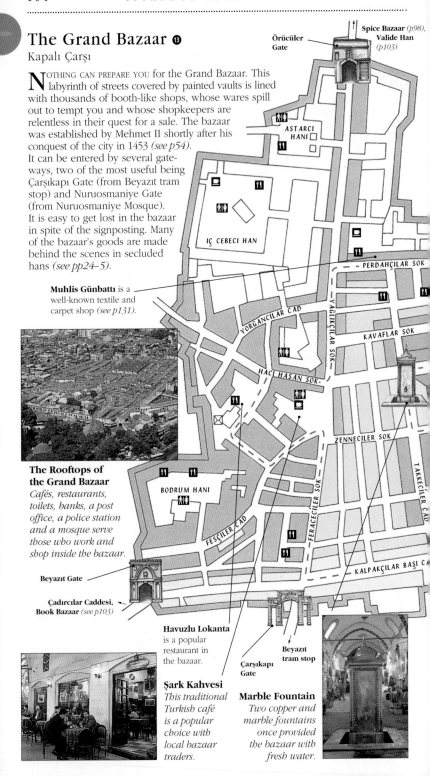

NOTHING CAN PREPARE YOU for the Grand Bazaar. This labyrinth of streets covered by painted vaults is lined with thousands of booth-like shops, whose wares spill out to tempt you and whose shopkeepers are relentless in their quest for a sale. The bazaar was established by Mehmet II shortly after his conquest of the city in 1453 (see p54). It can be entered by several gateways, two of the most useful being Çarşıkapı Gate (from Beyazıt tram stop) and Nuruosmaniye Gate (from Nuruosmaniye Mosque). It is easy to get lost in the bazaar in spite of the signposting. Many of the bazaar's goods are made behind the scenes in secluded hans (see pp24–5).

Spice Bazaar (p98), **Valide Han** (p103)

Örücüler Gate

ASTARCI HANI

IÇ CEBECI HANI

PERDAHÇILAR SOK

YORGANCILAR CAD

YAĞLIKÇILAR SOK

KAVAFLAR SOK

HACI HASAN SOK

ZENNECILER SOK

TAKKECILER CAD

FERACECILER SOK

BODRUM HANI

FESÇILER CAD

KALPAKÇILAR BAŞI C

Muhlis Günbattı is a well-known textile and carpet shop (see p131).

The Rooftops of the Grand Bazaar
Cafés, restaurants, toilets, banks, a post office, a police station and a mosque serve those who work and shop inside the bazaar.

Beyazıt Gate

Çadırcılar Caddesi, Book Bazaar (see p103)

Havuzlu Lokanta is a popular restaurant in the bazaar.

Çarşıkapı Gate

Beyazıt tram stop

Şark Kahvesi
This traditional Turkish café is a popular choice with local bazaar traders.

Marble Fountain
Two copper and marble fountains once provided the bazaar with fresh water.

Zincirli Han
This is one of the prettiest hans in the bazaar. Here a piece of jewellery can be made to your own choice of design.

VISITORS' CHECKLIST

Çarşıkapı Cad, Beyazıt.
Map 4 C4. 🚇 Beyazıt (for Çarşıkapı Gate), Çemberlitaş (for Nuruosmaniye Gate). 🚌 61B.
🕐 9am–7pm Mon–Sat.

The İç Bedesten is the oldest part of the bazaar. Once a warehouse, it also served as a place where jewellers could make and sell their wares.

The Oriental Kiosk was built as a coffee house in the 17th century and is now a jewellery shop.

Rugs on Display
Carpets and kilims *(see pp358–9) from all over Turkey and Central Asia are on sale in the bazaar.*

ZINCIRLI HAN

Mahmut Paşa Gate

AYNACILAR SOK

HALICILAR ÇARŞISI CAD

Money traders

AĞA SOK

İÇ BEDESTEN

MUHAFAZACILAR SOK

Gateway to the İç Bedesten
Though the eagle was a symbol of the Byzantine emperors (see pp50–51), this eagle, like the bazaar itself, postdates the Byzantine era.

KESECİLER CAD

TERZİ BAŞI SOK

SANDAL BEDESTENİ SOK

SANDAL BEDESTENİ

The Sandal Bedesteni dates from the 16th century and is covered by 20 brick domes supported on piers.

Nuruosmaniye Mosque, Çemberlitaş tram stop

Nuruosmaniye Gate

KEY

Souvenirs
Traditionally crafted items, such as this brass ewer, are for sale in the bazaar.

Kalpakçılar Başı Caddesi, the widest of the streets in the bazaar, is lined with the glittering windows of countless jewellery shops.

— Suggested route
☐ Antiques and carpets
☐ Leather and denim
☐ Gold and silver
☐ Fabrics
☐ Souvenirs
☐ Household goods and workshops
▬ Boundary of the bazaar

0 metres   40

0 yards   40

BEYOĞLU

OR CENTURIES Beyoğlu, a steep hill north of the Golden Horn, was home to the city's foreign residents. First to arrive here were the Genoese. As a reward for aiding the reconquest of the city from the crusader-backed Latin Empire in 1261, they were given the Galata area, which is now dominated by the Galata Tower. During the Ottoman period, Jews from Spain, Arabs, Greeks and Armenians settled in communities here. From the 16th century the European powers established embassies in the area to further their interests within the lucrative territories of the Ottoman Empire. The district has not changed much in character over the centuries and is still a thriving commercial quarter today.

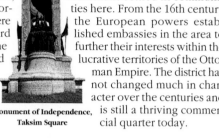

Monument of Independence, Taksim Square

SIGHTS AT A GLANCE

Historic Buildings and Monuments
Galata Tower ❸
Mevlevi Monastery ❷
Pera Palas Hotel ❶

Mosques and Churches
Nusretiye Mosque ❹

Quarters
Çukurcuma ❺
Taksim ❻

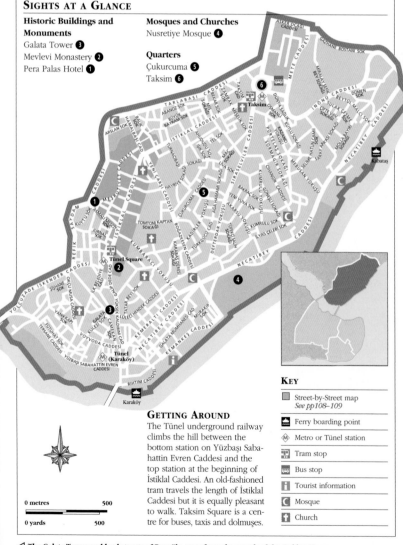

KEY

	Street-by-Street map *See pp108–109*
	Ferry boarding point
Ⓜ	Metro or Tünel station
	Tram stop
	Bus stop
ℹ	Tourist information
C	Mosque
✝	Church

0 metres   500
0 yards   500

GETTING AROUND
The Tünel underground railway climbs the hill between the bottom station on Yüzbaşı Sabahattin Evren Caddesi and the top station at the beginning of İstiklal Caddesi. An old-fashioned tram travels the length of İstiklal Caddesi but it is equally pleasant to walk. Taksim Square is a centre for buses, taxis and dolmuşes.

◁ The Galata Tower and backstreets of Beyoğlu, seen from the mouth of the Golden Horn

Street-by-Street: İstiklal Caddesi

Crest on top of the Russian Consulate gate

T HE PEDESTRIANIZED İstiklal Caddesi is Beyoğlu's main street. Once known as the Grande Rue de Pera, it is lined by late 19th-century apartment blocks and European embassy buildings whose grandiose gates and façades belie their use as mere consulates since Ankara became the Turkish capital in 1923 *(see p58)*. Hidden from view stand the churches which used to serve the foreign communities of Pera (as this area was formerly called), some still buzzing with worshippers, others just quiet echoes of a bygone era. Today, the once seedy backstreets of Beyoğlu, off İstiklal Caddesi, are taking on a new lease of life, with trendy jazz bars opening and shops selling hand-crafted jewellery, furniture and the like. Crowds are also drawn by the area's cinemas and numerous stylish restaurants.

★ Pera Palas Hotel
This hotel is an atmospheric period piece. Many famous guests, including Agatha Christie, have stayed here since it opened in 1892. Non-residents can enjoy a drink in the bar ❶

St Mary Draperis
is a Franciscan church dating from 1789. This small statue of the Virgin stands above the entrance from the street. The vaulted interior of the church is colourfully decorated. An icon of the Virgin, said to perform miracles, hangs over the altar.

★ Mevlevi Monastery
A peaceful garden surrounds this small museum of the Mevlevi Sufi sect (see p255). On the last Sunday of every month visitors can see dervishes perform their famous swirling dance ❷

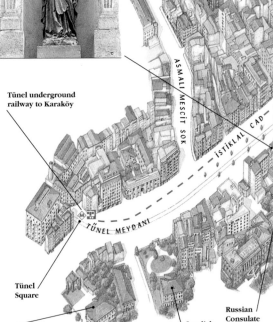

Tünel underground railway to Karaköy

ASMALI/MESCİT SOK

İSTİKLAL CAD

TÜNEL MEYDANI

Tünel Square

Russian Consulate

Swedish Consulate

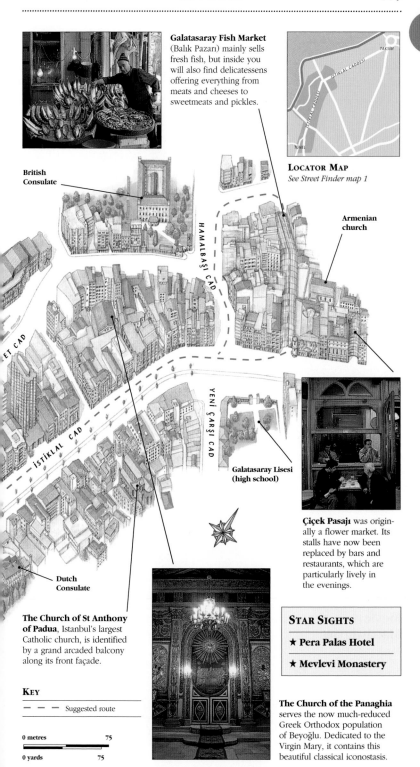

Galatasaray Fish Market
(Balık Pazarı) mainly sells
fresh fish, but inside you
will also find delicatessens
offering everything from
meats and cheeses to
sweetmeats and pickles.

LOCATOR MAP
See Street Finder map 1

**British
Consulate**

HAMALBAŞI CAD

**Armenian
church**

ET CAD

YENİ ÇARŞI CAD

İSTİKLAL CAD

**Galatasaray Lisesi
(high school)**

Çiçek Pasajı was originally a flower market. Its
stalls have now been
replaced by bars and
restaurants, which are
particularly lively in
the evenings.

**Dutch
Consulate**

**The Church of St Anthony
of Padua**, Istanbul's largest
Catholic church, is identified
by a grand arcaded balcony
along its front façade.

KEY

– – – Suggested route

| 0 metres | 75 |
| 0 yards | 75 |

STAR SIGHTS

★ **Pera Palas Hotel**

★ **Mevlevi Monastery**

The Church of the Panaghia
serves the now much-reduced
Greek Orthodox population
of Beyoğlu. Dedicated to the
Virgin Mary, it contains this
beautiful classical iconostasis.

The peaceful courtyard of the Mevlevi Monastery

Pera Palas Hotel ❶
Pera Palas Oteli

98–100 Meşrutiyet Cad, Tepebaşı.
Map 1 D3. 📞 *(0212) 251 45 60.*
🚇 *Tünel.* ♿ *by arrangement.*
📷 *by appointment only.*

THROUGHOUT the world
there are hotels that have
attained a legendary status.
One such is the Pera Palas
(see p326). Relying on the
hazy mystique of yesteryear,
it has changed little since it
opened in 1892, principally
to cater for travellers on the
Orient Express *(see p76)*.

It still evokes images of
uniformed porters and exotic
destinations such as Baghdad.
The Grand Orient bar serves
cocktails beneath its original
chandeliers, while the patis-
serie offers irresistible cakes
and a genteel ambience.

Former guests who have
contributed to the hotel's
reputation include Mata Hari,
Greta Garbo, Jackie Onassis,
Sarah Bernhardt, Josephine
Baker and Atatürk *(see p58)*.
A room used by the thriller
writer Agatha Christie can be
visited on request.

Mevlevi Monastery ❷
Mevlevi Tekkesi

15 Galip Dede Cad, Beyoğlu. **Map** 1
D3. 📞 *(0212) 243 50 45.* 🚇 *Tünel.*
🕐 *9:30am–4:30pm Wed–Mon.* 📷

ALTHOUGH SUFISM was banned
by Atatürk in 1925, this
monastery has survived as
the Divan Edebiyatı Müzesi,
a museum of *divan* literature

(classical Ottoman poetry). The
monastery belonged to the
most famous Sufi sect, known
as the Whirling Dervishes *(see
p255)*. The original dervishes
were disciples of the mystical
poet and great Sufi master
Celaleddin Rumi, known as
"Mevlâna" (Our Leader), who
died in the town of Konya,
south central Anatolia, in 1273.

Tucked away off a street
named after one of the great
poets of the sect, Galip Dede,
the museum centres on an
18th-century lodge, within
which is a beautiful octagonal wooden dance floor. Here,
for the benefit of visitors, the
sema (ritual dance) is performed by a group of latter-
day Sufi devotees on the last
Sunday of every month. At
3pm a dozen or so dancers
unfurl their great circular skirts
to whirl round the room in an

extraordinary state of ecstatic
meditation, accompanied by
haunting music.

Around the dance floor
are glass cases containing
a small exhibition of artifacts
belonging to the sect, including hats, clothing, manuscripts, photographs and
musical instruments. Outside,
in the calm, terraced garden,
stand the ornate tombstones
of ordinary members and
prominent sheikhs (leaders)
of the sect. Surrounding the
elegantly carved tombs is
a profusion of delicately
scented roses.

Galata Tower ❸
Galata Kulesi

Büyük Hendek Sok, Beyoğlu.
Map 5 D1. 📞 *(0212) 245 32 63.*
🚇 *Tünel.* 🕐 *9am–7pm daily.* 📷
Restaurant & Nightclub 🕐
8pm–midnight daily.

THE MOST distinctive silhou-
ette on the Galata skyline
is a 62-m (205-ft) high round
tower topped by a conical
roof. It was built in 1348 by the
Genoese as part of their
fortifications. Throughout the
Ottoman period the building
was used as a watchtower for
fires, but it has since been
converted to cater for tourism.
The top two floors, the 8th
and 9th, are occupied by a
restaurant and nightclub.
Sadly, the interior decor

The distinctive Galata Tower, as seen from across the Golden Horn

reflects few of the building's medieval origins.

You can reach the top of the tower either by lift or by way of a narrow spiral staircase. It is worth the climb simply to admire the fabulous panoramic view from the balcony, which encompasses the main monuments of Istanbul and, beyond, the Princes' Islands.

The window-filled dome and arches of Nusretiye Mosque

Nusretiye Mosque ❹

Nusretiye Camii

Necatibey Cad, Tophane. **Map** 1 E3.
🚌 25E, 56. ⬜ daily.

THE BAROQUE "Mosque of Victory" was built in the 1820s by Kirkor Balian, part of a renowned family of imperial architects. The ornate building, with decorative outbuildings and marble terrace, is more like a large palace pavilion than a mosque.

Commissioned by Mahmut II to commemorate his abolition of the Janissary corps in 1826 (see pp57), it faces the Selimiye Barracks (see p125) which housed the New Army that replaced the Janissaries. In the high-domed interior, the Empire-style swags and embellishments celebrate the sultan's victory. The marble panel of calligraphy around the interior of the mosque is particularly fine, as is the pair of *sebils* (kiosks for serving drinks) outside.

Çukurcuma ❺

Map 1 E4. 🚇 *Taksim.*

THIS CHARMING OLD quarter of Beyoğlu, radiating from a neighbourhood mosque on Çukurcuma Caddesi, has become an important centre for Istanbul's furnishings and antiques trades. Old warehouses and homes have been converted into shops and showrooms, where modern upholstery materials are piled up in carved marble basins and antique cabinets. Browsing can yield "treasures", from 19th-century Ottoman embroidery to 1950s biscuit boxes.

***Suzani* textiles (see p130) on sale in Çukurcuma**

Taksim ❻

Map 1 E3. 🚇 *Taksim.* 🚇 *Taksim.*
Taksim Art Gallery 📞 (0212) 245
20 68. ⬜ 11am–7pm Mon–Sat.

CENTRING ON THE vast, open Taksim Square (Taksim Meydanı), the Taksim area is the hub of activity in modern Beyoğlu. Taksim means "water distribution centre", and from the early 18th century it was from this site that water from the Belgrade Forest was distributed throughout the modern city. The original stone reservoir, built in 1732 by Mahmut I, still stands at the top of İstiklal Caddesi. In the southwest of the square is the Monument of Independence, sculpted by the Italian artist Canonica in 1928. "Independence" shows Atatürk (see p58) and the other founding fathers of the modern Turkish Republic.

Further up, on Cumhuriyet Caddesi, is the modern building of the **Taksim Art Gallery**. As well as temporary exhibitions it has a permanent display of Istanbul landscapes by some of Turkey's most important 20th-century painters.

At the far end of Taksim Park, north of Taksim Square, breathtaking views of Istanbul and the Bosphorus can be enjoyed from the bars on the top floor of the Ceylan Inter-Continental Hotel (see p326).

Fountain in the park at the centre of Taksim Square

FURTHER AFIELD

A WAY FROM Istanbul's city centre there are numerous sights worth visiting. Stretching from the Golden Horn to the Sea of Marmara, the Theodosian Walls are one of the city's most impressive monuments. Along the walls stand several ancient palaces and churches: particularly interesting is the Church of St Saviour in Chora, with its stunning Byzantine mosaics. If you follow the Bosphorus

Tiles depicting Mecca, Cezri Kasım Paşa Mosque, Eyüp

northwards it will bring you to Dolmabahçe Palace, an opulent fantasy not to be missed. Beyond it is peaceful Yıldız Park, with yet more beautiful palaces and pavilions. Not all visitors have time to see the Asian side of the city, but it is worth spending half a day here. Attractions include splendid mosques, a railway station and a small museum dedicated to Florence Nightingale.

SIGHTS AT A GLANCE

Mosques and Churches
Ahrida Synagogue ❶
Atik Valide Mosque ㉔
Church of the Pammakaristos ❸
Church of the Pantocrator ❼
Church of St John of Studius ❽
Church of St Saviour in Chora pp118–9 ⓮
Church of St Stephen of the Bulgars ❷
Eyüp Sultan Mosque ⓯
Fatih Mosque ❻
Greek Orthodox Patriarchate ❹

İskele Mosque ㉓
Kara Ahmet Paşa Mosque ⓬
Mosque of Selim I ❺
Şemsi Paşa Mosque ㉒

Historic Sights
Bosphorus Bridge ㉘
Fortress of Asia ㉛
Fortress of Europe ㉚
Haydarpaşa Station ㉖
Leander's Tower ㉑
Military Museum ⓲
Ortaköy ㉗

Pierre Loti Café ⓱
Selimiye Barracks ㉕
Shrine of Zoodochus Pege ⓫
Theodosian Walls ❿
Yedikule Castle ❾
Yıldız Park ⓴

Palaces
Beylerbeyi Palace ㉙
Complex of Valide Sultan Mihrişah ⓰
Dolmabahçe Palace pp122–3 ⓳
Palace of the Porphyrogenitus ⓭

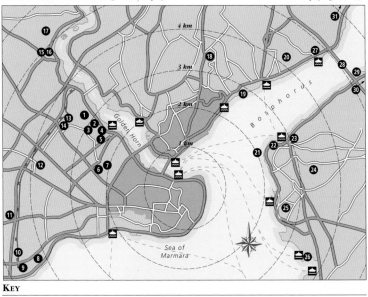

KEY

▢ Central Istanbul	═ Motorway	─ City walls
▢ Greater Istanbul	═ Main road	
⛴ Ferry boarding point	═ Other road	

0 kilometres 1
0 miles 1

◁ **Fountain in the grounds of the sumptuous Dolmabahçe Palace**

Ahrida Synagogue ❶
Ahrida Sinagogu

Gevgili Sok, Balat. 🚌 *55T, 99A.*
⬜ *by appointment only.* 📞 *Karavan Travel, (0212) 523 47 29.* 🚫

THE NAME OF the oldest and most beautiful synagogue in Istanbul is a corruption of Ohrid, the name of a town in the former Yugoslavia from which its congregation came.

Founded before the Muslim conquest of Istanbul in 1453, it has been in constant use ever since. The painted walls and ceilings, dating from the late 17th century, have been restored to their Baroque glory. Pride of place, however, goes to the central Holy Ark, which is covered in rich tapestries.

Visits are possible by prior arrangement with one of various specialist tour operators, such as Karavan Travel.

Church of St Stephen of the Bulgars ❷
Bulgar Kilisesi

85 Mürsel Paşa Cad, Balat.
🚌 *55T, 99A.* ⛴ *Balat.* ⬜ *9am–4pm daily.*

ASTONISHINGLY, this entire church was cast in iron, even the internal columns and galleries. It was created in Vienna in 1871, shipped all the way to the Golden Horn (*see p99*) and assembled on

The Church of St Stephen of the Bulgars, wholly made of iron

its shore. The church was needed for the Bulgarian community who had broken away from the authority of the Greek Orthodox Patriarchate just up the hill. Today, it is still used by this community, who keep the marble tombs of the first Bulgarian patriarchs permanently decorated with flowers. The church stands in a pretty little park dotted with trees, and which runs down to the edge of the Golden Horn.

Church of the Pammakaristos ❸
Fethiye Camii

Fethiye Cad, Draman. 🚌 *90, 90B.*
⬜ *prayer times only.* 📷

THIS BYZANTINE church is one of the hidden secrets of Istanbul. It is rarely visited despite the important role it

has played in the history of the city, and its breathtaking series of mosaics. For over 100 years after the Ottoman conquest it housed the Greek Orthodox Patriarchate, but was converted into a mosque in the late 16th century by Sultan Murat III.

The charming exterior is obviously Byzantine, with its alternating stone and brick courses and finely carved marble details. The main body of the building is the working mosque, while the extraordinary mosaics are in a side chapel. This now operates as a museum and officially you need to get permission in advance from Haghia Sophia (*see pp82–5*) to see it. However there is a chance that if the caretaker is around he may simply let you in.

Dating from the 14th century, the great Byzantine renaissance, the mosaics show holy figures isolated in a sea of gold, a reflection of the heavens. On either side are portraits of the Virgin Mary and John the Baptist beseeching Christ. They are overlooked by the four archangels, while the side apses are filled with other saintly figures.

Greek Orthodox Patriarchate ❹
Ortodoks Patrikhanesi

35 Sadrazam Ali Paşa Cad, Fener.
📞 *(0212) 521 19 21.* 🚌 *55T, 99A.*
⬜ *9am–5pm daily.* 📷

THIS WALLED COMPLEX has been the seat of the patriarch of the Greek Orthodox Church since the early 17th century. Though nominally head of the whole church, the patriarch is now shepherd to a diminishing Istanbul flock.

The main door to the Patriarchate has been welded shut in memory of Patriarch Gregory V, hanged here for treason in 1821 after encouraging the Greeks to throw off Ottoman rule at the start of the Greek War of Independence (1821–32). Turkish–Greek antagonism worsened with the Greek occupation of parts

Byzantine façade of the Church of the Pammakaristos

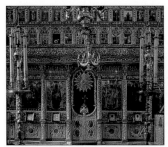

The ornate, gilded interior of the Church of St George in the Greek Orthodox Patriarchate

of Turkey in the 1920s *(see p58)*, anti-Greek riots in 1955, and the expulsion of Greek residents in the mid-1960s. Today the clergy at the Patriarchate is protected by a metal detector at the entrance.

The Patriarchate centres on the basilica-style Church of St George, dating back to 1720, yet the church contains much older relics and furniture. The patriarch's throne is thought to be Byzantine, while the pulpit is adorned with fine wooden inlay and icons.

Mosque of Selim I **❺**
Selim I Camii

Yavuz Selim Cad, Fener. 🚌 *55T, 90, 90B, 99A.* 🕐 *daily.*

THIS MUCH-ADMIRED mosque is also known locally as Yavuz Sultan Mosque: Yavuz, "the Grim", being the nickname the infamous Selim acquired. It is idyllic in a rather off-beat way, which does seem at odds with Selim's barbaric reputation.

The mosque, built in 1522, sits alone on a hill beside what is now a vast sunken parking area, once the Byzantine Cistern of Aspar. Sadly, it is rarely visited and has an air of neglect, yet the mosque's intimate court-yard gives an

İznik tile panel in the Mosque of Selim I

insight into Islam's concept of paradise.

The windows set into the porticoes in the courtyard are capped by early İznik tiles *(see p161)* made by the *cuerda seca* technique – each colour is separated during the firing process, affording the patterns greater definition. Similar tiles lend decorative effect to the simple prayer hall, with its fine mosque furniture *(see pp32–3)* and original, carefully painted woodwork.

Fatih Mosque **❻**
Fatih Camii

Macar Kardeşler Cad, Fatih. **Map** 4 A2. 🚌 *28, 87, 90, 91.* 🕐 *daily.*

A SPACIOUS OUTER courtyard surrounds this vast Baro-que mosque, the third major structure on this site. The first was the Church of the Holy Apostles, the burial place of most of the Byzantine emperors. Most of what you see today was the work of Mehmet Tahir Ağa, the chief imperial architect under Mustafa III. Many of the build-ings he constructed around the prayer hall, including eight Koranic colleges *(medreses)* and a hospice, still stand. The only surviving parts of Mehmet the Conqueror's mosque are the three porticoes of the court-yard, the ablutions foun-tain, the main gate into the prayer hall and, inside, the mihrab. Two exquisite forms of 15th-century decoration can be seen over the windows in the porticoes: İznik tiles and lunettes adorned with calli-graphic marble inlay. Stencilled patterns decorate the domes of the prayer hall, and parts of the walls are revetted with beautiful tiles.

The tomb of Mehmet the Conqueror stands behind the prayer hall, near that of his consort, Gülbahar. His sarcophagus and the turban decorating it are both appropriately large. It is a place of enormous gravity, always busy with supplicants.

If you pay a visit to the mosque on a Wednesday, you will also see the weekly market, which turns the streets around it into a circus of commerce. From tables piled high with fruit and vegetables to trucks loaded with unspun wool, this is a real spectacle.

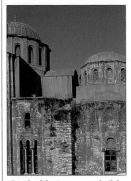

Church of the Pantocrator, built by Empress Irene in the 12th century

Church of the Pantocrator **❼**
Zeyrek Camii

İbadethane Sok, Küçükpazar. **Map** 4 B2. 🚌 *28, 61B, 87.* 🕐 *prayer times daily.* ♿

EMPRESS IRENE, the wife of John II Comnenus, founded the Church of the Pantocrator ("Christ the Almighty") during the 12th century. This hulk of Byzan-tine masonry was once the centrepiece of one of Istan-bul's most important religious foundations, the Monastery of the Pantocrator. The complex included an asylum, a hospice and a hospital. Now a mosque, it boasts a magnificent figur-ative marble floor and is composed of three interlinked chapels. A caretaker may let you in outside prayer times in the afternoon.

Church of St John of Studius ⑧

İmrahor Camii

İmam Aşir Sok, Yedikule.
🚌 80, 80B, 80T. 🚉 Yedikule.

I STANBUL'S OLDEST surviving church, St John of Studius, is now merely a shell consisting of its outer walls, but you can still get an idea of the original beauty of what was once part of an important Byzantine institution.

The church was completed in AD 463 by Studius, a Roman patrician who served as consul during the reign of Emperor Marcian (450–57). Originally connected to the most powerful monastery in the Byzantine Empire and populated with ascetic monks, in the late 8th century it was a spiritual and intellectual centre under the rule of Abbot Theodore, who is now highly venerated in the Greek Orthodox Church as St Theodore. The most sacred relic housed in the church was the head of St John the Baptist, until its removal by the soldiers of the Fourth Crusade *(see p50-51)*. The reigning emperor would visit the church each year for the Beheading of the Baptist feast on 29 August.

In the 15th century the church housed a university and was converted into a mosque. The building was abandoned in 1894 after it was damaged by an earthquake. The church is a perfect basilica, with a single apse at the east end, preceded by a narthex and a courtyard. It has a magnificent entrance portal, with carved Corinthian capitals and a sculpted architrave and cornice, but it is empty inside.

The battlements of Yedikule Castle, an Ottoman addition to the walls

Yedikule Castle ⑨

Rumelihisarı Müzesi

Yahya Kemal Cad 42, Rumelihisarı.
📞 (0212) 263 53 05. 🚌 80, 93T.
🕐 9:30am–4:30pm Thu–Tue.

Y EDİKULE, the "Castle of the Seven Towers", is built onto the southern section of the Theodosian Walls and displays both Byzantine and Ottoman features because it was built in stages over a long period of time. Its seven towers are joined by thick walls to make a five-sided fortification. The two square marble towers built into the great land walls once flanked the Golden Gate (now blocked up), which consisted of three maginficent golden

Carving of the Byzantine eagle over Yedikule Gate

portals. The gate was built by Emperor Theodosius I in AD 390 as the triumphal entrance into the thriving medieval city of Byzantium.

In the 15th century, Sultan Mehmet II (the Conqueror) completed Yedikule Castle by adding three round towers and connecting curtain walls. After viewing the castle from the outside, you can enter through a doorway in the northeastern wall. The tower to your left as you enter is the *yazılı kule*, "the tower with inscriptions". It was used as a prison for foreign envoys and others who fell out of favour with the sultan. Its name is derived from the names and epitaphs which many of these doomed individuals carved into the walls. Some of these morbid inscriptions are still visible.

The northern of the two towers flanking the Golden Gate was a place of execution. Among those who met their end here was the 17-year-old Sultan Osman II, who was dragged off to Yedikule by his own Janissaries in 1622, after four years of misrule.

The walkway around the ramparts is accessible via a steep flight of stone steps and offers good views of the land walls, the Marble Tower to the south, nearby suburbs and the bordering cemeteries.

Ruins of the Church of St John of Studius

Theodosian Walls ❿
Teodos II Surları

From Yedikule to Ayvansaray.
Ⓜ *Ulubatlı.* 🚊 *Topkapı.*

WITH ITS 11 fortified gates and 192 towers, this great chain of double walls sealed Constantinople's landward side against invasion for more than a thousand years. Extending for a distance of 6.5 km (4 miles) from the Sea of Marmara to the Golden Horn, the walls are built in layers of red tile alternating with limestone blocks. They can be reached by metro, tram or train, but to see their whole length you will need to take a taxi or dolmuş *(see pp386–7)* along the main road that runs outside them.

The walls were built by Theodosius II in AD 412–22. They endured many sieges, and were only breached by Mehmet the Conqueror in May 1453 *(see p54)*, when the Ottomans took Constantinople. Successive Ottoman sultans continued to maintain the walls until the end of the 17th century.

Controversially, parts of the walls have been rebuilt, but the new sections do give an idea of how the walls used to look. Many of the gateways are still in good repair, but a section of walls was demolished in the 1950s to make way for a road. The Charsius Gate (now called Edirnekapı), Silivrikapı, Yeni Mevlanakapı and other original gates still give access to the city. The Yedikule Gate (which stands beside the castle of the same name) has an imperial Byzantine eagle carved above its main archway.

Silivrikapı, one of the gateways through the Theodosian Walls

Shrine of Zoodochus Pege ⓫
Balıklı Kilise

3 Seyit Nizam Cad, Silivrikapı.
📞 *(0212) 582 94 56.* 🚊 *Seyitnizam.*
🚌 *93T.* ⏰ *8am–4pm daily.*

THE FOUNTAIN OF Zoodochus Pege ("Life-Giving Spring") is built over Istanbul's most famous sacred spring, which is believed to have miraculous powers. The fish in it are said to have arrived by miracle shortly before the fall of Constantinople *(see p54)*. They are believed to have leapt into the water from a monk's frying pan on hearing him declare that a Turkish invasion of the fortified town was as likely as fish coming back to life. The spring was probably the site of an ancient sanctuary of Artemis.

Kara Ahmet Paşa Mosque ⓬
Kara Ahmet Paşa Camii

Undeğirmeni Sok, Fatma Sultan.
⬜ *Prayer times only.* Ⓜ *Ulubatlı.*
🚊 *Topkapı.* 🚌 *93T.*

ONE OF THE most worthwhile detours along the city walls is the Kara Ahmet Paşa Mosque, which is also known as Gazi Ahmet Paşa. This lovely building, with its peaceful leafy courtyard and graceful proportions, is one of the imperial architect Sinan's *(see p101)* lesser known achievements, which he built in 1554 for Kara Ahmet Paşa, a grand vizier of Süleyman the Magnificent *(see p55)*.

The courtyard is surrounded by the cells of a *medrese* and a *dershane*, or main classroom. Attractive apple-green and yellow İznik tiles *(see p161)* dating from the mid-1500s grace the porch, with blue-and-white tiles on the east wall of the prayer hall. Outside the city walls is tiny Takkeci İbrahim Ağa Mosque, which dates from 1592 and has some particularly fine İznik tile panels.

Palace of the Porphyrogenitus ⓭
Tekfur Sarayı

Şişehane Cad, Edirnekapı. 🚌 *87, 90, 126.*

ONLY GLIMPSES of the former grandeur of the Palace of the Porphyrogenitus (sovereign), during its years as an imperial residence, are discernible from the sketchy remains. Its one extant hall, now open to the elements, has an attractive three-storey façade in typically Byzantine style. It was most likely built in the late Byzantine era as an annexe of the Blachernae Palace. These palaces became the principal residences of the imperial sovereigns during the last two centuries before the fall of Constantinople to the Ottomans in 1453.

During the reign of Ahmet III (1703–30) the last remaining İznik potters *(see p161)* moved to the palace and it became a centre for tile production. Cezri Kasım Paşa Mosque in Eyüp has some very fine examples of these tiles.

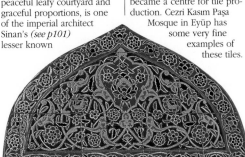

Tilework over *medrese* doorway at Kara Ahmet Paşa Mosque

Church of St Saviour in Chora 🚇
Kariye Camii

Scene from the
Life of the Virgin

SOME OF THE VERY FINEST Byzantine mosaics and frescoes can be found in the Church of St Saviour in Chora. Little is known of the early history of the church, although its name "in Chora", which means "in the country", suggests that the church originally stood in a rural setting. The present church dates from the 11th century. From 1315 to 1321 it was remodelled, and the mosaics and frescoes were added by Theodore Metochites, a theologian, philosopher and one of the elite Byzantine officials of his day.

View of St Saviour in Chora

THE GENEALOGY OF CHRIST

THEODORE METOCHITES, who restored St Saviour, wrote that his mission was to relate how "the Lord himself became a mortal on our behalf". He takes the *Genealogy of Christ* as his starting point: the mosaics in the two domes of the inner narthex portray 66 of Christ's forebears.

The crown of the southern dome is occupied by a figure of Christ. In the dome's flutes are two rows of his ancestors: Adam to Jacob ranged above the 12 sons of Jacob. In the northern dome, there is a central image of the Virgin and Child with the kings of the House of David in the upper row and lesser ancestors of Christ in the lower row.

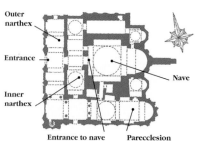

Mosaic showing Christ and his ancestors, in the southern dome of the inner narthex

THE LIFE OF THE VIRGIN

ALL BUT ONE of the 20 mosaics in the inner narthex depicting the *Life of the Virgin* are well preserved. This cycle is based mainly on the apocryphal Gospel of St James, written in the 2nd century, which gives an account of the Virgin's life. This was popular in the Middle Ages and was a rich source of material for ecclesiastical artists.

Among the events shown are the first seven steps of the Virgin, the Virgin entrusted to Joseph and the Virgin receiving bread from an angel.

THE INFANCY OF CHRIST

SCENES FROM the *Infancy of Christ*, based largely on the New Testament, occupy the semicircular panels of the outer narthex. They begin on

GUIDE TO THE MOSAICS AND FRESCOES

Outer narthex

Entrance →

Nave

Inner narthex

Entrance to nave   Parecclesion

Outer narthex looking east

KEY

- ☐ The Genealogy of Christ
- ☐ The Life of the Virgin
- ☐ The Infancy of Christ
- ☐ Christ's Ministry
- ☐ Other Mosaics
- ☐ The Frescoes

Outer narthex looking west

the north wall of the outer narthex with a scene of Joseph being visited by an angel in a dream. Subsequent panels include Mary and Joseph's *Journey to Bethlehem*, their *Enrolment for Taxation*, the *Nativity of Christ* and, finally, Herod ordering the *Massacre of the Innocents*.

The *Enrolment for Taxation*

CHRIST'S MINISTRY

WHILE MANY of the mosaics in this series are badly damaged, some beautiful panels remain. The cycle occupies the vaults of the seven bays of the outer narthex and some of the south bay of the inner narthex. The most striking mosaic is the portrayal of Christ's temptation in the wilderness, in the second bay of the outer narthex.

Theodore Metochites presents St Saviour in Chora to Christ

OTHER MOSAICS

THERE ARE three panels in the nave of the church, one of which, above the main door from the inner narthex, illustrates the *Dormition of the Virgin*. This mosaic, protected by a marble frame, is the best

preserved in the church. The Virgin is depicted laid out on a bier, watched over by the Apostles, with Christ seated behind. Other devotional panels in the two narthexes include one, on the east wall of the south bay of the inner narthex, of the *Deësis*, depicting Christ with the Virgin Mary and, unusually, without St John. Another, in the inner narthex over the door into the nave, is of Theodore Metochites himself, shown wearing a large turban, and humbly presenting the restored church as an offering to Christ.

THE FRESCOES

THE FRESCOES IN the parecclesion are thought to have been painted just after the mosaics were completed, probably in around 1320. The

VISITORS' CHECKLIST

Kariye Camii Sok, Edirnekapı.
 (0212) 631 92 41. 28,
86 or 90 then 5 minutes' walk.
 9:15am–4pm Thu–Tue.

most engaging of the frescoes – which reflect the purpose of the parecclesion as a place of burial – is the *Anastasis*, in the semidome above the apse. In it, the central figure of Christ, the vanquisher of death, is shown dragging Adam and Eve out of their tombs. Under Christ's feet are the gates of hell, while Satan lies before him. The fresco in the vault overhead depicts *The Last Judgment*, with the souls of the saved on the right and those of the damned to the left.

Figure of Christ from the *Anastasis* fresco in the parecclesion

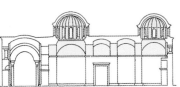

Inner narthex looking east

Parecclesion and outer narthex looking south

Inner narthex looking west

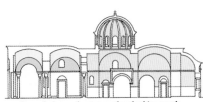

Parecclesion and outer narthex looking north

Visitors at the tomb of Eyüp Ensari, Mohammed's standard bearer

Eyüp Sultan Mosque ⑮
Eyüp Sultan Camii

Cami-i Kebir Sok. 📞 (0212) 564 73 68. 🚌 39, 55T, 99A. 🕐 daily.

MEHMET THE Conqueror built the original mosque on this site in 1458, five years after his conquest of Istanbul, in honour of Eyüp Ensari. That building fell into ruins and the present mosque was completed in 1800, by Selim III.

The mosque's delightful inner courtyard features two huge plane trees on a platform. This was the setting for the Girding of the Sword of Osman, part of a sultan's inauguration in the days of Mehmet the Conqueror.

Opposite the mosque is the tomb of Eyüp Ensari himself, said to have been killed during the first Arab siege of Constantinople in the 7th century. The tomb dates from the same period as the mosque and its decoration is in the Ottoman Baroque style.

Complex of Valide Sultan Mihrişah ⑯
Mihrişah Valide Sultan Külliyesi

Seyit Reşat Cad. 🚌 39, 55T, 99A. 🕐 9:30am–4:30pm Tue–Sun.

MOST OF THE northern side of the street leading from Eyüp Mosque's northern gate is occupied by the largest

Baroque *külliye (see p32)* in Istanbul, although unusually it is not centred on a mosque. Built for Mihrişah, mother of Selim III, the *külliye* was completed in 1791.

The complex includes the ornate marble tomb of Mihrişah and a soup kitchen, which is still in use today. There is also a beautiful grilled fountain *(sebil)*, from which an attendant once served water and refreshing drinks of sweet sherbet to passersby.

Pierre Loti Café ⑰
Piyer Loti Kahvesi

Gümüşsuyu Cad, Balmumku Sok 5, Eyüp. 📞 (0212) 616 23 44. 🚌 39, 55T, 99A. 🕐 8am–midnight daily.

THIS FAMOUS CAFÉ stands at the top of the hill in Eyüp Cemetery, a 20-minute walk up Karyağdı Sokağı from Eyüp Mosque, from where it commands sweeping views down over the Golden Horn. It is named after the French novelist, Julien Viaud, a French naval officer, popularly known as Pierre Loti, who frequented the café during his stay here in 1876. Loti defiantly fell in love with a married Turkish woman and wrote an autobiographical novel, *Aziyade*, about their affair. The café is prettily decked out with 19th-century furniture and the waiters wear period outfits.

Period interior of the Pierre Loti Café

Military Museum ⑱
Askeri Müze

Vali Konağı Cad, Harbiye. **Map** 1 F1. 📞 (0212) 233 27 20. 🚌 46H. 🕐 9am–5pm Wed–Sun. **Mehter Band performances** 3–4pm Wed–Sun.

ONE OF ISTANBUL'S most impressive museums, the Military Museum traces the history of the country's conflicts from the conquest of Constantinople in 1453 *(see p54)* through to modern warfare. The building used to be the military academy where Atatürk studied from 1899 to 1905. His classroom has been preserved as it was then.

The museum is also the main location for performances by the Mehter Band *(see p23)*, formed in the 14th century during the reign of Osman I *(see p54)*. Until the 19th century the muscians were Janissaries, who accompanied the sultan into battle and performed songs about hero-ancestors and battle victories. The band had a wide influence and is thought to have provided some inspiration for Mozart and Beethoven.

Some of the most striking weapons on display on the ground floor are the curved daggers *(cembiyes)* carried at the waist by foot soldiers in the 15th century. These are ornamented with plant, flower and geometric motifs in relief and silver filigree. Other exhibits include 17th-century copper head armour for horses and Ottoman shields

An Ottoman curved dagger (*cembiye*) displayed in the Military Museum

made from cane and willow covered in silk thread.

A moving portrayal of trench warfare is included in the section concerned with the ANZAC landings of 1915 at Chunuk Bair on the Gallipoli peninsula *(see p168–9)*, and upstairs is a spectacular exhibit of the tents used by sultans on their campaigns.

From the nearby station on Taşkışla Caddesi you can take the cable car across Maçka Park to Abdi İpekçi Caddesi in Teşvikiye. Some of the best designer clothes, jewellery, furniture and art shops in the city are here *(see pp130–131)*.

Dolmabahçe Palace ⓳

See pp122–3.

Yıldız Park ⓴

Çırağan Cad, Beşiktaş. **Map** 3 D2.
🚌 25E, 40. ⬜ *dawn to dusk daily.*
🚗 *for vehicles.*

YILDIZ PARK was originally laid out as the garden of the first Çırağan Palace. It later formed the grounds of **Yıldız Palace**, an assortment of buildings from different eras now enclosed behind a wall and entered separately from Ihlamur-Yıldız Caddesi. The palace is a collection of pavilions and villas built in the 19th and 20th centuries. Many of them are the work of the eccentric Sultan Abdül Hamit II (1876–1909, *see p57*), who made it his principal residence as he feared a sea-borne attack on Dolmabahçe Palace *(see pp122–3)*. The main building in the entrance courtyard is the State Apartments (Büyük Mabeyn), dating from the reign of Sultan Selim III (1789–1807). Around the corner, the **City Museum** (Şehir Müzesi) has a

display of Yıldız porcelain. The Italianate building opposite is the former armoury, or Silahhane. Next door to the City Museum is the **Yıldız Palace Museum**, housed in what was the Marangozhane (Abdül Hamit's carpentry workshop), and containing a changing collection of the palace's art and objects.

Further on is Yıldız Palace Theatre (completed in 1889 by Abdül Hamit), now a museum. The theatre's restored interior is mainly blue and gold, and the stars on the domed ceiling refer to the palace's name: yıldız means "star" in Turkish. Backstage, the former dressing rooms contain theatre displays, including original costumes and playbills.

The lake in the grounds is shaped like Abdül Hamit's *tuğra (see p28)*. A menagerie was once kept on the lake's islands where some 30 keepers tended tigers, lions, giraffes and zebras.

Several other little pavilions dot Yıldız Park, which, with its many ancient trees and exotic shrubs, is a very popular spot for picnics. As the park is situated on a hill, and it is a fairly long climb to the top, you may prefer to take a taxi up to the Şale Köşkü (Chalet Villa) and walk back down past the other sights.

Şale Köşkü is one of the most impressive in the park and built by Abdül Hamit. Although its façade appears as a whole, it was in fact built in three stages.

The Malta and Çadır pavilions were built during the reign of Abdül Aziz who

ruled from 1861–76. Both of them formerly served as prisons but are now open as cafés. Malta Pavilion, also a restaurant, is a favoured haunt of locals on Sundays.

Mitat Paşa, reformist and architect of the constitution, was among those imprisoned in Çadır Pavilion, for instigating the murder of Abdül Aziz. Meanwhile, Murat V and his mother were locked away in Malta Pavilion for 27 years after a brief incarceration in the Çırağan Palace.

In 1895 the Imperial Porcelain Factory began production here, to satisfy the demand of the upper classes for chic European-style ceramics. The unusual building was designed to look like a stylized medieval castle of Europe, complete with several turrets and portcullis windows. The original household items such as sugar bowls, vases and plates that were produced here usually depict idealized scenes of the Bosphorus and other local spots. Examples of these items can today be seen in various museums and palaces all over Istanbul.

City Museum
☎ *(0212) 258 53 44.*
Yıldız Palace Museum
☎ *(0212) 258 30 80.*

A bridge in the grounds of Yıldız Palace

Dolmabahçe Palace ⑲
Dolmabahçe Sarayı

Sèvres vase at the foot of the Crystal Staircase

Sᴜʟᴛᴀɴ ᴀʙᴅᴜ̈ʟ ᴍᴇᴄɪ̇ᴛ built Dolmabahçe Palace in 1856. As its designers he employed Karabet Balyan and his son Nikoğos, members of the great family of Armenian architects who lined the Bosphorus *(see pp126–7)* with many of their creations in the 19th century. The extravagant opulence of the Dolmabahçe belies the fact that it was built when the Ottoman Empire was in decline. The sultan financed his great palace with loans from foreign banks. The palace can be visited only on a guided tour, of which two are on offer. The best tour takes you through the Selamlık (or Mabeyn-i Hümayun), the part of the palace that was reserved for men and which contains the state rooms and the enormous Ceremonial Hall. The other tour goes through the Harem, the living quarters of the sultan and his entourage. If you want to go only on one tour, visit the Selamlık.

★ **Crystal Staircase**
The apparent fragility of this glass staircase stunned observers when it was built. In the shape of a double horseshoe, it is made from Baccarat crystal and brass, and has a polished mahogany rail.

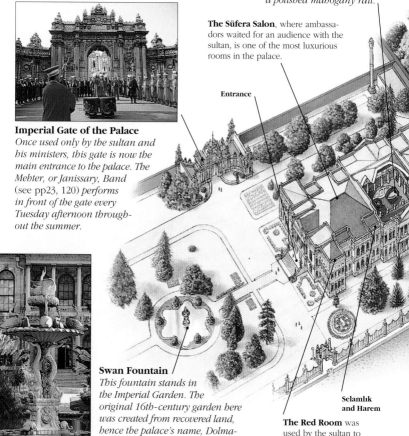

The Süfera Salon, where ambassadors waited for an audience with the sultan, is one of the most luxurious rooms in the palace.

Entrance

Imperial Gate of the Palace
Once used only by the sultan and his ministers, this gate is now the main entrance to the palace. The Mehter, or Janissary, Band (see pp23, 120) performs in front of the gate every Tuesday afternoon throughout the summer.

Swan Fountain
This fountain stands in the Imperial Garden. The original 16th-century garden here was created from recovered land, hence the palace's name, Dolmabahçe, meaning "Filled-in Garden".

Selamlık and Harem

The Red Room was used by the sultan to receive ambassadors.

★ **Ceremonial Hall**
This magnificent domed hall was designed to hold 2,500 people. Its chandelier, reputedly the heaviest in the world, was bought in England.

VISITORS' CHECKLIST

Dolmabahçe Cad, Beşiktaş.
Map 2 B4. ☎ (0212) 236 9000.
🚌 25E, 40. ◯ 9am–4pm
(last adm) Tue, Wed & Fri–Sun
(Oct–Feb: last adm 3pm).
⬤ the first day of religious
festivals. 🎫 📷 📹 🚻

**The Zülvecheyn,
or Panorama
Room**

Blue Salon
On religious feast days the sultan's mother would receive his wives and favourites in the Harem's principal room.

Harem

The Rose-coloured salon was the assembly room of the Harem.

Reception room of the sultan's mother

Main shore gate

Atatürk's Bedroom
Atatürk (see p58) died in this room at 9:05am on 10 November 1938. All the clocks in the palace, such as this one near the crystal staircase, are stopped at this time.

Sultan Abdül Aziz's bedroom
had to accommodate a huge bed built especially for the 150-kg (330-lb) amateur wrestler.

★ **Main Bathroom**
The walls of this bathroom are revetted in finest Egyptian alabaster, while the taps are solid silver. The brass-framed bathroom windows afford stunning views across the Bosphorus.

STAR FEATURES

★ **Ceremonial Hall**

★ **Crystal Staircase**

★ **Main Bathroom**

Leander's Tower, on its own small island in the Bosphorus

Leander's Tower ㉑
Kız Kulesi

Üsküdar. **Map** 6 A3. 🚢 *Üsküdar.*
📞 *(0216) 342 47 47.*

LOCATED ON AN ISLET offshore from Üsküdar, the tiny, white Leander's Tower is a well-known Bosphorus landmark, dating from the 18th century. In more recent years the tower has served as a quarantine centre during a cholera outbreak, a lighthouse, a customs control point and a maritime toll gate. It was refurbished in 1999, however, and it is now a restaurant and offshore disco.

In Turkish the tower is known as the "Maiden's Tower" after a legendary princess, confined here after a prophet foretold that she would die of a snakebite. The tower's English name derives from the Greek myth of Leander, who swam the Hellespont (the modern-day Dardanelles, *see pp168–9*) to see his lover, priestess Hero.

Şemsi Paşa Mosque ㉒
Şemsi Paşa Camii

Sahil Yolu, Üsküdar. **Map** 6 A2.
🚢 *Üsküdar.* ⭘ *daily.*

THIS IS ONE OF the smallest mosques to be commissioned by a grand vizier (Ottoman prime minister). Its miniature dimensions combined with its picturesque waterfront location make it one of the most attractive little mosques in the city. It was built in 1580 by the architect Sinan *(see p101),* at the request of Şemsi Ahmet Paşa, who succeeded Sokollu Mehmet Paşa.

The mosque's garden, overlooking the Bosphorus, is surrounded on two sides by the theological college or *medrese (see p32),* with the small mosque on the third side and the sea wall on the fourth. The mosque itself is also quite unusual in that the tomb of Şemsi Ahmet Paşa is joined to the main building, divided from the interior by a grille.

Dome in the entrance to Atik Valide Mosque

İskele Mosque ㉓
İskele Camii

Hakimiyeti Milliye Cad, Üsküdar.
Map 6 B2. 🚢 *Üsküdar.* ⭘ *daily.*

ONE OF ÜSKÜDAR'S most prominent landmarks, the İskele Mosque (also known as Mihrimah Sultan Mosque),

Fountain set into the platform below the İskele Mosque

takes its name from the ferry landing where it stands. A massive structure on a raised platform, it was built by Sinan between 1547 and 1548 for Mihriman Sultan, favourite daughter of Süleyman the Magnificent. Without space to build a courtyard, Sinan constructed a large protruding roof which extends to cover the *şadırvan* (ablutions fountain) in front of the mosque.

Atik Valide Mosque ㉔
Atik Valide Camii

Çinili Camii Sok, Üsküdar. **Map** 6 C3.
🚌 *12C (from Üsküdar).* ⭘ *prayer times only.*

THE ATİK VALİDE MOSQUE, set on the hill above Üsküdar, was one of the most extensive mosque complexes in the whole of Istanbul. The name translates as the Old Mosque of the Sultan's Mother, as the mosque was built for Nur Banu, the wife of Selim II ("the Sot") and the mother of Murat III. She was the first of the sultans' mothers to rule the Ottoman Empire from the Harem *(see p71).* Sinan completed the mosque, which was his last major work, in 1583. It has a wide shallow dome which rests on five semidomes, with a flat arch over the entrance portal.

The interior is surrounded on three sides by galleries, the undersides of which retain the rich stencilling typical of the period. The mihrab apse is almost completely covered with panels of fine İznik tiles *(see p161),* while the mihrab itself and the *minbar* are both made of sculpted marble. Side aisles were added in the 17th century, while the grilles and architectural trompe l'oeil paintings on the royal loge in the western gallery date from the 18th century.

Outside, a door in the north wall of the courtyard leads down a flight of stairs to the *medrese* (theological college), where the *dershane* (classroom) projects out over the street below, supported by an arch. The *şifahane* (hospital), built around a central courtyard just east of the mosque, is also worth a visit.

Selimiye Barracks **㉕**
Selimiye Kışlası

Çeşmei Kebir Cad, Selimiye.
Map 6 B5. *Harem*. 12.

Haydarpaşa Station, terminus for trains arriving from Anatolia

THE SELIMIYE BARRACKS were originally made of wood and completed in 1799 under Selim III, who was sultan from 1789 to 1807. They were built to house the "New Army" that formed part of Selim's plan for reforming the Imperial command structure and replacing the powerful Janissaries *(see pp56–7)*. The plan backfired and Selim was deposed but the barracks were, nevertheless, a striking symbol of Constantinople's military might, perhaps becoming even more so when they were rebuilt in stone in 1829 by Mahmut II. The building still houses Istanbul's First Army Division and is off limits to the public.

The Florence Nightingale Museum is found within the Selimiye Barracks. It still contains some of the original furniture and the famous lamp which gave her the epitaph "Lady of the Lamp." Visits must be arranged in advance by faxing the Army Headquarters, (0216) 333 10 09.

Nearby are two other sites worth seeing – the Selimiye Mosque and the British War Cemetery (also known as the Crimean Memorial Cemetery). The mosque was built in 1804 and is set in a lovely courtyard. The Cemetery, south on Burhan Felek Caddesi, contains the graves of men who died in the Crimean War, World War I battles at Gallipoli *(see pp168–9)* and during World War II in the Middle East.

Haydarpaşa Station **㉖**
Haydarpaşa Garı

Haydarpaşa İstasyon Cad. 📞 (0216) 348 80 20. 🚊 Haydarpaşa or Kadıköy. ⏰ 8am–6pm daily.

THE WATERFRONT location and grandeur of Haydarpaşa Station, together with the neighbouring tiled jetty, make it the most impressive point of arrival or departure in Istanbul. Built on land reclaimed from the sea, the station is surrounded by water on three sides – a unique feature.

The first Anatolian railway line, which was built in 1873, ran from here to İznik *(see p160)*. The extension of this railway was a major part of Abdül Hamit II's drive to modernize the Ottoman Empire. Lacking sufficient funds to continue the project, he applied for help to his German ally, Kaiser Wilhelm II. The Deutsche Bank agreed to invest in the construction and operation of the railway. In 1898 German engineers were contracted to build the new railway lines running across Anatolia and beyond into the far reaches of the Ottoman Empire. At the same time a number of stations were built.

Construction on Haydarpaşa, the grandest of these, started in 1906. Its two German architects, Otto Ritter and Helmut Conu, chose to build on a grand scale, using a neoclassic German style. The station was completed in 1908.

FLORENCE NIGHTINGALE

The British nurse Florence Nightingale (1820–1910) was a tireless campaigner for hospital, military and social reform. During the Crimean War, in which Britain and France fought on the Ottoman side against the Russian Empire, she organized a party of 38 British nurses. They took charge of medical services at the Selimiye Barracks in Scutari (Üsküdar) in 1854. By the time she returned to Britain in 1856, at the end of the war, the mortality rate in the barracks had decreased from 20 to 2 per cent, and the fundamental principles of modern nursing had been established. On her return home, Florence Nightingale opened a training school for nurses.

A 19th-century painting of Florence Nightingale in Selimiye Barracks

The Bosphorus Trip

Ceremonial gate, Çırağan Palace

ONE OF THE GREAT PLEASURES of a visit to Istanbul is a cruise up the Bosphorus. It is relaxing and offers an excellent vantage point from which to view the city's famous landmarks. You can go on a pre-arranged guided tour or take one of the small boats that tout for passengers at Eminönü. But there is no better way to travel than on the official trip run by Turkish Maritime Lines *(TDİ, see p381)*. Laden with sightseers, the TDİ ferry makes a round-trip to the upper Bosphorus two or three times daily, stopping at six piers along the way, including a leisurely stop at Anadolu Kavağı for lunch. You can return to Eminönü on the same boat or make your way back to the city by bus, dolmuş or taxi.

LOCATOR MAP

Sadberk Hanım Museum
Housed in two yalıs (see p31), this private museum contains ethnographic displays and a private archaeology collection.

Fortress of Europe
Situated at the narrowest point on the Bosphorus, this fortress was built by Mehmet II in 1452 as a prelude to his invasion of Constantinople.

Dolmabahçe Palace
This opulent 19th-century Baroque palace is a symbol of Ottoman grandeur.

View of the City
As the ferry departs, you have a view of many of the old monuments of Istanbul, including Süleymaniye Mosque.

Rumeli
Kavağı

Anadolu
Kavağı

Anadolu Kavağı
*The last stop on the trip brings you to this
village and a ruined 14th-century
Byzantine fortress, the Genoese Castle.*

VISITORS' CHECKLIST

Map 5 D2. *The TDİ ferries
operate between the major terminals every 20 or 30 minutes
(but the service is more limited
on the upper reaches of the
Bosphorus). Alternatively, organized private tours last around
2–3 hours and turn back just
before the Fatih Sultan Mehmet
Bridge. Book and board just west
of the Eminönü ferry piers. Hotels
can arrange a tour aboard a
luxury cruise boat.*
*TDİ, Eminönü Pier 3 (Boğaz
Hattı), (0212) 522 00 45/46.*

Huber
Köşkü

Beykoz

Yeniköy

Paşabahçe

İstinye

Çubuklu

Kanlıca

Fatih Sultan
Mehmet Bridge

Fortress
of Asia

dilli

Beykoz
*Beykoz is the largest
fishing village along the
Asian shore. Situated
in the village square
is this fountain dating
from 1746.*

Yeniköy
*Handsome 19th-
century yalıs line the
waterfront of this
ancient village. It was
invaded by Cossacks
who crossed the Black
Sea in 1624.*

Fortress of Asia
*Fifty years older than the Fortress of Europe, this fortress
was built by Sultan Beyazıt I just before the failed
Ottoman siege of Constantinople in 1396–7.*

0 kilometres 2
0 miles 1

KEY

Motorway
Main road
Other road
Ferry boarding point
--- Route of Bosphorus trip
Viewpoint

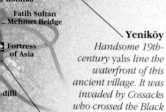

The Bosphorus suspension bridge between Ortaköy and Beylerbeyi

Ortaköy ㉗

Map 3 F2. ▦ 25E, 40, 41.

CROUCHED AT the foot of the Bosphorus Bridge, the suburb of Ortaköy has retained a village feel. Life centres on İskele Meydanı, the quayside square, which was until recently busy with fishermen unloading the day's catch. Nowadays, though, Ortaköy is better known for its lively Sunday market, which crowds out the square and surrounding streets, and its shops selling the wares of local artisans. It is also the location for a thriving bar and café scene, which in the summer is the hub of Istanbul's nightlife (see pp132–3).

Mecidiye Mosque, Ortaköy's most impressive landmark, is located on the waterfront. It was built in 1855 by Nikoğos Balyan, who was also responsible for Dolmabahçe Palace (see pp122–3).

Ortaköy's fashionable waterfront square and ferry landing

Bosphorus Bridge ㉘
Boğaziçi Köprüsü

Ortaköy and Beylerbeyi. **Map** 3 F2. ▦ 200, 202 (double deckers from Taksim).

SPANNING the Bosphorus between the districts of Ortaköy and Beylerbeyi, this was the first bridge to be built across the straits that divide Istanbul and separate Europe from Asia. It was inaugurated on 29 October 1973, to coincide with the 50th anniversary of the founding of the Turkish Republic (see p58). It is 1,074 m (3,524 ft) long, and is the world's ninth longest suspension bridge. It reaches 64 m (210 ft) above the water.

The Bosphorus is especially popular in summer, when cool breezes waft off the water.

Beylerbeyi Palace ㉙
Beylerbeyi Sarayı

Abdullah Ağa Cad, Beylerbeyi Mahallesi, Asian side. 🛈 (0216) 321 93 20. ▦ 15 (from Üsküdar), 10 (from Beşiktaş). 🚢 from Üsküdar. 🕐 May–Sep: 9am–5pm Tue–Wed & Fri–Sun; Oct–Apr: 9am–4pm Tue–Wed & Fri–Sun. 📷 ✎

DESIGNED IN the Baroque style of the late Ottoman period, Beylerbeyi Palace was built between 1861 and 1865 by members of the Balyan family under the orders of Sultan Abdül Aziz. A previous palace had stood here, and the gardens were already laid out by Murat IV in 1639. As the Ottoman empire withered, palaces proliferated in a flourish of grandeur and showmanship. Abdül Aziz had Beylerbeyi built as a pleasure palace to entertain dignitaries and royalty. The Empress Eugénie of France (wife of Napoleon III) was a guest at the palace in 1869 on her way to the opening of the Suez Canal. The Duke and Duchess of Windsor also visited Beylerbeyi. The fountains, baths and colonnades were meant to impress, as were the lovely frescoes of Ottoman warships.

To keep himself distracted, Aziz had a zoo built and, apparently, delighted in the flocks of ostriches and several Bengal tigers. The zoo is no longer there, but the palace has recently been refurbished and restored to some of its former elegance.

Third-but-last of the line of sultans, the autocratic Abdül Hamit II spent six years as a prisoner in an anteroom of the palace and died there, virtually forgotten, after being deposed in 1909.

There are superb views of the palace from the Bosphorus, from where the two prominent bathing pavilions – one for the Harem and the other for the selamlık (the men's quarters), can best be seen.

The most attractive room is the reception hall, which has a pool and fountain. Running water was popular in Ottoman houses for its pleasant sound and cooling effect in the heat. The crystal chandeliers are mostly Bohemian.

Ornate landing at the top of the stairs in Beylerbeyi Palace

The Fortress of Europe, built by Mehmet the Conqueror to enable him to capture Constantinople

Fortress of Europe 🕥

Rumeli Hisarı

Yahya Kemal Cad, European side. ☎ *(0212) 263 53 05.* 🚌 *25E, 40 and 41 (from Taksim Square).* ⏰ *9am–5pm Thu–Tue.* 📷

THIS FORTRESS was built by Mehmet the Conqueror in 1452 as his first step in the conquest of Constantinople *(see p54)*. Situated at the narrowest point of the Bosphorus, the fortress controlled a major Byzantine supply route. Across the straits is Anadolu Hisarı, or the Fortress of Asia, which was built in the 14th century by Beyazıt I.

The Fortress of Europe's layout was planned by Mehmet himself. While his grand vizier *(see pp56–7)* and two other viziers were each responsible for the building of one of the three great towers, the sultan took charge of the walls. Local buildings were torn down to provide the stones and other building materials. One thousand masons laboured on the walls alone. It was completed in four months – a considerable feat, given the steep terrain.

The new fortress was soon nicknamed Boğazkesen – meaning "Throat-cutter" or "Strait-cutter". It was garrisoned by a force of Janissaries *(see pp56–7)*. These troops trained their cannons on the straits to prevent the passage of foreign ships. After they had sunk a Venetian vessel, this approach to Constantinople was cut off.

Following the conquest of the city, the fortress lost its importance as a military base and was used as a prison, particularly for out-of-favour foreign envoys and prisoners of war. The structure was restored only in 1953.

Today it is in excellent condition and is a pleasant place for an afternoon outing. Some open-air theatre performances are staged here during the Istanbul Festival of Arts and Culture *(see p35)*.

Fortress of Asia 🕥

Anadolu Hisarı

Riyaziyeci Sokak (on the harbour front), Asian side.

LIKE ITS comrade-in-arms across the water, the Fortress of Asia, built directly opposite, offers commanding views over the Bosphorus. It was built 50 years earlier by Mehmet II's grandfather,

Sultan Beyazıt I (1389–1402). It was the Sultan's strategic trump card in his attempt to defend Constantinople from the haughty Venetians, who walked a tightrope between consolidating their territorial ambitions and trying to avoid conflicts that might threaten the riches of their lucrative Ottoman trade, which mainly involved silks, spices, cottons and dyes, as well as sugar.

In spite of the value of the fortress as a deterrent, a low-level war took place between the Venetians and the Ottomans, lasting from 1463 to 1497. Genoa and Florence skilfully manoeuvred to fill the trade gap, in exchange for generous trade agreements from the Ottomans.

The Fortress of Asia is closed to the public, but its exterior is well worth seeing. Take a Bosphorus boat trip *(see pp126–7)*, arriving at the harbour, and sit in the park, where the view of the castle can best be appreciated.

BIRDS OF THE BOSPHORUS

In September and October, thousands of white storks and birds of prey fly over the Bosphorus on their way from their breeding grounds in eastern Europe to wintering regions in Africa. Large birds usually prefer to cross narrow straits like the Bosphorus rather than fly over an expanse of open water such as the Mediterranean. Among birds of prey on this route you can see the lesser spotted eagle and the honey buzzard. The birds also cross the straits in spring on their way to Europe but, before the breeding season, they are fewer in number.

The white stork, which migrates over the straits

SHOPPING IN ISTANBUL

ISTANBUL'S SHOPS and markets, crowded and noisy at most times of the day and year, sell a colourful mixture of goods from all over the world. The city's most famous shopping centre is the massive Grand Bazaar. Turkey is a centre of textile production, and Istanbul has a wealth of carpet and fashion shops. If you prefer to do all your

Contemporary glass vase

shopping under one roof, head for one of the city's modern shopping malls. Wherever you shop, be wary of imitations of famous brand products – even if they appear to be of a high standard and the salesman maintains that they are authentic. Be prepared to bargain where required: it is an important part of a shopping trip.

GENERAL INFORMATION

MOST SHOPS TRADE from 9am to 8pm Monday to Saturday, and markets open at 8am. Large shops and department stores open later in the morning. The Grand Bazaar and Spice Bazaar are open from 8:30am to 7pm. Malls are open from 10am to 10pm seven days a week. Details on payment, VAT exemption and buying antiques appear on pp354–5.

CARPETS AND KILIMS

IN THE GRAND BAZAAR (see pp104–105), **Şişko Osman** has a good range of carpets, and **Galeri Şirvan** sells Anatolian tribal *kilims* (rugs).

The Cavalry Bazaar has many kilim shops, and **Hazal**, in Ortaköy, stocks a fine collection of kilims. **Sümerbank**, in Beyoğlu, has a good selection of handmade carpets.

FABRICS

IN ADDITION to carpets and kilims, colourful fabrics in traditional designs from all over Turkey and Central Asia are widely sold. **Sivaslı Yazmacısı** sells village textiles, headscarves and embroidered cloths. **Muhlis Günbattı** has rare Central Asian textiles, Uzbek and Turkmen *suzanis* (large hand-appliqued cloths), silk ikats, Ottoman kaftans, as well as carpets.

LEATHER

TURKISH LEATHERWEAR, while not always of the best quality hides, is durable, of good craftsmanship and reasonably priced. The Grand Bazaar is full of shops selling leather goods. **B B Store**, for example, offers a good range of ready-to-wear and made-to-order garments, and **Desa** has an extensive range of both classic and fashionable designs.

JEWELLERY

THE GRAND BAZAAR is the best place to find gold jewellery – it is sold by weight, with only a modest sum added for craftsmanship. The daily price of gold is displayed in the shop windows. Other shops in the same area sell silver jewellery, and pieces inlaid with precious stones. **Urart** stocks collections of unique gold and silver jewellery inspired by the designs of ancient civilizations. **Antikart** specializes in restored antique silver jewellery.

HOW TO BARGAIN

In up-market shops in Istanbul, bargaining is rare. However, in the Grand Bazaar and the shops located in or around the old city (Sultanahmet and Beyazıt) haggling is a must, otherwise you may be cheated. Bazaar shopkeepers, known for their abrasive insistence, expect you to bargain. Take your time and decide where to buy after visiting a few shops selling similar goods. The procedure is as follows:

• You will often be invited inside and offered a cup of tea. Feel free to accept, as this is the customary introduction to any kind of exchange and will not oblige you to buy.

• Do not feel pressurized if the shopkeeper turns the shop upside down to show you his stock – this is normal practice and most salesmen are proud of their goods.

• If you are seriously interested in any item, be brave enough to offer half the price you are asked.

• Take no notice if the shopkeeper looks offended and refuses, but raise the price slightly, aiming to pay a little more than half the original offer. If that price is really unacceptable to the owner he will stop bargaining over the item and turn your attention to other merchandise in the shop.

Haggling over the price of a carpet

Brightly decorated candle lanterns in the Grand Bazaar

POTTERY, METAL AND GLASSWARE

SHOPS IN THE Grand Bazaar are stocked with traditional ceramics, including pieces decorated with exquisite blue-and-white İznik designs *(see p161)*. Other types of pottery come from Kütahya, which makes use of a free style of decoration, and Çanakkale, which features more modern designs. With its large stock of plates, bowls, Turkish coffee cups and vases, **May** is one of the best places. For a modern piece of Kütahya ware, visit **Mudo Pera** which stocks pieces by master potter, Sıtkı Usta. Most museum shops also sell a good range of pottery, including reproduction pieces.

The Grand Bazaar and the Cavalry Bazaar are centres of the copper and brass trade and offer a huge selection.

For glassware, **Paşabahçe**, the largest glass manufacturer in Turkey, offers the best range, and some exquisite, delicate pieces with gilded decoration.

HANDICRAFTS

IDEAL GIFTS AND souvenirs include embroidered hats, waistcoats and slippers, inlaid jewellery boxes, meerschaum pipes, prayer beads, alabaster ornaments, blue-eye charms to ward off the evil eye, *nargiles* (bubble pipes) and reproductions of icons. At the Istanbul Crafts Centre you can see calligraphers at work. **Rölyef** in Beyoğlu, the Book Bazaar and **Sofa** sell antique and reproduction calligraphy, as well as *ebru* (marbled paintings) and reproductions of Ottoman miniatures.

FOOD, DRINK, HERBS AND SPICES

THE SPICE BAZAAR *(see p98)* is the place to buy nuts, dried fruits, herbs and spices, jams, various herbal teas, and even exotic delicacies such as caviar. The Galatasaray Fish Market is excellent, as are various shops specializing in particular foods.

International names alongside Turkish shops in Akmerkez

SHOPPING MALLS

ISTANBUL'S MODERN shopping malls contain cinemas, "food courts", chic cafés and hundreds of shops. The most popular are **Akmerkez** in Etiler, **Galleria**, next to the yacht marina in Ataköy, and **Carousel**, close to Galleria, in Bakırköy. Seasonal sales take place mainly in clothes shops, but also in department stores and some speciality shops.

ENTERTAINMENT IN ISTANBUL

ISTANBUL OFFERS A great variety of leisure pursuits, ranging from arts festivals and folk music to belly dancing and nightclubs. The most important cultural event is the series of festivals organized by the Istanbul Foundation for Culture and the Arts between March and November. Throughout the year, traditional Turkish music, opera, ballet, Western classical music and plays are performed at the Atatürk Cultural Centre, Cemal Reşit Rey Concert Hall (CRR) and some other venues around the city. Beyoğlu

Belly dancer, Galata Tower

is the main centre for entertainment of all kinds. This area also has the highest concentration of cinemas in the city, and numerous lively bars and cafés. Though Konya *(see pp250–51)* is the home of the religious dervish order, productions of the mystical whirling dervish dance are staged at the Mevlevi Monastery in Beyoğlu once a month. Ortaköy, on the European shore of the Bosphorus, is another very popular venue for dining, music and dancing. For a trip to the beach on a hot day, the Princes' Islands *(see p158)* are best.

ENTERTAINMENT GUIDES

A BI-MONTHLY magazine in English, *The Guide* lists cultural events and activities in the city. Entertainment information and contact numbers are available in the English *Turkish Daily News*, as well as Turkish Airlines' in-flight magazine and the Turkish daily newspaper *Hürriyet*.

Entertainment guides available in Istanbul

FESTIVALS

FIVE MAJOR ANNUAL festivals (theatre, film, music and dance, jazz, and a biennial fine arts exposition) are organized by the Istanbul Foundation for Culture and the Arts. All tickets can be obtained via telephone from the **Istanbul Festival Committee** or at the individual venues themselves.
Istanbul also hosts the Yapı Kredi Arts, Akbank Jazz, and Efes Pilsen Blues festivals in autumn each year.
During festivals a special bus service runs between show venues and the city centre.

CLASSICAL MUSIC AND DANCE

EACH SEASON the Istanbul State Opera and Ballet companies, State Symphony Orchestra and State Theatre perform a wide repertoire of classical and modern works in

Taksim's purpose-built, 900-seat **Atatürk Cultural Centre** (**AKM**). These are very popular events and early booking is thus essential. The **Cemal Reşit Rey Concert Hall** (**CRR**) also stages Western classical music concerts and hosts music and dance groups. Concerts are also held at smaller venues in the city. Contact the Sultanahmet Tourist Office *(see p79)* for details.

BOOKING TICKETS

TICKETS FOR all AKM and CRR performances can be bought a week in advance from their respective box offices. The information desks of the larger department stores and shopping centres may also sell tickets. Payment is usually by cash.

ROCK AND JAZZ

AN INCREASING number of Istanbul's clubs and bars plays good live music. **Hayal Kahvesi** is a bar dedicated to jazz, rock and blues and has an outdoor summer venue in Çubuklu. The **Q Club**, in the grounds of the Çırağan Palace Hotel Kempinski, is an exclusive jazz bar. The

Rock House Café in Ortaköy has live bands on some weeknights. Other venues are **Mojo** (live rock) and **Sappho** (jazz and Turkish pop).

TRADITIONAL TURKISH MUSIC AND DANCE

TRADITIONAL TURKISH music performed at the CRR includes Ottoman classical, mystical Sufi and Turkish folk music. Summer recitals of Turkish music are organized in the Basilica Cistern *(see p86)*, which has wonderful acoustics. The Sultanahmet Tourist Office has details.
Fasıl is a popular form of traditional music that is best enjoyed live in *meyhanes* (taverns) such as **Ece**, **Kallavi 20** and **Hasır**. It is performed on the *kanun* (zither), as well as *tambur* and *ud* (both similar to the lute). **Galata Tower** restaurant is an alternative venue for Turkish folk music and dance, while belly dancing is a nightclub attraction in Beyoğlu.

Folk dancing at the Kervansaray venue

Other places featuring top performers of traditional art are **Kervansaray**, **Orient House** and **Manzara**.

NIGHTCLUBS

A TOP NIGHTCLUB is the luxurious, summer-only **Club 29**. **Majesty**, a bar-restaurant complex, has a delightful outdoor balcony. Avoid seedy-looking clubs in the Beyoğlu district. These have been known to coerce clients into paying extortionate bills.

CINEMAS AND THEATRE

T HE LATEST foreign films are on circuit at the same time as in the rest of Europe, albeit with Turkish subtitles.

Alkazar, **Emek** and **Beyoğlu** show mainly art-house films. The first show is half-price. Many cinemas offer half-price tickets on Wednesdays, and

Classical concert in the church of Haghia Eirene (see p72)

students with a valid student card are entitled to discounts.

Theatres stage local and international plays, but only in Turkish. The theatre season runs from September to June.

SPORTS

M AIN FIVE-STAR hotels have good swimming pools and welcome non-residents

for a fee. Turks are fanatical about football: **Beşiktaş**, **Fenerbahçe** and **Galatasaray** are the top sides.

Horse races take place at **Veli Efendi** racecourse on weekends and Wednesdays.

CHILDREN

T HOUGH ISTANBUL IS NOT an obvious destination for children, they are always made welcome. Yıldız Park *(see p121)* has much to offer, and **Tatilya** theme park *(see p361)*, 35 km (22 miles) west of Istanbul, has rides, shops and a simulation cinema.

LATE-NIGHT TRANSPORT

T HE LAST late-night buses and dolmuşes leave the Taksim area at midnight, but taxis are available all night. For more information on getting around Istanbul, *see pp384–7.*

DIRECTORY

ISTANBUL FESTIVAL COMMITTEE

📞 *(0212) 293 31 33.*

CLASSICAL MUSIC AND DANCE

AKM
Taksim Meydanı, Taksim.
Map 1 B3.
📞 *(0212) 251 56 00.*

CRR
Gümüş Sok, Harbiye.
Map 1 C1.
📞 *(0212) 231 51 03.*

ROCK AND JAZZ

Hayal Kahvesi (Beyoğlu)
Büyükparmak Kapı Sok 19, Beyoğlu.
Map 1 B4.
📞 *(0212) 243 68 23.*

Mojo
Büyükparmak Kapı Sok 26, Beyoğlu. **Map** 1 B4.
📞 *(0212) 243 29 27.*

Q Club
Çırağan Palace Hotel Kempinski, A Blok, Beşiktaş.
Map 3 D3.
📞 *(0212) 236 24 89.*

Rock House Café
Dereboyu Cad 36–8, Ortaköy. **Map** 3 F2.
📞 *(0212) 227 60 10.*

Sappho
İstiklal Cad 14, Bekar Sok, Beyoğlu. **Map** 1 B4.
📞 *(0212) 245 06 68.*

TRADITIONAL TURKISH MUSIC AND DANCE

Ece
Tramvay Cad 104, Kuruçeşme.
📞 *(0212) 265 96 00.*

Galata Tower
Büyükhendek Cad, Galata.
Map 1 A1.
📞 *(0212) 245 11 60.*

Hasır
Beykoz Korusu, Beykoz.
📞 *(0216) 322 29 01.*

Kallavi
Kallavi Sok 20, Beyoğlu.
Map 1 A4.
📞 *(0212) 251 10 10.*

Kervansaray
Cumhuriyet Cad 30, Harbiye.
Map 1 C2.
📞 *(0212) 247 16 30.*

Manzara
Conrad Hotel, Yıldız Cad, Beşiktaş. **Map** 2 C3.
📞 *(0212) 227 30 00.*

Orient House
Tiyatro Cad 27, Beyazıt.
Map 4 C4.
📞 *(0212) 517 61 63.*

NIGHTCLUBS

Club 29
Paşabahçe Yolu 24, Çubuklu, Beykoz.
📞 *(0216) 322 28 29.*

Majesty
Muallim Naci Cad 10/2, Salhane Sok, Ortaköy.
Map 3 F3.
📞 *(0212) 236 57 57.*

CINEMAS

Alkazar
İstiklal Cad 179, Beyoğlu.
Map 1 B4.
📞 *(0212) 293 24 66.*

Beyoğlu
İstiklal Cad 140, Halep Pasajı, Beyoğlu. **Map** 1 B4.
📞 *(0212) 251 32 40.*

Emek
İstiklal Cad, Yeşil Çam Sok 5, Beyoğlu. **Map** 1 B4.
📞 *(0212) 249 50 92.*

SPORTS

Beşiktaş FC
Spor Cad 92, Beşiktaş.
Map 2 A4.
📞 *(0212) 227 87 80.*

Fenerbahçe FC
Kızıltoprak, Kadıköy.
📞 *(0216) 345 09 40.*

Galatasaray FC
Hasnun Galip Sok 7, Galatasaray. **Map** 1 B4.
📞 *(0212) 251 57 07.*

Veli Efendi Hipodromu
Osmaniye, Bakırköy.
📞 *(0212) 543 70 96.*

CHILDREN

Tatilya
E5 Motorway, Beylikdüzü.
📞 *(0212) 852 05 13.*

STREET FINDER

THE MAP REFERENCES that are given throughout this section refer to the maps on the following pages. Some small streets with references may not be named on the map. References are also given for hotels *(see pp324–6)*, restaurants *(see pp342–5)*, shops *(see pp130–31)* and entertainment venues *(see*

Commuters at a tram stop

pp132–3). The map provided below shows the area covered by the six maps, and the key lists the symbols that are used. The first figure of the reference tells you which map page to turn to; the letter and number indicate the grid reference. The map on the inside back cover shows public transport routes.

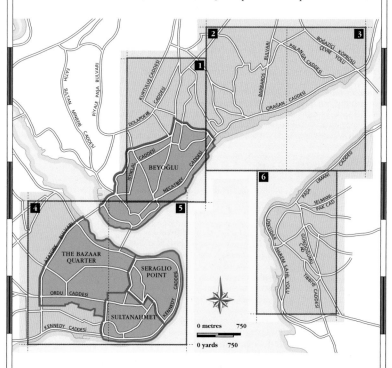

KEY TO STREET FINDER

▮ Major sight	**D** Dolmuş terminus	═══ Railway line
▮ Place of interest	🚖 Taxi rank	─── Tram line
▮ Other building	ℹ Tourist information	▬▬▬ Motorway
⚓ Ferry boarding point	**H** Hospital	∙∙∙ Pedestrian tunnel
⚓ Sea bus boarding point	🚓 Police station	─── City wall
🚉 Railway station	🛁 Turkish baths	**SCALE OF MAPS**
Ⓜ Metro or Tünel station	**C** Mosque	**1-6**
🚊 Tram stop	✡ Synagogue	
🚡 Cable car station	✝ Church	0 metres 250
🚌 Main bus terminus	⊠ Post office	0 yards 250

Map labels visible: BEYOĞLU, THE BAZAAR QUARTER, SERAGLIO POINT, SULTANAHMET, ORDU CADDESİ, KENNEDY CADDESİ, İSTİKLÂL CADDESİ, NECATBEY, DOLAPDERE, PYALE PAŞA BULVARI, FATİH SULTAN MİNARELİ CADDESİ, KURTULUŞ CADDESİ, BARBAROS BULVARI, PALANGA CADDESİ, BOĞAZİÇİ KÖPRÜSÜ, ÇEVRE YOLU, ÇIRAĞAN CADDESİ, PAŞA LİMANI CADDESİ, SELMANİ PAK CAD, ÜSKÜDAR HAREM SAHİL YOLU, GÜNDOĞUMU CAD, TIBBİYE CADDESİ

0 metres   750
0 yards   750

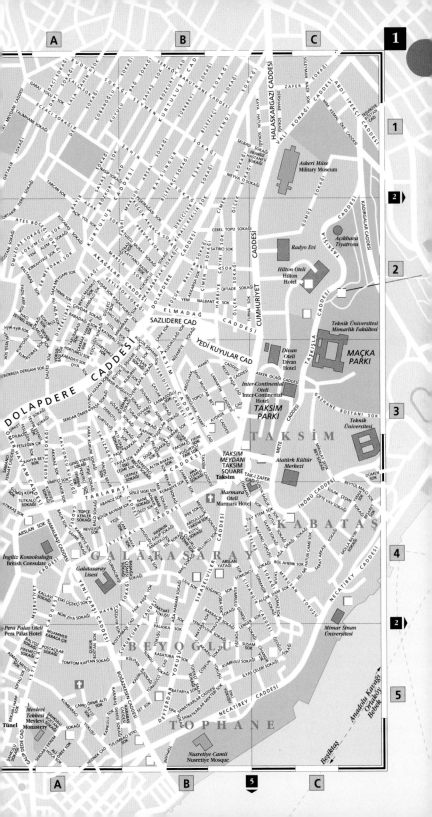

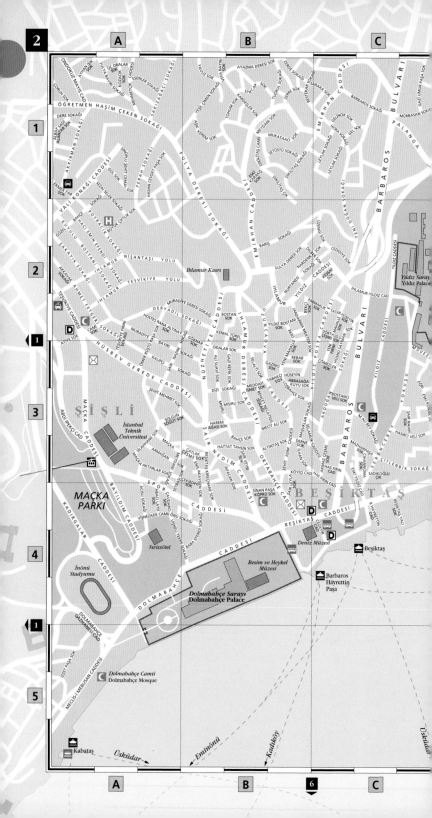

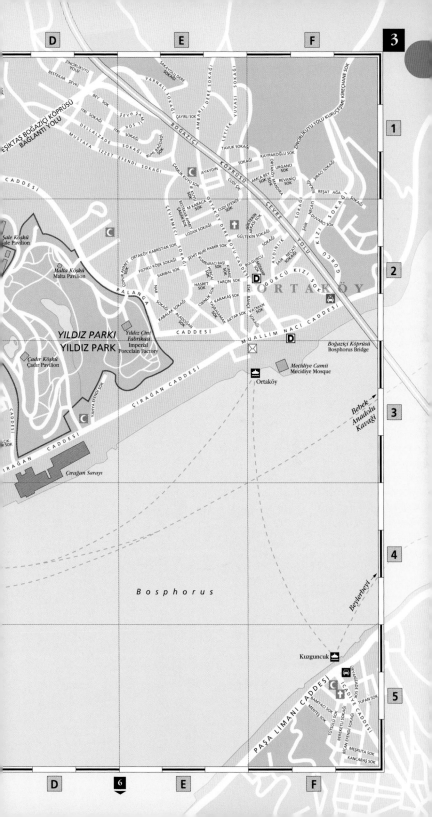

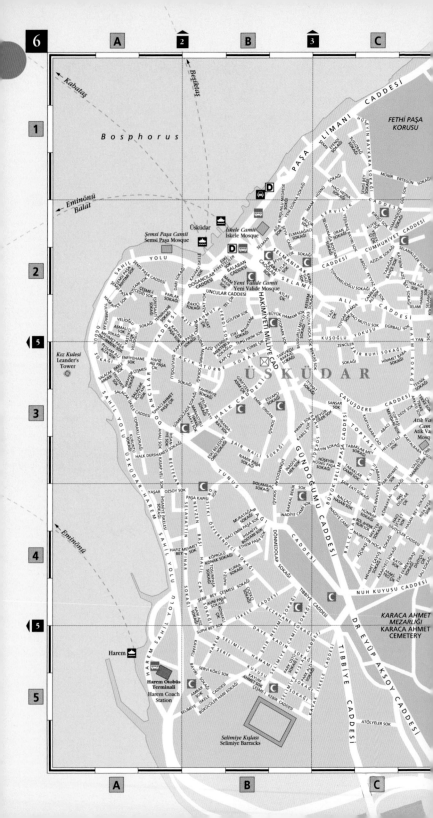

Street Finder Index

IN TURKISH, Ç, Ğ, İ, Ö, Ş and Ü are listed as separate letters in the alphabet, coming after C, G, I, O, S and U, respectively. In this book, however, Ç is treated as C for the purposes of alphabetization and so on with the other letters. Hence Çiçek follows Cibinlik as if both names began with C. Following standard Turkish practice we have abbreviated Sokağı to Sok, Caddesi to Cad and Çımazi to Çık.

N

O

P

R

S

TURKEY REGION BY REGION

Turkey at a Glance

TURKEY OCCUPIES THE rugged Anatolian plateau, an
arid upland region that is encircled by the mighty
Taurus and Pontic mountain systems. The country's
unrivalled wealth of historic sights includes Istanbul –
the capital of three empires, as well as the ruins
of classical sites such as Ephesus, Hierapolis and
Aphrodisias. In the interior of the country are the
unique cave cities and churches of Cappadocia.
The eastern provinces of Turkey are less frequently
visited, but offer such spectacular attractions as
Lake Van, Armenian churches and the enigmatic
stone heads at the summit of Mount Nemrut.

Istanbul's skyline *is defined by
the silhouettes of great mosques
such as Süleymaniye Mosque (see
pp100–101), built by the architect
Sinan in the 16th century.*

War Memorials
*on the Gallipoli
Peninsula (see
pp168–9) salute
the bravery of the
soldiers who fought
and died here in
World War I.*

ISTANBUL
(See pp60–145)

THRACE AND THE
SEA OF MARMARA
(See pp150–69)

THE BLACK SEA
(See pp260–75)

ANKARA AND WESTERN
ANATOLIA
(See pp236–59)

THE AEGEAN
(See pp170–203)

MEDITERRANEAN
TURKEY
(See pp204–35)

0 kilometres 50

0 miles   25

The Castle of St Peter *(see pp196–7)
guards the harbour at Bodrum. The
castle was built by the Knights of St
John in the 15th century, using stones
taken from the ruins of the celebrated
Mausoleum of Halicarnassus.*

The Mevlâna Museum *(see pp252–3) is a
place of pilgrimage that contains the tombs
of important Mevlevi Dervish mystics. Nearby
is the Selimiye Mosque, an emblem of Konya.*

◁ **The picturesque town of Mardin, near the Syrian border**

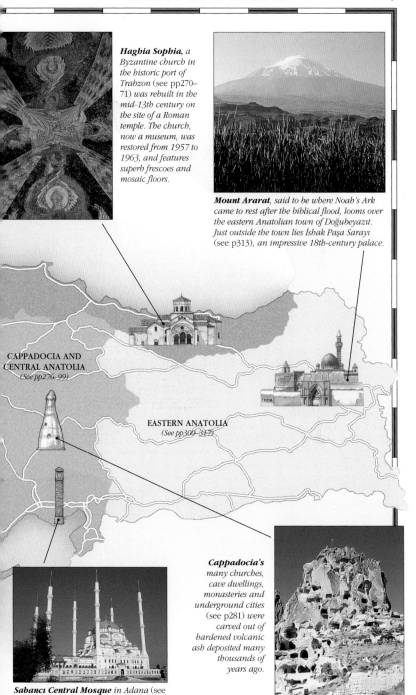

Hagbia Sophia, *a Byzantine church in the historic port of Trabzon (see pp270–71) was rebuilt in the mid-13th century on the site of a Roman temple. The church, now a museum, was restored from 1957 to 1963, and features superb frescoes and mosaic floors.*

Mount Ararat*, said to be where Noah's Ark came to rest after the biblical flood, looms over the eastern Anatolian town of Doğubeyazıt. Just outside the town lies İshak Paşa Sarayı (see p313), an impressive 18th-century palace.*

CAPPADOCIA AND CENTRAL ANATOLIA
(See pp276–99)

EASTERN ANATOLIA
(See pp300–317)

Cappadocia's *many churches, cave dwellings, monasteries and underground cities (see p281) were carved out of hardened volcanic ash deposited many thousands of years ago.*

Sabancı Central Mosque *in Adana (see pp230–31) is one of the largest mosques in the Islamic world. The Ottoman-era clocktower is an older landmark of this fast-growing southern city.*

Thrace and the Sea of Marmara

*S*TANDING AT A NATURAL CROSSROADS, *Istanbul makes a good base for excursions into the neighbouring areas of Thrace and the Sea of Marmara. Whether you want to see great Islamic architecture, immerse yourself in a busy bazaar, relax on an island or catch a glimpse of Turkey's rich birdlife, you will find a choice of destinations within easy reach of the city.*

On public holidays and at weekends nearby resorts are crowded with Istanbul residents taking a break from the noisy city. For longer breaks, they head for the Mediterranean or Aegean, so summer is a good, quiet time to explore the Thrace and Marmara regions.

The country around Istanbul varies immensely from lush forests to open plains and, beyond them, impressive mountains. The Princes' Islands, where pine forests and monasteries can be toured by a pleasant ride in a horse-drawn carriage, are also just a short boat trip away from the city. A little further away, the lakeside town of İznik is world famous for its ceramics. This art form, which reached its zenith in the 16th and 17th centuries, is one of the wonders of Ottoman art, and original pieces are highly prized.

To the northwest, near the Greek border, is Edirne, a former Ottoman capital. It is visited today for its mosques, especially the Selimiye. Edirne also stages Kırkpınar grease-wrestling matches every July when enthusiastic crowds flock to enjoy the contest and the accompanying folk festival.

South of the Sea of Marmara is the pretty spa town of Bursa. Originally a Greek city, it was founded in 183 BC. The first Ottoman capital, it has some fine architecture and also maintains the tradition of the Karagöz shadow puppet theatre. Near the mouth of the straits of the Dardanelles lie the ruins of the legendary city of Troy, dating from about 3600 BC. North of the Dardanelles are cemeteries commemorating the thousands of soldiers killed in the battles fought over the Gallipoli Peninsula during World War I.

Boats in Burgaz Harbour on the Princes' Islands, a short ferry ride from Istanbul

◁ The Green Tomb of Mehmet I in Bursa, one of the city's best-known landmarks

Exploring Thrace and the Sea of Marmara

ISTANBUL IS THE JEWEL of the Thrace and Marmara region, but places like Edirne and Bursa – and others within a radius of about 250 km (150 miles) – each have their own history and importance, with some fine museums and mosques. Şile, located on the Black Sea coast, is a day's outing from Istanbul, as is the quaint hamlet of Polonezköy. Bird parks, the superb tiles of İznik, along with the spas and ski slopes around Bursa give the Marmara area the edge for variety. A visit to the World War I battlefields and cemeteries of the Gallipoli Peninsula is a moving experience.

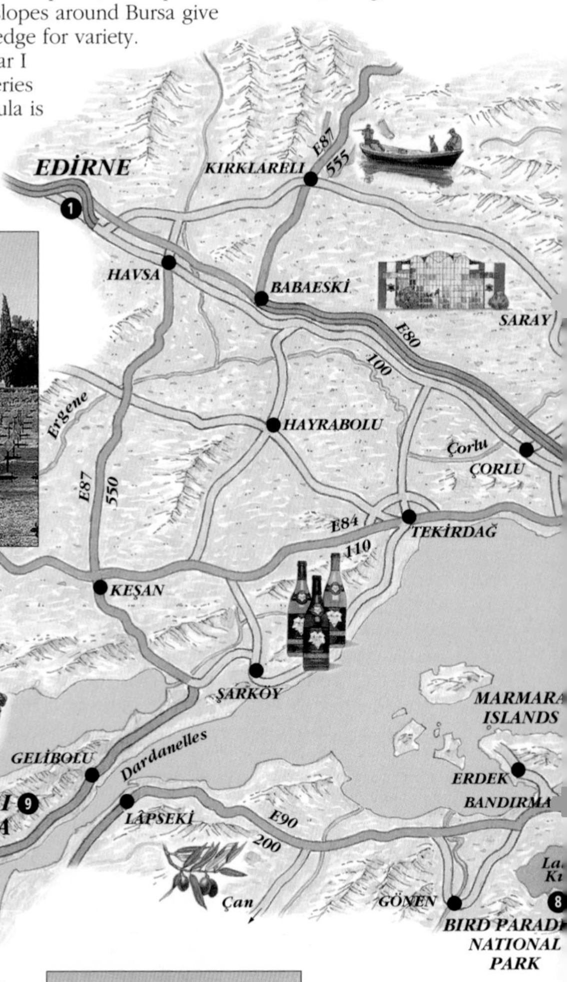
EDİRNE
1
KIRKLARELİ
E87
555
HAVSA
BABAESKİ
SARAY
E80
100
Ergene
HAYRABOLU
Çorlu
ÇORLU
E87
550
E84
110
TEKİRDAĞ
KEŞAN
ŞARKÖY
MARMARA ISLANDS
GELİBOLU
Dardanelles
ERDEK
BANDIRMA
GALLIPOLI 9
PENINSULA
LÂPSEKİ
E90
200
ECEABAT
Çan
GÖNEN
8
BIRD PARADISE NATIONAL PARK

French war cemetery, Gallipoli Peninsula

Sights at a Glance

Bird Paradise National Park 8
Bursa pp162–7 7
Edirne pp154–7 1
Gallipoli Peninsula pp168–9 9
İznik 5
Polonezköy 3
Princes' Islands 2
Şile 4
Uludağ National Park 6

Bird Paradise National Park – an area rich in protected wildlife

Key

- Motorway
- Main road
- Minor road
- Scenic route
- River
- Viewpoint

GETTING AROUND

The Trans European Motorway (TEM) system means that a six-lane superhighway bypasses the hub of Istanbul using the Fatih Sultan Mehmet Bridge over the Bosphorus. On this toll road, the Istanbul to Ankara journey takes about 3 hours. The E80, which runs parallel to the TEM road, is still known as the E5 (or E-Beş). Car ferries (no reservations required) commute frequently between Gebze and Yalova. A sea bus service (advance booking essential) does the Yenikapı (central Istanbul) to Bandırma run in a few hours. From Istanbul, local and intercity trains depart from Sirkeci Station on the European side and Haydarpaşa Station on the Asian side. Ferries depart from the Eminönü ferry piers in Istanbul to four of the Princes' Islands and from Kabataş, near the Dolmabahçe Palace, to the islands on the south coast of the Sea of Marmara.

Children walking up a picturesque street in an old quarter of Bursa

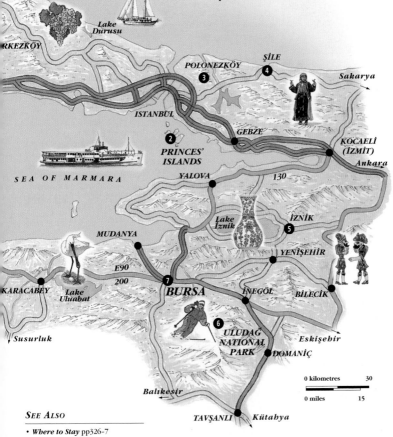

SEA OF MARMARA

RKEZKÖY

Lake Durusu

POLONEZKÖY **3**

ŞİLE **4**

Sakarya

ISTANBUL

GEBZE

KOCAELİ (İZMİT)

Ankara

PRINCES' ISLANDS **2**

YALOVA

130

İZNİK **5**

Lake İznik

YENİŞEHİR

MUDANYA

E90

BİLECİK

KARACABEY

Lake Uluabat

200

BURSA **7**

İNEGÖL

Susurluk

ULUDAĞ NATIONAL PARK **6**

DOMANİÇ

Eskişehir

Balıkesir

TAVŞANLI

Kütahya

0 kilometres 30

0 miles 15

SEE ALSO

• *Where to Stay* pp326–7

• *Where to Eat* p345

Edirne **①**

STANDING ON THE RIVER TUNCA near the border with Greece, Edirne is a provincial university town that is home to one of Turkey's star attractions, the Selimiye Mosque *(see pp156–7)*. As this huge monument attests, Edirne was historically of great importance. It dates back to AD 125, when the Emperor Hadrian joined two small towns to form Hadrianopolis, or Adrianople. For nearly a century, from 1361 when Murat I took the city until Constantinople was conquered in 1453 *(see p54)*, Edirne was the Ottoman capital. The town has one other claim to fame – the annual grease-wrestling championships in July.

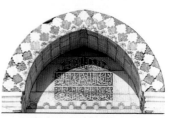
Entrance arch, Mosque of the Three Balconies

Entrance to Beyazıt II Mosque viewed from its inner courtyard

☾ Beyazıt II Mosque
Beyazıt II Külliyesi
Yeni Maharet Cad. ◯ *daily.* **Health Museum** ☏ *(0284) 212 09 22.*
◯ *9am–5:30pm Mon–Fri &*
9:30am–5:30pm Sat–Sun. 📷 ♿
Beyazıt II Mosque stands in a peaceful location on the northern bank of the Tunca River, 1.5 km (1 mile) from the city centre. It was built in 1484–8, soon after Beyazıt II succeeded Mehmet the Conqueror *(see p54)* as sultan.

The mosque and its courtyards are open to the public. Of the surrounding buildings in the complex, the old hospital, which incorporated an asylum, has been converted into the **Health Museum**. Disturbed patients were treated in this asylum – a model facility for its time – with water, colour and flower therapies. The Turkish writer Evliya Çelebi (1611–84) reported that singers and instrumentalists would play soothing music three times a week. Overuse of

hashish was one of the most common afflictions. The colonnaded inner mosque courtyard, unlike most later examples, covers three times the area of the mosque itself. Inside, the weight of the impressive dome is supported on sweeping pendentives.

☾ Mosque of the Three Balconies
Üç Şerefeli Camii
Hükümet Cad. ◯ *daily.* ♿
Until the fall of Constantinople, this was the grandest building of the early Ottoman state. It was finished in 1447 and takes its name from the three balconies which adorn its southeastern minaret – at the time the tallest in existence. In an unusual touch, the other three minarets of the mosque are each of a different design

and height. Unlike its predecessors in Bursa *(see pp162–7)*, the mosque has an open courtyard, a feature that set a precedent for the great imperial mosques of Istanbul. The interior plan was also innovative. With minimal obstructions, both the *mihrab* and *minbar* can be seen from almost every corner of the prayer hall.

☾ Old Mosque
Eski Cami
Talat Paşa Asfaltı. ◯ *daily.* ♿
The oldest of Edirne's major mosques, this is a smaller version of the Great Mosque in Bursa *(see p164)*. The eldest son of Beyazıt I, Süleyman, began the mosque in 1403, but it was his youngest son, Mehmet I, who completed it in 1414.

A perfect square, the mosque is divided by four massive piers into nine domed sections. On either side of the prayer hall entrance there are massive Arabic inscriptions proclaiming "Allah" and "Mohammed".

GREASE-WRESTLING

The Kırkpınar Grease-Wrestling Championships take place annually in July, on the island of Sarayiçi in the Tunca River. The event is famed throughout Turkey and accompanied by a week-long carnival. Before competing, the wrestlers don knee-length leather shorts *(kıspet)* and grease themselves from head to foot in diluted olive oil. The master of ceremonies, the *cazgır*, then invites the competitors to take part in a high-stepping, arm-flinging parade across the field, accompanied by music played on a deep-toned drum *(davul)* and a single-reed oboe *(zurna)*. Wrestling bouts can last up to two hours and involve long periods of frozen, silent concentration interspersed by attempts to throw down the opponent.

Wrestlers performing a ceremonial ritual before the contest

🏨 Rüstem Paşa Caravanserai

Rüstem Paşa Kervansarayı
İki Kapılı Han Cad 57.
☎ *(0284) 212 61 19.*

Sinan *(see p101)* designed this caravanserai for Süleyman's most powerful grand vizier, Rüstem Paşa, in 1560–61. It was constructed in two distinct parts. The larger courtyard, or han *(see pp24–5)*, which is now the Rüstem Paşa Kervansaray Hotel, was built for the merchants of Edirne, while the smaller courtyard, now a student hostel, was an inn for other travellers.

A short walk away, on the other side of Saraçlar Caddesi, is the Semiz Ali Paşa Bazaar. This is also the work of Sinan, and dates from 1589. It consists of a long, narrow street of vaulted shops.

🏛 Museum of Turkish and Islamic Arts

Türk ve İslam Eserleri Müzesi
Kadir Paşa Mektep Sok. ☎ *(0284) 225 11 20.* 🕒 *8:30am–noon & 1:30–5:30pm Tue–Sun.* 🎟

Edirne's small collection of Turkish and Islamic works of art is attractively located in the *medrese (see p32)* of the Selimiye Mosque.

The museum's first room is devoted to the local sport of grease-wrestling. It includes enlarged reproductions of miniatures depicting 600 years of the sport. These show the wrestling stars resplendent in their leather shorts, their skin glistening with olive oil.

Other objects on display include the original doors of the Beyazıt II Mosque. There are also military exhibits. Among them are some beautiful 18th-century Ottoman shields, with woven silk exteriors, and paintings of military subjects.

The tranquil 15th-century Muradiye Mosque

Visitors' Checklist

👥 *150,000.* 🚆 *Ayşekadın, (0284) 235 26 73.* 🚌 *E-5 exit at Highway Maintenance Depot, (0284) 226 00 20.* [D] *Rüstem Paşa Kervansaray Hotel.* [i] *Hürriyet Meydanı 17, (0284) 213 92 08.* 🛒 *Mon, Wed, Sat.* 🎪 *Grease-Wrestling (early–mid-Jul).*

[C] Muradiye Mosque

Muradiye Camii
Küçükpazar Cad. 🕒 *daily.* 🚫📷

What is today a tranquil mosque was first built as a *zaviye* (dervish hospice) in 1421 by Murat II, who dreamed that the great dervish leader Celaleddin Rumi *(see p252, 255)* asked him to build a hospice in Edirne. Only later was it converted into a mosque. Its interior is notable for its massive inscriptions, similar to those in the Old Mosque, and for some fine early 15th-century İznik tiles *(see p161)*. It may be locked outside prayer times.

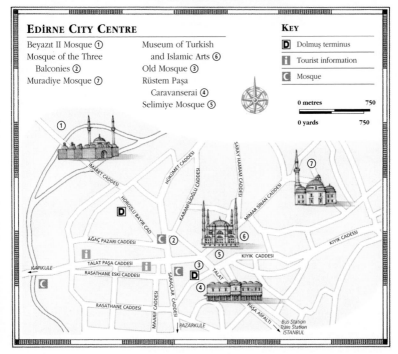

Edirne City Centre

Beyazıt II Mosque ①
Mosque of the Three Balconies ②
Muradiye Mosque ⑦
Museum of Turkish and Islamic Arts ⑥
Old Mosque ③
Rüstem Paşa Caravanserai ④
Selimiye Mosque ⑤

Key

[D] Dolmuş terminus
[i] Tourist information
[C] Mosque

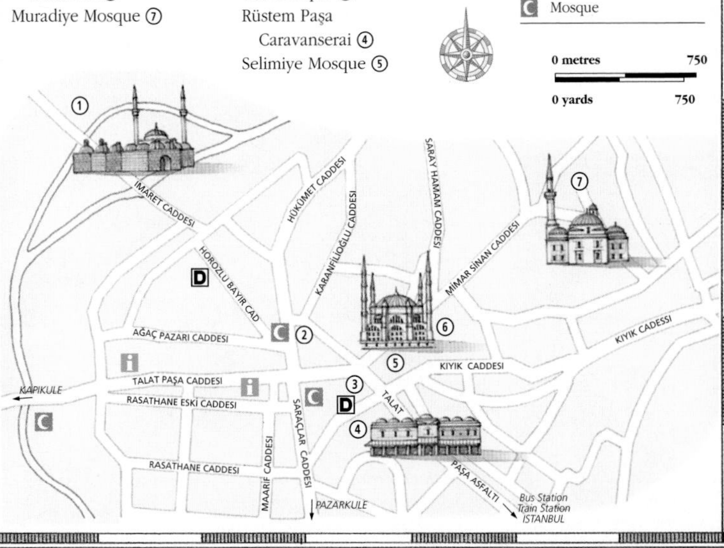

Edirne: Selimiye Mosque
Selimiye Camii

THE SELIMIYE IS THE GREATEST of all the Ottoman mosque complexes, the apogee of an art form and the culmination of a life's ambition for its architect, Sinan *(see p101)*. Built on a slight hill, the mosque is a prominent landmark. Its complex includes a *medrese* *(see p32)*, now housing the Museum of Turkish and Islamic Arts, a school and the Kavaflar Arasta, a covered bazaar.

Selim II commissioned the mosque. It was begun in 1569 and completed in 1575, a year after his death. The dome was Sinan's proudest achievement. In his memoirs, he wrote: "With the help of Allah and the favour of Sultan Selim Khan, I have succeeded in building a cupola six cubits wider and four cubits deeper than that of Haghia Sophia." In fact, the dome is comparable in diameter and slightly shallower than the building Sinan had so longed to surpass.

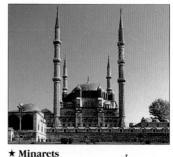

★ **Minarets**
The mosque's four slender minarets tower to a height of 84 m (275 ft). Each one has three balconies. The two northern minarets contain three intertwining staircases, each one leading to a different balcony.

Ablutions Fountain
Intricate, pierced carving decorates the top of the 16-sided open şadırvan (ablutions fountain), which stands in the centre of the courtyard. The absence of a canopy helps to retain the uncluttered aspect.

STAR FEATURES

★ **Minarets**

★ **Dome**

★ **Minbar**

The columns supporting the arches of the courtyard are made of old marble, plundered from Byzantine architecture.

Courtyard Portals
Alternating red and honey-coloured slabs of stone were used to build the striking arches above the courtyard portals. This echoes the decoration of the magnificent arches running around the mosque courtyard itself.

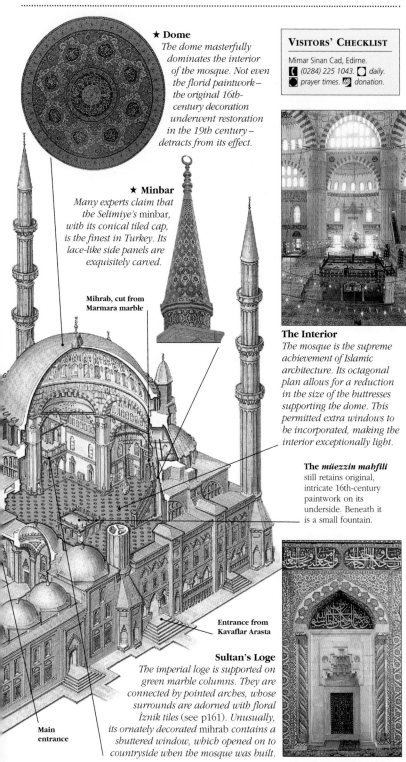

★ **Dome**
The dome masterfully dominates the interior of the mosque. Not even the florid paintwork – the original 16th-century decoration underwent restoration in the 19th century – detracts from its effect.

VISITORS' CHECKLIST

Mimar Sinan Cad, Edirne.
(0284) 225 1043. daily.
prayer times. donation.

★ **Minbar**
Many experts claim that the Selimiye's minbar, with its conical tiled cap, is the finest in Turkey. Its lace-like side panels are exquisitely carved.

**Mihrab, cut from
Marmara marble**

The Interior
The mosque is the supreme achievement of Islamic architecture. Its octagonal plan allows for a reduction in the size of the buttresses supporting the dome. This permitted extra windows to be incorporated, making the interior exceptionally light.

The müezzin mahfili
still retains original, intricate 16th-century paintwork on its underside. Beneath it is a small fountain.

**Entrance from
Kavaflar Arasta**

**Main
entrance**

Sultan's Loge
The imperial loge is supported on green marble columns. They are connected by pointed arches, whose surrounds are adorned with floral İznik tiles (see p161). Unusually, its ornately decorated mihrab contains a shuttered window, which opened on to countryside when the mosque was built.

Burgazada, one of the relaxed and picturesque Princes' Islands

Princes' Islands ❷
Kızıl Adalar

🏠 17,200. 🚢 from Eminönü or sea bus from Kabataş (European side) and sea bus from Kadıköy (Asian side). ℹ Town Hall, (0216) 382 70 71 and (0216) 382 78 56.

THE PINE-FORESTED Princes' Islands provide a welcome break from the bustle of the city and are just a short ferry ride southeast of Istanbul. Most ferries call in turn at the four largest of the nine islands: **Kınalıada, Burgazada, Heybeliada** and **Büyükada**.

Easily visited on a day trip, the islands take their name from a royal palace built by Justin II on Büyükada, then known as Prinkipo (Island of the Prince) in 569. In Byzantine times the islands became infamous as a place of exile, and also as the site of several monasteries.

In the latter half of the 19th century, with the inauguration of a regular steamboat service from Istanbul, many wealthy foreigners settled on the

Visitors strolling along a street in the village of Büyükada

islands. One who found the tolerant attitude to foreigners and generous morality attractive was Leon Trotsky, who lived in one of Büyükada's finest mansions from 1929 to 1933. Zia Gökalp (*see p308*), a key figure in the rise of Turkish nationalism, lived here during the waning years of the Ottoman era.

Büyükada is the largest of the Princes' Islands, and it attracts many visitors because of its lovely sandy beaches, outdoor summer culture and the Art Nouveau style of the wooden dwellings that have given the island much of its lingering Ottoman atmosphere. Both Büyükada and Heybeliada shun any form of motorized transport in favour of horse-drawn carriages or donkeys. At the top of Büyükada's wooded southern hill stands the Monastery of St George, built on Byzantine foundations.

Door to the Monastery of St George, Büyükada

Heybeliada, the second largest island, houses the imposing former Naval High School (Deniz Harp Okulu), built in 1942. Less touristy than Büyükada, this island offers lovely, tiny beaches and walks in pine groves. The island's northern hill is the stunning location of the Greek Orthodox School of Theology (built in 1841). The school itself is now closed, but its library, famous among

Orthodox scholars, is still open and worth a visit.

The smaller islands of Kınalıada and Burgazada are less developed and therefore more peaceful.

Polonezköy ❸

🏠 800. 🚌 221 from Taksim or 101 from Beşiktaş to Beykoz, then dolmuş. 🎪 Cherry festival (first two weeks of Jun).

POLONEZKÖY STILL REFLECTS clear signs of the Polish roots of its founders, who came here in 1842 fleeing Russian oppression. United by politics, Poles fought in Abdül Mecid I's army against Russia in the Crimean War (1853–56). Exempted from taxes for their efforts in the war, they settled in their namesake village. Unlike many people who came to Istanbul principally for trade, Poles came here in search of freedom and some of them converted to Islam. Polonezköy's old-world charm and culinary traditions are still there, but it has become very popular for a day's outing or a weekend break. Turks make up most of its current population.

There are excellent walks in the surrounding countryside and, even though villas and spas have sprung up, there are still several authentic restaurants serving Polish specialities, including the wild boar for which the town was once well known.

The surrounding beech forest, which also offers pleasant walks, has become a conservation area protected from further development.

Şile ❹

🏠 5,000. 🚌 from Üsküdar.

THE QUINTESSENTIAL Black Sea holiday village, Şile has several fine, sandy beaches and a large, black-and-white striped lighthouse high on a clifftop. In ancient times, the village, then known as Kalpe, was a port used by ships sailing eastward from the Bosphorus. Şile's lighthouse, the largest in Turkey, was built by the French for Sultan Abdül Aziz in 1858–9. Visiting it after dusk on a warm evening makes a pleasant outing. Apart from tourism, Şile is known for producing cotton, as well as a cool, loose-weave cotton cloth, known as *şile bezi*, which is sold in local shops.

İznik ❺

See pp160–61.

Uludağ National Park ❻

Uludağ Milli Parkı

[(0224) 211 42 85.] City bus marked "Teleferik" from Koza Park, then cable car to look-out point at Sarıalan. [ ] to Sarıalan, then dolmuş. [ ] daily. [ ] only for vehicles.

ONE OF A NUMBER of Turkish mountains to claim the title of Mount Olympus, Uludağ, at 2,540 m (8,340 ft), was believed by the Bithynians (of northwestern Asia Minor) to be the abode of the gods. In the Byzantine era, it was home to several monastic orders. After the Ottoman conquest of Bursa, Muslim dervishes *(p255)* moved into the abandoned monasteries. Nowadays, however, no traces of Uludağ's former religious communities remain.

Spring and summer are the best times for visiting Uludağ National Park, as its alpine heights remain relatively cool, offering a welcome escape from the heat of the lower areas. Visitors will find plenty of good opportunities for peaceful walking and picnicking.

The park includes about 670 sq km (258 sq miles) of woodland. As you ascend, the deciduous beech, oak and hazel gradually give way to juniper and aspen, and finally to dwarf junipers. In springtime, the slopes are blanketed with hyacinths and crocuses.

The main tourist season in Uludağ starts in November, when it becomes Turkey's most fashionable and accessible ski resort, with a reliable cable-car service and a good selection of hotels.

Osman Gazi *(see p54)* is supposed to have founded seven villages for his seven sons and their brides here. **Cumalıkızık**, on the lower slopes of Uludağ, is the most perfectly preserved of the five surviving villages and it is registered as a national monument. Among its houses are many 750-year-old half-timbered buildings.

Bursa ❼

See pp162–7.

Spoonbill wading in the lake at Bird Paradise National Park

Bird Paradise National Park ❽

Kuşcenneti Milli Parkı

[(0266) 735 54 22.] from the old bus station in Bandırma. [ ] sunrise to sunset daily. [ ] [ ]

AN ESTIMATED 255 species of birds visit Bird Paradise National Park at the edge of Kuş Gölü, the lake formerly known as Manyas Gölü. Located on the great migratory paths between Europe and Asia, the park is a happy combination of plant cover, reed beds and a lake that supports at least 20 species of fish. The park will delight amateur and professional birdwatchers alike, and a good field guide and some mosquito repellent will enhance the experience.

At the entrance to the park, there is a small museum with displays about various birds. Binoculars are provided at the desk and visitors make their way to an observation tower.

Two main groups of birds visit the lake: those that come here to breed (March–July), and those that pass by during migration, either heading south (November) or north (April–May). Among the birds that breed around the lake are the endangered Dalmatian pelican, the great crested grebe, cormorants, herons, bitterns and spoonbills. Over 3 million birds fly across the area on their migratory routes – storks, cranes, pelicans and birds of prey like sparrowhawks and spotted eagles. April and May are the best months to enjoy this area. Close to the main park area, there is a restaurant that serves fresh trout, and it is a good spot to break for lunch.

Uludağ National Park, a popular ski resort in winter

İznik ❺

🏛 20,122. 🚉 Yeni Mahalle, Yakup Sok. (0224) 757 25 83.
ℹ️ Belediye İşhanı, Kılıçaslan Cad, (0224) 757 19 33, (0224) 757 14 54.
📅 Wed. 🎪 İznik Flower and Summer Festival (1st or 2nd week of May); Liberation Day (28 Nov).

A CHARMING lakeside town, İznik gives little clue now of its former glory as a capital of the Byzantine Empire. Its most important legacy, however, dates from the 16th century, when its kilns produced the finest ceramics ever made in the Ottoman world.

The town first reached prominence in AD 325, when it was known as Nicaea. In that year Emperor Constantine (see p49) chose it as the location of the first Ecumenical Council of the Christian Church. The meeting produced the Nicene Creed, a statement of doctrine on the nature of Christ in relation to God.

The Seljuks (see p52) took Nicaea in 1081 and renamed it İznik. It was recaptured in 1097, during the First Crusade, on behalf of Emperor Alexius I Comnenus. After the Crusader capture of Constantinople in 1204 (see p53), the city served as the capital of the "Empire of Nicaea" for 50 years. In 1331, Orhan Gazi captured İznik and incorporated it into the Ottoman empire. İznik still retains

Grand domed portico fronting the Archaeological Museum

its original layout. Surrounded by the town walls, its two main streets are in the form of a cross, with minor streets running out from them on a grid plan. The walls still more or less delineate the town's boundaries. They were built in 300 BC by the Greek Lysimachus, then ruler of the town, but were frequently repaired by the Byzantines and, later, the Ottomans. Extending for some 3 km (2 miles), the walls are punctuated by huge gateways. The main one, Istanbul Gate (İstanbul Kapısı), marks İznik's northern limit. It is decorated with a carved relief of fighting horsemen and is flanked by Byzantine towers.

Istanbul Gate from within the town walls

One of the town's oldest surviving monuments, the ruined church of **Haghia Sophia**, stands at the intersection of the main streets, Atatürk Caddesi and Kılıçaslan Caddesi. An earlier version of the church was

the principal place of worship in Byzantine Nicaea. The current building was erected after an earthquake in 1065. The remains of a fine mosaic floor, and also of a Deësis (a fresco depicting Christ, the Virgin and John the Baptist), are protected from damage behind glass screens. Just off the eastern end of Kılıçaslan Caddesi, the 14th-century **Green Mosque** (Yeşil Camii) is named after the tiles covering its minaret. Unfortunately, the original tiles have now been replaced by modern copies of inferior quality. Opposite the mosque, the Kitchen of Lady Nilüfer (Nilüfer Hatun İmareti), one of İznik's loveliest buildings, now houses the town's **Archaeological Museum**. This imaret was set up in 1388 by Nilüfer Hatun, wife of Orhan Gazi, and served as a hospice for wandering dervishes. Entered through a spacious five-domed portico, the central domed area is flanked by two more domed rooms. The museum has displays of Roman antiquities and glass, as well as some recently discovered examples of Seljuk and Ottoman tiles.

🕌 **Haghia Sophia**
Atatürk Cad. 📞 (0224) 757 10 27.
🕐 9am–noon & 1–5:30pm daily. 🎫

🕌 **Green Mosque**
Müze Sok. 🕐 daily (except prayer times).

🏛 **Archaeological Museum**
Müze Sok. 📞 (0224) 757 10 27.
🕐 9am–noon & 1–5:30pm daily. 🎫

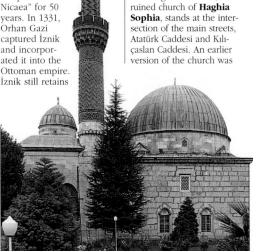

Green Mosque, named after the green tiles adorning its minaret

İznik Ceramics

İZNIK WAS ONE of two major centres (the other being Kütahya) where fine, painted and glazed pottery was fashioned during the Ottoman period. Pottery vessels, plates, and flat and shaped tiles were produced at İznik from the 15th to the 17th century. The last major commission was for 21,043 tiles of some 50 different designs for the Sultanahmet Mosque in Istanbul, completed in 1616. Early İznik pottery

16th-century İznik mosque lamp

is brilliant blue and white. The potteries reached their peak in the 16th century when the famous "tomato red" colour was fully developed. Today visitors can see it sparkle on the superb tilework of the 1561 Rüstem Paşa Mosque *(see p98)* in Istanbul. This period of İznik greatness in ceramic art coincided with the great period of design at the Nakkaşhane design studio in the Topkapı Palace *(see pp68–71)*.

***Chinese porcelain**, which was imported into Turkey from the 14th century and of which there is a large collection in Topkapı Palace, often inspired the designs used for İznik pottery. During the 16th century, İznik potters produced imitations of pieces of Chinese porcelain, such as this copy of a Ming dish.*

Rock and wave border pattern

***Cobalt blue and white** was the striking combination of colours used in early İznik pottery (produced between c.1470–1520). The designs used were a mixture of Chinese and Arabesque, as seen on this tiled panel on the wall of the Circumcision Chamber in Topkapı Palace. Floral patterns and animal motifs were both popular at this time.*

***Damascus ware** was the name erroneously given to ceramics produced at İznik during the first half of the 16th century. They had fantastic floral designs in the new colours of turquoise, sage green and manganese. When such tiles were discovered at Damascus, the similar İznik pots were wrongly assumed to have been made there.*

***Armenian bole**, an iron-rich red colour, began to be used around 1550, as seen in this 16th-century tankard. New, realistic tulip and other floral designs were also introduced, and İznik ware enjoyed its heyday, which lasted until around 1630.*

Miniature depicting potters

***Wall tiles** were not made in any quantity until the reign of Süleyman the Magnificent (1520–66). Süleyman used İznik tiles to refurbish the Dome of the Rock in Jerusalem.*
Some of the best examples are seen in Istanbul's mosques, notably in the Süleymaniye (see pp100–101), Rüstem Paşa Mosque and, here, in this example from the Blue Mosque (pp88–9).

Bursa

Basin, Museum of Turkish and Islamic Arts

THE CITY OF BURSA – known to Turks as *yeşil Bursa* ("green Bursa") – has tranquil parks and leafy suburbs set on the lower slopes of Mount Uludağ *(see p159)*. This disguises the vibrant commercial heart of the city, which is today made prosperous by automobiles, food and textiles, as it was by the silk trade in the 15th and 16th centuries. The Romans developed the potential of Bursa's mineral springs, and there are estimated to be about 3,000 thermal baths in the city today. In 1326 Bursa became the first capital of the Ottoman Empire after it succumbed to Osman *(see p54)*.

Bursa has been a provincial capital since 1841 and, despite its commercial centre, it has retained its pious dignity. No city in Turkey has more mosques and tombs. Paradoxically, it is also the home of the satirical shadow-puppet genre known as Karagöz *(see p26)*.

View over the rooftops of the city of Bursa

Yıldırım Beyazıt Mosque
Yıldırım Beyazıt Camii
Yıldırım Cad. ◯ *daily (except prayer times).*
This Mosque is named after Beyazıt I, whose nickname was "Yıldırım", meaning "thunderbolt". This referred to the speed with which he reacted to his enemies. Built in 1389, just after Beyazıt became sultan, the mosque at first doubled as a lodge for Sufi dervishes *(see p255)*. It has a lovely portico with five domed bays.

Inside, the prayer hall and interior court (a covered "courtyard" in Bursa mosques, which prefigures the open ones preferred by later Ottoman architects) are divided by an impressive arch. This rises from two *mihrab*-like niches. The walls of the prayer hall itself are adorned with several attractive pieces of calligraphic design *(see pp28–9)*.

Green Tomb
Yeşil Türbe
Yeşil Cad. ◯ *daily.* 🎨 *donation.*
The tomb of Mehmet I, which stands elevated among tall cypress trees, is one of the city's most prominent landmarks. It was built between 1414 and 1421.

The tomb is much closer to the Seljuk style of architecture than classical Ottoman. Its exterior is covered in green tiles – mainly 19th-century replacements for the original faïence. A few older tiles survive around the entrance portal. The interior, entered through a pair of superbly carved wooden doors, is simply dazzling. The space is small and the ornamentation, covering a relatively large surface area, is breathtaking in its depth of colour and detail. The *mihrab* has especially intricate tile panels, including a representation of a mosque lamp hanging from a gold chain between two candles.

The sultan's magnificent sarcophagus is covered in exquisite tiles and adorned by a long Koranic inscription. Nearby sarcophagi contain the remains of his sons, daughters and nursemaid.

Green Mosque
Yeşil Camii
Yeşil Cad. ◯ *daily (except prayer times).*
Bursa's most famous monument was commissioned by Mehmet I in 1412, but it remained unfinished at his death in 1421 and still lacks a portico. Nevertheless, it is the finest Ottoman mosque built prior to the conquest of Constantinople *(see p54)*.

The main portal is tall and elegant, with an intricately carved canopy. It opens into the entrance hall. Beyond this is an interior court with a carved fountain at its centre. A flight of three steps leads up from here into the prayer hall. On either side of the steps are niches for worshippers to leave their shoes. Above the entrance to the court is the sultan's loge *(see p33)*, resplendent in richly patterned tiles created using the *cuerda seca* technique. They are in beautiful greens, blues and

The distinctive and prominent Green Tomb of Sultan Mehmet I

yellows, with threads of gold that were added after firing. The tiling of the prayer hall was carried out by Ali Ibn İlyas Ali, who learned his art in Samarkand. This was the first time that tiles were used extensively in an Ottoman mosque, and it set a precedent for the later widespread use of İznik tiles *(see p161)*. The tiles covering the walls of the prayer hall, which is well lit by floor-level windows, are simple, green and hexagonal. Against this plain backdrop, the effect of the *mihrab* is especially glorious. Predominantly turquoise, deep blue and white, with touches of gold, the *mihrab*'s tiles depict flowers, leaves, arabesques and geometric patterns. The mosque's exterior was also once clad in tiles, but these have disappeared over time.

🏛 Museum of Turkish and Islamic Arts

Türk ve İslam Eserleri Müzesi
Yeşil Cad. ☎ *(0224) 327 76 79.*
● *currently closed for repairs, but the façade is worth seeing on its own. No date for the re-opening of the museum has yet been set.*

Façade of the Museum of Turkish and Islamic Arts

Visitors' Checklist

👥 *1,300,000.* ✈ *20 km (12 miles) NW of city centre.* 🚌 *Yeni Yalova Yolu, (0224) 261 54 00.* [D] *Atatürk Cad, near the State Theatre or behind Heykel.* [i] *Ulucami Parkı, Orhangazı Altgeçidi 1 (0224) 220 18 48.* 🎭 *International Bursa Festival (1st week of Jun–3rd week of Jul); International Karagöz Festival (2nd–3rd weeks of Nov).*

This interesting museum is housed in a fine Ottoman-era building, once the *medrese (see p32)* associated with the Green Mosque. A colonnade surrounds its courtyard on three sides. The cells leading off from this courtyard, once used by the students, are now exhibition galleries. Exhibits date from the 12th to the 20th centuries, and include Seljuk and Ottoman ceramics, elaborately decorated Korans and beautiful ceremonial costumes. One display features Turkish baths, complete with embroidered towels and silver bath clogs, and there is an authentic re-creation of a circumcision room.

Bursa City Centre

Alaeddin Mosque 7
Archaeological Museum 10
Green Mosque 3
Green Tomb 2
Hüsnü Züber House 9
Muradiye Mosque 8
Museum of Turkish and Islamic Arts 4
Tombs of Osman and Orhan Gazi 6
Tophane Citadel 5
Yıldırım Beyazıt Mosque 1

Key

- Street-by-Street area *See pp164–5*
- 🚌 Coach station
- [D] Dolmuş terminus
- [i] Tourist information
- ☪ Mosque

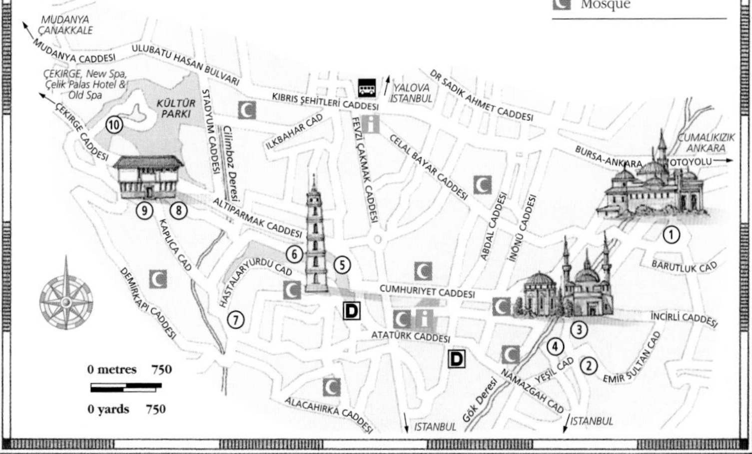
MUDANYA ÇANAKKALE
MUDANYA CADDESİ
ULUBATU HASAN BULVARI
ÇEKİRGE, New Spa, Çelik Palas Hotel & Old Spa
ÇEKİRGE CADDESİ
KÜLTÜR PARKI
STADYUM CADDESİ
Cilimboz Deresi
KIBRIS ŞEHİTLERİ CADDESİ
YALOVA İSTANBUL
DR SADIK AHMET CADDESİ
İLKBAHAR CAD
FEVZİ ÇAKMAK CADDESİ
CELAL BAYAR CADDESİ
CUMALIKIZIK ANKARA
BURSA-ANKARA OTOYOLU
ALTIPARMAK CADDESİ
KAPLICA CAD
ABDAL CADDESİ
İNÖNÜ CADDESİ
HASTALARYURDU CAD
BARUTLUK CAD
DEMİRKAPI CADDESİ
CUMHURİYET CADDESİ
İNCİRLİ CADDESİ
ATATÜRK CADDESİ
YEŞİL CAD
EMİR SULTAN CAD
NAMAZGAH CAD
Gök Deresi
ALACAHIRKA CADDESİ
İSTANBUL
İSTANBUL
0 metres 750
0 yards 750

Bursa: The Market Area

BURSA'S CENTRAL MARKET AREA is a warren of streets and Ottoman *hans* (warehouses). The area emphasizes the more colourful and traditional aspects of this busy industrial city and is a good place to experience the bustle of inner-city life. Here too you can buy the local fabrics for which the city is famous, particularly hand-made lace, towelling and silk. The silkworm was introduced to the Byzantine empire in the 6th century and, until recently, there was still a brisk trade in silk cocoons in Koza Han in June and July. Here you can also find hand-made, camelskin Karagöz puppets *(see p26)*.

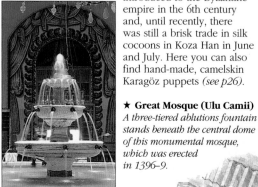

★ **Covered Bazaar**
The great bazaar, built by Mehmet I in the 15th century, consists of a long hall with domed bays, with an adjoining high, vaulted hall. The Bedesten is home to jewellers' shops.

★ **Great Mosque (Ulu Camii)**
A three-tiered ablutions fountain stands beneath the central dome of this monumental mosque, which was erected in 1396–9.

Şengül Hamamı Turkish baths

FEVZI ÇAKMAK CAD

Bey Han (also called Emir Han) was built as part of the Orhan Gazi Mosque complex, to provide revenue for the mosque's upkeep.

Cafés

KOZA PARKI

ATATÜRK CAD

Umur Bey Hamamı,
built by Murat II (1421–51), is one of the world's oldest Turkish baths. It now houses workshops.

Koza Park
The gardens in front of Koza Han, with their fountains, benches and shaded café tables, are a popular meeting place for locals and visitors throughout the day.

★ Koza Han

This is the most attractive and fascinating building in the market area. Since it was built in 1491 by Beyazıt II, it has been central to the silk trade.

Geyve Han is also known as İvaz Paşa Han.

Fidan Han dates from around 1470, when it was built by a grand vizier of Mehmet the Conqueror.

İçkoza Han

Flower Market
The numerous bunches of flowers for sale in the streets around the town hall make a picturesque sight in the midst of Bursa's bustling market area.

BORSA SOK

UZUN ÇARŞI CAD

ÇÖMLEK SOK

0 metres 40
0 yards 40

STAR SIGHTS

★ Great Mosque

★ Covered Bazaar

★ Koza Han

The Belediye, Bursa's town hall, is a Swiss chalet-style, half-timbered building that forms a surprising landmark in the centre of the city.

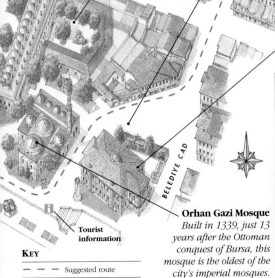

BELEDİYE CAD

Tourist information

KEY

– – – Suggested route

Orhan Gazi Mosque
Built in 1339, just 13 years after the Ottoman conquest of Bursa, this mosque is the oldest of the city's imperial mosques.

Exploring Bursa

The clocktower in Tophane

Tophane, the most ancient part of Bursa, is distinguished by its clock-tower, which stands on top of a hill. This area was formerly the site of the citadel and is bounded by what remains of the original Byzantine walls. It is also known as Hisar, which means "fortress" in Turkish. If you continue westwards for 2 km (1 mile), crossing the Cılımboz River, you come to the historic district of Muradiye. Çekirge (or "cricket") is Bursa's most westerly area. The origin of this name is not known, but the cool, leafy character of this suburb gives Bursa the tag of *yeşil*, or "green", by which it is known in Turkey.

Tophane

Tophane's northern limit is marked by the best-preserved section of the citadel walls, built on an outcrop of rock. At the top is a pleasant park, filled with cafés, which also contains the imposing clock-tower and the tombs of Osman and Orhan Gazi, the founders of the Ottoman dynasty.

delineated the entire circumference of the ancient city. However, Orhan encouraged Bursa's expansion and developed the present-day commercial heart of the city further to the east.

🛡 Tophane Citadel
Hisar

Osman Gazi Cad. ⏻ *daily.* ♿

The citadel walls can be viewed from a set of steps leading uphill from the intersection of Cemal Nadir Caddesi and Atatürk Caddesi. These steps end at the tea gardens above. The citadel fell into Ottoman hands when Orhan Gazi's troops broke through its walls. Later, he built a wooden palace inside the citadel and had the old Byzantine ramparts re-fortified. Until this era the walls had

⚰ Tombs of Osman and Orhan Gazi
Osman & Orhan Gazi Türbeleri

Ulu Cami Cad. ⏻ *daily.* 🎦 *donation.*

Osman Gazi began the process of Ottoman expansion in the 13th century (*see p52*) and attempted to capture Bursa. But it was his son, Orhan, who took the city just before Osman Gazi died. Orhan brought his father's body to be buried in the baptistry of a converted church and he himself was later buried in the nave. The tombs that can be seen today date from 1868.

🕌 Alaeddin Mosque
Alaeddin Camii

Alaeddin Mahallesi. ⏻ *daily.* ∅

The Alaeddin Mosque is the oldest in Bursa: it was built in 1335, only nine years after the city was conquered in 1326. It is in the form of a simple domed square, fronted by a portico of four Byzantine columns with capitals. The mosque was commissioned by Alaeddin Bey, brother of and vizier to Orhan Gazi.

Muradiye

Muradiye is a leafy, residential district of Bursa. Close to the Muradiye Mosque, the Hüsnü Züber House is a fine example of a traditional Turkish home. To the north is a park, among the attractions of which are a boating lake and the Archaeological Museum.

Tomb of Osman Gazi, the first great Ottoman leader

🕌 Muradiye Mosque
Muradiye Külliyesi

Murat II Cad. ⏻ *daily.* 🎦 *donation.*

This mosque complex was built by Murat II, the father of Mehmet the Conqueror (*see p54*), in 1447. The mosque itself is preceded by a graceful domed portico. Its wooden door is finely carved and the interior decorated with early İznik tiles (*see p161*). The *medrese* (*see p32*), next to the mosque, now serves as a dispensary. It is a perfectly square building, with cells surrounding a central garden courtyard. Its *dershane*, or main classroom, is richly tiled and adorned with an ornate brick façade.

The mosque garden, with its cypresses, well-tended flower beds and fountains, is one of Bursa's most tranquil retreats. Murat II was the last of the Ottoman sultans to be buried in Bursa and his mausoleum stands in the garden beside the mosque. The other 11 tombs in the garden are a reminder of the Ottoman code of succession, which recognized a future sultan as the strongest (or

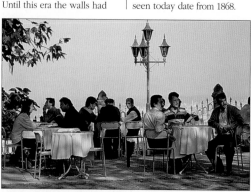

Popular café in the park above the ancient citadel walls in Tophane

Interior of Muradiye Mosque, showing the decorative *mihrab*

most cunning) male relative, even if not always the most suitable to rule. Competing male relatives could expect to be put to death or spend most of their lives in enforced solitary confinement, known as "the cage". This did not, however, prevent the ruling offspring from having an emotive memorial built for a deposed brother. Selim II ("the Sot"), for example, had an elaborate octagonal mausoleum built in Bursa for his older brother, Mustafa. The tomb's interior has some particularly striking İznik tile panels depicting flowers.

🏛 Archaeological Museum

Arkeoloji Müzesi
Kültür Parkı. ☎ (0224) 234 49 18.
⏰ 8:30am–noon & 1–5:30pm
Tue–Sun. ● Mon. 🌐
Finds dating from the 3rd millennium BC up to the Ottoman conquest of Bursa in 1326 are collected in this museum. The ceremonial armour accessories are the most interesting items, with the Roman glass a close second. There are a number of Roman statues and bronzes, as well as Byzantine religious objects and coins. The labelling of objects has recently been improved.

🏨 Hüsnü Züber House

Hüsnü Züber Evi,
Yaşayan Müze
Uzunyol Sok 3, Muradiye. ☎ (0224) 221 35 42 for opening times.
The Hüsnü Züber House is one of the most attractive and best-preserved Ottoman

mansions in Bursa and a study in vernacular architecture. The 150-year-old house was once a diplomatic guesthouse, then became the Russian consulate, but its present owner, the artist and author Hüsnü Züber, is struggling to maintain it as a private museum. Art exhibitions and concerts are held here, and the house is regularly open to the public. The owner himself is usually there on Sundays. The interior is attractive, but the most interesting features are the Anatolian motifs – about 600 according to the owner – applied to spoons, musical instruments and other objects using a pyrogravure process (engraving by burning). Textile museums have come here from around the world searching for design and print ideas.

Hüsnü Züber House, dating from the mid-19th century

Çekirge

The Çekirge area offers the most prominent and best developed of all the natural mineral springs *(kaplıca)* in Turkey. In the 6th century, Emperor Justinian *(see p49)* built a bath house here; his wife, Theodora, arrived later with a retinue of about 4,000. Çekirge also has some of the city's finest and most luxurious hotels. The spa culture and healthy mountain air are enhanced by some spectacular alpine vistas.

🔥 New Spa

Yeni Kaplıca
Mudanya Yolu 6. ☎ (0224) 236 69 68. ⏰ 5am–11pm (men) & 7am–11pm (women) daily.
Despite the name, the New Spa baths have a substantial pedigree. They were rebuilt in 1522 by Rüstem Paşa, grand vizier to Süleyman the Magnificent *(see p55)*.

🏨 Çelik Palas Hotel

Çelik Palas Otel
Çekirge Cad 79.
☎ (0224) 233 38 00.
This five-star hotel is a famous local icon. Built in 1933, it is the city's oldest, most prestigious spa hotel. Atatürk *(see p58)* frequented its baths, which are open to both sexes. Their centrepiece is an attractive circular pool in a domed marble room.

🔥 Old Spa

Eski Kaplıca
Çekirge Meydanı, Kervansaray.
☎ (0224) 233 93 00.
⏰ 8am–10:30pm daily.
The Old Spa baths were established by Sultan Murat I in the late 14th century and renovated in 1512 during the reign of Beyazıt II. Remnants of an earlier building, thought to date from the reign of Emperor Justinian, can also be seen. These include some Byzantine columns and capitals in the *hararet* (steam room) of the men's section *(see p77)*. The spa is adjacent to, and owned by, the new Kervansaray Termal Hotel. Refreshing spring water, said to cure certain skin diseases and rheumatism, bubbles into the central pool of both the men's and women's sections at a temperature of around 45°C (113°F).

Attractive, tranquil interior of the Old Spa baths

Gallipoli Peninsula 🄰
Gelibolu Yarımadası

Shell cases at Alçıtepe

WASHED BY THE Aegean Sea to the west, the Gallipoli Peninsula is bordered to the east by the Dardanelles, a strategic waterway giving access to the Sea of Marmara, the Bosphorus and the Black Sea. In ancient times, this deep channel was called the Hellespont. Today, the peninsula is an unspoiled area of farmland and pine forest, with some lovely stretches of sandy beach.

However, it was also the scene of one of the bloodiest campaigns of World War I, in which more than 500,000 Allied (Australian, British, French, Indian and New Zealand) and Turkish soldiers laid down their lives. The region has three museums, and is dotted with cemeteries and monuments. In 1973, the Gallipoli National Historic Park was created in recognition of the area's great historical significance.

Suvla Bay
On 7 August 1915, British troops landed here in an attempt to break the stalemate further south.

Suvla Point · Suvla Bay · Salt Lake · Küçükanafart
Nibrunesi Point · Limnea · Kemal
Anzac Cove
Aribururnu Cove
Z Beach (ANZAC)
War Cemeteries
Brighton Beach · Ses
Museum
Kaba

★ Kabatepe Information Centre
The centre is also a museum, with letters, photographs, shrapnel and other memorabilia relating to the Gallipoli campaign.

Kum Bay

Behr

Gözetleme

At Y Beach, ambiguous signals led to an unauthorized withdrawal on both sides.

KRITHIA (Alçıtepe)

War Cemeteri

Abide

Cape Helles Memorial

French Cemetery
A sombre obelisk and rows of striking black crosses honour the French troops who fell during the Anglo-French landing at Cape Helles on 25 April 1915.

The Çanakkale Şehitler Abidesi commemorates fallen Turkish soldiers.

0 kilometres

0 miles   2

Reconstructed Trenches
At some points, the Allied and Turkish trenches were no more than a few metres apart.

VISITORS' CHECKLIST

Gallipoli National Park. 🚢 from Çanakkale to Eceabat. 🚌 from Bursa and Istanbul. ◯ 8am–5pm daily (winter); 9am–6pm daily (summer). **Kabatepe Information Centre** ◖ (0286) 814 12 97. ◯ 8:30am–6pm daily. 🏛 **Mehmetcik Memorial** ◯ 9am–1pm & 2–6pm daily. 🎫 🏴 ANZAC Day (24–25 Apr).

★ Chunuk Bair
Various monuments honour the 28,000 men who died here on 6–9 August 1915.

Kumkoy

Büyükanafarta

Yalova

KEY

🚃	Major road
═	Other road
═	Minor road
⟋	River, lake or dam

Gallipoli attlefields

Bigali

Atatürk Statue

Chunuk Bair

ehmetcik Memorial   *Kilye Bay*

Eceabat (Maidos)

Atatürk Museum

Kilitibahir   *The Narrows*

Çanakkale

★ Mehmetcik Memorial
This memorial was unveiled in 1985. Atatürk's eulogy unites the fallen sons of Turkey (Mehmetcik) with the Allied dead ("Johnnies").

Dardanelles (Çanakkale Boğazı)

Kepez

THE GALLIPOLI CAMPAIGN 1915–16

After the start of World War I, Allied leaders developed a plan to seize the Dardanelles. This would give them control of Constantinople and diminish the threat of Russia gaining control of the strategic waterway. A naval assault was repulsed by Turkish shore batteries and minefields, so the order was given to land troops to secure the straits. At dawn on 25 April 1915 British and French troops landed at the tip of the Gallipoli Peninsula. Further north, a large force of ANZACs (Australia and New Zealand Army Corps) came ashore but met dogged opposition from the Turkish defenders. A second landing at Suvla Bay failed to win any new ground. Many soldiers died from disease, drowning or the appalling conditions of trench warfare. After nine months, the Allied force withdrew.

British troops landing under fire at Cape Helles

STAR FEATURES

★ **Chunuk Bair**

★ **Kabatepe Information Centre**

★ **Mehmetcik Memorial**

THE AEGEAN

ISCOVERING THE AEGEAN REGION *of Turkey takes visitors on a panoramic, classical journey, from Çanakkale on the Dardanelles (the ancient Hellespont) to the finger of land off Marmaris known as the Datça Peninsula. Together, the coast and hinterland tell a story spanning some 5,000 years of Greek and Roman history. This is where Homer's myths and heroes come to life.*

Here, it is easy to imagine the sculpture classes at Aphrodisias, the busy streets of ancient Ephesus or a medical lecture at the famous Asclepium at Pergamum (Bergama).

Most of modern-day Turkey was once part of the eastern Roman empire, known as Asia Minor. Many of the remote classical sites in the Aegean region formed part of ancient Caria, an independent kingdom whose boundaries roughly corresponded to the Turkish province of Muğla. Caria's origins are disputed but its resistance to Hellenization is well documented. The Carians prospered under Roman rule but retained some autonomy, with their sanctuary at Labranda, and Zeus as their deity. The Carian symbol, a double-headed axe, was inscribed on many buildings as a defiant trademark. The Mausoleum at Halicarnassus (modern-day Bodrum), built as the tomb of the Carian king Mausolus, was one of the Seven Wonders of the Ancient World.

The Aegean region contains many Christian sights. The Seven Churches of the Apocalypse, mentioned in the Book of Revelation, surround İzmir; the last resting place of the Virgin Mary is just outside Ephesus; St John's Basilica is in Selçuk and the castle of the Knights of St John still guards the harbour at Bodrum.

The Aegean's original tourist resorts, such as Kuşadası, Marmaris and Bodrum, have now matured, and offer superb facilities and sophisticated nightlife. Bodrum's Halikarnas disco has an international reputation, and Kuşadası is known for its shopping.

Roman arched gateway at the ruined city of Hierapolis, near Denizli

◁ The inviting yacht harbour at Marmaris

Exploring the Aegean

AROUND 26 MILLION people – roughly a third of Turkey's population – inhabit the Aegean region. Here, incomes are generally higher and the lifestyle more westernized than elsewhere in the country. Tourists are attracted to this area for its beaches, nightlife and yachting, but there are many other worthwhile sights from the green and fertile Menderes River Valley to the Roman city of Ephesus near Selçuk. Visitors can explore the countryside in day-trips from Marmaris to Knidos on the scenic Datça Peninsula.

SIGHTS AT A GLANCE

Temple of Trajan, Bergama (Pergamum)

GETTING AROUND
The Aegean region is well served by good roads and public transport. Dolmuşes ply the routes to the smaller towns and villages. Izmir and Bodrum both have airports with frequent connections to Istanbul. Izmir is also served by rail, with connections to the city's Adnan Menderes Airport. Ferry services link İzmir, Marmaris and Bodrum with ports in Greece and Italy.

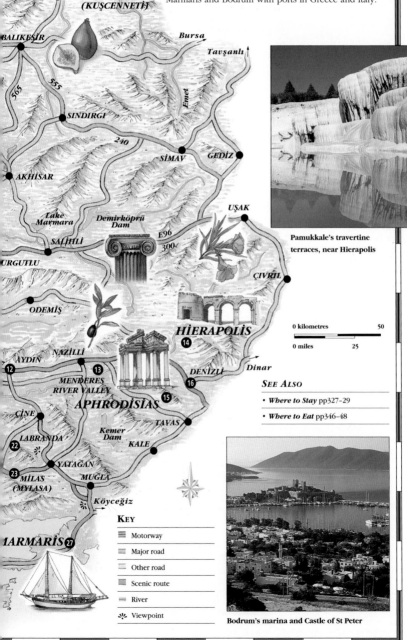

SUSURLUK

BIRD PARADISE
(KUŞCENNETİ)

BALIKESİR

Bursa

Tavşanlı

565

555

Emet

SINDIRGI

240

SİMAV

GEDİZ

AKHISAR

Lake
Marmara

Demirköprü
Dam

UŞAK

E96

300

SALİHLİ

URGUTLU

ÇİVRİL

ODEMİŞ

HİERAPOLIS
14

Pamukkale's travertine
terraces, near Hierapolis

0 kilometres   50

0 miles   25

NAZİLLİ

AYDIN
12

13

MENDERES
RIVER VALLEY

APHRODISIAS

DENİZLİ
16

Dinar

SEE ALSO

• *Where to Stay* pp327–29

• *Where to Eat* pp346–48

ÇİNE

LABRANDA
22

Kemer
Dam

TAVAS

KALE

YATAĞAN

MİLAS
(MYLASA)
23

MUĞLA

Köyceğiz

15

KEY

≣ Motorway

≣ Major road

≣ Other road

≣ Scenic route

≈ River

☆ Viewpoint

1ARMARIS 27

Bodrum's marina and Castle of St Peter

Çanakkale, a historic crossing point between Asia and Europe

Çanakkale ❶

🏛 76,420. 🚢 from Eceabat or Kilitbahir. 🚌 Atatürk Cad. 🚏 İskele Meydanı 27, (0286) 217 11 87. 🎭 Fri. 🎊 Navy Days (13–18 Mar), ANZAC Days (24–25 Apr), Sardine Festival (30–31 Jun).

ÇANAKKALE OCCUPIES the narrowest point of the straits called the Dardanelles, which are 1,200 m (3,937 ft) wide at this point. In 450 BC, the Persian King Xerxes built a bridge of boats here to land his troops in Thrace, and the final battles of the Peloponnesian War took place in these waters around 400 BC.

During his campaign to take Constantinople in 1453, Mehmet II (the Conqueror) built two fortresses to secure the straits: Kilitbahir (on the European side) and Çimenlik (in Çanakkale harbour).

Today, ferry services link Çanakkale with Kilitbahir and Eceabat on the other side. Çanakkale makes the most convenient base for tours of the Gallipoli battlefields *(see pp168–9)* across the straits.

The town has an attractive harbour, a naval museum and the landmark clock in the main square. Çanakkale means "pottery castle" and the town was once a centre for the production of high-quality kaolin for a flourishing ceramics industry. Today this type of clay is imported, but the vitreous enamel ware *(see p356)* made in Çanakkale remains one of Turkey's top export earners.

ENVIRONS: A few kilometres south of the town is the **Archaeological Museum**, which should not be missed.

🏛 Archaeological Museum
Arkeoloji Müzesi
Barbaros Mahallesi, Yüzüncü Yıl Cad.
📞 (0286) 217 67 40. ⏰ 8am–noon, 1–5pm daily. 🖼

Troy ❷

📍 İskele Meydanı 67, Çanakkale, (0286) 217 11 87. 🚌 from Çanakkale, then taxi. 🎊 Troy Festival (based in Çanakkale but includes Troy and environs, 10–18 Aug).

FEW AREAS OF Turkey have been as thoroughly excavated as Troy (Truva in Turkish). Nine different strata have yielded pieces of a history that runs from around 4000 BC until about AD 300. Troy was the pivot of Homer's *Iliad* and was where the decade-long Trojan War (13th century BC) was fought.

Reconstruction of the Trojan Horse

The site is known as **Hisarlık**, or "castle kingdom" in Turkish. The stonework and walls are impressive. Visible today are a defence wall, two sanctuaries (probably dating from the 8th century BC), houses from various periods and a Roman theatre. The site called the Pillar House at the southern gate may have been the palace of King Priam.

The site is well marked with 12 information points and some ongoing excavations. The most visible attraction is a large wooden Trojan Horse, a reconstruction of the device used by the Greeks to deceive and ultimately vanquish the Trojans, and a universal symbol of treachery today. In August each year, Turkish schoolchildren release a white dove from the Trojan Horse to celebrate peace.

🏛 Hisarlık
5 km (3 miles) from main E87 road. 🚌 from Çanakkale every 30/40 minutes. ⏰ 8am–7:30pm (5pm in winter) daily. 🖼 🔲 🔲

SCHLIEMANN'S SEARCH FOR ANCIENT TROY

The German-born Heinrich Schliemann – regarded by many as an unscrupulous plunderer and by others as an archaeological pioneer – nurtured a lifelong ambition to discover Homer's Troy. In 1873, three years after starting excavations at Hisarlık, he stumbled upon what he claimed to be King Priam's hoard of gold and silver jewellery. The over-eager explorer damaged the site, but his valuable find demonstrated that Greek civilization started 1,000 years earlier than previously believed. Part of the hoard, which was on display in a Berlin museum, vanished after World War II. It reappeared in the Pushkin Museum in Russia in 1996. Its return, authenticity and origins are still controversial.

Heinrich Schliemann's wife, wearing "Priam's" jewellery

Humpbacked Ottoman bridge on the outskirts of Behramkale

Behramkale ❸ (Assos)

🏛 3,000. 🚌 to Ayvacık, 19 km (12 miles) N, then dolmuş. 🚗 from Edremit or Çanakkale.

NESTLED ON THE SHORES of the Gulf of Edremit and sheltered by the Greek island of Lesbos, 10 km (6 miles) offshore, it is easy to see why Assos enjoyed the reputation of the most beautiful place in Asia Minor. Ancient Assos reached the pinnacle of its glory when Plato's protégé, Aristotle, founded a school of philosophy here in 340 BC. In the 2nd century BC, the town included not only the present citadel, with the remaining Doric columns of the Temple of Athena (built in the 6th century BC), but also the village of Behramkale, 238 m (781 ft) below.

St Paul is reputed to have passed through Assos on his third biblical journey, and the town is referred to in the Acts of the Apostles. After the fall of the Byzantine empire, the town's commercial fortunes declined, but today this charming and cultured retreat attracts many artists and scholars, who leave the bustle of the city and find a source of inspiration here.

As you come into the town, note the fine Ottoman bridge dating from the 14th century. There is also a mosque and a fort from this time, all built by Sultan Murat I. Residents of Assos favour houses with archways and overhanging balconies, and there are bougainvilleas everywhere.

Ayvalık ❹

🏛 4,200. 🚌 1.5 km (1 mile) N of town centre. ℹ Opposite the yacht harbour, (0266) 312 21 22. 🚢 Thu.

AYVALIK TAKES ITS NAME from *ayva*, the Turkish word for quince, but the fruit is only available in season (January and February). Of the many villages along the Aegean coast peopled by Greeks until 1923 *(see p58)*, Ayvalık is the one that has most retained the flavour of a bygone age. There are many stone houses, and the town's mosques betray their Greek Orthodox origins. A Greek church and a few Greek-speakers remain.

Ayvalık's appeal stems from its cobbled streets and leisurely lifestyle. The beach at Sarımsaklı (which means "garlic") and peninsula of Alibey (also known by its Greek name of Cunda) are within reach by road, but the ferry journey is more restful.

Bergama (Pergamum) ❺

See pp176–7.

Foça ❻

🏛 3,500. ℹ Atatürk Bulvarı 1 (entrance to Foça), (0232) 812 12 22. 🚌 from İzmir to Foça turnoff on main E87. 🚗 from junction of E87.

PHOCAEA, ANCIENT FOÇA, was probably settled around 1000 BC and was part of the Ionian League *(see p190).* Around 500 BC the Phocaeans were famed as mariners, sending vessels powered by 50 oarsmen into the Aegean, Mediterranean and Black Sea. There is a small theatre dating from antiquity at the entrance to the town. Near the centre of town, you will find an interesting stone tomb known as **Taş Küle**. There is also a restored Genoese **fortress**. But apart from a few *hamams* (Turkish baths), this is the extent of Old Foça.

ENVIRONS: 23 km (14 miles) up the coast is the town of Yenifoça (New Foça), with good campsites and beaches. The military presence in the area may have helped keep it off the tourist trail. Apart from summer weekends and holidays, it is an ideal place to escape the crowds. The area is known for its monk seal conservation programme, but these marine mammals are seldom seen.

Boats, old houses and up-market cafés in Foça's harbour

Bergama (Pergamum) 5

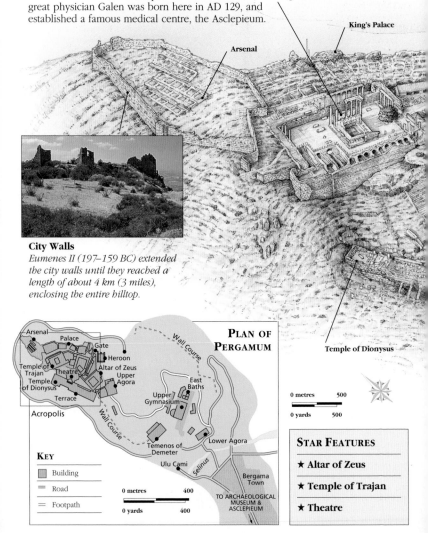

PERCHED ON A HILLTOP above the modern town of Bergama, the great acropolis of Pergamum is one of the most dramatic sights in Turkey. Originally settled by the Aeolian Greeks in the 8th century BC, it was ruled for a time by one of Alexander the Great's generals. The city prospered under the Pergamene dynasty founded by Eumenes I, who ruled from 263 to 241 BC, when this was one of the ancient world's main centres of learning. The last ruler of this dynasty, Attalus III, bequeathed the kingdom to Rome in 133 BC, and Pergamum became capital of the Roman province of Asia. The great physician Galen was born here in AD 129, and established a famous medical centre, the Asclepieum.

Statue of Hadrian, Bergama Museum

★ Temple of Trajan
Built of white marble, it was completed during Hadrian II's reign (AD 117–138).

King's Palace

Arsenal

City Walls
Eumenes II (197–159 BC) extended the city walls until they reached a length of about 4 km (3 miles), enclosing the entire hilltop.

Temple of Dionysus

PLAN OF PERGAMUM

Arsenal
Palace
Gate
Heroon
Temple of Trajan
Theatre
Altar of Zeus
Temple of Dionysus
Upper Agora
East Baths
Terrace
Upper Gymnasium
Acropolis
Wall Course
Temenos of Demeter
Ulu Cami
Lower Agora
Selinus
Bergama Town

TO ARCHAEOLOGICAL MUSEUM & ASCLEPIEUM

KEY

▭	Building
═	Road
═	Footpath

0 metres 400
0 yards 400

0 metres 500
0 yards 500

STAR FEATURES

★ Altar of Zeus

★ Temple of Trajan

★ Theatre

Library Ruins
Reputedly containing 200,000 parchment scrolls, many works from Pergamum went to its rival library in Alexandria as part of Mark Anthony's wedding gift to Cleopatra in 41 BC.

VISITORS' CHECKLIST

(0232) 631 28 83. from İzmir. 9am–6pm (7pm in summer) daily. There is much uphill walking, as the Acropolis and Asclepieum are 8 km (5 miles) apart. Allow a full day to tour the site.

Temple of Athena

The Heroon was a shrine built to honour the kings of Pergamum.

★ **Altar of Zeus**
One of Pergamum's largest temples, the first stone reliefs of the building were found in the 1870s. The altar was rebuilt in Berlin's Pergamum Museum.

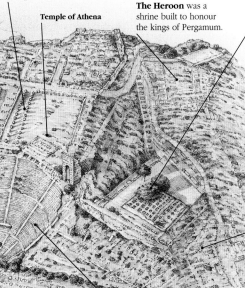

Upper Agora
The agora (marketplace) lay immediately below the Altar of Zeus. From here, a ramp led up to to the main city gate.

Theatre Terrace

★ **Theatre**
Constructed in the 3rd century BC, the theatre has 80 rows of seats and an estimated capacity of 10,000. The seats were constructed of andesite, and the royal box in the lower section of marble.

İzmir ❼

THE MOST WESTERN-LEANING of Turkish cities,
İzmir's position at the head of the Gulf of İzmir
(İzmir Körfezi) has given it a trading edge that
has lasted from the 3rd century AD to today.
For centuries, it was known as Smyrna, a name
possibly derived from the myrrh trees that
grow here. The city's origins are believed to
date back to 3000 BC, based on finds from
the Bayraklı Mound. Until 1922, the city had
a large Christian population, including
thousands of Greek Orthodox, most of
whom fled during the turmoil of the War of
Independence (see p58). As Turkey's third
largest city and the regional headquarters of NATO,
İzmir has a multicultural sophistication.

Konak Clock Tower

The Governor's Palace, in the centre of the city

Exploring İzmir

İzmir's broad boulevards are
balanced by leafy pedestrian
precincts. Buses, ferries and a
new Metro make it easy to
get around, or horse-drawn
carriages will do for the more
sedate tourist. To explore the
old quarter of İzmir, visit the
Konak district, to the west
of the city centre.

🏛 Archaeology Museum

Halil Paşa Cad, Bahri Baba Park İçi.
📞 (0232) 489 07 96. ⏱ 8:30am–
6pm (5pm in winter) Tue–Sun.
🎟 📷 with permission.
The main displays
consist of artifacts from
the Bayraklı Mound,
which was settled from
about 3000 to 300 BC.
The Byzantine glassware
is especially eye-catching,
but the highlight is the
Treasury (Hazine). It
is kept locked and the
guard may need to be
summoned, but the gold
jewellery dating from the
6th–3rd centuries BC
offers ample proof of
ancient artistic talent. The
Roman and Byzantine
imperial silver and gold
coins are well displayed.

🏛 Ethnographic Museum

Next to the Archaeology Museum.
📞 (0232) 489 07 96. ⏱ 8:30am–
noon & 1–5:30pm (5pm in winter)
Tue–Sun. 🎟
Housed in a former French
hospital, built in 1831, the
museum highlights local
crafts and skills – from
quilting and felt-making to
weapons and woodblock
printing. Bridal costumes,
glassware, an oven used
to fire blue beads (mavi
boncuk) and a replica of
İzmir's first apothecary shop.

🏯 Konak Clock Tower

Saat Kulesi
Konak Square. 🚌 any bus marked
"Konak".
Built in 1901, the clock
tower is the symbol of
İzmir. It was one of 58
built in Ottoman times
to encourage Turks
to adopt European
timekeeping habits.
İzmir's is one
of the finest
of these monu-
ments. Its ornate
decorative style

The Konak mosque, adorned with ceramic tiles from Kütahya

offers a strong contrast to the
exquisite simplicity of the tiny
Konak Mosque (Konak Camii)
that nestles beside it.

Kızlarağası Han

Look for signs off the N end of Fevzi
Paşa Cad. ⏱ 8am–9pm daily.
This typical Ottoman trading
complex (see pp24–5) has
been restored, with the
courtyard turned into a café.
There are craft and furniture
restoration workshops on
the upper floor. This is a
good place to purchase
handicrafts and copper.

St Polycarp Church

Necatibey Sok 2. 📞 (0232) 484 84
36. ⏱ 11:30am (Sun). Advance
notice suggested for other times.
The patron saint of İzmir, St
Polycarp was a Christian
martyr who gave us the
adage, "The spirit indeed
is willing, but the flesh is
weak." This is the
oldest Roman

KEY

🚆	Train station
⛴	Ferry boarding point
D	Dolmuş
ℹ	Tourist information
🚓	Police station
C	Mosque
⊠	Post office
♨	Turkish baths

Catholic church in İzmir and the seat of the Catholic archbishop. Permission to build a chapel to St Polycarp was granted in 1620 by Süleyman the Magnificent *(see p56)*. To the right of the altarpiece is a self-portrait of Raymond Peré, designer of the Konak Clock Tower.

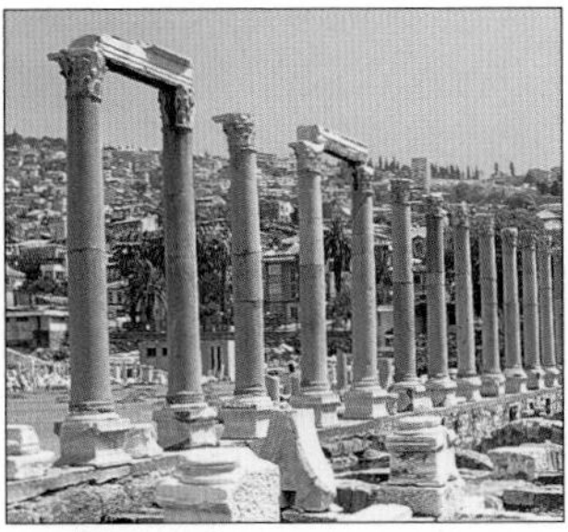

Corinthian columns in the Agora, the city market in Roman times

🏛 Agora

🕐 8:30am–noon & 1–5:30pm Tue–Sun. 🎫

The present remains of the Agora, the central market of the Roman city of Smyrna, date from about the 2nd century AD, when it was rebuilt by the Emperor Marcus Aurelius. There are several Corinthian columns with well-preserved capitols still standing, and enough arches, as well as part of a basilica (city hall), to give the flavour of a Roman town.

🏛 Velvet Castle

Kadifekale

🚌 from Konak Clock Tower marked "Kale", then on foot.

Also known as Mount Pagos, the Velvet Castle was built on Hellenistic foundations. Originally it had 40 towers, with numerous additions made by the Romans, Genoese and Ottomans over the centuries. The castle is a good spot for an afternoon's outing, and offers unsurpassed vistas over İzmir Bay.

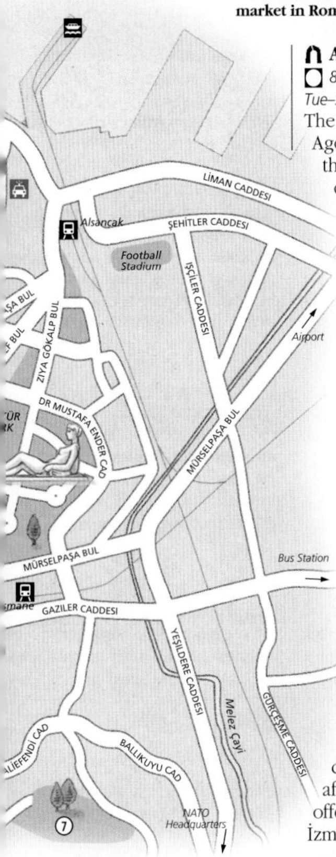

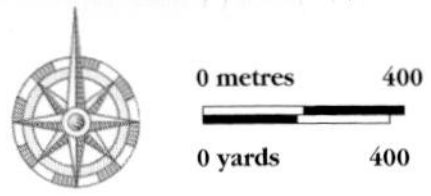

Visitors' Checklist

👥 2,800,000. ⛴ Alsancak, in the city centre. 🚆 Basmane, Eyül Meydanı 9; Alsancak, Ziya Gökalp Bulvarı, (0232) 464 77 95. ✈ Adnan Menderes, 12 km (8 miles) SE of city centre, (0232) 274 26 26. 🚌 8 km (5 miles) NE of city centre, (0232) 472 10 10. ℹ Gaziosmanpaşa Bulvarı 1, (0232) 445 73 90. 🎉 Liberation Day (9 Sep), International Arts Festival (10 Jun–10 Jul).

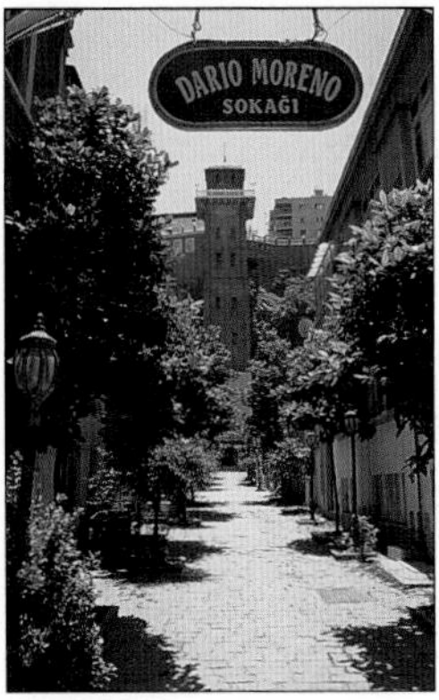

Dario Moreno Street, with the Asansör in the background

Asansör

🕐 24 hours (elevator). ☎ (0232) 261 26 26 (restaurant).

The Asansör is a working 19th-century elevator in the Karataş district. From its rooftop restaurant, there are fine views over the city.

Leafy Dario Moreno Street (Dario Moreno Sokaği) lies in a restored section of İzmir's old Jewish quarter. The street is named after a 1960s singer who was fond of the city.

Sights at a Glance

Agora ⑥
Archaeology Museum ①
Ethnographic Museum ②
Kızlarağası Han ④
Konak Clock Tower ③
St Polycarp Church ⑤
Velvet Castle ⑦

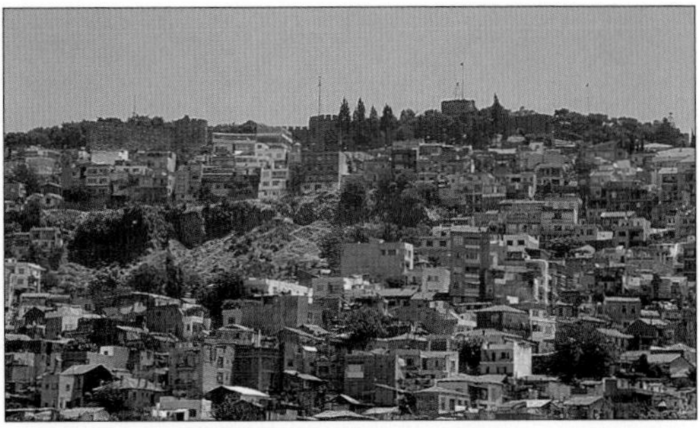

The Velvet Castle (Kadifekale), İzmir's ancient citadel

Çeşme ❽

🏛 21,120. 🚢 from Brindisi, Bari, Venice and Chios. 🚌 1 km (0.5 mile) S of ferry dock. 🚗 for local sights. ℹ İskele Meydanı 4, (0232) 712 66 53. 🛒 Wed and Sun; Sat (Alaçatı). 🎭 İzmir International Arts Festival (10 Jun–10 Jul).

THE TOWN'S MAIN FEATURE is the 14th-century Genoese Castle of St Peter, a powerful symbol of Italian Renaissance mercantilism. Sultan Beyazıt II (1481–1512) fortified the castle to counter attacks by both pirates and the Knights of St John, who operated from bases on the island of Rhodes and at Bodrum *(see pp196–7)*. The castle contains a **museum** with nautical exhibits. The hotel next to the harbour was formerly a *caravanserai (see pp24–5)*.

Unlike other more popular resorts, Çeşme is dedicated to promenading, yachting and the simpler pleasures of life. There are several fine restaurants, and the cosmopolitan, tolerant atmosphere attracts world-class performers, who come here for the month-long İzmir International Arts Festival.

The long peninsula around Çeşme is serviced by a fast, six-lane highway from İzmir. However, you can still take the old road, stopping at beaches in Ilıca or spending an afternoon at Alaçatı, the windsurfing capital of Turkey, where wind energy supplies a quarter of the town's power requirements.

🏛 **Museum**
Çeşme Castle. ◻ 9am–noon & 1–5:30pm Tue–Sun. 🎟

Çeşme waterfront, with the Castle of St Peter above the town

Selçuk ❾

🏛 25,000. 🚆 from İzmir or Denizli. 🚌 Atatürk Cad. ℹ Agora Çarşısı 35, (0232) 892 63 28, (0232) 892 69 45. 🌐 www.selcukephesus.gen.tr. 🛒 Sat. 🎭 Camel Wrestling (3rd and 4th week in Jan).

VISITORS OFTEN BYPASS Selçuk on their way to Ephesus, but it deserves a stopover. The town is dominated by a 6th-century Byzantine citadel (Ayasoluk Hill) with 15 well-preserved towers. Nearby are the remains of a Byzantine church and a Seljuk mosque. You enter the citadel through a Byzantine gate. At the foot of the hill is the Basilica of St John, built by the Emperor Justinian *(see p50)* in the 6th century on the site of an earlier shrine. It is believed to contain the tomb of St John the Evangelist, who spent his later years at Ephesus during the 1st century. Restoration has brought back some of the basilica's former glory, and there are some fine frescoes in the chapel.

The **Ephesus Museum** is one of Turkey's best. Marble and bronze statues and frescoes are beautifully displayed, and exhibits include a sculpture of Artemis, jewels and numerous artifacts thought to have come from the nearby Artemision, the ancient Temple of Artemis (one of the Seven Wonders of the Ancient World). Today, the ruins of the Artemision are waterlogged.

The İsa Bey Mosque (also known as the Selim Mosque), an ornate 14th-century Seljuk mosque, is located near the museum. It is not always open to visitors but the exterior calligraphy and inlaid tilework are worth a visit.

🏛 **Ephesus Museum**
Behind Tourism Information Office. 📞 (0232) 892 60 10. ◻ 8:30am–noon & 12:30–5pm daily. 🎟

ENVIRONS: The former Greek village of Şirince, 8 km (5 miles) east of Selçuk, has a peaceful air that is welcoming after the bustle of Ephesus.

At Çamlık is the **Open-Air Steam Train Exhibition**, a museum run by Turkish State Railways. There are more than 24 steam locomotives and other railway vehicles on display at the site.

Open-Air Steam Train Exhibition
Çamlık, 12 km (7 miles) S of Selçuk on the E87. 🎟

Byzantine gateway in Selçuk, at the foot of Ayasoluk Hill

Ephesus ❿

See pp182–3.

Kuşadası **⓫**

🏛 42,500. 🚢 from Samos.
🚌 from Selçuk, Söke and İzmir.
🚏 1 km (0.5 mile) S of town centre
on Söke road. ℹ Liman Cad 13,
(0256) 614 11 03. 📅 Fri.

KUŞADASI IS A frequent port
of call for luxury cruise
liners. Only Bodrum and
Istanbul can match it for fast-
paced, hedonistic nightlife.

The town's name, meaning
"bird island", is taken from an
islet, known as Pigeon Island,
tacked onto the mainland by
a causeway. A 14th-century
Genoese fort reveals the
town's commercial origins.

**ENVIRONS: Dilek Peninsula
National Park** protects the
last of Turkey's wild horses
and rare Anatolian cheetahs.
The military presence has
ensured that the area has
been left undisturbed. Hike to
the summit of Samsun Dağı
(ancient Mount Mycale) for
fine views of the peninsula.

🦌 Dilek Peninsula
National Park
Dilek Yarımadası Milli Parkı
18 km (11 miles) W of Söke. 🚌 from
Kuşadası or Söke. ℹ (0256) 646 10
79. 🕐 8am–6pm daily. 🎫 extra for
vehicles.

Camel wrestling, a popular event in Aydın

Aydın **⓬**

🏛 143,561. 🚏 700 m (0.5 mile) S
ot town centre 🚆 from İzmir and
Denizli. ℹ Dörtyol Mevkii, (0256) 211
28 42. 📅 Tue. 🎪 Camel Wrestling
(Jan), Aphrodisias Culture and Fine Art
Festival (May), Fig Festival (1st week in
Sep), Chestnut Festival (Dec).

KNOWN IN ROMAN times as
Tralles, Aydın's tranquil
appearance stems from long
periods of prosperity. It was
known variously as Caesarea
and Güzelhisar before falling
under Ottoman rule in the
late 14th century. Frequent
earthquakes have meant that
there are few ruins to be
seen, and the region is still
subject to tremors. Aydın
suffered badly during the War
of Independence (see p58).

The region is famous for
its figs (incir), black olives,
cereals, and cotton,
and Aydın is a leading
exporter of snails and
salmon. In the 1920s,
Atatürk (see p58)
targeted the region as
the focus of a new
state-owned cotton
industry. Today, raw
cotton and ready-to-
wear clothing remain
Turkey's biggest
export commodities.
Nowadays, Aydın is a peaceful
town with a **museum** and
several distinctive mosques.

🏛 Museum
W of the gardens
ℹ (0256) 225 22 59. 🕐 9am–noon
& 1:30–5pm Tue–Sun. 🎫

Menderes River
Valley **⓭**

ONE OF TURKEY'S main grain-
growing regions, and a
major producer of fruit and
cotton, the Menderes Valley
is made up of the Büyük
Menderes (Great Meander)
and Küçük Menderes (Lesser
Meander) rivers, with a wide
alluvial plain in between. The
S-shaped bends formed by
the slow-moving Büyük
Menderes below Aydın have
given us the word "meander".

Nysa, a Seleucid foundation
dating from around 280 BC,
presents a lovely sight as you
approach from Sultanhisar
(just to the south). There is a
theatre overlooking a tributary
of the Büyük Menderes, and a
a gymnasium, library, agora
and council house. The whole
city is built in and over a
ravine (although the bridge is
in poor condition). Its claim
to fame was as a sanctuary to
Pluto, god of the underworld.

At **Tire**, north of Aydın, lie
the remains of a number of
caravanserais (see pp24–5)
dating from the 14th and 15th
centuries. In the wake of the
capture of Constantinople in
1453, Mehmet II (see p54)
ordered the removal of the
inhabitants of Tire, as part of
the effort to repopulate the
capital. There is a dramatic
domed bazaar building here
and a lively bazaar is still held
each week on Tuesdays.

The yacht marina at Kuşadası, one of the largest on the Aegean coast

Ephesus ❿

EPHESUS IS ONE OF THE GREATEST ruined cities in the western world. A Greek city was first built here in about 1000 BC and it soon rose to fame as a centre for the worship of Cybele, the Anatolian Mother Goddess. The city we see today was founded in the 4th century BC by Alexander the Great's successor, Lysinachus. But it was under the Romans that Ephesus became the chief port on the Aegean. Most of the surviving structures date from this period. As the harbour silted up the city declined, but played an important role in the spread of Christianity. Two great Councils of the early Church were held here in AD 431 and 449. It is said that the Virgin Mary spent her last days nearby and that St John the Evangelist came from the island of Pátmos to look after her.

Statue of Artemis

Restored Mural
Murals in the houses opposite the Temple of Hadrian indicate that these were the homes of wealthy people.

★ **Library of Celsus**
Built in AD 114–117 by Consul Gaius Julius Aquila for his father, the library was damaged first by the Goths and then by an earthquake in 1000. The statues occupying the niches in front are Sophia (wisdom), Arete (virtue), Ennoia (intellect) and Episteme (knowledge).

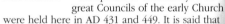

The Commercial Agora was the main marketplace of the city.

The brothel was adorned with a statue of Priapus, the Greek god of ferility.

Private houses featured murals and mosaics.

Temple of Domitian

| 0 metres | 200 |
| 0 yards | 200 |

THE HOUSE OF MARY

According to the Bible, the crucified Jesus asked St John the Evangelist to look after his mother, Mary. John brought Mary with him to Ephesus in AD 37, and she spent the last years of her life here in a modest stone house. The house of the Blessed Virgin is located at Meryemana, 8 km (5 miles) from the centre of Ephesus. The shrine, known as the Meryemana Kultur Parkı, is revered by both Christians and Muslims, and pilgrims of both faiths visit the shrine, especially on 15 August every year.

The house of the Blessed Virgin

STAR FEATURES

★ **Library of Celsus**

★ **Temple of Hadrian**

★ **Theatre**

★ **Theatre**
Carved into the flank of Mt Pion during the Hellenistic period, the theatre was later renovated by the Romans.

VISITORS' CHECKLIST

3 km (2 miles) W of Selçuk, on Efes Müzesi Uğur Mumcu Sevgi Yolu. ☎ *(0232) 892 60 10 (museum).* ℹ *Selçuk tourist office, (0232) 892 69 45.* 🚌 *from Selçuk.* ◯ *8:30am–5:30pm (6:30pm summer) daily.*

The *skene*
(stage building) featured elaborate ornamentation.

★ **Temple of Hadrian**
Built to bonour a visit by Hadrian in AD 123, the relief marble work on the facade portrays mythical gods and goddesses.

Marble Street
was paved with blocks of marble.

Gate of Hercules
The gate at the entrance to Curetes Street takes its name from two reliefs showing Hercules draped in a lion skin. Originally a two-storey structure, and believed to date from the 4th century AD, it had a large central arch with winged victories on the upper corners of the archway. Curetes Street was lined by statues of civic notables.

The **Odeon** (meeting hall) was built in AD 150.

Baths of Varius

Colonnaded Street
Lined with Ionic and Corinthian columns, the street runs from the Baths of Varius to the Temple of Domitian.

The impressive two-storey façade of the Library of Celsus ▷

Hierapolis ⑭

Necropolis

IN HELLENISTIC TIMES, the thermal springs at Hierapolis made the city a popular spa. Today, the ruins of Hierapolis still draw visitors, who come to swim in its mineral-rich pools and to see the startling white travertine terraces of nearby Pamukkale.

Founded by Eumenes II, king of Pergamum *(see pp176–7)*, the city was noted for its textiles, particularly wool. Hierapolis was ceded to Rome in 133 BC along with the rest of the Pergamene kingdom. The city was destroyed by an earthquake in AD 60, and was rebuilt and reached its peak in AD 196–215. Hierapolis fell into decline in the 6th century, and the site became partially submerged by water and deposits of travertine.

Necropolis

★ **Arch of Domitian**
The main thoroughfare of Hierapolis was a wide, colonnaded street called the Plateia, which ran from the Arch of Domitian to the south gate.

Site of early theatre

Baths and church

Agora

Pool
The popular bathing pool, littered with fragments of marble columns, may be the remains of a sacred pool associated with the Temple of Apollo.

Church

Nymphaeum

Site museum in Roman baths

PAMUKKALE

The spectacular white travertine terraces at Pamukkale, next to Hierapolis, have long been one of Turkey's most popular (and photographed) sights. The terraces form when water

Travertine terraces, Pamukkale

from the hot springs loses carbon dioxide as it flows down the slopes, leaving deposits of limestone. The layers of white calcium carbonate, built up in steps on the plateau, have earned the name of Pamukkale (cotton castle). To protect them from damage, the terraces are now off-limits to visitors.

6th-century basilica

VISITORS' CHECKLIST

19 km (12 miles) N of Denizli
(0258) 272 20 77. from
Izmir, get off at Denizli. from
Denizli. 8am–6pm (7pm in
summer) daily. additional fee
for parking. Pamukkale
Festival (music and folklore
performances, late May/early Jun).

Necropolis

*The largest ancient graveyard in Anatolia, with more than
1,200 tombs, the necropolis (one of two at Hierapolis)
contains tumuli, sarcophagi and house-shaped tombs
from the Roman, Hellenistic and early Christian periods.*

The octagonal rotunda was paved in marble.

The crypt is believed to have contained the body of St Philip.

★ **MARTYRIUM OF ST PHILIP**

Built in the 5th century AD, on the site where the apostle was crucified and stoned in AD 80, the building measures 20 m (65 ft) per side. The side arcades were used as accommodation.

Eight-sided chambers were separated by eight polygonal spaces.

Entrance chambers were paved with limestone.

★ **Theatre**
*The well-preserved theatre,
built in 200 BC, could seat
20,000. However only
30 rows of seats have
survived. Shown here is the
skene, or stage building.*

STAR FEATURES

★ **Arch of Domitian**

★ **Martyrium of St Philip**

★ **Theatre**

0 metres 125

0 yards 125

Aphrodisias ⓯

Marble frieze in the museum

THE SITE OF APHRODISIAS was a shrine as early as 5800 BC, when Neolithic farmers came here to worship the Mother Goddess of fertility and crops. At some point, the site was dedicated to Aphrodite, goddess of love, and was given the name Aphrodisias during the 2nd century BC.

For centuries it remained little more than a shrine, but when the Romans defeated the Pontic ruler Mithridates *(see p48)* in 74 BC, Aphrodisias was rewarded for its loyalty and prospered as a cultural and artistic hub known for its exquisite marble sculptures. During the Byzantine era, the Temple of Aphrodite became a Christian basilica. Gradually, the city faded into obscurity, later becoming the Turkish village of Geyre.

★ **Stadium**
The stadium is one of the best preserved structures of its kind from the classical era.

★ **Temple of Aphrodite**
Fourteen columns of the temple have been re-erected. The lateral colonnades shown here became the nave of the Christian basilica.

Gable ends were surmounted by statues, called *akroteria.*

The stepped platform was built on a stone foundation.

The west cella was used as a treasury.

PLAN OF APHRODISIAS

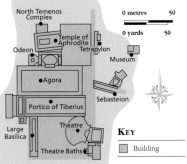

North Temenos Complex

Temple of Aphrodite

Odeon

Tetrapylon

Museum

Agora

Sebasteion

Portico of Tiberius

Large Basilica

Theatre

Theatre Baths

0 metres   50
0 yards   50

KEY
▢ Building

STAR FEATURES
★ **Stadium**
★ **Temple of Aphrodite**
★ **Tetrapylon**

★ **Tetrapylon**
*One of the jewels of Aphrodisias,
this 2nd-century gateway was
reconstructed with four groups
of Corinthian columns.*

VISITORS' CHECKLIST

Between Aydın and Denizli,
40 km (24 miles) S of E87
highway to Geyre. **(** (0256) 448
80 86 (museum). **(** 9am–6pm
daily. **⬛ ⬛ ⬛ ⬛** when
excavations in progress.

Sculptures
*Works produced by
the city's famous
school of sculpture
were exported as far
afield as North
Africa and Rome.
Some are exhibited
in the museum.*

Fluted columns
were constructed
from marble
drums that were
quarried nearby.

★ **TEMPLE OF APHRODITE**
Completed in the 1st century AD, the
temple was the heart of Aphrodisias.
It was later converted for Christian
worship, with walls and colonnades
dismantled and reused to enlarge
and modify the building.

The cult statue
of Aphrodite stood
in the cella.

The Atatürk Ethnography Museum
in Denizli

Denizli ⓰

🏠 270,000. **ℹ** behind provincial
government building, (0258) 264 39
71 and 261 33 93.

DENIZLI IS OFTEN thought of
as a tourist backwater,
but the town has little need
to pander to visitors. It is a
thriving agricultural centre, a
centre for carpet production
and one of Turkey's major
textile towns, continuing a
prosperous trade begun as far
back as Roman times. Today,
Aegean cotton fibres fetch
more on world markets than
many other spun cottons.

Denizli, literally translated as
"with sea", takes its name from
the many springs that feed the
River Lycus. In pre-Roman
times, another city linked with
water, Hydrela, was located
here. Denizli is a good base
for touring the ancient sites of
Hierapolis and Pamukkale
(see pp186–7), the latter being
about 22 km (16 miles) away.

The town was conquered
by the Seljuks in the 11th century and came under Ottoman
rule in 1428. At some point in
between, when Denizli was
known as Ladik, it seems that
the inhabitants of nearby
Laodiceia moved here after
their own city was ravaged by
one of the many earthquakes
that have marked this region.

The **Atatürk Ethnography
Museum** has some interesting
local folk art and decorative
artifacts on display. Denizli's
Great Mosque (Ulu Camii) is
also worth a visit.

**Atatürk Ethnography
Museum**
Kayalık Cad, Saraylar Mah 459
Sok 10. **(** (0258) 241 08 66.
(9am–5:30pm all year round. **⬛**

Theatre
*Completed in 27 BC, structural changes were made in
AD 200 to make it suitable for gladiatorial spectacles.*

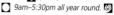

The Temple of Athena at Priene, a superb example of Ionian architecture

Priene ⑰

D from Söke or Milas to Güllübahçe.
○ 8am–7pm (5pm in winter) daily.

THE ANCIENT CITY of Priene has a breathtaking setting between the Büyük Menderes River and Mount Mykale. Like Miletus and Ephesus *(see pp182–3)*, it was a member of the Ionian League, a group of 12 city-states believed to have been settled by Greek colonists before 1000 BC.

Laid out by the architect Hippodamos of Miletus in about 450 BC, Priene is in a good state of preservation. The Temple of Athena, built in the 4th century BC in honour of the city's patron goddess, is considered one of the great achievements of Ionian architecture. The work was supervised and financed by Alexander the Great *(see pp46–7)* when he occupied the city. Because of Priene's strong Greek ties, it was not viewed with favour by the Romans. Its importance declined and by Byzantine times it had been abandoned. This neglect has meant that Priene is one of the most intact Hellenistic settlements to be seen. The theatre, dating from the 3rd century BC, could seat 5,000

people. The bouleuterion (council chamber) could hold 640 delegates. There is also a stadium, complete with starting blocks for athletes, and sanctuaries to Demeter and Kore. The lower gymnasium walls are adorned with schoolboy graffiti from 2,000 years ago!

Miletus ⑱

D from Söke or Milas. 🚗 take the road that descends to Didyma, turn W at the village of Akköy, 7km (4 miles) from the main road.

ALTHOUGH LESS impressive than Priene, Miletus was more renowned for its art, politics and trade than many other Greek cities. Known as Milet today, it was once the principal port of the Ionian League, and flourished as a

İlyas Bey Mosque, built in the 15th century at Miletus

centre for art and industry. In Roman times it supplied wool and textile dyes to the wool trade in Ankara *(see p240)*. One of its sons, the scientist and mathematician Thales – known as one of the Seven Sages of Antiquity – correctly forecast a total eclipse of the sun in 580 BC.

The Persians took control of the Ionian cities in the mid-6th century BC. Miletus led a revolt against Persian rule in 500–494 BC, but in 479 BC succumbed to the tyrannical Persian king, Darius. It was rebuilt by the Romans.

Of the surviving buildings, the finest is the 15,000-seat theatre, dating from AD 100. Over the centuries, Greeks, Romans and Byzantines all made alterations to the structure. The bouleuterion (council chamber) was built in 175–164 BC during the reign of the Seleucid king, Antiochus IV Ephiphanes. The well-preserved Baths of Faustina date from AD 43, and were named for the wife of Emperor Marcus Aurelius. The complex includes a palaestra (gymnasium), and there is a stadium nearby. The Baths of Faustina was a model for the development of the Turkish bath, or *hamam (see p77)*. It is also worth strolling around the stadium, nymphaeum (reservoir) and shrine of Apollo Delphinius (built in 500 BC).

Incongruously, a mosque reposes amid the ruins of ancient Miletus. The İlyas Bey (or Balat) Mosque was built in 1403 by İlyas Bey, emir (ruler) of the Beylik of Menteşe. It celebrated his return from exile at the court of the Mongol ruler Timur, also known as Tamerlane *(see p53)*, after Timur's invasion of Anatolia in 1402. The mosque is built of brick and both white and coloured marble that was taken from Roman Miletus. There is splendidly detailed carving on the marble window grilles, screen and prayer niche *(mihrab)*, and the use of coloured marble on the façade is impressive. The dome measures 14 m (45 ft) in diameter and was the largest built during the Beylik period *(see p53)*. İlyas Bey died the year after the mosque was completed and is buried in the adjacent tomb (dated 1404). The mosque is a beautiful early forerunner of the Ottoman *külliye (see p32)*, a building style that flourished during the 16th century. The *külliye* combined social welfare and residential functions with facilities for Islamic worship.

The Temple of Apollo in Didyma, with its ornate carved columns

Didyma ⓳

🚌 from Söke or Milas to Yenihisar. 🚢 from Bodrum twice a week in summer (check first). 🛈 (0256) 811 45 30, (0256) 811 57 07. 🕐 9am–7pm (5pm in winter) daily. 🖾

Head of Medusa, Didyma

THE PRIME REASON to visit Didyma (modern Didim) is for the Temple of Apollo, built in the 7th century BC to honour the god of prophecy and oracles. By 500 BC, the shrine at Didyma was one of the leading oracles of the Greek world. It even had a sacred spring. Branchid priests, who were reputedly connected to the great oracle at Delphi, were in charge of the shrine. Marble from nearby Lake Bafa *(see p192)* was used to build the temple.

A carved relief of the head of Medusa, with its serpentine curls, has become almost synonymous with Didyma.

The well below the Medusa head was the place where arriving pilgrims would purify themselves before approaching the oracle. It is now roped off to prevent accidents.

In its heyday, the Temple of Apollo featured 108 Ionic columns. Only three are still intact. However, the surviving stumps are still impressive.

The Temple of Apollo was destroyed by Persians in the mid-6th century BC, but was restored around 350 BC by Alexander the Great. With the coming of Christianity, the temple was converted into a church and Didyma became a bishopric. In 1493, an earthquake destroyed the temple and Didyma was abandoned. The Ottomans renamed it Yenihisar (new castle) in the 18th century.

The impressive theatre at Miletus, capable of seating 15,000 in Roman times

Lake Bafa ⑳

25 km (16 miles) W of Söke. **D** *via Söke or Milas.* 🎿 ☐ ♨ ⛱ 🚶

C ONSIDERED ONE OF the most picturesque landscapes in Turkey, the Lake Bafa area is the setting for several classical gems, with the peaks of Mount Latmos as a backdrop. Rising to 1,500 m (4,915 ft), the mountain is aptly known as Beş Parmak (five fingers).

In ancient times, Lake Bafa was an arm of the sea. When silt eventually closed the gulf, the port of **Herakleia**, near the eastern shore of the lake, was left landlocked. The same process was responsible for the decline of Miletus and Priene *(see pp190–91)*. Lake Bafa is brackish and supports many species of fish.

Herakleia, also known as Herakleia-under-Latmos, occupies a dramatic setting at the lakeside. Its fortifications, towers and well-preserved Temple of Athena are tangible vestiges of its former status. In such settings, legends are fostered: a young shepherd, unrequited love and eternal sleep are part of local lore. A shrine to the shepherd-hero, Endymion, can be visited near the lake. There are some difficult-to-reach monasteries high up the mountain.

Herakleia
10 km (6 miles) from Camiçi (by car on track). ⛴ *from Lake Bafa.*

ENVIRONS: Euromos, located to the southeast of Lake Bafa, wholly deserves its reputation as having one of the best preserved temples in Turkey. Euromos was, in fact, an

Lake Bafa, an arm of the Aegean in ancient times

amalgamation of several cities, including Herakleia, owing allegiance to Milas *(see p193)*. In time, rivalries emerged between them, and Euromos (meaning "strong" in Greek) turned out to be politically fickle. Like many cities of ancient Caria, it opted to ally itself with Rome and Rhodes, not Greece.

⋔ Euromos
12 km (7 miles) NW of Milas. **D** *from Selimiya to Milas.* ☐ *8am–7pm (5pm in winter).*

Altınkum ㉑

4 km (3 miles) S of Didyma. ⚔ *2,300.* **D** *via Priene and Miletus.*

T HE PROTECTED sandy bay of Altınkum offers a relaxing spot to unwind, especially after a day spent tramping around classical ruins. Most day trips to Priene, Miletus and Didyma *(see pp190–91)* end up here. In fact, locals generally refer to the area as Didyma, or Didim (on bus

The popular beach at Altınkum

schedules, for example). Like many idyllic retreats that have experienced rapid growth, Didyma's success has spilled over to nearby towns. Charter groups and tours flock to Altınkum and it can be very busy in summer. This was one of Turkey's original camping venues. As it grew, pensions opened, and Turkish families began to flock here for sun and sand. There is not much else here – for anything more, you will have to go to Yenihisar (ancient Didyma). Few people know how to enjoy themselves as much as Turks, and Altınkum finds them in full holiday mode.

Labranda ㉒

15 km (9 miles) N of Milas on unsurfaced track (by car, taxi, or on foot from Milas). ☐ *8am–7:30pm (5pm in winter).*

G ETTING TO LABRANDA is certainly worth the effort for those who persevere. This Carian sanctuary nestles high on the mountains above Milas, at an impressive elevation of 610 m (2,000 ft), giving good views of the surrounding area. From early times, it fell under the jurisdiction of Milas (Mylasa). The remains of the sacred way leading there are one of the sights to note.

Despite being damaged by several fires and earthquakes, the remains of a stadium have been uncovered by Swedish archaeologists. Baths and a fountain house (which may have been a water storage depot) date from about the 1st century BC and the area still boasts an abundant source of spring water. The most interesting buildings are three androns (banqueting halls), the second built by Mausolus (*see p194*), who ruled from nearby Milas.

The chamber tombs and sarcophagi, although pillaged, are unusual and reveal much about ancient burial practices.

Milas (Mylasa) ㉓

🏛 *42,000.* ✈ *13 km (8 miles) SW of town, (0252) 523 01 01.*
🚌 *Intercity buses to Bodrum.*
ℹ *at airport, (0252) 523 00 66.*

The Gümüşkesen Mausoleum, a Carian monument in Milas

THE ORIGINS OF Milas are uncertain and the many theories are largely unsubstantiated. What is clear is that its most notewothy and prosperous period was when it was capital of Caria and the administrative seat for the Persian satrap (subordinate ruler), Mausolus. Like most Carian cities, Milas was ruled in turn by the Persians, Alexander the Great, the Romans and the Byzantines before finally falling under Ottoman control in 1425.

Local carpet in Milas

The remains of the ancient city lie within the present town centre. The first thing you notice is the two-storey **Gümüşkesen** (silver moneybag) **Mausoleum**, a structure of uncertain age. The lower floor is the actual tomb, with an aperture in the roof to provide sustenance to the deceased. The town's most intact monument is the handsome Baltılı (Axe) Gate.

As an administrative seat, Milas issued regulatory decrees, notably concerning money. Inscriptions dating from the 3rd century AD list detailed regulations that ban illegal conversions from imperial (Roman) to local money and black-market money dealings.

Save some time for modern Milas, which has some charming timber houses with lattice-work shutters. The town is justly famed for its carpets, characterized by soft neutral and beige tones.

ENVIRONS: Yatağan, site of a thermal power station and known for its environmental pollution, has little to offer, but two interesting sights are located in the area. **Stratonikeia** was founded in 295 BC. It was apparently named after the wife of Seleucas I, king of Syria. The ruins to be seen – an agora (marketplace), a rather unkempt Hellenistic theatre with seating for 10,000 and the Temple of Sarapis – are in the village of Eskihisar on the 330 road, south of the city.

The town's small museum houses mainly Roman finds but includes a Mycenaean mug from about 1000 BC.

Lagina is located northwest of Yatağan and is best known for its association with the cult of Hecate, the Greek goddess of darkness and sorcery. The gate of the temple precinct dates from between 125 and 80 BC. The Temple of Hecate would have stood here but the site has not yielded major finds.

🏛 **Stratonikeia**
20 km (12 miles) W of Milas.
🚌 *Own transport.* 🅳 *on main Yatağan–Milas road.* 🅱
🏛 **Lagina**
15 km (9 miles) N of Yatağan.
🚌 *Own transport essential.*

Güllük ㉔

🏛 *5,600.* 🅳 *from Milas, 28 km (17 miles) SE of Güllük, then 8 km (5 miles) to town.*

THIS IS A LOVELY bay and harbour with a genuine nautical atmosphere and lots of accommodation. The real reason for coming to Güllük is to see the site of ancient **Iasus**, with its elaborate wall, 810 m (2,658 ft) long, built during the 5th century AD.

The fortunes of Iasus were tied to fishing. Bronze-Age finds from here bear detailed inscriptions that have shed new light on the lifestyles of the ancients. Legends of boys frolicking with dolphins also originated here.

Almost opposite Güllük on the main 330 road is the site of Cindya. To the south is the ancient Barbylia (modern Varvil Bay), a town that grew wealthy by trading in salt.

🏛 **Iasus**
🚢 *by boat from Güllük to Kıyıkışlacık.* 🚌 *18 km (11 miles) from main Milas road.*

The large ruined theatre at Stratonikeia

Bodrum ㉕

BODRUM IS THE MODERN NAME for the ancient Dorian city of Halicarnassus, location of the famous Mausoleum built by Mausolus (375–53 BC), ruler of ancient Caria, who made the city his capital. The city walls, also built by Mausolus, were almost destroyed during Alexander the Great's siege in the 4th century BC. Herodotus, the father of written history, was born here in 484 BC, as was Dionysius, the great rhetoric teacher of the 1st century BC. Modern Bodrum was the first Turkish town to experience a tourist boom, its major sight being the 15th-century Castle of St Peter *(see pp196–7)*, now a museum of nautical archaeology.

Carian statue in the castle

The busy harbour, attracting cruising yachts of all sizes

Exploring Bodrum

Bodrum is subtly divided by the Castle of St Peter into a bustling, vehicle-free eastern sector with beaches and a quieter western hub which borders the yacht harbour. Dolmuşes make transport easy. Those marked "Şehir İçi" (inner city) stop at all major points. Boat trips to nearby beaches are also available from the harbour.

🎵 Halikarnas Disco

Cumhuriyet Cad, No 178.
⬜ Apr–Sep. 📞 (0252) 316 80 00.
🖥 www.halikarnas.com.tr.

Located at the water's edge with a view of the Castle of St Peter, open-air Halikarnas is one of the most famous nightclubs in Turkey and an emblem of hedonistic nightlife. With a capacity of 5,000, Halikarnas offers a spectacular laser light show and the very best DJs (both Turkish and international). The open-air cabaret, revue and musical acts feature top performers. Every age group succumbs to the magic of this lively nightclub. Smart dress is required.

🛁 Bodrum Hamam

Cevat Şakir Cad, Fabrika Sok (opposite the bus station).
⬜ 6am–10pm daily. 📞 (0252) 313 41 29. 🖥 www.hamam.com.

Linked to the Çemberlitaş Baths in Istanbul, the Bodrum Hamam is housed in a lovely old stone building. Service is highly professional, emphasizing cleanliness and an authentic Turkish bath experience.

The superb and renowned Turkish bath

Masseurs are well-trained and you are bound to feel like a "new penny" when you exit. The owners claim a 500-year lineage. The hamam runs a shuttle that will collect and return you, suitably pampered.

⚓ Old Dockyard (Tersane) and Arsenal Point

W of the marina entrance at the end of Neyzen Tevfik Cad.
⬜ dawn to dusk.

The ancient dockyard on the end of Arsenal Point is part of the effort to restore Bodrum's walls. Its position, opposite the Castle of St Peter, overlooks the main harbour. The dockyard was built in the 18th century, when the Ottoman sultans made an attempt to revive the empire's naval strength. Attractions include a cistern, an Ottoman Tower on the west side of the harbour, a graveyard, fortification to protect the shipyard and a grand tomb built in 1729 to commemorate Cafer Paşa, who was a naval hero and prominent city patron.

♉ Mausoleum

Turgut Reis Cad (corner of Hamam Sok). ⬜ 8am–noon & 1:30–5pm Tue–Sun.

The massive Mausoleum of Halicarnassus was one of the Seven Wonders of the Ancient World. Named for Mausolus, ruler of Caria, and intended as his tomb, work on the structure began in 355 BC, two years before he died. It was completed by his wife, Artemisia, the only woman to rule Caria. The Mausoleum stood 41 m (134 ft) in height, and comprised a podium, a colonnade of 36 columns and a pyramid, the whole topped by a horse-drawn chariot statue. It was probably these superb sculptures that made the Mausoleum so celebrated in its day. The tomb stood for about 1,500 years but, by 1402, when the Knights of St John arrived in Bodrum, it had fallen into ruin and many of its stones were used in the construction of the Castle of St Peter. Since the 1960s, Danish

The scant remains of the great
Mausoleum

archaeologists have excavated
and partially reconstructed
the base of the Mausoleum.

Don't miss the exhibition
rooms on your left as you
enter the site. The three-
dimensional models and
reconstructions are the most
interesting displays here.

⋔ Antique Theatre

Kıbrıs Şehitler Cad (N of the
Mausoleum). ◯ *dawn to dusk.*
Little remains of the ancient
city of Halicarnassus, but the
theatre on the south slopes
of the Göktepe district is
one of the more intact sites.
Excavations began here in
1973 and restoration still
goes on. Dating from the
4th century BC, the theatre

consists of a stage building,
an orchestra and rows of
seating. It was probably
used more for gladiatorial
fights than for theatrical
performances. The unusual
balustrades in the orchestra
may have been put there to
protect spectators!

⋔ Myndos Gate

Cafer Paşa Cad.
The Myndos Gate was the
western exit from ancient
Halicarnassus, and led to the
Lelegian town of Myndos,
today known as Gümüşlük
(see p198), named after
the silver *(gümüş)* mines
there. Bodrum's city walls

The Myndos Gate, the western portal of the
city in ancient times

VISITORS' CHECKLIST

🏠 35,180. ✈ at Milas, (0252)
536 65 65. 🚌 Cevat Şakir
Caddesi, (0252) 316 26 37.
ⓘ Barış Meydanı, (0252) 316 10
91. 🛒 Thu & Fri for food and
produce. Tue for textiles &
clothes. 🎉 Bodrum Yacht Week
(3rd week in Oct).
Ⓦ www.halikarnassos.com

date from 365 BC and were
probably built by Mausolus.
They extended for some
7 km (4.3 miles), protecting
the town on three sides. The
Myndos Gate originally had
two monumental towers,
made of andesite
blocks, on each side
of a courtyard. Most
of the walls were
demolished by
Alexander the Great
when he laid siege to
the town in 334 BC.
A restoration project,
begun in 1998 and
sponsored by two
large communications
companies, has been
the most successful
effort to date.

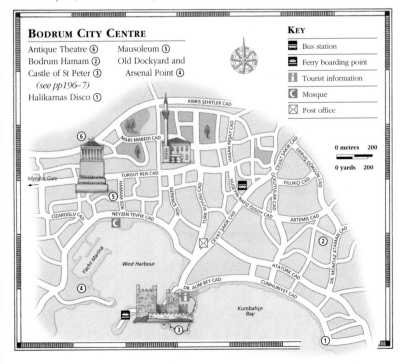

BODRUM CITY CENTRE

Antique Theatre ⑥   Mausoleum ⑤
Bodrum Hamam ②   Old Dockyard and
Castle of St Peter ③   Arsenal Point ④
  (see pp196–7)
Halikarnas Disco ①

KEY

🚌 Bus station

⛴ Ferry boarding point

ⓘ Tourist information

Ⓒ Mosque

⊠ Post office

0 metres   200
0 yards   200

KIBRIS ŞEHITLER CAD

MARS MABEDI CAD

HASAN REŞAT CAD

CEVAT ŞAKIR CAD

DERVİŞ GÖRGÜN CAD

⑥

Myndos Gate

TURGUT REIS CAD

ÜÇKUYULAR CAD

YILLIKÇI CAD

HAMAM SOK

GERENCE SOK

TÜRK KUYUSU CAD

HÜSEYIN NAFİZ ÖZSOY CAD

ARTEMIS CAD

⑤

CIZAROĞLU CAD

NEYZEN TEVFİK CAD

Ⓒ

CEVAT ŞAKIR CAD

DR. MÜMTAZ ATAMAN CAD

⊠

②

Yacht Marina

West Harbour

④

ATATÜRK CAD

DR. ALIM BEY CAD

CUMHURİYET CAD

ⓘ

③

Kumbahçe
Bay

①

Castle of St Peter

Heraldic relief carving

ODRUM'S MOST DISTINCTIVE landmark is its castle, begun in 1406 by the Knights of St John *(see p227)*. It five towers represented the nationalities of its formidable inhabitants. When Süleyman the Magnificent conquered Rhodes in 1523, both Bodrum and Rhodes came under Ottoman rule and the knights left for Malta. Neglected for centuries, the castle became a prison in 1895 and was damaged by shells from a French warship during World War I. In the early 1960s, it was used to store artifacts found by local sponge divers. This led to a fruitful Turkish-American partnership to restore the castle and put on display the spectacular undersea treasures found around Turkey. The innovative reconstructions of ancient shipwrecks and their cargoes have brought the museum international acclaim.

German Tower
This is one of two towers that are open to the public.

Gatineau Tower

Spanish (or Snake) Tower

Glass Hall
The Mycaenean beads and Damascus glass date from between 15 BC and AD 11. Syrian glass ingots, used in the production of various glass items, date from the 14th century BC.

Land-facing battlements

★ Glass Shipwreck Hall
A steel frame supports the original timbers of a Fatimid-Byzantine ship thought to have sunk in 1025. The glass shards and ingots, among other finds, make this a time capsule of the era.

Outer entrance

Castle moat

STAR FEATURES

★ Amphora Exhibit

★ Glass Shipwreck Hall

★ Late Bronze-Age Shipwrecks

★ Amphora Exhibit
Earthenware jars and pots were used to transport oil, wine and dry foods in ancient times. Pointed bases allowed for upright storage in layers.

View of the Castle Across the Harbour
Medieval engineers ensured that the castle was virtually immune to attack. It even had secure water supplies.

VISITORS' CHECKLIST

In Bodrum harbour. (0252) 316 25 16. 8:30am–12:30pm & 1:30–6pm. Allow a minimum of 2–3 hours. Mon (also Sat & Sun for Glass Shipwreck Hall and Carian Princess Hall). several exhibits charge an additional entry fee. www.bodrum-info.org.

French Tower

Italian Tower

English Tower
Construction of this edifice, also known as the Lion Tower, was partly financed by public contributions.

Carian Princess Hall

Chapel and Eastern Roman Shipwreck

★ Late Bronze-Age Shipwrecks
Ancient nautical life and trade are captured in this life-size replica of a ship that sank off Kaş (see p214) in the 14th century BC.

The Commander's Tower
forms the inner entrance to the castle and details some World War I history.

Diver recovering amphorae from the floor of the Mediterranean

DIVING FOR TREASURE

Many underwater treasures were originally found by sponge divers working at depths of 40–50 m (131–164 ft), and the painstaking scientific recovery work often involved more than 20,000 dives by teams of experts. An able and enthusiastic archaeologist, Oğuz Alpözen, is now the museum director. The partnership between the museum and the Institute of Nautical Archaeology has made Bodrum a showpiece of historical treasures beautifully preserved in their last port of call.

Bodrum Peninsula Tour [26]

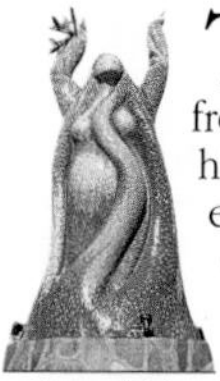

Friendship statue, Turgut Reis

THE BODRUM PENINSULA was originally peopled by the Lelegians, migrants from mainland Greece who maintained historic ties to the Carians. There were eight Lelegian cities, dating from as early as the 4th or 5th century BC. Myndos was the most prominent, but Pedasa offers the most to see.

Today, the Bodrum Peninsula is renowned as a holiday paradise. Its secluded bays are ideal for yachting, watersports and getting away from it all. The windmills to be seen on the hills were once used to grind grain. The terrain varies from lush coniferous forests to rocky cliffs and sandy coasts. The coastline claimed many ancient ships and some of their treasures are displayed in Bodrum's Castle of St Peter *(see pp196–7)*.

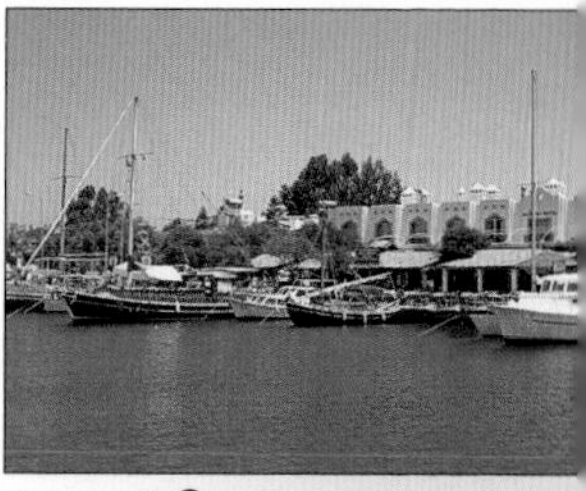

Yalıkavak [6]
Formerly an important sponge-fishing port, Yalıkavak is an ideal spot for a meal. Local delicacies include sea beans and stuffed marrow flowers.

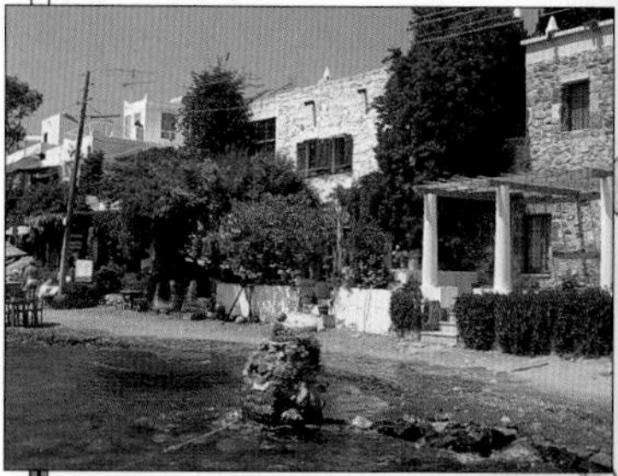

Gümüşlük (Myndos) [5]
Gümüşlük occupies the site of ancient Myndos, founded by King Mausolus *(see pp194–5)* in about 350 BC. The remains of a sunken city lie offshore.

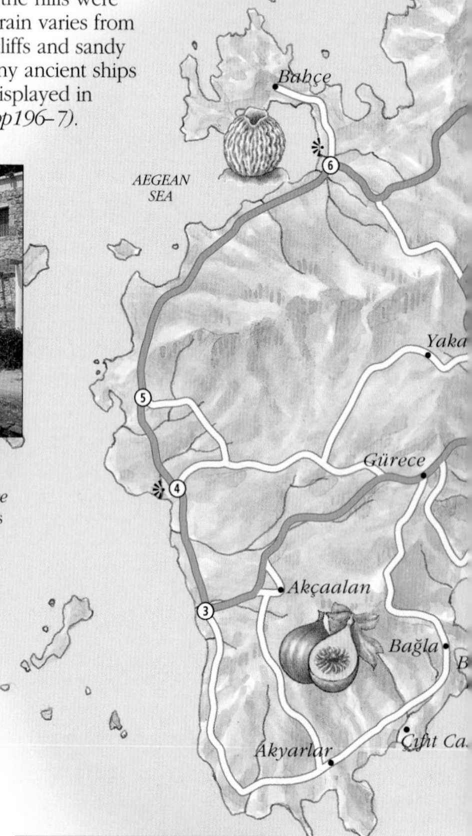
Bahçe
AEGEAN SEA
Gürece
Akçaalan
Bağla
Akyarlar

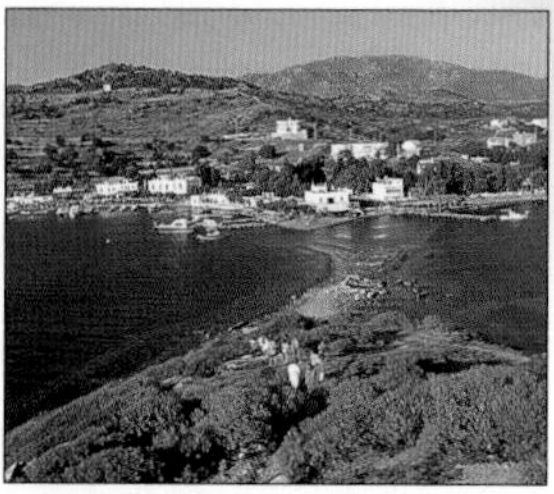

Kadıkalesi [4]
The town takes its name from *kadı*, (Arabic for "judge"), after a former resident. The old Greek church (now a private residence) on the hill is probably the most intact Greek building in the area. Tangerine groves are a beautiful sight, either in blossom or bearing fruit, and there are superb views of the nearby islets.

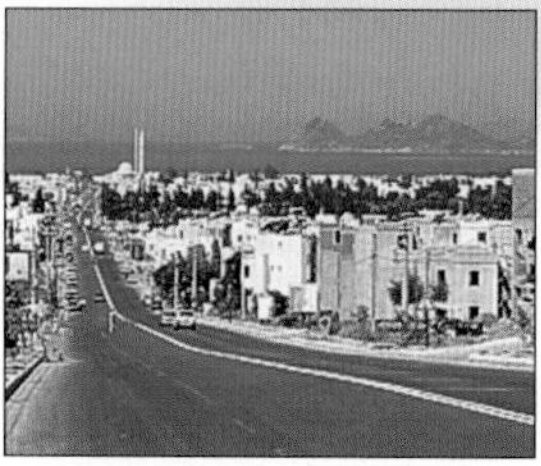

Turgut Reis [3]
The town is named after a famous Ottoman admiral and naval hero. The rich alluvial soil is perfect for growing figs, which abound in this area.

KEY

■ Tour route

= Other road

☆ Viewpoint

Göl Türkbükü ⑦

Two neighbouring towns, Gölköy and Türkbükü, amalgamated their names in 1999. Watersports are a speciality here. The area is a hideaway for celebrities, and boasts two of Turkey's most prestigious small hotels, Ada (see p328) and Maça Kızı.

Küçük Tavşan Island

Gölköy

Yuk. Gölköy

Torba

Mustafa Paşa Tower

Bodrum

330

Gümbet

İç Island

Karaada Island

Pedasa ①

Though difficult to reach, Pedasa is worth the journey. The ruins cover about 2.5 sq km (1 sq mile), and show a typical Lelegian town. Extensive research and restoration is being done on the site, which includes the remains of a citadel, main gate, rampart walls and castle keep.

| 0 kilometres | 5 |
| 0 miles | 2.5 |

Ortakent ②

This inland village boasts the imposing 17th-century Mustafa Paşa Tower, which was recently refurbished. It is one of the easiest sights to reach on the peninsula, and has abundant water and lovely orchards.

TIPS FOR DRIVERS

Tour length: 100–120 km (63–75 miles), with paved roads and two-way traffic most of the way. The tour can be done by dolmuş, but it is then more difficult to see the ancient sites.
🛈 Turgut Reis, (0252) 382 39 33. Turgut Reis is the only major town, with a number of petrol stations and amenities.
When to go: Any time of year.

Marmaris ㉗

Waterside statue of Atatürk

LIKE MOST OF THE RESORTS along the Aegean coast, it is difficult to envisage Marmaris as the quaint fishing village it used to be. The stretch of beach, now lined with hotels, extended to the main street until the 1990s. Marmaris was extensively damaged by an earthquake in 1957, which destroyed most of the old town. Today the rebuilt (and greatly expanded) town is a top holiday destination. Ancient inscriptions indicate that Marmaris was once the Dorian city of Physcus, attached to the city of Lindos and part of the island state of Rhodes. Süleyman the Magnificent *(see pp56–7)* assembled a mighty fleet here in 1522 to prepare for his conquest of Rhodes, at which time he regained possession of the Datça Peninsula *(see pp202–203)* and had Marmaris Castle rebuilt.

strolling along the street to observe those who want to be observed. Some of the bars have been nicely done up and, decibels aside, this is not an unattractive area. There are also a number of hotels and pensions in the area, but visitors in search of rest and relaxation would do better to look elsewhere.

Restored Greek houses in the Old Quarter near the harbour

Exploring Marmaris

Few places can compete with Marmaris' exclusive setting in a sheltered bay rimmed with oleanders, liquidambar trees and pine forests. All major attractions are located within a few metres of the seafront and can be reached on foot. The harbour and quay extend along a beach walkway that runs the length of the town.

Netsel Marina

📞 *(0252) 412 27 08 and 412 14 39.*
FAX *(0252) 412 53 51.*
Turkey's largest and most luxurious marina has it all – parking, top-class restaurants, entertainment, bars, excellent shops and plenty of service facilities such as banks, ATMs and travel agents. All major currencies and credit cards are accepted for mooring, refuelling and other marina services. Among several yacht

brokerage firms here, **Gino Marine** will organize luxury charter cruises to give you a view of Marmaris from the water. There is berthing for over 750 yachts up to 40 m (130 ft) in length.

The Netsel call sign on VHF channel 06 is "Port Marmaris". Marmaris is a safe anchorage, with no underwater currents, sandbanks or rocks, and can be approached night and day in most weather conditions.

Gino Marine

📞 *(0252) 412 27 08.*
FAX *(0252) 412 53 51.*

🍸 Bar Street

Hacı Mustafa Sokağı
Most tourist towns have their bars and pubs concentrated on a couple of streets. Those in Marmaris occupy much of Hacı Mustafa Sokağı. Despite the noise, it is always worth

🏛 Greek Revival Houses in Old Quarter

Tepe Mahallesi.
The Old Quarter around the Castle is by far the most charming part of Marmaris. Many houses that were either abandoned or derelict have now been restored to their original appearance. Most belong to professional people who seem to be accustomed to strangers peeking into a shady courtyard or admiring a handsome brass knocker. Karaca Restaurant, just outside the entrance to the Castle, has a well-preserved interior. From the top terrace of the restaurant, you will get a wonderful view of the town and its numerous delightful "barbecue" chimneys. See if you can spot the one and only remaining original Greek chimney from here. As you wander the cool and shady lanes above the bustle of the harbour, you could find yourself wishing that some of Turkey's other coastal resorts had retained the same quaint neighbourhood appeal as this corner of Marmaris.

Netsel Marina, offering a complete service to touring yachts

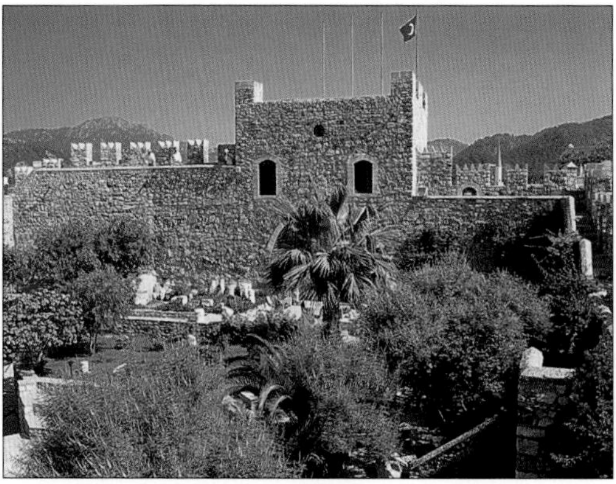

The Castle, incorporating a nautical museum

🏛 Castle and Museum

☎ *(0252) 412 14 59.* 🕐 *8am–noon & 1–5:30pm Tue–Sun.* 🎟

The original castle was rebuilt by Süleyman the Magnificent in 1522 after his successful campaign against Rhodes. Today, the restored structure is a museum housing a small collection of nautical items. There are also inscriptions and sculptures displayed in the courtyard. More engaging for most visitors, however, will be the panoramic view of the harbour and old Greek houses under renovation.

🛒 Bazaar

Entrance from Kordon Caddesi and the street beside the tourist office.

You may find a unique item among the tourist bric-a-brac offered up for sale in the bazaar, among the leather goods, jewellery, herbs, spices and teas. A delicious local speciality is Marmaris honey, which is produced along the scenic Datça Peninsula *(see pp202–203)*. Both pine *(çam)* or flower *(çiçek)* honey are fragrant, thick and dark. By the end of October the last of the honey and fresh summer produce will have been sold.

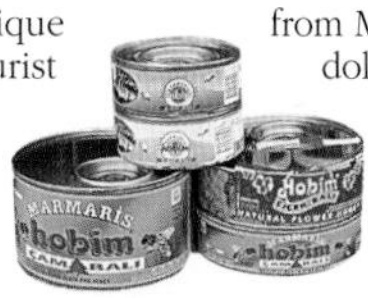

Marmaris honey

VISITORS' CHECKLIST

👥 *35,000.* ⛴ *from Rhodes.* ✈ *Dalaman, 120 km (75 miles) E of town, (0252) 792 52 91.* 🚌 *NE of town centre on Muğla road.* ℹ *İskele Meydanı (central harbour), (0252) 412 10 35.* 🛒 *Fri.* 🎉 *Yacht Race Week (Nov).*

ENVIRONS: A number of large holiday villages are located in **İçmeler**, about 6 km (4 miles) around the bay from Marmaris. Transport to and from Marmaris is easy, as dolmuşes make the trip on a regular basis. İçmeler lacks the quaint atmosphere of an old Turkish town, as do many parts of Marmaris, but many visitors (particularly families with children) prefer the more up-to-date facilities and much cleaner beaches that are found here.

MARMARIS TOWN CENTRE

Bar Street ②
Bazaar ⑤
Castle and Museum ④
Greek Revival Houses in Old Quarter ③
Netsel Marina ①

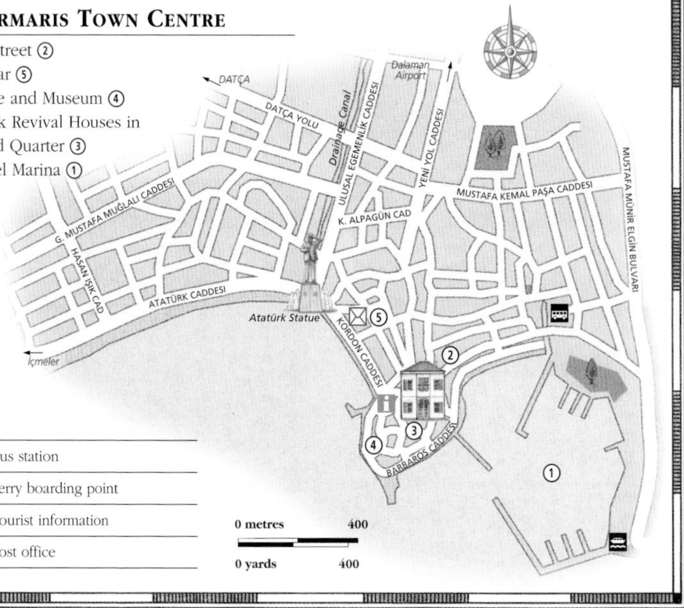

KEY

🚌 Bus station
⛴ Ferry boarding point
ℹ Tourist information
✉ Post office

Datça Peninsula Tour ㉘

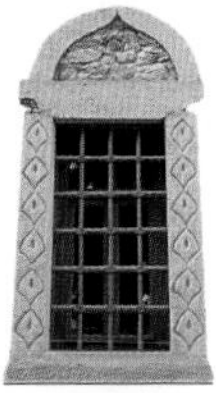

Restored window in Eski Datça

THE NARROW FINGER of the Datça Peninsula, pointing westward from Marmaris, lies at the place where the Mediterranean and the Aegean meet. Locals claim that the air is rich in oxygen, thanks to the prevailing wind *(meltem)* and the mixing of salinity levels and current patterns in the sea.

The route along the peninsula follows narrow and twisting roads, affording glimpses of the sea though pine-clad gullies. At the western tip, about 35 km (21 miles) west of Datça, lie the ruins of Knidos, one of the most prosperous port cities of antiquity. In its heyday it was home to an eminent medical school. Here, you can lunch on seafood, and swim in the sheltered bay.

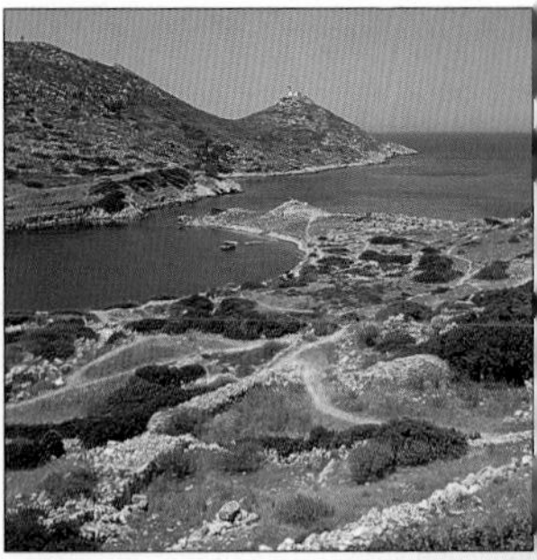

Knidos ⑤
This port was the site of a shrine of Aphrodite, dating from about 360 BC. The remains of a theatre, agora, houses and a round temple are visible today.

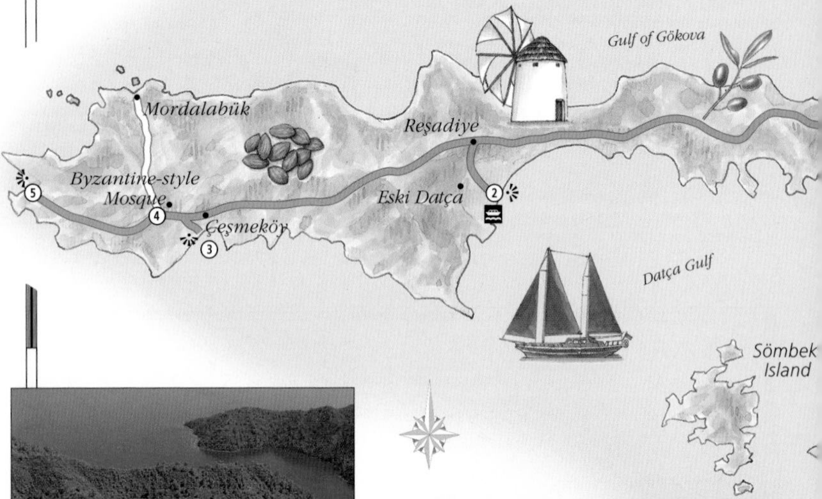

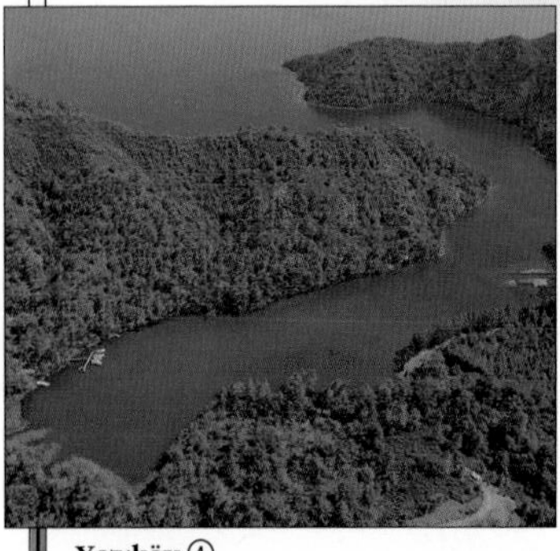

Yazıköy ④
The western half of the peninsula consists of rugged, pine-clad mountains dotted with olive and almond groves. The village of Yazıköy, at the end of the paved portion of the road, lies deep in the olive-growing region.

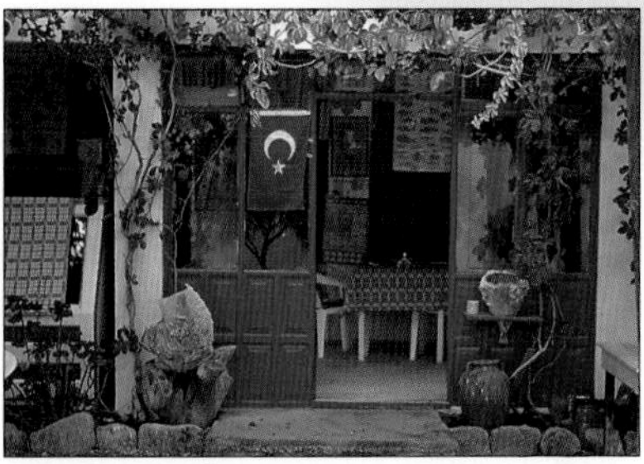

Palamut Bükü ③
This bay can also be reached by boat from Datça, and offers a long, tranquil pebble beach lapped by brisk, clear water. Palamut Bükü is a good spot for lunch, with several simple but good fish restaurants.

Orhaniye/Keçibükü ⑥
On the way back to Marmaris, take the Bozburun road to Orhaniye (turn right just after Değirmenyanı), and continue on for about 7 km (4 miles) to Keçibükü. Lovely sea views make the little town an idyllic place to stop.

Bençik ①
This, the narrowest point of the peninsula, is a mere 800 m (2,600 ft) wide. Locals used to call it *Balıkaşıran* (the place where the fish pass over).

Tips for Drivers

Tour length: Day trip (or 2 hours' drive) from Marmaris, west on the main road, about 62 km (39 miles) from Marmaris to Datça, and 21 km (13 miles) from Datça to Knidos. Sections of the road to Knidos are in poor condition – care is advised. Boat tours run from Marmaris to Knidos, with various stops.
When to go: Spring, when the almond trees are in blossom
Where to stay: Campsites are available at Çubucak Forest Campsite and Inbükü Camping Ground. ⬛ Both sites are closed May–Oct.

Key

▬	Tour route
=	Other road
⬛	Boat trips
☀	Viewpoint

Datça ②
The small town of Datça has a busy yacht harbour, and many shops and restaurants. A few kilometres inland is the old town, Eski Datça, with many lovely stone houses.

MEDITERRANEAN TURKEY

TURKEY'S MEDITERRANEAN COAST *is synonymous with turquoise seas, sun and blue skies, and has a wealth of ancient remains. Originally colonized by the Greeks and later ruled by the Romans, the region is littered with well-preserved classical sites. However, Hittites, Seljuks, Ottomans, Armenians and even the Crusaders have all left their distinctive imprints upon these shores.*

The highlands of Lycia, between Fethiye and Antalya, were the seat of an impressive civilization whose distinctive stone tombs – both free-standing and cliff-hewn – still dot the landscape. At ruined cities such as Pınara, Myra and Xanthos, it is possible to glimpse the achievements and scale of the Lycian civilization.

The city of Antalya, an important gateway to the Mediterranean region, boasts a spectacular cliff-top setting and quaint walled quarter. It is also a good base for visits to the romantic mountain-top ruins of the Pisidian capital of Termessos and the monumental Roman remains at Perge and Aspendos. Bustling Side, with its temples of Apollo and Athena, is renowned for stunning sunsets.

The Cave of St Peter in Antakya and St Paul's well in Tarsus – birthplace of the Apostle – are reminders of the role of Christianity in fostering the area's cultural and religious diversity.

The short French protectorate era (1918–39) in the Hatay, in the far southeast, left a European colonial legacy in urban planning and local architecture. This corner of the Mediterranean region contains the multicultural cities of İskenderun and Antakya (ancient Antioch on the Orontes), where the Arab-Syrian influence is clearly visible. Antakya is also renowned for its Roman mosaics.

An ancient Lycian tomb rising above the placid waters of a coastal inlet

◁ Mamure Castle near Anamur, a well-preserved crusader castle

Exploring the Western Mediterranean Coast

SEPARATED FROM the dry Anatolian plateau by the Taurus Mountains, the Mediterranean coast of Turkey is dominated by plunging cliffs and headlands interspersed with fertile alluvial flood plains, and fringed in places with fine sandy beaches. Throughout the region, the many civilizations that have shaped Turkey left their mark on cities, harbours, roads and rivers. To leave your own footprints, venture along the Lycian Way from Fethiye to Antalya, now rated as one of the world's top treks, or take the "Blue Voyage" on a traditional *gület* (wooden yacht).

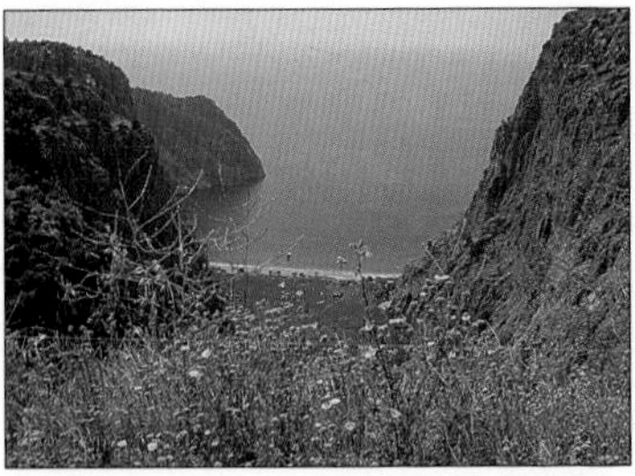

Butterfly Valley, near Ölü Deniz

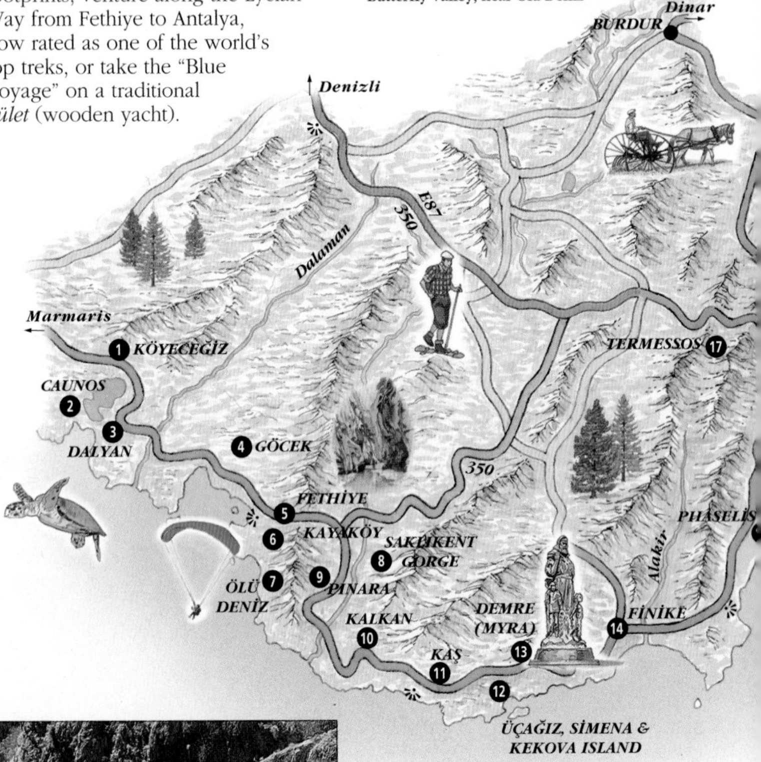
Dinar
BURDUR
Denizli
E87
350
Dalaman
Marmaris
1 KÖYCEĞİZ
CAUNOS 2
3 DALYAN
4 GÖCEK
350
FETHİYE 5
6 KAYAKÖY
8 SAKLIKENT GORGE
ÖLÜ DENİZ 7
9 PINARA
KALKAN 10
KAŞ 11
12 ÜÇAĞIZ, SİMENA & KEKOVA ISLAND
DEMRE (MYRA) 13
14 FİNİKE
Alakır
TERMESSOS 17
PHASELIS

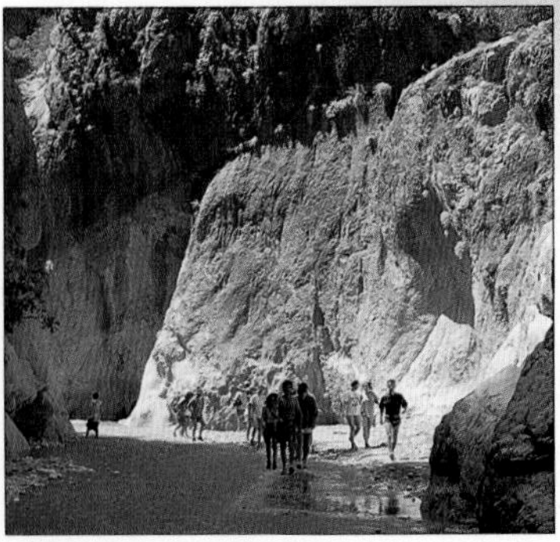

Hiking in Saklıkent Gorge

GETTING AROUND

Antalya's Bayındır International Airport is gradually opening up direct access to European destinations. From here, fast main roads run east and west, parallel to the coast. The modern coast road hugs the cliffs in places, but only the 30-km (19-mile) stretch from Demre to Finike can be considered truly challenging. With only a few exceptions, all the main sights and attractions are easily accessible by bus and dolmuş.

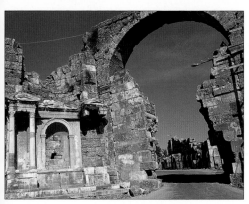

The Vespasian Monument, a Roman fountain in Side

SIGHTS AT A GLANCE

Alanya **22**
Anamur and Anemurium **23**
Antalya pp218–19 **16**
Aspendos p221 **20**
Caunos **2**
Dalyan **3**
Demre (Myra) **13**
Fethiye **5**
Finike **14**
Göcek **4**
Kalkan **10**
Kaş **11**
Kayaköy **6**
Köyceğiz **1**
Ölü Deniz **7**
Perge **18**
Phaselis **15**
Pınara **9**
Saklıkent Gorge **8**
Side pp224–5 **21**
Selge **19**
Termessos **17**
Üçağiz, Simena and Kekova Island **12**

KEY

≡ Motorway
▭ Major road
▭ Other road
▭ Scenic route
▭ River
☀ Viewpoint

SEE ALSO

• *Where to Stay* pp329–31

• *Where to Eat* pp348–50

The picturesque yacht harbour at Antalya

Exploring the Eastern Mediterranean Coast

THE MEDITERRANEAN COASTLINE east of Alanya is much less populous (and visited) than the western portion, but offers sights every bit as diverse. These include the bird-watcher's paradise of the Göksu Delta, several Armenian and Crusader castles, and the important Hittite site of Karatepe. The region also has a decidedly Middle Eastern flavour: the further east you go, the more lively and colourful the bazaars become and the foods tingle with stronger spices. This influence is most apparent in the southeast, around İskenderun and Antakya. Turkey's fourth largest city, Adana, is the main centre in the area. It has a subtropical climate, which receives rainfall mainly during the autumn and winter months.

Remnants of the Temple of Zeus, Silifke

SEE ALSO

• *Where to Stay* pp329–31

• *Where to Eat* pp348–50

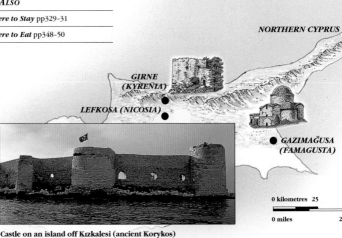

Castle on an island off Kızkalesi (ancient Korykos)

Konya

Göksu

715

● **MUT**

KIZKALESİ ㉕

Anamur

SİLİFKE ㉔

Anamur

NORTHERN CYPRUS

**GİRNE
(KYRENIA)** ●

LEFKOŞA (NICOSIA) ●

**GAZIMAĞUSA
(FAMAGUSTA)** ●

0 kilometres   25

0 miles   25

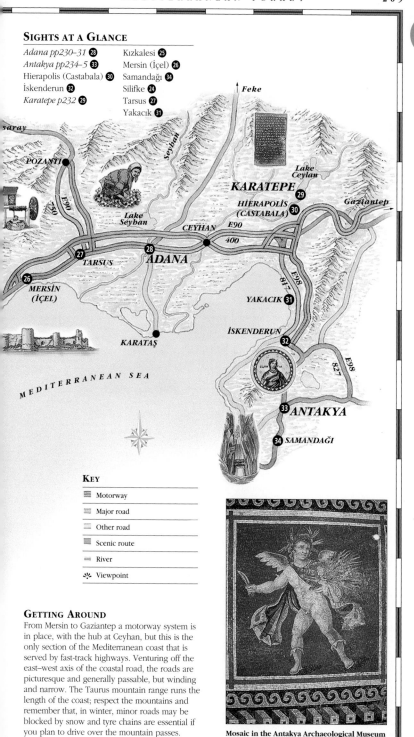

SIGHTS AT A GLANCE

POZANTI

KARATEPE

HİERAPOLİS
(CASTABALA) 30

Gaziantep

Lake
Ceylan

Lake
Seyhan

CEYHAN

E90
400

TARSUS 27 28 ADANA

MERSİN 26
(İÇEL)

YAKACIK 31

İSKENDERUN 32

KARATAŞ

MEDITERRANEAN SEA

33 ANTAKYA

34 SAMANDAĞI

KEY

- Motorway
- Major road
- Other road
- Scenic route
- River
- Viewpoint

GETTING AROUND

From Mersin to Gaziantep a motorway system is
in place, with the hub at Ceyhan, but this is the
only section of the Mediterranean coast that is
served by fast-track highways. Venturing off the
east–west axis of the coastal road, the roads are
picturesque and generally passable, but winding
and narrow. The Taurus mountain range runs the
length of the coast; respect the mountains and
remember that, in winter, minor roads may be
blocked by snow and tyre chains are essential if
you plan to drive over the mountain passes.

Mosaic in the Antakya Archaeological Museum

Lake Köyceğiz, a haven for water birds

Köyceğiz ❶

30 km (19 miles) N of Dalyan.
🚶 7,200. 📍 (0252) 262 47 03.

INDEPENDENT Menteşe clans governed this area even after the beginning of Ottoman rule in 1424. By the late 1830s, when the English archaeologist Charles Fellows visited the area, the power of the family had declined, however. Currently, the family *konak* (manor house) is under restoration. Another manor, once the centre of a cotton estate belonging to the *khedive* (viceroy) of Egypt, is now the Dalaman state farm. Many people in Köyceğiz village are descended from African slaves brought here to work on cotton plantations. A plantation of *liquidambar orientalis*, the tree used to produce church incense, survives as a reminder of a once-important local industry.

The reed-fringed lake of Köyceğiz, 10 m (33 ft) deep in places, is home to many water birds, including the rare Smyrna kingfisher.

Caunos ❷

6 km (4 miles) from Dalyan.
📞 (0252) 284 20 44. ⏰ Apr–Sep.
🎟 included in price of boat tour.

THE ANCIENT CITY of Caunos bordered the kingdoms of Lycia and Caria. Although a Carian foundation, its culture shared aspects of both states. The local tombs are Lycian *(see p215)* in style, but were in fact carved by the Carians. Like Xanthos, capital of Lycia, Caunos resisted the Persian general, Harpagus, during the 6th century BC, for which many citizens of Caunos were slaughtered in a final sally. The city was re-established and Hellenized, especially by the Carian ruler, Mausolus *(see pp194–5)*. Caunos welcomed Alexander the Great, but after his death came under the rule of Rhodes. It won independence from Rome, but after supporting Mithridates against the Romans, the city was punished by return to Rhodian rule. Caunos was known both for its figs and malarial mosquitoes. It was a major seaport until the harbour silted up.

Turtle Statue in Dalyan

At the site are defensive walls built in the 4th century BC, a theatre dating from the 2nd century BC, a temple to Apollo and a Roman bath. There is a Doric temple and an agora (marketplace) with a nymphaeum (fountain) thought to have been built to honour Emperor Vespasian.

Dalyan ❸

13 km (8 miles) from the main D400 road. 🚶 6,600. ✈ Dalaman, 25 km (16 miles) E of Dalyan, (0252) 792 52 91. 🚌 Ortaca, 13 km (8 miles) NE of Dalyan. 🅳 entry road to Dalyan, (0252) 284 24 58. 🛈 (0252) 284 42 35. 🎭 Caretta (turtle) Festival (end Aug–early Sep). 🛍 Sat.

THIS BUSTLING RESORT takes its name from the Dalyan River (Dalyan Çayı), meaning "fishing weir", which flows through the town. Although the town is a fast-growing tourist centre, fishing has long been the mainstay of the local economy. Over the years, the town replaced ancient Caunos as a fishery when the latter's harbour became choked by silt. A new weir built on the river, together with a fish-processing plant, means that you can enjoy the delicious local red roe caviar, which comes in a pot sealed with beeswax. Local fish is available at waterside eateries. The threatened loggerhead turtle *(see p211)* has become a symbol of Dalyan, drawing increasing numbers of visitors to the area. This came about in 1986, when conservationists managed to persuade civic authorities to protect the turtles' breeding ground from development. Since then, local people have adopted the loggerhead turtle as a motif for the town. The Turtle Statue (Kaplumbağa Heykeli) on Cumhuriyet Meydanı is a

The resort town of Dalyan, by the tranquil Dalyan River

tangible symbol of Dalyan's new passion for conservation.

On the eastern bank of the Dalyan River are two rows of tombs cut into the cliffs. Constructed for the citizens of Caunos, the tombs are mainly of the house type and date from the 4th century BC, (see p215), with Ionic columns and triangular pediments. Most have a small chamber with three stone benches to accommodate the dead. The surviving inscriptions are mainly in Latin, for the tombs were re-used during Roman times. They are fenced off and must be viewed from some distance away. The rock tombs can be reached by river-boat tours, which depart from the Dalyan Sea Co-operative.

ENVIRONS: A short distance upriver from Dalyan (about 10 minutes by boat) lie the **mud baths** of Ilıca. With a constant temperature of 40°C (104°F), they are reputed to be beneficial for rheumatism and gynaecological disorders, and are certainly relaxing. Beyond Ilıca, at Sultaniye Kaplıcaları, on the shores of Lake Köyceğiz, a domed building lined with marble surrounds a natural pool where water wells up at 39–41°C (102–106°F). Locals report that, after the Adana earthquake of 1998, the water at the bathhouse gave off a plume of sulphur gas and that the water changed colour and appeared gassy.

Turtle Beach (İztuzu Plajı), which partly bars the mouth of the Dalyan River, has for centuries been a refuge for

Yachts moored in Göcek's harbour

breeding loggerhead turtles and is now a protected area. Until recently, the significance of this endangered species was poorly understood. The beach is now closed to tourists at night so that the young turtles are not attracted by the bright lights, which would lead them away from the life-giving sea.

Staying on the beach after dark is forbidden, so you are unlikely to catch a glimpse of the turtles, but you may see blue crabs. The best way to get to the beach is to take a boat from the river bank near the centre of Dalyan. There are full-day tours to the beach that take in both Caunos and the mud baths at Ilıca.

◑ Mud Baths
Çamurlu Kaplıcası
◖ (0252) 284 20 35. **◗** Apr–Oct.
◪ ▢

✗ Turtle Beach
İztuzu Plajı
12 km (7.5 miles) from town centre.
▦ from Dalyan (40 min): depart before 10:30am, return between 3pm and sunset. **◪** for car park only.

Göcek **❹**

23 km (14 miles) E of Dalaman.
▦ 1 km (0.5 mile) from town centre.
ℹ Club Marina (private yacht club), (0252) 645 18 00; municipal yacht club, (0252) 645 19 38.

NEAR THE PASS of the same name, and just south of the main D400 road, Göcek is now a major yachting centre. Popularized by Prince Charles and former Turkish president, Turgut Özal, the town has a remarkable concentration of up-market facilities, including a luxury hotel and several striking waterside housing developments. The public marinas have berths for about 350 boats, with a further 200 berths available in a secluded private marina. Near the tip of the peninsula can be seen the ruins of the Roman town of Lydae, with two mausolea and a fort.

LOGGERHEAD TURTLES

The loggerhead turtle (Caretta caretta) has become closely associated with Dalyan, where soft sand and a tranquil south-facing beach provide an ideal nesting ground.

Loggerhead turtles can mate several times in a season. Between May and September, the females arrive *en masse* to drag themselves up onto the beaches where they themselves hatched. There they laboriously dig a pit and lay their eggs above the tide line. The sand keeps the eggs at an even temperature until they are ready to hatch.

Loggerhead turtle (Caretta caretta)

Kayaköy, once the prosperous Greek community of Levissi but abandoned in 1923

Fethiye ❺

🏃 52,000. ✈ Dalaman, 50 km (31 miles) NW of town. 🚌 2 km (1 mile) E of town centre. ⛴ from Rhodes. 🅸 İskele Karşısı, No. 1, (0252) 614 15 27 and 612 19 75. 🗓 Fri.

A MEDIUM-SIZED market town and agricultural centre, Fethiye fringes a sheltered bay with a large harbour, making it a good place for scuba diving and boating. Holiday facilities range from the resort sprawl of Çalış, just north of the town, to the upmarket Hillside Beach Club, which holds an annual waterskiing competition.

Modern Fethiye stands on the ruins of the Lycian city of Telmessus. Earthquakes in 1856 and 1958 levelled most of the ancient edifices, which included a temple of Apollo, but a Roman theatre near the harbour survives. Cut into the cliffs above the town's market are several Lycian temple tombs *(see p215)*, some from the 4th century BC. Charles Texier, a 19th-century French explorer, carved his initials on one of these tombs.

Fethiye Museum displays artifacts from the half-flooded ruins of Letoön *(see p214)*, including stelae which scholars used in their efforts to decode the Lycian language.

🏛 Fethiye Museum
Fethiye Müzesi
Off Atatürk Cad.
📞 (0252) 614 11 50. 🕓 8:30am–5pm Tue–Sun. 📷

Lycian tombs cut into the cliffs above Fethiye

Kayaköy ❻

10 km (6 miles) SW of Fethiye. 🅳 from Fethiye or Ölü Deniz.

D ERELICT KAYAKÖY, formerly known as Karmylassos, then Levissi, was a thriving Greek town until it was abandoned in the exchange of populations that took place in 1923 *(see p58)*. About 400 roofless houses stand on the hillside overlooking a fertile plain. The Orthodox church of Panayia Pyrgiotissa is now undergoing restoration and is becoming a focus of movements for peace and international reconciliation. A few of the old houses have been sympathetically restored, but most are abandoned, with plaster peeling from the stone walls. An old paved *kaldıran* (mule trail) running through the village makes for pleasant walking. There have been proposals to use the attractive site as a venue for weddings.

Ölü Deniz ❼

20 km (12 miles) S of Fethiye. 🏃 1,200. 🅳 from Fethiye. 🅸 Tourism Co-operative, (0252) 617 04 38, (0252) 617 01 45.

M ADE FAMOUS IN THE 1970s by visitors from Britain, the inviting beach and lagoon at Ölü Deniz (which means dead sea – because of the calm water) now adorn many posters promoting Turkish travel. The land behind the restaurant-fringed beach has been appropriated for hotels, pensions and camp sites. The adjoining mountain, Baba Dağı, is the jump-off point for paragliders, who soar over the lagoon. Ölü Deniz also marks the start of the Lycian Way, Turkey's first long-distance walking route, which ends just short of Antalya.

Saklıkent Gorge 🖲

30 km (18 miles) E of Fethiye.
D from Fethiye and then on foot.
summer only.

The beautiful lagoon and beach at Ölü Deniz

SAKLIKENT GORGE cuts into the rugged flank of the 3,016-m (9,895-ft) Gömbe Akdağı, and delivers a rushing stream of pure limestone-filtered water. From the restaurants at the base of the gorge, which specialize in trout from local trout farms, you can walk for a few hundred metres into the gorge on platforms built over the torrent. Bougainville Travel of Kaş (see p365) organizes abseiling trips into the gorge. These involve scrambling over rocks to cross the waterfalls that tumble down the walls.

If you enter by road and footpath, along the flank of Akdağı, there is quite a steep descent, but this brings you to the trout farms. At Saklıkent,

7 km (4.5 miles) from the main D400 road, consider a meal at one of the trout restaurants, which have low tables placed over the water. Enjoy the cool air before you return to sea level – when the temperature is 40°C (104°F) at the coast, Saklıkent is very refreshing.

Also in the area is the ruined city of Tlos, one of the oldest and most important Lycian cities. Hittite records from the 14th century BC refer to a settlement called Tlawa, which was probably Tlos. Built on a hill, with a commanding view over the

valley of the Eşen River (Eşen Çayı) – known in ancient times as the Xanthos – the main Lycian/Roman remains consist of tombs hewn from rock, as well as a stadium, gymnasium and palaestra, and baths. In Byzantine times, Tlos was a bishopric, and the churches at the site were most probably former temples. The acropolis was used until the 19th century, when it was the stronghold of a pirate known as Kanlı Ali Ağa (Bloody Ali).

Agencies in Fethiye and Kaş offer tours of both Saklıkent Gorge and Tlos.

Catwalk built over the water in Saklıkent Gorge

BUTTERFLY VALLEY

From Ölü Deniz, it is a short boat ride to Butterfly Valley (Kelebek Vadisi), a flat-bottomed valley enclosed by towering cliffs. The valley was named for the migratory *Euplagia quadripunctaria*, commonly known as the Jersey Tiger, a spectacular red, black and white tiger moth

Euplagia quadripunctaria

that colonizes the valley by the thousand during the summer. Other species are present year-round, with some unique to the area. A 20-minute trek leads to a waterfall from the mill stream at Faralya, which cascades into the valley, providing damp conditions for the butterflies and supporting a variety of plants. No permanent buildings are allowed on or behind the beach, but a wooden bar-restaurant supplies beer and food to those wishing to camp. Alternative access is by steep path from Faralya, the village perched 600 m (1,968 ft) above, but this route is not recommended since the path is dangerous.

Tombs cut into the rock at Pınara

Pınara ❾

50 km (31 miles) E of Fethiye.
◯ 9am–5:30pm Tue–Sun. 📷

ONE OF THE MOST important cities of ancient Lycia, Pınara, whose name means "round", is situated on and around a huge circular plug of rock above the village of Minare, some 5 km (3 miles) west of the main D400 road. The entrance is about 3 km (2 miles) along an unpaved track that is passable by car.

The rock face is honey-combed with tombs, mainly square holes, which must have been sealed after use. The acropolis is approached by steps carved into the rock. A well-preserved theatre is cut into the hillside below, with baths nearby. The agora (marketplace) lies just above the ticket office.

Visitors strolling through the picturesque streets of Kalkan

Kalkan ❿

🏠 6,800. 🚌 at junction with main coast road. 🛍 Thu.

THE VILLAGE OF Kalkan has been permanently inhabited only since the eradication of malaria-bearing mosquitoes in the 1950s. In earlier times, the local people avoided the pests by migrating in summer to the *yayla* (summer pasture) of Bezirgan, above the village. The core of stone, Greek-style houses built around the harbour has now been augmented by modern colour-washed villas on the hills. Good accommodation and a choice of restaurants make it an ideal base from which to explore the ancient Lycian cities of Xanthos, Letoön and Patara.

Xanthos (now Kınık), the ancient capital of the Lycian League (*see p215*), is 30 minutes by bus west of Kalkan, just before the bridge spanning the Eşen River. The site is extensive and spectacular, and includes superb examples of Lycian tombs. A bilingual Greek-Lycian pillar found at the site helped researchers to decipher the Lycian language.

Letoön, site of the temples of Leto, Artemis and Apollo, was a cult centre favoured by Alexander the Great. Now partly flooded, the evocative ruins are a peaceful wildlife enclave frequented by frogs, kingfishers and terrapins.

Patara was once the major port of the Lycian League. Damaged by severe earthquakes in AD 141 and AD 240, its harbour silted up.

Kaş ⓫

🏠 5,300. ✈ Dalaman, 155 km (96 miles) NW of town, or Bayındır Intl Airport (Antalya), (0242) 330 36 00, 210 km (130 miles) NE of town. 🚌 Fethiye Cad. 🚹 5 Cumhuriyet Meydanı, (0242) 836 12 38. 🛍 Fri. 🎭 Kaş/Lycia Festival (last week in Jun).

KAŞ WAS BUILT adjoining a long, narrow peninsula, over the ancient port city of Antiphellos (port of Phellos), and was noted for its cork oaks. In 1839, it was so tiny and impoverished that the English archaeologist Charles Fellows (who excavated the nearby Lycian site of Xanthos) had to cross to the island of Castellorizo to buy chickens to eat. Today, the situation is reversed: the islanders buy their chickens at Kaş market on Fridays. The harbours are filled with scuba-diving boats and yachts making trips to the Blue Cave and the sunken city at Kekova (*see p216*), with hotels and pensions along the waterfront. Uzun Çarşı, the shopping street, is lined with carpet and leather shops and bars, and is dominated by a Lycian sarcophagus from the 5th century BC.

"Hand of Fatma" door knocker, Kaş

The tourism information office in the main square can provide information on the annual Kaş/Lycia Festival, which makes good use of the tiny Hellenistic theatre located on the peninsula road just west of the town.

Fishing boats and touring yachts in the harbour at Kaş

Lycian Tombs

ANCIENT LYCIA, a federation of 19 independent cities, lay in the mountainous area between modern Fethiye and Antalya.

Burials must have had an important role in the beliefs of the Lycians, for they cut hundreds of tombs into cliff faces and crags that can be seen throughout the area. They were probably copies of domestic architecture, intended as houses for the dead. Most have carved doors, beam ends, pitched roofs and prominent lintels – typical of construction in wood.

During the 4th century BC, the rulers of Xanthos (modern Kınık) produced some of the most remarkable tombs, combining Greek and Persian styles. One of the most famous of these, the Nereid Monument, is now in the British Museum in London.

Tomb relief

The house tomb *of one to three storeys, shown here at Tlos, was carved into solid rock. A sliding slab door opened into an inner chamber. Some tombs had exterior porticoes with carvings.*

The doorway of a house tomb often featured a sliding slab.

House tombs at Myra, *near Demre, feature richly carved façades. The elaborate reliefs on some of the tombs still bear traces of paint applied by the original builders.*

Rock cut away to make a roof space

Sarcophagus placed atop the pillar base

The freestanding temple tomb had a temple façade and a portico, from which a door led to a grave chamber with benches for the dead.

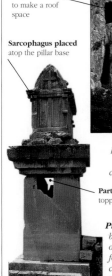

Partly hollow base topped by a stepped lid

Pillar tombs *(on a stepped base or built directly on rock) are the oldest Lycian tombs. These are found only at Xanthos, the chief city of Lycia, and Apollonia. This example is from Xanthos.*

Prominent lid ridge

"Beam ends" used to open the lid of the sarcophagus

Stepped base

Sarcophagus tombs had a stepped base, a lower grave chamber (called a hyposorion), a flat plate for the coffin and a lid. The pitched, rounded lid symbolized a house roof, and had a prominent ridge. From 500 BC to AD 300, elaborate "saddlebacked" sarcophagus tombs were produced.

Varnished charter vessels and quaint fishing boats share the little harbour at Üçağız

Üçağız, Simena and Kekova Island ⑫

38 km (24 miles) E of Kaş.
🏠 1,800. ⛴ from Demre or Kaş.

THE PICTURESQUE waterfront village of Üçağız ("Three Mouths") is a 19-km (12-mile) drive south of the D400, just east of Kaş. Dolmuşes will drop you at the main road, from where you will be able to walk into the village.

Built on the site of (and using stones from) the Lycian town of Teimiussa, houses, restaurants and pensions front a sheltered bay with three openings to the sea. There are some signs of subsidence, probably as a result of an earthquake that took place in about AD 530. Submerged saddleback tombs (see p215)

can be seen at the Lycian site of Aperlae and the village of Kale (ancient Simena) nearby, where a castle built in around 1440 surrounds a tiny theatre cut into the rock. A pleasant stroll along the coast via the marked Lycian Way leads to its rarely visited twin.

Diving is not permitted in the bay enclosed by Kekova Island (Kekova Adası), but you can sail over remains of ancient buildings.

Demre (Myra) ⑬

🏠 19,200. ⛴ 100 m (100 yards) from main square. ❶

THE ANCIENT CITY of Myra and the port of Andriake, 3 km (2 miles) southwest of Demre, date from around the 5th century BC, and grew rich

on coastal trade, supplying incense (derived from the *liquidamber orientalis* tree) to Egypt and Constantinople. The modern town of Demre, officially known as Kale, lies about 2 km (1 mile) from the ruins of Myra.

The most popular parts of Myra are the theatre and two cliffs carved with spectacular house tombs. When Charles Fellows visited the site in 1840, the paint on the tombs was still visible and letters of the inscriptions were picked out in red and blue. The oldest part of Myra was on the acropolis hill, with a 5th-century-BC defensive wall. Myra's water supply ran in channels cut into the wall of the Demre gorge. Hot sulphur springs at Andriake provided natural cures, and baths were fed by both sources.

Nearby Sura, 5 km (3 miles) to the west, features a temple that adjoined a whirlpool in the sea. From here, priests threw skewers of meat into the waves; predictions were made according to which fish took the food. The beach between Andriake and Sura is a deserted haven for wildlife.

THE REAL SANTA CLAUS

Nicholas, the 4th-century Bishop of Myra, was famed for his unfailing generosity and piety. He was beatified, and legend established him as the patron of fishermen and children, and the town as a place of pilgrimage. (He is also the patron saint of bakers, brewers and brides.) There are two statues of St Nicholas (Noel Baba in Turkish) in Demre: one is a gift from the Russian Orthodox Church, and is mounted on a revolving pedestal. The saint's myrrh-impregnated bones were buried on his church's premises. Although this church was destroyed by the Arabs in 809, the bones survived and were moved to Bari, Italy, in 1087. The church at Demre was rebuilt by a Russian prince in the 19th century. Demre is also the headquarters of the St Nicholas Foundation.

Statue of St Nicholas in Demre

Carved mask relief from the theatre at Myra

Finike ⑭

22,000. off D400 highway.
from Rhodes. Sat.

FINIKE IS A MARKET town
located at the foot of the
Gülmez Dağları, a long spur
of the Taurus Mountains, and
on the banks of the Karasu
(Black Water) River.

In ancient times, Finike was
known as Phoenicus. The
original harbour, once noted
for its export of the timber
that was used in building the
Ottoman fleet, is now buried
under silt, and a modern
yacht harbour has replaced it.
In Byzantine times, the surrounding mountains were a
source of cedar of Lebanon
(used in shipbuilding), but
the tree is rarely found in
these parts today.

Finike has since prospered
through the export of citrus
fruit and other produce. Its
fertile orchards brim with
orange and lemon trees, and
the town's logo is an orange.

To the north lie the ruins of
Limyra, with a theatre, many
tombs and a monument to
Gaius Caesar, adopted son of
the Emperor Augustus, who
died here on his way back
from Armenia in 44BC.

Not much is known about
the early history of **Olympos**,
although it was an influential
member of the Lycian League.
The site is reached by a dirt
track through a narrow gorge
with a seasonally dry river
bed. The ruined city occupies
a charming setting adjoining a
4-km-long (3-mile) beach. To
the south is an extensive
necropolis, including unique
square tombs with sliding
doors. A theatre, baths and
landing stages also occupy
the south bank. The northern
side has an acropolis, more
tombs, a temple dating from
the time of Emperor Marcus
Aurelius and a Byzantine
bathhouse. The whole site is
starred with anemones in
spring; kingfishers whirr over
the stream and ducks nest in
the reeds.

At the northern end of the
beach, past Çıralı and at an
altitude of 300 m (984 ft), are
two outcrops of volcanic
rock, where escaping natural

Escaping natural gas burning near Olympos

gas is permanently alight. The
flame is known as Yanartaş
(burning stone). In ancient
times, the fire was guided upwards to light a beacon that
would warn ships at sea of
impending danger. There is
also a Byzantine church here,
which was probably once a
temple of Vulcan.

According to myth, this
mountain is where the hero
Bellerophon, mounted on the
winged horse, Pegasus, killed
the three-headed Chimaera by
pouring molten lead into the
monster's mouth.

⛰ Olympos
11 km (7 miles) E of main D400 road
from café on D400, or taxi. 🏍

Phaselis ⑮

40 km (24 miles) SW of Antalya.
daily. 🏖 🏛

DECKED WITH FLOWERS in
spring, the ruined city of
Phaselis is a popular stopping
place for cruise yachts.

The Lycian port city was
sold to Greek settlers from
Rhodes by a local shepherd in
the 7th century BC. They built
an extensive town with three
harbours around an acropolis
on a headland. The canny
Phaselians, noted for their
skill in trade and commerce,
invited Alexander the Great to
winter here in 333 BC, even
presenting him with a golden
crown in return for valuable
protection. Phaselis became a
pirate stronghold before it
was absorbed into the Roman
province of Lycia-Pamphylia
in AD 43. It survived Arab
raiding, only to be eclipsed
by Antalya in Seljuk times.

Most of the ruins date from
the Roman era. They include
a theatre, two sets of baths,
an agora, an aqueduct leading
from Mount Olympos and a
marble gateway erected in
honour of Emperor Hadrian.

The north harbour at Phaselis, with Mt Olympos in the background

Antalya

Mask
carved in
relief

Aℕᴛᴀʟʏᴀ's ᴘᴏᴘᴜʟᴀᴛɪᴏɴ has increased rapidly since the tourism boom began in the late 1980s. Mountains, beaches and the seaside setting are the obvious magnets, and the city is now one of Turkey's premier resort areas. Antalya (ancient Attaleia) was founded by Attalus II, a king of Pergamum, in 159 BC.
The city prospered during the Roman, Byzantine and Seljuk eras before coming under Ottoman rule in 1390. The most important remains are the Roman city walls and the imposing Hadrian's Gate.

Roman marble sculpture from the Antalya Archaeological Museum

The attractive old harbour, showing remnants of the city walls

Exploring Antalya
Antalya's broad, palm-lined boulevards and interesting Old Town (Kaleiçi) make it a pleasant place to explore. The beaches, parks, excellent shops and lively cultural scene make it a focal point of the Mediterranean coast.
Antalya has one speciality not found anywhere else in Turkey – *hibeş*, a hot, spicy sesame-oil dip.

Aqualand
Dumlupınar Bulvarı, Konyaaltı.
(0242) 238 56 00. May–Oct: 10am–6pm daily.
A water-based theme park run in partnership with a Spanish company, Aqualand features huge, brightly coloured chutes, slides and a wave pool. The park also has a disco, restaurant and baby play area.

Pyramid Congress Centre
Yeni Yüzyıl Bulvarı.
(0242) 243 76 40 (during conferences only).
The Pyramid Congress Centre (also known as AKM), a copy of I M Pei's Louvre extension

in Paris, was built in 1996 as a venue for a four-yearly World Forestry Congress. It can hold 3,000 delegates, and is home to a variety of congresses, trade fairs and concerts. The centre is often confused with the Culture Centre, which lies 200 m (650 ft) away, towards the Sheraton Hotel.

Antalya Archaeological Museum
Kenan Evren Bulvarı, Konyaaltı
(0242) 238 56 88.
9am–6:30pm Tue–Sun.
with prior permission.
The museum, perched on the cliffs 2 km (1.25 miles) west of the city centre, is the true jewel of Antalya. It houses a unique collection of Roman marble sculptures dating from the 2nd century AD, many of them from nearby Perge (*see p220*). The statues and friezes are displayed in the new green-marble Perge hall.
Displays also include Bronze-Age urn burials, silver found in Phrygian

tumulus burials, relics of St Nicholas (*see p216*) and a collection of early Byzantine church silver. There is also an ethnography section. If your time in Antalya is limited, save it for this – one of the handful of Turkish museums that is truly outstanding. The newly renovated Sarcophagi Hall and Gallery of the Gods are also recommended viewing. Don't miss the sarcophagus dog called Sephanos.

Yacht Harbour
Yat Limanı
Yeşil Cad. (0224) 327 76 79.
8am–5pm Tue–Sun.
In the 1990s, Antalya built a new harbour 10 km (6 miles) west of the city to replace its historic old harbour, which had become overcrowded due to the surge in tourism. The new harbour is also the site of Antalya's fish market. The picturesque old harbour is now used mainly for *gulet* (*see p206*) tours to Rat Island or the waterfalls at Lara. The waterfront is lined with restaurants and is a pleasant place to stroll or people-watch. Antalya's harbour won an award some years ago for its attractive setting, plan and use of resources.

Fluted Minaret
Yivli Minare
A 13th-century minaret dating from the reign of Seljuk Sultan Alaeddin Keykubad (*see p250*), this has become the symbol of Antalya. The red bricks were once decorated with turquoise tiles. The adjoining mosque is still used, and just above is the Fine Arts Gallery, built over a former mosque.

The Fluted Minaret

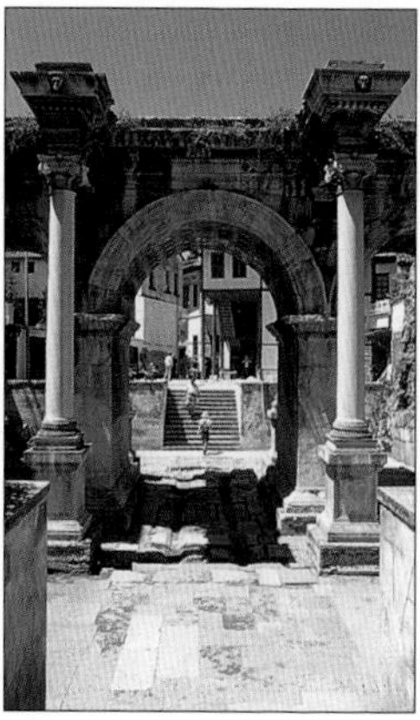

Hadrian's Gate, with the deep wheel ruts clearly visible

🏛 Clock Tower

Saat Kulesi

Cumhuriyet Cad

This local landmark was built in 1244 and marked the upper limit of the Old Town. Its sombre appearance indicates that the tower was once part of the city's defensive system.

🏛 Hadrian's Gate

Hadrian'in Kapısı

Atatürk Cad.

Built to honour the visit of Emperor Hadrian in AD 130, Hadrian's Gate consists of three arched gateways fronted by four Corinthian columns. For years, the structure was encased in the Seljuk city wall and was uncovered only in the 1950s. Restoration work has been carried out and the pavement between the arches stripped back to the Roman level, showing clearly the wheel ruts cut into the stone.

🏛 Truncated Minaret

Kesik Minare

Hesapçı Sok.

The Truncated Minaret is the landmark decapitated tower next to the ruins of what has been, variously, a Greek temple, the Church of St Peter and a mosque. The tower was badly damaged by fire in 1851. Various architectural styles, especially on the capitals, give clues to its past. You cannot go inside, as railings surround the site, but it is worth a look.

🌳 Karaalioğlu Park and Hıdırlık Tower

Located on the southeastern side of the harbour, the park has a variety of mature exotic trees in which wild ring-necked parakeets nest. It also has tea gardens with fabulous views over the Gulf of Antalya, Mount Tahtalı and the distant Beydağlar Mountains.

The circular Hıdırlık tower dates from the 2nd century BC, and was a lighthouse in Roman times. Locals linger here to watch the setting sun.

Visitors' Checklist

👥 1,850,000. ✈ Bayındır Intl, 12 km (8 miles) E of city, (0242) 330 36 00. ⛴ from Venice. 🚌 4 km (2.5 miles) N of city centre, (0242) 331 12 50. [D] Doğu Garajı. ℹ Cumhuriyet Cad, (0242) 343 27 60. 🎭 Aspendos Festival (2nd week Jun–1st week Jul), Golden Orange Film Festival (1st week Oct).

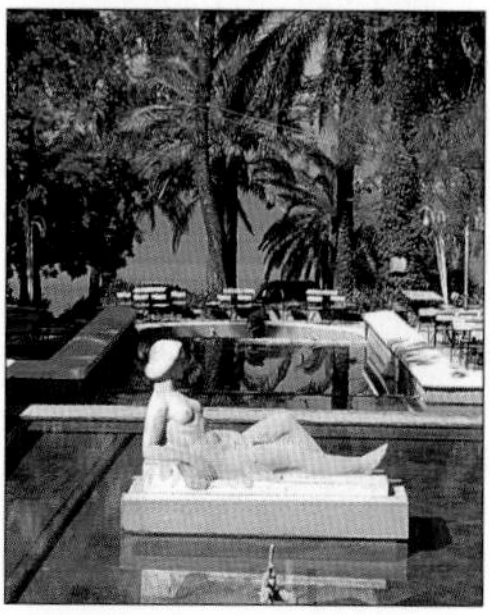

Tea garden beside a reflecting pool in Karaalioğlu Park

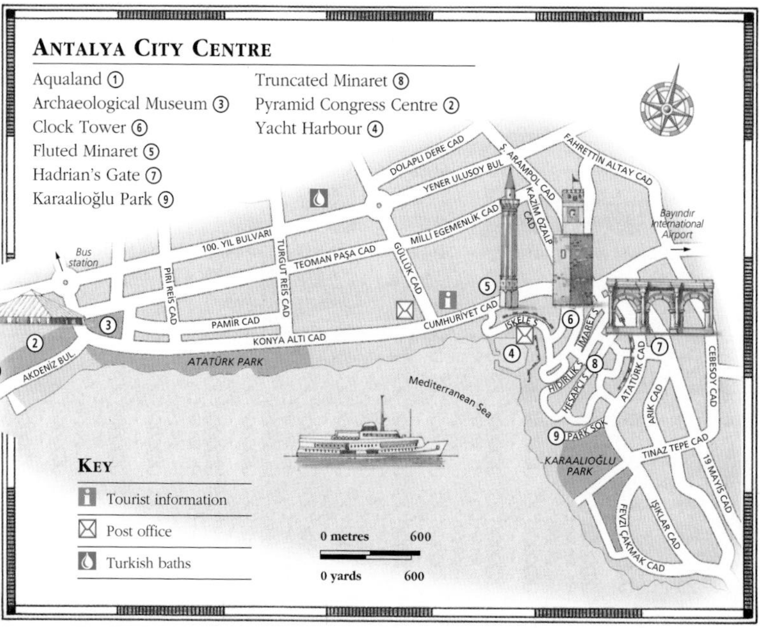
ANTALYA CITY CENTRE
Aqualand 1
Archaeological Museum 3
Clock Tower 6
Fluted Minaret 5
Hadrian's Gate 7
Karaalioğlu Park 9
Truncated Minaret 8
Pyramid Congress Centre 2
Yacht Harbour 4
DOLAPLI DERE CAD
YENER ULUSOY BUL
S. ARAMPOL CAD
KAZIM ÖZALP CAD
FAHRETTIN ALTAY CAD
Bayındır International Airport
MILLI EGEMENLIK CAD
100. YIL BULVARI
Bus station
TEOMAN PAŞA CAD
GÜLLÜK CAD
TURGUT REİS CAD
PIRI REİS CAD
PAMIR CAD
KONYA ALTI CAD
CUMHURIYET CAD
İSKELE S
İMARET S
ATATÜRK PARK
AKDENIZ BUL.
Mediterranean Sea
HIDIRLIK S
HESAPÇI S
ATATÜRK CAD
ARIK CAD
CEBESOY CAD
PARK SOK
KARAALIOĞLU PARK
TINAZ TEPE CAD
19 MAYIS CAD
IŞIKLAR CAD
FEVZI ÇAKMAK CAD
KEY
Tourist information
Post office
Turkish baths
0 metres 600
0 yards 600

Termessos ⑰

35 km (22 miles) NW of Antalya;
9 km (6 miles) off the main road.
◯ 7:30am–7:30pm daily.

Termessos was built by the Solymians in a strategic position on the shipping route to the Aegean. The Greek historian Arrian (around AD 95–180) said of the location that "the two cliffs make a sort of natural gateway so that quite a small force can, by holding the high ground, prevent an enemy from getting through". The city's formidable natural defences convinced Alexander the Great not to attempt to take the city during the 4th century BC.

The main buildings visible today are a theatre, the defensive walls below the gymnasium, the gymnasium itself, the temples of Hadrian and Zeus, an odeon (for musical performances), cisterns in the agora, the stoas (covered walk) of Attalos and Osbaras, and the temple of Artemis. A large necropolis extends upwards as far as a modern fire-watch tower on the hill. You can walk from the gymnasium down to sea level along the old road, ending in a gorge.

Termessos lies in Güllük Dağ National Park, which includes an area for breeding wild goats and deer, and may be the last refuge of the Anatolian lynx. The area is also known for its butterflies.

The remains of the Hellenistic Gate at Perge

Perge ⑱

18 km (11 miles) NE of Antalya.
◯ 9am–7:30pm daily.

Located on the Kestros River (modern-day Aksu), Perge was once a wealthy city. It declined in Byzantine times, and was abandoned in the 7th century. However, it still presents an impressive sight. The theatre is currently undergoing restoration: its frieze of Neptune with sea creatures can be seen in the Archaeological Museum in Antalya (see p218). The huge stadium is largely intact.

A pair of Hellenistic towers marks the entry to the city. The towers front a courtyard with a fountain. On the left, baths with hypocaust (underfloor heating) systems face a colonnaded agora. A water channel leads from a second fountain on the acropolis hill

into a channel down the centre of the columned main street, an arrangement that helped to cool the air in summer. Plancia Magna, the city's benefactress, was buried outside the walls; a marble statue of her is in the Antalya Archaeological Museum.

Selge ⑲

105 km (65 miles) NE of Antalya.
◯ daily.

The village now occupying the site gives no idea of the former importance of Selge. Founded by Calchas of Argos (who also founded Perge), it was the first Pisidian city to mint coins, in the 5th century BC. Coins from Selge were used until the 5th century AD. The classical geographer Strabo cites olives, wine and medicinal plants as sources of revenue. Selge seldom features in classical histories, but we know from the Greek historian Polybius that, in 218 BC, when Selge was at war with the city of Pednelissos, it was able to field an army of 20,000 men. Selge was defeated in this war and had to pay tribute to its enemy. However, it regained prosperity and independence and flourished, especially in the 2nd century AD.

Visible today are a theatre, a stadium, a large temple to Zeus, a smaller one to Artemis, and a cistern. The site, with its spectacular mountain surroundings and cool air, is now part of the Köprülü Çayı National Park.

The theatre at Termessos, with seating for more than 4,000 people

Aspendos ⑳

Carving on theatre seat

ASPENDOS, LOCATED ON the Euromedion River (now the Köprülü River), was once the easternmost city of the kingdom of Pergamum *(see pp176–7)*. In Roman times it became an important trading centre. Today, its main attraction is a beautifully preserved Roman theatre, built in around AD 162 by the architect Zeno. The structure is enclosed by a stage building that once had a timber canopy. The theatre hosts the annual Aspendos Opera and Ballet Festival (mid-June–early July). Aspendos also has a remarkable aqueduct, and numerous remains.

VISITORS' CHECKLIST

50 km (31 miles) E of Antalya.
☐ 8am– 7pm (summer);
8:30am–5pm (winter) daily.
● early closing (4pm) for
festival performances (Jun).
☐ in Belkıs village.
♿ ground level only.

Arched Gallery
Running right round the top of the theatre, the restored gallery provided patrons with an all-weather vantage point.

★ **Theatre**
The theatre, which can seat 12,000, was maintained by the Seljuks and traces of 13th-century paint still adorn the stage building.

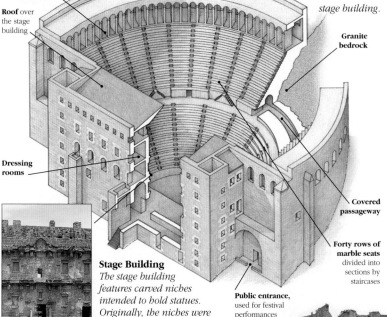

Roof over the stage building

Granite bedrock

Dressing rooms

Covered passageway

Forty rows of marble seats divided into sections by staircases

Stage Building
The stage building features carved niches intended to hold statues. Originally, the niches were separated by columns.

Public entrance, used for festival performances today

★ **Aqueduct**
The aqueduct, built in around AD 100 by the architect Tiberius Claudius Italicus, incorporated a 1-km (0.5-mile) siphon system.

STAR FEATURES

★ **Aqueduct**

★ **Theatre**

Side ㉔

T HE CLASSICAL GEOGRAPHER STRABO tells us that Side (whose name means pomegranate) was settled by Greek colonists from Aeolia, near Smyrna (modern İzmir), in the 7th century BC. In the 2nd century BC, Side became a centre for pirates, who made large profits from slave trading. Under the Romans, it remained an important slave market. Excavations have shown that the city was burned by Arab raiders in the 7th century, but it revived under the Seljuks. During the 1920s, Side was resettled by Muslims returning from Crete.

Statue of Hercules

The partially reconstructed Temple of Apollo

∩ Temples of Apollo and Athena

At sunset, the marble columns and re-erected pediments of the temples of Apollo and Athena frame superb views of the Gulf of Antalya. Around the temples is a basilica, built later in a contrasting rough aggregate stone. The Medusa heads of the friezes date from the 2nd century AD.

∩ Theatre

⏱ 9am–10pm daily (later in summer).
🎟 at theatre, grants entrance to the whole site, reduction after 5pm.

Almost entirely freestanding, Side's large theatre was built on arches over Hellenistic foundations during the 2nd century AD. The lower seats are partially supported by the hillside, but the upper seats rest entirely on huge arches.

This was the largest theatre in Pamphylia, and could hold 17,000 spectators. There are 29 rows of seats above and 29 below the main lateral aisle. Changes to the structure of

The tranquil harbour, cradled by the remains of ancient breakwaters

Exploring Side

The busy resort of Side is an ideal place to take in ancient ruins, beaches and shopping without venturing too far afield. It is a haven for shoppers, with its leather, jewellery and souvenir stores and many bars and eateries in summer. Pedestrianization, the small pensions and quaint, family-run facilities have enabled the town to retain its "village" charm. Its monuments lend discipline and historic value to the narrow streets.

⊞ Harbour

Side occupies a peninsula that terminates in a small harbour. The remains of moles built in antiquity are visible in places offshore. From here, you can take a luxurious boat trip up the Manavgat River (Melas in ancient times), see a waterfall and a stop for some lunch at a trout restaurant.

GOLFING IN BELEK

Between Side and Antalya lies the purpose-built golfing resort of Belek. Here, there are four 18-hole courses, all beautifully landscaped through mature pine forests and offering considerable contrast, ranging from a links course to one set amid lakes and huge trees. The Belek courses operate in close partnership with excellent five-star hotels and have golf professionals who speak a variety of languages. The Mediterranean region's mild winter and early spring make this the most attractive time to visit. Several tournaments are held here each year.

Typical landscaped golf course

Waterfall on the Manavgat River, upstream from the town

◁ Ölü Deniz, with its curving beach and a *gulet* (wooden yacht) in the foreground

The large Roman theatre, built on Hellenistic foundations

remains of Roman shops leading to the main street. A local tractor pulls an open bus, saving visitors the walk from the bus station.

the building permitted the orchestra pit to be flooded in order to enact naval dramas. The stage building had two storeys, decorated, as at Perge (see p220), with friezes of the story of Dionysus. These are currently being displayed in the nearby agora or museum garden while restoration work is carried out on them.

🏛 Vespasian Monument, Arch and Colonnaded Street

The arched gateway that marks the entrance to Side from its neighbour, Manavgat, blocks most vehicular traffic. Next to the arch is a fountain adorned with carved basins, dedicated to the Emperor Vespasian. From here runs a colonnaded street lined with plain granite columns and the

🏛 Museum in Roman Bathhouse

((0242) 753 10 06. ◯ 9am–12pm & 1:30–6:30pm (5pm in winter) Tue–Sun. ☑

The museum occupies a charming setting – the largest of Side's baths – and includes a number of superb marble sarcophagi, a trio of statues known as the Three Graces and another statue showing Hercules holding the golden apples of the Hesperides. There are also elegant portrait heads and tiny carvings that include a house complete with dog peering around the door. The garden features a cupola with maze decoration and many friezes.

The Vespasian Monument, with a carved pediment and inscription

VISITORS' CHECKLIST

🏙 22,000. ✈ Antalya, 70 km (43 miles) NE of Side. 🚌 on main coast road in Manavgat, 2 km (1 mile) E of main entrance. ℹ Side Yolu Üzeri, Manavgat, (0242) 753 12 65. ♦ Sat.

The Three Graces, Museum in Roman Bathhouse

🏛 Aqueduct, Nymphaeum and City Walls

The Romans installed an impressive water-supply system. Outside the main gate was a nymphaeum (ornamental fountain), which was fed by a two-storey aqueduct running on arches for 30 km (19 miles) from the Melas (now the Manavgat) River. Clay pipes were used to distribute water to homes from the city cisterns.

Outside the massive Roman city walls are necropoli, with examples of temple tombs.

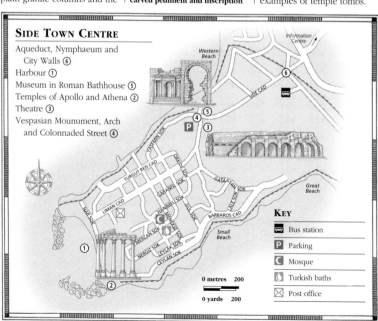

SIDE TOWN CENTRE

Aqueduct, Nymphaeum and City Walls ⑥
Harbour ①
Museum in Roman Bathhouse ⑤
Temples of Apollo and Athena ②
Theatre ③
Vespasian Monument, Arch and Colonnaded Street ④

Information Centre

Western Beach

SIDE CAD

⑥

⑤
④
③

P

YASEMİN SOK

ERENLER CAD

TURGUT REİS CAD

GARANFİL SOK

BRİTOL SOK

GACLAYAN SOK

TALİ SOK

Great Beach

NUR SOK

LİMAN CAD

HANIMELİ SOK

MERCAN SOK

GÜL SOK

BARBAROS CAD

Small Beach

NERGİS SOK

LALE SOK

LEYLAN SOK

CEYLAN SOK

①

②

0 metres 200
0 yards 200

KEY

🚌 Bus station

P Parking

C Mosque

⬙ Turkish baths

⊠ Post office

The Red Tower, dominating the harbour at Alanya

Alanya ㉒

🏃 110,000. ✈ 3 km (2 miles) W of city centre. ℹ Damlataş Cad 1 (near the cave), (0242) 513 12 40. 🎭 Wed & Fri. 🎫 International Triathlon (Sep).

THE PROMONTORY and castle of Alanya are visible for miles and offer superb views of beaches and mountains. Now a large modern resort, in Roman times Alanya was called Coracesium, and was a stronghold of the pirates who menaced the grain fleets on their passage to Rome. After the defeat of the pirates in 65 BC, Coracesium became a thriving city. The Seljuk ruler, Alaeddin I Keykubad, made Alanya his winter residence and fortified it heavily.

A double line of defensive walls mount the promontory to enclose the Citadel (Kale), inside which is a Byzantine church. Punctuated by towers and gates, the walls are still in good condition. It takes about an hour to walk to the top, but there is an hourly bus service.

The harbour is commanded by the 35-m-high (115-ft) Red Tower (Kızılkule), a hexagonal structure built by Alaeddin Keykubad I in 1226 and now restored. The Red Tower protected Alanya's strategic dock-yard, or *tersane*, which could accommodate five ships under construction at once. In Seljuk times, the plentiful local forests provided ample timber for shipbuilding and even for export.

The garden of the **museum** has a collection of farming tools as well as items from Pamphylian sites in the area. A Phoenician inscription from the 6th century BC shows the development of lettering from its cuneiform origins.

Atatürk visited Alanya for a few days in 1935. The owner of the house where he stayed turned it into a museum. The ground floor has photographs and Atatürk memorabilia, and the upper floor displays the furniture of a typical Alanya house in Republican times.

There are several caves around the base of the cliffs, including a phosphorus cave, a pirate cave and a lovers' cave. The best known is the stalactite-hung **Damlataş Cave**, said to provide relief from asthma. The internal temperature registers a steady 23°C (73°F). Access is from the western beach, behind the Damlataş restaurant.

🏛 Museum
Hilmi Balcı Cad, Damlataş Cad.
📞 (0242) 513 12 28 and 513 71 16.
🕐 9am–noon & 1:30–6:30pm. 🎫
🛖 Damlataş Cave
Damlataş Mağarası
🕐 6–10am for spa patients & 10am–7pm for the public. 🎫

ENVIRONS: Near Ehmedek, a village where local women sell silk and lace handicrafts, is a *bedesten* (trading hall) converted into a hotel, with high-arched rooms around a courtyard. There is a pool, a vaulted hall and cisterns below. Nearby is the restored 16th-century Süleymaniye Mosque and a 13th-century *türbe* (tomb).

Anamur and Anemurium ㉓

110 km (68 miles) SE of Alanya. 🚌 on the coast road. ℹ at the bus station.

THE TOWN OF ANAMUR is bisected by the D400 coastal road, with the town centre to the north and the harbour to the south. There are good beaches and important turtle nesting sites here, and more to see at ancient Anemurim, located on a coastal headland – the southernmost tip of Turkey – west of the modern town.

Anemurim ("Place of the Winds"), first noted by the classical geographer Strabo (63 BC–AD 23), was founded in the 1st century AD, and thrived under the Byzantines. It was battered by an earth-quake in around 580, and after the Arabs took Cyprus in 649, the city became vulnerable and was abandoned. It was never resettled, so many of the old Roman and Byzantine houses and tombs remain in good condition, particularly the mosaics and frescoes.

ENVIRONS: On the coast road 2 km (1 mile) east of Anamur lies **Mamure Castle**, known to locals as "Marble Castle". Built over a Byzantine fort, the castle was occupied by the Crusaders. Rebuilt by Alaeddin Keykubad I, it was used by the Karamanoğlu dynasty and garrisoned by the Ottomans. Today, the fortress is often used as a film set.

⌂ Mamure Castle
Mamure Kalesi
🕐 9am–5:30pm daily. 🎫

The large baths complex at Anemurium

The Crusades in Turkey

MEDITERRANEAN TURKEY is closely associated with the impact of the Crusades – the military campaigns mounted from the late 11th century onwards, in order to wrest the Holy Land from Muslim control.

The crusader armies marched through Anatolia to reach the Holy Land, capturing cities such as Edessa (Şanlıurfa) and Antioch (Antakya). The period reached its nadir with the sack of Constantinople by a crusader army in 1204 *(see p50)*.

The military orders – the Knights Templar, Hospitaller Knights of St John and the Teutonic Order – were active all along the coast. The most prominent symbol of their presence is the Castle of St Peter at Bodrum *(see p196–7)*.

A crusader knight

COASTAL FORTRESSES

Mamure Castle, near Anamur, is one of the best-preserved crusader castles on the southern coast of Turkey. The Ottomans expanded the castle and used it until 1921.

The 36 towers are still intact.

Crenellated walls

The castle is surrounded on three sides by the sea.

Shallow moat

Great Court

Death of Friedrich II
The Holy Roman Emperor drowned near Silifke in 1290. Silifke itself was held by the Knights of St John in 1211–66.

The Siege of Antioch 1095
Captured from the Seljuks during the First Crusade after a seven-month siege, Antioch (Antakya) became the seat of the Principality of Antioch, one of the three main Crusader kingdoms. It fell to the Mamelukes in 1284.

Insignia of the Templar order

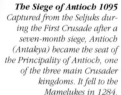

The Capture of Rhodes
After taking Rhodes in 1310, the Knights of St John moved operations to Smyrna (now İzmir) in 1344. When Smyrna was lost to the Mongols, the knights moved down the coast to Bodrum.

The Knights Templar
The order was active in the Amanus Mountains and around Antioch (Antakya). The knights safeguarded the route into Syria.

The Knights of St John
The crests of English, French and German crusaders are carved into the walls of the Castle of St Peter at Bodrum.

Grand Master of the Teutonic Knights
The Teutonic Order held castles in Cilicia, in the Crusader-aligned Kingdom of Lesser Armenia (1198–1375).

Corinthian columns of the Temple of Zeus Olbia at Uzuncaburç

Silifke ㉔

🏠 *105,000.* 🚌 *İnönü Cad.*
ℹ️ *Göksu Mahallesi, Gürten
Bozbey Cad 6, (0324) 714 11 51.*
⚫ *weekends.* 🎭 *Folklore and
Culture Festival (3rd week in May).*

FOUNDED AS SELEUCIA by one
of Alexander the Great's
generals, Silifke lies on an
important route to Konya and
the interior by way of the
Göksu River valley. A temple
of Jupiter, with its surviving
columns topped by stork's
nests, a Byzantine cistern and
a Roman bridge can still be
seen today. St Paul passed
through here, and Thecla, his
disciple, founded an underground church about 5 km
(3 miles) east of Silifke. This
is currently being restored. A
Byzantine castle is accessible
from the Konya road and,
9 km (6 miles) to the north,
is a monument that points to
where the Holy Roman
Emperor Frederick Barbarossa
drowned on 10 June 1190
while attempting to ford the
deep Göksu River during the
Third Crusade.

Silifke Museum, 1 km
(0.5 mile) west of the town,
houses the Gülnür hoard, a
superb collection of 5,200
silver and gold coins dating
from the reign of Alexander
the Great.

🏛 Silifke Museum
Taşucu Cad. ☎ *(0324) 714 10 19.*
⏰ *8am–noon & 1:30–5pm Tue–Sun.*
♿

ENVIRONS: At **Uzuncaburç**,
about 28 km (17 miles) north
of Silifke, lie the remains of
an impressive Roman city.
Inhabited from Hittite times,
the city was called Olba by
the Greeks and Diocaesarea
by the Romans.

Beside the road are several
temple tombs, complete with
sarcophagi, which are worth a
look. The centrepiece is the
Temple of Zeus, with about
30 massive peristyle columns.
However, the walls of the
cella (which would have
enclosed the statue of Zeus)
were removed when the
building was converted into a
church. Other sights include a
charming Greek theatre and
two city gates. Also worth
exploring are a Hellenistic
tower, the necropolis and a
pyramid-roofed mausoleum.
Apple orchards and fig trees
surround the ruins today.

⋔ Uzuncaburç
⏰ *9am–6pm daily.* 🏞 🛗 🚻

**The romantic sea castle, off the
coast near Kızkalesi**

Kızkalesi ㉕

KIZKALESI IS SITUATED where
the narrow coastal strip
opens out onto the Çukurova
plain. Its chief landmarks are
two castles, one on the shore,
and its sister, 200 m (656 ft)
out to sea. Local fishermen
will ferry you over to explore
the ruins. The 12th-century
castle on the shore was built
on the ancient site of Korykos
from the stones of Greek and
Roman buildings preceding it.

In the early 19th century, a
lighthouse marked the end of
a mole leading from the sea
castle, which lay on an island.
Legend has it that a jealous
father confined his daughter
to this sea-bound castle, but

BIRDS OF THE GÖKSU DELTA

South of the main coast road near Silifke, where the Göksu
River reaches the sea, 145 sq km (56 sq miles) have been
designated as a region of outstanding environmental
importance. The two lagoons are home to migrating and
permanently residing water birds, including Dalmatian
pelicans, pygmy cormorants, marbled and white-headed
ducks, ospreys and terns.
The marshlands provide
food for wagtails, egrets
spoonbills and squacco,
grey and purple heron.
The best times to see the
birds are at dawn and
dusk in spring and
autumn. Bird-watchers
need their own transport
to tour the delta, which
is also an important
nesting area for logger-
head and green turtles.

Nesting storks, Göksu Delta

the fortress was more likely built for protection from the Mediterranean's fierce pirates.

Three km (2 miles) east of Kızkalesi are the ruins of **Elaiussa Sebaste**, bisected by the main road. The area around the theatre is under excavation by an Italian team. There is a Byzantine church and harbour buildings to the south of the road. The town must have been important in classical times, for no less than three aqueducts and numerous reservoirs were built to supply it with water. Four km (3 miles) further along the coast is Kanlıdivane ("Place of Blood"), a huge chasm 60 m (197 ft) deep, into which prisoners were thrown to their deaths. There are several churches and a Hellenistic tower around the the chasm, which features carvings in niches in the side, and has become a haven for local wildlife. From this point onwards, the coast abounds in ancient ruins, although the population is sparse until you reach the holiday villages associated with Mersin.

⋔ Elaiussa Sebaste
◯ 9am–6pm daily. ⬚

Mersin (İçel) ㉖

🏚 750,000. 🚌 NE of city centre (service buses from train station). 🚉 (0324) 238 32 71. 🚏 İstiklal Cad NE of city centre, (0324) 238 16 48. ⛴ Near tourist office in the harbour area. 🛈 İsmet İnönü Bul 5, (0324) 238 32 71.

Mersin is a harbour city with relatively few tourist attractions. The main reason to stay here is to catch a ferry to Northern Cyprus. Accommodation is plentiful and restaurants varied, with good fish and fast food. Mersin's **museum** has recently been renovated and contains local archaeological remains.

Mersin means "myrtle" in Turkish, referring to the shrub found all along the coast. The city's new official name is İçel (the name of the province of which it is the capital).

Compared to other Turkish cities, Mersin is fairly young,

The spectacular Selale Waterfall on the Tarsus River, outside Tarsus

and was first incorporated in 1852, with a cosmopolitan population of Turks, Greeks and Armenians. The Turkish government had plans to turn Mersin into a strategic port, but this never happened.

In 1989, the government initiated a housing scheme here for nomads displaced by ethnic fighting in the eastern provinces. But the transition to city life has been hard for these people, and many remain jobless. Mersin has the transient feel of a port, which many believe stems from the city not having enjoyed the benefits of a structured Ottoman administration.

About 12 km (8 miles) west of Mersin lie the ruins of Pompeiopolis, where the remains of a harbour and a column-lined street that date from the 2nd century AD survive. In 1812, Captain Francis Beaufort described this street, the city gates, a substantial theatre and a "beautiful harbour with parallel sides and circular ends" as being on the whole so imposing that even "the most illiterate seaman in the ship could not behold it without emotion".

🏛 Mersin Museum
Republic Square, Halkevi Binası.
📞 (0324) 231 96 18. ◯ 9am–noon & 1:30–4:30pm Tue–Sun. ⬚

Tarsus ㉗

🏚 21,300. 🚌 Drop-off point at Cleopatra's Gate. 🚉 from Adana.

Although St Paul is referred to in the Bible as "the man from Tarsus", this does not mean that there is a lot to see in the town. The museum has moved to a new cultural centre, near an excavated portion of the old city. Here, a section of Roman street, complete with stoas (covered walkways), has been exposed to a depth of 2–3 m (6.5–10 ft) below today's street level. In the back streets of the town is a covered well, named after St Paul, which is still a place of pilgrimage.

St Paul's well, Tarsus

Tarsus once controlled the Cilician Gates, a strategic pass through the Taurus Mountains into the Anatolian interior. The route is now bypassed by a new motorway carrying oil tankers and other truck traffic to Ankara and beyond.

Adana ㉘

ADANA IS AN IMPORTANT manufacturing centre, with its origins rooted in commerce and trade. The city lies on the Seyhan River, which is spanned by a Roman bridge. This bridge marks the lowest possible ford over the river, which bisected a crucial extension of the

Shield from the Ethnography Museum

Silk Route through the Cilician Gates. The pass linked the coast with the interior of Anatolia. Adana was ruled by the Arabs, Seljuks, Armenians and Mamelukes until it was captured by the Ottomans in 1515. After World War I it fell into French hands, until the War of Independence *(see p58).*

Exploring Adana

Adana's old quarter includes metal workshops, an 18th-century church and a clock tower. The Roman Stone Bridge, restful park and stunning Central Mosque are all worth visiting, and the city makes a comfortable base if you are travelling further east.

Be sure to sample Adana's speciality kebab, which is made of highly spiced minced meat pressed onto a skewer and grilled. This is served with *şalgam*, a cooling blood-red drink made from carrot and turnip juice, or *aşlama*, a liquorice drink.

🏛 Ethnography Museum

Etnografya Müzesi
İnönü Cad (off Ziyapaşa Bulvarı).
((0322) 363 37 17. **◯** 8:30am–noon & 1:30–5pm Tue–Sun. 🖼
The museum is housed in a former church situated to the west of the old town, and

Colourful traditional *kilim* (rug) in the Ethnography Museum

includes a reconstruction of an old Adana house. There is a collection of ceremonial weaponry and firearms, while the displays of copper kitchenware illustrate a prominent local trade. Tents, carpets and textiles complete the display.

The Archaeological Museum, with local finds displayed outside

🏛 Archaeological Museum

Adana Müzesi
Fuzuli Sok 10. **(** (0322) 454 38 55.
◯ 8:30am–noon & 1:30–5pm (5:30pm in summer) Tue–Sun.
🖼 👪
The museum contains objects from excavations of local late-Hittite sites, as well as Hellenistic and Roman remains from in and around the city. A highlight is the natural crystal figure of a Hittite god, Tarhunda, clad in a pointed hat, together with Eastern Anatolian Urartian belts from around 600 BC.

There is also a gold and silver ram-headed bracelet and a gold ring bearing the head of a woman. The fine Achilleus marble sarcophagus, from the 2nd century AD, has lively battle scenes; another sarcophagus is adorned with standing draped women. A Roman mosaic shows animals listening to lyre music.

☪ Sabancı Central Mosque

Merkez Camii
Fuzuli Cad (near the Roman Stone Bridge). **◯** daily (except during prayer times). 🖼 donation.
Completed in 1998, this is Turkey's largest mosque and rivals most in the Middle East for sheer size. The principal dome is 32 m (105 ft) high. The architectural style of the mosque follows that of the Blue Mosque *(see p88)* in Istanbul and Edirne's Selimiye Mosque *(see p154).* Only the Sabancı and Blue mosques feature the hallowed six minarets. All work on the mosque, down to state-of-the-art wireless acoustics, was carried out by Turkey's most prestigious craftsmen.

The massive Sabancı Central Mosque, with its six minarets

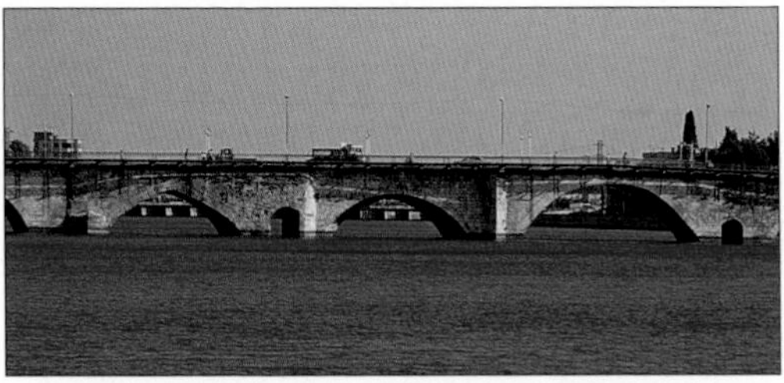

The Roman Stone Bridge, still in use after more than 18 centuries

Roman Stone Bridge

Taş Köprü

The graceful, 14-arch Roman Stone Bridge over the Seyhan River is 319 m (1,056 ft) long. Built in the 2nd century AD, during the reign of Emperor Hadrian, the bridge may be one of the oldest still used by vehicular traffic. It originally had 21 arches, but only 14 of these are visible and in use today. The bridge has been restored several times, first by Emperor Justinian in the 6th century and later under the Ottomans.

[C] Great Mosque

Ulu Camii

Abidinpaşa Cad. 🕒 *daily (except during prayer times).* $ *donation.*

The Great Mosque was built in 1507 by Halil Bey, the emir of the powerful Ramazanoğlu family, who was given lands by the Seljuk sultan, Alp Arslan, after he defeated the Byzantine army at the battle of Manzikert in 1071 *(see p52)*. The bands of black and white stone are a typical feature of Syrian religious architecture. Halil Bey's tomb, inside the mosque, is decorated with tiles made in İznik and Kütahya, as well as mosaics. The eight-cornered minaret is a particularly striking feature.

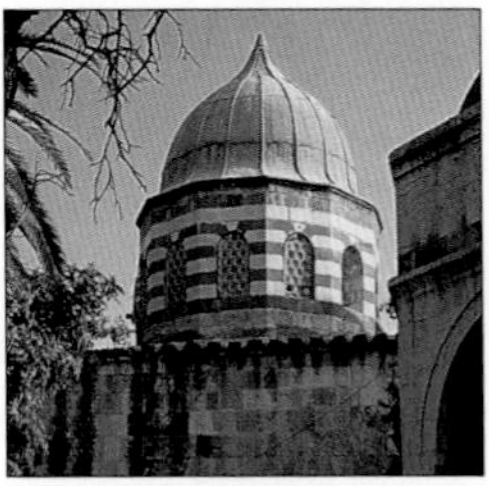

The Great Mosque, decorated with black and white marble

Visitors' Checklist

👥 *2,300,000.* ✈ *Şakirpaşa, 3 km (2 miles) W of city centre.* 🚌 *6 km (4 miles) W of city centre, (0322) 428 20 47.* 🚆 *N end of Ziya Paşa Cad, (0322) 453 31 72.* [D] *Atatürk Cad, Osman Gazi Cad.* ℹ *Atatürk Cad 13, (0322) 363 14 48.* 🎭 *Altın Koza Art and Culture Festival (dates vary annually).* 🛍 *daily.*

🛍 Covered Bazaar

Near the clock tower on Ali Münif Cad. 🕒 *dawn to dusk, daily.*

Adana's medieval-looking clock tower was built in late Ottoman times. It overlooks the Covered Bazaar, where handicrafts, trinkets and food items are sold. Near the Covered Bazaar is the Çarşı Hamamı, a beautiful, domed Turkish bath with an exquisite marble interior. The baths are open to all.

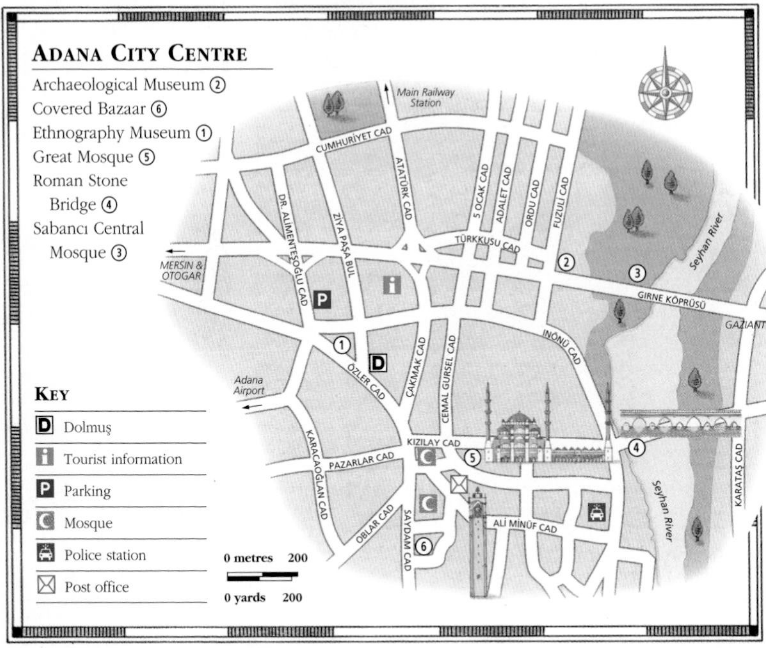
ADANA CITY CENTRE
Archaeological Museum ②
Covered Bazaar ⑥
Ethnography Museum ①
Great Mosque ⑤
Roman Stone Bridge ④
Sabancı Central Mosque ③
Main Railway Station
CUMHURİYET CAD
ATATÜRK CAD
5 OCAK CAD
ADALET CAD
ORDU CAD
FUZULİ CAD
DR. ALİMENTEŞOĞLU CAD
ZİYA PAŞA BUL
TÜRKKUŞU CAD
MERSIN & OTOGAR
GİRNE KÖPRÜSÜ
GAZİANTEP
Seyhan River
İNÖNÜ CAD
ÖZLER CAD
ÇAKMAK CAD
CEMAL GÜRSEL CAD
Adana Airport
KARACAOĞLAN CAD
KIZILAY CAD
PAZARLAR CAD
KARATAŞ CAD
ALİ MÜNİF CAD
OBLAR CAD
SAYDAM CAD
KEY
Dolmuş
Tourist information
Parking
Mosque
Police station
Post office
0 metres 200
0 yards 200

Karatepe **㉙**

KARATEPE is a late Hittite fortress dating from the 9th century BC built on a hill beside the Seyhan River. It was discovered by the German archaeologist H T Bossert in 1946. When Bossert's team excavated the site, they found two entrances. Each was lined with relief carvings and featured an inscription in both ancient Phoenician and Hieroglyphic Hittite. As the

Monumental stone lion

Phoenician language had already been deciphered, this turned out to be a vital clue to the interpretation of the hieroglyphic form of the Hittite language, which was found to be close to Luwian, another ancient Anatolian language.

The pleasant hilltop site, next to a man-made lake, has several picnic areas and is well worth the 70-km (44-mile) drive from Adana.

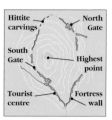

Karatepe Hill *juts into the waters of a lake created by the construction of the Aslantaş Dam. Water from the lake irrigates the fertile farmlands around Adana.*

Hittite carvings — **North Gate**
South Gate — **Highest point**
Tourist centre — **Fortress wall**

KARATEPE FORTRESS

The Karatepe site *is believed to have been the fortified residence of the Hittite king of Adana, Azatiwatas. Entry was through formal gateways, one of which is shown at right. Each was lined with orthostats (carved relief panels). The gateways are now roofed to protect the ancient stonework.*

Orthostat (relief panel)

Carved lion figure

The orthostats *consist of carvings of sacrificial, hunting and feasting scenes. There are numerous figures of gods and sphinxes, interspersed with scenes of ordinary people, all done in a cheerful cartoon style.*

Warrior figure

Relief carvings *at Karatepe show influences from a number of cultures, including Assyria and ancient Egypt. Because of this, archaeologists believe the carvings were executed by foreign craftsmen recruited by King Azatiwatas to work on the site.*

The remains of the theatre at Hierapolis (Castabala)

Hierapolis (Castabala) ③⓪

22 km (14 miles) N of Osmaniye.
◯ 8am–noon & 2–5pm daily.

ON THE ROAD leading to the Hittite site of Karatepe, take some time to see the ancient Roman city of Hierapolis (Castabala) – not to be confused with the other Hierapolis (see pp186–7), near Denizli. Hierapolis (Castabala) was mentioned by the elder Pliny (AD 23–79) around AD 70. There is a colonnaded street, theatre, baths and a hill fortress.

Yakacık ③①

22 km (14 miles) N of İskenderun.
 in the town hall. ◯ 8am–5pm daily.

YAKACIK (ANCIENT PAYAS) is the site of the Sokollu Mehmet Paşa complex. This is not well known, even though the local municipality, which runs the site with great enthusiasm, claims that many thousands of visitors come here each year. The complex features all the amenities beloved by Ottoman travellers – mosque, baths, caravanserai and theological college. The caravanserai was built in 1574 for Muslims making the *haj*

(pilgrimage to Mecca). It was the brainchild of Sokollu Mehmet Paşa, one of the most enlightened grand viziers ever to serve the Ottoman state. A Serb who rose to power from humble beginnings, Sokollu Mehmet Paşa served under three sultans between 1564 and 1579. It was under his initiative that Sultan Selim II (1524–74) seized Cyprus from the Venetians in 1571. However, Selim's fondness for the island's wine earned him the nickname of "the Sot" and proved to be his undoing, as

Massive Atatürk memorial statue on the promenade at İskenderun

he allegedly slipped in the bath while inebriated and never regained consciousness.

İskenderun ③②

 166,000. Atatürk Cad, (0326) 616 36 31. İstasyon Cad, (0326) 614 00 49. İskele Cad, (0326) 613 54 00. Atatürk Bulvarı 49/B, (0326) 614 16 20. İskenderun Culture and Fine Arts Week (1st week in Jul).

THE CITY of İskenderun, (formerly Alexandretta), was originally founded to commemorate Alexander the Great's victory over Persian emperor Darius at the Battle of Issus in 332 BC (see pp46–7). It was a major trading centre in Roman times, and is still an important port. The people of İskenderun are proud of their multicultural city and of its remaining Christian and Jewish communities. The surviving Armenian, Catholic, and Orthodox churches are hidden in the backstreets, along with mosques. None are particularly old, but all will welcome visitors on Sundays. The promenade, with its attractive French colonial architecture, is a favourite place for an evening stroll.

Antakya ③

Mosaic in the Archaeological Museum

ANTAKYA WAS FOUNDED (as Antioch) by the Seleucids in 300 BC, and was their capital. Later, it became the third-largest city of the Roman Empire, and an important Christian centre. Antioch was devastated by earthquakes in the 6th century and fell into Arab hands in 628. Although recaptured by the Byzantines, its role was gradually displaced by the rise of Constantinople. In 1098, Antakya was captured by the Crusaders after a seven-month siege, and became capital of the Principality of Antioch. It passed to the Mamelukes in 1268 and the Ottomans in 1516, and eventually slipped into decline.

Exploring Antakya

Antakya is located on the Asi (Orontes) River. After World War I, it was part of French-ruled Syria until a plebiscite in 1939 (*see p59*) returned it to Turkey, together with the rest of the Hatay Province. The city's mixed population, Arab cultural influence and vestiges of French colonial rule give Antakya a distinct character. You are likely to hear Arabic spoken, and many local dishes, such as *şam oruğu*, a wheaten ball filled with minced meat and walnuts, have Arabic origins.

The Grotto where St Peter preached to the early Christians

∩ St Peter's Grotto

🕐 9am–noon & 1:30–6:30pm (flexible for group tours) Tue–Sun.

This cave church is thought to have been founded by St Luke. It is named, however, after Peter, who was in the forefront of the early church movement from his headquarters in Antioch. Rebuilt by the Crusaders, it is partially floored with mosaic, and the remains of frescoes can be seen. A tiny spring in the church was used for baptisms. The church was repaired in the 19th century by Capuchin monks, who are now its custodians. A festival is held here annually on 29 June.

Near the church is a relief portrait carved into the hillside. This is thought by some to be a representation of Charon, the boatman who conveyed the dead to Hades. However, the image is more likely to be that of a member of the Seleucid dynasty, founders of the city.

Two other churches are still functioning in the city. One is a Capuchin chapel on Kurtuluş Caddesi, the other a Greek Orthodox church near the Rana Bridge.

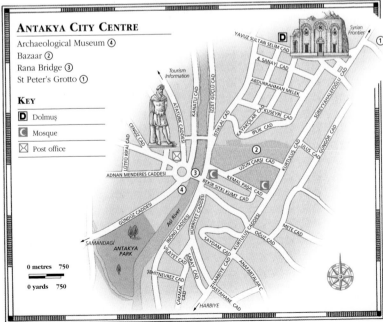

ANTAKYA CITY CENTRE

Archaeological Museum ④
Bazaar ②
Rana Bridge ③
St Peter's Grotto ①

KEY

D Dolmuş
C Mosque
⊠ Post office

0 metres 750
0 yards 750

A cobbler at his work bench in the Bazaar

Bazaar

🕐 9am–9/10pm Mon–Sat.

A warren of streets to the east of the Rana Bridge houses Antakya's bazaar. Here, you can see *hans* (warehouses) dating from Ottoman times, in which skilled metalworkers are hard at work. Donkeys are a common sight in the streets around the bazaar, and the aroma of exotic foods fills the air. The line of shops facing the Rana Bridge sell *künefe*, a pudding made of cream cheese and spun wheat, all in a honey sauce and served piping hot. This is only one of the local specialities to be savoured in the city. Many restaurants are in the bazaar.

Habibi Neccar Camii is a mosque converted from a Byzantine church, which itself succeeded a classical temple. The minaret was added in the 17th century. It is a place of pilgrimage in honour of a local saint, whose head is reputedly buried beneath it.

Rana Bridge

Antakya is bisected by the Asi River (known as the Orontes in ancient times, when it was a major focus of settlement). The two halves of the city are joined by the Rana Bridge, built by the Romans during the 3rd century AD. Near this landmark lies the site of the Golden Oratory church, built by Emperor Constantine I (in around AD 280–337).

VISITORS' CHECKLIST

🏠 150,000. 🚌 *Abdürrahman Melek Cad, NE of town centre, (0326) 214 91 97.* 🛈 *Saray Caddesi, Vilâyet Binası, 4 Kat, (0326) 216 06 10.* 🎭 *St Peter's Catholic Church Festival (29 Jun).* 🎪 *Mon–Sat.*

🏛 Archaeological Museum

Gündüz Cad 1. 📞 *(0326) 214 61 68.* 🕐 *8:30am–noon & 1:30–5pm (8am–noon & 1:30–6pm in winter) Tue–Sun.* 🌐 *www.hatayarkeolojimuzesi.com*

This museum was originally built by the French to store finds unearthed by foreign excavations when the Hatay Province was part of the French protectorate of Syria.

Today, the museum houses an impressive collection of Roman mosaics, surpassed only by the finds at Gaziantep recovered from Zeugma (*see p307*). The Antakya mosaics were found all over the province, though many come from the ancient pleasure gardens of Daphne (modern-day Harbiye). Executed in a lively, libertine style, the mosaics portray the deeds of Thetis, Orpheus, Dionysus, Hercules and other mythical figures. The museum also has a coin collection, displays of palaeolithic objects and Hittite sculptures from Carchemish and other sites in northern Syria. The nearby park is a peaceful refuge from the city.

Statue in the Archaeological Museum

ENVIRONS: South of Antakya lies **Harbiye**, famed for its forests of cypress and laurel, and for its waterfalls and trout streams. In antiquity, the valley was known as Daphne, after the mythical "queen of the nymphs" pursued by Apollo, and was a popular resort. However, the ruins of the temple to Apollo and the ancient pleasure gardens have all disappeared. Reachable by dolmuş from Antakya, there are several good restaurants here, and local gift shops sell the popular laurel soap.

Samandağı 🈠

25 km (15 miles) SW of Antakya.
🚌 *local dolmuş from Antakya.*

SOUTHWEST OF Antakya lies Samandağı, a modest, largely Arabic-speaking resort town near the border, where you will feel that you have already entered Syria. There are a couple of hotels and seaside restaurants along the somewhat scruffy beach.

North of the town is the site of Seleucia ad Piera (modern-day Çevlik), founded as the port of Antioch in around 300 BC. This was the site of an important temple to Zeus, which still stands above the coast and affords grand views over the sea.

Because ancient Antioch lay at the junction of important trading routes, Seleucia ad Piera became a major port, but the danger posed by the region's periodic but devastating floods led Emperor Vespasian to commission a tunnel to divert floodwaters from the town. The **Titus Tunnel** (Titus ve Vespasianyus Tüneli), completed by Vespasian's son, Titus, is an impressive cutting running 1,300 m (4,265 ft) through solid rock. The tunnel is 7 m (23 ft) high and 6 m (20 ft) wide.

Titus Tunnel

25 km (16 miles) SE of Antakya.
🕐 *daily.* 🎫 *Only in summer.*

The Titus Tunnel, a flood-control project built by the Romans

ANKARA AND WESTERN ANATOLIA

ANKARA, THE BUSTLING CAPITAL *of Turkey, can appear rather soulless and cold in its modernity as it rises from the plains of Western Anatolia. When Atatürk chose it as his capital in the 1920s, his determination to westernize led him to commission the German architect, Hermann Jansen, to build a thoroughly new city. Today, most tourists visit Ankara for its outstanding museums.*

No doubt the most fascinating sight in Ankara is the superb Museum of Anatolian Civilizations, housing the greatest collection of Hittite antiquities in the world. The Hittite civilization flourished in central Anatolia during the second millennium BC, and for some time their empire almost rivalled that of ancient Egypt. The exquisite relief carvings and statues conjure up an intriguing picture of a civilization about which relatively little is known. Also worthy of a visit is the impressive Atatürk Mausoleum, the great leader's enduring symbol of immortality.

The western approach to Ankara winds over monochrome, flat, steppe country. Near Polatlı – the easternmost point reached by Greek forces in 1922 during the War of Independence – lies Gordion, capital of the ancient kingdom of Phrygia and seat of the legendary King Midas. The more picturesque route runs northwest from Ankara through the forests and mineral springs of Kızılcahamam National Park.

Much of the area encompassed by Eşkişehir and Afyon is inhospitable and forbidding. By comparison, the Lake District forms a welcome oasis with an abundance of birds attracted by its reeds and marshlands. Lake Eğirdir is an unspoiled resort area.

Kütahya owes its existence to an illustrious tile-making tradition on which the town still relies today.

Konya is the cultural gem of Western Anatolia. Its Seljuk architecture and the impressive Mevlâna Museum, home of the whirling dervish sect, make it one of the country's most visited sights. Konya's Karatay Museum houses an important tile collection.

Sunflowers thrive on the rolling Anatolian plain

◁ **Anıtkabir, Atatürk's colossal Mausoleum in Ankara**

Exploring Ankara and Western Anatolia

WESTERN ANATOLIA may seem somewhat bleak and inhospitable, yet the vast steppes, remote towns and salt lakes have much to offer the visitor. This is also where Turkey's administrative heart beats. Ankara, the efficient modern capital, has excellent transport links to the rest of the country and is a good starting point for tours of the region. Southeast of the pious city of Konya, former capital of the Seljuk Sultanate of Rum, lies the Bronze-Age site of Çatalhöyük, widely regarded as the world's earliest urban settlement.

Houses painted in pastel shades, Afyon

SIGHTS AT A GLANCE

Afyon **6**
Ankara pp240–47 **1**
Beyşehir **4**
Çatalhöyük **3**
Çavdarhisar **11**
Eğirdir **5**
Eskişehir **9**
Konya pp250–253 **2**
Kütahya pp258–9 **10**
Şehitgazi Valley **8**
Sivrihisar **7**

KEY

≡ Motorway

▬ Major road

▬ Secondary road

▬ Other road

▬ Scenic route

~ River

☼ Viewpoint

Sunset at tranquil Lake Eğirdir

0 kilometres   50

0 miles   25

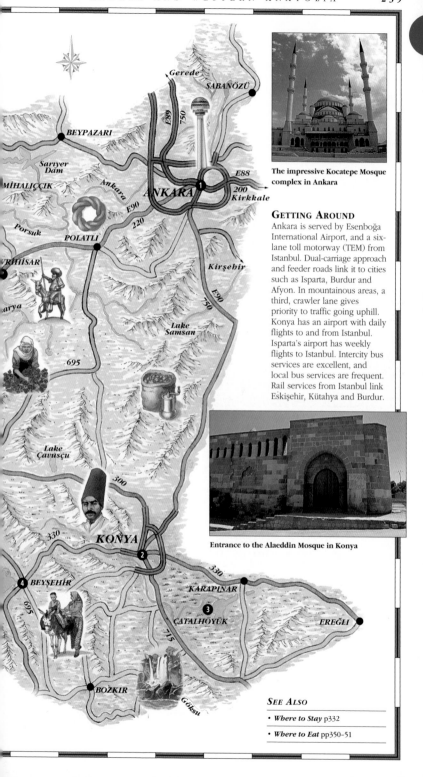

The impressive Kocatepe Mosque complex in Ankara

GETTING AROUND

Ankara is served by Esenboğa International Airport, and a six-lane toll motorway (TEM) from Istanbul. Dual-carriage approach and feeder roads link it to cities such as Isparta, Burdur and Afyon. In mountainous areas, a third, crawler lane gives priority to traffic going uphill. Konya has an airport with daily flights to and from Istanbul. Isparta's airport has weekly flights to Istanbul. Intercity bus services are excellent, and local bus services are frequent. Rail services from Istanbul link Eskişehir, Kütahya and Burdur.

Entrance to the Alaeddin Mosque in Konya

SEE ALSO

- *Where to Stay* p332

- *Where to Eat* pp350–51

Ankara ❶

ANKARA, the modern capital of the Turkish Republic, occupies a strategic location on the east–west route across the Anatolian steppe. Believed to have been the site of a Hittite city, there is evidence of Phrygian settlement here in 1200 BC, when it was known as Ancyra. The city was occupied by the Lydians and Persians before its absorption into the Roman Empire in 24 BC. Annexed by the Seljuks in 1073, the city played a military and commercial role until Byzantine times. At this time, wool from the Angora (Ankara) goat became a major export. When Atatürk chose Ankara as the new capital in 1923, land values boomed and developments spread out across the surrounding hills.

Hittite bronze deer

View of Ankara, a modern capital with attractive, wide boulevards

Exploring Ankara

A new metro, state theatres and good museums combine with lush parks and good shopping in the Ulus/Hisar district to ensure a pleasant visit. Buses and dolmuşes cover the main routes in the city.

↑ Roman Baths
Hamamları
Çankırı Cad, Ulus. 📞 (0312) 310 72 80. 🚌 Ulus. ⏰ 8:30am–12:30pm & 1:30–5:30pm daily. 🎫
Very little remains to be seen of these 3rd-century Roman baths. With the trademark features of *frigidarium* (cold room), *tepidarium* (warm room) and *caldarium* (hot room), these baths were built to honour Asclepius, the Greek god of medicine.

↑ Temple of Augustus and Rome
Augustus Tapınağı
Ulus. 🚌 Ulus. ⏰ daily.
This temple was built in about 20 BC by King Pylamenes of Galatia to honour a visit by the great Roman emperor, Augustus. The inscription on the outer walls is one of the few surviving testaments to authenticate Augustus's accomplishments. The temple became a Byzantine church in the 4th century AD.

Adjoining the temple are the mosque (dating from 1425) and tomb of **Hacı Bayram Veli** (1352–1429), founder of the Bayrami religious sect. The fine Seljuk wooden interior, in particular, is worth seeing. Some renovation work was done in the 17th century by the famous architect Mimar Sinan (*see p101*).

Nearby is the **Column of Julian**, reaching 15 m (49 ft) and dating from AD 362. The column commemorates a visit by this Roman emperor.

🕌 Hacı Bayram Veli
🚌 Ulus. ⏰ daily (except during prayer times). 🎫 donation appreciated.

↑ Column of Julian
Jülyanüs Direği. 🚌 Ulus.

🏛 Museum of the War of Independence
Kurtuluş Savaşı Müzesi
Cumhuriyet Bulvarı, Ulus. 📞 (0312) 310 71 40. 🚌 Ulus. ⏰ 9am–noon & 1–5pm Tue–Sun. 🎫 (students, soldiers and teachers free).
The attractive museum building, with its overhanging eaves, once served as the Grand National Assembly. A collection of photographs, ephemera and documents records the events that led up to the founding of the Republic (1919–23). Although captions are in Turkish, the exhibits are fairly self-explanatory.

🏛 Republic Museum
Cumhuriyet Müzesi
Cumhuriyet Meydanı.
📞 (0312) 310 53 61. 🚌 Ulus. 🚇 Ulus. ⏰ 9am–noon & 1–5pm Tue–Sun. 🎫 (students, soldiers and teachers free).
The displays in the museum celebrate the advances and achievements that the Turkish Republic has made since its inception in 1923. Most of the labels are in Turkish.

Bazaars and Markets
🚌 Ulus. ⏰ 9:30am–5:30pm daily.
The most interesting and "authentic" shopping districts are in the Ulus/Hisar area. The streets to look for are Salman Sokak, Konya Sokak and Çıkrıkçılar Sokak. Markets cater to tourists and sell a wide range of jewellery, carpets, herbal remedies, spices, iron and copper trinkets, as well as various textiles. Also look out for the Bakırcılar Çarşısı (Copperworkers' Bazaar) on Salman Sokak.

Local flea markets and produce markets are held in most districts at least once a week. One of the best takes place on Saturdays on Konya Sokak in the Ulus area.

A typical shop selling old carpets in the Hisar area

🏛 Ethnography Museum

Etnoğrafik Müzesi

Talat Paşa Bulvarı. ☎ (0312) 311 95 56. 🚌 Ulus. 🕐 8:30am–12:30pm & 1:30–5:30pm Tue–Sun. 🎟

Set in a pretty, white marble kiosk (summerhouse), with beautiful Ottoman interiors, and carpets and mosque woodwork dating from Seljuk times onwards, the museum offers a charming record of Turkish costume and handicrafts through the years.

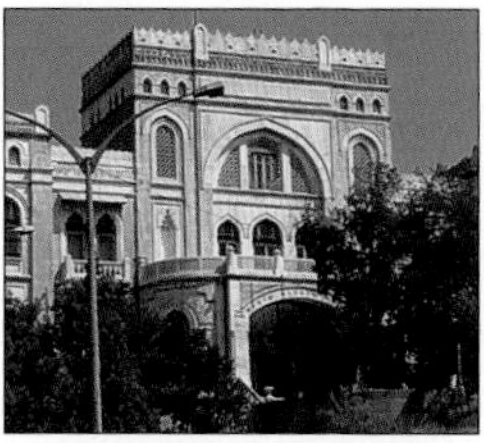

Painting and Sculpture Museum, commissioned by Atatürk

🏛 Painting and Sculpture Museum

Resim ve Heykel Müzesi

Talat Paşa Bulvarı, Opera Meydanı, Ulus. ☎ (0312) 311 82 64. 🚌 Samanpazari. 🕐 9am–noon & 1–5:30pm Tue–Sun. 🎟

The Painting and Sculpture Museum houses a collection of post-revolutionary Turkish art which is significant chiefly as a historical record. Behind the museum there is a small concert hall heavily draped in red velvet where exponents of *sanat müziği* (improvised vocal classical music) usually perform Ottoman court music on Friday evenings.

🏛 Turkish Grand National Assembly

T.B.M.M. (Türkiye Büyük Millet Meclisi)

İsmet İnönü Bul. ☎ (0312) 420 67 42. 🚌 Bakanlıklar. 🕐 9:30am–5pm daily. 🎟 No entrance fee but passport or identity card required.

This impressive complex, housing the legislature, is of a pre-World War II German design, with square columns and colonnades, spacious corridors and heavy woodwork. Set in a well-kept, stately park, it is a haven of cathedral-like calm amid the roar of the Ankara traffic. The public are not allowed to witness parliamentary debates. Many foreign embassies and consulates are also located in the area.

Visitors' Checklist

👥 3,631,612. ✈ Esenboğa International Airport, (0312) 428 02 00. 🚆 Talatpaşa Bul, (0312) 311 06 20. 🚌 Bahçelerarası Cad, Söğütözü, (0312) 224 10 00. [M] east–west Ankaray line and north–south Metro line, with various stops, both operate from 6:15am–midnight. ℹ Gazi Mustafa Kemal Bulvarı 121, Tandoğan, (0312) 231 55 72. 🛒 daily in Ulus and Kale. 🎭 Film Festival (late Apr–early May); Cartoon Festival (2nd week in May); International Ankara Music Festival (last week in May).

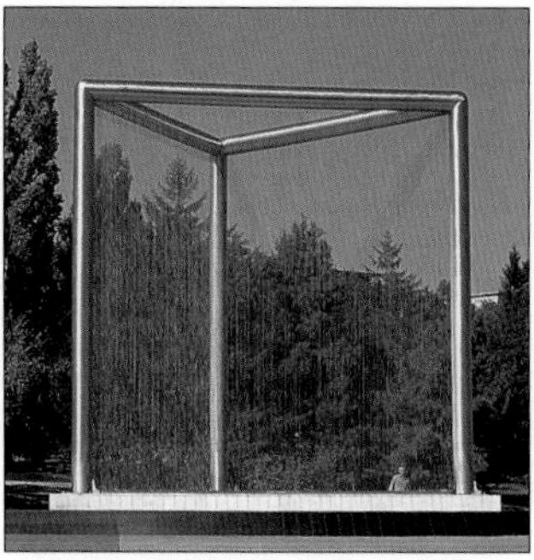

Triangular fountain outside the Turkish Grand National Assembly

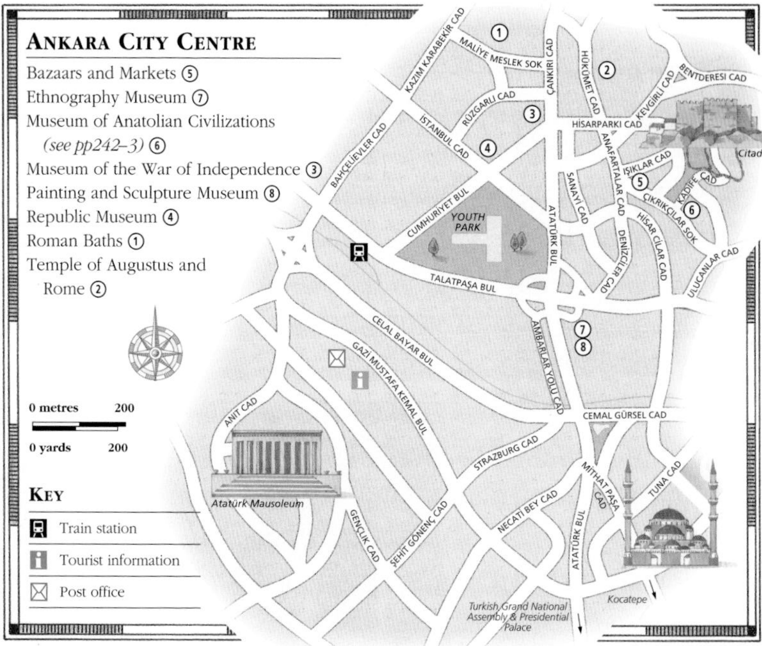

ANKARA CITY CENTRE
Bazaars and Markets 5
Ethnography Museum 7
Museum of Anatolian Civilizations (see pp242–3) 6
Museum of the War of Independence 3
Painting and Sculpture Museum 8
Republic Museum 4
Roman Baths 1
Temple of Augustus and Rome 2
0 metres 200
0 yards 200
KEY
Train station
Tourist information
Post office
KAZIM KARABEKİR CAD
MALİYE MESLEK SOK
ÇANKIRI CAD
HÜKÜMET CAD
BENTDERESİ CAD
KEVGİRLİ CAD
RÜZGARLI CAD
İSTANBUL CAD
HİSARPARKI CAD
Citadel
ANAFARTALAR CAD
IŞIKLAR CAD
KADİFE CAD
ÇIKRIKÇILAR SOK
HİSAR CILAR CAD
BAHÇELİEVLER CAD
CUMHURİYET BUL
YOUTH PARK
SANAYİ CAD
ATATÜRK BUL
DENİZCİLER CAD
ULUCANLAR CAD
TALATPAŞA BUL
CELAL BAYAR BUL
GAZİ MUSTAFA KEMAL BUL
AMBARLAR YOLU CAD
CEMAL GÜRSEL CAD
ANIT CAD
Atatürk Mausoleum
STRAZBURG CAD
MİTHAT PAŞA CAD
TUNA CAD
NECATİ BEY CAD
GENÇLİK CAD
ŞEHİT GÖNENÇ CAD
Turkish Grand National Assembly & Presidential Palace
Kocatepe

Museum of Anatolian Civilizations
Anadolu Medeniyetleri Müzesi

Turkey's most outstanding museum occupies two renovated Ottoman-era buildings and is situated in the Atpazarı (horse market) district of the city, below the citadel. The museum, which was named European Museum of the Year in 1997, displays the achievements of Anatolia's many diverse cultures. Exhibits range from simple Paleolithic stone tools to exquisite Hellenistic and Roman sculptures. The displays are laid out in chronological order, and include a statuette of the Mother Goddess from Çatalhöyük *(see p254)*, Bronze-Age treasures from the royal tombs at Alacahöyük *(see p294)* and superb Hittite sculptures and orthostat reliefs.

Urartian Lion Statuette
Unearthed at Kayalıdere, this small bronze lion shows the skill of the Urartian craftsmen.

Lecture theatre

Museum Entrance
The main displays are housed in the Mahmut Paşa Bedesten, a bazaar warehouse built in the 15th century.

★ **Serving Table**
Found at Gordion (see p247) in the tomb of Midas, this folding wooden table is an outstanding example of Phrygian craftsmanship from the end of the 8th century BC.

Entrance

Terracotta Cooking Pot
Neolithic peoples favoured the use of terracotta. This small pot and stand, found at Çatalhöyük (see p254), dates from approximately the 6th millennium BC.

STAR EXHIBITS

★ **Roman Head**

★ **Serving Table**

★ **Sphinx Relief**

★ Sphinx Relief
This well-preserved Neo-Hittite stone relief, dating from the 9th century BC, was found at Carchemish.

VISITORS' CHECKLIST

Saraçlar Sokak (below the Citadel). 📞 *(0312) 324 31 60.*
🚌 🚇 *Ulus.* ⏰ *8:30am–7pm daily (summer).*
⬤ *Nov–Apr: Mon.* ♿ 🚹 🛍

Ground floor

Main Gallery
The uncluttered layout of the interior provides the perfect setting for the vast range of historic collections.

Golden Bowl with Studs
This early Bronze-Age bowl from Alacahöyük dates from the 3rd millennium BC.

★ Roman Head
The spread of classical Greek and Roman civilization gave rise to more realistic works of art, such as this marble head.

Lower floor

Artifacts displayed in the museum gardens

KEY

☐	Temporary Display
☐	Urartian Period
☐	Phrygian Period
☐	Hittite Period
☐	Assyrian Colonies
☐	Early Bronze Age
☐	Chalcolithic and Neolithic
☐	Paleolithic
☐	Classical Period

Exploring Ankara

Visitors to ANKARA will notice the striking contrasts between the modern city centre and the old town. Wide, tree-lined boulevards, green parks, smart embassies, government buildings and universities make up the new administrative centre, while parts of the old town – particularly certain streets around the citadel – appear to be remarkably simple and traditional. Atatürk's mausoleum dominates the modern part of Ankara, symbolizing a fusion of ancient and modern concepts.

Chandelier inside the Kocatepe Mosque

🔒 Atatürk Mausoleum
Anıtkabir

Anıt Cad, Anıttepe. ☎ (0312) 231 79 75. 🚌 Anıttepe. 🚇 Tandoğan. ⏰ Jun–Sep: 9am–5pm daily; Oct–May: 9am–4pm daily. Sound and light show (summer). 📷

Ankara's most imposing site, the Atatürk Mausoleum, commands a hill to the west of the city. Construction of this monument, begun in 1944, was completed in 1953. To one side of the central courtyard, bronze doors open into the marble-lined hall and cenotaph, where visiting heads of state and vast numbers of ordinary Turks still come to pay their respects to Turkey's supreme leader. İsmet İnönü, second President of the Republic, is entombed opposite. A hall nearby houses some splendid vintage cars used by Atatürk, and visitors can also admire a display of personal possessions and gifts presented to Atatürk by fellow heads of state over the years.

Guard at the Atatürk Mausoleum

🏛 Presidential Palace
Cumhurbaşkanlığı Köşkü

Çankaya Cad. ☎ (0312) 440 72 10. 🚌 Çankaya. ⏰ 1–5pm Sun only. 📷 no entrance fee, but passport or identity card required.

Set in a formal garden, the residence is not open to the public, but visitors can view Atatürk's house, which is now a museum, within the grounds. The father of the Turkish republic moved here in 1921 and this is where he planned the direction his country would take in years to come. The house has a slightly sombre atmosphere. The ground floor is decorated in a classic Ottoman fashion, while the upstairs living quarters provide visitors with a glimpse of Atatürk's lifestyle and personal tastes.

Atatürk Boulevard
Atatürk Bulvarı

Ankara's premier boulevard links the old city with the Presidential Palace and the official government buildings. Along the way is the original home of the Red Crescent (Kızılay), the Islamic equivalent of the Red Cross, as well as Turkey's first department store, Gima.

🔒 Kocatepe Mosque
Kocatepe Camii

Olgunlar Sok. 🚌 Kocatepe. 🚇 Kızılay. ⏰ daily (except during prayer times). 📷 donations appreciated.

Kocatepe Mosque is a landmark in Ankara. One of the world's largest mosques, it is a four-minaret replica of the Blue Mosque (see pp88–9) in Istanbul. Underneath it is a western-style shopping centre called Beğendik, as well as a large car park.

🔒 Kavaklıdere and Çankaya
Ankara's up-market shopping areas cater for the diplomatic corps and government elite. The best can be found south of Kızılay in the suburbs of Kavaklıdere and Çankaya, where many foreign embassies are located. Going south on

The vast central courtyard and stark simplicity of Atatürk's mausoleum, housing his plain sarcophagus

Tunalı Hilmi Caddesi, parallel to Atatürk Bulvarı, you reach Kuğulu Park and Cinnah Caddesi. Both streets are studded with designer boutiques. Karum, opposite the park, is an exclusive shopping centre. Do not expect bargains here.

◼ Atakule

Atatürk Bulvarı terminates in Çankaya Caddesi. A short stroll down this lively street will take you to the impressive Atakule tower and shopping complex that overlooks Ankara's Botanical Gardens. In good weather, the restaurant at the top of the 125-m-high (410-ft) tower affords excellent views over the city.

♣ Citadel

Hisar

Hisarparkı Cad. ▦ *Hisar.* ◯ *daily.*
The Hisar, or Byzantine citadel, dominates the northern end of Ankara. The walls enclose a ramshackle collection of wooden houses, with some passable restaurants, several carpet shops and junkyards filled with antiques and collectables. Salman Sokak, or "Copper Alley", lives up to its nickname, with plenty of old and new copper pieces on offer. You will find bargains and bric-à-brac here, but few real treasures.

Youth Park

Gençlik Parkı

Atatürk Bulvarı. ▦ *Opera or Ulus.* ⓜ *Ulus.* ◯ *dawn to dusk daily.*
The Youth Park just south of Ulus is Ankara's liveliest and most popular area for urban recreation. It has an artificial lake, where small boats can be hired. There are also a few pleasant cafés, where tea is served in a *samovar* (double-tiered pot) at tables overlooking the lake. And, of course, there is a funfair *(luna park),* a sports stadium, tennis courts and a swimming pool.

The lovely Korean Garden, on the other side of Cumhuriyet Bulvarı, commemorates the oft-forgotten combat role played

Vintage steam engine at the Open-Air Steam Locomotive Museum

by Turkish soldiers during the Korean War (1950–54). The 45-m-high (148-ft) Parachute Tower here was once popular with daredevils willing to pay for leaping from its heights.

🏛 Turkish Railways Open-Air Steam Locomotive Museum

Açık Hava Buharlı Müzesi

Ankara Gar Sahası, Celâl Bayar Bulvarı Üzeri. 【 *(0312) 309 05 15.* ◯ *9am–6pm daily.* ▨
This open-air museum close to the Ankara Railway Station is bound to appeal to a broad audience, and not simply those visitors interested in steam traction. It should not be confused with the Turkish Railways (TCDD) Museum inside the station. Atatürk's personal railway carriage, a gift from Adolf Hitler, can be seen adjacent to the main station concourse. The open-air collection of steam-driven giants, located

Sign at
Atatürk Farm

across the railway tracks to the left, includes several old German models used during the invasion of Russia in World War II. There are also several post-war US models.

In the event that you find the museum closed, ask the railway personnel in the station building to arrange for someone to open it for you.

♞ Atatürk Farm and Zoo

Atatürk Orman Çiftliği

Çiftlik Cad. 【 *(0312) 211 01 70.* ▤ *Gazi.* ◯ *9am–5pm Tue–Thu & Sat–Sun.*
Ankara's many parks were established in the early years of the republic, since Atatürk believed that parks and natural recreation areas were part of his country's heritage.

His farm on the outskirts of Ankara is one such peaceful retreat from the city's hectic pace and noise, and makes a good destination for people who are travelling with children.

Apart from a replica of Atatürk's boyhood home in Salonika (modern Thessaloniki), there are large leafy grounds and orchards to explore and enjoy.

Much of the produce that can be sampled at the farm, such as ice cream, yoghurt, milk and meat rolls, are made on site. There is also a brewery where visitors can sample a glass of locally made beer.

The farm grounds adjoin the railway line. It is most convenient to take the suburban train to Gazi Station and make your way from there.

Boating on the pleasant lake in Youth Park

Ankara: Further Afield

Basin used at spa baths

LIFE IN THE TURKISH CAPITAL is enhanced by a number of green belts situated around the outskirts of the city. Here, the focus is on outdoor and leisure activities. These are made possible by the proximity of forests, ski centres, thermal spas and some attractive picnic areas. Most forest areas and parks are open from dawn to dusk; a guardian or ranger is generally in attendance and a small fee will be charged for vehicles. Taking your own vehicle is recommended for maximum enjoyment; the centres are clearly marked off the main roads. Note that camping is restricted to designated areas only. Most of the attractions listed here are day outings from Ankara, but if you want to "take the waters" at a spa, plan to spend a few days.

A pleasant outdoor swimming pool at Kızılcahamam

The town of Kızılcahamam, with the blue spa building on the left

🎿 Diamond Head
Elma Dağı
23 km (14 miles) E of Ankara on the Sivas road. 🎿
Located at an altitude of 1,855 m (6,085 ft), this is the nearest ski centre to Ankara. On snowy weekends the slopes are crowded with locals skiing, skating and tobogganing. Although the season here is limited and the runs short and busy, Diamond Head makes a good place to practise before heading eastwards to try the more challenging runs at Palandöken *(see p317)*.

🌲 Soğuksu National Park
Soğuksu Milli Park
82 km (51 miles) N of Ankara.
🎫 *(0312) 736 11 15 (national park office).* 🎿
If you like walking and trekking in a beautiful and safe forest area, this is the ideal place to go. The forest park, situated at an altitude of

975 m (3,200 ft), has picnic places and well-marked hiking trails, and offers a relaxing retreat from the city.

The region's many natural hot mineral springs have been developed to create spa resorts. One of the best of

Shady forest footpath in the Soğuksu National Park

these is **Kızılcahamam**. Of all the thermal spas scattered around Ankara, it is also the most suited to tourists. There are comfortable hotels and other facilities for visitors who want to stay for a few days. Some treatments involve not only bathing in, but also drinking, the mineral-rich waters, which contain bicarbonate, chloride, sodium and carbon dioxide, and are said to have curative properties.

🎿 Bolu
137 km (85 miles) NE of Ankara. Take toll motorway (E89) from Ankara to Istanbul, or highway (no toll) E80.
🎫 *(0374) 212 22 54.*
The Bolu area is known for its deciduous forests and a steep mountain pass, which affords splendid views of the area. At Kartalkaya, 42 km (26 miles) east of the town of Bolu, there is a pleasant ski centre open from December to March.

🎿 Gölbaşı Lake and Çubuk Dam
25 km (16 miles) S of Ankara along the E90 towards Konya.
If you enjoy picnicking, these areas make a pleasant weekend trip. Both Gölbaşı and the Çubuk Dam are popular with Turkish families for day outings, weekend picnics and informal waterside lunches. There are also some excellent lakeside restaurants.

🌊 Haymana Hot Springs
Haymana Kaplıca
60 km (38 miles) S of Ankara.
🎫 *contact hotels directly for bookings.* 🎪 *Hot Springs Festival (3rd week in Jun).*
Haymana is one of six thermal spas within easy reach of Ankara, and its history extends as far back as Roman times.

Municipal water fountain in the centre of Haymana

It is worth coming here for the relaxing atmosphere and to experience the feeling of physical well-being after a good soak. At Haymana, the waters emerge at 45°C (113°F) and you can smell the calcium, magnesium, sodium and bicarbonate. There are several good hotels here, providing a wide range of facilities.

Infidel's Castle

42 km (26 miles) NE of Haymana
☐ daily.

A sight worth visiting in this region is the **Infidel's Castle** (Gavur Calesı). Strategically perched on a sheer cliff, it consists of an underground cult tomb with two adjoining tomb chambers, and was discovered in 1930. Although this is thought to be a Hittite site, there is doubt about the dating of the stone relief figures of gods and goddesses on the walls, since these do not have the characteristic conical headgear shown in other Hittite relief carving.

Polatlı and Gordion

70 km (43 miles) W of Ankara.
intercity bus between Ankara and Afyon, getting off at Polatı. Take a taxi or one of the infrequent dolmuşes from there.

The village of Yassıhöyük stands on the site of Gordion, the capital of ancient Phrygia, dating from around the 8th century BC. There are several sights worth seeing here, and you can easily tour the site in the course of a day trip from Ankara. If you wish to stay over, however, the nearby town of **Polatlı**, some 18 km (11 miles) to the southeast is

well supplied with hotels and some good restaurants.

Gordion was famous as the seat of the legendary King Midas, whose touch was said to have turned everything to gold. Legend has it that this power turned on Midas when he touched his daughter, as well as his food and drink. The problem was solved only when the god Dionysus took pity on him and granted him a cure. It is thought that Midas took his own life in 695 BC after a crushing military defeat.

Phrygia reached its zenith in the middle of the 8th century BC, but Gordion was made famous again by Alexander the Great (see pp46–7). In 333 BC, after wintering in Lycia, Alexander led his army northward from Sagalassos to Gordion. Here, he came upon and cut the Gordion knot (see p47), fulfilling a prophecy that whoever loosed the bond would become the ruler of the known world.

Today, little remains of the palace, but about 80 burial mounds of Phygrian kings have been excavated in the Gordion area over the past 40 years. The most interesting of these is the **Midas Tomb** (Midas Tümülüsü), which lies within the grounds of the **Gordion Museum** (Gordion Müzesi). The large mound is thought to cover the chamber in which the king was buried,

Phrygian mosaic, Gordion Museum

and is 50 m (164 ft) in height. When archaeologists opened the tomb they found the skeleton of a man of around 60 years of age, who is now believed to be another king from the same dynasty.

The acropolis has also been excavated, and shows layers of civilization from the Bronze Age to Greek and Roman times. Although the acropolis gives an idea of the size and extent of the historic settlements in the region, most of the mosaics found there have been moved and are now kept in the museum. In other places, simple roof structures have been erected to protect excavated mosaics from the elements.

The Gordion Museum was established in 1963, and has been nominated for several awards over the years. It displays Bronze Age, Hittite, Hellenistic, Greek and Roman finds, but its displays concentrate on the Phrygian period, and feature many superbly crafted artifacts. The exhibits include ceramics, woodwork and several bronze vessels found in the Midas Tomb, as well as musical instruments and more.

Midas Tomb

☐ 8am–5pm daily.
Gordion Museum
9 km (5 miles) N of the town.
(0312) 638 21 88. ☐ 8am–5pm Tue–Sun.

Entrance to the burial mound said to house the tomb of King Midas

The distinctive green-tiled dome of the Mevlâna Museum in Konya ▷

Street-by-Street: Konya ❷

K ONYA IS SET ON A HIGH, BLEAK plain in the middle of the Anatolian steppe. Known throughout Turkey for its pious inhabitants and strong Islamic leanings, this ancient city has an increasingly modern and prosperous appearance. Konya has been inhabited since Hittite times. It was known as Iconium to the Romans and Byzantines. The city's heyday was in the 12th century, when it was the capital of the Seljuk Sultanate of Rum.

Samovar for sale in the park

At the heart of the city lies the circular Alaeddin Park (Alaeddin Parkı), a low hill dominated by the Alaeddin Mosque, Konya's largest. It was finished in 1220 by Alaeddin Keykubad I (1219–36), the greatest and most prolific builder of the Seljuk sultans.

Villa of Sultan Kılıç Arslan
A concrete arch covers the remains of this Seljuk landmark. Nearby are tea gardens.

★ Konya Fair
This amusement park is a popular rendezvous for the people of Konya.

ALAEDDIN BULVARI

The Seminary of the Slender Minaret, now housing the Museum of Wood and Stone Carving, is named for its elegant tiled minaret.

0 metres	80
0 yards	80

Ottoman House
Gracious three-storey houses with projecting balconies are typical of middle-class homes built during the late Ottoman period.

STAR SIGHTS

★ **Alaeddin Mosque**

★ **Karatay Museum**

★ **Konya Fair**

★ Karatay Museum
Housed in the Great Karatay Seminary, a 13th-century Seljuk theological school, the Karatay Museum has a superb collection of ceramics and tiles.

VISITORS' CHECKLIST

🚶 1,943,757. ✈ 25 km (15 miles) NW of city centre, (0332) 235 46 49. 🚆 20 km (12 miles) N of city centre, (0332) 351 20 32. 🚌 Ferit Paşa Cad, (0332) 332 36 70. 🛈 Mevlâna Cad 65, (0332) 351 10 74. 🎭 Mevlâna Festival (9–17 Dec). 🔓 daily.

★ Alaeddin Mosque
The mosque is set in beautiful wooded surroundings on a site that has been used since prehistoric times.

ANKARA CAD

ALAEDDIN BULVARI

Tiled *mihrab*
The mihrab in the Alaeddin Mosque is adorned with some of the finest Seljuk tilework.

Car Park

KEY

– – – Suggested route

Mevlâna Museum
Mevlâna Müzesi

The entrance to the museum, with the famous green-tiled dome

THE CITY OF KONYA has close links with the life and work of Celaleddin Rumi, or Mevlâna, the 13th-century founder of the Mevlevi dervish sect – better known as the "whirling" dervishes *(see p255)*. Rumi developed a philosophy of spiritual union and universal love, and is regarded as one of the Islamic world's greatest mystics. He settled in Seljuk-ruled Konya and is believed to have died here in 1273.

The museum is an enlargement of the original dervish lodge *(tekke)*. It contains the tomb of Rumi, the ceremonial hall *(semahane)*, and displays of memorabilia and manuscripts. There are also galleries for spectators and musicians.

Entrance

★ Ablutions Fountain
Used in the dervish cleansing ritual, the ablutions fountain (şadırvan) is pleasantly cooling on hot days.

Hürrem Sultan Mausoleum

Cemetery

Dervish Life
Life-like mannequins clad in authentic dress illustrate the spiritual aspects of the daily life of an initiate in the lodge.

STAR EXHIBITS

★ Ablutions Fountain

★ Mevlâna's Tomb

★ Semahane

Mother-of-Pearl Case
This finely worked case is said to contain the beard of Mevlâna.

VISITORS' CHECKLIST

Selimiye Cad, Mevlâna Mahallesi.
((0332) 351 12 15.
☐ summer: 9am–6pm
Tue–Sun; noon–5pm Mon.
● Mon (winter).

Prominent female members of the Mevlâna order are buried in this graveyard.

Verandah

★ Semahane (Ceremonial Hall)
Once the setting for the whirling ceremony, the Semahane now houses museum displays.

Musical Instruments
Instruments used by the dervishes include this ud, *finely worked in ivory with a mother-of-pearl fretboard.*

★ Mevlâna's Tomb
Gilded calligraphy adorns the walls around the sarcophagus. The tombs of Rumi's father and other dervish leaders are nearby.

KEY

☐ Dervish Lodge
☐ Administrative Offices
☐ Dervish Assembly Chamber
☐ Monumental Fountain
☐ Recitation Room
☐ Mescid-Chapel Mosque
☐ Semahane (Ceremonial Hall)
☐ Tombs of Çelebi

Çatalhöyük ❸

Own transport or taxi from Konya recommended. Turn left to Çumra, from the Karaman/Mersin road.

DATING FROM as early as 7000 BC, Çatalhöyük is universally regarded as one of the world's earliest urban settlements. It was originally discovered and excavated by James Mellaart in 1958. Research resumed in 1997, after a 30-year interval.

It is thought that roughly 10,000 people lived here in flat-roofed square houses with rooftop entrances and high windows. The city was the focus of a culture that produced an array of mural decoration, decorative textiles and pottery.

Visitors can enter the site only when accompanied by an official museum guide. The **Çatalhöyük Museum** displays the latest finds, and there are "virtual reality" exhibits in houses and shrines. Artifacts displayed in the museum are reproductions; the originals are either in museums in Konya or the superb Museum of Anatolian Civilizations *(see pp242–3)* in Ankara.

Bronze bowl found at Çatalhöyük

🏛 **Çatalhöyük Museum**
📞 *(0332) 452 57 20.* ⭘ *8am–5pm daily.* 🎫

Eğirdir Lake, a tranquil haven for naturalists

Beyşehir ❹

👤 *67,872.* 🚌 *frequent buses from Konya, or intercity buses to Burdur.*

BEYŞEHIR IS THE LARGEST of the fresh-water lakes in what is known as Turkey's Lake District, and the third largest in the country. Its shallow waters contain carp, perch and pike. The town of the same name, at the southeastern corner of the lake, features an unusual combined weir and bridge.

One of the main reasons for coming to Beyşehir is to see the **Eşrefoğlu Mosque** (Eşrefoğlu Camii), dating from 1297. The wooden interior, with its 48 wooden columns and *mihrab* (prayer niche) decorated with cut tiles, is among the finest examples of this type of architecture remaining from the Beylik period *(see p53)*.

C Eşrefoğlu Mosque
Beside the bus station, NW after crossing the weir-bridge. ⭘ *prayer times, but a guardian will let visitors in at other times.* 💰 *donation.*

Eğirdir ❺

👤 *40,817.* 🚏 *daily to Istanbul via Afyon, (0246) 311 46 94.* 🚌 *(0246) 311 40 36.* ℹ️ *2 Sahil Yolu, (0246) 311 43 88.* 🛒 *Thu.* 🎉 *Apple Festival (Sep).*

RINGED BY MOUNTAINS rising to 3,000 m (9,842 ft), Eğirdir Lake makes a good base for walkers, birders and flower enthusiasts. When the snow melts in May, the hills display many flowering bulbs, orchids and become a stop-over for migrating birds. Yeşil Ada (green island) is linked to the mainland by a causeway, and has a number of cheerful family restaurants.

ENVIRONS: Antiocheia-in-Pisidia is famous as the place where St Paul first preached to the Gentiles. The ruins of the city include the basilica of St Paul, a synagogue, Roman theatre, baths and a superb aqueduct.

Davraz Ski Centre is operational from December to April. There is also a 50-bed ski lodge at Çobanisa, 27 km (17 miles) from Isparta, with a chairlift to the north face of the mountains.

Davraz Ski Centre
📞 *(0246) 218 44 38, for the most up-to-date information.*

The unusual wooden interior of the Eşrefoğlu Mosque

The Whirling Dervishes

THE MEVLEVI ORDER, better known as the Whirling Dervishes, was founded by the Sufi mystic, Celaleddin Rumi, also called Mevlâna. He believed that music and dance represented a means to induce an ecstatic state of universal love and offered a way to liberate the individual from the anxiety and pain of daily life. His greatest work, the six-volume *Mesnevi*, consists of 25,000 poems that were read in the *tekkes* (lodges) of the order.

Celaleddin Rumi

Central to the practice of the dervishes is the *sema*, or whirling ceremony. This consists of several parts, each with its own meaning. Love is the central theme of the mystical cycle of the *sema*, which symbolizes the sharing of God's love among earthly beings. For man, the dance is a spiritual ascent to divine love. The *sema* combines both spiritual and intellectual elements, emphasizing self-realization and the ultimate goal, which is perfect union with God.

Conical headdress

Black cloak

Clothing
Clothing worn for the sema *has symbolic meaning. The headdress, for example, stands for the tomb of the ego.*

Ud
Duvar
Cymbals
Ney

Musical accompaniment *is highly symbolic: the* ney *(reed flute) represents the breath of God.*

THE SEMA RITUAL

The *sema* consists of five parts, the first three of which are prayers, greetings, and musical improvizations. The ritual then moves into four salutes *(selams)*: truth through knowledge, the splendour of creation, total submission before God and coming to terms with destiny.

Whirling *is the climax of the* sema. *Its selams (salutes) represent stages during the rapture of submission to God.*

The wide white skirt *symbolizes the ego's shroud.*

The movement concludes *with a bow, signifying the return to a state of subservience.*

The dervishes greet one another *and salute the soul, which is "enslaved" by shapes and bodies.*

The dervishes extend their arms, *to allow divine energy to enter the right palm, move through the body, and pass out through the left palm into the earth.*

Verses from the Koran *are read after the dance, including a prayer for the peace of all souls.*

Cobbled street in the old quarter of Afyon

Afyon ➏

🏠 *801,829.* 🚌 *İsmet İnönü Cad, (0272) 212 09 63.* 🚉 *(0272) 213 00 22.* ℹ️ *Valilik Binası, Kat 3, Suite 333, (0272) 213 54 47.*

THE WORD AFYON means "opium", and it is difficult not to miss the fields of white and dark purple opium poppies if you visit the area in May. Opiates are extracted for medicinal purposes at a factory in nearby Bolvadın, using the special poppy straw method. The town museum has exhibits detailing various methods of opiate extraction.

Other local products are a white, soft marble, which is found in huge slabs along the roadsides and is used for everything from gravestones to kitchen basins. Afyon Kaymağı, a rich clotted cream, is typically served on small metal trays and eaten with honey for breakfast.

Towering over the town is a 225-m (738-ft) crag that can be reached by climbing 700 steps. The Hittites and Byzantines may have used its commanding position for a fortress, but exact dates are speculative.

The Seljuks left the greatest mark on Afyon's history. The major Seljuk building is the **Great Mosque** (Ulu Camii), completed in 1272. It features a geometric ceiling and 40 wooden columns, some with traces of paint on the capitals.

The **Archaeological Museum** contains a collection of largely Roman artifacts, which were excavated from around Isparta, Uşak, Burdur and Kütahya.

Afyon was Atatürk's headquarters for the final stages of Turkey's War of Independence *(see p58)*, which reached a climax with the victory over the advancing Greek army at Dumlupınar on 26 August 1922. The **Victory Museum** (Zafer Müzesi), known more for its classical Anatolian architecture than for its contents, recalls the heady days of national liberation. Most of the top Republican commanders stayed in this building during the campaign. There is also a war memorial at nearby Dumlupınar.

🎫 **Great Mosque**
Ulu Camii
Köşe Dee Sok. ⬜ *during prayer, or ask the guardian on duty to let you in.* 💰 *donation.*

🏛 **Afyon Archaeological Museum**
Kurtuluş Cad 96. 📞 *(0272) 215 11 91.* ⬜ *8am–noon & 1–5:30pm Tue–Sun.* 💰

🏛 **Victory Museum**
Zafer Müzesi
In front of the Governor's Building. 📞 *(0272) 212 09 16.* ⬜ *9am–noon & 1–5pm Tue–Sun.*

Sivrihisar ➐

🏠 *32,600.* 🚌 *along the E90 from Polatlı, then dolmuş to the town.*

SIVRIHISAR IS THE ANCIENT town of Justinianopolis, built by Emperor Justinian *(see p49)* to guard the western route to Ancyra (ancient Ankara). The modern town is spread out at the foot of a crag, on which lie the remains of the original Byzantine fortress. The Great Mosque (Ulu Camii), built in 1247, is an excellent example of a Seljuk mosque. Some of its 67 wooden pillars have intricately carved and painted capitals. A warren of pretty Ottoman houses surrounds the mosque, and the Sivrihisar area is famous for fine handwoven kilims.

ENVIRONS: 14 km (9 miles) to the south of Sivrihisar lie the ancient ruins of **Pessinus**, near the modern village of Ballıhisar (honey castle). During the 3rd century BC, Pessinus was an important Phrygian cult centre but was abandoned in around AD 500 or 600. Sights include the scant remains of a temple of Cybele, the Anatolian mother goddess. However, nothing is left of the stadium and theatre. At one time, it is believed that there were over 360 springs here, and the remains of hydraulic works can still be seen. The site is open to the public and access is free, if not easy.

The "forest of columns" in the Great Mosque in Sivrihisar

The Tomb of King Midas (left), cut from solid rock

Şehitgazi Valley ❽

🏛 *32,600.* 🚍 *or on foot.*

THE VILLAGE OF Şehitgazi is named after Şehit Battal Gazi, an Arab commander and martyr (*şeyit*), or "warrior of the faith", who died during the siege of Afyon in about AD 750. His large tomb, and that of the Byzantine princess who fell in love with him, are housed in a beautiful *tekke* (monastery complex), built by Hacı Bektaş Veli (*see p293*) about 10 km (6 miles) to the northwest of the town centre.

The main attraction of the valley is the monumental tomb (5th or 6th century BC) of King Midas at Midasşehir, or Yazılıkaya. The tomb lies 65 km (40 miles) south of Eskişehir in a marvellous, open-air setting. The site is open from dawn to dusk and you can wander freely here and in the small museum.

Aslantaş, 35 km (22 miles) north of Afyon, was a major Phrygian cult centre. There are other Phrygian sites at Kümbet and Aslankaya, but the roads here are unpaved and there are few visitors.

Eskişehir ❾

🏛 *872,650.* 🚆 *from Istanbul and Ankara, (0222) 231 13 65.* 🚌 *(0222) 225 80 94.* ℹ️ *Valilik Binası, ground floor, (0222) 230 17 52.* 🎭 *International Yunus Emre Culture and Fine Arts Week (6–10 May), Meerschaum Festival (3rd week Sep).* 🍴 *most days.*

COMMANDING THE MAIN ROAD from Istanbul to Ankara, Eskişehir (ancient Dorylaeum)

has prospered from trade for centuries, but has also been ravaged by passing armies. It was badly damaged during the War of Independence and has few historical monuments. Today, it is a major railway junction, as well as the home base of the Turkish air force.

Eskişehir is also a mining centre, with supplies of borax, chrome and manganese, as well as meerschaum (or "sea foam"), a soft, porous, heat-resistant, light white clay used to make elaborate carved tobacco pipes (*see p356*), which are popular among visitors to Turkey. The **Meerschaum Museum** (Lületaşı Müzesi) has displays of historic pipes and old photos of the mines. You can watch carvers at work on Sakarya Caddesi, and purchase pipes and other decorative items made from meerschaum.

Meerschaum pipe

🏛 **Meerschaum Museum**
Lületaşı Müzesi
İki Eylül Cad. 📞 *(0222) 233 05 82.* 🕐 *10am–5pm daily.* 🎫

Kütahya ❿

See pp258–9.

Çavdarhisar (Aezani) ⓫

60 km (37 miles) SW of Kütahya. 🚐 *infrequent dolmuş to and from Kütahya.* 🕐 *9am–noon & 1–5pm daily.* 🎫

THE PHRYGIAN SITE at Aezani (today's Çavdarhisar) does not feature on most tourists' itineraries, but a visit here will be highly rewarding.

Aezani reached its zenith in the 2nd century AD, when it was transformed from a minor Phrygian settlement into a large, thriving city and sanctuary of Zeus, ruler of the gods. At this time, the legend of Zeus's birth in the nearby cave at Steunos reinforced the belief in pagan culture, even though such cult worship was at that time being challenged elsewhere by early Christian communities. Today, the cave can be reached only with a four-wheel-drive vehicle.

The most impressive re-mains are of the Temple of Zeus, built during the reign of Emperor Hadrian (AD 117–138). There is a crypt underneath the temple that is believed to have been the seat of the cult of Cybele, the mother goddess of Anatolia.

The scattered remains of a theatre, municipal gymnasium and stadium are visible today. These were envisaged on a scale that would rival cities like Ephesus or Pergamum. However, Aezani's influence had begun to wane by the 3rd century AD. In 1970, an earthquake demolished much of the site. Some fine mosaics of Phrygian gods can be seen in the ruins of the bathhouse and gymnasium.

Remains of the well-preserved Temple of Zeus at Aezani

Kütahya ⑩

KÜTAHYA'S EARLIEST inhabitants were the Phrygians in the 7th century BC. Alexander the Great called the city Kotaeon and used it as his headquarters as he advanced on Gordion *(see p247)* in 332 BC. The Byzantines later occupied the fortress on the acropolis hill until it fell to the Seljuks. Kütahya's golden age was under Sultan Selim I (the Grim; 1512–20), when ceramic craftsmen from Persia were settled here. In 1833, the breakaway ruler of Egypt, Paşa Muhammad Ali, occupied Kütahya. In 1922, Greek forces were routed near here, marking a turning point in the War of Independence *(see p58)*. Today, this is a peaceful and devout town and most shops shut during prayer times on Fridays. The numerous splendid period houses hint at untapped tourist potential.

Tilework at the main water fountain

The double-walled fortress, built by the Ottomans

The Dumlupınar monument, honouring Turkish war dead

Exploring Kütahya

Almost all of the town's sites can be seen on foot. Allow at least an afternoon to see the scores of mansions and townhouses.

Between the 15th and the 17th centuries, Kütahya was the rival of İznik *(see pp160–61)* in the painting and glazing of tiles and ceramics. By the early 20th century, the local ceramic industry had all but vanished. Now, Kütahya is again the focus of a revival of this skilled art. The town is acclaimed for beautiful hand-painted ceramic items, and workshops are found in many of the back streets.

The Dumlupınar monument, 50 km (31 miles) south of the town, is also worth visiting. It commemorates the soldiers who fell in the decisive battle of the War of Independence.

🏛 Kossuth House Museum

Kossuth Evi Müzesi
Macar Sokak (off Gediz Cad).
☎ (0274) 223 62 14. ⏱ 8am–noon & 1–6pm Tue–Sun. 🖼 🔲
This house/museum complex was the home of Hungarian freedom fighter, Lajos Kossuth (1802–94), who sought refuge in Turkey after leading an unsuccessful revolt to free his homeland from the rule of the Hapsburgs in 1848. Kossuth and his family stayed here as the guests of the Ottoman government in 1850–51, and the 19th-century stone-and-wood house where they lived has changed remarkably little since that time.

The statue of Kossuth in the rose garden was erected in 1982, and Hungarians renew friendship ties here annually on 5 April. The house is also referred to as "the House of the Hungarian Patriot".

⛪ Fortress

Kale
Proceed up Gediz Cad from the Kossuth House Museum.
The ruined fortress resembles many other Ottoman-period citadels. Not much is known about its history, but the Kütahya-born historian and traveller, Evliya Çelebi (1811–82), wrote that it had 70 towers. One of the few remaining ones is now under extensive restoration. Most people come here for the delightful revolving restaurant, **Döner Gazino**, at the top.

Döner Gazino

⏱ dawn to dusk daily.

🏛 Kütahya Tile Museum

Kütahya Çini Müzesi
Gediz Cad. ☎ (0274) 223 69 90.
⏱ 8am–noon & 1:30pm–5:30pm Tue–Sun. 🖼 🔲
Since 1999, the Tile Museum has been housed in a restored 15th-century soup kitchen *(imaret)* located behind the Great Mosque (Ulu Camii). This is one of Turkey's most attractive small museums. The displays focus on tiles, vases, ewers and decorative porcelainware produced in the town from the 14th century to the present, and are arranged around a typical ornamental pool *(şadırvan)*.

Restored mosque soup kitchen, now housing the Kütahya Tile Museum

C Great Mosque
Ulu Camii

End of Cumhuriyet Cad, Börekciler Mahallesi. ☐ *daily, except at prayer times.* ☒ *donation.*

This is the biggest mosque in Kütahya, but not the oldest. Building started under Sultan Yıldırım Beyazıt early in the 15th century, but it was not finished until the time of Mehmet II (1451–81). Many of the marble columns come from Aezani *(see p257)*. The Sakahanesi (watersellers' square) near the mosque is a popular local gathering place.

Bazaars
☐ *9am–6pm Mon–Sat.*

Kütahya's bazaars occupy two buildings. The Grand Market (Büyük Bedesten) was built in the 14th century and stands on Çemberciler Caddesi. The 15th-century Small Market (Küçük Bedesten) is just next

Spices and pulses for sale outside the Grand Market

to it on Kavafiye Sokak (Shoemaker's Street). Don't miss the vaulted ceilings. Today, the bazaars sell chiefly vegetables and second-hand goods. More specialized traders overflow into the surrounding streets.

Interior of the Great Mosque showing the women's balcony

🏛 Kütahya Archaeology Museum
Kütahya Arkeoloji Müzesi

Gediz Cad, Börekciler Mahallesi. ☎ *(0274) 224 07 85.* ☐ *9am–1pm & 1:30–5:30pm Tue–Sun.* ☒

Adjoining the Great Mosque, the museum is housed in the mosque's former seminary, the Vacidiye Medresesi, built in 1314 by a local ruling clan. The museum was restored in

VISITORS' CHECKLIST

🏠 *220,000.* 🚉 *İstasyon Cad, (0274) 223 61 21.* 🚌 *Atatürk Bulvarı, (0274) 224 33 00.* 🅸 *Hükümet, (0274) 223 19 62.* 🎭 *Dumlupınar Fair, Turkey's largest handicraft fair (last three weeks of Jul); Culture and Tourism Fair (mid-Jul for three days).* 🛒 *Wed and Sat on Belediye Sok (central area). Local market (Thu) along Gediz Cad.*

1999, and its centrepiece is a stunningly beautiful Amazon tomb dating from the 2nd century AD, found at Aezani in 1990. The displays also include fossils, Phrygian terracotta toys, Roman glass and sculptures and delicate earthenware figurines.

🏠 Historic Kütahya Manor Houses
Tarihi Kütahya Konakları

The town's spacious period houses date mainly from the 18th and 19th centuries. All are derelict and so only the exteriors can be seen. They usually have three storeys, projecting balconies and front and back entrances. Look near the Ulu Camii on Ahi Erbasan Sokak (in Gazi Kemal Mahallesi) and Germiyan Sokak for typical examples.

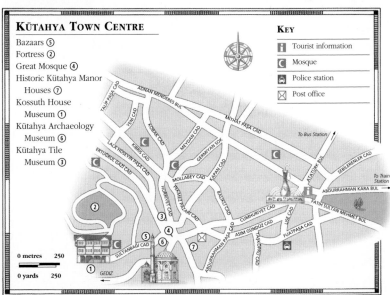

KÜTAHYA TOWN CENTRE

Bazaars ⑤
Fortress ②
Great Mosque ④
Historic Kütahya Manor Houses ⑦
Kossuth House Museum ①
Kütahya Archaeology Museum ⑥
Kütahya Tile Museum ③

KEY

🅷 Tourist information
🅲 Mosque
🚓 Police station
⊠ Post office

To Bus Station
To Train Station

0 metres 250
0 yards 250

THE BLACK SEA

A
LTHOUGH IT IS THE *least visited part of Turkey, the Black Sea region is one of the loveliest, most scenic and culturally authentic areas of the country. Take some time to explore the hidden treasures of this diverse region, which include the beautiful ports of Amasra and Sinop, the historic coastal city of Trabzon, and Safranbolu, a gem of Ottoman architecture and a UNESCO World Heritage Site.*

Until the 1920s, the Black Sea coast was strongly influenced by Greek culture. Its major city, Trabzon, was once capital of a Byzantine state ruled by the Comnene family. The Genoese and Venetians were also active along the coast, as can be seen from the many ruined castles.

For travellers with an interest in religion and history, the region has many Christian sites to explore. Chief among these are Trabzon's church of Haghia Sophia and the Sumela Monastery, as well as the Georgian churches and monasteries in the Artvin area.

This is Turkey's wettest region, and the climate is moist and moderate even in summer. From the coastal highway, the coastal plain rises to lush tea and hazelnut plantations, virgin forests and the Pontic mountain ranges, which form an almost unbroken barrier. The peaks around Çamlıhemşin attract trekkers and mountaineers from all over the world.

The local people are down-to-earth and industrious. Smallholdings are common, and many of the owners have retained their Caucasian origins and traditions. Temel and İdris are popular Black Sea boys' names. Temel is Turkey's archetypal slow learner, and is often the butt of jokes.

A Black Sea sardine known as *hamsi* is the symbol of the region and the nickname for its people.

The centre of Trabzon, around the historic castle

◁ Mosque on the shore of Uzungöl, a glacial lake in the foothills of the Pontic Mountains

Exploring the Black Sea

WITH ITS MILD, damp climate, the Black Sea region is suitable to visit all year round. The best time to go is in springtime, when the mountain valleys are carpeted with wild flowers. The high peaks of the coastal mountains are known for their luxuriant pine forests, alpine lakes and racing rivers which descend to the coastal plain. In the extreme northeast, the Kaçkar range is the highest of the Pontic mountain chain, which defines the region. These mountainous areas receive heavy snowfalls in winter.

Safranbolu and Sumela Monastery are the outstanding sights of the region. There are many villages where locals still practise Ottoman-era crafts: Devrek, for example, is renowned for its decorative wooden canes.

Picturesque Amasra, built on a rocky promontory

SİNOP

Altınkaya Dam

010

KASTAMONU ②

Gökırmak

030

Amasya

AMASRA ①

755

SAFRANBOLU
②

065

DEVREK

GEREDE

Şile   SAKARYA
(ADAPAZARI)

E80 BOLU

100

Ankara

İstanbul

Tarakb

0 kilometres   50

0 miles   25

KEY

≡ Motorway

≡ Major road

≡ Secondary road

≡ Other road

≡ Scenic route

— River

❄ Viewpoint

Government House at Safranbolu, now undergoing restoration

GETTING AROUND

Renting a car, or even a four-wheel-drive vehicle, is probably the best way to see the Black Sea coast. This option offers the flexibility to explore minor roads and lanes. Take the central highway only when necessary, or risk missing much of what the region has to offer.

Samsun and Trabzon are both served by non-stop flights from Istanbul and Ankara. Intercity buses run daily, or more frequently, to the major centres. Otherwise, visitors must rely on local minibuses, erratic dolmuşes or foot. Take walking shoes and rain gear in any season. Don't expect to find the same sophisticated, scheduled transport as in other parts of Turkey. But if you are adventurous and flexible, a Black Sea journey will be highly rewarding.

Breathtaking Sumela Monastery

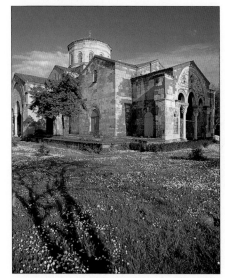

Haghia Sophia, a well-preserved Byzantine church in Trabzon

SIGHTS AT A GLANCE

SEE ALSO

• *Where to Stay* p333

• *Where to Eat* pp351–2

The small harbour at Amasra, with its Roman bridge and watch tower

Amasra ❶

🏛 7,675. 🚌 Atatürk Meydanı.
ℹ Büyük Liman Cad.

THE PICTURESQUE and tranquil town of Amasra is located about 15 km (9 miles) from Bartın. In the 6th century BC, Amasra was called Sesamus, and its inhabitants were known as Megara. By the 9th century, Amasra was of sufficient importance to be designated a bishopric. It was destroyed by Arab raiders, and then rebuilt in the 12th century by the Genoese. They recognized the trading advantages that Amasra could give them and rented the castle and harbour from the Byzantines. The two fortresses built by the Genoese during the 14th century can still be seen today. One overlooks the main harbour and the other – no more than the remains of a small tower – sits at the harbour mouth. Amasra came under Otto-man rule in 1460.

Interesting places to see in the town include the **Fatih Mosque**, a former Byzantine church, and the 19th-century **İskele Mosque**. Some portions of the Byzantine city walls are still standing, as is a Roman bridge in the harbour.

🄲 **Fatih Mosque**
In the town centre. ⭕ daily (except during prayer times).
🄲 **İskele Mosque**
On the harbour. ⭕ daily (except during prayer times).

Safranbolu ❷

See pp268–9.

Kastamonu ❸

🏛 60,000. 🚌 10 min walk N of town centre. ℹ Nasrullah Meydanı, (0366) 212 01 62. 🗓 Wed & Sat.
🎭 Atatürk Hat Festival (23–30 Aug), Garlic Festival (1st week Sep).
🎡 near Daday at Çömlekciler.

KASTAMONU is well known for outdoor activities as well as for crafts. The pastures of nearby Daday offer some of the very finest trail riding in all of Turkey. The local women are famed for hand-printed tablecloths and upholstery fabrics made from cotton and flax. Other specialities of the area include colourful knitted wool socks and fruit jams.

During the 11th century, Kastamonu was controlled by the powerful Comnene family, rulers of Trabzon (see

Carved wooden implements, Amasra

pp270–71). Indeed, the town's name probably comes from Castra Comneni (Latin for "camp of the Comnenes"). The town fell under Ottoman rule in 1459. During this era, the region around Kastamonu produced rice, iron, cotton fabrics and mohair, mostly for export. Kastamonu Castle was built by the Byzantines in the 12th century and was kept in good repair by the Seljuks and Ottomans. Today, its remains serve as a fire tower and lookout point.

Displays at the Kastamonu **Ethnographic Museum** include Byzantine and Greek mementos and 17th-century agricultural tools. There is a library on the first floor and a coin display. The building itself is of historic importance, for it was here on 25 August 1925 that Atatürk delivered a famous speech forbidding the wearing of the fez (the old-fashioned conical felt hat).

The **Archaeology Museum**, which was recently repaired, displays finds from Byzantine and Ottoman times, and a selection of historical artifacts.

The town's main mosques are the Atabey Mosque (uphill, behind the Aşir Efendi Han shopping centre), with its 40 wooden pillars and stone door, and the İbni Meccar Mosque, built in 1353 by the Çandaroğulları family. This lovely mosque in stone and wood is also known as Eli güzel ("beautiful hand").

Mahmut Bey Mosque, containing a beautiful wooden interior

🏛 **Ethnographic Museum**
Hepkebirler Mah, Sakarya Cad.
 (0366) 214 01 49. ○ *9am–noon & 1pm–5:30pm Tue–Sun.*
🏛 **Archaeology Museum**
İsfendiyarbey Mahallesi, Cumhuriyet Cad 6. *(0366) 214 54 56.* ○ *9am–noon & 1pm–5:30pm Tue–Sun.*

ENVIRONS: The Mahmut Bey Mosque is located some 17 km (10 miles) northwest of Kastamonu in the village of Kasaba. For a small donation, the local *imam* (Muslim priest) will open the mosque. Inside the well-preserved building are some beautiful paintings and fine calligraphy.

Cide, Abana and İnebolu are all easy day trips from Kastamonu. Cide is a pretty, unspoiled fishing village, and Abana is renowned for its fish restaurants and good, clean swimming. İnebolu has some well-preserved houses.

About 63 km (39 miles) south of Kastamonu is **Ilgaz Mountain National Park**, reachable by dolmuş or your own transport. Visitors to the park can see bears, foxes and deer. There is also a deer breeding and research station. This area offers excellent skiing from November until March. A culinary speciality here is whole lamb, cooked *tandır* style (in a wood-fired clay oven) for four to five hours until the meat falls off the bone. The dish is traditionally eaten with the fingers.

Ilgaz Mountain National Park
 (0336) 212 58 71. ○ *all year.*
 for vehicles.

Samsun ❹

 355,000. *Yeni Vilayet Binası, Kat 4, (0362) 431 29 88.*
 from Ankara to Atatürk Bulvarı, (0362) 445 15 82. *Yeni Garajlar 1, (0362) 238 11 70.* *direct from Ankara or Istanbul; 8 km (5 miles) from Samsun on the Amasya road.*
 from Istanbul (30 hrs).
 Samsun Fair (Jul), Akdağı Annual Summer Migration Festival "Hıdrellez" (Jun or Jul depending on weather). *Sat.*

APART FROM producing the most popular cigarette brand in the country, Samsun also holds a proud place in Turkish hearts as the place where Atatürk came after his escape from Istanbul on 19 May 1919, to draw up plans for a Turkish republic. Today, this anniversary is celebrated as a national holiday, Youth and Sports Day.

Samsun has two good museums devoted to the revered memory of Atatürk and his legacy. The **Gazi Museum** occupies a former hotel where he stayed in 1919 and the **Atatürk Museum** has displays of his clothing, various personal items and a collection of photographs.

The **Archaeological and Ethnographic Museum** is a treasure-trove of antiquities from the surrounding villages. It has Bronze-Age artifacts as well as ceramics, bronze and brass implements, glass and mosaics dating from the Hittite, Hellenic, Roman and Byzantine eras. There is also

some beautiful gold and silver jewellery, as well as several fine, hand-written books and hand-woven kilims.

About 80 km (50 miles) southwest of Samsun in the **Havza** district are a number of thermal springs *(kaplıca)* that are very popular.

🏛 **Gazi Museum**
○ *9am–noon & 1pm–5:30pm Tue–Sun.*
🏛 **Atatürk Museum**
 (0362) 435 75 35. ○ *9am–noon & 1pm–5:30pm.*
🏛 **Archaeological and Ethnographic Museum**
Cumhuriyet Meydanı. *(0362) 431 68 28.* ○ *9am–noon & 1–5:30pm Tue–Sun.*

Atatürk and aides, Atatürk Museum

ENVIRONS: Near Bafra, about 40 km (25 miles) northwest of Samsun, excavations at a site called İkiztepe (twin hills) have revealed early Hittite bronze finds. The bronze items have been removed, but the site is open and there is no entrance fee. Hittite copper and bronze artifacts have also been uncovered at Dündartepe, 3 km (2 miles) outside Samsun, where excavations still continue.

Men's section at a thermal spring in the Havza area

Traditional Ottoman architecture in Safranbolu ▷

Street-by Street: Safranbolu **②**

Finely carved fountain (çeşme)

S AFRANBOLU'S MARKET AREA, a warren of narrow streets and merchant shops, has many restored Ottoman dwellings *(see p31)*. Because of its important architectural heritage, Safranbolu has been declared a World Heritage Site.

In Ottoman times, the town lay on a major trade route. Its many handsome three-storey stone-and-timber *konaks* (mansions) were erected by wealthy merchants and craftsmen. In summer they lived in the cool Bağlar district, and in winter they moved down to the more sheltered Çarşı (bazaar) quarter around the Kazdağı Mosque.

Köprülü Mehmet Paşa Mosque
The mosque, located near the massive Cinci Hanı, opened for worship in 1661.

★ **Cinci Hanı**
The 350-year-old Cinci Hanı, a refuge for travelling merchants, gives a good idea of the scale of commerce centuries ago.

Kastamonu

CINCI HANI

ŞEKERCİLER SOKAK

YUKARI ÇARŞI SOKAK

ARASI

The Covered Way
was formerly used by cobblers and shoemakers.

Cinci Hamamı
is a 17th-century Turkish bath still in use today.

★ **Kazdağı Mosque**
Located in the main square, the mosque was built in 1779.

Kiranköy

STAR SIGHTS
★ Cebeciler Konak
★ Cinci Hanı
★ Kazdağı Mosque

KEY

– – – Suggested route

Sundial
An interesting sundial occupies the shady courtyard of the Köprülü Mehmet Paşa Mosque.

VISITORS' CHECKLIST

🏠 22,000. ✈ 10 km (6 miles) SW of town centre in Karabük. 🚌 in Karabük. 🛈 Tourism Information Office, Arasta Çarşısı 7, (0372) 712 38 63. 🕓 Thu.

Shoemakers' Street
The name of this street recalls a local craft. During World War I the town made boots for the Ottoman army.

Grain Market

KUNDURACILAR SOKAK

ESKİ HAMAM SOKAK

CEBİCİ SOKAK

ARASTA SOKAK

MÜTFÜS SOKAK

★ **Cebeciler Konak**
The upper storey of the Cebeciler Konak shows typical wooden shutters and stencilled wall decorations made with natural dyes.

The Tourism Information Office
is in the *Arasta* (market) area.

Market Street
Restored konaks line the narrow Arasta Sokak (Market Street). Some of these old houses have been turned into atmospheric guest houses, complete with authentic decor and furniture.

0 metres   40

0 yards   40

Trabzon ❺

![Fresco, Gülbahar Mosque and Tomb]

Fresco, Gülbahar Mosque and Tomb

THE EARLIEST EVIDENCE of civilization in Trabzon dates from 7000 BC. Established as a Greek colony (with Amasra and Sinop), the town benefited from its position on the busy trade route between the Black Sea and the Mediterranean. It grew quickly and was a focal point for the Pontic kings.

At the beginning of the 13th century, the Comnene dynasty established a Byzantine state with its capital at Trabzon. During the Comnene era, the city gained a reputation as a beautiful, sophisticated cultural centre. The Genoese and the Venetians came here to trade, as Trabzon was the terminus of a northern branch of the Silk Route. In 1461, Trabzon fell under Ottoman rule.

Trabzon Castle, established in the 5th century BC

🏛 Church and Museum of Haghia Sophia
Aya Sophia Müzesi
Follow İnönü Cad. 📞 *(0462) 223 30 43.* ⏲ *8am–noon & 1–5:30pm Tue–Sun (8:30am–noon & 1–5pm Tue–Sun in winter).* 📷 🚫

This restored 13th-century Byzantine church situated just a few kilometres from the city centre, is by far the most impressive sight in Trabzon. It was originally built by the Comnene emperor, Manuel VII Palaeologus. In 1577, it reverted to a mosque and, after serving as an ammunition depot and also as a hospital in 1957, became a museum. The interior frescoes depicting scenes from the Old Testament are among the finest in Turkey. The patterned mosaics date from Byzantine times, and you can still see the original coloured marble covering of the floor. Restoration work on the old frescoes is intermittent.

🔓 St Anne's Church
Küçük Ayvasıl Kilisesi
Kahraman Maraş Cad.

An Armenian church built in the 9th century, St Anne's is now permanently closed, but the exterior is worth a look. The entrance is adorned with carved crucifixes and angels. Another Armenian church, St Basil's (Büyük Ayvasil), is also found in this area.

🏰 Trabzon Castle
Trabzon Kalesi
İç Kale Sok.

The castle is located on the flat-topped hill (*trapezus* in Greek) that gave Trabzon its name. Today, only a small portion of the castle walls remain, but the area originally had three distinct wards, each with its own mosque. The only one still standing is the Fatih Camii in the Ortahisar (middle castle) section. Before it became a mosque, this was the principal church of the Comnene dynasty and its dome was topped with gold. Sadly, the gold, like the mosaics and frescoes inside, is long gone.

🏰 Zağnos Bridge and Tower
Zağnos Köprüsü ve Kale Kule
Zağnos Cad.

Built in 1467, the Zağnos Bridge crosses the Kuzgun ravine. In Ottoman times, the bridge provided access to charitable institutions. The Zağnos Tower was formerly a much-feared prison. Today, there is little reminder of its grim past, and visitors can tour the site and enjoy a meal at the tower restaurant.

🅖 Gülbahar Mosque and Tomb
Gülbahar Hatun Camii
Tanjant Yolu. ⏲ *except during prayer times.*

Built in 1514 by Sultan Selim the Grim in memory of his mother, Gülbahar, this is one of the few mosques in the city that was not originally a church. Gülbahar was noted for her charity work, and the mosque was built as part of an *imaret*, an Ottoman social welfare institution consisting of a soup kitchen and hostel for students and the poor. The main place of worship was the black-and-white stone section, with its five cupolas. The mosque is all that remains of the complex. Just to the east is Gülbahar's octagonal tomb.

Fresco in Haghia Sophia, showing the Last Supper

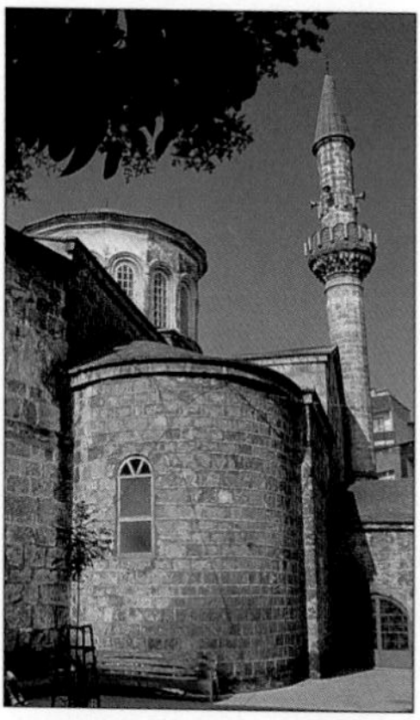

St Eugenius Church, turned into a mosque in 1461

St Eugenius Church

Yeni Cuma Camii

Follow signs from Fatih Hamami on Kasım Sok.

In the 14th century, this was the Church of St Eugenius, named for the martyred 5th-century archbishop of Carthage. In Ottoman times, the church was turned into a mosque. It is kept locked these days, but the guardian will open up for visitors.

Trabzon Museum

Uzun Sok, Zeytinlik Cad 10.

☎ (0462) 322 38 22. 🕘 9am–noon & 1–5:30pm Tue–Sun. 🎫

Trabzon Museum occupies a mansion built in the late 19th century for a Greek banker. The finely restored house is decorated in Baroque style and contains displays of local archaeology and ethnography.

Environs: A few kilometeres outside the centre of the city is **Atatürk's Villa**, an ornate three-storey mansion where Atatürk stayed several times after 1924. It was here that he made his will in 1937, the year before his death. The house was built in 1903, and is a typical example of upper-class Crimean architecture. The city of Trabzon presented it to Atatürk, and he left it to his sister, Makbule Atakan, at his death. The interior has been left almost undisturbed.

Atatürk's Villa

Atatürkün Köşkü

Soğuksu Cad, 4 km (2.4 miles) SW of city centre. *☎ (0462) 231 00 28. 🕘 8:30am–4:30pm daily. 👤 on inquiry at the entrance. 🎫*

Visitors' Checklist

👥 217,000. ✈ 8 km (5 miles) from city centre, (0462) 221 16 80. 🚌 Değirmendere, 3 km (2 miles) from city centre, (0462) 325 21 60. ⛴ from Istanbul and Rize. ℹ İskenderpaşa Mahallesi, Ali Nike Effendi Sok 1/A, (0462) 230 19 10. 🎉 Hıdrellez Summer Migration Festival (6 May). 🛒 daily.

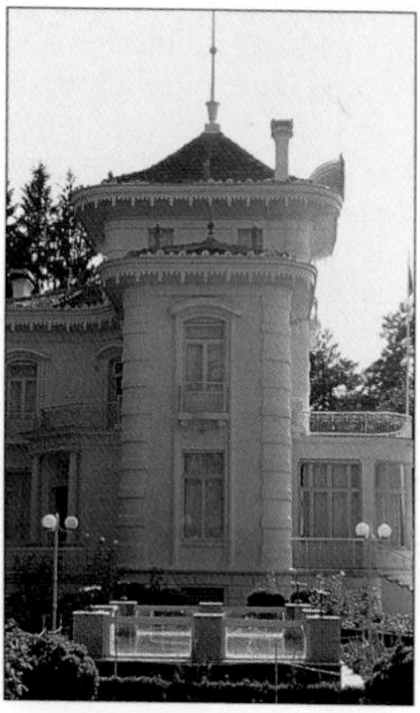

Atatürk's Villa, a handsome early 20th-century mansion

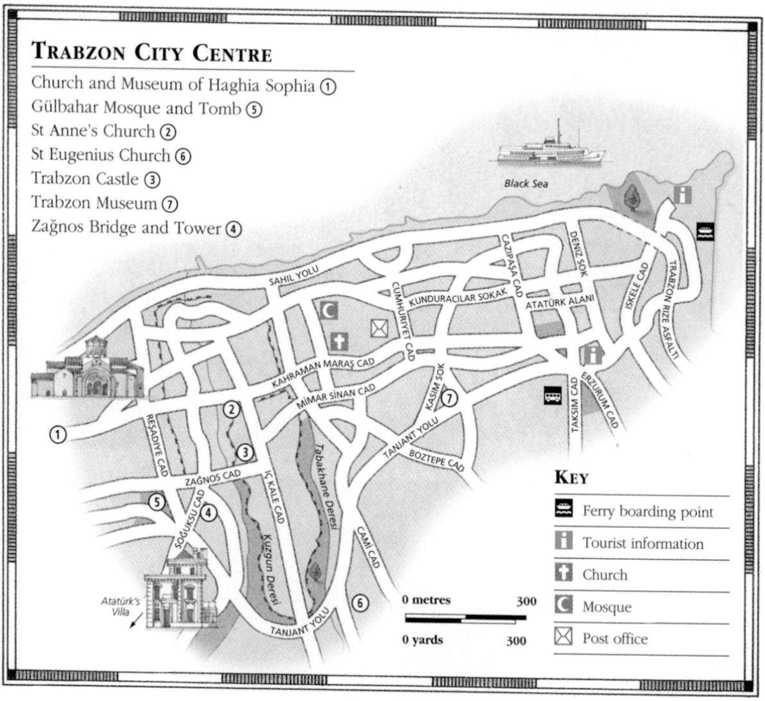
TRABZON CITY CENTRE
Church and Museum of Haghia Sophia 1
Gülbahar Mosque and Tomb 5
St Anne's Church 2
St Eugenius Church 6
Trabzon Castle 3
Trabzon Museum 7
Zağnos Bridge and Tower 4
Black Sea
SAHIL YOLU
CUMHURIYET CAD
KUNDURACILAR SOKAK
CAZIPAŞA CAD
DENIZ SOK
ATATÜRK ALANI
ISKELE CAD
TRABZON RIZE ASFALTI
KAHRAMAN MARAŞ CAD
MIMAR SINAN CAD
KASIM SOK
TAKSIM CAD
ERZURUM CAD
TANJANT YOLU
BOZTEPE CAD
REŞADIYE CAD
ZAĞNOS CAD
SOĞUKSU CAD
İÇ KALE CAD
Tabakhane Deresi
Kuzgun Deresi
CAMI CAD
TANJANT YOLU
Atatürk's Villa
0 metres 300
0 yards 300
KEY
Ferry boarding point
Tourist information
Church
Mosque
Post office

Sumela Monastery ❻

Sümela Manastırı

Monastery entrance

Sumela monastery sits high up on the cliffs of Mt Mela, southeast of Trabzon. It was founded in the 4th century by two Greek monks, Barnabas and Sophronius, who were guided to the site by an icon of a "black" image of the Virgin, allegedly painted by St Luke. After their deaths, Sumela became a place of pilgrimage. It was decorated with frescoes, and its treasures included priceless manuscripts and silver plates. The monastery was rebuilt several times – the ruins seen by today's visitors date largely from the 19th century.

In the Ottoman era, Sumela enjoyed the protection of the sultans, but it was abandoned and badly damaged during the War of Independence. In recent years, extensive restoration work has been carried out.

VISITORS' CHECKLIST

55 km (34 miles) SE of Trabzon in Altındere National Park. ☎ (0462) 512 29 03 (lower entrance) and (0462) 512 28 91 (upper entrance). ☐ May–Oct: 8am–6pm daily; Nov–Apr: 9am–3pm daily. ☑ ☐ ☐

★ **Frescoes**
Though badly damaged by vandals, lovely fresco panels cover the walls of the church.

Restoration
A fire in the 1920s left many of the monastery buildings roofless and exposed to the elements. Restoration work involves rebuilding the roof trusses and adding tiles.

★ **Living Quarters**
The cells used by the Greek Orthodox monks are ranged along the five-storey outside building overlooking the Altındere valley.

Forest Path
A 1-km (0.5-mile) path winds through pine forest to the often mist-shrouded monastery. It takes 30 minutes to make the ascent.

STAR FEATURES

★ **Frescoes**

★ **Living Quarters**

Zigana ❼

🎪 *Kadırga Festival: migration to high pastures and nomadic origins (usually held in spring and summer).*

AFTER VISITING the Sumela Monastery, travellers can return to Trabzon or continue further southwest to reach the spectacular alpine area known as Zigana and situated in the Kalkanlı Mountains. There is some skiing here, but only day trips are possible as there are no hotels.

Fog and snow cover the Zigana area for about seven months of the year, and it is usually damp here. Heavy winter snowfalls make access difficult and even dangerous.

To get to Zigana, you can drive through the 1,500-m (4,291-ft) mountain tunnel, the longest in Turkey.

A more challenging, but much more scenic route runs parallel to the main 885 road through Hamsiköy village. It is worth stopping here to sample the excellent local cuisine. The speciality is a nourishing, creamy rice pudding.

Gümüşhane ❽

🏠 35,000. 🛈 *Valilik Binası, Kat 3, (0456) 213 34 72.*

GÜMÜŞHANE (silver works) takes its name from the rich deposits of silver ore found here. In the late 16th century, silver was more valuable than gold. However, by the late 19th century, the silver industry had declined.

Before World War I, the area was a focus of conflict between the Russians and the

A ruined Byzantine church in the old section of Gümüşhane

Ottomans, for Gümüşhane occupied a strategic position on the trade route between Anatolia and Persia (Iran).

Here, visitors can explore the surrounding castles, and several mosques. The most interesting of these is the Süleymaniye (or Küçük) Camii. There are also eight *hamams* (Turkish baths), which cater for men and women.

Gümüşhane is renowned for its rosehip *(kuşburun)* syrup and sweet cherry jam *(kiraz reçeli)*.

Wild poppy near Bayburt

Bayburt ❾

🏠 41,000. 🛈 *Hükümet Binası, Kat 4, (0458) 211 44 29.* 🏛 *Mon.* 🎪 *Dedekorkut Cultural Festival (2nd week in Jul).*

SITUATED ON the Çoruh River, Bayburt is the capital of the smallest of Turkey's 78 provinces. Bayburt Castle was probably built in Byzantine times, but there is evidence of an older fortress on the site.

The castle has a violent history. It had to be rebuilt by the Byzantine Emperor Justinian and was repaired by both Seljuks and Ottomans

The Çoruh River, running through the fortress town of Bayburt

following various attacks. At its peak, there were 300 houses within the complex. Provision for daily needs included a bakery and flour mill. The community even produced its own paint.

Today, visitors can see a theological school, a mosque, *hamams* and kitchens, as well as a dervish lodge. The eastern corner contains the remains of a church built between the 8th and 14th centuries. On the hills at the southern edge of the city stand the twin mausoleums of Şehit (martyr) Osman and his sister. Osman Park, beside the river, is a good place to relax and enjoy a refreshing glass of tea.

About 20 km (12 miles) northwest of Bayburt are the remains of underground cities dating from Byzantine times. These are usually open to visitors. For details, inquire at the tea garden at the entrance or at the tourism office in the town centre.

Outside Bayburt, on the way to Aşkale and Erzurum, travellers must negotiate a spectacular mountain pass which rises to the dizzying height of 2,302 m (7,552 ft).

Village on the shores of Uzungöl (Long Lake)

Uzungöl ⑩

🚌 *tour bus from Trabzon or dolmuş from Of (90 min); dolmuşes are less frequent in the winter months.*

FOR MOUNTAIN SCENERY, few places in Turkey compare with this alpine lake, which was carved out during the Ice Ages. At an altitude of over 1,000 m (3,280 ft), Uzungöl (Long Lake) is a hidden gem surrounded by lush greenery and remote meadows.

At weekends, Uzungöl is popular with local people, who journey here by dolmuş from the coastal village of Of, but there is not much to do besides camping, hiking in the nearby hills, fishing and relaxing. The village has a few basic hotels, and the local lake trout is excellent.

Rize ⑪

🏛 *72,000.* 🚌 *0.8 km (0.5 mile) west of town.* ℹ *Valilik Binası, A Blok, Kat 5, (0464) 213 04 07.* 🛍 *Russian bazaar daily.* 🎉 *Tea Festival (3rd week Jun).*

IN ANCIENT TIMES, Rize was ruled by the Pontic kings *(see p298)* and was known as Rhizus. The name means rice, although the town is now better known for its tea.

Rize was strongly fortified by the Byzantines in the 6th century and later became part of the Comnene empire. Like Trabzon, it came under Ottoman control in 1461.

In Ottoman times, many people left Rize to seek work in Russia. There they learned the art of bread- and pastry-making, which they brought back with them when they returned. Today, many of Turkey's master pastry chefs and bakers come from Rize.

Visitors will notice many locals clad in the versatile *Rize bezi*, a light cloth made of silk, cotton or wool, in black and purple. It is mainly used as a head covering for women, but also doubles as a useful rain bonnet and a handy receptacle when the local women go out to gather tea leaves.

Corn bread, Hemşin Valley

The small **Rize Museum** is not outstanding, but has some displays of local life and lore.

🏛 **Rize Museum**
Piri Çelebi Mahellesi, PTT Arkası.
📞 *(0464) 214 02 35.* 🕐 *9am–noon & 1–5:30pm Tue–Sun.* 🎫

Hemşin Valley ⑫

42 km (26 miles) E of Rize.

EAST OF RIZE, the road turns off to the Hemşin Valley. A few kilometres further east is a second turning south to Çamlıhemşin. The road rises steeply and the air is filled with the smell of boxwood trees. This area lies deep within the Kaçkar Mountains (Kaçkar Dağları), at an altitude of 3,932 m (12,900 ft). This is one of Turkey's best areas for trekking and hiking. To the east is Ayder, a village known for its hot springs.

The local inhabitants, the Hemşin, were once Christian Armenians who subsequently converted to Islam. They delight in their seasonal and farming festivals, folklore traditions and colourful costumes, and still migrate to and from the high summer pastures.

A staple food of the valley is *mıhlama* (corn bread), made from corn grown on the coastal plain. The bread is served straight from the pan in which it was baked. Sometimes, *lor* (white, unsalted cheese) is added to *mıhlama*, which is often served hot for breakfast.

There are two castles near Çamlıhemşin. One is Kale-i Bala, above the village of Hisarcık Köyü, dating from

TURKISH TEA

Turkey's first tea plants were brought from Japan in 1878, but the industry did not take off until the 1930s. The moist climate of the Black Sea coast provides superb growing conditions. Rize is the centre of the Turkish tea industry, and the home of the country's Tea Institute (Çay Enstitüsü). To sample the best tea, look for *tomurcuk* (the flowering bud of the tea bush). Leaves from other parts of the plant are not as flavourful. Turks prefer the black tea sold in local markets; green tea is exported. Specialized fragrant teas are also produced, again mostly for export. Glasses, spoons, sugar and some good company are all part of enjoying Turkish tea, which is brewed in a double boiler. The leaves are scalded before brewing to impart an earthy, smoky flavour.

Turkish tea served in a typical "tulip" glass

200 BC. Further up the valley is the lonely Zilkalesi (Bell Castle) with eight ramparts overlooking the valley of the Storm River (Fırtına Çayı). Both are open to visitors and entrance is free.

There are some spectacular stone bridges, probably built by the Byzantines, spanning the Storm River, most notably at the village of Şenyuva.

Traffic and poor-quality roads make driving in the Hemşin Valley a challenge. A four-wheel-drive vehicle is recommended, particularly after rains. Local dolmuş traffic is casual and erratic.

The area is broken up by many steep valleys and narrow passes, and local people have devised an ingenious transport solution: the *vargel*, a cable car on a pulley system. It is powered by electricity (or people power, if no electricity is available). Used to carry goods, animals and people, the *vargel* is a practical, if quaint, solution and offers a bird's-eye view of the area.

Russian dolls for sale in Hopa, near the Georgian border

Hopa ⑬

🚌 on W bank of river.

HOPA IS THE LAST main town before the frontier with Georgia. It is a garrison town, and there is a strong military presence. Hopa was a major port in ancient times, and is still the main seaport (after Trabzon) on the eastern Black Sea coast.

Today, the town is dominated by the boat-building industry and a large thermal power station.

Bulls fighting at the Kafkasör Festival in Artvin

Artvin ⑭

🏛 20,000. 🛈 Camii Meydanı 10, (0466) 212 30 71. 🎪 Kafkasör Festival (Jun).

ARTVIN RECEIVES more rain than any other place in Turkey, so everything grows wonderfully here. The people of Artvin are known for their many festivals, which feature traditional dancing, games, music, food and costumes. The major annual celebration is the Kafkasör (Caucasian) Festival in June, featuring the spectacle of fighting bulls.

Around Artvin are a number of beautiful villages. Şavşat, about 55 km (34 miles) to the east on the road to Ardahan, is a lovely alpine hamlet. The road goes on to Veliköy and, 19 km (11 miles) further on, reaches the **Karagöl-Sahara National Park**, which has extensive forests and lakes.

🏞 Karagöl-Sahara National Park
📞 (0466) 531 21 37. ⏰ May–Oct daily. 🅿 for cars only. 🏨

Yusufeli ⑮

68 km (42 miles) S of Artvin or 150 km (93 miles) NE of Bayburt (difficult route). 🏛 4,000.

YUSUFELI IS A nature-lover's paradise, with some of the most rugged scenery in Turkey. As it is a designated conservation area, hunting is strictly controlled and many wild species are protected.

Yusufeli is becoming well known for whitewater rafting (*see p362*) on the challenging Çoruh River. The best time to go is in spring when the wild flowers are in bloom. There are outstanding opportunities for photography, particularly around the deep, icy lakes.

Around Yusufeli, there are many Georgian and Armenian churches and out-of-the way castles. Dört Kilise (Four Churches) is a few kilometres southwest of the town, while İşhan is a superb 11th-century church in the mountains east of Yusufeli off the main road (signposted to Olur). A track leads to the church.

The churning waters of the spectacular Çoruh River

CAPPADOCIA AND CENTRAL ANATOLIA

ENTRAL ANATOLIA *is one of Turkey's few completely landlocked regions. The ancient cities of Boğazkale and Alacahöyük reveal the Hittite presence in this area during the 1st and 2nd millennia BC. Most of the artifacts from these places are now housed in museums, but visitors can imagine the impact and extent of the impressive civilization that once flourished in the region.*

In the ancient Persian language, Cappadocia meant "land of beautiful horses", and in Roman times, brood mares from Cappadocia were so highly prized that a special tax was imposed on their sale.

Trying to describe Cappadocia in physical terms simply does not do justice to the air of mystery that pervades the area. Remarkable conical rock outcrops, called *peri bacaları* (fairy chimneys), are the region's most famous and characteristic feature. Carved into the rock are scores of hidden chapels adorned with exquisite frescoes – ample proof of the strength of the Christian faith that was established here by the 4th century AD.

Over the centuries, Central Anatolia has nurtured vast armies and great empires, and its history and prosperity have always been linked to the land and agriculture. Today, tourism has become the mainstay of the local economy, but the region still produces most of Turkey's cereal crops as well as grapes, vegetable oils and sugar beets. The diary of a 4th-century saint even records wine as a local product.

Kayseri, the major city, is known as much for its many varieties of cured beef *(pastırma)* as for its industrious but conservative inhabitants. A gentler side of the region is to be found near Amasya along the picturesque Yeşilırmak River.

Konaks (mansion houses) along the bank of the Yeşilırmak River

◁ **"Fairy chimneys" with caps, in the vicinity of Ürgüp**

Exploring Cappadocia and Central Anatolia

THE MAJESTIC JEWEL of Central Anatolia is the Cappadocia region, a bewitching landscape of spectacularly eroded tuff (hardened volcanic ash). Mount Erciyes (Erciyes Dağı), an extinct volcano, looms over this haunting panorama. Volcanic deposits have made this a fertile area for agriculture, with grapes, apricots, cherries, sugar beets and chickpeas grown locally.

The main Hittite sites in Asia Minor are found at Boğazkale and Alacahöyük. Often neglected, Kayseri is a treasure-trove of Seljuk history and should not be missed. The Pontic kings *(see p48)* once ruled in Amasya, an unspoiled town in the valley of the Yeşilırmak River. The region's varied sights complement the country crafts, such as carpet weaving and the beautiful decorative pottery produced around Avanos.

Uçhisar village, overlooked by cave dwellings

Hot-air balloon drifting over the eroded tuff landscape

SIGHTS AT A GLANCE

Aksaray **11**
Alacahöyük **16**
Amasya pp298–9 **18**
Boğazkale pp296–7 **15**
Bünyan **5**
Çorum **17**
Göreme Open-Air Museum pp284–5 **2**
Güzelyurt **9**
Hacı Bektaş **13**
Ihlara Valley **10**

Kayseri pp290–91 **4**
Kırşehir **12**
Mount Erciyes **6**
Mustafapaşa **3**
Nevşehir **1**
Niğde **8**
Sivas **20**
Soğanlı **7**
Tokat **19**
Yozgat **14**

Sabanözü
Ankara
Ankara
ALACAHÖYÜK **16**
190
BOĞAZKALE **15**
KIRIKKALE
Ankara
E88
200
765
260
Seyfe Lake
Ankara
KIRŞEHİR **12**
HACI BEKTAŞ **13**
E90
750
NEVŞEHİR
AKSARAY **11**
GÜZELYUR
10
IHLARA VALLEY
NİĞDE
ULUKIŞLA

The King's Gate at Boğazkale, in Hattuşaş National Park

KEY

≡ Motorway

▬ Major road

▬ Secondary road

▭ Other road

▪ Scenic route

▬ River

☼ Viewpoint

GETTING AROUND

Kayseri and Nevşehir are both served by intercity buses, as well as regular flights to and from Istanbul. Most of the main sights are a 40–60-minute drive on good paved roads from these centres. Minibuses and dolmuşes run frequently between major tourist attractions, but renting your own vehicle will give you the greatest flexibility. Some sights (even the underground cities) involve quite a bit of walking. Coach tours from centres throughout Turkey serve the region.

The Blue Seminary (Gök Medresesi) in Amasya

Rock Formations of Cappadocia

THE LANDSCAPE OF CAPPADOCIA was created around 30 million years ago, when erupting volcanoes blanketed the region with ash. The ash solidified into an easily eroded material called tuff, overlain in places by layers of hard volcanic rock. Over time, the tuff was worn away, creating distinctive formations, including the capped-cone "fairy chimneys" near Ürgüp.

Cappadocia covers a relatively small area – around 300 sq km (116 sq miles). It has become a popular area for tourists, and the area around Nevşehir, together with nearby Ürgüp and Göreme *(see pp282–5)*, offer the best opportunities to see the bewitching natural formations for which the region is celebrated.

LOCATOR MAP

☐ *Tuff formations*

Mushroom Shape
This "mushroom" rock, an unusual example of erosion, is located near Gülşehir.

EROSION AND WEATHERING

Cappadocia's extraordinary landscape is partly the result of erosion by water, wind and changes in temperature. Rainfall and rivers wear down the tuff and, like the wind, carry away loose material. In winter, extreme temperature changes cause the rocks to expand and contract and eventually to disintegrate.

Cavities below the hard layer are turned into dwellings.

FAIRY CHIMNEYS

The extraordinary formations pictured below are called "fairy chimneys" because early inhabitants of Cappadocia believed that they were the chimneys of fairies, who lived under the ground. Some of them reach heights of up to 40 m (130 ft).

Complete erosion wears away the protective caps and creates the conical shapes found in the Göreme Valley.

Elongated Shape
These columns are capped with layers of slightly harder material.

Pedestal Shape
Created when a lump of basalt rests atop a tuff column.

Cone Shape
Erosion thins tuff beneath the basalt cap, which then falls off.

Eroded Tuff Field
In the triangle defined by Nevşehir, Ürgüp and Avanos, the tuff layer was originally up to 100 m (328 ft) thick. As the older tuff continues to erode, younger cones are formed. This process has been taking place for around 10 million years.

Lava flows harden into a protective layer over the tuff.

Erosion widens cracks and fissures, separating sections from the main body and allowing for the development of strange shapes.

Underground cities

Cracks in the tuff layers allowed people to hollow out dwellings and churches.

Protective caps give a tubular shape to the eroded formation.

VOLCANOES OF ANATOLIA

Snowcapped Mount Erciyes, 20 km (13 miles) southwest of Kayseri

Volcanic activity in Central Anatolia is a product of the region's position *(see pp18–19)* at the boundaries of two of the tectonic plates that make up the Earth's crust. Mount Erciyes is the largest in a chain of extinct volcanoes created by the collision of the heavy Arabian with the lighter Anatolian Plate. The collision pushed magma to the surface, building up immense pressure and eventually causing Mounts Erciyes, Hasan and others to erupt, spewing forth enormous amounts of rock and lava that greatly altered the landscape of Central Anatolia. The Hittites *(see pp44–5)* worshipped snow-covered Mount Erciyes. They called it "Harkassos" (White Mountain).

Underground Cities
The softness of the tuff made it easy to excavate in order to create dwellings. In some places, as at Derinkuyu (above), whole cities were constructed underground. These settlements had living quarters, stables, wells, ventilation systems, churches and storage rooms.

Nevşehir **❶**

**Sunflower
from the
Nevşehir area**

A S THE CAPITAL OF CAPPADOCIA, Nevşehir makes a very good starting point for touring the region. Known as Nyssa in antiquity, the town has the Kurşunlu Mosque and *medrese (see p32),* dating from 1725, as well as a castle and a good museum. The surrounding tuff formations and troglodyte (underground) cities are the most popular attractions, but visitors are likely to leave the Nevşehir area with strong memories of sunflowers, chickpeas, donkeys and sugar beets, as well as apricots drying on rooftops. A striking feature of the Nevşehir area is its strong Christian leaning. As early as the 4th century, monks and hermits inhabited Cappadocia.

**Passageway in Derinkuyu,
showing "millstone" door**

Zelve

10 km (6.2 miles) NE of Nevşehir.
◯ May–Oct: 8:30am–7pm daily;
Nov–Apr: 8:30am–5:30pm daily. 🖼

A secluded monastic retreat, Zelve lies in a series of deep valleys and is dotted with rooms and caves on many levels. Metal walkways and stairs lead to less accessible chapels and hideaways which hold a few frescoes. In 1950 an earthquake shook the Çavuşın/Zelve area, and the cave dwellings remain somewhat unkempt today. The nature of the site will appeal to the fit and adventurous. Many of the caves and rooms are only accessed by clambering through dark holes and tunnels, so bring a torch and spare batteries.

Two small churches lie on the valley floor: the Üzümlü Kilise (Grape Church) and the Balık Kilise (Fish Church), both featuring ornate carvings. The latter is an Ottoman mosque, but with a stone steeple.

Derinkuyu

30 km (18.6 miles) S of Nevşehir.
◯ May–Oct: 9am–7pm daily;
Nov–Apr: 9am–5pm daily. 🖼

There are believed to be about 36 underground cities in this region, but only a few have been excavated. Of these, Derinkuyu (deep well) is the biggest, most popular and best lit. It is thought to have been home to around 20,000 people. The eight-level complex is 60 m (197 ft) deep. A long "transit" tunnel

was supposed to have linked Derinkuyu with a similar "ant hill" settlement at Kaymaklı, about 10 km (6 miles) away. At peak times (11am–3pm) the tunnels can get somewhat uncomfortably crowded – anyone who tries to backtrack will be very unpopular.

The first levels include a stable, wine-press and a large vault. Deeper down, there are living quarters, a kitchen and a church.

The heavy millstones recessed into the walls were, in fact, doors that could be rolled into place to seal off strategic areas of the settlement. Huge ventilation shafts still function, but damp is a problem. Living here for any extended period of time could not have been easy.

Spread over three valleys and with many fairy chimneys, Zelve was inhabited until 1952

House in Ürgüp dating from the period of Greek habitation

VISITORS' CHECKLIST

72,500. ✈ Kapadokya, (0384) 421 44 50.
🚌 Gülşehir Cad, Nevtur, (0384) 213 11 71 and 213 12 29.
Göreme Tur, (0384) 213 55 37 and 213 47 09. 🛈 in front of the State Hospital, (0384) 212 95 73. 🚴 Cappadocia Mountain Biking Festival (1st week Jul).

Ürgüp

12km (7 miles) E of Nevşehir.
🏙 15,000. 🛈 Parkı İçi, (0384) 341 40 59. 🍷 Wine/grape Festival (end Sep, early Oct).

Ürgüp is now so synonymous with the troglodyte cities built during Byzantine times that it is easy to overlook the town's Roman and Seljuk history. Ürgüp's ancient name was Assiana, and it was known as Başhisar under the Seljuks. Seljuk influence can be seen in the 13th-century remains of the Kadıkalesi (castle) and the Altıkapı Tomb. Near the Nükrettin Mausoleum is a library named after Tasinağa, a 19th-century town squire. Until 1923, when Turkey became a republic, the town had a large Greek population.

Ürgüp's **museum** contains ceramics and statues from pre-historic to Byzantine times, as well as displays of textiles, costumes, weapons and books.

Ürgüp is a convenient base to tour Cappadocia. There are plenty of pensions and hotels, yet the town has retained its village charm. This area has always been well known for its farm produce, particularly for grapes. Ürgüp-labelled wine is refreshing and light. In general, the white wines are more authentic and interesting than the reds.

Several local spots offer impromptu entertainment in the evenings.

🏛 Museum

Next to tourist office, at park entrance. ☏ (0384) 341 40 82. ⏰ 8am–noon & 1–5pm Tue–Sun. 🖾

Avanos

16 km (10 miles) NE of Nevşehir.
🏙 14,500. 🛈 Açık Pazar Yeri, (0384) 511 43 60.

Watered by the Kızılırmak (Red River), Avanos is a pretty, leafy town noted for its pottery and ceramics. Carpet-weaving and tapestry-making are equally important local skills.

In Roman times, Avanos was called Venessa. It fell under Ottoman suzerainty in 1466 along with Nevşehir. Today it is a typical country town, albeit with a lack of grand mosques or *medreses*. In the town centre is the Yeraltı (Ulu) Mosque, dating from the 15th century, and the Alaeddin Mosque, built by the Seljuks.

Ceramics and wine are the town's lifeblood. Visitors can purchase many serviceable pottery items, while exquisite porcelain designs are the stock in trade of places like Kaya Seramik Evi. These pieces are thrown by hand, then painted and glazed. The intricate designs are pains-takingly reproduced from the İznik originals (see p161), and even manage to capture the typical milky, opaque porcelain background.

Display of local wine from the Ürgüp area

About 5 km (3 miles) east of Avanos is Sarıhan, a Seljuk *han* or caravanserai (see p24) built in 1238 on the classic square plan. The repaired *han* gives a good idea of the accommodation facilities, as well as stables and a small mosque, available to traders making the long trek along the Silk Route (see pp24–5).

Shaping a jug in a pottery workshop in Avanos

Kaymaklı

20 km (12 miles) S of Nevşehir.
⏰ May–Oct: 9am–7pm daily; Nov–Apr: 9am–5pm daily. 🖾

Discovered in 1964, Kaymaklı is the second most important underground city in the region. It is believed to have housed thousands of people from the 6th to 9th centuries. Although five levels are open to visitors, experts believe Kaymaklı has eight levels. It is unclear when the first floor was originally excavated. The underground area is thought to cover an area of about 2.5 sq km (1 sq mile).

Being smaller and less crowded than many of the region's other underground cities, the rooms and their various functions seem more convincing. To appreciate the area as it was centuries ago, try to get there early.

Göreme Open-Air Museum ❷

THE GÖREME VALLEY HOLDS the greatest concentration of rock-cut chapels and monasteries in Cappadocia. Dating largely from the 9th century onwards, the valley's 30 or more churches were built by cutting rooms out of the soft volcanic tuff. Many of the churches feature superb Byzantine frescoes depicting scenes from the Old and New Testaments, and particularly the life of Christ and deeds of the saints. The cultural importance of the valley has been recognized by the Turkish government and they have restored and preserved the many caves to create the Göreme Open-Air Museum. UNESCO has declared the Göreme Valley a World Heritage Site.

Tokalı Church
The Tokalı Church, located near the entrance to the museum, contains some of the most beautiful frescoes in the Göreme Valley.

The walking route starts at the car park near the entrance.

★ Kızlar Monastery
Monks lived and worked in this hollowed-out formation. Ladders or scaffolding were probably used to reach the upper levels.

STAR SIGHTS

★ **Dark Church**

★ **Elmalı Church**

★ **Kızlar Monastery**

Camel Tours
Portions of the Göreme Valley and surrounding area can be viewed from atop a camel on guided tours.

★ Dark Church
A pillared church, built around a small courtyard, the Dark Church contains frescoes depicting the ascension of Christ.

VISITORS' CHECKLIST

15 km (9 miles) E of Nevşehir.
(0384) 271 21 67. Kayseri
Erkilet (90km from Nevesbir),
(0352) 337 54 94. 8am–6pm
daily (8am–5pm in winter).
additional fee for Buckle Church
and Dark Church.

Katherina Church

Çarıklı Church

Dining Hall

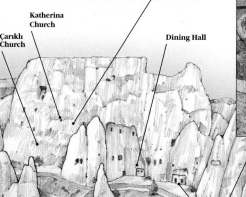

Yılanlı Church
The barrel-vaulted church has painted panels devoted to a number of saints.

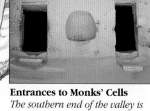

Entrances to Monks' Cells
The southern end of the valley is honeycombed with the tiny cells once occupied by monks.

★ Elmalı Church
Noted for the sophistication of its frescoes, the church dates from the 11th century.

Barbara Church
The church takes its name from a fresco on the west wall, which is thought to depict St Barbara. A seated figure of Christ occupies the central apse. Saints Georgius and Theodorus are depicted killing the dragon.

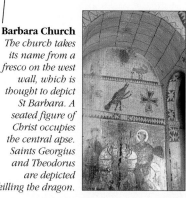

The Church of Constantine and Helen, in Mustafapaşa

Mustafapaşa ❸

6 km (4 miles) S of Ürgüp.
🏠 *3,800.*

FORMERLY KNOWN AS Sinasos, Mustafapaşa is a perfectly preserved Greek village, whose inhabitants left during the exchange of populations between Greece and Turkey in 1923. The houses have a wealth of carved stonework, wall paintings and reminders of the former inhabitants' lifestyles. Although some houses are neglected, the balconies and sculptured windows are sure to delight. Sadly, the 19th-century Church of Constantine and Helen in the town centre is in a particularly bad state. Of note are the monastery of St Nicholas and the Church of St Basil, the latter located outside the village.

Several pensions and a few hotels have been restored to their former Greek appearance.

Kayseri ❹

See pp290–91.

Bünyan ❺

35 km (22 miles) E of Kayseri.
🏠 *5,780.* 🎪 *Yoghurt Festival (18 May).*

BÜNYAN LIES EAST of Kayseri, off the main highway to Sivas. This is a good place for a relaxed outing for a few hours or an afternoon, and often features on sightseeing tours to the region.

The economic mainstay of the town is handicrafts, mainly the carpets handwoven by the women. You can see them at work on the looms and learn about the designs and the amount of work involved. A particular feature of carpets from Bünyan is the use of thin, high-tensile mercerized cotton to make bedspreads, floor rugs, and prayer mats. This ensures that the finished carpet always lies flat.

Mount Erciyes ❻
Erciyes Dağı

MOUNT ERCIYES, at a height of 3,916 m (12,848 ft), is Cappadocia's dominant natural landmark. Locals regard this extinct volcano with respect because of its role in shaping the landscape when it buried the area in volcanic dust and ash millions of years ago. The residual tuff – fine-grained, compressed volcanic ash – is the area's major geological feature *(see pp280–81)*. The calcium in the tuff enriches the soil, encouraging the growth of trees and vines.

Between the two peaks (Greater and Lesser Erciyes) are two lovely moraine lakes, Cora and Sarı. Mount Erciyes is also a ski centre *(see p362)* with a chairlift and a lodge. The season runs from November to May. Hiking is possible in summer, but you will need a guide and proper gear.

Soğanlı ❼

38 km (24 miles) S of Ürgüp.
🏠 *4,650.* ⏰ *8:30am–5:30pm daily.* 📷

THE MAIN ATTRACTION OF the Soğanlı Valley is that it is quiet and undisturbed. It is possible, even, to think of this valley as a microcosm of

Pigeon coops cut into the rocks at Soğanlı, marked with white rings to attract the birds

◁ **Troglodyte dwellings in the rock above the village of Uçhisar**

the whole Göreme Valley. There are six interesting churches to visit here, though it is thought that more than 100 flourished at one time. All six are in good condition and can be seen on foot during the course of a day trip.

The delicate, pastel tones of Soğanlı's frescoes differ from the harsher hues to be seen in the churches at Göreme, where ongoing restoration has produced stronger colours.

The distinctive, colourful cloth dolls sold throughout Cappadocia are produced by Soğanlı's handicraft industry.

Niğde

🏛 69,500. 🚌 *Emin Eşirgil Cad, 1 km (0.5 mile) from town centre.* 🚉 *end of İstasyon Cad, 1 km (0.5 mile) from town centre, (0388) 232 35 41.* 🛈 *Belediye Sarayı, (0388) 232 33 93.* 🛍 *Women's Handicraft Market (Sat).* 🎭 *Tepecuması Folklore and Country Festival (27 May).*

KNOWN IN HITTITE TIMES AS Nahita, Niğde survived 10th-century Arab raids better than its neighbours. Its position on a major trade route to the Mediterranean appealed to the enterprising Seljuks, and so Niğde flourished as a regional capital until the time of the Mongol invasions *(see p53)*.

White-headed duck

The Seljuks filled the town with fine architecture, notably the Alaeddin Mosque (1223), distinguished by its superb stonework, ornate portal and typical squat minaret, and the Great Mosque (Ulu Camii), which was built around 1335. There is also a Seljuk tomb, the Hüdavend Hatun Türbe, featuring the octagonal forms typical of Seljuk architecture.

Niğde's bazaar *(bedesten)*, with its fine clock tower, is a vestige of the town's heyday. The museum has sections on ethnography and Asian civilizations, and displays the mummified remains of a nun from the Ihlara Valley *(see p292)*.

Do try and taste Niğde's creamy sheep's cheese, which is traditionally sold wrapped in a goatskin. These local cheeses are called *tulum peynırı*, meaning "encased in a skin".

ENVIRONS: There are several interesting places near Niğde. The best are **Bor**, a carpet-weaving centre that lies 15 km (9 miles) to the southwest, and **Kemerhisar**, which is 20 km (12 miles) to the south. This Hittite site dates from about 1200 BC. At the site, you can see the arches of an aqueduct and a mineral spring.

The Byzantine monastery church at **Eski Gümüş**, about 9 km (6 miles) northeast of Niğde, was restored in the early 1990s and is one of the best-kept secrets in Turkey. The frescoes here are outstanding by any standards.

If you are a mountaineer, the **Aladağlar Mountains** offer some excellent climbing and include Demirkazık, the highest peak in the region. To reach the summit, the best starting point is the village of the same name, which lies 65 km (40 miles) east of Niğde. To the northeast of Niğde is **Sultansazlığı Bird Sanctuary**, which is considered to be Turkey's most important bird sanctuary after Lake Manyas (Kuşcenneti; *see p157)*. With a total area of

A narrow gorge in the spectacular Aladağlar Mountains, near Niğde

172 sq km (66 sq miles), the marshes are regarded as some of the largest and most important wetlands in Europe and the Middle East. Since 1993, the area has been protected under the terms of the Ramsar Convention, an agreement signed in Iran in 1971 to conserve wetlands and their resources. The reserve is a haven for around 300 species of bird, including ducks, flamingoes, terns, cranes, egrets and plovers. Partridges, swordbeaks, whimbrels and pelicans all come here to breed. The best bird-watching spot is the lookout at Ovaçiftlik, where there is also a museum.

🦆 Sultansazlığı Bird Sanctuary

70 km (44 miles) SW of Kayseri. 🕿 *(0352) 658 55 49.* 🕙 *5am–midnight daily.* 🅿

The Sultansazlığı Bird Sanctuary, a bird-watcher's paradise

Kayseri 4

DOMINATED BY Mount Erciyes, Kayseri has been fought over by Persians, Arabs, Mongols and Ottomans. Its most prosperous era was undoubtedly under the Romans – when it was known as Eusebeia/Mazaka and then Caesarea – but it also flourished under the Seljuks. At the junction of five roads, the city was a key point on the Roman road system, and the Romans established an imperial munitions factory here. By the 4th century Kayseri was a focal point of Christian life and faith. Its most famous cleric (and bishop) was St Basil the Great (around AD 329–379), who defended church doctrine against heretical movements.

Seljuk stone carving

Exploring Kayseri

Kayseri was once a prominent centre of education, and has many religious institutions, tombs and mosques to visit. Nowadays, textiles and sugar beet are the main industries, but the city is also known for fine carpets. In addition, the best *sucuk* (salami) in Turkey comes from here and the 20 varieties of *pastırma* (cured beef) are a regional speciality.

⬛ Twin-Turreted Theology Complex

Çifte Medresesi
Sinan Park. ☎ (0352) 231 35 65.
◯ 8am–noon & 1–5:30pm Tue–Sun.
The complex consists of two adjoining theological centres, the Gıyasiye Medresesi and the Şifahiye Medresesi. The Seljuks placed great emphasis on learning – this extended to anatomy and medicine. This was the first Seljuk academy of medicine and is now called the Gevher Nesibe Medical History Museum. Here you

can learn more about Seljuk medical practices. There is an operating theatre, consultant's offices and accommodation for psychiatric patients.

The architectural scheme incorporates arches, vaulted antechambers *(eyvan)* and an open courtyard.

Three Bazaars

Behind the Ulu Camii. ◯ *Sun.*
Kayseri's three bazaars offer a contrast to the city's wealth of tombs and mausoleums. The Covered Bazaar (Kapılı Çarşı) dates from 1859, but the other two, the Bedesten and Vizir Han, date from the 15th and 16th centuries respectively.

There are few places that capture the keen spirit of age-old trading better than the bazaars of Kayseri. All three are still patronized by local people and traders, who barter and haggle in a lively atmosphere. Many of the local specialities, such as textiles and carpets, can be bought in the bazaars.

Entrance to the Twin-Turreted Theology Complex

⬛ Citadel

Kale
The north wall and ramparts of the Citadel were built by the Emperor Justinian in the 6th century. However, little of the outer fortifications can be seen today. The black basalt structure originally had 195 bastions, and it is still an imposing sight – albeit as a shopping centre today.

⬛ Güpgüpoğlu Stately Home

Güpgüpoğlu Konağı
Tennuri Sok, Cumhuriyet Mahallesi.
☎ (0352) 222 95 16. ◯ 8:30am–noon & 1:30–5pm Tue–Sun. 📷
A family home built between 1417 and 1419, the house has been carefully preserved and restored to its former glory, with each room highlighting specific aspects of Ottoman life. There are guest rooms, a bridal chamber, meeting areas for family gatherings and men's and women's quarters. Notable features are the built-in cupboards *(yüklük)* for storing mattresses, and the kitchen area, which consists of a pantry and a large main kitchen *(tokana)*.

⬛ Huand Hatun Mosque Complex

Huand Hatun Camii ve Medresesi
Behind tourism information office.
◯ 9am–5:30pm daily.
This *külliye* (religious and educational institution adjoining a mosque) was one of the first mosque precincts the Seljuks built in Anatolia, although the

The 13th-century Citadel, now a busy shopping centre

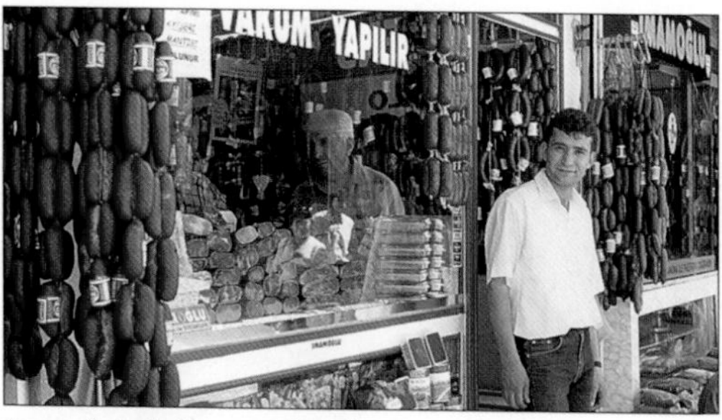
VAKUM YAPILIR

Owner of a typical *pastırma* (cured beef) shop in Kayseri

Visitors' Checklist

👥 794,225. 🚌 Osman Kavuncu Cad. 🚆 N end of Atatürk Bulvarı, 1 km (0.5 mile) from city centre, (0352) 231 13 13. ✈ Erkilet, (0352) 337 52 44. ℹ Kağnı Pazarı 61, Melihgazi, (0352) 222 39 03 and 231 92 95. 🎭 Culture and Art Week (1st week Apr), Kayseri Anatolian Exhibition (mid Jul–mid Aug), Pastırma Festival (15 Sep).

minaret was erected in 1726. The complex has a mosque, training centre and *hamam* (Turkish bath) for men and women, and also includes the subtantial mausoleum of Mahperi Huand Hatun, wife of Alaeddin I Keykubad *(see p250)*. Her inscription on the east door dates back to 1238.

Octagonal Tomb

Döner Kümbet

Talas Cad.

There are many grand tombs to be found all around Anatolia, but the elegance and pure simplicity of the Döner Kümbet makes it one of the most impressive. The tomb was constructed around 1250 as the final resting place of Şah Cihan Hatun, who was a Seljuk princess.

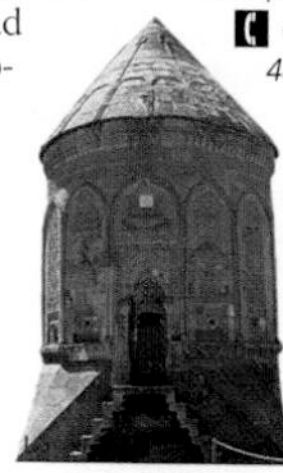

The Octagonal Tomb

Archaeology Museum

Arkeoloji Müzesi

Gültepe Mah. Kışla Cad 2.

☎ (0352) 222 21 49 and 232 48 12. 🕘 9am–noon & 1–5:30pm Tue–Sun. 💲

The museum consists of two large halls and a pleasant garden. The displays run in chronological sequence from the Bronze Age to the Byzantine period. By far the most valuable and interesting items to be seen are the series of cuneiform tablets documenting the commercial transactions of the Assyrian trading colony which flourished here during the late Hittite era *(see pp24–5)*.

Environs: Kültepe, formerly known as Kanesh or Kanış, and now Karum, is one of the most important Bronze-Age sites in Turkey. In the second millennium BC, Kültepe was the foremost Assyrian trading colony. Most of the objects found here can now be seen in the museum in Kayseri or in the Museum of Anatolian Civilizations in Ankara *(see pp242–3)*.

Kültepe

21 km (13 miles) NE of Kayseri on the Sivas highway. *☎ (0352) 289 32 32. 🕘 7am–5:30pm daily. 💲*

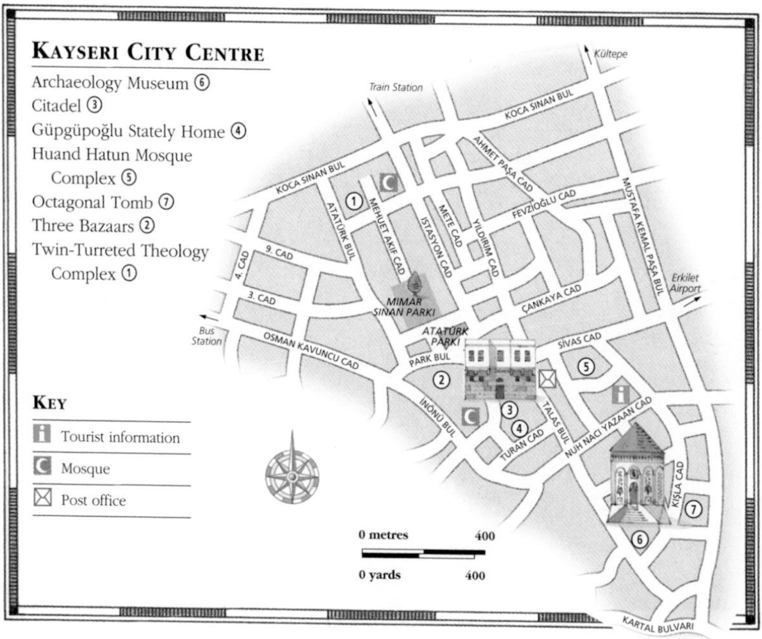
Kayseri City Centre
Archaeology Museum 6
Citadel 3
Güpgüpoğlu Stately Home 4
Huand Hatun Mosque Complex 5
Octagonal Tomb 7
Three Bazaars 2
Twin-Turreted Theology Complex 1
Key
Tourist information
Mosque
Post office
0 metres 400
0 yards 400
Kültepe
Train Station
Koca Sinan Bul
Ahmet Paşa Cad
Fevzioğlu Cad
Mustafa Kemal Paşa Bul
Atatürk Bul
Mehmet Akif Cad
İstasyon Cad
Mete Cad
Yıldırım Cad
9. Cad
4. Cad
3. Cad
Mimar Sinan Parkı
Çankaya Cad
Erkilet Airport
Bus Station
Osman Kavuncu Cad
Atatürk Parkı
Park Bul
Sivas Cad
İnönü Bul
Talas Bul
Turan Cad
Nuh Naci Yazaan Cad
Kışla Cad
Kartal Bulvarı

Güzelyurt ❾

28 km (17 miles) SE of Aksaray.
🚶 4,380. 🚌 infrequent from
Aksaray or Ihlara Valley.

GÜZELYURT MEANS "beautiful country" and is an apt description of the town and its environs. This is a popular area for horseback riding and mountain biking. The latter is a restful alternative to driving.

It is estimated that there were over 50 Greek Orthodox churches here once, though only a few endure today. The church of St Gregory of Nazianzus, one of the four founders of the Greek Ortho-dox church, has been con-verted into a mosque.

A government protection order is in force in Güzelyurt, so all restoration and con-struction work must conform to official guidelines.

The valley 4 km (2 miles) to the northeast of the town, also known as the Monastery Valley, has an abundance of rock-carved churches.

The **Karballa Hotel** used to be a monastery. The former monks' quarters have been converted into quaint rooms.

Karballa Hotel

On the main square. 📞 (0382) 451
21 03. @ karballa@hotmail.com.

Ihlara Valley ❿

TO MANY PEOPLE, the Ihlara Valley is more compelling than the rock churches and dwellings in the region. The setting is dramatic, with the Melindiz River winding along the canyon floor.

The main part of the valley lies between the village of Selime to the north and the town of Ihlara to the south. You could spend an entire day exploring the 15-km-long (9-mile) canyon.

Of the 60 or so original churches in the valley, which was known as Peristrema in Greek times, only about 10 can be seen and some of the interior frescoes are in less than pristine condition.

Most of the churches in the valley date from the 11th cen-tury. Their unusual names signify their use or a peculiar feature: Hyacinth, Black Deer, Crooked Stone and Dovecote. Many of the interior frescoes depict scenes from the lives of the saints, the lives of the ascetic monks, or punish-ments for wrongdoing.

It was once thought that a medical school, where the art of mummification was taught and practised, was located between the villages of Belisırma and Yaprakhisar.

The Eğri (Leaning) Minaret, built
by the Seljuks in the 13th century

Aksaray ⓫

🚶 153,000. 🚌 0.5 km (0.3 mile)
from main square. 🛈 Taşpazar
Mahallesi, Kadıoğlu Sok 1, (0382) 213
24 74 and 212 46 88.

IN ROMAN TIMES, Aksaray was known as Archelais, after Archelaus II, the last king of Cappadocia. By 20 BC, the kingdom had been reduced to a virtual protectorate of Rome and the king enjoyed only token status.

From the south, Aksaray is overlooked by the twin peaks of Mount Hasan (Hasan Dağı), an extinct volcano known as "little sister" to Mount Erciyes.

The spectacular Ihlara Valley, one of Central Anatolia's best hiking areas

Aksaray is close to the eastern end of the Tuz Gölü (Salt Lake). In Ottoman times, the lake brought prosperity to Aksaray as it was the main source of salt for almost the whole of Anatolia.

Aksaray might appear to be a sleepy base for tourists, but spare some time to view the fine Seljuk building styles and architecture, with vestiges of the original ochre-coloured sandstone. Worth seeing are the Great Mosque (1314), with its beautifully carved *minbar* (pulpit), and the **Zinciriye Medresesi**, a 14th-century Koranic school, that now serves as the museum.

Aksaray has its own leaning tower, the Eğri (Leaning) Minaret, on Nevşehir Caddesi. The minaret is part of the Kızıl (Red) Minare Mosque, which was built in 1236 during the reign of the great Seljuk Sultan Alaeddin I Keykubat *(see p250)*. The mosque was built on sand, which has shifted over time, causing the minaret to lean.

🏛 **Zinciriye Medresesi**
Muhsin Çelebi Sokak. [*(0382)* 213 16 67. ⬤ *8am–noon & 1–5pm daily.* 📷

Kırşehir ⑫

160 km (100 miles) SE of Ankara. 🏛 *83,450.* ℹ *Terme Cad, Ulucan I Apartman, Kat 1, (0386) 213 14 16.*

IN BYZANTINE TIMES, Kırşehir was known as Mokyssos. It prospered under the Seljuks, who renamed it Gülşehir, or Rose Town. One of the finest of the city's Seljuk buildings is the Cacabey Mosque, built in 1272 as an astrological observatory and theological college. The Alaeddin Mosque, built in 1230, and the Ahi Evran Mosque are also located in Kırşehir. The latter contains the tomb of Ahi Evran, founder of a *tarikât* (religious brotherhood) whose members helped to spread the message of Islam to the Christian communities of Anatolia.

Various artifacts from Kalehöyük, an important Hittite archaeological site 55 km (34 miles) to the north-west of Kırşehir, are on display in the excellent **Archaeology Museum**. Kalehöyük is one of the many Hittite centres that are being excavated in the area. The museum has more than 3,300 artifacts on display, including coins, ethnographic items and archaeological materials.

Another prime reason for visiting the area is a Japanese arboretum, the **Mikasonmiya Memorial Garden** (Mikasonmiya Anı Bahçesi). One of the largest and most pleasant parks in Turkey, it is planted with some 16,500 trees, made up of 33 different species.

🏛 **Archaeology Museum**
Ankara Cad (in the Culture Centre). [*(0386) 213 33 91.* ⬤ *9am–noon & 1–5pm daily.*
🌼 **Mikasonmiya Memorial Garden**
ℹ *Contact the Kırşehir tourist office, (0386) 213 1416, for opening hours.*

Hacı Bektaş ⑬

🏛 *9,348.* ℹ *Opposite the Museum, (0384) 441 36 87.* 📷 🎭 *Hacı Bektaş Veli Commemoration Festival (16–18 Aug).*

THE MYSTIC AND spiritual philosopher Hacı Bektaş arrived in this area from Iran, via Mecca, in the late 13th century, and founded a centre of learning. His ideas were an offshoot of the Shi'ite sect of Islam, and rested on a belief in natural harmony that was bolstered by mysticism and divine love. The teachings of Hacı Bektaş offered an approachable and compassionate alternative to the main current of Islam. The Bektaşi doctrine, as set out in his book the *Malakat*, is based on both Islamic and Christian principles. This made it a popular belief. He attracted many

Gravestone at Hacı Bektaş

Doorway into the tomb of Hacı Bektaş, in the third courtyard

devotees, most notably among the Janissaries, who were the elite fighting force of the Ottoman sultans *(see p56)*.

The **Hacı Bektaş Museum** (Pirevi, or "founder's house") is the chief attraction, along with the stunning wood carvings of the archaeological museum. Be sure you allow sufficient time to see the whole complex: there are tombs, courtyards, initiation cells, pools and a refectory (dining room) with authentic kitchen cauldrons. The tomb of Hacı Bektaş, in the third courtyard, has seven doors, and is particularly striking. Some of the inscriptions were done with natural dyes from the madder root, and later restored with oil-based paint.

Atatürk came through here in 1919 on his way from Sivas to Ankara; his visit is marked on 22 and 23 December each year. Admiration for the order did not prevent him banning all mystical sects and dervish lodges in 1925, because they were contrary to Turkey's secular state dogma.

The symbol of the order is the rose and blond onyx that is found in the area. It is known as Hacı Bektaş stone.

🏛 **Hacı Bektaş Museum**
Nevşehir Cad. [*(0384) 441 30 22.* ⬤ *8:30am–12:30pm & 1:30–5:30pm Tue–Sun.* 📷

The 19th-century clock tower in the main square in Yozgat

Yozgat ⓮

🏛 80,000. 🛈 İl Özel İdare Hizmet Binası, Kat 3, (0354) 212 64 23.
🚌 (0354) 212 41 15. 🚌 Tue.
🎭 Summer Folklore and Culture Festival (10–15 Jun).

RESEARCH SHOWS that there were settlements here as early as 3,000 BC. However, the tides of history barely affected Yozgat until it fell to the Ottomans in 1408 and the influential Çapanoğlu dynasty made the town their seat. The Çapanoğlus built or repaired many fine mosques, including the Ulu (Çapanoğlu) Camii. The **Yozgat Ethnographic Museum** is housed in a 19th-century *konak* (mansion), the Nizamoğülu Konağı.

In the centre of the town there is an interesting, though garish, clock tower built in 1897 by Ahmet Tevfikzade, the mayor of the town. Ask to see the mechanism if you are interested in timepieces.

🏛 **Yozgat Ethnographic Museum**
Emniyet Cad. 📞 (0354) 212 27 73.
🕐 8am–noon & 1–5pm Tue-Sun.

ENVIRONS: **Çamlık National Park**, located about 5 km (3 miles) south of Yozgat, covers 8 sq km (3 sq miles) of woodland, and has abundant fauna and flora, picnic areas and mineral springs.

🌲 **Çamlık National Park**
📞 (0354) 212 10 84. 🕐 daily.

Boğazkale ⓯

See pp296–7.

Alacahöyük ⓰

30 km (19 miles) SE of Çorum.

LOCATED BETWEEN Sungurlu and Çorum, Alacahöyük is the third and most important site (after Boğazkale and Yazılıkaya) in the Hattuşaş complex of Hittite sites in this region. Most of the artifacts found at the site are displayed in museums in Ankara *(see pp242–3)* and Çorum.

Excavations at Alacahöyük have yielded items ranging from the Chalcolithic period (5500 BC–3000 BC) up to the Phrygian period (750 BC–300 BC) – a staggering time span that makes the site one of Turkey's most important archaeological centres.

At the site itself, the Sphinx Gate is an imposing reminder of cult power, its half-man, half-animal statues displaying striking Egyptian influences.

The royal tombs can also be seen. The **Alacahöyük Museum** displays some of the earthenware pots that were used for burial rites.

🏛 **Alacahöyük Museum**
📞 (0364) 422 70 11. 🕐 8am–noon & 1–5pm Tue–Sun.

One of the carved sphinxes that guard the gate at Alacahöyük

Çorum ⓱

🛈 Yeni Hükümet Binası, A Blok, Kat 4, (0364) 213 85 02.
🎭 Hittite Festival (mid-Jun).

THE TOWN OF ÇORUM dates from Roman times, when it was known as Niconia. The surrounding area is rich in Hittite history, making it likely that the site was inhabited as early as 1400 BC. Throughout Turkey, the name of Çorum is associated with roasted chickpeas (*leblebi*), one of the many nuts that Turks munch compulsively. Locals say that Çorum's chickpeas are tastier

Shop in Çorum specializing in the famous local produce, chickpeas

and healthier than any others. Çorum makes a good base from which to tour two major Hittite sights, Boğazkale *(see pp296–7)* and Alacahöyük. Both are located to the south-west of the town.

The **Çorum Museum** has been renovated and sprawls over several buildings. It is a serious and informative place with many artifacts and ethno-graphic displays, among them very good Hittite objects.

🏛 **Çorum Museum**
Town centre. ☎ *(0364) 213 15 68.*
◯ *8:30am–noon & 1–5:30pm Tue–Sun.* 📷

Amasya ⑱

See pp298–9.

Tokat ⑲

🏨 *121,000.* ℹ *Valilik Binası, Kat. 3, (0356) 214 37 53.* 🚌 *2 km (1 mile) from main square, (0356) 214 22 20.* 🎉 *Pinecone Festival (mid-Sep).*

Tᴏᴋᴀᴛ ᴅᴇsᴇʀᴠᴇs a place on visitors' itineraries because there is a lot more to see here than ankle-high ruins. The Seljuks left the most to see, but the town is also known for resisting Ottoman rule. In protest at Ottoman authority, Turcoman tribesmen took to wearing red headgear, thus earning the name of Kızılbaşı (redheads), which became a term for "rebels".

The town flourished after Sultan Beyazıt I won control of trade routes to Erzincan. Trade caravans then began to use the Amasya–Tokat route, skirting Trabzon (Trebizond), to reach Bursa *(see pp162–7)*, the commercial jewel of the 15th and 16th centuries.

The Seljuks and Ottomans endowed Tokat with many fine buildings, especially the Blue Seminary (Gök Medrese) and two restored 19th-century Ottoman *konaks* (mansions): the Madımağın Celal'ın House and the Latifoğlu House. The two houses will easily detain you for some time. If time is limited, Tokat's interesting **Archaeological Museum** is the place to go.

The Heavenly Seminary in Sivas, showing filigree stonework

Tokat has a proud 300-year tradition of hand-printed textiles *(yazmacılık)*. The craft still thrives in the Gazi Emir Han near the business hub of Sulu Sokak. The town is also renowned for copper-working and ceramics in bold primary colours.

Specialities include *pekmez*, a delicious drink made from concentrated grape juice, and the full-bodied, fruity Karaman red wine.

🏛 **Archaeological Museum**
Gaziosmanpaşa Bulvarı 143.
☎ *(0356) 214 15 09.* ◯ *8:30am–noon & 1–5pm Tue–Sun.*

Environs: The ruined city of Sebastopolis is located 68 km (42 miles) southwest of Tokat. The modern name, Sulusaray (watery palace), comes from the thermal springs which bubble water at 50°C. Finds here include a city wall, bath chambers and a temple.

Shop selling hand-printed textiles in Tokat

Sivas ⑳

🏨 *255,000.* ℹ *Valilik Binası, (0346) 221 31 35.* 🚉 *İstasyon Cad, (0346) 221 10 91.* 🚌 *3 km (2 miles) SE of main square, (0346) 226 15 90.* 🎉 *Nevruz (21 Mar).*

Sɪᴛᴜᴀᴛᴇᴅ ᴀᴛ ᴀɴ ᴀʟᴛɪᴛᴜᴅᴇ of 1,275 m (4,183 ft), Sivas is the highest city in Central Anatolia. Known as Sebasteia in Roman times, its position on a caravan route made it an important trade centre.

Sivas boasts the cream of Seljuk architecture, with tiles, intricately etched stonework, star mosaics, honeycombed decorative motifs and bold blue hues all in evidence. The Heavenly Seminary (Gök Medresesi), built in the 1200s, and Twin Minaret Seminary (Çifte Minareli Medresesi), with its outstanding carved details, should not be missed. The Darüşşifası (Medical Hospice) housed a hospital. The Bürüciye Medresesi (1271) has a quiet courtyard and some excellent tilework.

The Sivas Congress (which consolidated Atatürk's plans to free Turkey from foreign domination) was held in a schoolroom here in 1919. The room is preserved in the **Ethnography Museum**.

Local artisans are known for long-stemmed wooden pipes, as well as for penknives and bone-handled knives.

🏛 **Ethnography Museum**
İstasyon Cad. ☎ *(0346) 221 04 46.*
◯ *8:30am–noon & 1–5:30pm Tue–Sun.* 📷

Bogazkale 🟠
Hattuşaş National Park

BOĞAZKALE IS THE MODERN name for the ancient Hittite capital city of Hattuşaş, built around 1600 BC on a strategic site occupied since the third millennium BC by a people known as the Hatti. An Assyrian trading colony was also active here early in the second millennium BC. It is one of the most important ancient sites to be found in Anatolia. The many thousands of clay and bronze tablets discovered here have provided scholars with a wealth of information about the ancient Hittite civilization.

The city occupies an extensive site bordered on three sides by steep ravines. Sections of the walls, including the impressive Lion's and King's gates, are still standing. The builders adapted the fortifications in masterly fashion to take advantage of topographical features.

Bronze Plaque
This plaque found at Boğazkale records a treaty between the Hittite king, Tudhaliyas IV, and another ruler.

Modern village of Boğazköy

Entry to excavation site

Yenice Citadel

★ **Lion's Gate (Aslanlıkapı)**
The Lion's Gate takes its name from the two lion statues that guarded the city over 3,000 years ago. The lions here are only replicas – the originals are now in the Museum of Anatolian Civilizations in Ankara (see pp242–3).

HITTITE CIVILIZATION

A people of Indo-European origin, the Hittites arrived in Anatolia from the Caucasus region around 2000 BC. Over the next few centuries, they built up a powerful state, with a capital at Hattuşaş (now known as Boğazkale). At its height, the Hittite kingdom controlled much of Anatolia, rivalling both Egypt and Babylon. Hittite art reached its peak between 1450 and 1200 BC, and Hittite artisans were renowned as superb carvers and metalworkers.

One of the twelve gods in stone relief at Yazılıkaya, near Boğazkale

0 metres   550
0 yards   550

The Sphinx Gate
(Yerkapı) is built into an artificial hill, and incorporates a tunnel 70 m (230 ft) in length.

VISITORS' CHECKLIST

Part of Çorum Museum, within
Hattuşaş National Park.
☎ (0364) 452 20 06.
◯ 8am–noon &.1pm–6pm
Tue–Sun (may open for groups
with advance notice). ▨

★ Great Temple (Büyük Mabet)
*One of the best preserved Hittite temples,
the Great Temple was built around 1400
BC, and was dedicated to the storm god,
Teshub. The temple complex contains
ritual chambers, administrative areas
and storage rooms.*

The Citadel (Büyükkale)
*The walled citadel was the seat
of government at Hattuşaş.
A monumental staircase led up
to three courts, one of which
contained the living quarters of
the royal household.*

Battlements,
probably made
of mud bricks

Rough stone
blocks

Corbelled archway

Sarı
Citadel

King's Gate

★ RECONSTRUCTION OF THE KING'S GATE
The King's Gate (Kral Kapı) was named after the
regal-looking Hittite war god on the stone relief
guarding the entrance. The city wall is built with
huge, roughly worked stone blocks, and totals about
7 km (5 miles) in length. The height of the stone
portion was about 6 m (20 ft). Like the other
structures in the city, this would have been overlaid
with sun-dried brick.

STAR FEATURES

★ Great Temple

★ King's Gate

★ Lion's Gate

Amasya ⑬

LYING IN A SECLUDED VALLEY of the Yeşilırmak River, Amasya has seen the passage of nine civilizations, from the Hittites to Ottomans. Its most prosperous era was as royal capital of the Roman kingdom of Pontus, when it was called Amaseia; the tombs cut into the cliffs above the town contain the graves of the Pontic kings. However, a glance at Amasya's many fine Ottoman buildings will confirm that the four centuries of Ottoman rule were equally illustrious. In the 15th century, Amasya was second only to Bursa in cultural and trading importance. By the 1800s, the city excelled as the empire's leading centre for Islamic education.

Bust in the Archaeology Museum

Exploring Amasya

Its dramatic location and air of tranquillity aside, Amasya is known for the tasty apples grown on the surrounding farms and for colourful hand-knitted socks. All main sights are conveniently accessible on foot. The citadel is the only exception, but it can be reached by car.

The Citadel, perched dramatically on a hilltop

🏛 Large-Doored Seminary

Büyük Ağa Medresesi
Zubediye Hanım Sok. ● *during lessons.*
The wonderful airy symmetry and octagonal plan of this complex, also known as the Kapıağası, are its outstanding features. It was built in 1488 by Hüseyin Agha, a private consort of Sultan Beyazıt II. The vaulted porticoes and domed rooms are now used by Koranic students, who adhere to exactly the same rigorous discipline as their predecessors did two or three centuries ago.

⛰ Citadel

Kale
Can be reached by 2-hour climb from the front, or by a road from behind.
The original Hittite fortress was reinforced by the Pontic king, Mithradates *(see p48)*. He built eight layers of walls, with 41 towers, to protect a self-sustaining complex with a palace, cisterns, storage areas, powder magazine and cemetery. From the Citadel there are stupendous views of the nearby Rock Tombs.

🪦 Rock Tombs

Kral Kaya Mezarları
Entrance under the railway line off Hazeranlar Sok. **(** (0358) 218 96 34. **◐** 8am–5pm (7pm in summer). 🖾
The tombs of the Pontic kings date from 333 BC to 44 BC, covering the Hellenistic and Roman periods. The Mirror Cave (Aynalı Mağrası), about 1 km (0.5 mile) from the main tombs, has a coloured painting showing the Virgin Mary and the Apostles.

The carved portal of the Teaching Hospital Complex

🏥 Teaching Hospital Complex

Daruşşifa/Bimarhane Medresesi
Atatürk Cad. **◐** 9am–6pm daily.
The outer walls of the original asylum date from 1308. The complex served as a medical research centre, a school for interns and a hospice for mental patients. Music and speech therapy were used to calm disturbed patients. The carved front portal is wonderfully detailed and represents a rare architectural remnant of the Ilhanid Persian empire of the 13th century. The building now houses a café and the offices of the local Music and Fine Arts Directorate.

🏛 Hazeranlar Mansion

Hazeranlar Konağı
Hattuniye Mahallesi. **(** (0358) 218 40 18. **◐** Tue–Sun. **●** Mon. 🖾
This restored mansion dates from 1865. It was built by a local treasury officer, Hasan Talat Efendi, in memory of his sister, Hazeran Hanım (Lady Hazeran). The layout, typical of the time, features separate areas for men and women. The carpets, from the late Ottoman period, are particularly fine.

The tombs of the Pontic kings, carved into the limestone cliffs

Konaks (mansion houses) along the Yeşilırmak River

🄲 Sultan Beyazıt Mosque and Theological College

Sultan Beyazıt II Külliyesi
Mustafa Kemal Paşa Cad. ⬤ *during prayer times.* 🖾 *donation.*

This was Amasya's primary theological complex, eclipsing all other places of religious learning. It was a product of the prosperity and social stability that prevailed under Sultan Beyazıt II (1481–1512). In that era, Muslim principles and obedience to the state were instilled at an early age. The wonderful domes and portals are inspirational in themselves, and the oak trees in the garden are said to be as old as the mosque itself.

🏛 Archaeology and Ethnography Museum

Arkeoloji ve Etnografik Müzesi
Mustafa Kemal Paşa Cad 91.
🄲 *(0358) 218 45 13.* ◯ *9am–noon & 1:30–5:30pm Tue–Sun.* 🖾

Recently opened after some extensive renovations, the museum is now well lit, its displays nicely labelled and the concept of space much enhanced. Notable is the bronze statue of the Hittite storm god, as well as Roman coins minted in Amasya.

The museum is best known for its collection of mummies, which were found in Anatolia and date from the Ilhanid period (around the 14th century). Previously housed in a dank tomb adjacent to the museum, these now have much more prominence in their new display cases.

The Sultan Beyazıt Mosque, completed in 1486, with its famous rose garden

VISITORS' CHECKLIST

🏚 *373,250.* 🚉 *2 km (1 mile) W of town centre, (0358) 218 12 39.* 🚍 *2 km (1 mile) NE of town centre, (0358) 218 80 12.* 🛈 *Atatürk Cad 39, (0358) 218 50 02.*

🄲 Blue Seminary

Gök Medresesi
Mustafa Kemal Paşa Cad (Torumtay Sok). ◯ *contact a guardian to let you in.* ⬤ *during prayer time.* 🖾 *donation.*

A theological complex dating from 1267, the Blue Seminary is typical of 13th-century Seljuk architecture. It was formerly used as a mosque and Koranic school, and takes its name from the turquoise/ blue tiles and glazed bricks used in its construction. The elaborately carved wooden doors contrasted with the austere interior and are now housed in the Archaeology and Ethnographic Museum.

Adjoining the complex is the Torumtay Türbe, a square tomb built in 1279 in memory of the Emir Torumtay, Seljuk governor of the province and founder of the seminary.

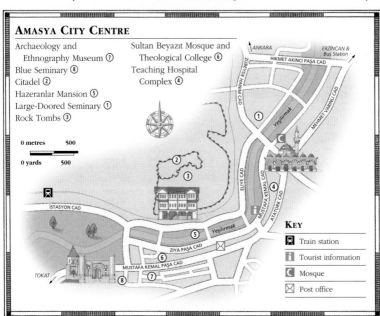

AMASYA CITY CENTRE

Archaeology and
  Ethnography Museum ⑦
Blue Seminary ⑧
Citadel ②
Hazeranlar Mansion ⑤
Large-Doored Seminary ①
Rock Tombs ③

Sultan Beyazıt Mosque and
  Theological College ⑥
Teaching Hospital
  Complex ④

0 metres   500

0 yards   500

ANKARA
ERZİNCAN & Bus Station
HİKMET AKINCI PAŞA CAD
ZÜBEYDE HANIM CAD
MEHMET VARİNLİ CAD
Yeşilırmak
①
ELYE CAD
②
③
İSTASYON CAD
MUSTAFA KEMAL CAD
ATATÜRK CAD
④
⑤ Yeşilırmak
ZIYA PAŞA CAD
⑥
MUSTAFA KEMAL PAŞA CAD
TOKAT
⑦
⑧

KEY

🚉 Train station

🛈 Tourist information

🄲 Mosque

⊠ Post office

EASTERN ANATOLIA

THE VAST, HIGH PLATEAU OF EASTERN TURKEY *is dominated by the extinct volcano of Mount Ararat (Ağrı Dağı), which soars to a height of 5,165 m (16,945 ft). The surface of Lake Van reflects the summits of the surrounding peaks. Trapped by the mountains, the lake has no outflow. In the south, the eastern extension of the Taurus range crumbles suddenly into the sun-baked Mesopotamian plain.*

The region is drained by two great rivers – the Euphrates (Fırat) and Tigris (Dicle) – as well as their tributaries. For centuries, the Euphrates demarcated the eastern frontier of the Roman and Byzantine empires. Today, the rivers have been harnessed by the Southeast Anatolian Project (GAP) to supply the southeastern part of the country with irrigation water and hydro-electric power.

This border zone has always been a cultural melting pot – Monophysite Christian Armenians and Syrians lived alongside Orthodox Greeks and later Arabs and Turks, while Kurds have long occupied the highlands.

Modern, bustling Gaziantep is the gateway from the southeast, leading to the golden apricot orchards of Malatya, the huge stone heads on the summit of Mount Nemrut (Nemrut Dağı), and Abraham's legendary birthplace at Şanlıurfa. Diyarbakır's austere basalt walls loom dramatically over the Tigris, guarding the road north to the interior plateau. Van was once the seat of the sophisticated Urartian kingdom. The rough frontier town of Doğubeyazıt was home to fiercely independent Kurdish princes. Kars, 10th-century capital of Armenia and access point for Ani, has been fought over many times by Russians and Turks. During World War I, Russian forces reached as far west as Erzurum, a Seljuk city with imposing medieval tombs and religious buildings, which guards the strategic highway into central Anatolia.

Snowcapped Mount Ararat, legendary resting place of Noah's Ark

◁ The remains of a 12th-century bridge over the Tigris River at Hasankeyif

Exploring Eastern Anatolia

FROM THE BAKING PLAINS of Upper Mesopotamia to the icy heights of Mount Ararat, this vast region of Turkey is relatively undeveloped and unspoiled, making it a natural target for the more adventurous traveller. It is a land of frontiers, from cold and lonely Kars – a short step away from Armenia – through the Turkish-Iranian border town of Doğubeyazıt, to the bustling bazaar city of Şanlıurfa close to Syria. Many peoples have lived in and fought over this land. Visitors can see Armenian churches and Kurdish castles, Arab houses, Syrian Orthodox monasteries and both Seljuk and Ottoman mosques vying with ruins from the Urartian and Roman eras. Late spring and early autumn are the best seasons to visit.

The citadel at Şanlıurfa

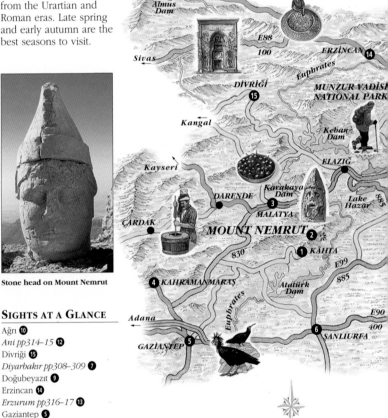

Stone head on Mount Nemrut

SIGHTS AT A GLANCE

0 kilometres　　80

0 miles　　40

SEE ALSO

KEY

- ▬ Motorway
- ▬ Major road
- ▬ Secondary road
- ▭ Other road
- ▬ Scenic route
- ➤ River
- ☼ Viewpoint

Seljuk tombs at Erzurum

Artvin

ARDAHAN
Lake
Çıldır

Yusufeli

KARS 11
ANİ
12 *Akyaka*

Rize

yburt

13 ERZURUM
HORASAN
AĞRI
10
E80
100
Lake
Balık

E80
100

Peri Suyu
950

DOĞUBEYAZIT
9

Murat
E99
975

300
Lake
Hacı
MURADİYE

Lake
Nazik
LAKE
VAN 8
VAN

TATVAN
Lake
Batman
E99
965
975

DİYARBAKIR
7
Tigris
BAYKAN

Tigris CİZRE

MARDİN
ESENDERE

GETTING AROUND

Comfortable intercity coaches connect all the
major cities in the region, and are reasonably
priced. For rural areas or out-of-the-way sites,
the best option is a locally hired taxi. Rental
cars are not widely available and driving conditions can be difficult, with bad, potholed
roads and heavy truck traffic in many areas.
Non-stop flights from Istanbul and Ankara
serve Erzurum, Malatya, Gaziantep, Diyarbakır
and Van. Rail travel between Erzurum and
Kars, and Malatya and Tatvan, on Lake Van,
is slow but scenically rewarding.

The island of Akdamar, in Lake Van

The Atatürk Dam, centrepiece of the GAP (Southeast Anatolian Project)

Kâhta ❶

43 km (27 miles) E of Adıyaman.
🛈 Mustafa Kemal Cad, Milli Park
Müdürlüğü Hizmet Binası, (0416)
725 50 07. 🎭 International Kâhta
Kommagene Festival (last week in Jun).

Locals like to claim that dusty Kâhta has become a seaside town now that the lake created by the **Atatürk Dam** (Atatürk Barajı) – the fourth largest in the world when it was completed in 1990 – laps at the town's eastern edge. Apart from a few hotels, Kâhta's main attraction is its proximity to Mount Nemrut (Nemrut Dağı), located 75 km (46 miles) to the northeast.

Environs: The Atatürk Dam, part of the GAP project, has intruded into the Euphrates basin's ancient past. Building of this and other dams has flooded important historic treasures and sites.

The oil town of **Adıyaman** is slightly further away from Mount Nemrut (about a half-hour drive west of Kâhta), and makes an alternative base.

Adıyaman
🛈 Atatürk Bul 41, (0416) 216 10 08.

Mount Nemrut ❷
Nemrut Dağı

See p306.

Malatya ❸

🏠 300,000. ✈ 4 km (2.5 miles) W
of city centre, off Turgut Özal Bul,
(0422) 238 47 68. 🚌 2 km (1 mile)
W of city centre, (0422) 212 40 40.
🚆 23 km (14 miles) W of city centre.
🛈 Valilik Binası, (0422) 323 30 25.
Culture Centre İstasyon Virajı No
35, (0422) 324 76 12. 🛍 daily.
🎭 Cherry Festival (18 Jun); Apricot
Festival (3rd week Jul).

Malatya is famous for its apricots, grown in the vast surrounding orchards. It was also the birthplace of two Turkish presidents: İsmet İnönü, Atatürk's right-hand man during the War of Independence; and Turgut Özal, an economist who served first as Prime Minister, and then President, from the mid-1980s (see p59).

**Apricot vendor in Malatya's
Apricot Bazaar**

Malatya is a pleasant and fairly prosperous town with a university and a military base, but makes a less convenient base than Kâhta for trips to Mount Nemrut.

The town's most interesting sights are its bazaars. The **Apricot Bazaar** specializes in locally grown and dried apricots. Trading takes place after the harvest, and during the Apricot Festival in July. Around the central mosque is the **Copper Bazaar**, a group of copper-beating workshops where you can buy hand-made trays, pots and vases.

When renovations finish, the **Archaeological Museum** will feature finds from Aslantepe, a Hittite site located 4 km (3 miles) northeast of Malatya, which was flooded as a result of the GAP project. Items including Hittite stone god statues, cuneiform seals, bone idols and early bronze swords were transferred to the museum. There are over 15,500 items spanning most historic periods. The Neolithic sculptures from 8000 BC are particularly impressive, as are the obsidian knives.

Local carpets and *kilims* (rugs) have distinctive features, such as the rectangular "tower bastion" motif. The *yedi dağ çiçeği* (seven-point flower) motif can be found on *kilims*. Carpets generally have simpler designs in strong, primary colours, with borders featuring stylized flowers, rams, medallions or dragons. Small hand-loomed carpets and goat-hair rugs are also found in and around Malatya.

Apricot Bazaar
New Malatya Quarter. ⬜ Mon–Sat.
Copper Bazaar
New Malatya Quarter. Adjoining the Apricot Bazaar. ⬜ Mon–Sat.
🏛 **Archaeological Museum**
Dernek Mahallesi, Kanal Boyu.
❏ (0422) 321 30 06. ⬜ Closed for refurbishment. 🈲

ENVIRONS: Eski Malatya, the old part of town, lies about 12 km (7.5 miles) north of the modern centre. A little village of 2,000 inhabitants has developed inside these walls, once an important Roman and then Byzantine stronghold. The 17th-century Silahtar Mustafa Paşa Caravanserai has been restored, but is now sadly neglected and visitors have to wander around among chickens and donkeys.

The much-restored **Great Mosque** (Ulu Camii) is built around a tiny courtyard, its graceful interior divided into separate summer and winter areas. The winter area is supported by massive pillars and enclosed by thick walls, while the summer section has a beautifully carved wooden pulpit, and amazing herringbone brick vaulting that was decorated with scattered turquoise tiles.

Copper tea pot from Malatya

⬛ Great Mosque
Ulu Camii
Opposite the bus station. ⬜ daily (except during prayer times).

Kahramanmaraş ❹

🏃 235,000. 🚌 W of main highway on Azerbaycan Bulvarı, (0344) 225 00 99. 🚏 Cumhuriyet Cad, (0344) 214 12 04. 🛈 Trabzon Cad, 9 Sok, Özgür Apartmanı, No 2/2, (0344) 212 65 90.

LIKE MANY OTHER towns in Turkey, Kahramanmaraş has a deceptive air of calm and tranquillity that conceals a turbulent past. The first part of its name (meaning "heroic") was added by Atatürk in recognition of the town's successful expulsion of French and British troops in 1920.

It is, however, often just called "Maraş", after its particularly famous product, Maraş Dondurması – a delicious type of ice cream containing gum arabic that is pounded or whipped into glutinous form. It is sold all over Turkey by costumed vendors. Locally, it is sold by the metre and cut with a knife. You can also buy it served in a cone.

As early as the 1940s, Kahramanmaraş was an important centre for shoe- and boot-making. However, due to an abundant supply of cotton (thanks to irrigation from the

The pleasant park below the citadel at Kahramanmaraş

GAP project), the area is now better known for its weaving and spinning mills.

The town's citadel, probably used as defence against Arab raiders in the 7th century, is now a popular tea garden and park. Two mosques, the Great Mosque and the Hatuniye Camii, date from the 15th- and 16th-century Beylik period. Their interiors feature fine wooden carvings.

The local **Archaeological and Ethnographic Museum** displays Hittite statues, ceremonial costumes, *kilims* and textile items from various eras.

🏛 **Archaeological and Ethnographic Museum**
Azerbaycan Bul. ❏ (0344) 223 44 87. ⬜ 9am–noon & 1–5:30pm Tue–Sun. 🈲

The 17th-century Silahtar Mustafa Paşa Caravanserai in Eski Malatya

Mount Nemrut ❷

Nemrut Dağı

Stone head of Zeus

THE HUGE STONE HEADS on the summit of Mount Nemrut (Nemrut Dağı) were built by King Antiochus I Theos, who ruled the Commagene kingdom between 64 and 38 BC. To glorify his rule, the king had three enormous terraces (east, west and north) cut into the mountaintop. Colossal statues of himself and the major gods (both Greek and Persian) of the kingdom were placed on the terraces, and the summit became a sanctuary where the king was worshipped. Today's visitors can still see the remains of the east and west terraces (not much is left of the north terrace), which also feature large, detailed stone reliefs.

The enigmatic site was discovered in 1881 by a German engineer, Karl Sester, but was not fully documented until the 1990s.

VISITORS' CHECKLIST

52 km (32 miles) from Kâhta,
84 km (52 miles) from Adıyaman
in Nemrut Dağı National Park.
(0416) 725 50 07.
May–Oct: 8am–8pm daily.
Nov–Apr.

★ **East Terrace**
The site affords superb views of the surrounding region. Behind the sanctuary rises a 50-m (165-ft) high mound rumoured to contain the tumulus of King Antiochus.

Lion
Eagle
Tyche
Zeus
Apollo
Hercules
Eagle
Lion

Head of Antiochus
The re-erected head of King Antiochus stands near the tumbled one of Tyche, Commagene goddess of fortune.

RECONSTRUCTION
This artists' impression depicts the East Terrace as it probably looked in the 1st century BC. The limestone figures were 8–10 m (26–33 ft) in height.

★ **Stone Reliefs**
This life-size relief carving of a lion surrounded by stars and a crescent moon is considered to be one of the oldest horoscope representations in the world.

STAR FEATURES

★ **East Terrace**

★ **Stone Reliefs**

Gaziantep ➎

🏛 882,000. 🚉 İstasyon Cad, (0342)
323 30 15. ✈ Sazgan, 18 km (11
miles) from city centre, (0342) 582 11
11. 🚌 2 km (1 mile) SE of city centre,
(0342) 323 27 47. ℹ 100, Yıl Atatürk
Kültür Parkı, (0342) 230 59 69.
📅 Pistachio Festival (1st week in Sep).

THE TOWN OF Gaziantep has
boomed in recent years,
mainly due to its proximity
to the Southeast Anatolian
Project (see p19). Olives and
grapes are grown around the
city, as are the pistachio nuts
for which Turkey is famous.

Originally known as Antep,
the town received its prefix
gazi (warrior) in honour of its
role in defeating the French
invaders in 1920.

The site has been occupied
since Hittite times. A crumbling
citadel with 36 towers looms
impressively over the town.
Originally a fortress built by
Emperor Justinian, the present
structure dates from Seljuk
times. Just below the citadel
is a bazaar where *usta* (craftsmen) produce and sell copperware and furniture inlaid with
mother-of-pearl, a craft for
which Gaziantep is famous.

The **Archaeological
Museum** houses interesting
artifacts from all phases of
Gaziantep's history. Among
prehistoric bones and Hittite
pottery are mosaics and other
items removed from the
Roman town of Zeugma
before that site was submerged
by the waters of the Birecik
Dam. In the nostalgia corner
is what is believed to be T E
Lawrence's motorcycle.

The Pool of Abraham in Şanlıurfa

The **Hasan Süzer Ethno-
graphy Museum** occupies a
fascinating 19th-century house.

🏛 **Archaeological Museum**
İstasyon Cad. 📞 (0342) 231 11 71.
🕐 8:30am–12:30pm & 1:30–4:30pm
Tue–Sun. 🈺
🏛 **Hasan Süzer
Ethnography Museum**
Eyüboğlu Mah, Hanifioğlu Sok 64.
📞 (0342) 230 47 21. 🕐 8:30am–
12:30pm & 1:30–4:30pm Tue–Sun. 🈺

Şanlıurfa ➏

🏛 580,000. 🚌 1 km (0.5 mile) W
of city centre. ✈ 6 km (4 miles) S
of city centre, (0414) 247 03 43.
ℹ Göller Mahallesi, Balıklı Göl Sok,
F-Blok, 3–4, (0414) 215 24 67.

THE CITY OF Şanlıurfa offers
visitors to this region the
most to see and should not
be missed. First settled by the
Hurri peoples around 5,500
years ago, it was occupied

by a succession of peoples,
such as the Hittites, Assyrians,
Greeks and Romans.

Alexander the Great named
it Edessa, and the Ottomans
renamed it Urfa. The city
acquired the prefix *şanlı*
(glorious) through the role
it played in resistance to the
French in 1920.

During Şanlıurfa's long
Christian history it was used
as a centre of the Nestorian
movement, and later became
the capital of a crusader state
(1097–1144). Churches, now
mosques, in the old town
include the Selahattin Eyubi
Camii, once the church of St
John. Many Armenians lived
in Urfa until 1920.

Most visitors, however,
come here to see the Gölbaşı
(lakeside) area at the foot of
the citadel. This pleasantly
landscaped garden contains
the Pool of Abraham, said to
be the site where the biblical
prophet was saved from the
vengeful Assyrian king,
Nimrod (Nemrut). A small
cave nearby is said to be the
birthplace of Abraham.

The stone covered bazaar,
or Kapalı Çarşı, is an Ottoman
structure, with designated
rows of streets devoted to
particular trades. Traditional
crafts and skills predominate,
and it is a good place to shop
for locally produced cloth.

Be sure to sample the local
specialities: *çiğ köfte* (raw
meatballs), once believed to
be a dish prepared for Hittite
kings; and *lahmacun* (a flat,
pizza-like bread topped with
spicy meat).

Roman mosaic, Archaeological Museum at Gaziantep

Diyarbakır ❼

Frieze, Great Mosque

Southeastern Turkey's liveliest city, Diyarbakır is situated on the edge of a high bank dropping down to the Tigris River. Its 6 km (4 miles) of black basalt walls encircle an old centre of cobbled streets and alleys, mosques, churches and mansions.

As the unofficial capital of Turkey's Kurdish-dominated southeast, political feelings can run high here. However, the inhabitants are generally warm and open to visitors, and justly proud of their atmospheric but economically deprived home city.

Diyarbakır is renowned for the gigantic watermelons sold in its markets. Watered by the Tigris River and fertilized with pigeon droppings, these can reach weights of up to 50 kg (112 lbs).

Exploring Diyarbakır

Most of the city's sights are concentrated in the central area and can be seen on foot. Walking alone around the walls is not recommended.

🏛 Archaeology Museum

Arkeoloji Müzesi

Elazığ Cad. ☏ (0412) 227 67 40. ⬤ 9am–noon & 1–5:30pm Tue–Sun. ✎

The most interesting section of this Archaeology Museum (situated outside the city walls, not far from the Harput Gate) is devoted to the Akkoyun and Karakoyun (White and Black Sheep). These Turcoman tribal groups ruled the region in the period between the decline of the Seljuks and the rise of the Ottomans.

🛏 Hasan Paşa Hanı

Gazi Cad. ⬤ daily. ⬤ Sun.

Located opposite the Great Mosque (Ulu Camii), and built by governor Verizade Hasan Paşa, the 16th-century *han* (see pp24–5) is still used by traders, and has some decent jewellery, carpet and antique outlets. The black basalt façade is dignified by a bold white limestone frieze.

⬤ Great Mosque

Ulu Camii

Gazi Cad. ⬤ daily. ⬤ during prayer times.

A fairly plain building with a basilica-plan style, the Great Mosque is the most significant building in Diyarbakır, and is regarded as one of the holiest places in the Islamic world.

The Great Mosque, originally built by the Arabs in the 7th century

It was built on the site of a church around AD 639 after the Arabs captured the city. In 1091–92, the Seljuk ruler Malik Şah remodelled the building, using the revered Great Ummayad Mosque in Damascus as a model.

The interior is spacious and austere, while the courtyard buildings are built from black basalt with bands of white limestone, faced with blind arches supported by Roman columns interspersed with Seljuk friezes. The mosque faces a Roman *stoa* (portico), topped by a library.

🏛 Ziya Gökalp Museum

Ziya Gökalp Müzesi

Ziya Gökalp Bul. ☏ (0412) 221 27 55. ⬤ 8:30am–noon & 1–5pm Tue–Sun. ✎

Ziya Gökalp, one of the chief ideologues of Turkish nationalism during the period of the Young Turks (see p57), was born in Diyarbakır. His house is now a museum.

Vendor offering one of the region's famous watermelons

⬤ Kasım Padişah Mosque

Dört Ayaklı Camii

Yeni Kapı Cad. ⬤ daily. ⬤ during prayer times. ✎ donation.

This was the last of the great mosques built under the reign of the Akkoyun (White Sheep) Turkomans. It is unusual for its free-standing minaret supported by four 2-m (6.5-ft) high basalt pillars carved from a single block of stone, known as the Dört Ayaklı Minare (four-legged minaret). It is said that your wish will be granted if you walk seven times around its pillars.

⬤ Behram Paşa Mosque

Behram Paşa Camii

Melik Ahmet Cad. ⬤ daily. ⬤ during prayer times. ✎ donation.

Built in 1572 on the orders of the governor, Behram Paşa, this centrally located mosque is the city's largest. The black basalt exterior is enlivened by white stone banding, and the interior is light and graceful. The central ceiling has a calligraphic frieze of inlaid mother-of-pearl.

Black-and-white banding on the Behram Paşa Camii

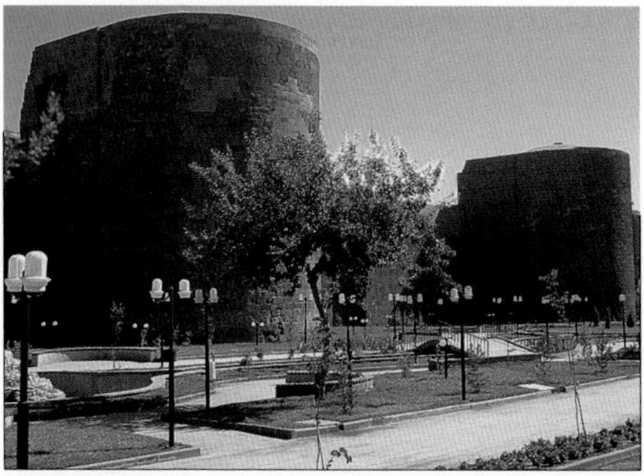

The impressive walls surrounding the old city

🏰 City Walls

Diyarbakır'ın Kalesi

The black walls encircling the city – said to be visible from space – were originally built by the Romans (who captured Diyarbakır from the Sassanids in the 3rd century AD), since the city lacked natural defences. The Byzantines added to the structure, but what can be seen today is mainly the work of Seljuks, who captured the city in 1088.

Constructed from blocks of black basalt, the walls are pierced by four major gates (Harput, Yenikapi, Mardin and Urfa) and studded with 72 towers. The walls are 12 m (39 ft) high and more than 5 km (3 miles) in length. It is possible to walk along the top for much of the way.

The most impressive views are from the southern walls, looking down over the Tigris River winding its way towards Iraq. The Tower of the Seven Brothers (Yedi Kardeş Burçu), located between the Mardin and Urfa gates and built in 1208, provides a particularly good vantage point.

Visitors' Checklist

👥 1,000,000. ✈ Kaplaner, 3 km (2 miles) SW of city centre.
🚆 1 km (0.5 mile) W of city centre, (0412) 221 87 87.
🚌 2 km (1 mile) NW of city centre, Ziya Gökalp Bulvarı.
ℹ Dağıkapı Burcu Giriş Bölümü, (0412) 221 78 40.
🎉 Watermelon Festival (Sep); Nevruz (21 Mar); Hıdrellez Festival celebrating spring migration (6 May, depending on weather).

Environs: The **Atatürk Villa** was given to the founder of the Turkish Republic in 1937 by the citizens of Diyarbakır. On display are period photographs and personal effects. It is situated a few kilometres south of the city, off the road to Mardin, and has expansive views of the Tigris and the Dicle Köprüsü (Tigris Bridge). Built in 1065 on the site of an older structure, the bridge spans the river in 10 arches.

🏛 Atatürk Villa

Atatürk Köşkü

◷ 8:30am–noon & 1:30–5pm daily. 🎫

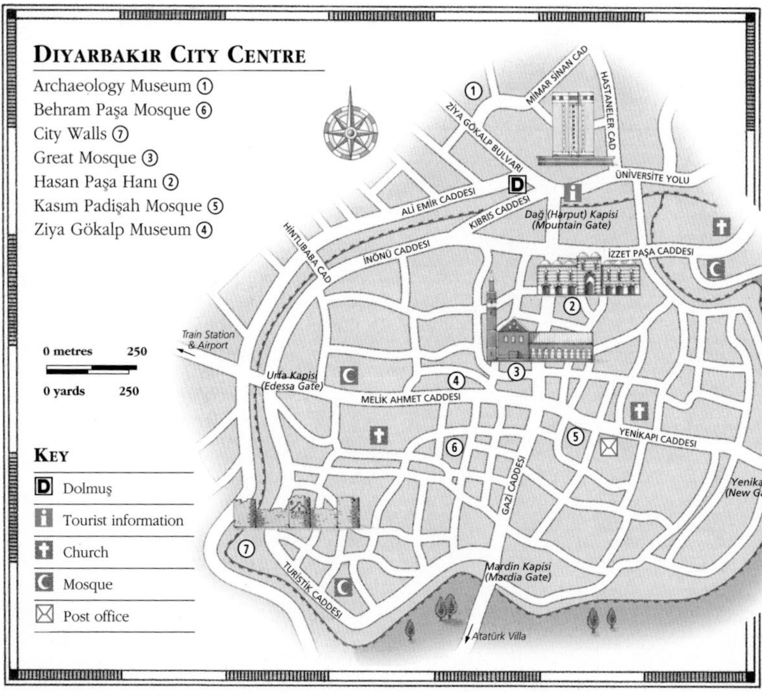
Diyarbakır City Centre
Archaeology Museum 1
Behram Paşa Mosque 6
City Walls 7
Great Mosque 3
Hasan Paşa Hanı 2
Kasım Padişah Mosque 5
Ziya Gökalp Museum 4
0 metres 250
0 yards 250
Key
[D] Dolmuş
Tourist information
Church
Mosque
Post office
MİMAR SİNAN CAD
HASTANELER CAD
ZİYA GÖKALP BULVARI
ÜNİVERSİTE YOLU
ALİ EMİR CADDESİ
KIBRIS CADDESİ
Dağ (Harput) Kapisi (Mountain Gate)
HİNTLİBABA CAD
İNÖNÜ CADDESİ
İZZET PAŞA CADDESİ
Train Station & Airport
Urfa Kapisi (Edessa Gate)
MELİK AHMET CADDESİ
YENİKAPI CADDESİ
Yenikapi (New Gate)
GAZİ CADDESİ
TURİSTİK CADDESİ
Mardin Kapisi (Mardia Gate)
Atatürk Villa

Lake Van ❽

156,000. ✈ 6 km (4 miles) S of city centre, (0432) 216 10 19. 🚌 İpek Yolu, NW of town centre, (0432) 223 15 45. 🚆 to Tatvan, (0432) 223 13 80. ⛴ 5 km (3 miles) from town centre. 🛈 Cumhuriyet Cad 223, (0432) 216 20 18.

THE STARTLINGLY BLUE waters of Lake Van (Van Gölü) mirror the surrounding peaks, the highest of which soars to a dizzying 4,058 m (13,313 ft). The lake is seven times larger than Lake Geneva and may be up to 400 m (1,312 ft) deep. Because it has no outlet, the lake has a salinity level well above that of sea water. It is so alkaline that locals do not need to use soap for washing. It is also lovely to swim in.

The Van basin was once the centre of the Urartian civilization (contemporaries and foes of the Assyrians). The remnants of their fortified capital straddle the imposing Rock of Van, located close to the eastern shore of the lake. A few kilometres away is the modern town of Van, a large but fairly undistinguished place. However, the small **Van Museum** contains many Urartian artifacts, including some fine gold jewellery.

🏛 **Van Museum**
Hacıosman Sok, Serefiye Mahallesi. 📞 (0432) 216 11 39. ☐ 9am–noon & 1–5:30pm Tue–Sun. 📷

ENVIRONS: Çavuştepe, 35 km (22 miles) southeast of Van, is another Urartian site.

The Rock of Van, with an ancient Urartian citadel at the summit

Worth seeing here is a palace, sacrificial altar and inscriptions. It is best visited en route to the stark and hauntingly beautiful 17th-century castle at Hoşap, 60 km (37 miles) from Van on the same road.

The high point of a visit to the Lake Van area is the exquisite 10th-century Armenian **Church of the Holy Cross** (Akdamar Kilesi), situated on a small island a few kilometres from the southern shore of the lake. The exterior of the church boasts a remarkable series of bas-relief carvings and friezes showing biblical scenes. Cruciform in plan, and just 15 x 12 m (49 x 39 ft) in size, the church is topped by a conical roof which rests on a cylindrical drum. Its classical beauty makes this one of the most photographed buildings in eastern Anatolia.

On the lake's northwestern shore are other attractions. There is the crescent-shaped crater lake on Nemrut Dağı (not the mountain with the statues near Kâhta) and the Seljuk cemetery and *kümbet* (domed tombs) at Ahlat. Both are worth a visit and can be accessed from the town of Tatvan, at the western corner of the lake.

The local cheese, *otlu peynir*, is worth trying if you can find it. A whole-milk cheese flecked with herbs, it is now rarely found outside the Van area. Another special feature of the area is the distinctive Van cat, a recognized feline breed that is pure white with one blue and one green eye.

Church of the Holy Cross
40 km (25 miles) SW of Van. ⛴ from Gevaş.

Doğubeyazıt ❾

42,873. 🚌 Belediye Cad, W of town centre.

SITUATED ON THE main road between Turkey and Iran, Doğubeyazıt is a half-hour drive from the border. There are two reasons for visiting this otherwise unremarkable frontier town: Mount Ararat and the İshak Paşa Sarayı.

Mount Ararat (Ağrı Dağı), Turkey's highest mountain, rises 5,165 m (16,945 ft) above the landscape. Although said to be the resting place of Noah's Ark, little evidence has ever been found to support

Frieze on the wall of the Church of the Holy Cross

◁ The 10th-century Armenian Church of the Holy Cross, on an island in Lake Van this claim. Access is difficult and prospective climbers need to obtain permission from the Ministry of Tourism in Ankara *(see p365)* in advance.

The impressive **İshak Paşa Sarayı** lies 8 km (5 miles) southeast of Doğubeyazıt. The fortress-like palace was constructed by an Ottoman governor in the late 18th century, although the mix of building styles (Ottoman, Persian, Armenian/Georgian and Seljuk) makes it difficult to attach an exact date. In Ottoman times, the palace lay on an important caravan route, explaining why such an opulent structure was erected in this lonely and remote part of the country.

The lavish arrangement of 366 rooms includes a harem with 14 bedrooms, *selamlık* (mens' quarters) and a small but beautiful mosque whose interior has been badly damaged over the years. Ottoman and Russian troops occupied İshak Paşa Sarayı at various times and showed little regard for its historic importance. Although major restoration work has recently been carried out, the results are rather controversial.

Nearby attractions, best visited on a dolmuş tour from Doğubeyazıt, are the sulphur springs at Diyadin, and the Meteor Çukuru (meteor crater), just before the Iranian border.

🏛 **İshak Paşa Sarayı**
📞 (0472) 312 69 09. ⏰ 9am–noon & 1–5:30pm Tue–Sun. 📷

Ağrı 🔟

🏨 89,400. 🚌 W side of town. ✈ (0472) 216 04 02. 🛈 Özel İdare Binası, Kat 4/12, (0472) 216 04 50/215 37 30.

THE LITTLE town of Ağrı (the name means "pain" in Turkish) is located 1,640 m (5,380 ft) above sea level. Its importance stems from its position on the main road to Iran. Although unremarkable, Ağrı has accommodation and makes a convenient staging post for Doğubeyazıt to the east, Erzurum to the west and Van to the south.

İshak Paşa Sarayı, on a hillside southeast of Doğubeyazıt

Kars 🔟

🏨 105,000. 🚌 2 km (1 mile) SE of town centre, (0474) 223 14 45. 🚂 off Cumhuriyet Cad, (0474) 223 43 99/43 98. ✈ (0474) 223 06 74. 🛈 Atatürk Cad, Milli Eğitim Hizmet Binası Kat 2, (0474) 212 68 65 and 68 63/68 17.

REMOTE BUT strategically very important, Kars is set on a grassy plain that is backed by distant peaks. The word *kar* means "snow" in Turkish and winters here are long and cold, while the spring and autumn rains turn streets to mud. The brief summer season is hot, dry and dusty.

Founded in the 10th century by the Armenian King Abas I, Kars was once a metropolis of around 100,000 inhabitants. In 1064, it was captured by the Seljuks, and subsequently came under Georgian and Ottoman rule. It was held by the Russians from 1878 to 1919, and the grid plan and numerous run-down Neo-Classical houses are reminders of their presence here.

The citadel (Kars Kalesi) was built by the Ottomans, as was the 15th-century Taş Köprü (stone bridge) over the River Kars. The 10th-century Armenian Church of the Apostles is a mixture of architectural styles and now houses the Havariler Museum.

The small **Archaeological Museum**, just east of the town centre, is surprisingly good, particularly its displays of *kilims* (rugs) and carpets.

Most visitors, however, visit Kars because they wish to see Ani *(see pp314–15)*, a ruined 11th-century Armenian city 43 km (27 miles) away to the east, on the border with Armenia. Permission to visit this haunting site must be obtained in advance from the tourist office in Kars.

Rail buffs will be intrigued and delighted to learn that old steam locomotives still regularly haul trains between Erzurum and Kars.

🏛 **Archaeological Museum**
Cumhuriyet Cad 365.
📞 (0474) 212 14 30. ⏰ 9am–noon & 1–5:30pm Tue–Sun. 📷

The citadel at Kars, overlooking a Turkish bath

Ani ⑫

THE RUINED CITY of Ani, on the border with Armenia, is one of the most evocative historical sites in Turkey. Set on a windswept, grassy plateau along the Barley River (Arpa Çayı), the site contains important remnants of Armenian architecture. In 961, Ani became the capital of the Bagratid kings of Armenia. It reached its apogee under King Gagik I (990–1020), when it was known as "the city of a thousand and one churches".

Slit window, Ani Cathedral

Sacked by the Turks in 1064, Ani recovered, only to be razed by an earthquake in 1319.

Due to its position in a sensitive border area, visitors must obtain a permit from the tourist office in Kars as well as security clearance from the police. Tickets to the site are available from the Archaeological Museum in Kars.

Church of St Gregory (of Gagik)

★ **Church of St Gregory (of Abugramentz)**
This twelve-sided rotunda is one of three churches dedicated to St Gregory.

View from Menücehr Mosque
This bridge, now ruined, spanned the Barley River (Arpa Çayı) in a single arch 30 m (32 yards) in length. The river demarcates the border between Turkey and Armenia.

City Walls

Maiden's Cast

Citadel
The Citadel is the oldest part of Ani and housed most of its residents until 961, when the Bagratids moved their capital here from Kars. It contains the ruined palace of the Bagratid kings, but is off-limits to visitors.

STAR FEATURES

★ **Ani Cathedral**

★ **City Walls**

★ **Church of St Gregory**

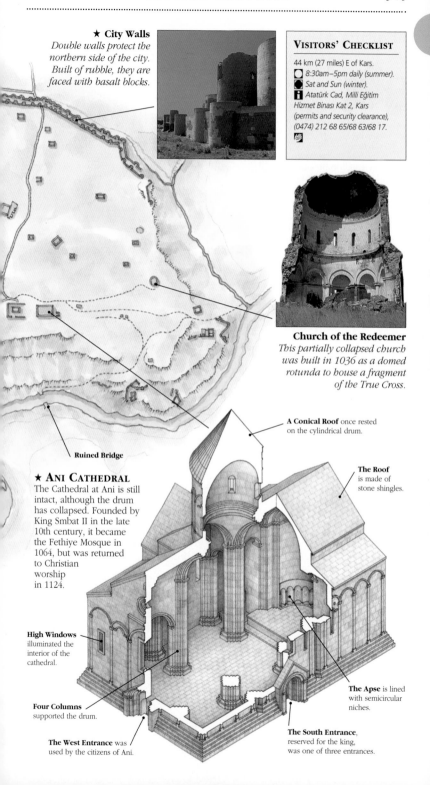

★ City Walls
Double walls protect the northern side of the city. Built of rubble, they are faced with basalt blocks.

VISITORS' CHECKLIST

44 km (27 miles) E of Kars.
🕘 8:30am–5pm daily (summer).
● Sat and Sun (winter).
ℹ Atatürk Cad, Milli Eğitim Hizmet Binası Kat 2, Kars (permits and security clearance), (0474) 212 68 65/68 63/68 17.

Church of the Redeemer
This partially collapsed church was built in 1036 as a domed rotunda to house a fragment of the True Cross.

A Conical Roof once rested on the cylindrical drum.

Ruined Bridge

The Roof is made of stone shingles.

★ ANI CATHEDRAL
The Cathedral at Ani is still intact, although the drum has collapsed. Founded by King Smbat II in the late 10th century, it became the Fethiye Mosque in 1064, but was returned to Christian worship in 1124.

High Windows illuminated the interior of the cathedral.

Four Columns supported the drum.

The West Entrance was used by the citizens of Ani.

The Apse is lined with semicircular niches.

The South Entrance, reserved for the king, was one of three entrances.

Erzurum ⓭

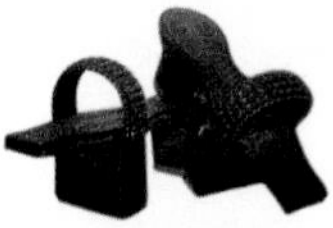

Sandals formerly used in the Turkish Baths

Sprawling across a vast plain at an altitude of almost 2,000 m (6,560 ft) and ringed by mountains, Erzurum is one of Turkey's coldest cities. It is also by far the most developed city in the region. Because it was located astride the main caravan route from India to Europe, and controlled the passage between the Caucasus and Anatolia, Erzurum was fought over and ruled by many peoples – Byzantines, Sassanids, Arabs, Armenians, Seljuk Turks, Mongols and Ottomans. Its most famous sights date from Seljuk times. Like Kars, the city was in Russian hands for over 40 years. In 1919, Atatürk's Nationalists met here to map out the frontiers of modern Turkey.

Exploring Erzurum

Erzurum has a university and a large garrison population. It also hosts a rough-and-ready horseback competition *(cirit)*, which involves throwing a spear at a target.

🏛 Archaeological Museum

Arkeoloji Müzesi

Yenişehir Cad 11. ☎ *(0442) 218 14 06.* ⏰ *9am–noon & 1–5:30pm Tue–Sun.* ♿

Exhibits range from Urartian metalwork and pottery to the jewellery and glassware of the Hellenistic and Roman eras.

💧 Turkish Baths

Erzurum Hamamı

Gülçü Kapısı Cad 10. ☎ *(0442) 218 12 98.* ⏰ *4am–midnight daily.*

Erzurum has several Turkish baths, most dating from the 19th century. This one (for men only) was built in the 1700s. Its eight vaulted domes are in a row near the hot pool.

☪ Yakut Seminary

Yakutiye Medrese

Cumhuriyet Cad. ⏰ *8:30am–noon & 1:30–5pm Tue–Sun.* ♿

Built in 1310 by Hoca Yakut, governor of the İlhan Mongols, this ornate Koranic school is widely regarded as the city's most beautiful building. The carved stonework around the entrance is very appealing and the short minaret has an elaborate lattice of brick and turquoise tiles.

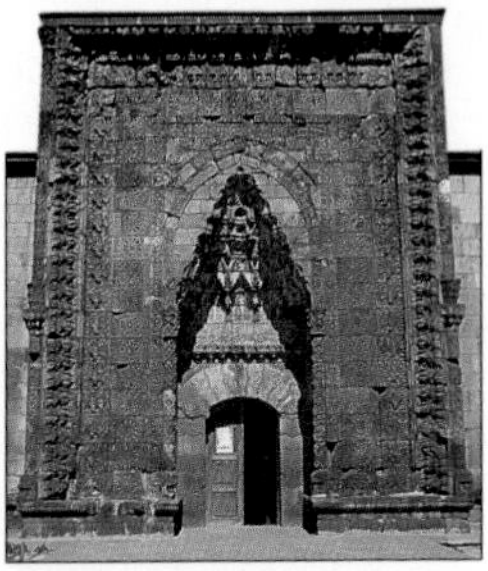

The ornate entrance portal of the Yakut Seminary

🏰 Citadel

Kale

N of Çifte Minareli Medresesi.

⏰ *8:30am–noon & 1:30–5:30pm daily (7pm in summer).* ♿

The citadel was built in the 5th century, during the reign of Byzantine Emperor Theodosius. It was restored in 1555 by Sultan Süleyman I (the Magnificent) and served as the eastern base of the Janissaries *(see p56)*. Inside is a ruined

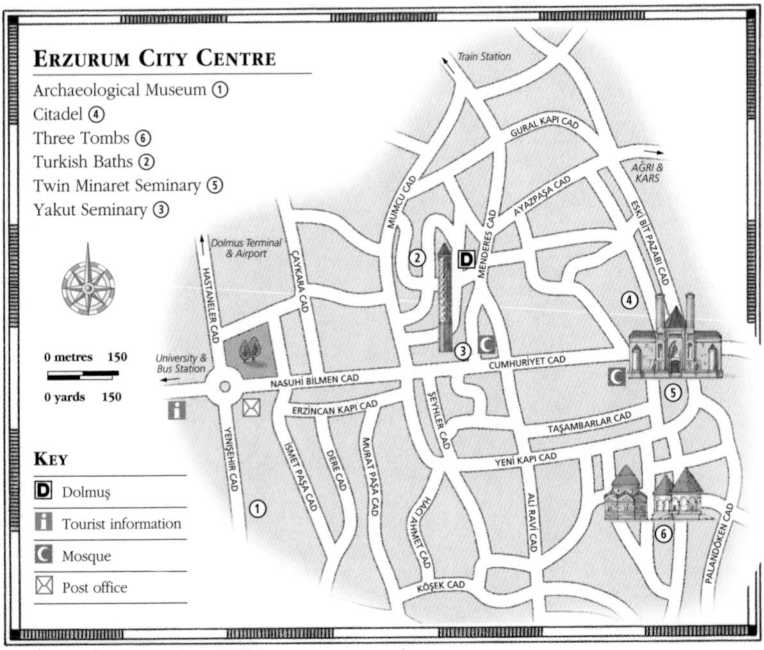

ERZURUM CITY CENTRE
Archaeological Museum 1
Citadel 4
Three Tombs 6
Turkish Baths 2
Twin Minaret Seminary 5
Yakut Seminary 3
0 metres 150
0 yards 150
KEY
Dolmuş
Tourist information
Mosque
Post office
Train Station
GURAL KAPI CAD
AĞRI & KARS
AYAZPAŞA CAD
MUMCU CAD
MENDERES CAD
ESKİ BİT PAZARI CAD
Dolmus Terminal & Airport
HASTANELER CAD
ÇAYKARA CAD
University & Bus Station
CUMHURİYET CAD
NASUHİ BİLMEN CAD
ERZİNCAN KAPI CAD
ŞEYHLER CAD
TAŞAMBARLAR CAD
YENİ KAPI CAD
YENİŞEHİR CAD
İSMET PAŞA CAD
DERE CAD
MURAT PAŞA CAD
HACI AHMET CAD
ALİ RAVİ CAD
PALANDÖKEN CAD
KÖŞEK CAD

VISITORS' CHECKLIST

🏙 750,289. ✈ 10 km (6 miles) NE of city centre, (0442) 218 19 04. 🚌 1 km (0.5 mile) NE of city centre. 🚉 1 km (0.5 mile) N of city centre. ℹ Cemal Gürsel Caddesi 9, (0442) 231 09 25 and 231 09 26. 🎭 Atatürk Congress and Festival (23 Jul). 📅 most days.

clocktower and also a mosque. There are fine views over the city from the walls.

ⓒ Twin Minaret Seminary
Çifte Minareli Medresesi
Cumhuriyet Cad. ⬜ 8am–5pm daily. 🎟

The two minarets that flank the soaring portal of the Çifte Minareli Medresesi have become the symbols of Erzurum. They are thought to have been built in 1253 on the authority of Huant Hatun, daughter of Seljuk Sultan Alaeddin Keykubad II. At the rear of the complex is the 12-sided cylinder tomb that contains her remains.

Twin Minaret Seminary

🏛 Three Tombs
Üç Kümbet
S of Twin Minaret Seminary. ⬜ daily.
Built by the Seljuks, the oldest of these conical mausoleums dates from the early 12th century. It is distinguished by the use of contrasting light and dark stone and by its truncated cone. Be sure to see the animal reliefs.

ENVIRONS: Erzurum has a reliable ski season that runs from November to May. Palandöken Ski Centre *(see p362)*, situated 8 km (5 miles) southwest of the city centre, has two hotels and six ski lifts serving 30 km (19 miles) of piste.

The gorge of the Euphrates (Firat) near Kemaliye

Erzincan ⓮

🏙 280,118. ℹ Fevzipaşa Cad, Yazıcıoğlu İşhanı 19/2, (0446) 223 06 75, 223 37 92 or 214 31 89.

ERZINCAN'S HISTORY has been marked by earthquakes, notably in 1939 and 1992. It was once considered one of Turkey's most impressive cities, but rebuilding work over the years has left it with few historic attractions.

Erzincan's specialities include decorative copperware and *tulum peyniri*, a cheese made from raw milk, and sold encased in a goat skin.

ENVIRONS: Altıntepe (Golden Hill), a Urartian site 27 km (17 miles) east of Erzincan, dates from around 700 BC. Many of the objects found here are now on display in Ankara's Museum of Anatolian Civilizations *(see p242–3)*. One of the best of these is a bronze cauldron with handles in the shape of bulls' heads.

The little town of **Kemaliye** (formerly known as Eğin) lies in the Munzur Mountains not far from Erzincan. Founded in the 11th century, Kemaliye's pebbled streets, wild streams and trim wooden buildings offer a charming snapshot of life in Ottoman times.

Carving detail, Divriği

The **Village Life Museum** in Ocakköyü, near Kemaliye, is the only private ethnographic museum in Turkey.

🏛 Village Life Museum
Köy Müzesi
Ocakköyü. ⓒ (0446) 754 40 65.
⬜ 9am–noon & 1–5pm Tue–Sun.

Divriği ⓯

🏙 18,000. 🚌 S of town centre, on road to Elazığ. 🚉 from Sivas, Erzincan or Malatya.

AFTER THE SELJUK victory at Manzikert (Malazgirt) in 1071 *(see p52)*, Divriği became the seat of the Mengüçek state and was ruled by the Mengüç family from 1142 to 1252. Among many fine buildings they left behind is the *külliye* (mosque-hospital complex), the best example of 13th-century Seljuk stonecarving in Turkey, and now a UNESCO World Heritage Site. The ornate portals of the **Süleyman Şah** or Kale mosque (built around 1229) and the adjoining *daruşşifa* (hospital) – easy to spot as you come into town – display exceptionally rich decoration.

Süleyman Şah
Şehir district. ⬜ 9am–5pm Mon–Fri.
● weekends.

Travellers' Needs

WHERE TO STAY

WHETHER YOU wish to stay in an Ottoman sultan's opulent palace, a quaint *yalı* (traditional wooden summer house) on the Bosphorus, or a comfortable, cosy family home, you can find the accommodation of your choice in Turkey. Camping has become popular, and the new interest in trekking holidays means that you can sleep under the stars. Turkey's hotels and guesthouses cater for a wide range of budgets and, in general, are found clustered around the main sightseeing areas: in Sultanahmet and Aksaray in Istanbul for instance. Some of the old towns, notably Safranbolu *(see pp268–9)*, offer accommodation in restored mansions and family homes around the historic town centre. The choice of hotels in Turkey's eastern provinces is more restricted because this area has not yet reached its full tourist potential. Apart from the better ones in main towns, lodgings tend to be spartan and can be overpriced. You can use the listings on pp324–35 to find a hotel that will suit your price range.

Doorman at Hilton Hotel

CHOOSING A HOTEL

MANY HOTELS in Turkey are rated by the Ministry of Tourism according to a star system, from one to five, with five stars being the most luxurious. Municipalities also use stars to rate their local accommodation, which can be confusing. Try not to base your choice exclusively on star ratings. Reputable hotels will allow you to see a room before you decide to stay. Hotel staff will often come to meet arriving buses and try to convince you to stay at their establishment.

Most hotels can be easily reached by public transport from the airport, bus or train station. With advance notice, most hotels will ferry guests to and from the airport. Many hotels in resort areas close from the end of October until March or April. Ask about this when you book, or look it up on the Internet. Most of the major hotels now have websites. Some hotels even advertise that they have a generator, ensuring that their services are not affected by Turkey's regular power cuts.

In southern coastal areas and inland plains, summer is hot and humid, so paying extra for an air-conditioned room can make a difference. Water shortages are a fact of life, so ask the smaller hotels if they have sufficient water. It also worth asking if the hotel has sufficient hot water.

Special License Hotels *(see p321)* are usually considered to be luxury establishments. Even if the listing says it is a *pansiyon* (pension), the comfort and décor will be first-rate, as well as the food. It is essential to book well in advance at these establishments and it is rare to find discounts here.

Lounge of the Ceylan Inter-Continental Hotel in Beyoğlu *(see p325)*

LUXURY HOTELS

MOST OF THE up-market international hotel chains are represented in Istanbul, Ankara and İzmir, as well as the other larger cities around Turkey. Almost all five-star hotels offer fine views over a city skyline, the Bosphorus, a dreamy coastal vista or some picturesque harbour scene.

Luxury hotels typically have swimming pools, fitness and health facilities, *hamams* (Turkish baths), saunas and conference facilities. Resort hotels and holiday villages, in particular, feature extensive nightly entertainment. Most hotels will gladly arrange city or boating tours and day trips to local attractions. You can, of course, also organize this yourself at a lower cost.

Many hotels have set aside non-smoking areas and make provision for disabled guests. This was unheard-of until quite recently.

The cosy Konak Melsa Hotel in Dalyan, on the Mediterranean *(see p330)*

◁ Ottoman-style slippers for sale in the Grand Bazaar in Istanbul *(see pp104–105)*

Club Lykia World holiday village, nestling in a cove near Ölü Deniz

HOLIDAY VILLAGES

THE COASTAL AREAS of Turkey have numerous holiday villages, self-contained resort complexes that offer a full range of holiday options for visitors, with access to their private stretch of beach. These may be more like mini-towns, but the lure of a holiday with all the frills and none of the concomitant worries continues to attract customers. Staying in a holiday village can be very economical, especially for families with children, as a great number of activities are included in the price of the holiday.

All the holiday villages offer programmes for children, as well as babysitting services and nightly entertainment programmes. Some, like the MIA Belpark Village near Belek *(see p330)* and Club Lykia World *(see p331)* near Ölü Deniz, cater for foreign diplomats and destination-management companies.

CHEAPER HOTELS

THERE IS A WIDE CHOICE of cheaper accommodation in Turkey, ranging from hotels and motels to family-run *pansiyons* (pensions). Some of the cheaper one-star hotels are not rated by the Ministry of Tourism, but by the local municipality, whose standards depend on the region. Therefore, when choosing one of the cheaper

hotels, take care not to base your decision on what you see in the newly renovated lobby; it is always best to see if the carpet runs past the first stairs. Most one-star hotels provide only minimal services, which could mean communal washing facilities. The safest bet would be to try to find a room in a *pansiyon*. Older ones are more like private houses with rooms to rent, but many of the newer ones are much like hotels in terms of services offered.

Hotel doorway, Selçuk

SPECIAL LICENSE HOTELS

SPECIAL LICENSE HOTELS are usually historic buildings that have been restored and transformed into quaint hotels. These do not fall under the auspices of the Turkish Ministry of Tourism and their facilities vary from grand luxury to the very basic. Most are found in the older quarters of Istanbul, and give guests a feeling for the lifestyle of the late Ottoman era. Many Special License Hotels are run by the **Turkish Touring and Automobile Club**, or TTOK *(see p383)*, which campaigns for the historic value of these buildings.

WHAT TO EXPECT

ALL HOTELS listed in this book were chosen because they provide comfortable, welcoming and secure accommodation. In the popular regions, front desk staff can be expected to speak English, but this is less likely in more remote areas. Hotel rooms cater for couples, with twin beds or a double bed and enough space to add a third if necessary.

Most multistorey hotels will have lifts but this will not be the case in older buildings converted into Special License Hotels. Facilities for wheelchair users are also found mainly in the more expensive hotels. Noise can be quite a problem in cities, even in the luxury hotels, so ask for a quiet room. It is perfectly in order to request hotel staff to put you in another room for any reason.

The price of the room will usually include breakfast. This will be either a set Turkish breakfast of fresh bread, butter, jam, soft white cheese, tomatoes, cucumbers and black olives, or a self-service buffet. In recent years, many hotels have begun to offer half board, with an evening meal thrown in. If you want to be independent, make this clear when you arrive. The evening meal may well turn out to be yet another buffet.

Yeşil Ev, a Special License Hotel *(see p324)*

The restored Sumengen and Historia hotels in Istanbul

PRICES AND DISCOUNTS

HOTEL PRICES are quoted per room (not per person) in US dollars, Euros or Turkish lira. Bargaining is perfectly acceptable, and discounts are often available if you pay in hard currency. Even luxury hotels will offer a discount to business travellers. Ask for the corporate rate. In general, your success in bargaining will depend on how busy the hotel is. If it is empty, as is often the case in winter, then you have some leeway for negotiation. You can expect to pay premium prices during religious or national holidays, however, when virtually all accommodation is booked.

BOOKING A ROOM

IT IS ALWAYS a good idea to book, especially in Istanbul or other large cities, and in the summer season between May and October. Telephone, fax and e-mail bookings are all accepted but, for peace of mind, try to confirm all your reservations and travel needs by fax. If you are travelling

with an organized tour, your agent should handle all the arrangements for you. Arriving in Turkey with a confirmed, written booking is always a good idea.

If you haven't pre-booked accommodation, or if you have changed your itinerary to get off the beaten track, visit any of the local tourist information offices to inquire about available accommodation. They will give you a list of local hotels, but leave it to you to make your choice and booking. Tourist offices can also give advice on approximate prices.

Don't be shy about looking around, seeing rooms and comparing prices.

CHECKING OUT AND PAYING

ALL GUESTS ARE expected to check out by noon, but on special request most hotels will agree to hold luggage for collection later.

Except for the very remote or most economical establishments, most hotels listed in this guide accept major international credit cards. Fewer will accept travellers' cheques, and may even charge a commission to cash them.

Value-added tax (VAT) is known as KDV in Turkish (*see p373*) and is generally included in the price of a room. When you register at a hotel, you will often be

asked for your credit card, which will then be swiped through an authorization machine. You will be asked to sign the form and the card must then be resubmitted for payment when your account is finally settled.

As with most hotels, tips for the staff are always very much appreciated and remembered. A few dollars is adequate for junior personnel, while a little more is called for if the front desk has done something special for you.

Remember that phone calls and minibar drinks are additional charges that increase your bill substantially.

Hotel guests relaxing by the pool

CHILDREN

IN MOST HOTELS, children up to the age of six years can stay in their parents' room at no extra charge. Many hotels also offer up to 50 per cent discount rates for 12–15-year-olds sharing a room with their parents. Cots for babies are willingly provided even by mid-range hotels. Children's menus are usually available in family resort areas and holiday villages. In Turkey, children generally are expected to eat when their parents do and they also tend to stay up late, particularly in the hot summer months.

HOSTELS AND STUDENT LODGINGS

TURKEY HAS MANY youth hostels, student lodgings and even a state-sponsored youth travel scheme for those who are travelling on a limited budget, such as university students and backpackers. The state-sponsored scheme was initiated in 2000 for

Luxurious double room at the Bosphorus Palace Hotel in Istanbul

students between the ages of 18 and 26, and requires the travellers concerned to be able to identify themselves with an International Student Identity or Youth Hostel Association card. Students have half-price access to selected hotels all over Turkey, as well as camp sites and university dormitories. The dormitories, however, are only available during university holidays. Entry to all Culture Ministry museums and sites is half the posted price. Full details are available from the **Student Travel Association General Directorate**, or Yurtkur, in Ankara, and the **Interyouth Hostel** in Istanbul.

CAMPING AND CARAVANNING

CARAVANNING and camping holidays are becoming increasingly popular and many new areas are being developed into well-equipped, highly organized camping grounds that provide ample space for tents or trailers, as well as ablution facilities.

In parts of the country, cosy, furnished bungalows may be available for self-catered forest holidays.

However, please note that camping is only allowed in designated areas, so be sure to check with the **Turkish Camping and Caravanning Association**, who will be able to provide you with a list of approved sites.

Parking a caravan or pitching a tent on any deserted beach, or simply pulling over to the side of the road in a caravan is discouraged.

A quaint, old-fashioned pension in the back streets of Selçuk

GUESTHOUSES

THIS IS A little-known type of accommodation in Turkey. The **Association for the Development of Tourist Guesthouses**, which is run by volunteers, gets requests for accommodation in all price ranges from all over the world. Even if municipalities or tourist information bureaux do not keep a list, patience is often rewarded, and excellent accommodation can nearly always be found.

SELF-CATERING

MOST CITIES AND towns in Turkey have apartment hotels for short-term rental. Pensions, too, often include cooking facilities, but these are usually shared with other guests. For tax reasons, not many self-catering apartments advertise openly, and word of mouth is the best way to locate these places. Some travel agents have lists of apartments, which they own and maintain, available for self-catering holidays.

Camping in the remote Kaçkar Mountains

DIRECTORY

HOTELS

Turkish Hotel Operators Union
Mete Cad, Mete Palas, Taksim, Istanbul.
(0212) 249 51 53 and 251 48 59.
FAX (0212) 252 16 64.

SPECIAL LICENSE HOTELS

Turkish Touring and Auomobile Club (TTOK)
(Turk Tur ve Otomobil Kulübü)
Oto Sanayi Sitesi Yanı 1, Seyrantepe Yolu, IV Levent, Istanbul.
(0212) 282 81 40.
FAX (212) 282 80 42.
www.turing@org.tr

STUDENT TRAVEL

Student Travel Association General Directorate
Yurtkur (Ministry of Tourism for Student Travel), Ankara.
(0312) 430 17 80.
www.kyk.gov.tr
webadmin@kyk.gov.tr

Interyouth Hostel
Caferiye Sok 6/1, Sultanahmet, Istanbul.
(0212) 513 61 50/51 and 522 95 01.

CAMPING

Turkish Camping and Caravanning Association
Bestekar Sok 62/12, Kavaklıdere, Ankara.
(0312) 466 19 97.

Filiz Sok 52, Kartaltepe, Bakırköy, Istanbul.
(0212) 662 46 15.

Mudaniye Cad, Ertürk Sok, Emek Apartman Altı F8/A, Bursa.
(0224) 253 02 82.

GUESTHOUSES

Association for the Development of Tourist Guesthouses
Cumhuriyet Bul, Elbir İşhanı 84/404, Alsancak, İzmir.
(0232) 425 72 73.

Choosing a Hotel

THE HOTELS IN THIS GUIDE have been selected from a wide price range for their good value or exceptional location, comfort and style. The chart highlights some of the factors which may influence your choice and gives a brief description of each hotel. Entries are listed by price category within the towns, with colour-coded thumbtabs to indicate the regions covered on each page.

ISTANBUL

	NUMBER OF ROOMS	CREDIT CARDS	CENTRAL LOCATION	RESTAURANT	SWIMMING POOL
SERAGLIO POINT: *The Kybele Hotel.* **Map 5 E4.** [$][$] Yerebatan Cad 35. ☎ *(0212) 511 77 66.* [FAX] *(0212) 513 43 93.* [W] *www.kybelehotel.com* @ *info@kybelehotel.com* A very intimate hotel near the Yerebatan Saray. Comfortable rooms beautifully decorated with antique furniture, glass lanterns and Turkish carpets. 🛏 ⛱ ❄	16	V MC AE DC	●	■	
SERAGLIO POINT: *Romance Hotel.* **Map 5 E3.** [$][$][$] Hüdavendigar Cad 7. ☎ *(0212) 512 86 76.* [FAX] *(0212) 512 87 23.* [W] *www.romancehotel.com* @ *romance@romancehotel.com* A pleasant hotel and a fairly new addition to the growing number of hotels in the Sirkeci area. It is situated near the train station, and is a short walk from Sultanahmet Square and most of the main attractions. 🛏 [24] [TV] ❄ 🏋 [P] ♿	63	V MC AE DC	●	■	
SULTANAHMET: *Side Hotel and Pension.* **Map 5 E4.** [$] Utangaç Sok 20. ☎ *(0212) 517 22 82.* [FAX] *(0212) 517 65 90.* [W] *www.sidehotel.com* @ *info@sidehotel.com* This family-run establishment, small and clean, offers low-budget accommodation in the heart of the historic centre of the city. There are hotel-style rooms, as well as cheaper, simpler ones with shared toilet facilities. The views of the Haghia Sophia and the Blue Mosque from the rooftop café are superb. 🛏 [TV] ❄	28	V MC	●		
SULTANAHMET: *Hotel Valide Sultan.* **Map 5 E4** [$][$] İshakpaşa Cad, Kutlu Gün Sok 1. ☎ *(0212) 517 65 58.* [FAX] *(0212) 638 07 05.* [W] *www.hotelvalidesultan.com* @ *vsultan@hotelvalidesultan.com* An exquisitely restored Ottoman-style hotel in traditional wood, close to the Topkapı Palace. Terrace restaurant and breakfast hall have excellent views of the Sea of Marmara, Haghia Sophia and the Blue Mosque. 🛏 ⛱ [24] [TV] ❄ [P]	17	V MC AE DC	●	■	
SULTANAHMET: *Pierre Loti Hotel.* **Map 5 D4.** [$][$] Piyerloti Cad 5. ☎ *(0212) 518 57 00.* [FAX] *(0212) 516 18 86.* [W] *www.pierrelotihotel.com* @ *info@pierrelotihotel.com* Named after the famous French novelist, the Pierre Loti Hotel is situated on the main road, a short walk from all the historical sights such as Topkapı Palace and the Archaeological Museum and the Grand Bazaar. 🛏 [24] [TV] ❄ ♿	36	V MC AE	●	■	
SULTANAHMET: *Yeşil Ev.* **Map 5 E4.** [$][$][$][$] Kabasakal Cad 5. ☎ *(0212) 517 67 85.* [FAX] *(0212) 517 67 80.* [W] *www.turing.org.tr* Yeşil Ev is set in the restored 19th-century wooden home of a former government minister in the heart of the old city, and near the historical monuments. There is a lovely quiet garden with lush evergreen trees. 🛏 ⛱ [24] [TV] ❄ ♿	19	V MC AE DC	●	■	
SULTANAHMET: *Four Seasons Hotel.* **Map 5 E3.** [$][$][$][$][$] Tevkifhane Sok 1. ☎ *(0212) 638 82 00.* [FAX] *(0212) 638 82 10.* [W] *www.fshr.com* Part of the international chain, and created from a century-old Neo-Classical Turkish prison, today this lovely hotel is the essence of understated luxury and elegance in the core of historic Istanbul. 🛏 ⛱ 💧 [24] [TV] ❄ 💼 🏋 [P] 🚭 ♿	65	V MC AE DC	●	■	
BAZAAR QUARTER: *Merit Antique.* **Map 2 B4.** [$][$][$][$][$] Ordu Cad 226, Laleli. ☎ *(0212) 513 93 00.* [FAX] *(0212) 512 63 90.* The four large buildings enclosing several courtyards that the hotel occupies today were built in 1918. Glass roofs turned them into elegant lobbies and dining rooms complete with birds, marble fountains and chandeliers. Grand spiral staircases lead up to the rooms. Caters for children. 🛏 [24] [TV] ❄ 🏋	272	V MC AE DC	●	■	●
BEYOĞLU: *Yeni Şehir Palas Hotel.* **Map 1 A4.** [$][$] Meşrutiyet Cad, Oteller Sok 1/3. ☎ *(0212) 252 71 60.* [FAX] *(0212) 249 75 07.* [W] *www.yenisehirpalas.com* @ *info@yenisehirpalas.com* Very popular hotel that seems to be filled all year round. The gargantuan breakfast is a star attraction. The highly recommended Vareli Wine Bar, under the same ownership, is attached to the hotel. 🛏 [24] [TV] ❄ 🏋 [P] 🚭 ♿	171	V MC AE DC	●	■	●

Price categories for a standard double room per night including breakfast and VAT:

$ under US$50
$$ US$50–US$100
$$$ US$100–US$150
$$$$ US$150–US$250
$$$$$ over US$250

CREDIT CARDS
Indicates which credit cards are accepted by the establishment (AE American Express, DC Diners Club, MC MasterCard, V Visa).

CENTRAL LOCATION
Reasonable walking distance from centre of town, main amenities and tourist attractions.

RESTAURANT
Restaurant on the premises, usually open to non-residents.

SWIMMING POOL
Hotel with an indoor or outdoor swimming pool.

	NUMBER OF ROOMS	CREDIT CARDS	CENTRAL LOCATION	RESTAURANT	SWIMMING POOL
BEYOĞLU: *Grace Hotel.* **Map 1 A4.** $$$ Meşrutiyet Cad No 38. (0212) 293 39 55. FAX (0212) 252 43 70. Located in a restored late Ottoman building in the heart of the business and entertainment centre. Close to the fish market, shopping area, restaurants and nightlife. Private nightclub in the basement.	52	V MC AE	●	■	●
BEYOĞLU: *Dilson Hotel.* **Map 1 B4.** $$$$ Sıraselviler Cad 49. (0212) 252 96 00. FAX (0212) 249 70 77. W www.dilson.com Centrally located hotel with dedicated and experienced staff to meet all your needs. Shaman World Music Club in the basement is a popular night spot for both guests and locals.	118	V MC AE DC	●	■	
BEYOĞLU: *Pera Palas Hotel.* **Map 1 A5.** $$$$ Mesrutiyet Cad 98, Tepebaşı. (0212) 251 45 60. FAX (0212) 251 40 89. W www.perapalas.com Once associated with the Orient Express and a legendary guest list, the hotel has now lost some of its atmosphere, but not its reputation. Still a landmark and an authentic experience in the old Pera quarter of Istanbul.	145	V MC AE DC	●	■	
BEYOĞLU: *Ceylan Inter-Continental.* **Map 1 C3.** $$$$$ Askerocağı Cad 1. (0212) 231 21 21. FAX (0212) 231 21 80. W www.interconti.com @ istanbul@interconti.com Luxurious five-star hotel recently allied to an international chain. Near the main shopping districts and business areas of Istanbul.	390	V MC AE DC	●	■	●
BEYOĞLU: *The Marmara Hotel.* **Map 1 B4.** $$$$$ Taksim Meydanı. (0212) 251 46 96. FAX (0212) 244 05 09. W www.themarmaraistanbul.com In the city's most frenetic hub, comfort and style reign, with panoramic views from the top-floor lounge bar. Don't miss the racy and cosmopolitan Marmara Café at street level. Offers all the luxury amenities.	387	V MC AE DC	●	■	●
FURTHER AFIELD: *Avlonya Hotel.* **Map 4 A4.** $$ Küçüklanga Cad 59. (0212) 529 54 08. FAX (0212) 585 94 32. The Avlonya Hotel caters mainly to business people visiting the Aksaray area. It is within reach of most of the sights, including Topkapı Palace, Haghia Sophia and the Grand Bazaar.	56	V MC AE DC	●	■	
FURTHER AFIELD: *Eysan Hotel* $$ Rıhtım Cad 26. (0216) 346 24 40. FAX (0216) 418 95 82. A well-appointed classic hotel on the quayside on the Asian shore of the Bosphorus, with sea views from all rooms. The dingy entrance is the only drawback to this hotel. There is also an excellent restaurant. Within walking distance of all amenities in the busy Kadıköy area.	48	V MC AE DC	●	■	
FURTHER AFIELD: *Harem Hotel.* **Map 6 B5.** $$ Ambar Sok 2. (0216) 310 68 00. FAX (0216) 334 77 30. @ harem@turk.net A small, family-run hotel situated close to the international sea port and the grandiose train station of Haydarpaşa. Children are catered for, and there is a games room and TV salon.	100	V MC AE		■	●
FURTHER AFIELD: *Dorint Park Plaza Istanbul.* **Map 1 B3.** $$$ Topçu Cad 23. (0212) 254 51 00. FAX (0212) 254 71 60. A hotel on a quiet side street not far from Taksim Square just outside Beyoğlu, offering professional service and luxury amenities. Baby-sitting facilities are available, there is a doctor on call, secretarial services, and a fitness centre and sauna.	178	V MC AE DC	●	■	●
FURTHER AFIELD: *Çınar Hotel* $$$$ Şevketiye Mah Fener Mevkii. (0212) 663 29 00. FAX (0212) 663 29 21. W www.cinarhotel.com @ cinarhotel@superonline.com Located in a leafy residential suburb bordering the Sea of Marmara, there are refreshing views from all rooms. Convenient for Atatürk Airport, this hotel has a relaxing personal charm not always associated with large establishments. 20 km (12 miles) from the city centre.	214	V MC AE DC		■	●

Price categories for a standard double room per night including breakfast and VAT:
$ under US$50
$$ US$50–US$100
$$$ US$100–US$150
$$$$ US$150–US$250
$$$$$ over US$250

CREDIT CARDS
Indicates which credit cards are accepted by the establishment (AE American Express, DC Diners Club, MC MasterCard, V Visa).

CENTRAL LOCATION
Reasonable walking distance from centre of town, main amenities and tourist attractions.

RESTAURANT
Restaurant on the premises, usually open to non-residents.

SWIMMING POOL
Hotel with an indoor or outdoor swimming pool.

	NUMBER OF ROOMS	CREDIT CARDS	CENTRAL LOCATION	RESTAURANT	SWIMMING POOL
FURTHER AFIELD: *Divan Hotel*. **Map 1 C3.** $$$$ Cumhuriyet Cad 2. (0212) 231 41 00. FAX (0212) 248 85 27. www.divanoteli.com.tr The Divan is almost an Istanbul institution. An uninteresting exterior does little justice to the hotel's fine service, comfort and one of the best dining rooms in Istanbul. Also offers a fitness centre and beauty salon.	180	V MC AE	●	■	●
FURTHER AFIELD: *Eresin Hotel Istanbul* $$$$ Millet Cad 186. (0212) 631 12 12. FAX (0212) 631 37 02. www.eresin.com The peaceful, low-key location and understated luxury attracts many visitors. Staff are well-trained and friendly.	241	V MC AE DC	●	■	●
FURTHER AFIELD: *Istanbul Princess Otel* $$$$ Büyükdere Cad 49. (0212) 285 09 00. FAX (0212) 285 09 51. www.istanbulprincess.com iprinces@istanbulprincess.com This is an ideal hotel for conferences and business meetings, but less interesting for tourists. All business facilities are available, and a secretarial service. Away from the bustle of Taksim but easy access to both the European and Asian sides of Istanbul.	305	V MC AE DC	●	■	●
FURTHER AFIELD: *Radisson Hotel* $$$$ Karayolu Uzeri E5 . (0212) 425 73 73. FAX (0212) 425 73 63. www.radissonsas.com Remote from the city, on a busy main artery, this concrete box hotel has little other than a health centre and jacuzzi to recommend it. However, it remains the only hotel in Istanbul adjacent to the airport complex and is useful for brief flight stopovers.	246	V MC AE DC		■	
FURTHER AFIELD: *Çırağan Palace Hotel Kempinski Istanbul* $$$$$ **Map 3 D3.** Çırağan Cad 84. (0212) 258 33 77. FAX (0212) 295 66 87. www.ciraganpalace.com ciragan@ciraganpalace.com.tr This 18th-century palace on the Bosphorus shore is now a hotel offering everything you would expect from a "Best Hotels in the World" listing. Special weekend, wedding and conference deals available. The Sunday Brunch at Bellini Restaurant is the best in Istanbul.	316	V MC AE DC	●	■	●
FURTHER AFIELD: *Hilton Hotel*. **Map 1 C2.** $$$$$ Cumhuriyet Cad, Harbiye. (0212) 315 60 00. FAX (0212) 240 41 65. www.hilton.com All you would expect from the world's most renowned international hotel chain. Set in lush gardens overlooking the Bosphorus Straits, with a concert hall. Close to the main business area.	498	V MC AE DC	●	■	●
FURTHER AFIELD: *Hyatt Regency Hotel*. **Map 1 F2.** $$$$$ Taşkışla Cad. (0212) 225 70 00. FAX (0212) 368 10 00. www.istanbul.hyatt.com A sumptuous hotel with sweeping views of the Bosphorus. Guests like the smart restaurants, lounges and bars, and the fully equipped business centre. Also has tennis courts, sauna and solarium.	360	V MC AE DC	●	■	●
FURTHER AFIELD: *Swissôtel Istanbul – The Bosphorus* $$$$$ **Map 2 A4.** Bayıldım Cad 2. (0212) 326 11 00. FAX (0212) 326 11 22. www.swissotel.com emailus.Istanbul@swissotel.com The hotel commands one of the premier scenic views over the Bosphorus from a wooded hilltop. Precision service as expected, and there is also a first-rate modern *hamam* (Turkish bath) if you are hesitant about the more traditional ones in Istanbul.	579	V MC AE DC	●	■	●

THRACE AND THE SEA OF MARMARA

	NUMBER OF ROOMS	CREDIT CARDS	CENTRAL LOCATION	RESTAURANT	SWIMMING POOL
BURSA: *Safran Otel* $$ Ortapazar Cad, Kale Sok 4. (0224) 224 72 16. FAX (0224) 224 72 19. Located in the city centre, this beautiful saffron-coloured restored mansion is close to all historical sights, in a quiet street away from the city noise.	10	V MC AE	●	■	

BURSA: *Almira Hotel* $$$$ · 235 · V MC AE DC
Ulubatlı Hasan Bulvari 5. (*(0224) 250 20 20.* FAX *(0224) 250 20 38.*
w *www.almira.com.tr* @ *reservation@almira.com.tr*
The bold and bulky exterior hides a cosy and comfortable interior. Poolside dining, shopping centre and Ottoman corner are special features. A few minutes' walk from many historical sights.

BÜYÜKADA: *Splendid Palace* $$$ · 70 · V MC
23 Nisan Cad 71. (*(0216) 382 69 50.* FAX *(0216) 382 67 75.*
Situated in a beautiful historic building close to the sea, and just minutes from the beach and town centre. Large garden restaurant and swimming pool. Children are catered for.

ÇEKIRGE: *Yıldız Thermal Hotel* $$ · 30 · V
Selvinaz Cad 1. (*(0224) 239 69 80.* FAX *(0224) 239 69 85.*
An elegant 1920s-style hotel with excellent facilities, notably two thermal baths with healing and therapeutic properties.

ÇEKIRGE: *Hotel Çelik Palas* $$$$ · 173 · V MC AE DC
Çekirge Cad 79. (*(0224) 233 38 00.* FAX *(0224) 236 19 10.*
A beautiful spa in the "Grand Hotel" tradition, with every conceivable luxury. This is one of Turkey's top spa resorts.

EDIRNE: *Hotel Rüstem Paşa Kervansaray* $$ · 79 · V MC
İki Kapalı Han Cad 57. (*(0284) 212 61 19.* FAX *(0284) 212 04 62.*
Constructed in the traditional Ottoman style of Mimar Sinan, this restored caravanserai is a city centre landmark. Caters primarily for groups of ten or more.

GALLIPOLI/DARDANELLES: *Boncuk Hotel* $$ · 48 · V MC
Gelibolu. (*(0286) 576 82 92.* FAX *(0286) 576 81 58.*
Situated right on the beach at Gelibolu. There are views of the Dardanelles from the balconies of this small hotel, as well as volleyball courts and games on the beach. Children are catered for.

HEYBELIADA: *Merit Halki Palace* $$$ · 45 · V MC AE DC
Refah Şehitleri Cad 94. (*(0216) 351 00 25.* FAX *(0216) 351 00 32.*
w *www.merithotels.com* @ *info@merithotels.com*
This wooden, château-style hotel has wonderful service and the "boutique" touches at which the Merit Group excels. It has access to the island's forest which offers recreation such as riding and cycling.

İZNIK: *Motel Burcum* $ · 30
Göl Sahil Yolu 12. (*(0224) 757 10 11.* FAX *(0224) 757 10 11.*
A small hotel situated on the lake shore a short walk from the centre of town. Some rooms have lake views. Camping is available in the garden.

ULUDAĞ: *Grand Yazıcı Hotel* $$$$ · 260 · V MC AE
Oteller 1. Gelişim Bölgesi. (*(0224) 285 20 56.* FAX *(0224) 285 20 48.*
w *www.grandyazici.com.tr* @ *sales@grandyazici.com.tr*
One of the best slope-side hotels. Convenient to ski lifts, with many après-ski activities and amenities.

ULUDAĞ: *Kervansaray Uludağ Hotel* $$$$ · 169 · V MC AE
Oteller 1. Gelişim Bölgesi. (*(0224) 285 21 87.* FAX *(0224) 285 21 93.*
In the heart of the skiing centre, this Swiss-style chalet hotel provides a fully equipped fitness centre, indoor and outdoor swimming pools and sauna. Children are catered for.

THE AEGEAN

ASSOS/BEHRAMKALE: *Assos Terrace Motel* $$ · 20 · V MC
Küçükkuyu Yolu, Kadırga Köyü. (*(0286) 764 02 85.* FAX *(0286) 764 02 84.*
w *www.assos.de/terrace/* @ *terrace@ttnet.net.tr*
A motel on the hillside near the beach, overlooking the harbour at Assos. All rooms have balconies and sea views. Offers canoeing, fishing and horse riding. Pets accepted and children welcome.

ASSOS/BEHRAMKALE: *Behram Otel* $$ · 17 · V MC
İskele Assos. (*(0286) 721 70 16.* FAX *(0286) 721 70 44.* w *www.behram-hotel.com*
A small and cosy hotel located in a restored old stone building on the harbour, with a warm atmosphere. Lovely waterfront restaurant. All rooms have central heating. Water sports and sailing available.

Price categories for a standard double room per night including breakfast and VAT:
$ under US$50
$$ US$50–US$100
$$$ US$100–US$150
$$$$ US$150–US$250
$$$$$ over US$250

CREDIT CARDS
Indicates which credit cards are accepted by the establishment (AE American Express, DC Diners Club, MC MasterCard, V Visa).

CENTRAL LOCATION
Reasonable walking distance from centre of town, main amenities and tourist attractions.

RESTAURANT
Restaurant on the premises, usually open to non-residents.

SWIMMING POOL
Hotel with an indoor or outdoor swimming pool.

Hotel	Number of Rooms	Credit Cards	Central Location	Restaurant	Swimming Pool
BODRUM: *Harmony Hotel* $$ Caferpaşa Cad. ☎ *(0252) 316 94 25.* [FAX] *(0252) 316 94 97.* [W] *www.bodrumharmony.com* A pleasant and popular hotel in a superb location right in the city centre, that overlooks a quiet courtyard and swimming pool, and is close to the beach. Children welcome. 👪 [24] [TV] ❄ [P]	34	V MC	●	■	●
BODRUM: *Seçkin Konaklar* $$ Neyzen Tevfik Cad 246. ☎ *(0252) 316 13 51.* [FAX] *(0252) 316 33 36.* [W] *www.seckinkonaklar.com* @ *garipbdr@superonline.com* Combines normal hotel rooms and self-catering apartments, amid flowering bougainvillea. Ultra comfortable. Many repeat visitors. 👪 [TV] ❄ ♿	35	V MC AE	●		●
BODRUM: *Hotel Marina Vista* $$$ Neyzen Tevfik Cad 226. ☎ *(0252) 316 02 56.* [FAX] *(0252) 316 23 47.* @ *marinavista@superonline.com* A serene and sophisticated nook in the hub of Bodrum. Good views, open-air atmosphere and a host of upmarket facilities. 👪 [24] [TV] ❄ 🏋	84	V MC AE DC	●	■	●
BODRUM: *Manastır Hotel* $$$$ Kumbahçe Mah Barış Sitesi Bodrum. ☎ *(0252) 316 28 54.* [FAX] *(0252) 316 27 72.* @ *manastir@unimedya.net.tr* One of Bodrum's prettiest medium-sized hotels. Many of the rooms have balconies and sea vistas. Games room and children's section. 👪 [24] [TV] ❄ [P]	59	V MC AE	●	■	●
BODRUM PENINSULA: *Ada Hotel* $$$$ Çataldibi Mevkii, Türkbükü. ☎ *(0252) 377 59 15.* [FAX] *(0252) 377 53 79.* [W] *www.adahotel.com* At the top end of an already classy enclave, Ada Hotel is more like a family home in a pretty garden setting. Mediterranean gourmet cuisine and an outstanding wine cellar. 👪 🖥 [24] [TV] ❄ 🍸 [P] ♿	13	V AE DC	 MC	■	●
ÇANAKKALE: *Anzac Hotel* $ Saat Kulesi Meydanı. ☎ *(0286) 217 77 77.* [FAX] *(0286) 217 20 18.* [W] *www.anzachotel.com* Drab to look at, but a landmark for backpackers and just about everybody else. Satisfies basic needs in comfort for budget-conscious travellers. Children are catered for. 👪 [24] [TV] [P]	27	V	● MC	■	
ÇEŞME: *Sheraton Çeşme Hotel, Resort and Spa* $$$$$ Ilıca. ☎ *(0232) 723 12 40.* [FAX] *(0232) 723 13 88.* [W] *www.sheraton.com* @ *info@sheratoncesme.com* Spa and therapy treatments are an outstanding feature to complement private beaches, wonderful cuisine and classical décor. Children are catered for. 👪 💧 [24] [TV] ❄ 🏋 🍸 [P] 🚭	373	V MC AE DC	●	■	●
DATÇA: *Uslu Apart Hotel* $$ İskele Mah Azmakbaşı Mevkii. ☎ *(0252) 712 80 08.* [FAX] *(0252) 712 80 10.* [W] *www.datcainfo.com/uslu/* @ *usluapart@hotmail.com* A clean apartment hotel right on the beach with lovely views over Datça Bay. Accommodation consists of two or three bedrooms, bathroom and kitchen. There is also a terrace bar and a snack bar. Offers most water sports, as well as *gulet* (two-masted traditional wooden boat) and yacht cruises. 👪 [TV] [P]	31	V MC			●
İZMIR: *Antik Han Hotel* $$ Anafartalar Cad 600. ☎ *(0232) 489 27 50.* [FAX] *(0232) 483 59 25.* A small hotel located in a beautifully restored Ottoman mansion in the centre of town, 14 km (9 miles) from the airport. Each room has a private bathroom and central heating. 👪 🖥 [TV] ❄ [P]	30	V MC AE	●	■	
İZMIR: *Ege Palas Hotel* $$ Cumhuriyet Bulvarı 210. ☎ *(0232) 463 90 90.* [FAX] *(0232) 463 81 00.* [W] *www.egepalas.com.tr* @ *egepalas@egepalas.com.tr* Luxury hotel in the centre of town equipped for both business people and vacationers. Close to all amenities and local transport. 👪 [24] [TV] ❄ 🍸 [P] ♿	112	V MC AE DC	●	■	●

İZMIR: *Hisar Hotel* $$ Fevzipaşa Bulvarı 153, Basmane. ☎ *(0232) 484 54 00.* [FAX] *(0232) 425 88 30.* Time-warp atmosphere, with friendly staff who always remember you. Ask for a quieter (and more modern) suite on the seventh floor for excellent value in the city centre. Children are catered for. 🚗 [24] [TV] ☰	63	V MC AE	●	■	
İZMIR: *Anemon İzmir* $$$ Mürsel Paşa Bulvarı 40. ☎ *(0232) 446 36 56.* [FAX] *(0232) 446 36 55.* [@] *info@anemonizmir.com* A fairly basic medium-sized hotel in the centre of town, 14 km (9 miles) from the airport. Close to all amenities and transport. 🚗 [TV] ☰ [P] ♿	101	V MC AE	●	■	
İZMIR: *İzmir Hilton* $$$$$ Gaziosmanpaşa Bulvarı 7. ☎ *(0232) 441 60 60.* [FAX] *(0232) 441 22 07.* [W] *www.hilton.com* A luxury five-star international hotel with legendary views over İzmir Bay. The Hilton has a well-deserved reputation as the city's premier meeting point. Pets accepted and children are catered for. 🚗 💧 [24] [TV] ☰ 🍸 🏋 [P] 🚭 ♿	381	V MC AE DC	●	■	●
KUŞADASI: *Anker Villas* $$ Kadıkalesi, Nazilli Sitesi 679. ☎ *(0256) 633 12 48.* [FAX] *(0256) 633 15 69.* [W] *www.ankervillas.com* [@] *contact@ankervillas.com* Self-contained villas, with two or three bedrooms, bathroom and kitchen. Rented weekly or monthly. Self-catering, but there are restaurants nearby. 🚗 [TV] ☰ [P]	50	V MC		■	●
KUŞADASI: *Öküz Mehmet Paşa Kervansaray* $$ ☎ *(0256) 614 41 15.* [FAX] *(0256) 614 24 23.* [W] *www.kusadasihotels.com/caravanserail/* [@] *caravanserail@kusadasi.net* One of the first authentic trading hans to be turned into a modern inn in Turkey. The Turkish/Oriental evening gala is hugely popular. 🚗 🍴 [24] [TV] ☰ [P] ♿	26	V MC AE DC	●	■	●
KUŞADASI: *The Grand Blue Sky International Hotel* $$$ Kadınlar Denizi. ☎ *(0256) 612 77 50.* [FAX] *(0256) 612 42 25.* [W] *www.grandbluesky.com* [@] *bluesky@grandbluesky.com* A luxury resort hotel situated on the beach. Offers water sports, ball games and fully equipped health and fitness facilities. 🚗 💧 [24] [TV] ☰ 🍸 🏋 [P] 🚭 ♿	325	V MC AE DC	●	■	●
MARMARIS: *Balcı Hotel* $ İnönü Cad 19. ☎ *(0252) 412 53 41.* [FAX] *(0252) 412 53 43.* A nice little hotel in the city centre close to all amenities and historical sights. All rooms have balconies. Children are welcome. 🚗 [TV] ☰ [P]	67	V MC	●	■	●
MARMARIS: *Laguna Hotel* $$ İçmeler. ☎ *(0252) 455 37 10.* [FAX] *(0252) 455 36 22.* [@] *reserv@lagunahotel.com* The package-holidaymaker's hotel with palm trees, sand and chaises longues beach-side and bar-side. Offers water sports, a games room, live entertainment and a sauna. Children welcome. 🚗 💧 [24] [TV] ☰ 🍸 🏋 [P] ♿	72	V MC		■	●
MARMARIS: *Nergis Hotel* $$$ Kemal Elgin Bulvarı. ☎ *(0252) 412 51 30.* [FAX] *(0252) 412 12 04.* [@] *nergishotel@superonline.com* An elegant medium-sized hotel right on the beach. All rooms have balconies and views of the sea. Children welcome. 🚗 [TV] ☰ 🍸 🏋 [P]	96	V MC	●	■	●
MARMARIS: *Elegance Hotels International Marmaris* $$$$ Uzunyalı Cad 130. ☎ *(0252) 412 81 01.* [FAX] *(0252) 412 20 05.* [W] *www.elegancehotel.com* [@] *elegancehotel@elegancehotel.com* A five-star luxury resort hotel right on the beach and a short walk from the city centre (2 km/1.2 miles). All water sports and activities available. There is also a nightclub and disco. Children are catered for. 🚗 💧 [24] [TV] ☰ 🍸 🏋 [P] ♿	190	V MC AE	●	■	●
SELÇUK: *Cenka Hotel* $ Atatürk Mah Kubilay Cad 24. ☎ *(0232) 892 31 30.* [FAX] *(0232) 892 34 90.* A medium-sized hotel with basic facilities in the centre of town. A 20-minute walk to the ruins of Ephesus and 5 km (3 miles) to the beach. 🚗 [TV] ☰ [P]	54	V MC	●	■	
SELÇUK: *Kalehan Hotel* $$ Atatürk Cad 49. ☎ *(0232) 892 61 54/21 69.* [FAX] *(0232) 892 21 69.* [W] *www.kalehan.com* [@] *erghir@superonline.com* A restored caravanserai located in the city centre, the Kalehan has Turkish hospitality down to a fine, but unpretentious, art and offers comfortable. accommodation. Popular with group tours. 🚗 🍴 [24] [TV] ☰ [P]	50	V MC	●	■	●

For key to symbols see back flap

Price categories for a standard double room per night including breakfast and VAT: $ under US$50 $$ US$50–US$100 $$$ US$100–US$150 $$$$ US$150–US$250 $$$$$ over US$250	**CREDIT CARDS** Indicates which credit cards are accepted by the establishment (AE American Express, DC Diners Club, MC MasterCard, V Visa). **CENTRAL LOCATION** Reasonable walking distance from centre of town, main amenities and tourist attractions. **RESTAURANT** Restaurant on the premises, usually open to non-residents. **SWIMMING POOL** Hotel with an indoor or outdoor swimming pool.			

MEDITERRANEAN TURKEY

Hotel	Number of Rooms	Credit Cards	Central Location	Restaurant	Swimming Pool
ADANA: *Zaimoğlu Hotel* $$ Özler Cad 22. (0322) 363 53 53. FAX (0322) 363 53 63. www.zaimoglu.com.tr One of the older hotels in town, this place is known for its hospitable staff and friendly atmosphere. Trips to the beach 45 km (28 miles) away can be arranged. Nightclub and late-night activities.	49	V MC AE		●	
ALANYA: *Boulevard Hotel* $$ Keykubat Cad 39. (0242) 513 11 33. FAX (0242) 513 72 22. www.boulevard-hotel.com Situated right on the beach, and close to the city centre and the castle ruins, this attractive hotel caters to vacationing families. Ball games and diving school available. There is also a doctor on call, billiards, table tennis, a TV room, and a playground for children. Pets accepted.	96	V MC AE	●	●	●
ANTAKYA: *Antik Beyazıt Hotel* $$ Hükümet Cad 4. (0326) 216 29 00. FAX (0326) 214 30 89. www.hotelguide.com.tr A small, elegant hotel situated in the city centre, a short walk from all the historical sights and amenities.	27	V MC AE	●		
ANTAKYA: *Büyük Antakya Hotel* $$$ Atatürk Cad 8. (0326) 213 58 58. FAX (0326) 213 58 69. Close to all the historically interesting sights and transport. Fully equipped meeting rooms and banquet halls. Nightclub and disco.	72	V MC AE	●	●	
ANTALYA: *Anı Pansiyon* $ Tabakhane Sok 26, Kaleiçi. (0242) 247 00 56. Comfortable and convenient, Anı Pension is more like a private house. Owner will cook meals on request. Children are welcome.	12		●	●	
ANTALYA: *Alp Paşa Hotel* $$$$ Barbaros Mah Hespacı Sok 30. (0242) 247 56 76. FAX (0242) 248 50 74. www.alppasa.com An attractive restored house in Kaleiçi (the old city centre), near all the historical sights. All rooms built around a central courtyard and pool. Traditional cuisine, folklore, and music evenings are a speciality.	62	V MC AE DC	●	●	●
ANTALYA: *Resort Dedeman Antalya* $$$$ Lara Yolu. (0242) 321 79 10. FAX (0242) 321 38 73. www.dedemanhotels.com The finest national chain of luxury hotels is right on the water, a little way out of town. A multitude of water sports, ball sports and entertainment facilities available. Children welcome.	483	V MC AE DC		●	●
BELEK: *Merit Arcadia Resort Hotel* $$$$ İskele Mevkii. (0242) 715 11 00. FAX (0242) 715 10 80. www.arcadiahotel.com Like a self-contained miniature village, with stunning décor. There is a private beach, aqua park and beauty salon.	463	V MC DC		●	●
BELEK: *MIA Belpark Village* $$$$ Belek Turizm Merkezi, İskele Mevkii. (0242) 715 13 00. FAX (0242) 715 13 17. www.antalya-ws.com/hotels/serik One of an international chain of resorts. Activities for children, and nightly entertainment. There is a doctor on call, baby-sitting service, indoor football, volleyball, water sports, boutique and car rental.	320	V MC AE DC	●	●	●
DALYAN: *Konak Melsa* $$ Köyceğiz Cad, Çavuşlar Mah. (0252) 284 51 04. FAX (0252) 284 39 13. konakmelsa@hotmail.com The highly professional Dutch-Turkish owners have done up this lovely little hotel in caravanserai style using local stone and carved wood. Quiet location and also features its own Internet café.	24	V MC	●		

DALYAN: *Club Alla Turca* $$$ | 60 | V MC
Gülpınar Mah. (0252) 284 46 16. FAX (0252) 284 43 87. @ info@cluballaturca.com
Situated in the centre of town, 12 km (7 miles) from İztuzu Beach. A quaint hotel set out in villa style among lovely gardens. Children welcome.

FETHIYE: *Area Otel* $ | 50 | V MC AE DC
Çalış Plajı Fethiye. (0252) 622 08 13. FAX (0252) 622 08 91.
Located on the beach front at Çalış Plajı, this hotel accepts pets and caters for children. Water and beach sports, include sailing and diving.

FETHIYE: *Prenses Hotel* $ | 60 | V MC
İskele Meydanı 7. (0252) 612 54 99. FAX (0252) 612 48 78.
Situated adjacent to the yacht basin, this small hotel offers a pretty setting. Each room has a balcony with views of the sea. Water sports and sailing nearby. The Ölü Deniz beach is 14 km (8.6 miles) away.

FETHIYE: *Montana Pine Resort* $$$$ | 159 | V MC
Hisar öncü. (0252) 616 71 08. FAX (0252) 616 64 51.
W www.montanapine.com
Situated on the lower slopes of Mount Babadağ and surrounded by pine forests, this Mediterranean chalet-style resort offers spectacular views. It is a short distance (3 km/2 miles) from the famous beach of Ölü Deniz. In-house activities for families and children.

GÖCEK: *Swissôtel Göcek Marina Resort* $$$$$ | 57 | V MC AE DC
Marina, Göcek. (0252) 645 27 60. FAX (0252) 645 27 67. W www.swissotel.com
All rooms have a private terrace overlooking Göcek Bay. Gourmet restaurants, plus the service and amenities one expects from a precision-run global group. Caters for children.

KALKAN: *Club Xanthos Hotel* $ | 70 | V MC AE
Kalamar Yolu. (0242) 844 23 88. FAX (0242) 844 23 55. W www.clubxanthos.com
A medium-sized hotel designed to resemble the surrounding crumbling ruins. Located near the beach, upper-floor rooms have views of the sea. Water sports and ball games available, and there is a play area for children.

KALKAN: *Dionysia Hotel* $ | 23 | V MC
Cumhuriyet Cad. (0242) 844 36 81. FAX (0242) 31 39.
A very small, quiet hotel in the centre of town with basic but clean facilities. All rooms have private bathrooms. Children are catered for.

KAŞ: *Gülşen Pansiyon* $ | 15 | V MC
Hastane Cad 23. (0242) 836 11 71. FAX (0242) 836 30 82.
One of the nicest family-run, budget pensions on the coast. Sea views, seaside terrace and beach. Caters for children.

KAŞ: *Sardunya Hotel* $ | 16 | V MC AE
Hastane Cad, 56. (0242) 836 30 80. FAX (0242) 836 30 82.
A stylish, comfortable hotel which feels like home, with the family on site and bustling around. Their own restaurant and private beach are across the road. This is a peaceful enclave in the busy town.

KAŞ: *Club Hotel Phellos* $$ | 81 | V MC
Doğruyol Sok 4 (0242) 836 19 53. FAX (0242) 836 18 90.
W www.hotelclubphellos.com.tr @ info@hotelclubphellos.com.tr
An attractive hotel close to the beach with lovely views of the sea. Comfortable rooms with bathrooms and balconies. Diving schools and water sports available.

ÖLÜ DENIZ: *Majestic Hotel* $ | 45 |
(0252) 617 02 08. FAX (0252) 617 03 65. W www.majestic-hotels.com
A smaller hotel near the beach and the Blue Lagoon that caters to vacationing families. Balconies overlook the courtyard and swimming pool. Ball and water sports available.

ÖLÜ DENIZ: *Club Lykia World* $$$$ | 824 | V MC
PO Box 102. (0252) 617 02 00. FAX (0252) 617 03 80. W www.lykiaworld.com
@ info@lykiaworld.com
A large holiday resort right on the beach with every water sport and outdoor activity available, including tennis, in-line skating, volleyball, surfing, sailing and paragliding. Nightclub and disco. Babies and young children catered for, with programmes for each age group.

Price categories for a standard double room per night including breakfast and VAT:
- **$** under US$50
- **$$** US$50–US$100
- **$$$** US$100–US$150
- **$$$$** US$150–US$250
- **$$$$$** over US$250

CREDIT CARDS
Indicates which credit cards are accepted by the establishment (AE American Express, DC Diners Club, MC MasterCard, V Visa).

CENTRAL LOCATION
Reasonable walking distance from centre of town, main amenities and tourist attractions.

RESTAURANT
Restaurant on the premises, usually open to non-residents.

SWIMMING POOL
Hotel with an indoor or outdoor swimming pool.

	NUMBER OF ROOMS	CREDIT CARDS	CENTRAL LOCATION	RESTAURANT	SWIMMING POOL
SIDE: *Perissia Hotel Side* $$$$ Bingeşik Mevkii Kumköy Yolu Üzeri PK 58. (0242) 753 39 50. FAX (0242) 753 39 60. www.perissiahotels.com.tr info@perissiahotels.com.tr A luxury hotel on the seaside with all sports facilities and activities. Water sports and nightly entertainment. Children welcome.	220	V MC		■	●

ANKARA AND WESTERN ANATOLIA

	NUMBER OF ROOMS	CREDIT CARDS	CENTRAL LOCATION	RESTAURANT	SWIMMING POOL
AFYON: *Grand Özer Thermal Hotel* $$$ Süleyman Gönçer Cad 12. (0272) 214 33 00. FAX (0272) 214 33 09. www.grandozer.com info@grandozer.com Up-market spa resort catering for many tastes, just 3 km (2 miles) from Afyon airport. Children are welcome.	116	V MC AE DC	●	■	●
ANKARA: *Başkent Hotel* $$ İstanbul Cad 28, Ulus. (0312) 310 90 80. FAX (0312) 310 92 93. An efficient, well-run hotel amid the bustle of Ulus.	56	V MC	●	■	
ANKARA: *Otel Aldino* $$$ Tunalı Hilmi Cad, Bülten Sok 22, Kavaklıdere. (0312) 468 65 10. FAX (0312) 468 65 17. www.hotelaldino.com aldino@ada.net.tr This smaller hotel located in the city centre is equipped with a Turkish bath and sauna. Massage facilities and gym available. Caters for children and pets.	56	V MC AE	●	■	
ANKARA: *Büyükhanlı Park Hotel and Residence* $$$$ Simon Bolivar Cad 32, Çankaya. (0312) 441 56 00. FAX (0312) 441 22 74. www.buyukhanliparkhotel.com info@buyukhanliparkhotel.com Situated in the city centre, this hotel caters to business people and holiday-makers. Conference facilities and sports centre. Beauty centre, sauna, steamroom, massage facilities and solarium available.	106	V MC AE DC	●	■	●
ANKARA: *Hilton Ankara* $$$$$ Tahran Cad 12. (0312) 468 28 88. FAX (0312) 468 09 09. www.hilton.com One of Ankara's landmark hotels in the chic part of the city. All the facilities for business and pleasure, including an indoor pool, fitness centre, sauna, Turkish bath and function halls.	323	V MC AE DC	●	■	●
KONYA: *Şifa Hotel* $ Mevlana Cad 55. (0332) 350 42 90. FAX (0332) 351 92 51. A small hotel in the centre of the city. The comfortable rooms are enhanced by an excellent breakfast, served on the terrace in summer.	32	V MC	●	■	
KONYA: *Hotel Balıkçılar* $$ Mevlana Alanı 1. (0332) 350 94 70. FAX (0332) 351 32 59. Almost next door to the Mevlâna Museum, they offer the services and facilities of bigger hotels. There is an excellent restaurant open during the evenings.	51	V MC	●	■	
KONYA: *Dündar Hotel* $$$ Kerkük Cad 34, Ferit Paşa Mah. (0332) 236 10 52. FAX (0332) 235 91 30. Still Konya's most prestigious hotel combining convenience and elegant service. Children are welcome.	107	V MC AE	●	■	
KÜTAHYA: *Hotaş Hotel* $ Menderes Cad, Akabe Sok 5. (0274) 224 89 90. FAX (0274) 224 20 24. A mid-range hotel close to the city centre, offering basic comforts and catering to a cross-section of tastes.	69	V MC	●	■	
LAKE DISTRICT (EĞIRDIR): *Atabey Hotel* $ Yeşil Ada Mah Cami Cad. (0246) 311 50 06. FAX (0246) 311 55 92. Situated on the water's edge with good views of the lake, this hotel is small and comfortable, with satellite TV in each room.	19	V MC	●	■	

LAKE DISTRICT (EĞIRDIR): *Hotel Eğirdir* $$ 63 V MC
Poyraz Sahil Yolu 2. ((0246) 311 49 92. FAX (0246) 311 42 19.
This recently restored hotel is cheerful and comfortable. Water sports, hiking and fishing can be arranged. ▦ TV ఉ

THE BLACK SEA

ARTVIN: *Demirkol Turistik Hotel* $$ 42 V MC
Bankalar Cad 16, Borçka. ((0466) 415 36 60. FAX (0466) 415 25 92.
A small hotel situated at the foot of the mountain in the centre of town. Close to all amenities and transport. Turkish bath, sauna and massage available. Trekking tours depart from here. ▦ ◐ 24 TV ▤ P

AYDER (ÇAMLIHEMŞIN): *Ahşap Pansiyon* $ 9
Yukarı Ambarlık Mevkii, Ayder Kaplıcaları (Ayder Hot Springs). ((0464) 657 21 62.
FAX (0464) 657 22 62.
Simple mountain chalet, open during summer only. For hardy trekkers, this offers breathless vistas of some of Turkey's most spectacular alpine scenery. ▦

RIZE: *Hotel Kaçkar* $ 29 V MC
Cumhuriyet Cad 101. ((0464) 213 14 90. FAX (0464) 217 73 98.
A lovely, cosy hotel that cannot be too highly recommended. It is very centrally located, right in the main square, and offers easy access to all the local sights. Children are welcome. ▦ 24 TV ▤ P ఉ

RIZE: *Hotel Dedeman Rize* $$$ 82 V MC AE
Alipaşa Köyü Mevkii. ((0464) 223 44 44. FAX (0464) 223 53 48.
W www.dedemanhotels.com
A national five-star hotel chain with luxurious surroundings and its own private beach. Fully equipped meeting rooms and banquet facilities. Also indoor swimming pool, fitness centre, and solarium. ▦ 24 TV ▤ ⏰ ♨ P

SAFRANBOLU: *Hotel Tahsin Bey Konağı* $ 16 V MC AE
Çeşme Mah Hükümet Sok 46. ((0370) 712 60 62. FAX (0370) 725 55 96.
Restored town house with lovely décor and stately atmosphere. The proprietors own the adjacent house too. ▦ ⏰ TV P

SAFRANBOLU: *Selvili Köşk* $ 7
Çeşme Mah Mescid Sok 23. ((0370) 712 86 46. FAX (0370) 725 22 94.
W www.hotelselvilikosk.com
A charming monument to Ottoman architecture and culture, this small villa, built in 1883, has simple comforts and a beautiful garden.
▦ ⏰ 24 TV

SAFRANBOLU: *Hotel Paşa Konağı* $$ 14 V MC AE
Kale Altı Sok. ((0370) 712 81 53. FAX (0370) 712 10 73.
Beautifully restored mansion with panelled bedrooms, traditional furnishings and fireplaces in every room. Glorious garden. ▦ ⏰ 24 TV ▤ P

SAMSUN: *Büyük Samsun Hotel* $$$ 112 V MC
Atatürk Bulvarı 629. ((0362) 432 49 99. FAX (0362) 431 07 40.
W www.buyuksamsunhotel.com.tr @ buyuksamsunhotel@tourismkey.com
Located on the main road, just 5 km (3 miles) from the airport, this hotel caters mostly to business travellers. Children are welcome. ▦ 24 TV ▤ ♨

TRABZON: *Horon Hotel* $ 44 V
Sıramağazalar Cad 125. ((0462) 326 64 55. FAX (0462) 321 66 28. W www.otelhoron.com.tr
A small, personal hotel situated near the old city and other historical sights, and only 3 km (2 miles) from the airport. ▦ 24 TV ▤

TRABZON: *Büyük Sumela Hotel* $$$ 115 V MC AE
Maçka. ((0462) 512 35 40. FAX (0462) 512 36 26. W www.buyuksumela.com
One of the region's best-known hotels, with a well-deserved reputation for quality. It enjoys a tranquil location some 20 km (12 miles) from the hustle and bustle of Trabzon's city centre and is surrounded by lush natural forests and carefully tended gardens. Very conveniently located for access to the Sumela Monastery (13 km/8 miles away). ▦ 24 TV ▤ ⏰ ♨ P ✉ ఉ

TRABZON: *Zorlu Grand* $$$$ 160 V MC AE DC
Maraş Cad 9. ((0462) 326 84 00. FAX (0462) 326 84 58. W www.zorlugrand.com
A spacious hotel in the middle of town that resembles an imperial palace, it is lavishly decorated with fine furniture and antiques. There is an attractive indoor swimming pool, as well as a sauna, a gym and a Turkish bath (*hamam*).
▦ ⏰ 24 TV ▤ ⏰ ♨ P

Price categories for a standard double room per night including breakfast and VAT:	CREDIT CARDS
$ under US$50	Indicates which credit cards are accepted by the establishment (AE American Express, DC Diners Club, MC MasterCard, V Visa).
$$ US$50–US$100	CENTRAL LOCATION
$$$ US$100–US$150	Reasonable walking distance from centre of town, main amenities and tourist attractions.
$$$$ US$150–US$250	RESTAURANT
$$$$$ over US$250	Restaurant on the premises, usually open to non-residents.
	SWIMMING POOL
	Hotel with an indoor or outdoor swimming pool.

CAPPADOCIA AND CENTRAL ANATOLIA

	Price	NUMBER OF ROOMS	CREDIT CARDS	CENTRAL LOCATION	RESTAURANTS	SWIMMING POOL
AMASYA: *Maden Hotel* Mustafa Kêmalpaşa Cad 5. (0358) 218 60 50. FAX (0358) 212 63 43. Central location, large airy rooms and polite staff keep this family-run hotel full on a regular basis. Children welcome.	$	40	V MC AE	●	■	
AMASYA: *Melis Hotel* Yeniyol Cad 135. (0358) 212 36 50. FAX (0358) 212 16 43. @ melisotel@hotmail.com A quaint little hotel filled with antique items. Congenial owner will arrange everything for you in Amasya.	$$	12	V MC	●		
GÖREME: *Kelebek Hotel and Pension* Aydınlı Mah. (0384) 271 25 31. FAX (0384) 271 27 63. W www.kelebekhotel.com Kelebek offers 25 rooms, some built into caves and others in traditional arched rooms. A look at the rooms on their website shows that comfort, décor and activities are first-rate here.	$$	25	V MC AE	●	■	
GÖREME: *Ottoman House* Orta Mah 36. (0384) 271 26 16. FAX (0384) 271 23 51. W www.indigoturizm.com.tr Ottoman House is as charming, homey a place as one could hope to find on holiday. Christmas, New Year and Easter packages. Excellent terrace restaurant.	$$	32	V MC AE	●	■	
KAYSERI: *Hotel Konfor* Atatürk Bulvarı 5, Düvenönü. (0352) 320 01 84. FAX (0352) 336 51 00. @ hotelkonfor@superonline.com This hotel is no exception to Kayseri's monochrome concrete tourist accommodation, but it does offer comfortable rooms, helpful staff and all-round cheerfulness.	$	44	V MC	●	■	
NEVŞEHIR: *Altınöz Hotel* Ragıp Üner Cad 23. (0384) 213 99 61. FAX (0384) 213 28 17. A deluxe hotel in the city centre close to all amenities and transport. Turkish bath *(hamam)*, sauna and massage available. Hot-air balloon rides over Cappadocia can be arranged by the hotel.	$$$	120	V MC AE DC	●	■	
NEVŞEHIR: *Peri Tower Hotel* Nar. (0384) 212 88 16. FAX (0384) 213 90 28. @ info@peritower.com Pseudo fairy-chimney exterior houses well-designed, luxurious rooms. Located in the ruins, 1 km (half a mile) from Nevşehir. All services and activities provided.	$$$	126	V MC AE		■	●
ORTAHISAR: *Burcu Kaya Hotel* (0384) 343 32 00. FAX (0384) 343 35 00. W www.burcukayaotel.com.tr This caravanserai-style hotel set in a pretty garden not far from the cave ruins has views of nearby Ihlara Valley's rolling green hills. Tours can be arranged. Children are catered for.	$$	82	V MC		■	●
SIVAS: *Sivas Büyük Hotel* İstasyon Cad. (0346) 225 47 62. FAX (0346) 225 23 23. Situated on the main road, this hotel has fully equipped conference facilities and is a good choice for visitors on business. Pets are accepted and children are catered for.	$$	114	V MC	●	■	
ÜRGÜP: *Dinler Hotel* Kayseri Cad 7. (0384) 341 30 30. FAX (0384) 341 48 96. W www.dinler.com This large hotel, situated in the city centre, is very comfortable and commands great views of the surrounding area. There is a disco at night.	$$$	172	V MC AE DC	●	■	●

ÜRGÜP: *Hotel Surban* $$$ | 31 | V MC
Yunak Mah PK 55. ☎ (0384) 341 46 03. FAX (0384) 341 32 23.
W www.hotelsurban.com.tr @ surban@hotelsurban.com.tr
The hotel and annex of five Seljuk-style houses are set against the cliffs, and a short walk from the town centre, shops, restaurants and nightlife. Accent on children and families. 🛏 🍽 24 TV 🗐 P

EASTERN ANATOLIA

DIYARBAKIR: *Class Hotel* $$ | 120 | V MC AE DC
Gazi Cad 101, Özdemir Mah. ☎ (0412) 229 50 00. FAX (0412) 229 25 99.
W www.diyarbakirclasshotel.com @ info@diyarbakirclasshotel.com
Diyarbakır's only five-star hotel. All services provided, including a vitamin bar and baby-sitting service. 🛏 💧 24 TV 🗐 🍴 🛁 P ♿

DIYARBAKIR: *Hotel Grand Kervansaray* $$$ | 45 | V MC AE DC
Gazi Cad, Deliller Han, Mardinkapı. ☎ (0412) 288 96 06. FAX (0412) 223 95 22.
W www.hotelkervansaray.com @ admin@hotelkervansaray.com
The hotel was a han during the 16th century and then later, a bazaar. It offers comfortable accommodation with all amenities. 🛏 🍽 💧 24 TV 🗐 🍴 🛁 ♿

ERZURUM: *Dedeman Palandöken Ski Centre* $$$$ | 180 | V MC AE DC
PO Box 115. ☎ (0442) 316 24 14. FAX (0442) 315 36 07.
W www.dedemanhotels.com @ hotels@dedeman.com.tr
Open in winter, November to February only, this hotel is right on the ski slopes of one of Turkey's most active ski areas. 🛏 24 TV 🗐 🍴 🛁 P

GAZIANTEP: *Hotel Kaleli* $$ | 70 | V MC AE
Hürriyet Cad, Güzelce Sok 50. ☎ (0342) 230 96 90. FAX (0342) 230 15 97.
Concrete comfort in the city centre. Functional hotel with adequate three-star facilities and a games (backgammon) room. 🛏 24 TV 🗐 🛁 ♿

GAZIANTEP: *Yesemek Hotel* $$ | 43 | V MC
İsmail Say Sok 4. ☎ (0342) 220 88 88. FAX (0342) 220 88 88.
Situated in the city centre, the box-brick eastern Anatolian exterior hides beautifully appointed rooms, a richly designed lobby and romantic dining room. Highly recommended. Children are catered for. 🛏 TV 🗐 🛁 ♿

GAZIANTEP: *Hotel Tilmen* $$$ | 58 | V MC
İnönü Cad 168. ☎ (0342) 220 20 81. FAX (0342) 220 20 91.
A medium-sized hotel in the middle of town, and 12 km (7 miles) from the Gaziantep Airport. Children are catered for. There are baby-sitting facilities and a doctor. The hotel provides tour guides on request. 🛏 24 TV 🗐 🛁 P

KAHRAMANMARAŞ: *Kazancı Hotel* $ | 36 | V MC
Kurtuluş Mah Garajlar Cad. ☎ (0344) 223 44 62. FAX (0344) 212 69 42.
A comfortable, small hotel just 1 km (half a mile) from the airport and in the city centre. Close to all amenities. Laundry service. 🛏 24 TV 🗐 P

KÂHTA: *Euphrat Hotel* $ | 52 | V MC
Nemrut Dağı, PO Box 14, Kâhta. ☎ (0416) 737 21 75. FAX (0416) 737 21 79.
Situated on the slopes of Mount Nemrut, just 9 km (6 miles) from the peak, with splendid views. Tours arranged daily. 🛏 TV

MALATYA: *Altın Kayısı Hotel* $$$ | 101 | V MC AE DC
İstasyon Virajı. ☎ (0422) 211 44 44. FAX (0422) 211 44 43. W www.altinkayisi.com
In the city centre, close to all amenities. Tours to Mount Nemrut and the surrounding historical monuments can be arranged. 🛏 24 TV 🗐 🍴 🛁 P

ŞANLIURFA: *Konuk Evi – Governor's Guest House* $ | 6 | V MC
Vali Fuat Bey Cad, Balıklıgöl. ☎ (0414) 215 93 77. FAX (0414) 215 30 45.
A charming 1890s mansion house built of "Urfa" stone around a courtyard. There is a lovely café situated in the garden. 🛏 🍽 TV 🗐 🛁 P

ŞANLIURFA: *Edessa Hotel* $$$ | 52 | V MC AE
Balıklıgöl Mevkii, Hasanpaşa Mevkii Karşısı. ☎ (0414) 215 99 11. FAX (0414) 215 55 89.
@ hoteledessa@superonline.com
It caters mainly to business people and conferences. Fax/modem and laptop lines in all rooms. Secretarial services available. 🛏 💧 24 TV 🗐 🛁 P

ŞANLIURFA: *Harran Hotel* $$$ | 99 | V MC
Atatürk Bulvarı. ☎ (0414) 313 28 60. FAX (0414) 313 49 18.
Close to all sights and amenities. Children are catered for. 🛏 24 TV 🗐 🛁 P

WHERE TO EAT

ESTAURANTS IN TURKEY range from the informal *lokanta* and kebab house, which are found on almost every street corner, to the gourmet restaurants of large luxury-class hotels. There are international restaurants in most major tourist centres. In Istanbul, restaurants purvey a wide variety of almost every style of cuisine, from French to Korean. Restaurants on the Mediterranean and Aegean coasts specialize in seafood dishes, and Cappadocia is famous for its grapes and wines. Interesting local dishes can be found

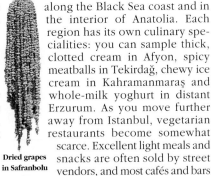

Dried grapes in Safranbolu

along the Black Sea coast and in the interior of Anatolia. Each region has its own culinary specialities: you can sample thick, clotted cream in Afyon, spicy meatballs in Tekirdağ, chewy ice cream in Kahramanmaraş and whole-milk yoghurt in distant Erzurum. As you move further away from Istanbul, vegetarian restaurants become somewhat scarce. Excellent light meals and snacks are often sold by street vendors, and most cafés and bars have a menu with light refreshments.

WHERE TO LOOK

GENERALLY, THE smartest and most expensive restaurants are to be found in the five-star international hotel chains all over Turkey. They always serve both Western and Turkish food.

The main roads and central business districts of most towns have a selection of fast-food eateries, cafés and inexpensive restaurants where the locals go to eat. Coastal resorts cater for all ages and tastes and offer dishes from all over the world. In the interior, most restaurants serve good, cheap regional food and cater for locals as much as tourists. Most towns have a number of cafés, patisseries and pudding shops. The latter specialize in *muhallebici* (traditional sweet milk puddings).

Slicing meat from a revolving grill for a döner kebab

The sumptuous Beyti Restaurant in Florya, Istanbul *(see p344)*

TYPES OF RESTAURANT

THE MOST COMMON type of restaurant in Turkey is the traditional *lokanta*. These establishments offer a variety of dishes, often listed on a board near the entrance. They serve *hazır yemek* (prepared food), usually consisting of hot meat and vegetable dishes that are displayed in a *bain marie*, or steam table. Other dishes on the menu may be *sulu yemek* (broth or stew) and *et* (meat – meaning grilled meat and kebabs).

Equally popular is the *kebap* or *ocakbaşı* (kebab house). In addition to grilled meats, most kebab houses serve the popular *lahmacun*, a thin dough base topped with fried onions, minced meat and tomato sauce. This dish is the Turkish version of pizza. Some also serve *pide*, a flatbread base served with various toppings such as eggs, cheese and salami.

In many areas, you can also find specialist *pide* restaurants.

If you have had too much to drink you may need a bowl of *işkembe* (tripe soup), the traditional Turkish cure for a hangover, before going to bed. *İşkembe* restaurants stay open until the early hours of the morning.

Fish restaurants are often concentrated along the same street, creating a lively atmosphere and making the street seem like one large restaurant. The meal typically consists of a selection of *mezes* (appetizers) *(see p340)*, followed by the catch of the day, which might include *palamut* (bonito), *sardalya* (fresh sardines) and *levrek* (sea bass). Also popular are Black Sea *hamsi* (a kind of anchovy), *istavrit* (bluefin) and *mezgit* (whiting). The Turks are proud of their local fish, and prefer to eat it in season. However, as fish is becoming scarcer and more expensive,

A trout restaurant on the river at Saklıkent

farmed fish has become more widely accepted, particularly *alabalık* (trout) and a type of bream known as *çupra*. Fish is served grilled or fried, and is usually accompanied by salad and *rakı (see p341)*, an anise-flavoured spirit.

A *meyhane* is more like a tavern, serving alcohol and *mezes*. These are cheap and convivial places, and often have live music. A *meyhane* is a good place to meet the locals and to get a taste of local foods and customs. By tradition, these establishments are a male preserve. They may not be suitable for unaccompanied women.

OPENING HOURS

FOR GOVERNMENT EMPLOYEES, lunch hour is from noon to 1pm, and many restaurants cater for them. But you will not find many set lunch hours throughout Turkey. Turks eat when they are hungry, without looking at the clock, and will simply drop in at the most convenient place they can find. Restaurants and kebab houses open at about

11am and stay open for business until the last customer leaves in the evening.

During Ramadan (Ramazan), Muslims fast from sunrise to sunset. As a result, many restaurants are closed during the day, or they may serve only a special *iftar* (fast-breaking) menu in the evening. More and more foreign restaurants are now appearing on the scene, and some of these close on Sundays, as they would in their native country. However, there are no firm guidelines on opening hours for such eating establishments, and most of them stay open longer than their counterparts in other countries. Seasonal restaurants are a different matter and many of Turkey's popular tourist resorts simply grind to a halt after 29 October to reopen around March or April, as soon as the weather improves. Some places open just for New Year's Eve *(see p37)*, which is always festive.

WHAT TO EXPECT

FOOD AND EATING are among life's finest pleasures, and nowhere more so than in Turkey. A meal is always an occasion and, for special meals, it is best to book. In large centres vegetarians can enjoy variety, and designer vegetarian restaurants seem to be

enjoying much interest. They do, however, become scarcer the further east you travel.

While most restaurants try to cater for non-smokers, there are no hard and fast rules on smoking in eating establishments, and so it is usually left up to the individual restaurant owner. It is, however, becoming increasingly common for restaurants to offer a smoke-free dining area.

When choosing a place to eat, remember that many of the cheaper restaurants and kebab houses do not serve alcohol. Also, many places will have a separate section for men only and another for families or women. These are designated by a sign with the words *aile salonu* (family room), where single men generally do not enter.

Turks are proud of their hospitality and service. Good service is always found in the upmarket restaurants that can afford well-trained, professional waiters and kitchen staff. You may find that the same standards do not apply in cheaper places. They often use raw recruits, many of whom rely on tips for their income. Be patient and bear in mind that it is natural for Turks to call a waiter by saying, "bakar mısınız" (service, please). The cheerfulness and enthusiasm of restaurant staff generally compensates for any minor shortcomings.

Drying chillis, Bodrum

SERVICE AND PAYING

THE MAJOR CREDIT CARDS are widely accepted, except in the cheaper restaurants, kebab houses, local *bufes* (snack kiosks) and some *lokantas*. Restaurants usually display the credit card sign or symbol on the entrance if they accept this form of payment. Value-added tax (KDV in Turkish) is always included in the bill, but the policy on service varies. Some places add 10 per cent or more to round up the bill while others leave it to the customer's discretion. Feel free to ask if you are unsure.

Waterside restaurant on Bird Island, near the Aegean resort of Kuşadası

What to Eat in Turkey

For almost five centuries, the peoples under Ottoman rule – in territories ranging from the Balkans to North Africa – contributed to the sophisticated cuisine that was created in the kitchens of Istanbul's Topkapı Palace *(see pp66–71)*. The influence of many cultures seeped into the fine foods of the Ottomans and spread throughout what is now Turkey, while some of today's staple dishes originated in Central Asia and were introduced by west-ward-migrating, nomadic Turks. Anatolia offers a varied culinary scene and, together with French and Chinese, ranks as one of the world's top three culinary traditions.

***Breakfast** in Turkey consists of feta-type cheese, tomatoes, olives and cucumber, as well as honey, jam, butter and bread, all served with tea.*

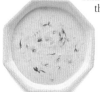

Yoğurt çorbası *is a yoghurt soup made with pulses or rice. Soups are eaten at any time of the day.*

Palamut
(Bonito)

Hamsi
(Anchovies)

Uskumru
(Mackerel)

Levrek
(Sea bass)

Kalkan
(Turbot)

Hamsi pilavı *is a Black Sea dish made with a mixture of anchovies and rice. It is one of many Turkish rice dishes.*

Levrek pilakisi *is a stew made with a combination of sea bass, onions and potatoes, flavoured with garlic.*

***Fish** is widely available in Istanbul, due to the city's proximity to the sea. During the winter months, oil-rich varieties of fish, such as bluefish and mackerel, are particularly plentiful in restaurants. The method of cooking can vary, but in most cases the fish is served either grilled or stewed.*

ANATOLIAN DISHES

The dishes of Anatolia are as varied as the regions in which they originated. Traditional and simple, they are often colourful and spicy.

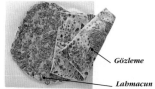

Gözleme

Lahmacun

Lahmacun and gözleme *are bread-based snacks. The first is a thin pizza-style snack. The second is folded over or rolled up.*

Fırında mantı *is a dish of noodle-dough parcels filled with meat. Other mantı dishes use the same dough.*

Karides güveç, *prawns with peppers and tomatoes topped with cheese, is just one of many kinds of* güveç *(stew).*

Bamya bastısı *is a popular okra and tomato stew which can be made with or without chunks of lamb.*

Döner kebab

Adana kebab

Şiş kebab

İskender kebab

Kebabs *may be meat, fish or vegetables. The most popular varieties are döner (sliced roast meat), şiş (cubes of meat grilled on a skewer), Adana (minced meat grilled on a skewer) and İskender, or Bursa, kebab (döner meat on bread with a rich tomato sauce and yoghurt).*

PALACE SPECIALITIES

The cooks of the Topkapı Palace kitchens created elaborate dishes during the days of the Ottoman Empire. Vegetables were stuffed or cooked in olive oil. Meat was grilled or roasted, seasoned and sometimes served with either a cream or tomato sauce.

İmam bayıldı, *literally "the imam fainted", is a dish of aubergines stuffed with tomatoes and onions.*

Pomegranate *(nar)*

Apricot *(kayısı)*

Cherries *(kiraz)*

Fig *(incir)*

Watermelon *(karpuz)*

Hünkar beğendili köfte *is meatballs "with sultan's delight": a purée of smoked aubergine with cheese.*

Karnıyarık *is a dish of aubergines, split open and stuffed with minced lamb, pine nuts and currants.*

Fresh fruit *in season is the ideal way to round off a Turkish meal. Watermelons, figs, pomegranates and apricots are among the most popular choices.*

SWEETS

Sweets are eaten throughout the day in Turkey, not just after a meal. They are sold in shops, on stalls and by street vendors. Some sweets are linked to religious feasts. Istanbul is renowned for its baklava.

Varieties of baklava

Turkish pastries are sticky sweets made from various types of pastry, coated with syrup and sometimes filled with nuts.

Tulumba

Tavuk göğsü kazandibi is a milk pudding made with shredded chicken breasts.

Aşure, also known as "Noah's pudding", is made with a combination of dried fruit and beans.

Fırında sütlaç, an oven-baked rice pudding which is served cold, is popular in Istanbul.

Mezes

Turşu (pickles)

A TURKISH MEAL OFTEN begins with *mezes* (starters), of which there are hundreds of different kinds – with new ones being created all the time. They range from simple combinations, such as plain white cheese with melon, to elaborately stuffed vegetables. Mezes are served in all Turkish restaurants and are often accompanied by raki. *Meyhanes (see p337)* often specialize in mezes from Anatolia and it is common to be offered a generous selection from a tray. Most mezes are served cold, although you can order hot ones too. Very few contain fish or meat, making them ideal for vegetarians.

Ekmek

Pide | *Simit*

Turkish bread *includes* ekmek *(white loaves) and* pide *(flat bread), which is often served with kebabs, and also eaten during religious festivals.* Simit *is a crisp, ring-shaped, savoury bread covered with sesame seeds.*

Cigar-shaped
Sigara böreği

Yalancı yaprak dolması **(stuffed vine leaves)**

Triangular
Muska böreği

Midye dolması **(mussel shells stuffed with rice)**

Böreks and Dolmas
Anything that can be stuffed is made into a dolma. *The most common are made with vine leaves, peppers and mussels.* Börek *(or* böreği*), a filled savoury pastry which is deep fried, can be stuffed with mince, spinach or cheese with herbs.*

Circassian chicken
*(*Çerkez tavuğu*) is a dish consisting of strips of chicken in a creamy walnut and bread sauce.*

COLD MEZES
Several mezes come in the form of purées and dips, often using yoghurt as a base. They are served with fresh, warm bread. Some of the most popular include *patlıcan salatası* (smoked aubergine purée), *haydari* (mint, garlic and yoghurt) and *tarama* (fish roe).

Patlıcan salatası **(smoked aubergine purée)**

Fava **(purée of broad beans)**

Tarama **(purée of fish roe)**

Haydari **(mint, garlic and yoghurt dip)**

Çoban salatası **(tomato, onion and cucumber salad)**

Lakerda, *finely sliced smoked tuna served with lemon, is a popular fish meze from the Black Sea.*

Fasulye piyazı *is a salad of haricot beans with olive oil and lemon juice. It is sometimes topped with boiled egg.*

Zeytinyağlı enginar, *artichoke hearts, is one of many choice vegetable dishes cooked in olive oil.*

What to Drink in Turkey

THE MOST COMMON DRINK in Turkey is tea (*çay*), which is normally served black in small, tulip-shaped glasses. It will be offered to you wherever you go: in shops and bazaars, and even in banks and offices. Breakfast is usually accompanied by tea, whereas small cups of strong Turkish coffee (*kahve*) are drunk mid-morning and also at the end of meals. Cold drinks include a variety of fresh fruit juices, such as orange and cherry, and refreshing syrup-based sherbets. Although Turkey does produce its own wine and beer, the most popular alcoholic drink is rakı, which is usually served to accompany mezes.

Fruit juice seller

SOFT DRINKS

BOTTLED mineral water (*su*) is sold in corner shops and served in restaurants everywhere. If you're feeling adventurous, you might like to try a glass of *ayran*, salty liquid yoghurt. *Boza* is made from bulgur wheat and is another local drink to sample. There is always a variety of refreshing, cold fruit and vegetable juices available. They include cherry juice (*vişne suyu*), turnip juice (*şalgam suyu*) and *şıra*, a juice made from fermented grapes.

Vişne suyu   **Ayran**

COFFEE AND TEA

TURKISH COFFEE is very dark, strong and served in tiny cups. It is ordered according to the amount of sugar required: *az* (little), *orta* (medium), *çok şekerli* (a lot). Ask for it especially, or the waiter may assume you want Nescafé. The ubiquitous daily drink is tea (*çay*), which is served with sugar, but without milk and comes in a small tulip-shaped glass. Most popular is the apple (*elma*) flavour, but there are also linden (*ıhlamur*), rose-hip (*kuşburnu*) and a delicious mint (*nane*) variety.

Traditional samovar for tea

Apple tea   **Limeflower tea**

ALCOHOLIC DRINKS

TURKEY'S NATIONAL alcoholic drink is rakı, a clear, anise-flavoured spirit that turns cloudy when water is added and is drunk with fish and mezes. The Turkish wine industry has yet to realize its full potential. Kavaklıdere and Doluca, the best-known brands, are overpriced for table wines. Villa Doluca is preferable. The İzmir-based producer Sevilen offers several interesting wines, such as Majestic, and an outstanding Merlot. Expect to pay high prices for imported wines and champagnes, which are found only in top-notch restaurants and bars. The locally brewed Efes Pilsen beer is excellent and also widely available on draught. Note that alcohol may not be served in some cheaper restaurants and kebab houses.

Rakı   **Beer**   **Red wine**   **White wine**

Turkish coffee is a very strong drink and an acquired taste for most people.

Sahlep is a winter drink made from orchid root.

Choosing a Restaurant

THE RESTAURANTS IN THIS GUIDE have been selected for their good value, interesting location and exceptional food. This chart lists additional factors which may assist your choice. Entries are alphabetical within price categories. The thumb tabs on the side of the page use the same colour coding as the corresponding regional chapters in the main section of this guide.

	Credit Cards	A la Carte Menu	Non-Smoking Section	Alcohol Available	Live Music
ISTANBUL					
SERAGLIO POINT: *Theodora Pub.* **Map** 5 E3. **$$** St Sophia Hotel, Alemdar Cad 2. **[** *(0212) 520 10 35.* Theodora Pub offers several outdoor terraces in summer and an English pub downstairs. Very busy and crowded. ☐ *noon–1am daily.* ▤ ▮	V MC AE DC	●		●	
SULTANAHMET: *Cennet.* **Map** 5 D4. **$** Divanyolu Cad 90. **[** *(0212) 513 14 16.* The building used to be a Turkish bath (*hamam*) but is now a bustling restaurant specializing in southeastern Turkish cuisine. Village women prepare *gözleme* (pancakes) and *börek* (savoury pastry) to order. ☐ *9am–11pm daily.* ▤ �V �		●			
SULTANAHMET: *Antique Gallery Café and Restaurant.* **Map** 5 E4. **$$** Yerebatan Cad, Söğüt Sok 18/B. **[** *(0212) 512 42 62.* Owned by the same family as the Kybele Hotel, the restaurant offers good Turkish food and service in a formal setting. Live *fasıl* music on a regular basis. ☐ *11am–midnight or later daily.* ▤ �V ▮ ▴	V MC AE DC	●		●	■
SULTANAHMET: *Kathisma.* **Map** 5 E5. **$$** Yeni Akbıyık Cad 26. **[** *(0212) 518 97 10.* Near the Blue Mosque, it serves international and Turkish dishes. Recognizable by the mosaic in the front entrance. ☐ *11am–2pm & 6:30–11pm daily.* ▤ �V ▮ ▴	V MC	●		●	
SULTANAHMET: *Medusa.* **Map** 5 E4. **$$** Yerebatan Cad 19. **[** *(0212) 511 41 16.* A popular restaurant offering good Turkish cuisine. Seating is a cushion on the floor covered in kilims and Turkish carpets. ☐ *11am–midnight daily.* ▴	V MC	●		●	
SULTANAHMET: *Mozaic Café Bar Restaurant.* **Map** 5 D4. **$$** Divanyolu Cad, İncili Çavuş Sok 1. **[** *(0212) 512 53 67.* An intimate little restaurant located on a quiet corner in the back streets of the old city. Mozaic serves an international menu and has outdoor tables in summer. ☐ *11am–2pm & 7pm–midnight.* ● *Sun.* ▤ �V ▴ ▮ ▴	V MC AE	●		●	
SULTANAHMET: *Rumeli Café.* **Map** 5 E4. **$$** Divan Yolu, Ticarethane Sok 8. **[** *(0212) 512 00 08.* Popular, with a good selection of dishes. If you like Ottoman cooking or have never tried it before, this is an obligatory stop. ☐ *9am–midnight daily.* �V ▴	V MC	●		●	
SULTANAHMET: *Hammam.* **Map** 5 E2. **$$$$$** Kennedy Cad, Sepetçiler Kasrı 3, Eminönü, Sarayburnu. **[** *(0212) 511 63 16.* Overlooking the Bosphorus, the building was previously the Foreign Press Centre. International and authentic Ottoman cuisine available. Reservations are required for Sunday brunch. ☐ *7:30pm–midnight Mon–Sat, 11am–3pm Sun* ▤ ▮ ▮ ▾	V MC AE DC	●	■	●	
BEYOĞLU: *İmroz.* **Map** 1 A4. **$$** Nevizade Sok. **[** *(0212) 249 90 73.* An historic Greek *meyhane*, and one of the oldest on the busy Nevizade Sokak near the fish market, İmroz is a favourite with locals. Mezes are the speciality but their grills and other foods are just as nice. ☐ *noon–1am daily.* �V ▴	V MC AE	●		●	■
BEYOĞLU: *Zencefil Café.* **Map** 1 B4. **$$** Kurabiye Sok 3. **[** *(0212) 244 40 82.* Serves authentic vegetarian cuisine using the freshest ingredients. Everything is light and wholesome, and their home-made breads are highly recommended. ☐ *9:30am–11pm daily.* �V ▾ *lunch only.*		●		●	
BEYOĞLU: *Haci Abdullah.* **Map** 1 A3. **$$$** Sakizağaci Cad 17. **[** *(0212) 293 85 61.* Housed in a former 1950's prison, this restaurant serves traditional Turkish and Ottoman cuisine. The *beğendi* kebab (spiced minced meat with yoghurt) is highly recommended. ☐ *10:30am–11pm daily.* ▤ �V ▴ ▾	V MC AE DC	●		●	

Price categories for a three-course meal for one, including tax and service:

[$] under US$5
[$][$] US$5–10
[$][$][$] US$10–20
[$][$][$][$] US$20-30
[$][$][$][$][$] over US$30

CREDIT CARDS
Indicates which credit cards are accepted (AE American Express, DC Diners Club, MC MasterCard, V Visa).

A LA CARTE MENU
Restaurant specializes in à la carte dishes.

NON-SMOKING SECTION
Restaurant has a non-smoking section.

ALCOHOL AVAILABLE
Indicates that the restaurant serves alcohol.

LIVE MUSIC
Background music is provided by musicians.

Restaurant	Credit Cards	A la Carte Menu	Non-Smoking Section	Alcohol Available	Live Music
BEYOĞLU: *Vareli Şarapbanesi (Vareli Wine House).* Map 1 A5. [$][$][$] Asmalı Mescit Mahallesi Oteller Sok 7/9 Tepebası. ☎ *(0212) 292 55 16.* The wine bar is part of the Yeni Şehir Palas Hotel. The food is outstanding. 🕒 *11am–3am daily.* ▤ [V] 🍸	V MC AE DC	●		●	■
BEYOĞLU: *Çatı.* Map 1 A5. [$][$][$][$] Orhan Apaydın Sok 20 (7th floor). ☎ *(0212) 251 00 00.* Çatı is one of Beyoğlu's gems. They have gained international recognition for their original and delicious dishes. Take a window seat for lovely views over the Bosphorus and old Istanbul. 🕒 *6pm–1:30am daily.* ● *Sun.* ▤ [V] [T] 🚸 🍸 ♿	V MC AE DC	●	■	●	■
BEYOĞLU: *Kallavi 20.* Map 1 A4. [$][$][$][$] Kallavi Sok 20, Tepebası. ☎ *(0212) 251 10 10.* The place is lively and friendly but may have peaked in popularity. The evening musical programme is great fun but the food less imaginative than the à la carte selection at lunchtime. 🕒 *11am–2pm & 7pm–midnight daily.* ♿ 🍴 *evenings only.*		●		●	■
BEYOĞLU: *Four Seasons Restaurant.* Map 1 A4. [$][$][$][$][$] İstiklal Cad 509. ☎ *(0212) 293 39 41.* A highly successful and popular restaurant that serves good continental and excellent Turkish foods. The setting is formal and the food beautifully presented, with service to match. 🕒 *noon–3pm & 7pm–midnight daily.* ▤ [T] 🍸 ♿ 🍴 *lunch only.*	V MC AE	●		●	
BEYOĞLU: *Sofra Restaurant London.* Map 1 A4. [$][$][$][$][$] Tarlabaşı Bulvarı 36. ☎ *(0212) 297 21 78.* The successful owner of Sofra in London has brought his style home to Istanbul with this innovative, contemporary, Ottoman-influenced cuisine. The food here is outstanding and the setting formal. In summer, the terrace has good views of the city. Reservations essential. 🕒 *noon–3pm & 7–11pm.* ▤ [V] [T] 🚸 ♿	V MC AE DC	●	■	●	
FURTHER AFIELD (ASIAN SHORE): *Cadde Restaurant* [$][$] Bağdat Cad 423, Şaşkınbakkal. ☎ *(0216) 385 19 02.* Delicious grills and kebabs in a non-epicurean area (although things are picking up here). Famous for its traditional İskender kebab. They will deliver to the house or hotel. 🕒 *11:30am–11pm daily.* ▤	V MC AE DC	●		●	
FURTHER AFIELD (ASIAN SHORE): *South China* [$][$] Moda Cad 251, Moda. ☎ *(0216) 348 38 51.* One of the city's many Chinese dine-in or take-out restaurants, South China has a large selection of freshly made dishes and is very popular with foreign residents. 🕒 *12:30pm–midnight daily.* 🍴	V MC	●		●	■
FURTHER AFIELD (ASIAN SHORE): *İskele Çengelköy Restaurant* [$][$][$] İskele Meydanı 20, Çengelköy. ☎ *(0216) 321 55 06.* One of the most popular fish restaurants in this leafy suburb, with the Bosphorus lapping almost at the entrance. The mezes are well prepared and fresh, and the fish is some of the best you will find. The service is willing and cheerful. 🕒 *noon–midnight daily.* [V] 🚸 🍸 ♿	V MC AE DC	●		●	
FURTHER AFIELD (ASIAN SHORE): *Katibim Restaurant.* Map 6 A2. [$][$][$] Şemsi Paşa Sahil Yolu 53, Üsküdar. ☎ *(0216) 310 90 80.* A family restaurant with an excellent view of the Bosphorus. Kebabs and mezes reign on the menu. There is an open-air terrace which is crammed in summer. 🕒 *8am–midnight daily.* 🚸	V MC AE DC	●		●	
FURTHER AFIELD (ASIAN SHORE): *İsmet Baba.* [$][$][$][$] İcadiye Cad 96–98, Kuzguncuk. ☎ *(0216) 333 12 32.* This well-established, family-run restaurant has been up and running since 1890. A variety of fresh fish from the Aegean, Black Sea and Mediterranean is on offer and the restaurant boasts a fantastic setting on the water's edge. 🕒 *noon–midnight daily.* ▤ [V]		●		●	

For key to symbols see back flap

Price categories for a three-course meal for one, including tax and service:

$ under US$5
$$ US$5–10
$$$ US$10–20
$$$$ US$20–30
$$$$$ US$30

CREDIT CARDS
Indicates which credit cards are accepted (AE American Express, DC Diners Club, MC MasterCard, V Visa).

A LA CARTE MENU
Restaurant specializes in à la carte dishes.

NON-SMOKING SECTION
Restaurant has a non-smoking section.

ALCOHOL AVAILABLE
Indicates that the restaurant serves alcohol.

LIVE MUSIC
Background music is provided by musicians.

Restaurant	Credit Cards	A la Carte Menu	Non-Smoking Section	Alcohol Available	Live Music
FURTHER AFIELD (ASIAN SHORE): *Olcay.* **Map 6 C1.** $$$ Paşalimanı Cad 62, Üsküdar. ☎ *(0216) 333 92 22.* A traditional *meyhane* with a feel of practised efficiency that makes dining a pleasure. Mezes and fish are their stock in trade and reservations are almost always required. ◯ *noon–11pm daily.* [V] 🍴$ *lunch only*	V MC	●		●	■
FURTHER AFIELD (ASIAN SHORE): *Sandal Balık Restaurant* $$$$ Mektep Sok 21–23, Moda, Kadıköy. ☎ *(0216) 338 36 78.* A small, modern and cosy fish restaurant that serves the freshest seafood and mezes. The memorable octopus salad and rich date dessert tempt many back for second helpings and repeat visits. ◯ *11am–3pm & 6–11:30pm daily.* ▤	V MC AE DC	●		●	
FURTHER AFIELD (BEBEK): *Mimi* $$$ 1 Cad 68. ☎ *(0212) 265 09 49.* Listen to live Greek music and dance the *sirtaki* while you dine on fine cuisine. The terrace is open in summer to accommodate more diners. This place is fun and attracts a rowdy, carefree crowd. ◯ *11am–3pm & 7pm–2am daily.* ▤ [T]	V MC AE	●	■	●	■
FURTHER AFIELD (BEBEK): *Yeni Kaptan Restaurant* $$$$ Beyaz Gül Cad 2. ☎ *(0212) 265 17 76.* One of Istanbul's best fish and seafood restaurants located on the Bosphorus. An excellent venue for trying out the real Turkish experience of eating fish while enjoying the view of the straits. ◯ *noon–3pm & 7:30pm–midnight.* ● *Mon.* ♿	V MC AE	●		●	
FURTHER AFIELD (BEBEK): *Mia Mensa* $$$$$ Kuruçeşme Cad 170/A. ☎ *(0212) 263 42 14.* A popular restaurant with a pretty garden on the shores of the Bosphorus. The menu is Italian and grappa and Sambuca are the favoured drinks. This is a very popular place and gets crowded with regulars. ◯ *noon–3pm & 7–11pm.* ● *Mon.* ▤ [T] [Y] ♿	V MC AE DC	●		●	
FURTHER AFIELD (BEBEK): *Tonoz* $$$$$ İnşirah Yokuşu 48. ☎ *(0212) 263 36 62.* A winter venue only, Tonoz is located in an old Genoese vault near the heart of Bebek. The speciality here is stuffed vegetables. The food is excellent and service keeps pace. ◯ *noon–11pm Oct–May.* ● *Sun.* [V] [Y]	V MC	●		●	■
FURTHER AFIELD (ETILER): *Casita Mantı* $$$ Nispetiye Cad 5 ☎ *(0212) 263 70 07.* A little late-night place in a lovely setting to eat soup and *mantı* (Turkish ravioli) after hours. They do other traditional dishes as well. It is possible to "celebrity spot" here on a regular basis. ◯ *24 hours daily.* [V]		●		●	
FURTHER AFIELD (ETILER): *Cilveli Meyhane* $$$$ Nispetiye Cad 24. ☎ *(0212) 268 66 61.* A boisterous *meyhane* where patrons frequently abandon their food and drinks to get up and dance. Excellent food. ◯ *noon–3pm & 7pm–1:30am daily.* ▤ [T]	V MC AE	●		●	■
FURTHER AFIELD (ETILER): *Dixie Station* $$$$$ Nispetiye Cad 24. ☎ *(0212) 265 05 51.* Istanbul's classiest suburb hosts an American-style restaurant, with overtones of the "Old South". Portions are hearty and so are prices. A few Turkish touches keep a wide range of customers happy. ◯ *7am–3am daily.* ▤ [V] [T] [Y]	V MC AE DC	●		●	
FURTHER AFIELD (FLORYA): *Beyti Restaurant* $$$$$ Orman Sok 33. ☎ *(0212) 663 29 90.* The winner of numerous awards, this elegant establishment is renowned for its excellent traditional cuisine. ◯ *11:30am–3pm & 7–11:30pm Tue–Sun.* ▤ [V] [T] 🚸	V MC AE DC	●		●	
FURTHER AFIELD (ORTAKÖY): *A La Turka* $$ Değirmen Sok 16. ☎ *(0212) 258 79 24.* A charming restaurant in the Ortaköy harbour, serving simple, well-cooked dishes like *dolma* and *köfte* at decent prices. There is a terrace in summer and the upstairs room is used for groups and meetings. ◯ *noon–10:30pm daily.* [V]	V MC AE	●		●	

FURTHER AFIELD (ORTAKÖY): *Bol Kepçe.* **Map** 3 F2. $$
Muallim Naci Cad 17/9. ☎ *(0212) 259 82 61.*
Popular with locals and serving wonderful home-cooked meals. Set back from the seafront. ○ *11am–1am Sun–Thu & noon–2am Fri and Sat.* 🧒 🍴$

FURTHER AFIELD (ORTAKÖY): *Myott* $$$
İskele Sok 14. ☎ *(0212) 258 93 17.*
Famous for its superb muesli with fruit and Italian coffees, Myott is a trendy and popular breakfast spot in Ortaköy. It was one of Istanbul's first Italian-style cafés and they do a superb brunch. ○ *9:30am–4pm.* ● *Mon.* 🍴$

FURTHER AFIELD (TAKSIM): *Evim Mantı* $$
Büyükparmakkapı Sok 2/1. ☎ *(0212) 293 40 25.*
An innovative menu which has dishes with Black Sea, Turkish and Italian influences. Warm salad in edible baskets is one of the most popular. The menu changes for lunch and dinner. ○ *10am–11pm.* ▤ [V] 🧒 ♿

FURTHER AFIELD (TAKSIM): *Nature and Peace* $$
Büyükparmakkapı Sok 21/23. ☎ *(0212) 252 86 09.*
One of Istanbul's first health food restaurants and still serving superb "natural" dishes. No red meat is served here. However, there is a good selection of fish, chicken and vegetarian dishes. ○ *11am–midnight.* ● *Sun.* ▤ [V] ♿

FURTHER AFIELD (TAKSIM): *Hacıabdullah Restaurant.* **Map** 1 A3. $$$
Sakızağacı Sok 17. ☎ *(0212) 293 85 61.*
Turkey's oldest licensed restaurant has been serving traditional Turkish meals since 1876. The chefs prepare over 125 speciality dishes daily. There is a family eating area upstairs. ○ *11am–11pm daily.* [V] 🧒

THRACE AND THE SEA OF MARMARA

BURSA: *Çiçek Izgara* $
Belediye Cad 15. ☎ *(0224) 221 65 26.*
Highlights Bursa's conventional tastes in grilled meats, salads, *pilav* and standard no-fuss fare. It is quite smart here, with good service. Women can comfortably come here together or on their own. ○ *11am–4pm & 6–9:30pm daily.* 🧒 ♿

BURSA: *Kebapcı İskender* $$
Ünlü Cad 7. ☎ *(0224) 221 46 15.*
One of the best-known and oldest kebab restaurants in Bursa. Families, tourists, women and teens mingle and munch the tasty kebabs for which the restaurant is famous. They serve nothing else. ○ *11am–9pm daily.* ▤ 🧒 ♿

BURSA: *Yusuf Restoran* $$
Kültürk Parkı içinde. ☎ *(0224) 234 49 67.*
Some of Bursa's best food is found here in a lovely nook in the Culture Park. The speciality is *tandır* lamb but there is a huge selection of mezes, grilled meats, vegetarian dishes and salads. Tables spill into the garden and it brims with families in the evenings and at weekends. ○ *noon–1am daily.* [V] 🧒 ♿

EDIRNE: *Lalezar* $
Karaağaç Yolu. ☎ *(0284) 213 06 00.*
Lovely relaxed place on the river Meriç serving mezes, fish and kebabs. Try to get a table next to the river. To reach here, take the Karaağaç dolmuş from Edirne. ○ *11am–1:30am daily.* 🧒 ♿

İZNIK: *Kenan Çorba ve Izgara Salonu* $
Atatürk Cad (near Haghia Sophia). ☎ *(0224) 757 02 35.*
A cool and leafy location, near all the sights. This is the place for a simple but satisfying meal in İznik. The specialities are soup and grills, but everything is cheerful and delicious here. ○ *9:30am–11:30pm daily.*

POLONEZKÖY: *Leonardo* $$
Köyiçi Sok 32. ☎ *(0216) 432 30 82.*
A restored country house serving Turkish and continental dishes. The garden is one of the best features. Buffet/smorgasbord fare is on offer at weekends. ○ *11am–11pm daily.* [V] 🧒 🍸 🍴$ *weekends only.*

PRINCES' ISLANDS/BÜYÜKADA: *Birtat* $$
Gülistan Cad 10. ☎ *(0216) 382 68 41.*
The restaurant offers fresh grilled fish and meat, and very tasty mezes. Their angel-hair dessert with warm cheese *(künefe)* is particularly good. Outdoor tables are available. ○ *11:30am–midnight daily.* [V] 🧒 🍸 ♿ 🍴$ *lunch only.*

Bol Kepçe	V MC			●	
Myott					
Evim Mantı	V MC AE DC	●			
Nature and Peace	V MC	●			
Hacıabdullah Restaurant	V MC AE	●		●	
Çiçek Izgara		●			
Kebapcı İskender		●			
Yusuf Restoran	V MC	●		●	
Lalezar	V MC AE	●			■
Kenan Çorba ve Izgara Salonu		●			
Leonardo	V MC AE	●		●	
Birtat	V MC AE DC	●		●	

Price categories for a three-course meal for one, including tax and service:

$ under US$5
$$ US$5–10
$$$ US$10–20
$$$$ US$20–30
$$$$$ over US$30

CREDIT CARDS
Indicates which credit cards are accepted (AE American Express, DC Diners Club, MC MasterCard, V Visa).

A LA CARTE MENU
Restaurant specializes in à la carte dishes.

NON-SMOKING SECTION
Restaurants has a non-smoking section.

ALCOHOL AVAILABLE
Indicates that the restaurant serves alcohol.

LIVE MUSIC
Background music is provided by musicians.

THE AEGEAN

	Credit Cards	A la Carte Menu	Non-Smoking Section	Alcohol Available	Live Music
ASSOS/BEHRAMKALE: *Kervansaray Hotel* $$$$ Behramkale Köyü İskelesi. ☎ *(0286) 721 70 93.* The best place for a good meal. Fish from the Aegean is their speciality but the cold and hot mezes are also excellent. There is a good selection of other dishes at reasonable prices. ○ *noon–3pm & 6:30pm–midnight daily.* ● *Oct–May.* ▤ [V] 🧒 🍸 ♿	V MC AE DC	●	■	●	
BODRUM: *Gemibaşı Restaurant* $$ Neyzen Tevfik Cad 176. ☎ *(0252) 316 12 20.* Cheap, cheerful, close to the harbour and with wonderful, freshly prepared Turkish fare. Tables overflow onto the street and it is always full. Single women can comfortably come here for an evening meal. ○ *noon–11pm.* [V] ♿	V MC	●		●	
BODRUM: *Kocadon* $$$$ Saray Sok 1 (off Neyzen Tevfik Cad). ☎ *(0252) 316 37 05.* The décor and atmosphere rival the cuisine at this smart, imaginative restaurant. The seafood is unforgettable. One of Bodrum's landmark eateries. ○ *7pm–midnight daily.* [V] ⛱ ♿	V MC AE DC	●		●	
BODRUM: *The Garden* $$$$ Cumhuriyet Cad 80. ☎ *(0252) 316 56 38.* As the name suggests, the interior décor of this restaurant is reminiscent of a botanical garden. Mediterranean cuisine is on offer here. Try the *tandır* (lamb) or enjoy a drink at the open-air bar. ○ *9am–4am daily.* ▤ [V] 🧒 🍸 ♿ 🍴$	V MC DC	●	■	●	■
BODRUM: *Hadigari* $$$$$ Dr. Alim Bey Cad, 34 Sok 2. ☎ *(0252) 313 90 87.* One of Bodrum's top restaurants, it also serves an interesting mixture of Turkish main courses with a medley of starters including Black Sea dishes. The seafood "steamboat" is a delight and presentation is everything. Excellent wine list. Music on Saturday and Sunday only. ○ *11am–5am daily.* ⛱	V MC AE DC	●		●	■
BODRUM: *Trança* $$$$$ Cumhuriyet Cad 36. ☎ *(0252) 316 66 10.* For location, this cannot be beaten. The dedicated owner knows his customers and offers a first-class selection of seafood (including lobster), steak, stews and vegetarian dishes. The upper terrace offers a splendid panorama of Bodrum. ○ *11:30am–1:30am daily.* [V] 🍸	V MC AE DC	●		●	
BODRUM PENINSULA: *Çimentepe* $$ Geriş Altı, Yalıkavak. ☎ *(0252) 385 42 37.* Standard Turkish fare enhanced by the lovely vista from the terrace. Unusual specialities are sea beans *(deniz börülcesi)* and stuffed marrow flowers *(kabak çiçeği dolma).* ○ *11am–midnight daily, later on weekends.* [V] 🍸 ♿	V MC AE	●		●	■
BODRUM PENINSULA: *Alara* $$$ Feribot İskelesi Torba. ☎ *(0252) 367 21 34.* Dream setting on the quay in a quiet, upmarket village. Simple but nicely cooked Turkish food and a few continental efforts but fish is the most obvious choice here. ○ *8:30am–midnight daily.* ● *Oct–May.* [V] ♿		●		●	
ÇANAKKALE: *Anzac Hotel* $$ Saat Kulesi Meydanı 8. ☎ *(0286) 217 77 77.* This is a cheap and cheerful place. Open to hotel guests as well as non-residents, they serve light snacks and a few more substantial meals, appealing to a global range of hungry backpackers. ○ *8:30am–1:30am daily.* 🍸	V MC	●		●	
ÇEŞME: *Körfez* $$$ İskele Meydanı (Yacht Harbour). ☎ *(0232) 712 67 18.* Many dishes are available at this attractive harbour-front restaurant but they excel at fish, seafood and mezes. ○ *11:30am–2pm daily.* [V] 🧒	V MC AE	●		●	■

Datça: *Akdeniz* $$$ Yat Limanı. ☎ *(0252) 712 44 99.* This restaurant overlooks the yacht harbour from an upper-floor terrace. Guests can enjoy creative Turkish cuisine leaning away from the traditional fare. 🕐 *11am–midnight daily.* 🍸 ♿	V MC	●		●	
İzmir: *Bonjour Café & Restaurant* $$$ 1387 Sok 3, Alsancak. ☎ *(0232) 421 64 14 .* In business for over 40 years, Bonjour is thriving in its new location. The food is very good, and some classic Californian "designer food" touches have drifted across the Atlantic. Brilliant desserts make up for the less interesting wines on offer. 🕐 *noon–midnight daily. Disco until 3am.* ▤ [V] 🍸 ♿ *summer terrace only.*	V MC AE DC	●		●	■
İzmir: *Fiori* $$$ Sht Nevret Bul. 7, Alsancak. ☎ *(0232) 464 60 40.* Situated in the city centre, this popular Italian restaurant serves good Italian and Spanish cuisine. Specials include Shrimp Paella and flambé dishes of various meats with cognac. 🕐 *1:30pm–midnight daily.* ▤ [V] 🚸 🍸	V MC	●		●	
İzmir: *La Folie* $$$ Alsancak Şehit Nevres Bulvarı 5/A. ☎ *(0232) 463 58 58.* Always packed, with a mixture of locals and ex-pats. Their Mediterranean dishes are fresh and colourful. They do not serve rakı, but all other alcoholic drinks are available. 🕐 *11am–3pm & 5:30–11pm daily.* ▤ ♿ 🍴$ *lunch only.*	V MC AE DC	●		●	
İzmir: *Deniz Restaurant* $$$$$ Atatürk Cad 188/B, Alsancak. ☎ *(0232) 422 06 01.* A classy and smart restaurant enjoying a wonderful location on the Kordon, overlooking İzmir Bay. Continental and international dishes with fish and seafood are available as well as Turkish specialities. 🕐 *11:30am–midnight daily.* 🍸 ♿	V MC AE	●	■	●	
Knidos: *Aphrodit* $$ Yat Limanı (harbour front). Situated next to the ruins and overlooking the water, Aphrodit has a restaurant monopoly in this remote enclave. There are no menus; you eat what you see but they serve adequate Turkish fare. They often arrange evening barbeques for visiting sailing crews. 🕐 *11am–11pm daily.* ● *Oct–May.*				●	
Kuşadası: *Kazım Usta* $$$ Balıkcı Limanı (Fisherman's harbour). ☎ *(0256) 614 12 66.* Right on the harbour, they do outstanding mezes here. The fish is also excellent and beautifully cooked and served. 🕐 *11:30am–midnight daily.* ♿		●		●	
Kuşadası: *Macit Et Lokantasi* $$$ Çevre Yolu. ☎ *(0256) 618 02 72.* Situated on the main highway with a bird's-eye view of the harbour from the garden. You will find the finest southeast-style Turkish meat dishes in the district here. 🕐 *11:30am–midnight daily.* ▤	V MC AE DC	●		●	
Marmaris: *Taraça* $$$ Tepe Mahallesi 30 Sok 11. ☎ *(0252) 411 39 99.* Opposite the entrance to the castle, this restaurant in an old restored Greek house serves a mixture of contemporary and traditional Turkish foods with some original culinary touches. 🕐 *10:30am–1am daily.* ▤ [V] 🍸	V MC AE DC	●		●	■
Marmaris: *La Campana* $$$$ Netsel Marina. ☎ *(0252) 412 55 57.* Run by a mother-and-daughter team, a subtle blend of of Italian and Turkish flavours characterizes this very professional restaurant that attracts flocks of international yachtsmen. 🕐 *11:30am–1:30am daily.* ▤ [V] [T] 🍸	V MC AE DC	●		●	
Marmaris: *Antique Café and Bar* $$$$$ Netsel Marina. ☎ *(0252) 413 29 55.* Meals that taste as good as they look. The table settings are artistic, and the European culinary touches are enhanced by fresh, local ingredients. 🕐 *noon–3pm & 7pm–2am daily.* ▤ [V] [T] 🍸 ♿	V MC AE DC	●	■	●	
Marmaris: *Birtat Restaurant* $$$$$ Yacht Harbour Barbaros Cad. ☎ *(0252) 412 10 76.* This is one of scores of restaurants lining the harbour, but Birtat has been pleasing clients since 1964 with creative seafood and fish specialities, and excellent grilled meats. 🕐 *noon–1:30am daily.* [V] ♿	V MC AE DC	●		●	

Price categories for a three-course meal for one, including tax and service:

Ⓢ under US$5
ⓈⓈ US$5–10
ⓈⓈⓈ US$10–20
ⓈⓈⓈⓈ US$20–30
ⓈⓈⓈⓈⓈ over US$30

CREDIT CARDS
Indicates which credit cards are accepted (AE American Express, DC Diners Club, MC MasterCard, V Visa).

A LA CARTE MENU
Restaurant specializes in à la carte dishes.

NON-SMOKING SECTION
Restaurant has a non-smoking section.

ALCOHOL AVAILABLE
Indicates that the restaurant serves alcohol.

LIVE MUSIC
Background music is provided by musicians.

	CREDIT CARDS	A LA CARTE MENU	NON-SMOKING SECTION	ALCOHOL AVAILABLE	LIVE MUSIC
SELÇUK: *Gökdağ Restaurant* ⓈⓈⓈ Atatürk Cad Aydın-İzmir Asfaltı 34. 〖 (0232) 892 67 77. One of Selçuk's most popular places. They specialize in meat dishes and *çöp şiş* but will lay on a sumptuous buffet and smorgasbord for groups. ◯ 7am–midnight daily. ▤ 🍴 for open buffet.	V MC AE DC	●		●	

MEDITERRANEAN TURKEY

	CREDIT CARDS	A LA CARTE MENU	NON-SMOKING SECTION	ALCOHOL AVAILABLE	LIVE MUSIC
ADANA: *Taşköprü Restaurant* Ⓢ Seyhan Cad 21. 〖 (0322) 359 94 65. One of the more popular of the many medium-priced restaurants in Adana. Standard but appetizing fare of kebabs, salads, *pide* (flat bread with toppings) and soups on order. They make good chips. ◯ 11am–2am Mon–Sat. ▤ 🅥 ♿	V MC AE DC	●		●	■
ADANA: *Zümrüt 3 Et Lokantası* ⓈⓈ İnönü Cad 135/C 3. 〖 (0322) 363 39 98. A budget place for both Turkish fast food and more leisurely meals. ◯ 24 hours daily. 🍴	V MC	●			
ALANYA: *Janus Restaurant and Café Bar* ⓈⓈⓈ Rıhtım Girişi (entrance to the harbour). 〖 (0242) 513 26 94. In a house at the harbour entrance, Janus serves reasonable Turkish and continental specialities and drinks throughout the day. It becomes a nightclub after midnight with canned music and dancing. ◯ 11am–3am daily. ▤ 🅨	V MC AE	●		●	■
ANTAKYA: *Antakya Ev Restoran* ⓈⓈ Silahli Kuvvetli Cad. 〖 (0326) 214 13 50. Eating in this restored Antakya house is a delight. Serves mainly regional foods like kebabs and grills. ◯ 11:30am–3:30pm & 7pm–midnight Mon–Sat. 🅥	V MC	●		●	
ANTAKYA: *Sultan Sofrası* ⓈⓈ İstiklâl Cad. 〖 (0326) 213 87 59. An outstanding and beautifully cooked selection of regional foods awaits you here. Very popular and is usually quite busy. ◯ 10:30am–11pm daily. 🅥 🍴	V MC	●		●	
ANTALYA: *Bayülgen* ⓈⓈ Teoman Paşa Cad 10. 〖 (0242) 247 54 74. A first-rate kebab salon with a designer look. The *künefe* (angel-hair dessert) is some of the best you will find outside the chef's home town of Gaziantep. ◯ 10:30am–midnight daily. 🍴	V MC	●			
ANTALYA: *Garage* ⓈⓈ Işıklar Cad 2/B. 〖 (0242) 243 23 49. A stylish, colourful place popular with trendy youth. They serve good pizza, pasta and schnitzels to a hip crowd surrounded by car bodies and chrome. ◯ 11am–midnight daily. ▤ 🅥 🚼 🅨	V MC AE	●		●	
ANTALYA: *Parlak Restaurant* ⓈⓈ Kazım Özalp (Şarampol) Sok Zincirli Han 7. 〖 (0242) 241 91 60. Known as much for their good service and hospitality as for their enduring speciality of spit-roasted chicken, Parlak is always popular and busy. ◯ 11:30am–midnight daily. 🅥 ♿	V MC AE DC	●			
ANTALYA: *7 Mehmet* ⓈⓈⓈ Hasan Subaşı Kültür Parkı 333. 〖 (0242) 241 16 41. Well-known for business lunches, special occasion meals or for anybody who loves consistently good Turkish food. The staff have been there for years, and the food is excellent. ◯ 11:30am–midnight daily. ▤ 🅥 🚼 🅨 ♿	V MC AE DC	●		●	
ASPENDOS: *Aspendos Restaurant* ⓈⓈⓈ On the road to the theatre, Belkıs. 〖 (0242) 735 70 88. Near the Aspendos ruins, the family-run restaurant offers seafood and classic Turkish dishes. ◯ noon–10pm daily (later during the Aspendos Festival). 🅥 🍴	V MC	●		●	

ASPENDOS: *Belkıs Restaurant* $$$ Belkıs Köyü. ☎ *(0242) 735 72 63.* Imaginative food right next to the river. Many foods are cooked or steamed in earthenware pots. It is a good place for a meal before or after seeing the ruins at Aspendos or during the Festival. 🕐 *8:30am–4pm & 5:30–midnight daily.* [V] 🍸 ♿	*V* *MC* *AE*	●		●	
DALYAN: *Şelâle* $$ Maraş Mahallesi. ☎ *(0252) 284 32 90.* In a rustic, lush setting near the river, the restaurant serves pleasing standard Turkish dishes and simple snacks. 🕐 *10am–10pm daily.* 🚸 🍸 ♿	*V* *MC*	●		●	
DALYAN: *Beyazgül Restaurant* $$$ Maraş Mahallesi Balıkhane Sok 26–28. ☎ *(0252) 284 23 04.* In a superb location on the Dalyan river, the restaurant and motel have been going for 15 years and the food, service and atmosphere are as good as ever. It also caters to non-residents. 🕐 *8am–11pm daily.* ☰ [V] 🚸 🍸 ♿		●		●	
DALYAN: *Riverside* $$$ Maraş Cad. ☎ *(0252) 284 31 14.* Opposite the Lycian tombs, they have a wide choice of Turkish foods but they will insist you try their fish and meze courses. 🕐 *11am–midnight daily.* 🍸 ♿	*V* *MC*	●		●	
FETHIYE: *Şadırvan* $$ Çarşı Meydanı (village square), Ovacık. ☎ *(0252) 616 61 40.* Set in a tranquil sanctuary in a pine forest off a dirt track on the Ölü Deniz–Fethiye road, the restaurant serves standard Turkish fare. There is outside dining in summer and a fireplace in winter. 🕐 *noon–10:30pm daily.* 🍴	*V* *MC*	●		●	
FETHIYE: *Meğri Lokantası* $$$ Çarşı Cad 13/A. ☎ *(0252) 614 40 47.* Located in a converted warehouse in the bazaar, Meğri is popular with both tourists and locals. They serve traditional Turkish food, and good fish dishes. Vegetarian dishes cooked to order. 🕐 *11:30–3pm & 6pm–midnight daily.* ☰ [V] 🚸	*V* *MC* *AE* *DC*	●		●	
FETHIYE: *Meğri 1* $$$ Eski Camii Gecidi Likya Sok 8–9. ☎ *(0252) 614 40 46.* Set in a traditional, old stone building, this restaurant offers a wide variety of Mediterranean and French cuisine. Specials include *buğulama*, a steamed fish dish. 🕐 *9am–2am daily.* ☰ [V] 🚸 🍸 🍴	*V* *MC* *AE*	●	■	●	
FETHIYE: *Rafet* $$$ Kordon Boyu. ☎ *(0252) 614 11 06.* One of Fethiye's oldest and most established restaurants. They serve classic Turkish dishes, kebabs, mezes and excellent fish. There is a lovely quiet garden at the back. 🕐 *11am–midnight daily.* [V] 🍸 ♿ 🍴	*V* *MC*	●		●	
FETHIYE: *Yacht Restaurant* $$$ Yat Limanı (Yacht harbour). ☎ *(0252) 614 70 14.* This place is known for a 20-course Turkish banquet accompanied by belly dancers and Turkish folk musicians. It is popular with groups (reservations in advance are essential). 🕐 *8–10:30am, noon–3pm & 7pm–1:30am daily.* 🍴	*V* *MC* *DC*			●	■
GÖCEK: *Verandah Restaurant* $$$$$ Göcek Marina Resort. ☎ *(0252) 645 27 60.* In a class of its own and in an area not known for cuisine, the Verandah serves outstanding Mediterranean food in beautiful surroundings. Their speciality is the salmon *pide* (flat bread with toppings). 🕐 *7pm–midnight daily.* ☰ [V] 👔 🍸 ♿	*V* *MC* *AE*	●	■	●	
KALKAN: *Korsan (The Pirate)* $$$ Yalıboyu Mahallesi. ☎ *(0242) 844 36 22.* On the waterfront in Kalkan, this restaurant is popular with British ex-pats for its charm and hospitality. The menu offers international and alternative Turkish cuisine, fish, mezes and grills. 🕐 *11am–3pm & 6pm–midnight daily.* [V] 🚸 🍸 ♿	*V* *MC* *AE*	●		●	■
KALKAN: *Patlıcan* $$$ Marina, Yalıboyu Mahallesi. ☎ *(0242) 844 33 32.* The menu features Ottoman classics but with international cordon bleu touches. They also do a first-class English breakfast. 🕐 *8:30am–midnight daily.*	*V* *MC* *AE* *DC*	●	■	●	
KAŞ: *Sympathy Restaurant* $$ Uzunçarşı Gürsoy Sok 11. ☎ *(0242) 836 24 18.* The owner cooks classic Ottoman dishes to perfection. *Çerkez tavuğu* (walnut chicken) is a masterpiece and everything is beautifully served. Excellent service and professionalism. 🕐 *11am–midnight daily.* [V] 🍸 ♿	*V* *MC*	●		●	

For key to symbols see back flap

Price categories for a three-course meal for one, including tax and service:

$ under US$5
$$ US$5–10
$$$ US$10–20
$$$$ US$20–30
$$$$$ over US$30

Credit Cards
Indicates which credit cards are accepted (AE American Express, DC Diners Club, MC MasterCard, V Visa).

A la Carte Menu
Restaurant specializes in à la carte dishes.

Non-Smoking Section
Restaurant has a non-smoking section.

Alcohol Available
Indicates that the restaurant serves alcohol.

Live Music
Background music is provided by musicians.

Restaurant	Credit Cards	A la Carte Menu	Non-Smoking Section	Alcohol Available	Live Music
Kaş: *Dolphin Café and Restaurant* $$$ Sandikçı Sok 18. ☎ *(0242) 836 35 38.* This restaurant serves excellent grilled meat dishes and the freshest seafood and fish. Good vegetarian dishes and dreamy views over the harbour from a raised panoramic terrace. ○ *May-Oct: 10am–1am daily.* ● *Nov–Apr: Mon–Thu.* [V] 🍸 🚸 ♿	V MC	●		●	
Kaş: *Chez Evy* $$$$ Terzi Sok 4. ☎ *(0242) 836 12 53.* Chez Evy rivals the best small restaurants of provincial France, and Evy herself is a gourmet cook. French menu with superb steaks and often featuring wild boar. Crème caramel is always on offer. In summer, you eat in the garden, in winter indoors by the fireplace. ○ *7pm–1am Tue-Sun.* [V] 👔 🚸 🍸		●		●	
Kaş: *Mercan Restaurant* $$$$ Yacht Harbour. ☎ *(0242) 836 12 09.* They do everything well here, although service gets frenetic at times. Fish is the speciality but is not cheap. In the summer, tables adjoin the harbour. ○ *11am–midnight daily.* [V] 🚸 ♿	V MC AE DC	●		●	
Ölü Deniz: *Buzz Beach Bar and Grill* $$$ Deniz Camp. ☎ *(0252) 617 04 50.* Excellent Turkish cuisine in a seafront restaurant set in a shady vineyard garden. Also open for breakfast, snacks, dessert and meals throughout the day. Comprehensive cocktail menu. ○ *8am–2am daily.* ● *Oct–May.* ▤ 🍸 ♿	V MC AE DC	●		●	
Ölü Deniz: *White Dolphin (Beyaz Yunus)* $$$$ Belceğiz. ☎ *(0252) 617 00 68.* Unbeatable sunset views from the outdoor terrace restaurant. This is the finest eatery in the Fethiye region and has kept up its reputation for Mediterranean food and seafood specialities for years. Not always cheap but excellent value for money. ○ *noon–2:30pm & 6:30pm–midnight daily.* ▤ 👔 🍸 ♿	V MC	●		●	
Side: *Bavaria House* $$$ Yasemin Sok 22. ☎ *(0242) 753 30 44.* Turkish and German cuisine is available at this traditionally-decorated eaterie. The *testi* kebab (lamb) is a speciality. ○ *9am–4am daily.* ▤ [V] 🚸 🍴$	V MC	●	■	●	
Side: *Moonlight* $$$ Barbaros Caddesi. ☎ *(0242) 753 14 00.* Tables are set right at the water's edge near Side's east beach. Fish and seafood are the most tempting on the menu, but grills and vegetarian dishes are also available. ○ *noon–3pm, 6:30pm–midnight daily.* [V] 🍸 ♿	V MC	●		●	
Side: *Soundwaves* $$$ Küçük Plajı üstü. ☎ *(0242) 753 10 59.* This restaurant is located in a quiet and pretty area, and the cooking and service are of a high standard. Seafood is recommended but they do steak perfectly on the grill, as well as several dishes flambéed at the table. ○ *6:30pm–1am daily.* 🍸		●		●	

Ankara and Western Anatolia

Restaurant	Credit Cards	A la Carte Menu	Non-Smoking Section	Alcohol Available	Live Music
Ankara: *Boyacızade Konağı* $$ Berrak Sok 7–9, Ulus. ☎ *(0312) 310 25 25.* Convenient to the citadel and one of its most popular restaurants, turning out decent local dishes at great prices. Wonderful city views and congenial atmosphere. ○ *11am–midnight daily.*	V MC AE DC	●		●	
Ankara: *Metin* $$$ Aladdin Cad. Cumhuriyet Meydani. ☎ *(0332) 351 52 12.* Enjoy traditional Turkish cuisine in this simple, modern restaurant. Specials include *etsal* (lamb cooked with cheese and vegetables). ○ *24 hrs daily.* ▤ [V] 🚸 🍸 ♿ 🍴$	V MC AE DC		■	●	■

ANKARA: *Zenger Pasa Konagi* $$$
Kaleidi, Doyran Sok 13, Kaleici. ☎ *(0312) 311 70 70.*
This restaurant is set in a wonderful old, historic building and serves
traditional Turkish cuisine. Specials include *kuzu kapama* (oven-baked lamb).
🕐 *10:30am–11:30pm daily.* 📋 V 🔥 Y ♿ ¶⊖¶

V
MC

ANKARA: *Atakule Dönen Restaurant and Café* $$$$
Çankaya. ☎ *(0312) 440 74 12.*
If you like food with a view, this is the best place in Ankara. Dishes include a
variety of Turkish and some international fare. On weekends it is advisable to
reserve a table. 🕐 *noon–11:30pm daily.* 📋 V 🔥 Y

V
MC
AE

ANKARA: *Washington* $$$$
Nenehatun Cad 97, Gaziosmanpaşa. ☎ *(0312) 445 02 12.*
A top international restaurant. Steaks are classic, but everything is beautifully
presented and served. The *gravad lax* starter is superb and there is an excellent
wine list. 🕐 *noon–midnight daily.* 📋 V 🔥 Y ¶⊖¶ *lunch only.*

V
MC
AE
DC

ESKIŞEHIR: *Şömine Kebap Salon* $$
2 Eylül Cad 37. ☎ *(0222) 231 97 26.*
This is the best of the bunch in the crush of Kebab Alley. The restaurant
is nicely decorated and the food is authentic. It is usually crowded.
🕐 *10:30am–midnight daily.*

V
MC

ESKIŞEHIR: *Hayal Kahvesi* $$$
Ismet Inönü Cad 115/A. ☎ *(0222) 320 82 20.*
This restaurant offers a wide variety of Mediterranean cuisine including a good
choice of fresh fish. Housed in an old building with traditional interior
décor. 🕐 *noon–2am daily.* 📋 V Y ¶⊖¶

V
MC

KONYA: *Mevlana Sofrası* $$
Şehit Nazımbey Cad 1/A, Civar Mahallesi. ☎ *(0332) 353 33 41.*
Private rooms for 5 to 50 people with low-level tables, linen serviettes and
various courses of local Konya dishes at economic prices. A summer terrace
overlooks the Mevlâna rose garden. Sema (Dervish) performances arranged for
groups of 10 or more. 🕐 *noon–midnight daily.* V

V
MC
AE
DC

KONYA: *Gülbahçesi Konya Mutfağı* $$
Gülbahçesi Cad, Aşcıbaşı Sok. ☎ *(0332) 353 07 68 .*
This municipality-run restaurant serves outstanding, authentic Konya
cuisine in quiet, cool surroundings (on the outdoor terrace in summer)
and with a fine view of the Mevlâna and its rose garden *(gülbahçe).*
Reasonable prices for high-quality food and service. 🕐 *noon–midnight daily.*
V ¶⊖¶ *for group reservations only.*

V
MC
AE
DC

KÜTAHYA: *Harlek* $$
Ilica. ☎ *(0274) 245 23 77 .*
Standard Turkish fare, including all kinds of meat grills and kebabs, is available
at this traditional Turkish eatery. 🕐 *7am–10am & noon–midnight daily.* 📋 🔥 ¶⊖¶

V
MC
AE

THE BLACK SEA

RIZE: *Konak* $
Palmiye Sok 2 (Piri Kelebi Mahallesi). ☎ *(0464) 214 44 26.*
Superb eating on the Black Sea coast. Historic mansion restored by archaeologist-
turned-restaurateur serves trout, stews, grills, burgers and pizza. Also offers
desserts and *mıhlama* (corn bread). 🕐 *11am–midnight daily.* V 🔥

V
MC
DC

RIZE: *Kalegon Dağ Evi Tesisleri* $$
Ayder, Çamlıhemşin. ☎ *(0464) 657 21 22.*
Outdoor eating on a rustic terrace in the mountains, caters to families and
passing hikers. Traditional Black Sea dishes as well as trout and grilled meats.
Outstanding views. 🕐 *11am–midnight daily.* ● *Oct–May.* V 🔥

V
MC

RIZE: *Nazlı Çiçek Alabalık Dinlenme Tesisleri* $$
Ayder, Çamlıhemşin. ☎ *(0464) 657 21 30.*
You eat grilled fresh trout here in the bracing mountain air. Salads, meat dishes
and a few baked desserts are also available. 🕐 *11am–10pm daily.* ● *Oct–May.*

SAFRANBOLU: *Kadıoğlu Şehzade Sofrası* $$
Çeşme Mahallesi, Arasta Sok 8. ☎ *(0370) 712 50 91.*
Offers the best choice of grills, stews, salads, şiş kebabs and a few vegetarian
dishes in Safranbolu, a town shy on culinary talent. 🕐 *noon–2pm & 6pm–
midnight daily.* 📋 V 🔥 Y

V
MC
AE

<table>
<tr><td colspan="2">

Price categories for a three-course meal for one, including tax and service:

$ under US$5
$$ US$5–10
$$$ US$10–20
$$$$ US$20–30
$$$$$ over US$30

</td><td>

CREDIT CARDS
Indicates which credit cards are accepted (AE American Express, DC Diners Club, MC MasterCard, V Visa).

A LA CARTE MENU
Restaurant specializes in à la carte dishes.

NON-SMOKING SECTION
Restaurant has a non-smoking section.

ALCOHOL AVAILABLE
Indicates that the restaurant serves alcohol.

LIVE MUSIC
Background music is provided by musicians.

</td></tr>
</table>

	CREDIT CARDS	A LA CARTE MENU	NON-SMOKING SECTION	ALCOHOL AVAILABLE	LIVE MUSIC
SAFRANBOLU: *Konağı* $$ Baba Sultan Mahallesi Naip Tarla Sok 4. ☎ *(0370) 712 81 53.* Meals are served in the bar or garden. Choose the garden if you wish to avoid the high-pitched bar music. Fixed menu of soup, *köfte* (meatballs), salad and dessert is basic but adequate. ○ *noon–2pm & 7pm–midnight daily.* ▣ ▦ ▦ ▦	V MC AE DC			●	
SAMSUN: *Buyuk Samsun Oteli* $$$ Ataturk Bulvari 629. ☎ *(0362) 432 49 99.* Turkish and Blak Sea Cuisine is available in this traditionally decorated restaurant. Specials include *labana sarmasi* (cabbage leaves stuffed with mince meat), *misir ekmegi* (corn bread) and *guymak* (fried corn with cheese). ○ *24hrs daily.* ▤ ▣ ▦ ▦	V MC	●		●	■
SAMSUN: *Samdan* $$$ Çakırlar Köprüsü, Altınkum. ☎ *(0362) 467 09 25.* A wide variety of seafood, meat dishes and vegetarian options are available here. The cuisine is traditional Black Sea and Turkish and the décor is modern. ○ *11am–3am daily.* ▤ ▣ ▦ ▦ ▦	V MC AE	●	■	●	■
TRABZON: *Meydan Kebap Salon* $ Gazipaşa Cad (opposite Meydan Park). ☎ *(0462) 321 02 03.* Well-cooked kebabs are served by friendly staff in this basic eaterie. ○ *11am–midnight daily.* ▤ ▦ ▦	V MC	●			
TRABZON: *Tad Pizza and Burger* $ Town Hall Square (Belediye Karşısı) 11. ☎ *(0462) 321 12 38.* This restaurant offers the usual range of hamburgers, chips, spaghetti and salad but they also make excellent *aşure* (Noah's pudding). ○ *7am–midnight daily.* ▤ ▣ ▦ ▦ ▦		●			
TRABZON: *Volkan 2 Lokantası* $ Atatürk alanı 8. ☎ *(0462) 322 47 31.* Basic but adequate, clean *lokanta* (eatery) serving starters, grills and kebabs. ○ *8am–midnight daily.* ▦ ▦	V MC	●			
CAPPADOCIA AND CENTRAL ANATOLIA					
AMASYA: *Konak Fast Food* $$ Ziya 4 Paşa Bulvarı 13. ☎ *(0358) 212 41 58.* For snacks, toast, soft drinks and light meals, accompanied by juke-box music, itis Amasya's version of trendiness. Tourists and locals hang out here and there is a good view of the river from the first-floor balcony. ○ *9am–midnight daily.*		●			
BOĞAZKALE: *Hattuşaş Restorant* $$ Atatürk Cad. ☎ *(0364) 452 20 13.* This establishment serves basic fare and is situated in the town centre (not near the site). It mostly caters for groups who have come to tour the Boğazkale site. ○ *9:30am–8pm daily.*		●			
GÖREME: *Ottoman House* $$$ Uzundere Sok 25. ☎ *(0384) 271 26 16.* The restaurant is on a pretty terrace in a quiet part of town. It is open to non-residents and they do a nice selection of basic Turkish dishes, usually a fixed-price menu consisting of soup, main meat course, salad and dessert in a friendly and relaxed atmosphere. ○ *24hrs daily.* ▣ ▦ ▦	V MC AE DC	●	■	●	
KAYSERI: *İskender Lokantası* $ Millet Cad 5. ☎ *(0352) 232 36 16.* Memorable İskender kebab served in a courtyard around an ornamental pool. They also do grilled meats and spicy Adana kebabs very nicely. The restaurant is highly recommended. ○ *10am–10pm daily.* ▤	V MC AE DC	●			

KAYSERI: *Altıntepe Turistik Tesisleri* $$ | V MC AE DC | ● | | ● | ■
Altıntepe Mah Yukarı Eriklet. 【 *(0352) 344 23 23.*
Quite far from Kayseri, but worth it. Serves traditional Turkish *dolma* (stuffed dishes), grills, seafood, and Kayseri local fare like *mantı* (ravioli) and *pastırma* (cured sausage). Traditional music every night. ◯ *8am–2am daily.* 🖿 ⓥ 🏃 🍷

SIVAS: *Sivas Büyük Hotel* $$$ | V MC AE | ● | | ● | ■
İstasyon Cad. 【 *(0346) 225 47 62.*
This is about the best hotel in town and the restaurant serves decent and well-prepared food in an area not known for cuisine. ◯ *11:30am–10:30pm daily.* 🖿 🍷

ÜRGÜP: *Şömine* $$$ | V MC
Cumhuriyet Meydanı (main square). 【 *(0384) 341 84 42.*
Şömine offers refined Turkish and continental cooking with a few romantic touches, as well as outside dining. ◯ *noon–3pm & 6:30pm–midnight daily.* ⓥ 🍷

EASTERN ANATOLIA

DIYARBAKIR: *Sarmaşık Ocakbaşı Aile Et Lokantası* $ | V MC AE DC | ●
Dağkapı Kıbrıs Cad 31. 【 *(0412) 224 25 97.*
Serves typical nomadic fare of hearty kebabs, stuffed peppers and yoghurt dishes. Soft drinks are available, but you may be offered a yoghurt drink called *ayran*. There is a family salon for mixed couples. ◯ *11am–10:30pm daily.*

DIYARBAKIR: *Öz Selim Amcanın Sofra Salonu* $$ | | ●
Kurt İsmailpaşa 1 Sok, Demiray Apartman. 【 *(0412) 222 16 16.*
One of the city's better restaurants. Grilled meat over open coals is a speciality, but ask for it well done. ◯ *10:30am–midnight daily.* ⓥ 🍽 *lunch only.*

ERZURUM: *Güzelyurt Restorant* $$$ | V MC | ● | | ●
Cumhuriyet Cad. 【 *(0442) 218 15 14.*
This place has been going since before 1922 and it is almost Erzurum's only choice (outside of hotel dining) for upmarket food or drink. They do good grills, fish, stews and salads. ◯ *10am–midnight daily.* 🖿 ⓥ 🍷

GAZIANTEP: *Atakan Et Lokantası* $$ | V MC | ●
Karagöz Cad 21, Şahinbey. 【 *(0342) 220 80 50.*
Typical *lokanta* serving eastern Anatolian dishes. The best is to have the kebab, *lahmacun* (thin dough rolled with spicy tomato topping and baked) or *döner* (meat, fish or chicken grilled on vertical spit). The *burmalı kadayıf* (pastry dessert) alone is worth the visit. ◯ *11:30am–11pm daily.* 🍽 *lunch only.*

GAZIANTEP: *Tahsin Usta Restaurant* $$ | V MC | ●
Suburcu Cad 14/A. 【 *(0342) 220 89 30.*
A spacious family restaurant serving kebabs, *lahmacun* (Turkish pizza) and the sweet desserts so beloved in Gaziantep. ◯ *11am–midnight daily.* 🖿 🍽

GAZIANTEP: *Şeflerin Yeri Mazıcıoğlu Turistik Et Lokantası* $$$ | V MC AE | ● | | ●
Milli Egemenlik Bulvarı, Şehitkamil. 【 *(0342) 321 80 55.*
Located outside Gaziantep, catch a taxi to get here. There is an assortment of different regional foods like *simit* or *soğan kebabı*. Open buffet breakfast on Sundays. ◯ *11:30am–midnight daily.* 🖿 ⓥ 🏃 🍷 🍽

MALATYA: *Melita Restaurant* $$ | V MC | ●
Turfanda İş Hanı (off Atatürk Cad). 【 *(0422) 322 43 00.*
Serves kebabs, mezes and filling meat dishes. It is about the biggest and best place to eat out in Malatya. ◯ *11:30am–midnight daily.* 🖿 ⓥ 🍽 *lunch only.*

ŞANLIURFA: *Urfa Sofrası* $ | | ●
Atatürk Bulvarı (opposite the indoor sports salon). 【 *(0414) 315 61 30.*
Good basic food at rock-bottom prices. You will come here because you are hungry, not for romantic dining or the atmosphere. ◯ *9am–10:30pm daily.*

ŞANLIURFA: *Tandır Et Lokantası* $$ | V MC | ●
Fuar Cad 14. 【 *(0414) 215 53 78.*
Cheap and cheerful. The house speciality is oven-baked *(tandır)* kebabs. Other dishes are available but the meat is especially good here. The restaurant has its own car park. ◯ *7:30am–midnight daily.* 🖿 🍽

ŞANLIURFA: *Hotel Harran* $$$ | V MC | ● | | ●
Atatürk Bulvarı. 【 *(0414) 313 28 60.*
This is one of Urfa's best hotels and their restaurant is open to non-residents for local and international fare, with a bit of finesse. Great views from the roof-top terrace. ◯ *11:30am–midnight daily.* 🖿 🍷 🍽

SHOPPING IN TURKEY

EVEN IF YOU are not a shopper by nature, the varied and unusual selection of gifts found in Turkey's markets will easily tempt you. The grand shops and teeming streets of Istanbul are a world away from the ateliers and craft shops of smaller towns in rural areas. Outside Istanbul, you will also find bargaining *(see p130)* a less cut-throat pursuit. However, you are

Colourful Kütahya ware

sure to encounter high-pressure sales pitches wherever you travel. The weekly market is a unique aspect of regional shopping. These markets are a holdover from the days of trading caravans, when shops as we know them did not exist. Traders still pay taxes to have a market stall, as they did 400 years ago. And the *zabıta* (municipal market police) still control weights, measures and prices.

Upmarket clothing boutique in Bodrum

OPENING HOURS

IN LARGE CITIES, shops are usually open from 9am to 7 or 8pm. But hours can be much extended in tourist and coastal areas, where many shops will stay open until midnight, seven days a week, particularly in summer, when the daytime heat discourages all but the most dedicated shoppers. Out of season, these places often close for extended periods so that the owners can relax after the long hours of summer trade.

In general, opening hours are much more flexible in rural areas. If you find a shop closed, you can ask where the owner is and it will not take long before someone tells him/her that there is a potential customer. Note that some shops may close during Muslim religious holidays.

HOW TO PAY

MOST SHOPS that cater to tourists will be happy to accept foreign currency. If you can pay in cash, you can

usually get a discount on the more expensive goods. Exchange rates are often displayed in shops, and appear in daily newspapers.

Credit cards are widely accepted for purchases (except in markets and smaller shops), and most vendors do not charge a commission. Visa, MasterCard and American Express are the most common, Diners Club less so. Vendors who accept credit cards may try to tell you that they will not be reimbursed for the transaction for several days, and ask you to pay a small compensatory commission. Resist this, and insist on paying without a commission. It is common for a vendor to ask you to go to the bank with him to draw the money out on your credit card. There is nothing wrong with this, but you will pay interest on your card for a

cash advance. Note that very few shops in Turkey now accept travellers' cheques.

In rural markets, you will be expected to pay in cash. Some merchants will happily accept foreign currency.

Merchants in bazaars and markets expect customers to bargain. If you see something you want to buy, offer half the asking price. Increase the offer slightly if the merchant resists. He will then indicate whether he thinks that the bargaining should continue.

VAT EXEMPTION

WITH TURKEY'S KDV (value-added tax) rate at 18 per cent, it seems a good idea to claim back tax. In practice, it is only worth the effort for a large purchase. There is an inbuilt resistance to foreign currency leaving Turkey. Even though the procedure looks clear-cut, you will encounter many difficulties and may not get your money in the end.

Fresh herbs and spices, sold by weight at Kadıköy Market in Istanbul

Locally produced copper and brassware in the old quarter of Safranbolu

BUYING ANTIQUES

BEFORE PURCHASING antique items, it is important to know what can and cannot be taken out of Turkey. The rule is that objects which are over 100 years old may be exported only with a certificate stating their age and granting permission to remove them from the country. Museums issue these certificates, as does the Culture Ministry in Ankara, who will also authenticate the correct age and value of an object, if necessary. The shopkeeper from whom you bought your goods will often know which

Ornate ceramic vase and saucer

museum will be authorizing your purchases for export. In theory, a seller should register with a museum all goods that are over 100 years old. In practice, sellers usually only seek permission after a particular item has been sold. In the past, antiques could be removed from Turkey without a certificate. Although this has changed, the export of antiques is not forbidden, as some believe. If the relevant authorities permit your purchase to be exported, you can either take it with you or send it home, whether or not it is over 100 years old. Do take note, however, that

taking antiques out of Turkey without proper permission is regarded as smuggling, and is a punishable offence.

Van cats and Kangal dogs have recently been included in this category.

HOW TO SEND PURCHASES HOME

IF YOU HAVE bought items from a reputable and trustworthy supplier, he will have an arrangement with an international courier company who can ship goods to your home address. Try to get your own copy of any shipping documents and an air waybill number. Do not use the post office (PTT) to send such items. Be aware that there are also some disreputable dealers, especially in carpets, who will either substitute an inferior item in place of the one you have bought or who will fail to send the goods. Beware of traders who advise you to ignore official rules.

SIZES AND MEASURES

TURKEY USES continental European sizes for clothes and shoes. Food and drink are sold in metric measures.

DIRECTORY

HANDICRAFTS AND GIFTS

Galeri Sarpedon
Hotel Pirat, Marina, Kalkan.
☎ (0242) 844 28 49 and 844 35 40.

Evcim
Netsel Marina Shopping Mall D-03, Marmaris.
☎ (0252) 412 06 26.
FAX (0252) 411 13 55.

Sibel Düzen
Hükümet Cad, Kaş.
☎ (0242) 836 19 54.
@ sibelduzel@turk.net.

Ceşni Turkish Handicrafts
Tunalı Hilmi Cad,

Ertuğ Pasajı 88/44, Ankara.
☎ (0312) 426 57 87.

JEWELLERY AND PRECIOUS STONES

Ece Jewellery
Uzun Çarşısı 5, Kaş.
☎ (0242) 836 21 40.

Oktay Aktaş Art Gallery
Iskele Mahallsei, Yalı Cad, Datça, Marmaris.
☎ (0252) 712 37 34.
FAX (0252) 712 26 53.

CARPETS AND KILIMS

Stella Yildiz Carpets and Kilims
Iskele Cad, Datça, Marmaris.

☎ (0252) 712 97 62.
FAX (0252) 712 36 85.
@ stella@egenet.com.tr.

Gallery Shirvan
Halıcılar Sok 50, Kapalıçarşı (Grand Bazaar) Istanbul.
☎ (0212) 522 49 86.

Kaş and Carry
Bahçe Sok 3/A, Kaş.
☎ (0242) 836 16 62.
FAX (0242) 836 23 89.

HAND-WORKED COPPERWARE

L'Orient
İçbedesten, Şerif Ağa Sok 22–23, Kapalıçarşı (Grand Bazaar), Istanbul.
☎ (0212) 520 70 46.

LINENS

Özdilek
Bursa.
☎ (0224) 211 52 00.
FAX (0224) 211 52 44.

Afyon (on main highway junction of Ankara and Afyon road).
☎ (0272) 252 54 00.

SPICES AND HERBS

Ayfer Kaun
Mısır Çarşısı (Spice Market) 7, Istanbul.
☎ (0212) 522 45 23.

Ucuzcular Kimya Sanayii
Mısır Çarşısı (Spice Market) 51, Istanbul.
☎ (0212) 520 64 92.

What to Buy in Turkey

WHEN IT comes to shopping, nothing can compare with Istanbul's bustling bazaars, markets, shops and stalls. In contrast, the rural markets have an unhurried feel and unique products that often don't travel much beyond provincial boundaries, such as stout walking sticks made in Devrek (near Zonguldak), ceremonial pipes produced in Sivas and the angora goat-hair bedspreads and rugs made in Siirt. Markets are lively and colourful, and the best places to find handmade items that are produced in small quantities.

Meerschaum pipe head

Copper goblets

Copperware
Antique copperware can be very expensive. Newer items, however, are also available, at more affordable prices.

Antique copper water ewer

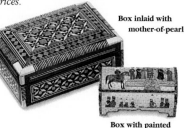

Pipes
Classic, beautifully crafted nargiles (bubble pipes) are still used by some Turkish men. They can make very attractive ornaments, even if you do not smoke.

Evil-eye pendants

Box inlaid with mother-of-pearl

Box with painted scenes on bone inlay

Jewellery
Turkey produces stunning gold jewellery in original designs. Silver is also popular, and rings and necklaces are often set with precious stones. A simple blue glass eye (boncuk) is said to ward off evil.

Inlaid Wood
Jewellery boxes crafted from wood or bone, and then inlaid or painted, make unusual souvenirs. Backgammon players will be delighted at the delicate, inlaid rosewood backgammon (tavla) sets available in markets and shops around Turkey.

Ceramics
Ceramics are an important artistic tradition. The style varies according to the area of origin. İznik, Kütahya and Çanakkale are famous for ceramic production, but Avanos is also known for hand-painted pottery and porcelain.

Green jugs from Çanakkale

Blue and white decorated ceramic plate

Glassware

This elegant lamp is an example of the blue and white striped glassware called çeşmibülbül, which is made in the famous Paşabahçe works. The firm makes many utilitarian designs as well as an up-market range in fine lead crystal. Paşabahçe glassware makes a wonderful gift.

Leather Goods

Shoes, handbags, briefcases and other leather accessories are good buys, as are jackets. For high-fashion, Istanbul is the place. Desa Deri is a good name all over Turkey. For accessories, look for the Matraş or Tergan brands.

Textiles

Hand-woven cloths, including ikat work (where the cotton is dyed as it is woven), and fine embroidery are just some of the range of textiles that can be bought. Turkey is also a leading producer of top-quality garments and knitwear. Bathrobes and towels are of high quality. Look for the Altınyıldız label for finest woollens and fabrics by the metre or yard.

Çeşmibülbül **lamp**

Cotton *ikat*
work

Embroidered scarves known as *oyalı*

Hand-printed *yazma* **(shawls) from Tokat**

Local Delicacies

Delicious sweets such as halva, Turkish delight and baklava are always popular. Many fragrant spices, as well as dried fruit and nuts are sold loose by weight in most markets and tourist shops throughout Turkey.

Halva

Nuts in honey

Turkish delight

Dried red peppers and aubergines

Mulberries

Sunflower and pumpkin seeds

Apricots

Chickpeas

Almonds

Pistachios

Turkish Carpets and Kilims

THE ANCIENT SKILL of weaving rugs has been handed down from generation to generation in Turkey. Rugs were originally made for warmth and decoration in the home, as dowry items for brides, or as donations to mosques. There are two main kinds of rug: carpets *(halı)*, which are knotted, and kilims, which are flat-woven with vertical (warp) and horizontal (weft) threads. Many foreign rugs are sold in Turkey but those of Turkish origin come in a particularly wide range of attractive colours. Most of the carpets and kilims offered for sale will be new or almost new; antique rugs are rarer and far more expensive.

A carpet may be machine-made or handmade. Fold the face of the rug back on itself: if you can see the base of the knots and the pile cannot be pulled out, it means that it is handmade.

Wool is the usual material for making a rug, although some carpets are made from silk.

CARPET
This reproduction of a 16th-century Uşak carpet is known as a Bellini double entrance prayer rug.

Weaving a Carpet
Wool for rugs is washed, carded, spun and dyed before it is woven. Weaving is a cottage industry in Turkey; the women weave in winter, leaving the summer months for farming duties.

RUG-MAKING AREAS OF WESTERN TURKEY

The weaving industry in Turkey is concentrated into several areas of production, listed below. Rug designs are traditional to their tribal origins, resulting in a wide range of designs and enabling a skilled buyer to identify the area of origin.

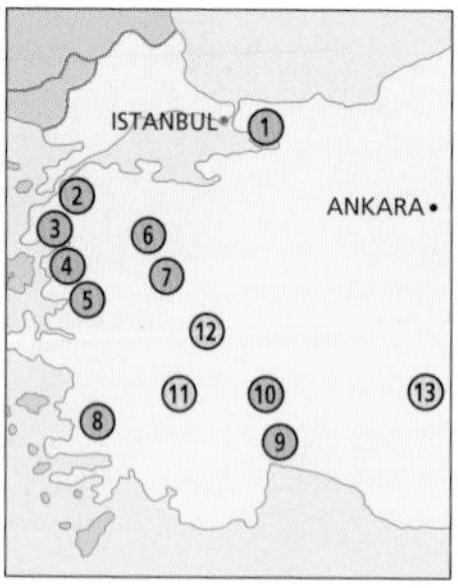

CARPETS

1. Hereke
2. Çanakkale
3. Ayvacık
4. Bergama
5. Yuntdağ
6. Balıkesir
7. Sındırgı
8. Milas
9. Antalya
10. Isparta

KILIMS

11. Denizli
12. Uşak

CARPETS AND KILIMS

13. Konya

Indigo

Madder

Camomile

Dyes
Before chemical dyes were introduced in 1863, plant extracts were used: madder roots for red; indigo for blue; and camomile and other plants for yellow.

The **"prayer design"** is inspired by a *mihrab*, the niche in a mosque that indicates the direction of Mecca *(see pp32–3)*.

The tree of life motif at the centre of the kilim is symbolic of immortality.

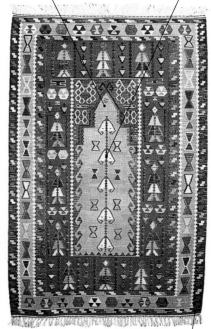

KILIM

Kilims are usually made using the slit-weave technique by which a vertical slit marks a colour change.

The width of a rug is limited by the size of the loom. Most rugs are small because a large loom will not fit into a village house.

BUYING A RUG

Before you buy a rug, look at it by itself on the floor, to see that it lies straight – without waves or lumps. Check that the pattern is balanced, the borders are of the same dimensions, and the ends are roughly the same width. The colours should be clear and not bleeding into one another. Bargaining is essential *(see p130)*, as the first price given is likely to be at least 30% higher than the seller really expects.

Buying a good-quality old rug at a reasonable price, however, is a job for an expert. The age of a rug is ascertained from its colour, the quality of the weaving and the design. Check the pile to make sure that the surface has not been painted and look for any repairs – they can easily be seen on the back of the rug. The restoration of an old carpet is acceptable but the repair should not be too visible. Make sure the rug has a small lead seal attached to it, proving that it may be exported, and ask the shop for a receipt.

Kilim pieces are used to make a variety of smaller craft objects, also for sale in carpet shops.

Burdock motif

Chest motif

Motifs

The recurring motifs in rugs – some of them seemingly abstract, others more figurative – often have a surprising origin. For instance, many are derived from marks that nomads and villagers used for branding animals.

Motif from wolf track, crab or scorpion

Modern motif of a human figure

ENTERTAINMENT IN TURKEY

ALMOST EVERY town and village in Turkey enjoys an annual celebration – be it grease wrestling, bull butting or simply an agricultural festival where farmers can show off their new tractors. Some of these events hark back to ancient seasonal rites, such as the Giresun Aksu Festival on the Black Sea in May. Even though most of these activities are aimed at locals, you are sure to be made welcome or even be a guest of honour.

Football souvenir

Spectator sports have a very long history in Turkey. In classical times, the many amphitheatres of Anatolia hosted wrestling matches, circuses and risqué theatricals which were entertainment as much as sport. Today, the average Turk identifies more with football (soccer) than any other type of sport. Visitors will soon notice the coloured banners and car horns blasting in support of favourite teams such as Beşiktaş, Galatasaray and Fenerbahçe.

ENTERTAINMENT GUIDES

A NUMBER OF magazines list events and entertainment in Istanbul and elsewhere in the country. Visitors to Istanbul, Antalya and Bodrum should look for *The Guide*, while *The Gate* magazine is available free at airports. Turkish Airlines also has its own publication called *Skylife*. The quarterly Istanbul magazine, *Jazz*, is a good source of information on various local jazz clubs, events and musicians.

Bodrum events guide

CINEMA, THEATRE AND MUSIC FESTIVALS

TURKEY HAS a large cinema-going public. Most films are shown in their original language with Turkish subtitles. The top film event, the **Golden Orange Film Festival**, is held annually in

Golden Orange Film Festival poster

Antalya *(see p218–9)*. Other items on the arts calendar are the **International Opera and Ballet Festival** *(see p35)* held at Aspendos, as well as a series of Istanbul events that focus on theatre, classical music, film and jazz. Among these is the Istanbul Theatre Festival in May *(see Istanbul Festivals p132)*. An international arts biennale is scheduled for 2003 and 2005.

Music festivals, many held under the umbrella of the **Pozitif** collective, include the Akbank Jazz Festival, which is held during April and May in Istanbul, Ankara and other cities; the touring Efes Pilsen Blues Festival, which happens in autumn, and the Fuji Film World Music Days that takes place in Istanbul. There are occasional concerts in the amphitheatre at Ephesus.

DISCOS, NIGHT CLUBS AND BELLY DANCING

YOU WILL find huge, open-air discos in most summer resorts – Bodrum's Halikarnas *(see p194)* is the best known, with pillars and torchlight reminiscent of ancient times.

Despite a somewhat seedy reputation – especially in the back alleys of Istanbul – belly dancing *(see p23)* is outdoor family entertainment for Turks at seaside resorts in summer, and this is where you are likely to see the most authentic displays. Special tourist floor shows at hotels and holiday villages in

Halikarnas disco in Bodrum

season frequently include folk dancing and traditional music. Sufi whirling dervishes often put on performances for visitors, especially during the Mevlâna Festival in Konya in December *(see p37)*.

SPECTATOR SPORTS

ALTHOUGH football *(futbol)* is hugely popular, grease wrestling, or *yağlı güreş*, is Turkey's most time-honoured sport *(see p152)*. The main event is the four-day festival at **Kırkpınar**, near Edirne, in June. Wearing nothing but *kıspet* (black leather trousers soaked with olive oil), up to 1,000 men compete according to weight groups.

Camel wrestling *(see p37)* takes place every January and February. The biggest camel wrestling festivals are in Selçuk and around İzmir.

The Camel Classic Motor Racing series, which is held in the summer months, starts in Istanbul and follows a circuit that includes most of the western resort areas.

The major events on the horse racing calendar include

the Gazi Race, held at the **Veli Efendi Hippodrome** in Istanbul at the end of June, and the Presidential Cup in Ankara at the end of October.

The Mediterranean coastal town of Alanya *(see p226)* is the venue for the **Alanya International Triathlon** (swimming, cycling and foot races) in October. The world-famous **Istanbul Eurasia Marathon** usually takes place in September.

THEME PARKS

THEME PARKS are growing in popularity in Turkey. The exciting **Aqualand** water park *(see p219)* in Antalya provides a variety of thrills and controlled spills that will appeal to visitors of all ages.

Some of the big holiday villages around Kemer or Alanya even have their own mini theme parks tucked away within the hotel complex, but access to these is usually reserved for resident guests only.

Istanbul's **Tatilya** *(see p133)* is modelled on Walt Disney World.

Folk dancers performing at Ephesus

TRADITIONAL TURKISH MUSIC AND DANCE

TRADITIONAL Turkish music is regularly performed at the Cemal Reşit Rey Concert Hall in Istanbul. In summer, recitals of Turkish music are occasionally organized in the Basilica Cistern *(see p86)*, which has wonderful acoustics.

Traditional *Fasıl* music *(see pp22–3)* is best enjoyed live in *meyhanes* (concert halls) such as Ece, Kallavi and Hasır in Istanbul. *Fasıl* is performed on instruments which include the violin, *kanun* (zither), *tambur* and *ud* (both similar to the lute).

CHILDREN

CHILDREN are welcome and will be fussed over almost everywhere. However, there are relatively few attractions that have been planned with children in mind. Beaches and theme parks are good bets, and holiday villages always have programmes for children. In Istanbul, there are large parks at Yıldız *(see pp124–5)* and Emirgan *(see p141)*. Also near Emirgan is Park Orman, with picnic areas, a pool and theatre.

Rides at Tatilya theme park, near Istanbul

OUTDOOR ACTIVITIES AND SPECIALIST HOLIDAYS

Turkey's geographical and climatic diversity presents almost limitless possibilities for outdoor enthusiasts. Anatolian winters are ideal for skiers and mountaineers, and the long, hot Mediterranean summers are perfect for yacht cruises, diving and windsurfing. Although

Lycian Way marker

spring and autumn are quite short, the temperate conditions are pleasant for walking and cycling. Turkey also has many options for themed holidays suitable for individuals or groups with particular interests, or those who prefer a more in-depth slant on historic events or sporting activities.

WALKING AND TREKKING

Turkey's spectacular basalt and limestone mountain ranges provide ample opportunity for hiking. The first marked long-distance trek, the Lycian Way, was opened in 1999 along the Mediterranean coast (see p206). In central Turkey, the landscape of Cappadocia, with its celebrated "fairy chimneys" (see pp280–81), also has several signposted walks. A lack of detailed maps makes solo ventures difficult elsewhere.

Among the best areas for day walks and treks are the mountains of Lycia on the Mediterranean coast, as well as the Turkish Lake District around Eğirdir (see p254) and the Bolkar and Aladağlar ranges (part of the Taurus Mountains). In the northeast, the Kaçkar Mountains, with glaciers, lakes and peaks rising to 3,932 m (12,900 feet), offer excellent longer treks, albeit for a short season. The highest peak in Turkey is Mount Ararat (see p312–13), near the eastern border with Armenia, rising to 5,165 m (16,945 feet). Ararat has been

reopened after being off-limits for some time. Adventure outfits like **Exodus**, **Upcountry** and **World Expeditions** can organize guided treks. Those who wish to set out on their own can obtain the necessary permits from the **Ministry of Tourism** in Ankara.

MOUNTAINEERING, CLIMBING AND CANYONING

Turkey's mountain ranges offer excellent opportunities for serious climbers. Deep snow makes ski mountaineering in the Aladağlar and Kaçkar regions a good option for ski mountaineering. The **Söbek Turizm** agency can organize treks and guides. **Bougainville** and **Get Wet** offer canyoning excursions.

SKIING

Turkey's most popular ski centre is Uludağ, near Bursa (see p159). It has many lifts, a range of runs and views over the Sea of Marmara. Kartal, between Istanbul and Ankara, offers newer facilities and less crowded runs. Near

Isparta, the newly opened Davraz ski centre has a 50-bed hotel and a 1-km (0.5-mile) chairlift. Erciyes, near Kayseri has a hotel, reliable snowfalls and long runs. Palandöken (see p317) near Erzurum, combines a long season with good runs and accommodation.

Duru Turizm will make bookings at most ski resorts.

The rapids of the Çoruh River are only for experienced rafters

WHITEWATER RAFTING

In the northeast, the Çoruh River has Grade-5 rapids and is the ideal testing ground for serious rafters. Several overseas agencies offer trips. In contrast, day trips on the Köprülü River (between Antalya and Side) are suitable for families and novices. Many local agencies operate through the hotels or from Antalya city centre. Both **Alternatif Turizm** and **Adrift** offer Çoruh rafting tours; **Mithra Tourism** and others run day tours on the Köprülü River.

CYCLING

For the serious mountain biker (see p385), overseas agencies offer tours lasting several days, often starting high in the Taurus Mountains

The popular Palandöken ski resort near Erzurum

Parasailing above the Mediterranean coast near Ölü Deniz

and following forestry trails down to the Mediterranean coast. The spectacular eroded landscape of Cappadocia is a good area for day cycle hire, as it is relatively compact and the roads are generally safe and quiet. **Bougainville** and **Exodus** offer mountain bike tours; **Argeus** rents cycles and arranges tours.

HORSE RIDING AND PONY TREKKING

CAPPADOCIA'S trails weave through valleys and up-lands. **Bagana Ranch** near Antalya offers excellent accom-modation, lessons and trail ri-ding. In Istanbul, the **Klassis Golf and Country Club** has an indoor ring and jumping facilities. The best place for trail riding is the Equestrian Centre at Daday, a village near Kastamonu (see p264).

SAILING AND CRUISING HOLIDAYS

THE AEGEAN and western Mediterranean coasts are perfect for cruises aboard comfortable *gulets* (traditional wooden sailing vessels). One-or two-week cruises (called "blue voyages") are an excuse to relax, swim and sunbathe, with occasional forays ashore for shopping or dining. Those with a historical bent can combine one of these cruises with visits to the many fasci-nating ancient sites along the coast, guided by an expert in Greek and Roman history. The chain of marinas, each about a day's sailing apart, also offer secure moorings

and facilities for private yachts. **Arya Yachting** in Bodrum or the UK's **Alternative Travel Group** offer cruises; and **Westminster Classic Tours** and **Martin Randall** have cruises with lectures and site visits.

DIVING

MARMARIS, BODRUM, Fethiye Kaş and Alanya are all leading diving resorts, with warm water and excellent visibility. Here, qualified scuba instructors accredited to the Professional Association of Diving Instructors (PADI) take novices through their an internationally recognized diving certificate course. **Bougainville**, the **European Diving Centre** and **Alter-natif Turizm** can be recom-mended. **Bougainville** is one of the few agencies offering professional coaching for dis-abled divers. Some diving schools also arrange outings for sea kayakers.

BEACHES

TURKEY'S Mediterranean, Aegean and Black Sea coasts have many beaches, offering a wide range of seaside pursuits. Conditions are generally warm, though the Black Sea can be rough at times, with big waves. The Bodrum peninsula has ideal conditions for sailing and dinghy racing. Water-skiing, water parasailing and jet skiing are offered at major beachside hotels and resorts. The best place for swimming, water-skiing and windsurfing near Istanbul is the Princes' Islands (see p158). It is no longer possible to swim in the sea closer to Istanbul owing to heavy pollution.

HOTEL-BASED SPORTS

FIVE-STAR hotels in the major resorts have good hard tennis courts. Most four- and five-star hotels also organize table tennis, billiards, archery, step dancing and aerobics; even some three-star hotels offer beach volleyball and excellent swimming pools.

GOLF

THE MILD winter and early spring make golf a year-round sport in Turkey. There are four purpose-built courses at Belek, east of Antalya (see p224). **Palmiye Tours** can arrange tailor-made tours for amateurs or championship golfers. Near Istanbul, the **Kemer** and **Klassis** country clubs offer first-rate courses.

Diving school in Marmaris, offering courses at all skill levels

HISTORICAL AND CULTURAL TOURS

GIVEN TURKEY'S wealth and variety of historic sites, it is no surprise that these are what attract most visitors to the country. Tourists who wish to visit ancient and classical sites can do so in the company of an expert in the field. The classical sites of the west and south, Ephesus *(see pp182–3)* and Pergamum *(see pp176–7)* in particular, draw large crowds of visitors, especially in the summer months. Others now under excavation, such as Sagalassos and Aphrodisias *(see pp188–9)*, are also very impressive and may be less congested. Some sites, such as Patara and Xanthos *(see p214)* – whose chief tombs are now on view in the British Museum – can be visited as part of a *gulet* tour *(see p363)*.

Istanbul deserves careful exploration, particularly its churches, mosques and museums. Since the major sites in Istanbul and around Göreme in Cappadocia are situated fairly close together, walking tours are an attractive option.

Much more recent history is movingly commemorated on the Gallipoli peninsula *(see pp168–9)*, site of some of the fiercest and most tragic battles of World War I. **British Museum Traveller** and **Andante Travels** run tours of the classical sites. Andante and **Martin Randall** offer cultural tours of Istanbul. **Troy-Anzac** have been arranging tours to the Dardanelles and Gallipoli for 30 years.

Memorial cemetery, Gallipoli

WILDLIFE TOURS

TURKEY'S DIVERSE habitats support many endemic plant species, especially of orchids and bulbs, with tulips being perhaps the best-known examples. This diversity, coupled with the country's pivotal position along migration routes between Europe, Asia and Africa, assures the presence of numerous bird species from three continents. In spring and autumn, over 200 species can be spotted in the course of a two-week holiday. DHKD, a local conservation group, records observations and works to preserve habitats such as wetlands. In-depth birding holidays are available from **Greentours**.

Marble head of Athena

The House of the Virgin Mary, near Ephesus *(see p182)*

RELIGIOUS TOURS

MODERN-DAY pilgrims can follow in the footsteps of the Apostle Paul, whose faith led him from Tarsus to Ephesus and beyond. Visitors can tour the "Seven Churches" founded by Paul, and see the small house near Ephesus where the Virgin Mary is said to have spent her last days.

There are also quite a few Armenian and Greek Orthodox churches in Istanbul *(see p114)* that are still active. In southeastern Turkey, there are haunting Syrian Orthodox churches and monasteries.

Both **Pacha Tours** and **Rainbow Tours** offer specialist itineraries that trace the wanderings of St Paul.

A bird hide in the Göksu Delta, near Silifke

RAIL TOURS

TURKEY'S RAIL NETWORK *(see pp380–81)* is extensive, but has slow trains and outdated rolling stock. However, the old-fashioned couchettes and dining carriages offer a relaxed, interesting way to see the country.

For rail buffs, there is an open-air rail museum at Çamlık, near Selçuk *(see p180)*, with well-marked displays and fine examples of vintage steam locomotives.

The most popular rail trips are from Istanbul to Kars, close to the Armenian border, and from Istanbul to Van in the southeast (which includes a ferry crossing of Lake Van). Both journeys take around three days, and are better undertaken in shorter hops. The Dutch company **SNP Reiswinkel** offers tours of the Istanbul–Kars route, with day breaks for exploration on foot.

OTHER SPECIALIST HOLIDAYS

SEVERAL OPERATORS offer more specialized holidays that involve particular pursuits such as photography, or painting and sketching.

Several other companies have begun to use Turkey's relaxed holiday atmosphere and natural beauty to offer breaks which include such activities as yoga, massage, tai chi and meditation.

Professionally led courses and programmes are available at **Huzur Vadisi**, inland from Göcek, and at the **Gölköy Centre** near Bodrum.

DIRECTORY

MINISTRY OF TOURISM

(For general information and trekking permits)
İsmet İnönü Bul 5,
Bahçelievler, Ankara.
☎ (0312) 212 83 00.
FAX (0312) 213 98 00.

ADVENTURE TRAVEL COMPANIES

Bougainville
İbrahim Serin Cad, Kaş.
☎ (0242) 836 37 37.
W www.bougainville-turkey.com

Exodus
9 Weir Road, London,
SW12 OLT, UK.
☎ (44) 020 8675 5550.
FAX (44) 020 8673 0779.

WALKING AND TREKKING

Exodus
(see Adventure Companies)

Upcountry
PK 745, Antalya.
☎ (0242) 243 11 48.
FAX (0242) 241 00 39.
W www.lycianway.com

World Expeditions
441 Kent St, Sydney,
NSW 2000, Australia.
☎ (61) 2 9264 3 36.
FAX (61) 2 9261 19 74.

MOUNTAINEERING, CLIMBING AND CANYONING

Sobek Turizm
İstasyon Cad 42, Niğde.
☎ (0388) 213 21 17.

Get Wet
☎ (0242) 753 40 71.

SKIING

Duru Turizm
Cumhuriyet Cad 245–7,
Harbiye, İstanbul.
☎ (0212) 246 50 60.
@ turkia@duru.com.tr

WHITEWATER RAFTING

Adrift
127 High St,
Hungerford RG17 0DL, UK.
☎ (44) 1488 684 509.

Alternatif Turizm
Çamlık Sok, Marmaris.
☎ (0252) 413 59 94.
W www.alternatifraft.com

Mithra Tourism
Kılıçaslan Mah,
Hesapçlı Sok 7.
FAX (0242) 247 65 53.
W www.mithratravel.com

CYCLING

Argeus
İstiklal Cad 13, Ürgüp.
☎ (0384) 341 46 88.
W www.argeus.com.tr

Bougainville & Exodus
(see Adventure Companies)

HORSE RIDING AND PONY TREKKING

Bagana Ranch
near Antalya.
☎ (0242) 425 22 70.
FAX (0242) 425 20 55.
@ bagana@antnet.net.tr

Klassis Golf and Country Club
Seyman Köyü, Altıntepe
Mevkii, Silivri (W of
İstanbul).
☎ (0212) 748 46 00.
FAX (0212) 748 46 43.

SAILING AND CRUISING HOLIDAYS

Alternative Travel Group
69–71 Banbury Road,
Oxford OX2 6PE, UK.
☎ (44) 1865 315 678.
FAX (44) 1865 315 697.

Arya Yachting
Caferpaşa Cad, Mildos
Evleri 25/1, Bodrum.
☎ (0252) 316 15 80.
FAX (0252) 316 50 59
W www.arya.com.tr.

Martin Randall
Barley Mow Passage, Chiswick, London W4 4PH, UK.
☎ (44) 20 8742 3355.
FAX (44) 20 8742 1066.
W www.martinrandall.com

Westminster Classic Tours
Suite 120, 266 Banbury
Road, Summertown,
Oxford OX2 7DL, UK.
☎ (44) 1865 728 565.
FAX (44) 1865 728 575.

DIVING

Alternatif Turizm
(see Whitewater Rafting).

Bougainville
(see Adventure Companies)

European Diving Centre
PK 26 48301, Fethiye.
☎ (0252) 614 97 71.
@ europeandiving@superonline.com

GOLF

Kemer Golf and Country Club
Göktürk Beldesi,
Kemerburgaz, İstanbul.
☎ (0212) 239 77 70.
W www.kg-cc.com

Klassis Golf and Country Club
Seyman Köyü, Altıntepe
Mevkii, Silivri.
☎ (0212) 748 46 00.
FAX (0212) 748 46 43.

Palmiye Tours
Işıklar Cad 57, Antalya.
☎ (0242) 243 15 00.
W www.pamfilya.com.tr

HISTORICAL AND CULTURAL TOURS

Andante Travels
Winterbourne Dauntsey,
Salisbury SP4 6EH, UK.
☎ (44) 1980 610 555.
FAX (44) 1980 610 002.

British Museum Traveller
46 Bloomsbury St, London
WC1B 3QQ, UK.

☎ (44) 20 7323 88 95.
FAX (44) 20 7580 86 77.

Martin Randall
(see Sailing and Cruising)

Troy-Anzac Tours
Yalı Cad 2, Çanakkale.
☎ (0286) 217 58 90.
W www.troyanzac.com

WILDLIFE TOURS

Greentours
High St, Longnor, Buxton
SK17 0PG, UK.
☎ (44) 1298 83563.
@ info@greentours.co.uk

RELIGIOUS TOURS

Pacha Tours
156 Broadway, Suite 316,
New York 10036, USA.
☎ (1) 212 764 40 80.
FAX (1) 212 764 56 42.

Rainbow Tours
Fevzi Paşa Bul 138/601,
Çankaya, İzmir.
☎ (0232) 446 16 38.
FAX (0232) 441 41 83.

RAIL TOURS

SNP Reiswinkel
Groesveekseweg 181,
Nijmegen, Netherlands.
☎ (30) 024 360 52 22.
FAX (30) 024 360 14 22.

OTHER SPECIALIST HOLIDAYS

Fotografevi
(photographic tours)
Tütüncü Çıkmazı 6,
Galatasaray, Beyoğlu.
☎ (0212) 251 05 66.

Gölköy Centre
☎ (0252) 257 72 07.

Huzur Vadisi
United Kingdom
☎ (44) 1970 626 821.

Jenny McGuire
(painting and sketching)
Kaş and Marmaris.
@ freespirit@shabakah.net.sa

SURVIVAL
GUIDE

PRACTICAL INFORMATION

MANY FIRST-TIME VISITORS to Turkey expect the country to be sedate and reserved due to the influence of Islam, so the exuberant and lively character of Turkish life comes as a pleasant surprise. Observing a few customs and learning some basic Turkish words or phrases will get you off to a good start. Show respect for the laws of the country,

Official sign to a tourist sight

as well as for religious differences, culture and class structure. Although you may not agree with the beliefs or politics, opinions are the least acceptable way to promote friendships. With very few exceptions, Turks are uninhibited when it comes to friendship and hospitality and will welcome any effort to appreciate their lifestyle and respect their traditions.

VISAS

THE VISA situation changes frequently, depending on political circumstances. Most tourist visas are issued for three calendar months, and bar the holder from working at any job. Overstaying the three-month limit incurs a fine, which can escalate alarmingly. Most tourist visas can be obtained at the airport or overland entry point, but the visa process is more complicated if you arrive by sea. Citizens of some countries need to obtain visas before arrival. For up-to-date requirements, contact the Turkish consulate or embassy in your country.

Customs service emblem

CUSTOMS

ONLY AIRPORTS and main road entry points offer full customs service. At major ports or marinas, customs hours are 8:30am–5:30pm weekdays. If you arrive or leave outside these hours in your own yacht or on a ferry, where a visa is required, you will have to pay a fee to activate a customs official.

Import limits are generous, with a few exceptions. You can buy duty-free items at the airport on entering Turkey. However, it is often more economical to buy cartons of cigarettes and local spirits from retail stores rather than from the duty-free shops.

Visitors over 18 years can bring in generous amounts of coffee, perfume (5 bottles), spirits (5 litres/185 fl oz) and cigarettes (500).

There is no limit on the amount of foreign currency or Turkish lira you can bring into the country, but on leaving you may take out a maximum of US$5,000 (or Turkish lira equivalent). In practice, though, this rule is rarely enforced.

Turkey is extremely strict regarding drugs. Sniffer dogs are in use at Atatürk Airport in Istanbul and will be used at other airports in the future.

You need to have a permit if you wish to take antiquities out of Turkey (see p355). Any high-value items, such as a car, will be entered in your passport at the customs entry point. You have to take the same item with you when you leave Turkey. Contact the Turkish consulate or embassy in your country for full details on what can and cannot be brought into Turkey.

If you have a car entered in your passport, you will not be allowed to make a day trip to neighbouring Greek islands.

ETIQUETTE

TURKS TEND TO dress smartly. In eastern areas, women usually cover their arms and legs in public. Although it is a matter of choice, increasing numbers of women cover their heads. Visitors are not expected to follow suit, but some Turks may be offended at exposed limbs. Mosques have strict dress codes (see p33).

Traditional rules of etiquette and hospitality still play an important part in Turkish society. Even though the persistence of carpet sellers can be annoying, always try to remain polite but firm. At all times show respect for Atatürk (see p58), whose picture you will see in offices, shops and public places.

Gay and lesbian visitors are unlikely to experience problems, but overt displays of affection are best kept to a minimum in Muslim countries. Homosexual culture is not new to Turkey, and Istanbul in particular has a lively gay scene.

Wearing the veil, a matter of personal choice for Turkish women

◁ **Boats in the harbour at Alanya, with the 13th-century Red Tower in the background**

Bazaar shops in Kayseri, Cappadocia

LANGUAGE

EVEN IF YOU learn only a few Turkish words, the effort will be worth it. Turks will respect any attempt at their difficult language. In cities, English-speakers can always be found. Menus are printed in several languages, and most shopkeepers can speak one other language.

PUBLIC CONVENIENCES

PUBLIC TOILETS are marked *Bay* for men and *Bayan* for women. A fee is usually charged for use. If you are squeamish about using the old-fashioned squat toilets, you can go to any restaurant, hotel or café and ask to use their modern flush toilets. Some motorway service areas have pristine washroom facilities for which there is no charge.

Sign for a public toilet

SMOKING

SMOKING IS NOW prohibited in government offices, on public transport, including dolmuşes and intercity buses (except for the driver), on all Turkish Airlines domestic flights and inside airport terminals. Restaurants are beginning to have sections for non-smokers and some hotels maintain non-smoking floors.

OPENING HOURS

TURKEY GENERALLY follows western working hours. Banks and offices are open from 9am to 5pm, although half-hour variations are common. Government offices close between noon and 1pm; so do some banks. Most official businesses are closed on weekends. In tourist areas, however, post offices often stay open seven days a week and until late at night.

Officially, museums are open from 9am to 5pm, but in practice opening hours vary considerably, as does the statutory closure day during the week. Some smaller establishments close for an hour at lunch time. Major museums are usually open all year round, but some small sites may close in winter. Local tourist offices know the latest information and visitors should double-check opening times before setting out on any sightseeing expedition.

TIME

TURKEY IS TWO HOURS ahead of Greenwich Mean Time, and clocks are synchronized to daylight saving time with the rest of Europe.

ELECTRICITY

TURKEY'S ELECTRICAL current is 220–240 volts AC. Plugs have two round pins, but two separate diameters, which fit all local sockets and most European two-pin plugs. Bring a universal adaptor for other voltages.

Power cuts are a fact of life, particularly outside the cities.

DIRECTORY

CONSULATES IN ISTANBUL

Australia
Tepecik Yolu 58, Etiler.
((0212) 257 70 50.

Canada
İstiklal Cad 373/5, Beyoğlu.
((0212) 251 98 38.

New Zealand
Level 24, Maya Akar Centre, Büyükdere Cad 100/102, Esentepe.
((0212) 275 29 89.

United Kingdom
Meşrutiyet Cad 34, Tepebaşı.
((0212) 293 75 40.

United States
Meşrutiyet Cad 104/108, Tepebaşı.
((0212) 251 36 02.

CUSTOMS INFORMATION

The main customs office (ask for Alo Gümrük) in Ankara will answer queries in English. Their informative website details items that can be brought into Turkey.

((0312) 311 79 71.

w www.gumruk.gov.tr

w www.turkey.org (for general information on visas and entry requirements).

TURKISH EMBASSIES AROUND THE WORLD

Australia
60 Mugga Way, Red Hill, Canberra, ACT, 2603.
((2) 62 95 02 27.

Canada
197 Wurtemburg Street, Ottawa, Ontario KIN 8L9.
((613) 789 40 44.

United Kingdom
43 Belgrave Square, London, SWIX 8PA
((44) 207 393 02 02.

United States
2525 Massachusetts Ave NW, Washington, DC, 20008,
((202) 612 67 40.

Personal Security and Health

Emblem of the Turkish police

For the sensible visitor, Turkey is as safe to visit as anywhere else. Bear in mind that the country has undergone rapid social change in a relatively short period, and urban centres bulge with people who have recently abandoned traditional ways of life. Unemployment is high, and there is a huge gap between rich and poor. Health care is of a high standard, with a thriving private health sector alongside the state-run system. It is essential to keep basic immunization up to date before you travel. Turkey is not as hygiene-conscious as you might expect an Islamic country to be.

POLICE

There are a number of police forces in Turkey, with responsibilities varying from traffic control to rapid response motorcycle units (Dolphin Police). The Jandarma, who are attached to the army, are responsible for policing rural areas. Special tourism police *(Turizm Polisi)* operate in Istanbul. In smaller towns, the *Emniyet Polisi* (Security Police) carry out law-enforcement duties.

Badge of Dolphin rapid-reaction unit

It is obligatory to carry some form of identification with you in Turkey. Police or Jandarma carry out spot checks on cars, buses and trucks. A passport or driving licence is usually sufficient.

Police officers are usually very helpful, but should you need help, the first place to contact is your embassy. Most countries have missions in Ankara and some have consulates in Istanbul *(see p369)*, İzmir or Antalya.

PERSONAL SECURITY

Do not wander off into lonely places, wherever you are. Do not pick up hitchhikers or offer to take people you don't know across the border. Never act as a courier for anyone else, into or out of Turkey.

Turkey has lower levels of crime than other countries. However, this is not the case in Istanbul, where crime is rising. Be vigilant and always know where your wallet and passport are. Pickpockets abound, although violence against foreigners is rare.

Women are no more at risk in Turkey than anywhere else. It makes sense, however, if possible, to travel with friends or in a group, and to stay in built-up areas.

Several provinces that were formerly under emergency rule (OHAL) are reopening to tourism. The areas of Siirt, Mardin, Hakkari, Şırnak, Diyakbakır and Batman are still under martial law; check with your embassy on the latest developments in these areas before planning a trip.

TURKISH TRADITIONS

The army, Atatürk and the Turkish flag are three of the fundamental symbols of Turkish identity. Disrespect towards any of these is seen as an insult to the state.

PHOTOGRAPHY

Always ask permission before taking photographs in any public places or of individuals. Taking photos of military installations is strictly forbidden.

HEALTH AND HYGIENE

Bottled spring water

Before arriving in Turkey, be sure that your basic inoculations (diphtheria, polio, typhoid and tetanus) are all up to date. Check with your doctor about hepatitis A and hepatitis B. Malaria persists in the east; use the best medication available, and remember to continue it for the required period after your trip.

Some visitors experience digestive upsets due to the amount of oil used in Turkish cooking. Try to eat lightly for the first few days and keep alcohol intake to a minimum.

Bottled water is safer to drink than tap water. Drink plenty of water or fruit juices.

Grilled meat is sometimes served lightly cooked. Ask for it *iyi pişmiş* (well cooked). In summer, avoid foods that may have been sitting in the sun.

Security policeman

Traffic policeman

Dolphin policeman

Turkish Security Police *(Emniyet Polisi)* patrol car

State ambulance in Istanbul

HOSPITALS

THE TURKISH health system has public and private hospitals. Private hospitals are well equipped and staffed, and are on the whole more comfortable than the state hospitals. Private hospitals may run their own ambulance services. Doctors at private hospitals are more likely to speak foreign languages.

It is strongly recommended that you take out both travel and medical insurance before you leave, or a policy that incorporates both. It may also be useful to have a policy that covers repatriation in an emergency. The state health system has few reciprocal agreements with other countries. You have to pay for treatment and then claim the amount back from your insurance company. State and private medical facilities accept major credit cards.

PHARMACIES

MOST NON-PRESCRIPTION medications are available from an *eczane* (pharmacy or chemist) at reasonable prices. Visitors are allowed to bring into the country sufficient quantities of medications that are required regularly.

Turkish pharmacists are well-trained and professional; most are also trained to give *iğne* (injections). Every area district has a *nobetci eczane* (duty pharmacist) outside normal business hours. The name is usually posted in a pharmacy window or, sometimes, as in Taksim Square in Istanbul, it is displayed prominently on an electronic billboard.

Condoms are readily and easily available in almost all pharmacies, even if not on display. Ask for a *prezervatif*.

ANIMALS AND INSECTS

BY FAR THE worst pests are mosquitoes, particularly in coastal areas. Many local repellents are available, such as Esem-Mat. Immunization clinics are the best place to buy anti-mosquito supplies. The Turkish for mosquito is *sivrisinek* (sharp fly).

At the seaside, watch out for a sea anemone known as *karadikiş* or *deniz kestanesi* (sea chestnut) clinging to the rocks. If you step on one, do not try to extract the quills; seek medical attention right away. In rocky terrain, look out for scorpions and snakes.

Don't approach, encourage or pet stray animals. If you are hiking in remote areas, you may come across shepherd dogs. These look fierce but are rarely aggressive unless you come between the dog and his flock.

Typical sign for a pharmacy in Istanbul

DIRECTORY

EMERGENCY NUMBERS

Police (emergency)
155.

Ambulance
112.

Jandarma
156.

Fire
110.

Tourism Police
Yerebatan Cad 6
Sultanahmet, Istanbul.
(0212) 527 45 03 and 528 53 69.

HOSPITALS

Admiral Bristol (American Hospital) in Istanbul
Güzelbahçe Sok 20,
Nişantaşı, Istanbul.
(0212) 231 40 50.

German Hospital
Sıraselviler Cad 119,
Taksim, Istanbul.
(0212) 293 21 50.

International Hospital
Istanbul Cad 82,
Yeşilköy, Istanbul.
(0212) 663 30 00.

Bayındır Medical Centre
Kızılırmak Mahallesi, 28 Sok
2 Söğütözü, Ankara.
(0312) 287 90 00.

Ahu Hetman Hospital
167 Sokak 3, Marmaris.
(0252) 413 14 15.

Fethiye Private Letoon Hospital
Antalya Yolu Taris Sokak, Fethiye.
(0252) 646 51 51.

Antalya International Hospital
Kızıltoprak Mahallesi,
933 Sokak 6, Antalya.
(0242) 311 15 00.

Özel Hayat Hastanesi
Şekerhane Mahallesi,
Yayla Yolu Civarı, Alanya.
(0242) 512 42 51/44 38.

Banking and Currency

THERE IS NO LIMIT on the amount of currency (foreign or Turkish) you can bring into Turkey. Many establishments accept major foreign currencies, but you should have a reasonable amount of Turkish lira with you as well. The rate usually goes up, so try not to exchange money before you need it. The exchange rate within Turkey will be much higher than abroad. Exchange rates for the main currencies are shown daily in the newspapers and on television and occasionally hit the headlines. Visitors will have few problems in paying by credit card, using automated teller machines (ATMs) or negotiating other money matters.

Cash dispenser with instructions in a range of languages

BANKS

BANKING HOURS run from Monday to Friday, 9am to 12:30pm, and from 1:30 to 5:30pm. Some banks, such as Garanti Bankası, remain open over the lunch hour and are experimenting with Saturday trading. Queues are long in banks and you have to take a number and wait for service.

Several Turkish banks have outlets at airports, offering a full range of banking services. If you are leaving Turkey by air, note that there are no banking facilities after you have passed through the customs and security check.

CHANGING MONEY

EXCHANGE BUREAUX (*döviz para*) are found in most towns, and this is the most reliable way to change money at a reasonable rate of exchange. These offer the best rates for foreign currencies, usually without the tedium of queuing at a bank. Rates are displayed daily on an electronic board. Exchange bureaux are usually open Monday to Saturday, but if you go before about 10am you will get the previous day's exchange rate.

Hotels, some shops and other retail outlets will change money for you, but the rate will not be to your advantage. If you are bargaining for an item, remember that foreign currency is acceptable, if not

Rates of exchange outside a *döviz*

preferable, and makes a good bargaining lever. It is always a good idea to bring some foreign notes with you.

CREDIT CARDS AND DEBIT CARDS

ATMS ARE FOUND all over Turkey, even in remote, small towns. They are often located at an outer entrance to a bank, to provide 24-hour service. Machines accept Visa and MasterCard (Access) and American Express, as well as debit cards for many international banks, such as HSBC and Citibank. Before leaving, ask your bank if its card is accepted internationally. It may be necessary to activate this service if you have not used it before.

The most versatile ATMs are those with the Cirrus or Plus interbank logo. You can usually take out funds up to your daily credit limit. However, state-run banks such as İş Bankası usually issue a maximum of 50 million Turkish lira in a single transaction, no matter which card you use.

You can use credit cards all over Turkey to pay for almost anything, including intercity bus tickets, car rental and meals. Smaller establishments may not take cards in winter, even if they do so in summer.

There is no commission on credit cards; even places that used to charge it, such as petrol stations, now display signs saying *kredi kartı*

komisyonu sıfırdır (without commission). If you buy an airline ticket from a travel agent, however, they will charge about 3 per cent commission on the fare.

TRAVELLER'S CHEQUES

ATMS HAVE practically made these obsolete. The only place to cash traveller's cheques without fuss is at the arrivals terminal at Atatürk International Airport. Some banks will oblige, but will charge a hefty commission.

TAX

VALUE-ADDED tax (KDV in Turkish) is included in all prices. It is currently 18 per cent. If you need a receipt for purchases, ask for a *fiş*; if you require an invoice, ask for a *fatura*. For information on tax refunds, see p354.

CURRENCY

THE CURRENCY of Turkey is the Turkish lira, abbreviated to TL. There are no smaller units. The lira has one of the lowest unit values in the world, with inflation currently at 70 per cent per annum. It may be useful to carry a small calculator as you will be dealing with millions of lira at a time. High-denomination banknotes cannot always be changed in smaller shops, so try to carry a range of notes. Small change is now practically worthless.

Banknotes

Turkish banknotes come in denominations ranging from 100,000 TL to 20 million TL, all bearing the head of Atatürk on one side. Some of the higher denomination notes are similar in colour and can easily be confused – take extra care when handling them and be wary of unscrupulous traders, who may try to exploit their similarity.

100,000 lira

250,000 lira

500,000 lira

1 million lira

5 million lira

10 million lira

Coins

Coins range from 25,000 TL to 250,000 TL. Those shown here (at their actual sizes) are for 25,000 TL and 50,000 TL. A smaller 50,000 TL coin, and 100,000 and 250,000 TL coins are also now in circulation.

25,000 lira

50,000 lira

Communications

**PTT sign on a
letter box**

THE TELEPHONE AND POSTAL services in
Turkey used to operate as a single
unit until 1996, when they were split
up to create Türk Telekom (telephone)
and the PTT (the postal service). Each
remains a government monopoly. The
Turkish administration has invested
heavily in the communications sector
and even remote villages have fibre-
optic telephone lines. Most major cities enjoy high-
speed Internet access. New-style phones are rapidly
replacing older ones in all the large cities. Note that
the older phones use different cards.

Post offices, or PTTs, can be used for sending letters
and making telephone calls. Many also change foreign
currency. Although the PTT has been neglected when
compared with the telephone system, the service is
reliable and it is rare for letters or parcels to go astray.

USING A CARD PHONE

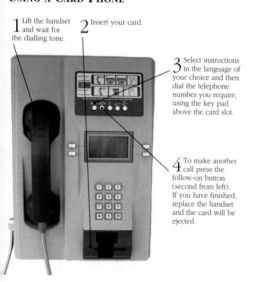

1 Lift the handset
and wait for
the dialling tone.

2 Insert your card.

3 Select instructions
in the language of
your choice and then
dial the telephone
number you require,
using the key pad
above the card slot.

4 To make another
call press the
follow-on button
(second from left).
If you have finished,
replace the handset
and the card will be
ejected.

**Akıllı phonecards, featuring
portraits of historical figures**

buy one from a post office,
ask to have it tested before
you pay for it. Staff will run
it through a demo telephone.
Note that the telephone token
(jeton), formerly in wide use,
is now almost obsolete.

Akıllı (smart) phonecards
are rigid, and are accepted
only by the new-style phones.

Some telephones in airports
or luxury hotels will accept
credit cards such as Visa and
MasterCard. Generally, local
telephones are programmed to
accept local credit cards only.

MOBILE PHONES

TURKEY'S TWO MAIN mobile
(cellular) phone operators
are Turkcell and Telsim. Turkcell has roaming agreements
with over 120 countries on the
900 MHz band, which means
that most people in Europe,
Africa or Asia can use their
existing cellphone and subscri-
ber identification module (SIM
card) via this network. If you
need to key in Turkcell's GSM
network selection number ma-
nually, the number is 28601.

North American cellular
phones operate on different
frequencies and wireless standards, so you will need a dual
or tri-band handset to use

USING PUBLIC
TELEPHONES

TELEPHONE CALLS can be
made either from public
call boxes, post offices or
small but convenient telephone "boutiques". Mobile
(cellular) phones have helped
to relieve some of the congestion at public call boxes,
which are usually grouped in
main squares, at transport
hubs or near post offices. The
most economical way to telephone locally or internationally is by using a phonecard.

Flexible cards for the old-style
phones come in units of 30,
60, 100, 120 and 180. These
can be purchased from
all post offices and, for
an additional charge,
from street sellers and
kiosks. After you pick
up the receiver, the
display screen will
prompt you to select
the language of your
choice, and insert your
card. A panel then shows the
number of units remaining on
your card. Note that phonecards can be unreliable; if you

**Mobile phone
company
logo**

them in Turkey. Many
people prefer to use a
prepaid card, known
as Hazır Kart. Pre-paid
subscribers now vastly
outnumber post-paid
ones and the service is
much more economi-
cal, even if less tech-
nologically oriented.
Your pre-paid SIM card can
be topped up at the well-
marked outlets which are
found all over Turkey.

COUNTRY DIRECT SERVICE

IF YOUR LOCAL telephone company has a direct-access calling card, you can use this from Turkey (including pay telephones and hotels) to contact an operator in your own country. Calls will be billed to your home number at your local international tariff (and discount) rate. As Turkish telephone rates are relatively expensive, it is well worth obtaining details about country-direct services from your telephone provider.

REACHING THE RIGHT NUMBER

• Istanbul is divided into two area codes:
0212 (European side)
0216 (Asian side)
• To call a number on the same side of Istanbul, dial only the seven-digit number. To call the other side, dial as intercity.
• To call another city in Turkey, dial the four-digit area code before the seven-digit number, for example: 0224 for Bursa.
• To call Turkey from abroad, the country code is 90, omit the zero of the local area code, followed by the seven-digit number.
• For international calls, dial 00 followed by the country code: Canada 1; Republic of Ireland 353; United Kingdom 44; US 1; South Africa 27; Australia 61; New Zealand 64.

OPERATOR SERVICES

Directory Enquiries
[118.

Inter-City Operator
[131.

International Operator
[115.

Wake-Up Call Service
[135.
Note: only international operators are guaranteed to speak English.

An Internet café in İzmir, one of thousands all over Turkey

INTERNET ACCESS

INTERNET CAFÉS have sprung up all over Turkey. If you need to find one, ask at the local tourist office. Charges are only a few dollars for an hour of browsing; for e-mail access, you will be charged for the time used. Travel agents will sometimes let you use their Internet facilities.

Foreign newspapers and magazines on sale in Ankara

NEWSPAPERS AND MAGAZINES

MANY ENGLISH-LANGUAGE publications are available in major centres in Turkey via newsagents or Dünya outlets. Foreign-language newspapers are available the following day from newsstands. Weekly magazines such as *Time* and *Newsweek* are readily found, even if less prominently, outside Istanbul and Ankara.

POSTAL SERVICES

POSTCARDS OR LETTERS sent from Turkey to Europe or North America automatically go via air mail. Letters, postcards and smaller packages are weighed at post offices and charged according to a price scale which may or may not be on display.

The PTT has a monopoly on all mail, and post offices are the only places to send and receive any mail. Outside Istanbul, the PTT acts for the customs office by collecting duties on parcels. Fees are levied arbitrarily on incoming mail and parcels, and even sometimes on *poste restante* letters. If you are sending a package, leave it open for inspection. Mail is delayed for weeks when items have to be opened, inspected and signed by customs. Do not send anything valuable or urgent by post. Tourist offices sometimes receive mail for visitors; this option usually ensures that such items are received promptly and intact.

Letters between Turkey and Europe average 7–10 days in transit. For other continents, count on 14 days or more. Many people use APS (Acele Posta Servisi), a recorded-delivery service, which takes two or three days within Turkey but can be pricey for international delivery. All the major international courier services operate in Turkey.

Postage stamps in 500,000, 300,000, 250,000 and 750,000 lira denominations

TRAVEL INFORMATION

Emblem of Turkish Airlines

THE EASIEST WAY to get to Turkey is to fly directly to Istanbul. Turkish Airlines (THY) has regular, direct flights from 113 destinations in Europe, North America and Asia and has proved a reliable carrier over the years. Several major European carriers, including Lufthansa and KLM, fly direct, while Air Canada and American Airlines also have routes to Istanbul. A new international airport on the Asian side of Istanbul has been completed, but is not yet in service.

Turkish Airlines operates an extensive domestic network, with routes focused on Istanbul or Ankara. Flights between İzmir and Antalya, or Erzurum and Samsun, for example, will invariably go via Istanbul or Ankara.

ARRIVING BY AIR

MOST VISITORS will arrive at Istanbul's Atatürk Airport (Atatürk Havalimani). For onward travel within Turkey, you will have to change to a domestic THY flight. Atatürk Airport has a separate terminal for domestic flights.

Major European carriers, such as Lufthansa, KLM, Air France and British Airways, all have at least one flight daily to Istanbul. American Airlines, Air Canada, Quantas and other international carriers also serve Istanbul, though not always by direct flight.

May to October is peak season, but flights tend to fill up during school or religious holidays (including the annual Muslim pilgrimage to Mecca, the date of which varies with the lunar calendar).

ATATÜRK AIRPORT

PASSENGERS ARRIVE at the *dış hatları* (international) terminal. If you are travelling on to another destination in Turkey, you will be taken as a transit passenger to the *iç hatları* (domestic) terminal.

The spacious modern arrivals hall at Atatürk Airport

Procedures for passengers in transit are confusing and not standardized, so it pays to be vigilant and to ask questions. THY staff are usually on hand as you exit the aircraft.

Depending on which airline or charter company you are flying with, you clear customs *(gümrük)* either in Istanbul or at your final destination. There are few customs formalities for foreigners entering Turkey. Remember that you can buy duty-free goods upon entry. For further details on custom allowances, see p368.

If you have cleared customs in Istanbul and are continuing your journey as a domestic passenger, a shuttle *(minibüs)* service will take you to the domestic terminal. There is a small charge for the inter-terminal shuttle bus. Note that taxis are generally reluctant to make the five-minute journey.

CHARTER FLIGHTS AND PACKAGE HOLIDAYS

ARRIVING ON A charter flight is generally a cheaper option, and most charter flights land in Istanbul. Two operators, Sun Express and Öger Tours, fly direct to Bayındır International Airport in Antalya. Sun Express runs regular direct charter flights to Antalya from Frankfurt and London in partnership with Turkish Airlines. Öger Tours operates from Hamburg, with a stop at Munich.

The western Mediterranean region is served by Dalaman Airport, which handles mainly short take-off and landing (STOL) charter flights from western Europe. Turkish Airlines runs limited regular flights between Istanbul and Dalaman all year round. The new Bodrum-Milas Airport is convenient for many Aegean destinations.

Taxi rank outside the domestic terminal at Atatürk Airport

DOMESTIC AIR TRAVEL

ALL MAJOR CENTRES in Turkey are linked by the Turkish Airways network. A recent innovation now makes it possible to book seats on domestic flights from outside Turkey. This can be done either over the Internet or by going to a Turkish Airlines sales office. You will save money if you pay for flight reservations after your arrival in Turkey.

The national carrier runs summer and winter schedules to its 35 local destinations, and adds extra flights for the busy summer season. Only the major cities have non-stop flights, though. Other flights go via Ankara or Istanbul, or there may be one direct flight per day, with others involving flight transfers. Summer and winter schedules are available from all THY regional and international offices, as well as on the Internet.

A Turkish Airlines Airbus A-340 taking off

FLYING WITHIN TURKEY

IF YOU ARE TAKING A DOMESTIC flight, you have to be at the airport an hour before the flight leaves. If you have no baggage to check, you can arrive later. If this the case, go to the counter displaying the *el bagajı* (hand luggage) sign. Try to go through the security check as early as possible, as this gets extremely busy. For security reasons, you will be required to identify your bags to the baggage handling crew before being allowed to take your seat on the aircraft.

On domestic flights, there is not much difference between business class and economy. If economy class is full, you will usually be able to purchase a ticket in business class at a higher price, but both classes offer identical three-abreast seating and a boxed snack. There is no smoking on any domestic flight, and usually no alcohol is served.

AIRPORT TRANSFERS

TO GET TO AND FROM Atatürk Airport, you will have to rely on the Havaş ground handling service *(see p387)*. Havaş services run regularly from the north side of Taksim Square *(see p111)*. At other airports, Havaş handles Turkish Airlines flights (both incoming and outgoing), but usually only to the domestic terminal. Taxis are the only other option. For information on car rental, see p382.

Major hotels will send a private driver if you request this in advance. The driver will display your name on a board so you can see it as you leave the customs area.

Travellers relaxing at a snack bar at İzmir's Adnan Menderes Airport

---

DIRECTORY

TURKISH AIRLINES

Atatürk Bulvarı 154,
Kavıklıdere, Ankara.
☎ (0312) 428 02 00.
FAX (0312) 428 16 81.
@ thyank@ttnet.net.tr

Cumhuriyet Cad 199–201,
3rd floor,
Harbiye, Istanbul.
☎ (0212) 225 05 56
(ticket sales).
☎ (0212) 663 63 63.
(reservations).

FAX 0212 240 2984.
@ agunaydin@thy.com

The THY website has an online timetable. Domestic flight reservations can be made at this address.
W www.turkishairlines.com
@ turkishairlines@thy.com

Flight booking can also be done online. At present, only domestic flights can be booked in this way.
W www.turkish-flt booking.com

OTHER CARRIERS SERVING TURKEY

Air Canada
W www.aircanada.ca

American Airlines
W www.americanairlines.com

British Airways
W www.british-airways.com

KLM (Royal Dutch Airlines)
W www.klm.com

Lufthansa
W www.lufthansa.com

INFORMATION

Atatürk Airport
☎ (0212) 663 64 00.

Bayındır International Airport
Antalya.
☎ (0242) 330 36 00.
☎ (0312) 398 01 00.
W www.aytport.com

Esenboğa Airport
Ankara.
☎ (0312) 428 02 00.

Travelling By Bus and Dolmuş

Varan bus company logo

FEW ENTERPRISES in Turkey are as well-developed or efficient as its intercity bus travel service. Bus or coach is the most comfortable way of getting to just about any destination in the country, and even beyond. For a more informal travelling experience, and over shorter distances, a *dolmuş* (shared taxi or minibus) is the most cheerful, versatile and cheapest way to get around. Travelling in a dolmuş may seem a bit intimidating, but if you state your destination clearly to the driver, you should enjoy the journey.

Innsbruck, Salzburg and Vienna. Varan have also teamed up with the Greater Istanbul Metropolitan Council to co-ordinate services with the Istanbul Sea Bus Service (IDO). This makes it possible to book either through Varan, the ferry services or their combined services. You can book online in English on the company website. Details of schedules and seasonal fares are also available. You can even use your mobile phone to get booking and schedule information via WAP protocol.

Bus passengers visiting a roadside craft stall in Cappadocia

TRAVEL BY BUS

THE PROFUSION of coach or long-distance bus companies gives the impression that bus travel is a highly competitive business. In fact, the entire industry operates on a franchise system: bus companies maintain relatively uniform fares based on petrol (gas) prices and the inflation rate. The system ensures that bus operators share revenue.

The leading intercity coach firms are **Kâmil Koç**, **Varan** and **Ulusoy**. They run regular schedules with teams of well-trained drivers, comfortable vehicles, on-board refreshments and videos. Most buses stop for 30 or 40 minutes every four hours or so, and some companies even operate their own immaculate service areas. Journeys of more than 10 hours tend to be made overnight.

Kâmil Koç, the oldest of these three companies, enjoys a reputation for reliability and safety. Ulusoy have linked up with Dedeman Hotels to offer a 50 per cent discount to their passengers who stay at a

hotel in the Dedeman chain. As you move eastwards in Turkey, the intercity bus network becomes sparser, with services offered by just a few local firms. These buses are just as comfortable, but the distances are greater and the passengers and their parcels decidedly "eastern".

BOOKING AND SPECIAL SERVICES

WHEN TRAVELLING by bus, it is essential to book your tickets in advance, particularly on weekends or during any school or religious holidays *(see p36)*. Several bus firms have now set up facilities for online booking and payment.

Varan run regular services to Athens and other European destinations such as Bologna,

ON THE BUS

SEATING ON BUSES is allocated on a same-sex basis, with exceptions made for married couples. Alcohol and smoking *(see p369)* are not allowed. The only person exempt from the no-smoking rule is the bus driver, but the modern air-control systems mean that you will probably not notice.

Intercity bus interior, with reclining seats

INSURANCE

THE LEADING bus companies offer travel insurance, but the proverbial small print, in fact, details a limit on claims.

BUS STATIONS

IN ALMOST ALL Turkish cities, the *otogar* (bus station) is now located well away from the city centre. Typically, the

Luxury bus operated by Kâmil Koç

Bodrum bus station, with buses from several different companies

company you are travelling with provides a free shuttle service from city-centre pick-up points to the main *otogar* to board the bus. The exception is in Bursa, where the municipality runs a shuttle service to and from the central terminal from convenient pick-up points all over the city.

The main intercity *otogar* in Istanbul is called **Esenler**, and is located 10 km (6 miles) northwest of the city centre. There is another bus station at **Harem**, on the Asian side of the Bosphorus, generally served by buses travelling to and from Esenler.

TRAVEL BY DOLMUŞ

IN ISTANBUL, a dolmuş means two things: a shared taxi that follows a fixed route and departs when full *(see p384)*, and the cream-coloured (or sometimes blue) minibuses which follow fixed routes according to hectic schedules

D

DOLMUŞ

Sign for a dolmuş stop

and are generally chock-a-block with passengers. These are particularly convenient for getting to areas outside the city centre. In the past, dolmuş passengers would travel in huge 1950s-vintage Chrysler or Chevrolet cars. Today minibuses or sport utility vehicles (SUVs) have largely replaced these enormous, fuel-hungry dinosaurs.

Outside Istanbul, however, a dolmuş simply means a minibus. These tend to be cream-coloured, and serve numerous points in the city centre. Dolmuş stops are indicated by rectangular blue signs bearing a large "D" on a white panel. Destinations are also shown on the front or side of the vehicle, and these relate to *mahallesi* (districts) rather than streets.

Dolmuş fares are cheaper than the normal bus prices. Payment is by

Turkish lira in cash, not tickets or electronic smart tickets. Note that if you sit in the front, you will be responsible for passing fares and change to and fro from passengers to the driver.

The best thing about travel by dolmuş is that you can usually alight wherever you want. Say "Müsait bir yer'de" (at the next convenient point) or "İnecek var" (somebody wants to get off). Dolmuşes can often get uncomfortably crowded, but drivers know city areas intimately and can generally drop you off right at your required stop.

Typical dolmuş as seen on routes in all large towns and cities of Turkey

DIRECTORY

BUS STATIONS

Esenler
(International Istanbul Bus Terminal)
Bayrampasa, Istanbul.
◷ *5am–midnight daily.*
☏ *(0212) 658 00 36.*

Harem
On the Asian side of the Bosphorus. Best for eastern destinations.
☏ *(0216) 333 37 63.*

BUS COMPANIES

Ulusoy
☏ *(0212) 471 71 00 (Istanbul).*
☏ *(0312) 286 53 30 (Ankara).*
☏ *(0242) 331 13 13 (Antalya).*
☏ *(0232) 472 06 07 (İzmir).*
Ⓦ *www.ulusoyotobus.com*

Kâmil Koç
Genel Müdürlük,

İnönü Cad, Kâmil Koç, İş Merkezi 16, Kat 4, Bursa.
☏ *(0212) 658 20 00 12 11 (Istanbul).*
☏ *(0242) 261 50 00 (Bursa).*
☏ *0252 614 19 73 (Fethiye).*
☏ *(0242) 836 19 49 (Kaş).*
☏ *(0252) 412 06 30 (Marmaris).*

Varan
☏ *(0212) 658 02 70*

(Istanbul).
☏ *(0312) 224 00 43 (Ankara).*
☏ *(0232) 472 03 89-90 (Izmir).*
☏ *(0242) 331 11 11 (Antalya).*
☏ *(0252) 316 78 49 (Bodrum).*

National call centre.
☏ *(0212) 251 74 74.*
Ⓦ *www.varan.com.tr*
@ *hkisi@mail.varan.com.tr*

Travelling by Train and Ferry

Insignia on a TDİ ferry

T URKEY'S STATE-OWNED RAILWAY SYSTEM is not as up-to-date as other European rail networks, but train travel is worth considering, especially if you have time. Most of Turkey's boat traffic is centred on Istanbul's busy waterways. Going by ferry, however, is not the same as a genuine cruise with a private yacht company (see p363). Car ferries from ports in Italy go to several Turkish coastal towns. Arriving by ferry from Brindisi or Venice is a leisurely, if not overly luxurious, experience, but for those who enjoy longer journeys a ferry can be a more memorable and relaxing option than travelling by the usual road or air routes.

Haydarpaşa Station, terminus for trains from Anatolia

TRAVEL BY TRAIN

T URKEY'S NATIONAL railway system is run by **Turkish State Railways** (**TCDD** or Türkiye Cumhuriyeti Devlet Demiryolları). It is not necessary to travel far in Turkey to see that the country is ideally suited to train travel, and that there is excellent potential for sight-seeing and touring by train. However, the country's rail network has suffered from a lack of new investment. There are a number of scenic tours to Kars, Lake Van, the Southeast Anatolian Project (GAP) and the Black Sea, but these have generally not been planned with the needs of tourists in mind. If time is not a factor and you want to experience a bit of nostalgic meandering, luxuriating in the old-fashioned couchettes and dining cars, then you

Side plate of a locomotive

will be quite delighted by this mode of travel.

Remember that rail travel, like the rest of Turkey, is divided into Thrace (Europe) and Anatolia (Asia). For the bulk of journeys to and from Istanbul, you will be arriving and departing from Haydarpaşa Station (see p125) on the Asian shore of the Bosphorus. Trains serving European destinations leave from

Sirkeci Station (see p76) near the Galata Bridge.

All rail trips can be booked on the TCDD website. However, tickets must be collected from the departure station by the end of the same day. Credit cards are accepted at most intercity train stations.

RAIL ROUTES

T HE TURKISH State Railways network consists of main and regional lines. There are rail links between all of the major cities. However, apart from the upmarket Mavi Tren (Blue Train), which travels between Istanbul and Ankara, most train services are slow and atmospheric.

The Taurus Mountains, which slice Turkey laterally, presented an insurmountable barrier to railway engineers, so there is no rail line along the southern Aegean and Mediterranean coasts. If you want to go to Antalya by train, for example, you have to get off the train at Burdur and continue the 100 km (62 miles) or so to Antalya by bus or taxi. Although much cheaper than other forms of travel, train journeys are also generally much slower.

SERVICE

M EALS ON TURKISH trains are delightful. TCDD dining carriages often have white linen and silver service, and so deserve more than a brief mention. Food is impeccably presented, delicious and, unlike airlines, there are no restrictions on the serving of alcohol. When you purchase

Sleeper carriage on the Ankara–Istanbul express

Car ferry crossing the Dardenelles from Çanakkale

Kos; Bodrum to Datça; Antalya to Girne (Northern Cyprus); Fethiye to Rhodes; Finike to Rhodes (day visits only, with obligatory same-day return). Note that these are commuter ferry services used by locals and are not necessarily scenic or tourism-oriented. Local tourist offices can provide the latest information.

ISTANBUL FERRIES

WHETHER THEY are commuter ferries, high-speed catamarans (sea buses) or car ferries, all of Istanbul's ferry services are run by the Greater Istanbul Municipality in partnership with Turkish Maritime Lines (TDİ) or other operators. For information on ferry services in and around Istanbul, see p385.

Sea bus (Deniz Otobüs) at a ferry dock in Istanbul

your ticket, make sure that it includes the meal service, if it is available. You can choose the time you want to eat and, once on board, your dining time will be announced.

If you plan to travel to the eastern provinces, note that certain services may be scaled down or not available at all. When you book, make sure you check what services will be provided on the train.

RAIL TOURS

SEVERAL FOREIGN tour group operators offer interesting and scenic rail package tours through the Anatolian interior. Such tours combine visits to the major tourist sights with the use of bus and air travel to provide variety and save time where necessary. For more details on specialized rail tours, see p364.

FERRIES

FERRY SERVICES are operated by the government-owned **Turkish Maritime Lines** (TDİ or Türkiye Denizcilik İşletmesi). TDİ ferries follow routes between the ports of Alanya, Brindisi, Çeşme, Girne (Northern Cyprus), Istanbul, İzmir, Taşucu and Venice. Contact TDİ or one of its authorized agents for the most up-to-date information.

In addition to TDİ, there are a number of local ferries, often privately owned, which operate on the following routes: Istanbul to Trabzon (Mondays only); Marmaris to Rhodes (many services daily by catamaran or hydrofoil); Bodrum to

---

DIRECTORY			

TRAIN INFORMATION

Turkish State Railways (TCDD)
Talat Paşa Bulvarı,
06330 Gar, Ankara.
[(0312) 309 0515, ext 336 and (0312) 311 06 20.

Istanbul (7am–midnight)
[(0216) 348 8020, ext 336.
w www.tcdd.gov.tr
An English-language portal has full information on rail routes, timetables, services, fares, authorized ticket agents, discounts, contact details and many special features.

TRAIN RESERVATIONS

Istanbul
Haydarpaşa Station,
8am–6pm (trains to Asia).
[(0216) 336 04 75.

Sirkeci Station
7am–midnight (trains to Europe).
[(0212) 527 0050/1.

Ankara
[(0312) 309 0515.

FERRY INFORMATION

Turkish Maritime Lines (TDİ)
Rıhtım Cad, Merkez Han 4, Karaköy, Istanbul.
[(0212) 245 5366 (with English menu options).

FERRY RESERVATIONS

[(0212) 249 92 22 and 293 74 54 (Istanbul).
[(0212) 244 02 07 (general information).
[(0242) 241 11 20 and 241 26 30 (Antalya).
[(0232) 464 88 89 and 464 88 64 (İzmir).

TDİ AGENTS OUTSIDE TURKEY

Alternative Travel & Holidays
146 Kingsland High Street, London E8 2NS, UK.
[(44) 207 249 98 00.
w www.alternative turkey.com

Pacha Tours
18 rue Godot de Mauroy 75, Paris, France.
[(33) 1 40 22 04 20.

Venice
[(39) 041 520 8819 and 522 95 44.

GENERAL TRAVEL INFORMATION AND BOOKINGS

w www.neredennereye. com
This is a simple and up-to-date web-based Turkish transport directory in six languages. It is excellent for rail and ferry timetables and booking information, and also covers bus and air travel.

Travelling by Car and Bicycle

Rental agency logo

BOTH IN TERMS of independence and convenience, you will see far more of the country by car than any other method of touring, although Turkey's high road accident rate may deter some drivers. You can rent a car from one of the international rental firms or bring your own vehicle or caravan.

Turkey is a large country, and places that may appear close on a map can take much longer than expected to reach. Apart from the Trans European Motorway (TEM) system around Istanbul and Ankara, and a motorway network around İzmir, there are few fast highways.

The rugged terrain and long distances make cycling a strenuous way to see the country. However, cyclists will benefit from their curiosity value, and are certain to encounter helpful, friendly people during their journey.

CAR RENTAL

BEFORE CONTACTING one of the well-known car rental agencies, inquire about fly-drive options. These are often more economical than local car rental, and you can pay in your own currency before you depart for Turkey.

To rent a car, you need to have a local driving licence (or an international one) and your passport. To avoid having to pay a large deposit, use a credit card. Drivers must be over 18 years of age.

Make sure you read the fine print on the rental contract: insurance cover may exclude windscreen damage or even theft. Keep your vehicle's *rhusat* (documents) with you at all times and do not leave them unattended in the car. The car will be given to you with an empty tank and you return it the same way. Most hotels can arrange car rental for you.

BRINGING YOUR OWN VEHICLE

IF YOU ENTER Turkey in your own vehicle, you need to have a valid driving licence and a Green Card to denote international insurance coverage. Documents relating to the car, such as proof of purchase or chassis number, are not required but can be useful. Officially, cars can be brought in for a period of six months, but customs officers often apply arbitrary decisions. Your car will be stamped into your passport on entry and then out again, provided you exit Turkey with the same vehicle. You cannot make day trips to neighbouring Greek islands if you have a car stamped in your passport. The same rules would apply when you bring your motorcycle.

FUEL

PETROL (GAS) IS EASILY obtainable, and is sold in leaded octanes of normal and super, and *kurşunsuz* (unleaded). Filling stations do a full service and will usually wash the windscreen too. There are no self-service facilities. Credit cards are accepted without commission *(see p372)*.

Many vehicles now run on Otogaz (liquid petroleum gas), which is cheaper than regular petrol. Top-up outlets have mushroomed, usually at established petrol stations and motorway service areas.

Truck refuelling at a large petrol station near Konya

RULES OF THE ROAD

VEHICLES DRIVE on the right and distances are shown in kilometres. Turkish road signs and icons conform to the international standard. It is compulsory to wear a seatbelt. Rules of the road are loosely interpreted, but are slowly being enforced to higher standards. The police frequently stop cars to check identification; showing a passport or driving licence will usually suffice.

TÜRKIYE
(50)
(90)
(120)
Urban and motorway speed limits

Look out for pedestrians, animals, tractors and vehicles without lights. Vehicles often reverse on the motorway hard shoulder if they have overshot their exit. Drivers making a left turn often veer to the right and wait for traffic to pass. Don't assume that you have the right of way: drivers often give way to vehicles entering from the right, even on minor roads. As in many countries, truck drivers rule the road. Park only in designated areas. Tow-away zones are indicated by a breakdown-van sign.

Intercontinental traffic crossing the Bosphorus Bridge

EMERGENCIES

IF YOU HAVE an accident, call the police and do not move your vehicle, even if others tell you to do so. Ambulances arrive less quickly than the police, and heavy city traffic can slow their progress. Many Turks display blood group details prominently; in case of a serious accident, this is a sensible precaution.

On secondary roads, local people will generally be very helpful if you have a flat tyre or breakdown. On the motorway system around Istanbul, there are emergency callboxes located every few kilometres, and these will connect you to the police. A local firm called Tur Assist handles recovery services. The **Touring and Automobile Association of Turkey** (TTOK), known simply as Turing, can provide detailed advice on driving in Turkey, transit documents and assistance with breakdowns, accidents and insurance. Your consulate or embassy can be helpful in the event of even a minor emergency.

REPAIRS

ALTHOUGH SPARE PARTS can be hard to get in Turkey, Turks are renowned for their ability to fix almost anything (this goes for bicycles, too). Most towns have a designated Sanayi area (industrial zone) or a specialized Oto Sanayi (automotive repair zone) to handle repairs. The standard may not be what you are used to, but it will be enough to get you on your way again.

CYCLING IN TURKEY

IT IS NOT DIFFICULT to bring a bicycle to Turkey. It will be entered in your passport by customs at the entry point, and you must take it with you when you exit or if you want to visit a Greek island. Bring extra inner tubes and any spares that may be required on a long-distance tour. It is

Mountain biking in Kalkan, on the Mediterranean coast

possible to rent bicycles in Turkey, but this is generally a seasonal activity found in the busier coastal areas.

Roadside emergency telephone

GETTING AROUND

BECAUSE DETAILED, small-scale maps of Turkey have largely been phased out, your biggest problem will be how to find your way on country roads or to out-of-the-way places. While rural roads make for great adventures, the potholes can be a hazard. Villagers can advise on road conditions in their region, but try to base yourself in a large town where information may be more reliable and available in your own language. Tourist offices or travel agents will also be able to help.

Aegean and Mediterranean coastal areas are the best for cycling; even if you have a stiff uphill climb, there are exhilarating opportunities for freewheeling. Cappadocia is less well known for cycling, but the off-road trails and tracks are more accessible than the coastal areas and the terrain is flatter. Finding your way on unmarked routes will likely present the greatest challenges. Most cycling tours are arranged by travel agents and local tour operators. Bougainville of Kaş *(see p362)* offers mountain biking tours locally and in Cappadocia.

Keep in mind that Turkish drivers may show very little consideration for cyclists.

DIRECTORY

CAR HIRE

Avis
Kısıklı Cad 26 81180 Altunizade, Istanbul.
((0216) 474 18 00.
Hilton Hotel Arcade, Elmadağ.
((0212) 246 52 56.
Atatürk Airport.
((0212) 662 08 52 (domestic terminal).
((0212) 663 06 46 (international terminal).
w www.avis.com.tr

Hertz
Atatürk Airport.
((0212) 663 64 00.
Istanbul (Harbiye).
((0212) 241 53 23.

Budget
Istanbul (Taksim).
((0212) 253 92 00.

Europcar
Atatürk Airport.
((0212) 663 07 46.
Istanbul (Taksim).
((0212) 254 77 10.

Sixt-Sun Rent a Car
Atatürk Airport.
((0212) 663 25 87.
Reservation Centre.
((0216) 318 90 40.
@ sixt@sunrent.com
w www.sunrent.com
Bayındır International Airport, Antalya.
((0242) 330 30 90.

CUSTOMS

The website of the Customs Ministry has information about bringing a private vehicle into Turkey.
w www.gumruk.gov.tr

INFORMATION AND ASSISTANCE

Touring and Automobile Association of Turkey (TTOK)
I Sanayi Sitesi, Çamlık Cad, IV Levent, Istanbul.
((0212) 282 81 40.
@ turing@turing.org.tr
w www.turing.org.tr

GETTING AROUND ISTANBUL

THERE CAN BE FEW CITIES IN the world that enjoy the variety and choice of transport that is available in bustling Istanbul. However, chronic traffic congestion can make it difficult to get around quickly. The city stretches some 150 km (93 miles) from Tekirdağ in the west almost to İzmit in the east. However, visitors rarely appreciate the real extent of the sprawling metropolis, as most of

Street sign at a junction in central Sultanahmet

the major tourist attractions are confined to compact districts like Sultanahmet, Beyoğlu and Taksim.

Travelling on Istanbul's various modes of public transport can be an exhilarating experience. For instance, the number 40 bus follows a route from Taksim to Tarabya along the Bosphorus, and reveals a side of the city not shown by a Bosphorus boat tour (see pp126–7).

ISTANBUL ON FOOT

THE DEVELOPMENT OF semi-pedestrianized areas, such as İstiklal Caddesi and central Sultanahmet, has made it possible to walk with ease in parts of Istanbul. Visitors can also tour some of the city's backwaters – the antiques shops of Çukurcuma, near Galatasaray, or Eyüp (see p120) – without meeting too much traffic.

Wherever you walk in Istanbul, bear in mind that traffic only stops at pedestrian crossings controlled by lights; always make use of pedestrian overpasses and underpasses.

Sign for a pedestrian underpass

Istanbul, like any major city, has parts that visitors should avoid. If you want to walk through neighbourhoods that are off the usual tourist track, seek the advice of locals and try to avoid walking in unfamiliar streets after dark.

TAXIS

TAXI CABS ARE ubiquitous in Istanbul, and fares are cheap in relation to other major European cities. Taxis operate day and night, and can be hailed in the street or found at taxi ranks. Restaurant and hotel staff can always phone for a taxi.

Cabs are bright yellow, with the word "taksi" on a sign on the roof. They take up to four passengers. In all licensed taxis the fare is charged according to a meter. The daytime (gündüz) fare applies between 6am and midnight; the night-time (gece) rate is 50 per cent higher. If you cross the Bosphorus Bridge in either direction the bridge toll will automatically be added to the fare. The normal procedure for tipping taxi drivers is just to round up the fare to the nearest convenient figure.

Most taxi drivers do not speak much English, if any. You may also find that some drivers are not familiar with routes to lesser-known sights, so it is a good idea to know which part of the city you want to visit and to carry a map with you at all times. It is also advisable to have the name and address of your destination written down in Turkish for you to show.

DOLMUŞES

DOLMUŞES ARE a useful way of getting around outside the city centre. These are the shared taxis with fixed routes. They are cheaper than regular taxis and more frequent than the buses. The word dolmuş means "full", because drivers usually wait until every seat is taken before they set off.

Dolmuş ranks are marked by a blue sign with a black "D" on a white background. A main centre for dolmuşes is Taksim. Unlike taxis, they do not add bridge tolls to the standard fare.

For more information on dolmuş travel, see p379.

USEFUL DOLMUŞ ROUTES IN ISTANBUL

Taksim – Ataköy
(from Şehit Muhtar Bey Caddesi)
Taksim – Eminönü
(from Lamartin Caddesi)
Taksim – Kadıköy
(from Lamartin Caddesi)
Taksim – Topkapı
(from Abdülhak Hamit Caddesi)
Beşiktaş – Taksim
(from Beşiktaş Caddesi)
Eminönü – Topkapı
(from Sobacılar Caddesi)
Kadıköy – Üsküdar
(from Haydarpaşa Rıhtım Caddesi)
Kadıköy – Bostancı
(from Kumluk Meydanı)
Üsküdar – Beykoz
(from Paşa Limanı Caddesi)
Beşiktaş – Sarıyer
(from Barbaros Bulvarı)
Yedikule – Edirnekapı
(along the city walls, changing at Topkapı Gate)

34 TAD 37

Licensed Istanbul taxi cab with its registration number on the side

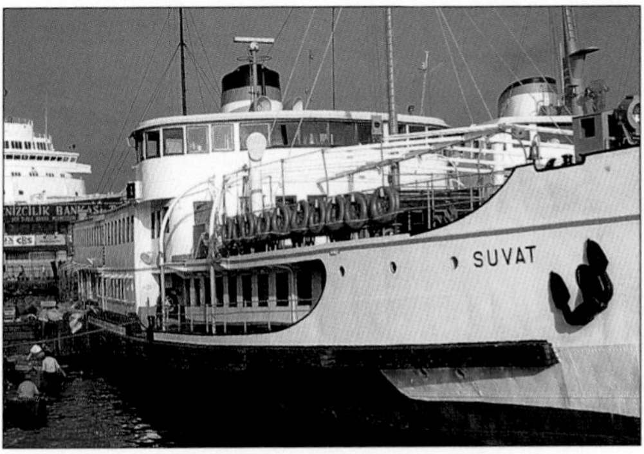
SUVAT
Large commuter ferries docked at the Eminönü ferry piers

FERRIES

PASSENGER AND CAR ferries ply the Golden Horn and the Bosphorus, linking the Asian and European sides. These are known as *vapur*, and are operated by **Turkish Maritime Lines** (TDİ) *(see p381)*. Fast catamarans, or Deniz Otobüsü (sea buses), also use these routes. These services are operated by the municipal-owned **Istanbul Sea Bus Service** (İDO). There are ferry terminals at Karaköy, Eminönü, Beşiktaş and Ataköy on the European side. The quays at Üsküdar, Harem, Kadıköy and Bostancı serve the Asian side *(see map below)*. Commuter ferries run every 15 or 20 minutes, with sea buses less frequent. To explore other alighting points along the Bosphorus, be sure to look at a timetable from TDİ or İDO, as stops along the upper reaches of the Bosphorus can be infrequent. Don't rule out the option of taking a boat up one side of the Bosphorus and coming back by bus.

From the western side of the Galata Bridge, there are a number of firms offering short, inexpensive excursions up the Bosphorus. These are full of local people, and make for a thoroughly rewarding experience. If you decide to book a private cruise through a tour company, be sure to use a reputable one, such as **Hatsail Tourism**.

FERRY TICKETS

FOR ALL LOCAL ferry journeys, you can purchase a flat-fare ticket *(jeton)* from the booth *(gişe)* at the ferry pier or at a slightly higher price from the unofficial street vendors who sit nearby.

To enter the pier, put the *jeton* into the slot beside the turnstile, and then wait in the boarding hall for a boat.

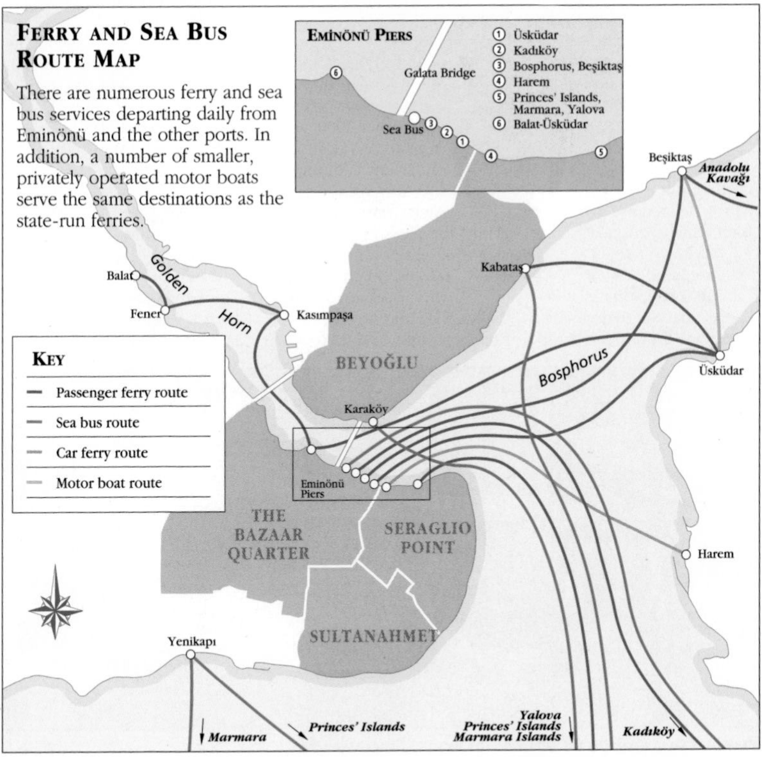
FERRY AND SEA BUS ROUTE MAP
There are numerous ferry and sea bus services departing daily from Eminönü and the other ports. In addition, a number of smaller, privately operated motor boats serve the same destinations as the state-run ferries.
EMİNÖNÜ PIERS
Galata Bridge
Sea Bus
① Üsküdar
② Kadıköy
③ Bosphorus, Beşiktaş
④ Harem
⑤ Princes' Islands, Marmara, Yalova
⑥ Balat-Üsküdar
KEY
Passenger ferry route
Sea bus route
Car ferry route
Motor boat route
Beşiktaş
Anadolu Kavağı
Kabataş
Balat
Golden Horn
Fener
Kasımpaşa
BEYOĞLU
Bosphorus
Üsküdar
Karaköy
Eminönü Piers
THE BAZAAR QUARTER
SERAGLIO POINT
Harem
SULTANAHMET
Yenikapı
Marmara
Princes' Islands
Yalova
Princes' Islands
Marmara Islands
Kadıköy

Municipal buses at the Eminönü bus station

GETTING AROUND BY BUS

ISTANBUL'S TWO inner-city bus companies, IETT and Halk Otobüsü, are both run by the Greater Istanbul municipality. IETT alone has over 2,600 buses covering hundreds of routes. Both companies operate from strategic, central terminals, and routes serve suburbs as much as 50 km (31 miles) outside the city core. Destinations are marked on the front of the bus, with the route shown on the side. Bus shelters are located all over the city. Few bus drivers speak English, but they are invariably patient and polite – even in the worst traffic jams.

Halk Otobüsü services require a cash payment upon entry; IETT buses require a ticket which you must buy before you alight. Tickets can be bought from the small square booths near the main areas, or at a small premium from the many street sellers or kiosks. Buy a *tam bilet* (full-fare ticket) for your journey. Double-decker buses, which are usually green and much more comfortable, require double fare, as do any routes over the Bosphorus bridges. Both IETT and Halk Otobüsü services accept the electronic ticket, AKBIL, which can be purchased at bus terminals and topped up at strategic points. Note that you cannot top up electronic tickets at street kiosks.

METRO

ISTANBUL'S UNDERGROUND system, known simply as the Metro, opened in September 2000, and runs from Taksim to 4. Levent. Although it has only six stops, the Metro relieves some of the pressure on the streets north of Taksim. Tokens, purchased upon entry, operate the turnstiles. The line runs deep underground, and there are at

Sign for the Metro

least two escalators before you reach the platform. Wait in the middle of the platform to board the carriages, as the train takes up only a fraction of the platform length.

TRAMWAYS

THE EXTENSIVE TRAM system is perhaps the most under-rated of Istanbul's people movers. Variously known as the *hafif tren* (light railway) or *hızlı tramvay* (speedy tramway), it is even referred to as the Metro (although it bears no resemblance to the new underground trains). The main tramway line runs from Eminönü, taking in Sultanahmet and the Grand Bazaar area, to Zeytinburnu, with a branch line extending from Aksaray to Yenibosna. This line serves the Esenler *otogar* (intercity bus station). Note that you must alight at the Otogar stop to reach the bus station.

The tramway system is fast and clean, and makes it easy to reach main areas of the city. The newer cars are air-conditioned. Like all traffic in Turkey, tramways run on the right-hand side of the road.

TÜNEL AND İSTIKLAL STREET TRAM

A PULLEY-OPERATED cable car, known simply as Tünel, runs underground from the Galata Bridge at Karaköy up to the Tünel end of İstiklal Caddesi in Beyoğlu. Built by French engineers and opened in 1875, it requires a token

Modern tram at a stop in Sultanahmet, the heart of historic Istanbul

The vintage İstiklal Street tram at Taksim Square

(jeton) purchased from the stall at the entrance. Commuters use this to climb the hill from the Golden Horn. The Tünel is open until 9pm.

From Tünel, you can board a refurbished trolley car to take you the 1 km (just under a mile) up to Taksim Square, with frequent stops along bustling İstiklâl Caddesi. The line is known as *nostaljik tramvay* (old tram).

TRAIN

THE SUBURBAN TRAIN network is lacking in romance and has been superseded by more efficient (and cleaner) means of transport. On the European side, one line follows the Sea of Marmara coast from Sirkeci Station down to Florya. On the Asian shore, services run from Haydarpaşa Station out to İzmit. You can cross the Bosphorus by ferry and alight at Haydarpaşa to step directly onto the train.

Suburban trains depart every half hour or so, and are used mainly by commuters, but can be useful if you need to get to a specific district. Access to the platform is through an automated gateway, which is activated by a token *(jeton)*. You will probably encounter many hawkers, who board and alight at each station.

AIRPORT TRANSFERS

THERE ARE not many options available for transfers to and from Atatürk Airport. The ground handling service, **Havaş**, runs a shuttle bus service to and from the city

centre. Other than this, there are only taxis. There are no public transport facilities servicing the inner airport complex. Taxis to the centre of Istanbul have become more regulated of late, and display daytime prices (about US$12) as well as nightime fares, which are double. The lack of public transport poses a problem, but Havaş offers an efficient and economical service. Havaş buses run continuously on the half-hour from 6:30am until about 11:30pm. Services leave from outside the arrivals concourse and are clearly marked. They go to Taksim Square, with stops at the Bakırköy Sea Bus Terminal and Aksaray. The fare is about US$3.50 for the 25-km (15-mile) journey. If you want the driver to stop along the route, he will sometimes oblige if it is a convenient stopping point. The Havaş bus also goes to the *otogar* (bus station) at Esenler but the service is very erratic. Havaş are not allowed to take passengers directly from the *otogar* to the airport.

Another option is to take city bus number 96-T from Taksim Square. This goes frequently to Atatürk Airport, but stops near the airport entrance, not at the terminals.

Airport shuttle bus bearing the Havaş logo

DIRECTORY	SEA BUSES	PRIVATE CRUISES	TRAIN INFORMATION
FERRY INFORMATION	**Istanbul Sea Bus Service (İDO)**	**Hatsail Tourism**	
	Kennedy Cad, Yenikapı	Cumhuriyet Cad, Erk Apt	**Haydarpaşa Station**
Turkish Maritime Lines (TDİ)	Feribot Iskelesi, Eminönü.	14, Elmadağ, Istanbul.	☎ *(0216) 336 04 75.*
Rıhtım Cad, Merkez Han	☎ *(0212) 517 96 96.*	☎ *(0212) 241 62 50.*	
4, Karaköy,	*(Information line)*	☎ *(0212) 246 70 03.*	**Sirkeci Station**
Istanbul.	☎ *(0266) 516 12 12.*	☒ *www.hatsail.com*	☎ *(0212) 527 00 51.*
☎ *(0212) 245 53 66*	*(Bandirma).*		
(with English menu	☎ *(0212) 660 90 01*	**METRO AND TRAMWAY INFORMATION**	**AIRPORT TRANSFERS**
options).	*(Bakiröy).*		
☒ *(0212) 249 53 91.*	☎ *(0216) 410 66 33*		**Havaş**
☒ *www.tdi.com.tr*	*(Bostancı).*	Hızlı Tramvay	☎ *(0212) 663 64 00.*
	☒ *www.ido.com.tr*	☎ *(0212) 568 99 70.*	

General Index

Historical sights (cont.)
Sublime Porte, Seraglio Point (Istanbul) 65, 66, **73**
Theodosian Walls (Istanbul) 113, **117**
Tomb of Sultan Mahmut II, Sultanahmet (Istanbul) 79, **91**
Yedikule Castle (Istanbul) 113, **116**
Yıldız Park (Istanbul) 113, **121**
Historical and cultural tours 364
directory 365
History of Turkey **40–59**
Hittite civilization **296**
Hittite Festival (Çorum) 35
Hittites 14, **44–5**
Sphinx Relief 243
Hopa 263, **275**
Horse riding and pony trekking 363
directory 365
Hospitals 371
Hostels and student lodgings 322
Student Travel Association General Directorate 323
Hotels in Turkey
Booking a room 322
Checking out and paying 322
Children 322
Choosing a hotel 320
Holiday Villages 321
Hotel listings **324–35**
Luxury hotels 320
Prices and discounts 322
Special License Hotels 321
Turkish Hotel Operators Union 323
House of Mary (Meryemana Kültür Parkı) **182**
Houses, Ottoman **73**, 250, 268, 269 295
Huand Hatun Mosque Complex (Huand Hatun Camii ve Medresesi) (Kayseri) 290
Hünkar mahfili (loge in mosque) 33
Hürrem Sultan Mausoleum, Mevlâna Museum (Konya) 252
Hüsnü Züber House (Hüsnü Züber Evi, Yaşayan Müze) (Bursa) 167

I

Iasus 193
İbrahim Müteferrika 103
İbrahim Paşa 87
İç Bedesten, Grand Bazaar (Istanbul) 105
İçmeler (holiday villages) 201
İftariye Pavilion, Topkapı Palace (Istanbul) 69
Ihlara Valley 278, **292**
İkiztepe (Hittite excavations) 265
Ilgaz Mountain National Park (Kastamonu) 265

İlyas Bey Mosque (Miletus) 191
İmaret, Süleymaniye Mosque, Bazaar Quarter (Istanbul) 100
Imperial costumes exhibition, Topkapı Palace (Istanbul) 69, 70
Imperial Gate, Dolmabahçe Palace (Istanbul) 122
Imperial Mint (Darphane-I Amire), Seraglio Point (Istanbul) 65, 67, **72**
Imperial Porcelain Factory (Istanbul) 121
Infancy of Christ (mosaics) 118
Infidel's Castle (Ankara) 247
Inoculations 370
Inside a mosque 32–3
Prayer times 33
Visiting 33
Insurance 371
International Bodrum Cup Regatta 36
International Film Festival (Istanbul) 34, 361
International İzmir Festival 35
International Opera and Ballet Festival (Aspendos) 35
Internet access 375
Ionian League 175, 190
Ionian Renaissance 45
İshak Paşa Sarayı (Doğubeyazıt) 312
İskele Mosque (Amasra) 264
İskele Mosque (İskele Camii) (Istanbul) 113, **124**
İskenderun 209, **233**
Islam 15
beliefs and practices 33
calligraphy 28
mosques 32–3
Ramazan (Ramadan) 33, 36
Islamic art **28–9**
Istanbul Crafts Centre (Mehmet Efendi Medresesi) 79, 81, **86**
Istanbul Festival of Arts and Culture 35
Istanbul
climate 38
hotels 324–6
map 62–3
Street Finder 134–45
see also Bazaar Quarter, Beyoğlu, Seraglio Point, Sultanahmet
Istanbul, Further Afield
Sights at a Glance 113
İstiklal Caddesi, Beyoğlu (Istanbul) 108–109
İzmir (Smyrna) 172, **178–9**
Agora 179
Archaeology Museum 178
Asansör 179
Ethnographic Museum 178
hotels 328
Kızlarağası Han 178
Konak Clock Tower 178

İzmir (cont.)
Konak district 178
Konak Mosque 178
map 178–9
Sights at a Glance 179
St Polycarp Church 178
Treasury 178
Velvet Castle 179
İznik (Nicaea) 152, **160**
Archaeological Museum 160
hotels 327
İznik ceramics **161**
İznik tiles 151
Atik Valide Mosque (Istanbul) 124
Blue Mosque (Istanbul) 88, 161
Kara Ahmet Paşa Mosque (Istanbul) 117
Mosque of Selim I (Istanbul) 115
Muradiye Mosque, Bursa 166
Muradiye Mosque, Edirne 155
New Mosque (Istanbul) **98**
Prince's Mosque (Istanbul) **99**
Rüstem Paşa Mosque (Istanbul) **96**
Sokollu Mehmet Paşa Mosque (Istanbul) **92**

J

Janissaries **56**, 129
Jazz 132, 360
Jewellery 130, 356
Jews 114, 233
Justinian (emperor) 50–51

K

Kaaba (Mecca) 33
Kabatepe Information Centre (Gallipoli Peninsula) 168
Kaçkar Mountains National Park 21
Kadıkalesi, Bodrum Peninsula 198
Kafkasör Culture and Arts Festival (Artvin) 35, 275
Kahramanmaraş 302, **305**
Archaeological Museum 305
hotels 335
Kâhta 302, **304**
hotels 335
Kalenderhane Mosque (Kalenderhane Camii), Bazaar Quarter (Istanbul) 75, 95, **99**
Kalkan 207, **214**
hotels 331
Kalpakçılar Başı Caddesi, Grand Bazaar (Istanbul) 105
Kara Ahmet Paşa Mosque (Kara Ahmet Paşa Mosque) (Istanbul) 113, **117**
Karaalioğlu Park and Hıdırlık Tower (Antalya) 219
Karagöl-Sahara National Park 275
Karagöz shadow puppet theatre 26, 151, 162

Acknowledgments

DORLING KINDERSLEY would like to thank the following people whose contributions and assistance have made the preparation of this book possible:

MAIN CONTRIBUTOR

SUZANNE SWAN graduated from Queen's University in Kingston, Ontario, Canada, and has lived in Turkey since 1990. She was contributing editor of *Antalya, the Guide* for two years and contributed to many articles and books on Turkey, including *Globetrotter Travel Guide to Turkey* and *Insight Guide to the Turkish Coast*. She is now the Turkish correspondent for World Trades Publishing Ltd.

CONTRIBUTORS AND CONSULTANTS

DOMINIC WHITING, a freelance writer-photographer, lived in Turkey for four years. He wrote *Footprints Turkey Handbook*, was a co-author of Time Out's *Istanbul City Guide*, and updated the *DK Eyewitness Guide to Istanbul*.

DR CAROLINE FINKEL is an Ottoman historian and academic researcher who lives in Istanbul.

DR BIANKA RALLE has an MA in German Studies and worked in journalism as well as teaching and training programmes for developing countries. She was a consultant on Turkey for the Organization for Economic Cooperation and Development (OECD) before entering academic publishing, and has a special interest in Turkish history and literature.

KATE CLOW was educated in the UK, but completed her MBA at Istanbul University in 1991 and stayed in Turkey. She has contributed to the *Rough Guide to Turkey*, *Top Treks of the World* and *Cornucopia Magazine*, and is the originator of the Lycian Way walk.

TERRANCE DUGGAN walked from Greece to Egypt in 1988–89, in the footsteps of Alexander the Great. A scholar and painter, he has written widely on Islamic and Turkish culture and art. His paintings of Seljuk and Ottoman designs have been exhibited in London, Istanbul and Italy.

TERRY RICHARDSON studied classics at Sheffield University, England. He has contributed to *Rough Guide to Turkey* and *Footprints Guide* and photographed for *Cornucopia Magazine* and *The Lycian Way*.

NILÜFER TÜNAY has a degree in Communication Technology, worked in the Turkish media sector and represented *Sea Trades Magazine* in Turkey. She is now retired.

MOLLY MCNAILLY-BURKE was Turkish correspondent for the *Irish Times* and a contributor to the *Insight* and *Columbus Guides*. She now lives in Hertfordshire, England.

RONNIE ASKEY-DORAN edited a satirical broadsheet in Istanbul and now lives in her native Australia.

CHRISTOPHER GARDNER is a botanist and horticulturist who lives in England.

ROSIE AYLIFFE lived in Turkey for three years while working as a freelance writer in Istanbul. She was one of the authors of *Rough Guide to Turkey*, and contributed to the *Rough Guide to France*, Time Out's London guides and the *DK Eyewitness Guide to Istanbul*.

ROSE BARING is a travel writer who has spent many months exploring Istanbul. She was co-author of *Essential Istanbul* (AA) and *DK Eyewitness Guide to Istanbul*.

BARNABY ROGERSON has travelled and lectured extensively in the eastern Mediterranean. With Rose Baring he co-wrote *Essential Istanbul* (AA) and contributed to other AA and Cadogan guides, as well as *DK Eyewitness Guide to Istanbul*.

CANAN SILAY was a journalist on the Turkish daily, *Hürriyet*, and then editor of *Istanbul, The Guide* for many years. She has contributed to several books on Turkey, including the Insight guides to Istanbul, Turkey and the Turkish coast.

ADDITIONAL CONTRIBUTORS

Sean Fraser, Lisa Greenstein, Alfred LeMaitre.

ADDITIONAL CARTOGRAPHY

Globetrotter Travel Maps; Haluk Inci, İki Nokta.

DESIGN AND EDITORIAL ASSISTANCE

Tarryn Berry, Leizel Brown, Jo Cowen, Lellyn Creamer, Claudia Dos Santos, Emily Hatchwell, Jacky Jackson, Simon Lewis, Irene Lyford, Ian Midson, Marisa Renzullo, Gerhardt van Rooyen, Reinette van Rooyen.

PROOFREADER AND INDEXER

Pat Barton.

ADDITIONAL PHOTOGRAPHY

DK Studio/Steve Gorton, Dave King, Ian O'Leary, Clive Streeter.

PUBLISHING MANAGER

Kate Poole

MANAGING EDITOR

Helen Townsend

DTP DESIGNER

Jason Little

CARTOGRAPHER

Casper Morris

SPECIAL ASSISTANCE

DORLING KINDERSLEY would like to thank staff at museums, mosques, churches, government departments, shops, hotels, restaurants, transport services and other organizations in Turkey for their help.

Particular thanks are due to: Dr Oğuz Alpözen, Bodrum Museum; İbrahim Baştutan; Emine Bilirgen, Topkapı Palace, Istanbul; Erol Çakir, İzmir Archaeology Museum; Süleyman Çakır; Sühelya Demirci, Sivas Museum; Hikmet Denizli; The Museum of Anatolian Civilisations, Ankara; Ercihan Düzgünoğlu, TÜRSAB, Istanbul; Veysel Ediz, Çorum Museum; Dr Donald Frey, Institute of Nautical Archaeology, Bodrum; Iclal and Muzaffer Guler; Ali Harmankaya, Side Museum; Kaili Kidner and Lars-Eric Möre, Göreme; Joanna March and Hülya Soylu, Turkish Tourist Office, London; Güney Paksoy, Yedikule and Rumeli Hisar Museums; Feyza Sürücü, Ministry of Tourism, Ankara; Ertan Tezgör, Turkish Grand National Assembly, Ankara; Feridun Ülker, Presidential Palace, Ankara; Ürcel Üzerin, Bursa Archaeological Museum;

Varan Turizm; Üsküdar Folklore and Tourism Society (ÜFTUD), Kırklareli region; Neco Yoksulabakan.

The following staff of provincial tourist offices were very helpful: Reşit Akgüneş, Diyarbakır; Nebahat Alkaya, Bodrum; Bülent Aslan, Amasya; Ayten Aydın, Dalyan; Mustafa Aydın, Kaş; Nurten Celikkaptan, İzmir; Polat Cengis, Çeşme; Ali Fuat Er, Amasya; Fadime Hanim, Sivas; Yaşar Gül, Kastamonu; Yücel Güneş, Nevşehir; Mehmet Hacıağaoğlu, Side; Hüsnü Küçükaslan, Tokat; Murat Keleş, Amasya; Mustafa Kurt, Amasya; Ferhat Malcan, Kaş; Halis Öğüt, Konya; Şentürk Özdemiş, Erzurum; Sare Özdemir, Safranbolu; Safiye Portal, Safranbolu; Kadir Savçı, Çanakkale; Cennet Tazegül, Kars; Ahmet Tazegül, Erzurum; Yüksel Unal, Samsun; Mevlut Uyumaz, Afyon; Erdal Uzun, Kütahya; Zübeyir Yılmaz, Antakya; İbrahim Yakup, Çorum; Garip Yıl, Osmaniye; Zeki Bey, Işak Paşa Saray, Doğubeyazıt.

Other associations and individuals whose assistance was invaluable: Faik Akın, Turkish Airlines, Istanbul; Çetin Akant, Pedasa/Bodrum; Baki Akpınar, Göreme; Ali Baba Rent a Car, Kaş; Dr Şakir Aktaş, Kaş; Ali Baysan, Foto Ali, Kaş; Ahmet Burcu, Istanbul; Hasan Dağlı, Kaş; Zafer Emeksiz, Payas/Yakacık Municipality; Ali and Nazife Gülşen, Kaş; Cengiz Güzelmeriç, Kaş; Prof. Dr Wilhelm Gernot, Würzburg University; Kamil Koç Otobüs İşletmeleri A.Ş., Bursa; Ahmet Karaşahin, Adana; Lars-Eric Möre, Kapadokya Balloons, Göreme; Kerim Mat, Alanya; Abdullah Muslu, Kaş; Myriam Hanim, St Polycarp Church, İzmir; Dr Munise Ozan, Kaş; Muhammed Özcan, Kaş; Aydın Özmen, Turkish Central Bank, Ankara; Cihat Şahin, Fethiye; Diler Şaşmaz, DHL, Antalya; Mustafa and Sultan Soylu, Kaş; Tahsin Bey Konak Hotel, Safranbolu; İsmail Tezer, Kayseri Governor's Office; Ömer Tosun, Ottoman House, Göreme; Tuğrul Bilen Unal, Turkish State Mint, Istanbul; Osman Uvuç, Kayseri Esnaf; Veysel Bey, İznik Municipality; Bayram Yıldırım, Bodrum; Özkan Yaşar, Kaş; Yenişehir Palas Hotel, Istanbul; Hüsnü Züber, Bursa.

PHOTOGRAPHY PERMISSIONS
DORLING KINDERSLEY would like to thank the following for their kind permission to photograph at their establishments: General Directorate of Monuments and Museums; Ministry of Culture; Ministry for Religious Affairs; İstanbul Valiliği İl Kültür Müdürlüğü; İstanbul Valiliği İl Müftülüğü; Milli Saraylar Daire Başkanlığı and Edirne Valiliği İl Müftülüğü.

PICTURE CREDITS
t = top; tl = top left; tlc = top left centre; tc = top centre; trc = top right centre; tr = top right; cla = centre left above; ca = centre above; cra = centre right above; cl = centre left; c = centre; cr = centre right; clb = centre right below; cb = centre below; crb = centre right below; bl = bottom left; b = bottom; bc = bottom centre; bcl = bottom centre left; br = bottom right; d = detail

The publisher would like to thank the following individuals, companies, and picture libraries for their kind permission to reproduce their photographs:

A TURİZM YAYINLARI: Topkapı Palace 70cr, 84tr; Archaeological Museum 74bc, 75tr. ADVERTISING ARCHIVES: 108tr; AISA ARCHIVO ICONGRAFICO, S.A., BARCELONA: 69bl, 71tl, 119tc; HAKKI AKDEĞIRMAN: 233t; AKG PHOTO: 58cr; Erich Lessing 3c, 47tl/bl; Haghia Sophia, Istanbul *Emperor Constantine IX Monomacbus*, mosaic detail from south gallery 40; Musée du Louvre *The Abduction of Helena* by

Guido Reni 43cr; National Museum of Archaeology, Naples *Battle of Alexander*, Roman mosaic from Pompeii 46–47; Bibliothèque Nationale, Paris from the *Djamil el Tawarik* 53cr; British Library, from the *Westminster Abbey Psalter* 53bl, 227t; Bibliothèque Nationale, Paris from *Avis directif pour faire la passage d'Outremer* by Jean Mielot (1455) 54bl; Topkapı Palace Museum *Map of the World* (detail) by Piri Reis (c.1513) 55tr; Erich Lessing/Künsthistorisches Museum, Vienna *Portrait of Süleyman the Magnificent* (c.1530), circle of Titian 55cr; Museo Civic Correr, Venice *The Battle of Lepanto*, Venetian 55br. ANCIENT ART AND ARCHITECTURE COLLECTION LTD: 51cr. AQUILA PHOTOGRAPHICS: Hanne and Jens Eriksen 159tr; D. Robinson 21bl; Juan Martín Simón 289c. PAUL ARTUS 17t; ATLAS GEOGRAPHIC: Zafer Kizilkaya 28cl, 198bl, 202bl, 203tl/cr; TAHSIN AYDOĞMUS: 7cr, 28tl, 30tl, 51bl, 81cr, 82tr, 85bl, 88tr, 96tl, 96tr, 119c/cr, 280cl, 281bl.

BRIDGEMAN ART LIBRARY, London: British Library, detail from the *Catalan Atlas* (1375) 24cl; Yale Center for British Art, Paul Mellon Collection *Caravan at Mylasa* (1845) by Richard Dadd 25tr; Topkapı Palace Museum *Aristotle Teaching*, from *The Better Sentences and Most Precious Dictions* 52tr; Stapleton Collection *Osman I* by John Young 54cl; Topkapı Palace Museum *Süleyman the Magnificent at the Battle of Mobacs in 1526* (1588), by Lokman 54–5; Victoria and Albert Museum, London: 161cbl/cbr; © THE TRUSTEES OF THE BRITISH MUSEUM: 161cla; DIRECTORATE OF MUSEUMS, BURSA: 162tl; REG BUTLER: 17t.

ÇALIKOĞLU REKLAM TURİZM VE TICARET LTD.: 133tc; CHRISTEL CLEAR PICTURE LIBRARY: © Detlef Jens 36tl; CORBIS: Dave Bartruff 183t; Gerard Degeorge 8–9; Nick Wheeler 182tl; Adam Woolfitt 2–3; MANUEL ÇITAK: 109cr, 131tr; SYLVIA CORDAIY PHOTO LIBRARY: © Anthony Bloomfield 27cl; © James de Bounevialle 20tr; © Dorothy Burrows 378cl, 382cr, 385t; © Gable 19cr, 215cr; P.S. Linfoot 34bl; © Jonathan Smith 13c, 27tc, 34ca, 58bc, 213tr, 361tr; © Chris Taylor 19bl, 215cl; Edward Wareham 387t; Julian Worker 20cl.

C.M. DIXON PHOTO RESOURCES: 74tr.

ABBIE ENOCK: 17br; MARY EVANS PICTURE LIBRARY: 9c, 45t, 45c, 46tl, 46cl, 48c, 48bl, 49c, 49bc, 49br, 51br, 52c, 54br, 55tl, 56tc, 56bc, 57tc, 57bl, 57br, 58tr, 58cl, 61c, 147, 169b, 174b, 227cl/cr/bl/bca/br, 319c, 367c.

FFOTOGRAFF: © Nick Tapsell 148t; FIRST ARMY HQ, ISTANBUL: 125b; DR DONALD FREY: 197bc.

CHRIS GARDNER: 20tl/cr/clb/br, 21tl/cr; ARA GÜLER: Mosaics Museum 87c; Topkapı Palace Museum 71cr, 91tr, 161bl; 359t; ŞEMSI GÜNER: 123tr.

SONIA HALLIDAY PHOTOGRAPHS: Bibliothèque Nationale, Madrid 51tr; engraved by Thomas Allom, painted by Laura Lushington 71br; Topkapı Palace Museum 86b; ROBERT HARDING PICTURE LIBRARY: David Holden 150; Michael Jenner 69br; J.H.C. Wilson 123br; Adam Woolfitt 19tr, 21cl, 33cl, 101tr, 151; HULTON GETTY IMAGES: 22br, 23tl, 59tc; THE HUTCHISON LIBRARY: © Robert Francis 27bl, 379b; © Maurice Harvey 386b; © John Hatt 62tl; © Jeremy Horner 26bl; © Joan Klatchko 186b, 233b; © Tony Souter 28b, 29bl, 134.

HANAN ISCHAR: 183b; ISTANBUL LIBRARY: 76b.

MICHAEL JENNER PHOTOGRAPHY: 183cr.

ALI KABBAS: 7c, 26tr, 29tc, 30b, 37b, 121tl, 255t; Museum of Turkish and Islamic Arts, Istanbul, from *Hadiqat al-Su'ada* (17th century), Baghdad 29br; GÜROL KARA: 104cl; İZZET KERRİBAR: 1, 4–5, 12, 14b, 15tr/c, 18cl, 20bl, 25b, 26tl/cr/br, 28ba, 28–9, 31tr/bl, 44cl, 60–61, 62bl/br; 64, 66tl, 72tr, 118tl, 122tr, 128br, 133t, 146–7, 149tl, 182tr, 193b, 205, 206b, 218tl/tr, 228b, 255cbr, 263t/b, 266–7, 272tr/bc, 277, 281cr, 294tr, 310–11, 336bl, 361cl, 364c, 366–7; KIPPA NATURE PHOTO AGENCY: H. Glader 21bra; J. van Holten; 21bc; E. Pott 21br.

JOSÉ LUCZYC-WYHOWSKA: 358cr, 359cl/cr/bl/blc/brc/br.

MAGNUM: Topkapı Palace Museum/Ara Güler 63c, 69tl; ALBERTO MODIANO: 19br, 26cl, 157b; with approval of ÜFTUD (Üsküdar Folklore and Tourism Society, Kırklareli region) 27bcr, 34tc; MUSEUM OF ANATOLIAN CIVILIZATIONS, Ankara: 41tc, 41bl, 41br, 42tc, 42cr, 42bl, 42br, 43tc, 43bl, 43br, 44bl, 44bc, 45bc, 45br, 47ca, 48tl, 48br, 49tc, 242tr/bc, 243tl/cr/cl, 296tr.

NATURAL HISTORY MUSEUM, LONDON: 213b. NETWORK PHOTO-GRAPHERS: Gerard Sioen/Rapho 7tr, 215c, 222–223, 313t.

GÜNGÖR ÖZSOY: 6br, 157tl/tr, 300, 301.
PHOTO ACCESS PHOTOGRAPHIC LIBRARY: Harvey Lloyd 22–3;

PHOTOBANK: Adrian Baker 56bl, 170, 382bl; Jeanetta Baker 14t, 34cb, 184–5, 190t, 191tr, 191b, 198cl, 364bl; Peter Baker 27tr, 174t, 176tr, 177b, 182cl/bl, 192b, 318–9, 337bl, 381t; PICTURES COLOUR LIBRARY LTD.: 24bl, 173t, 224bl, 358cl; PLANETARY VISIONS LIMITED: 11b.

NEIL SETCHFIELD: 94, 148bl, 194cl, 274b, 337cr, 354cl; GEORGE SIMPSON: 37cr; JEROEN SNIJDERS: 13b, 15bl, 116tr, 354b, 386tl; REMY SOW: 320cl; JEFF SPIBY: 211b.

GOLKHAN TAN: 22tl/cl/c/cr/r/bl/bc, 196cbl, 197cbr; TRAVEL INK: Marc Dubin 23b, 187b, 192t, 323b; Abie Enock 322tl; Ken Gibson 171; Simon Reddy 37t; TRIP PHOTOGRAPHIC LIBRARY: 153; TURKISH AIRLINES: 377t.

ANDREW WHEELER: 31cl, 54tl, 336t, 355t; PETER WILSON: 70c, 85cl, 85tr, 89tl, 118cl.

Front endpaper: all special photography except ROBERT HARDING PICTURE LIBRARY: David Holden tl; GÜNGÖR ÖZSOY: br; PHOTOBANK: Adrian Baker tcl.

JACKET
Front - CORBIS, Adam Woolfitt b; DK PICTURE LIBRARY, Clive Streeter c; Linda Whitwam cl; IZZET KERIBAR main image. Back - DK PICTURE LIBRARY, Alistair Duncan b; GETTY IMAGES, Chris Sanders t. Spine - IZZET KERIBAR.

All other images © Dorling Kindersley. For further information, see: **www.dkimages.com**

DORLING KINDERSLEY SPECIAL EDITIONS

Dorling Kindersley books can be purchased in bulk quantities at discounted prices for use in promotions or as premiums.
We are also able to offer special editions and personalized jackets, corporate imprints, and excerpts from all of our books, tailored specifically to meet your own needs.

To find out more, please contact:
(in the United Kingdom) – SPECIAL SALES, DORLING KINDERSLEY LIMITED, 80 STRAND, LONDON WC2R ORL; TEL. 020 7753 3572;

(in the United States) – SPECIAL MARKETS DEPT., DORLING KINDERSLEY PUBLISHING, INC., 375 HUDSON STREET, NEW YORK, NY 10014.

Phrase Book

PRONUNCIATION

Turkish uses a Roman alphabet. It has 29 letters: 8 vowels and 21 consonants. Letters that differ from the English alphabet are: **c**, pronounced "j" as in "jolly"; **ç**, pronounced "ch" as in "church"; **ğ**, which lengthens the preceding vowel and is not pronounced; **ı**, pronounced "uh"; **ö**, pronounced "ur" (like the sound in "further"); **ş**, pronounced "sh" as in "ship"; **ü**, pronounced "ew" as in "few".

IN AN EMERGENCY

Help!	**İmdat!**	*eem-dat*
Stop!	**Dur!**	*door*
Call a doctor!	**Bir doktor çağrın!**	*beer dok-tor chah-ruhn*
Call an ambulance!	**Bir ambulans çağrın!**	*beer am-boo-lans chah-ruhn*
Call the police!	**Polis çağrın!**	*po-lees chah-ruhn*
Fire!	**Yangın!**	*yan-guhn*
Where is the nearest telephone?	**En yakın telefon nerede?**	*en ya-kuhn teh-leh-fon neh-reh-deh*
Where is the nearest hospital?	**En yakın hastane nerede?**	*en ya-kuhn bas-ta-neh neh-reh-deh*

COMMUNICATION ESSENTIALS

Yes	**Evet**	*eh-vet*
No	**Hayır**	*b-'eye'-uhr*
Thank you	**Teşekkür ederim**	*teh-shek-kewr eh-deh-reem*
Please	**Lütfen**	*lewt-fen*
Excuse me	**Affedersiniz**	*af-feh-der-see-neez*
Hello	**Merhaba**	*mer-ba-ba*
Goodbye	**Hoşça kalın**	*bosh-cha ka-luhn*
Good morning	**Günaydın**	*gewn-'eye'-duhn*
Good evening	**İyi akşamlar**	*ee-yee ak-sham-lar*
Morning	**Sabah**	*sa-bah*
Afternoon	**Öğleden sonra**	*ur-leh-den son-ra*
Evening	**Akşam**	*ak-sham*
Yesterday	**Dün**	*dewn*
Today	**Bugün**	*boo-gewn*
Tomorrow	**Yarın**	*ya-ruhn*
Here	**Burada**	*boo-ra-da*
There	**Şurada**	*shoo-ra-da*
Over there	**Orada**	*o-ra-da*
What?	**Ne?**	*neh*
When?	**Ne zaman?**	*neh za-man*
Why?	**Neden**	*neh-den*
Where?	**Nerede**	*neh-reh-deh*

USEFUL PHRASES

How are you?	**Nasılsınız?**	*na-subl-sub-nubz*
I'm fine	**İyiyim**	*ee-yee-yeem*
Pleased to meet you	**Memnun oldum**	*mem-noon ol-doom*
See you soon	**Görüşmek üzere**	*gur-rewsh-mek ew-zeb-reh*
That's fine	**Tamam**	*ta-mam*
Where is/are ...?	**... nerede?**	*... neh-reh-deh*
How far is it to ...?	**... ne kadar uzakta?**	*... ney ka-dar oo-zak-ta*
I want to go to ...	**... a/e gitmek istiyorum**	*... a/eb geet-mek ees-tee-yo-room*
Do you speak English?	**İngilizce biliyor musunuz?**	*een-gee-leez-jeb bee-lee-yor moo-soo-nooz?*
I don't understand	**Anlamıyorum**	*an-la-mub-yo-room*
Can you help me?	**Bana yardım edebilir misiniz?**	*ba-na yar-duhm eh-deb-bee-leer mee -see-neez?*

USEFUL WORDS

big	**büyük**	*bew-yewk*
small	**küçük**	*kew-chewk*
hot	**sıcak**	*sub-jak*
cold	**soğuk**	*soh-ook*
good/well	**iyi**	*ee-yee*
bad	**kötü**	*kur-tew*
enough	**yeter**	*yeb-ter*
open	**açık**	*a-chubk*
closed	**kapalı**	*ka-pa-lub*
left	**sol**	*sol*
right	**sağ**	*saa*
straight on	**doğru**	*dob-roo*

near	**yakın**	*ya-kuhn*
far	**uzak**	*oo-zak*
up	**yukarı**	*yoo-ka-rub*
down	**aşağı**	*a-shab-ub*
early	**erken**	*er-ken*
late	**geç**	*gech*
entrance	**giriş**	*gee-reesh*
exit	**çıkış**	*chub-kubsh*
toilets	**tuvaletler**	*too-va-let-ler*
push	**itiniz**	*ee-tee-neez*
pull	**çekiniz**	*cheb-kee-neez*
more	**daha fazla**	*da-ba faz-la*
less	**daha az**	*da-ba az*
very	**çok**	*chok*

SHOPPING

How much is this?	**Ne kadar?**	*ney ka-dar*
I would like ...	**... istiyorum**	*... ees-tee-yo-room*
Do you have ...?	**... var mı?**	*... var muh?*
Do you take credit cards?	**Kredi kartı kabul ediyor musunuz?**	*kreb-dee kar-tub ka-bool eb-dee-yor moo-soo-nooz?*
What time do you open/ close?	**Saat kaçta açılıyor/ kapanıyor?**	*Sa-at kach-ta a-chub-lub-yor/ ka-pa-nub-yor*
this one	**bunu**	*boo-noo*
that one	**şunu**	*sboo-noo*
expensive	**pahalı**	*pa-ba-lub*
cheap	**ucuz**	*oo-jooz*
size (clothes)	**beden**	*beb-den*
size (shoes)	**numara**	*noo-ma-ra*
white	**beyaz**	*bay-yaz*
black	**siyah**	*see-yah*
red	**kırmızı**	*kuhr-muh-zub*
yellow	**sarı**	*sa-rub*
green	**yeşil**	*yeb-sheel*
blue	**mavi**	*ma-vee*
brown	**kahverengi**	*kah-veh-ren-gee*
shop	**dükkan**	*dewk-kan*
till	**kasa**	*ka-sa*
bargaining	**pazarlık**	*pa-zar-lubk*
That's my last offer	**Daha fazla veremem**	*da-ba faz-la veb-reb-mem*

TYPES OF SHOP

antiques shop	**antikacı**	*an-tee-ka-jub*
bakery	**fırın**	*fub-rubn*
bank	**banka**	*ban-ka*
book shop	**kitapçı**	*kee-tap-chub*
butcher's	**kasap**	*ka-sap*
cake shop	**pastane**	*pas-ta-neb*
chemist's/ pharmacy	**eczane**	*ej-za-neb*
fishmonger's	**balıkçı**	*ba-lubk-chub*
greengrocer's	**manav**	*ma-nav*
grocery	**bakkal**	*bak-kal*
hairdresser's (ladies)	**kuaför**	*kwaf-fur*
(mens)	**berber**	*ber-ber*
leather shop	**derici**	*deb-ree-jee*
market/bazaar	**çarşı/pazar**	*char-sbub/pa-zar*
newsstand	**gazeteci**	*ga-zeb-teb-jee*
post office	**postane**	*pos-ta-neb*
shoe shop	**ayakkabıcı**	*'eye'-yak-ka-bub-jub*
stationer's	**kırtasiyeci**	*kubr-ta-see-yeb-jee*
supermarket	**süpermarket**	*sew-per-mar-ket*
tailor	**terzi**	*ter-zee*
travel agency	**seyahat acentesi**	*say-ya-bat a-jen-teb-see*

SIGHTSEEING

castle	**hisar**	*bee-sar*
church	**kilise**	*kee-lee-seb*
island	**ada**	*a-da*
mosque	**cami**	*ja-mee*
museum	**müze**	*mew-zeb*
palace	**saray**	*sar-'eye'*
park	**park**	*park*
square	**meydan**	*may-dan*
theological college	**medrese**	*med-reb-seb*
tomb	**türbe**	*tewr-beb*
tourist information office	**turizm danışma bürosu**	*too-reezm da-nubsb-mab bew-ro-soo*
tower	**kule**	*koo-leb*
town hall	**belediye sarayı**	*beb-leb-dee-yeb sar-'eye'-ub*
Turkish bath	**hamam**	*ba-mam*

TRANSPORT

airport	**havalimanı**	*ba-va-lee-ma-nuh*
bus/coach	**otobüs**	*o-to-bewss*
bus stop	**otobüs durağı**	*o-to-bewss doo-ra-uh*
coach station	**otogar**	*o-to-gar*
minibus	**dolmuş**	*dol-moosh*
fare	**ücret**	*ewj-ret*
ferry	**vapur**	*va-poor*
sea bus	**deniz otobüsü**	*deh-neez o-to-bew-sew*
station	**istasyon**	*ees-tas-yon*
taxi	**taksi**	*tak-see*
ticket	**bilet**	*bee-let*
ticket office	**bilet gişesi**	*bee-let gee-sheh-see*
timetable	**tarife**	*ta-ree-feh*

STAYING IN A HOTEL

Do you have a vacant room?	**Boş odanız var mı?**	*bosh o-da-nuhz var muh?*
double room	**iki kişilik bir oda**	*ee-kee kee-shee-leek beer o-da*
room with a double bed	**çift kişilik yataklı bir oda**	*cheeft kee-shee-leek ya-tak-luh beer o-da*
twin room	**çift yataklı bir oda**	*cheeft ya-tak-luh beer o-da*
for one person	**tek kişilik**	*tek kee-shee-leek*
room with a bath	**banyolu bir oda**	*ban-yo-loo beer o-da*
shower	**duş**	*doosh*
porter	**komi**	*ko-mee*
key	**anahtar**	*a-nah-tar*
room service	**oda servisi**	*o-da ser-vee-see*
I have a reservation	**Rezervasyonum var**	*reb-zer-vas-yo-noom var*
Does the price include breakfast?	**Fiyata kahvaltı dahil mi?**	*fee-ya-ta kah-val-tuh da-heel mee?*

EATING OUT

A table for ... please	**... kişilik bir masa lütfen**	*... kee-shee-leek beer ma-sa lewt-fen*
I want to reserve a table	**Bir masa ayırtmak istiyorum**	*beer ma-sa 'eye'-uhrt-mak ees-tee-yo-room*
The bill please	**Hesap lütfen**	*beh-sap lewt-fen*
I am a vegetarian	**Et yemiyorum**	*et yeh-mee-yo-room*
restaurant	**lokanta**	*lo-kan-ta*
waiter	**garson**	*gar-son*
menu	**yemek listesi**	*ye-mek lees-teh-see*
fixed-price menu	**fiks menü**	*feeks meh-new*
wine list	**şarap listesi**	*sha-rap lees-teh-see*
breakfast	**kahvaltı**	*kah-val-tuh*
lunch	**öğle yemeği**	*ur-leh yeh-meh-ee*
dinner	**akşam yemeği**	*ak-sham yeh-meh-ee*
starter	**meze**	*meh-zeh*
main course	**ana yemek**	*a-na yeh-mek*
dish of the day	**günün yemeği**	*gewn-ewn yeh-meh-ee*
dessert	**tatlı**	*tat-luh*
rare	**az pişmiş**	*az peesh-meesh*
well done	**iyi pişmiş**	*ee-yee peesh-meesh*
glass	**bardak**	*bar-dak*
bottle	**şişe**	*shee-sheh*
knife	**bıçak**	*buh-chak*
fork	**çatal**	*cha-tal*
spoon	**kaşık**	*ka-shuhk*

MENU DECODER

badem	*ba-dem*	almond
bal	*bal*	honey
balık	*ba-luhk*	fish
bira	*bee-ra*	beer
bonfile	*bon-fee-leh*	fillet steak
buz	*booz*	ice
çay	*ch-'eye'*	tea
çilek	*chee-lek*	strawberry
çorba	*chor-ba*	soup
dana eti	*da-na eh-tee*	veal
dondurma	*don-door-ma*	ice cream
ekmek	*ek-mek*	bread
elma	*el-ma*	apple
et	*et*	meat
fasulye	*fa-sool-yeh*	beans
fırında	*fuh-ruhn-da*	roast
fıstık	*fuhs-tuhk*	pistachio nuts
gazoz	*ga-zoz*	fizzy drink
hurma	*boor-ma*	dates
içki	*eech-kee*	alcohol
incir	*een-jeer*	figs
ızgara	*uhz-ga-ra*	charcoal grilled

kahve	*kab-veh*	coffee
kara biber	*ka-ra bee-ber*	black pepper
karışık	*ka-ruh-shuhk*	mixed
karpuz	*kar-pooz*	water melon
kavun	*ka-voon*	melon
kayısı	*k-'eye'-uh-sub*	apricots
kaymak	*k-'eye'-mak*	cream
kıyma	*kuhy-ma*	minced meat
kızartma	*kuh-zart-ma*	fried
köfte	*kurf-teh*	meatballs
kuru	*koo-roo*	dried
kuzu eti	*koo-zoo eh-tee*	lamb
lokum	*lo-koom*	Turkish delight
maden suyu	*ma-den soo-yoo*	mineral water (fizzy)
meyve suyu	*may-veh soo-yoo*	fruit juice
midye	*meed-yeh*	mussels
muz	*mooz*	banana
patlıcan	*pat-luh-jan*	aubergine
peynir	*pay-neer*	cheese
pilav	*pee-lav*	rice
piliç	*pee-leech*	roast chicken
şarap	*sha-rap*	wine
sebze	*seb-zeh*	vegetables
şeftali	*shef-ta-lee*	peach
şeker	*sheh-ker*	sugar
su	*soo*	water
süt	*sewt*	milk
sütlü	*sewt-lew*	with milk
tavuk	*ta-vook*	chicken
tereyağı	*teh-reh-yab-ub*	butter
tuz	*tooz*	salt
üzüm	*ew-zewm*	grapes
vişne	*veesh-neh*	sour cherry
yoğurt	*yob-urt*	yoghurt
yumurta	*yoo-moor-ta*	egg
zeytin	*zay-teen*	olives
zeytinyağı	*zay-teen-yab-uh*	olive oil

NUMBERS

0	**sıfır**	*sub-fuhr*
1	**bir**	*beer*
2	**iki**	*ee-kee*
3	**üç**	*ewch*
4	**dört**	*durt*
5	**beş**	*besh*
6	**altı**	*al-tub*
7	**yedi**	*yeb-dee*
8	**sekiz**	*seb-keez*
9	**dokuz**	*dob-kooz*
10	**on**	*on*
11	**on bir**	*on beer*
12	**on iki**	*on ee-kee*
13	**on üç**	*on ewch*
14	**on dört**	*on durt*
15	**on beş**	*on besh*
16	**on altı**	*on al-tub*
17	**on yedi**	*on yeb-dee*
18	**on sekiz**	*on seb-keez*
19	**on dokuz**	*on dob-kooz*
20	**yirmi**	*yeer-mee*
21	**yirmi bir**	*yeer-mee beer*
30	**otuz**	*o-tooz*
40	**kırk**	*kubrk*
50	**elli**	*eb-lee*
60	**altmış**	*alt-muhsh*
70	**yetmiş**	*yet-meesh*
80	**seksen**	*sek-sen*
90	**doksan**	*dok-san*
100	**yüz**	*yewz*
110	**yüz on**	*yewz on*
200	**iki yüz**	*ee-kee yewz*
1,000	**bin**	*been*
100,000	**yüz bin**	*yewz been*
1,000,000	**bir milyon**	*beer meel-yon*

TIME

one minute	**bir dakika**	*beer da-kee-ka*
one hour	**bir saat**	*beer sa-at*
half an hour	**yarım saat**	*ya-ruhm sa-at*
day	**gün**	*gewn*
week	**hafta**	*baf-ta*
month	**ay**	*'eye'*
year	**yıl**	*yubl*
Sunday	**pazar**	*pa-zar*
Monday	**pazartesi**	*pa-zar-teb-see*
Tuesday	**salı**	*sa-lub*
Wednesday	**çarşamba**	*char-sham-ba*
Thursday	**perşembe**	*per-sbem-beb*
Friday	**cuma**	*joo-ma*
Saturday	**cumartesi**	*joo-mar-teb-see*

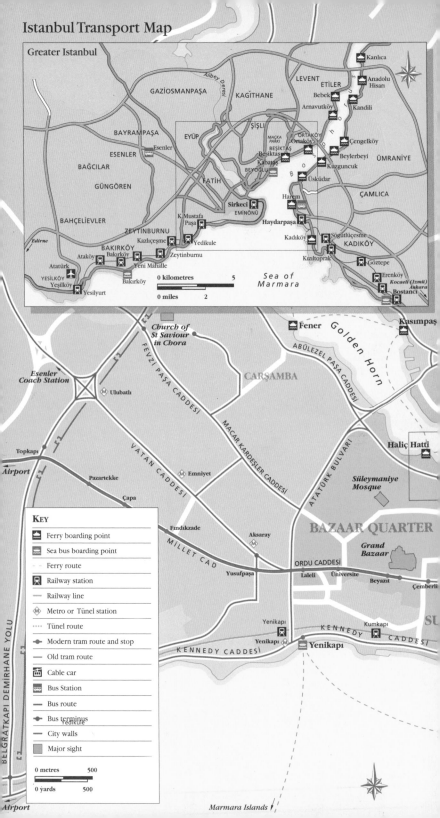